Spatial vision is that field of science which deals with the problem of inferring the structure of the world from vision. This problem can be divided into many separate tasks, such as extracting information about three-dimensional objects, or object recognition.

This book is a collection of invited papers presented at the 1991 York Conference on Spatial Vision in Humans and Robots. From computational models to explicit biological models of spatial processing, to neural networks, these papers bring together the biological and computational aspects of spatial image processing in a unique way. The book provides a snapshot of the state of the art in the understanding of spatial vision.

This collection will be of interest to biological researchers investigating how the brain solves spatial problems, as well as to researchers in robotics and computer vision systems.

Spatial Vision in Humans and Robots

Spatial Vision in Humans and Robots

The Proceedings of the 1991 York Conference
on Spatial Vision in Humans and Robots

Edited by

Laurence Harris
York University
North York, Ontario

Michael Jenkin
York University
North York, Ontario

CAMBRIDGE
UNIVERSITY PRESS

Published by the Press Syndicate of the University of Cambridge
The Pitt Building, Trumpington Street, Cambridge CB2 1RP
40 West 20th Street, New York, NY 10011-4211, USA
10 Stamford Road, Oakleigh, Victoria 3166, Australia

First published 1993

Printed in the United States of America   .

Library of Congress Cataloging-in-Publication Data

York Conference on Spatial Vision in Humans and Robots (1991:
    Toronto, Canada)
      Spatial vision in humans and robots: the proceedings of the 1991
    York Conference on Spatial Vision in Humans and Robots / edited by
    Laurence Harris, Michael Jenkin.
          p. cm.
      Includes bibliographical references and index.
      ISBN 0-521-43071-2
      1. Space perception — Congresses.   2. Robot vision — Congresses.
    I. Harris, Laurence (Laurence Roy), 1953–   .   II. Jenkin, Michael
    (Michael Richard MacLean), 1959–   .   III. Title.
    QP491.Y67   1991
    152.14′2 — dc20   92–40728
                                                                CIP

A catalog record for this book is available from the British Library

ISBN 0-521-43071-2 hardback

This book is dedicated to the future,

Lucy (2), William (1) and Joanna (10) Harris,

Emma (6) and Sarah (5) Jenkin.

Preface

This book came out of a conference of the same title which took place at York University, Toronto, Canada, from the 19th–22nd June, 1991.

We would like to thank the conference sponsors

The Human Performance in Space Laboratory of the Institute of Space and Terrestrial Science.

The Information Technology Research Centre.

The Department of Computer Science, York University.

The National Science and Engineering Research Council (Canada).

York University President's NSERC Fund.

Faculty of Pure and Applied Science, York University.

Neither the conference nor this book would have occurred without the sterling efforts of Prof. Ian P. Howard, Prof. David M. Regan and the secretarial assistance of Teresa Manini.

Contents

Preface vii

Foreword xi

Contributors xvii

1 Spatial vision in humans and robots   1
   Laurence Harris and Michael Jenkin

2 Spatial vision models: problems and successes   9
   Stanley A. Klein

3 On cytochrome oxidase blobs in visual cortex 33
   John Allman and Steven W. Zucker

4 Linear subspace methods for recovering
   translational direction 39
   Allan D. Jepson and David J. Heeger

5 Demodulation: a new approach to texture vision 63
   John Daugman and Cathryn Downing

6 What makes a good feature? 89
   Allan D. Jepson and Whitman Richards

7 Hand-printed digit recognition using
   deformable models 127
   Christopher K. I. Williams, Michael D. Revow and
   Geoffrey E. Hinton

8 The role of color in spatial vision 149
   Karen K. De Valois and Frank L. Kooi

9 Nonlinear processes in pattern discrimination
   and motion perception .161
   Hugh R. Wilson

10 **Will robots see?** 185
     Stanley A. Klein

11 **3D object recognition and matching: on a result
     of Basri and Ullman** 203
     Tomaso Poggio

12 **Surface interpolation networks** 211
     Alex P. Pentland

13 **Uncertainty models for $2\frac{1}{2}$-D and 3-D surfaces** 229
     Richard Szeliski

14 **An orientation based representation for
     contour analysis** 249
     *Deborah Walters, Krishnan Ganapathy and
     Frouke van Huet*

15 **Detection and discrimination of motion-defined
     and luminance-defined two-dimensional form** 281
     David Regan

16 **An inhibitory beam for attentional selection** 313
     John K. Tsotsos

17 **Bayesian models, deformable templates and
     competitive priors** 333
     Allan J. Yuille and J. J. Clark

18 **Cycloversion, cyclovergence and perceived slant** 349
     Ian P. Howard

19 **Model of visual motion sensing** 367
     David J. Heeger and Eero P. Simoncelli

20 **Some recent findings in early vision
     and focal attention** 393
     Bela Julesz

References 409

Index 445

Foreword

"Developments of recent decades require new formulations that include but transcend the hierarchical principle of brain organization. Prominent among them is the concept that the brain is a complex of widely and reciprocally interconnected systems and that the dynamic interplay of neural activity within and between these systems is the very essence of brain function." ... "An important feature of such distributed systems, particularly those central to primary sensory and motor systems, is that the complex function controlled or executed by the system is not localized in any one of its parts. The function is a property of the dynamic activity within the system: it resides in the system as such."[1]

The most important aspect of human sight is spatial vision, that is the ability to see external objects and discriminate their different shapes. Everyday life places heavy demands on spatial vision — reading road signs or instructions on the printed page, urban driving in rain or heavy fog, crossing a busy street — and the penalty for failing to see or recognize an object is often severe. The familiarity of these demands blinds us to the remarkable discrimination and reliability of everyday spatial vision, such as our ability to recognize one out of possibly thousands of faces stored in memory.

Our understanding of the neural processing that underlies spatial vision has advanced dramatically during the last two decades although, as brought out time and again in this book, this understanding is as yet fragmentary and shallow. The formidable challenge of spatial vision research can be appreciated when we see it as an endeavor to understand functional principles and physiological operations of a rather substantial part of the human brain, a structure containing some 10^{10} neurons, each of which receives up to thousands of connections from other neurons, and whose state continually changes. In this light, the dramatic advances in our understanding of spatial processing in the brain that we have seen over the last 20 years speak, not only to the scientific skills and technical ingenuity of scientists, but also to an intrinsic order and regularity in the functional organization of this astronomically complex network of brain cells.

[1] Mountcastle (1979), p. 26

It is widely assumed that, at an early stage in visual processing, retinal image features are first partitioned into discrete 'packages', each package corresponding to a different external object. Because of the effortless ease and accuracy with which the visual pathway usually carries out retinal image partition, the formidable difficulty of the task was not fully recognized until recently, when computer scientists attempted to instruct machines to recover the external objects in the visual environment from TV camera images of those scenes. This research area, reviewed in Chapters 11, 12, 13, 14 and 17 is basic to the design of what has been called "seeing robots" and to the design of machines for recognizing, for example, written symbols such as numbers (Chapter 7) and abnormal blood cells. Chapter 5 describes an intriguing alternative to fingerprint identification of individuals that, in contrast to fingerprinting, can be carried out remotely and unknown to the individual being investigated. This technique is based on computer discrimination of inter-individual differences in the eye's iris patterning.

Between the areas of computer vision and human visual psychophysics there is a two-way interplay that has been of mutual benefit to both areas. Chapters 4, 6, and 19 illustrate the role of computer scientists in the generation of psychophysical models of human vision, both in identifying how information about the visual environment is represented in the retinal image, and in formulating algorithms that would allow the information to be extracted. On the other hand, in the human visual pathway we have a physical structure that already for a great many years has been able, not only to detect and recognize objects but also perform many other extremely advanced visual functions — and with no apparent effort. In this sense, many of the major problems of robot vision have already been solved. Here, the psychophysicist has aided the computer scientist by experimentally teasing out the methods used by the human visual system to recover environmental information, and then expressing these methods in the form of algorithms.

Much of current vision research can be regarded as systems analysis, though even the most complex nonlinear systems treated in textbooks on systems analysis seem comparatively straightforward when compared with the human visual pathway. As is the case for any other system, our understanding of the human visual system is embodied in quantitative models of one kind or another. Here we should back-track a little to note that there are two complementary ways of describing a system. First, a complete description of the function of the system as-a-whole in the form of a mathematical model that allows the system's output to be calculated for any arbitrary input or combination of inputs. In principle, there may be several alternative mathematical models that are equally satisfactory and cannot be differentiated by comparing the system's output with its input. In practice, systems analysts must often restrict themselves to incomplete mathematical models, each of which allows the output of the system to be predicted over only a restricted range of the inputs to the system. The second level of description is structural, and can be expressed in the form of a structural model. For our present purpose it is important to bear in mind that a system of interconnected nonlinear parts may possess properties (system properties) that are not evident in any of the individual parts. Although a particular system property may be degraded or destroyed by removing some individual part of the system, it does not follow that the particular system property is located in that part of the system; in the extreme case, the property may have no specific location within the system, being a property of the system as-a-whole. A second relevant point is that the mathematical model of the system as-a-whole may be formulated as a hierarchical sequence of these stages, but the sequence of these stages may bear little relationship to the sequence of parts in the structural description of the system.

In vision research, a complete model of the function of the system as-a-whole would be a quantitative psychophysical model that, given an arbitrary visual input to the eye, would allow a subject's behavioral responses (e.g. a button press) to be predicted — at least in statistical terms. A complete model of this kind is, however, a distant ambition.

Admittedly, in the sensory and cognitive literature there is no shortage of metaphors posing as scientific hypotheses. Nor is there any shortage of self-styled models that are not formulated quantitatively and are difficult to subject to experimental test in such a way that sharp refutation is possible. Plentiful also are so-called models that, although quantitative, amount to little more than curve fitting and re-descriptions of data.

All the current psychophysical models of the system as-a-whole that not only go beyond re-description of data, but also satisfy the refutability criterion for a valid scientific hypotheses have the comparatively modest aim of providing a quantitative, though incomplete, representation of the visual system that allows behavioral responses to a severely restricted range of visual inputs to be predicted from a quantitative specification of these visual inputs. Even though limited in their aims, such models commonly feature parallel processing combined with multiple hierarchical stages, at least some of which are nonlinear. Perhaps the most familiar example of success in developing a restricted psychophysical model is provided by the psychophysical studies of color matching and photometry using the 2° foveally-viewed field that led to the CIE specifications of color and luminance. The history of this early research, and especially the contributions of Wright and Guild, can almost be regarded as a progressive restriction of the stimulus variables to the point that the psychophysical model predicted data with precision for any normally-sighted subject. It may not be coincidental that a number of currently-active psychophysicists, including at least three of the contributors to this book, had early training in color theory, and have subsequently showed no hesitation in attempting to generalize to other sub-modalities some of the powerful ideas, such as the concepts of the line element, the parallel orthogonal color channels, additivity, and the opponent process, that were originally created within the context of color theory.

In this book Chapters 2 and 9 exemplify this restricted, quantitative approach to mathematical modeling, limited here to the area of spatial vision. These chapters illustrate the clear rationale, sharp logic, mathematical strength and solid quantitative experimental methods that are required to create the nontrivial yet refutable hypotheses that allow progress towards this deceptively simple aim of generating a restricted psychophysical model.

Clearly, in order to segregate the retinal image of an object from the retinal image of that object's surroundings, the object's retinal image must differ visually in some way from the image of its surroundings. It is known that the human visual pathway can utilize several kinds of difference. In particular, the eye can distinguish an object from its surroundings (i.e. achieve figure-ground segregation) when the retinal images are identical except for a difference in luminance, or color, or texture, or binocular disparity or velocity, and it is known that any one of these factors is sufficient. The great majority of empirical studies on the detection and spatial discrimination of objects have been restricted to targets defined by differences in luminance such as, for example, luminance gratings and bright lines, and theoretical efforts to define the necessary and sufficient conditions for figure-ground segregation have been largely restricted to this case. Nevertheless, all the cues listed above are commonly available and are presumably utilized in the everyday battle to survive in our visually-complex and dangerous world, so that further knowledge of these modes of seeing may well be of immediate practical value in, for example aviation and highway safety. At a theoretical level, models of spatial discrimination such as vernier acuity and orientation discrimination have been restricted to data obtained with luminance-defined targets. These models are challenged by findings that some spatial discriminations can be approximately similar for luminance-defined targets and for comparable targets defined by motion alone or color alone. Chapter 8 reviews recent work on spatial vision for an object that is revealed only by a color contrast; the luminance, motion and depth of such an object is identical to those of its surroundings. Chapter 15 reviews research on spatial vision for a object that is revealed only by motion contrast; the luminance, color and depth of such an object is identical to those of its surroundings.

It is self-evident that even a restricted psychophysical visual model must take account of all the effective inputs to the visual system. So far we have assumed that all the effective inputs are visual. However, this is not necessarily so. The subject's criterion level is one nonvisual input that it can make a nonsense of an inadequately-designed psychophysical experiment. Signal detection theory and forced-choice methods were originally introduced to enable experimenters to control this variable. Attention, discussed in Chapters 16 and 20, is another nonvisual input that cannot safely be ignored in visual psychophysics. Finally, eye position can interact with retinal image information to affect visual perception. This third nonvisual input is discussed in Chapter 18.

We now turn from a functional description of the visual system as-a-whole to a structural description of the same system. The richness of structural description of the human visual pathway in nonhuman primate has seen dramatic advances in recent years. This is partly due to the introduction of new techniques but, more particularly, is a result of the imaginative way in which a number of neuroscientists have used their outstanding experimental capabilities in combining two or more techniques. Three examples convey the flavor of these advances: combining the anatomical cytochrome oxidase (CO) technique with single cell recording to demonstrate how functional properties differ for neurons within and between CO blobs; combining animal psychophysics with microstimulation to demonstrate reversible changes in the behavioral processing of motion produced by stimulation of cortical area MT in alert monkey; combining animal psychophysics with single cell recording in alert trained monkey to reveal the effects of nonvisual inputs (attention and the monkeys task) on the visual properties of single cells in prestriate cortical areas. Chapter 3 describes an attempt to relate the color and orientation timing properties of single cells in and between CO blobs to corresponding functions of the system as-a-whole.

It is a formidable problem to relate (a) the functional psychophysical properties of the visual system as-a-whole to (b) the structure of the visual pathway and the properties of its several parts. For example, it has been shown that the visual pathway of nonhuman primate contains multiple visual cortical areas, and that many (perhaps 20) subcortical nuclei receive visual inputs. Furthermore, there are rich reciprocal interconnections, not only between cortical visual areas but also between prestriate visual cortex and subcortical nuclei, and some of these interconnections descend from central brain locations toward the eye as far as as the striate cortex and even beyond. As was emphasized by Mountcastle in his 1979 essay, in such a system there might be little relationship between the early-to-late sequence of processing stages in a psychophysical model and the peripheral-to-central sequence of neural structures and, furthermore, the location of any given psychophysical stage might be distributed throughout the structural system.

D. Regan
York University, May 1992

Contributors

John Allman
Division of Biology
California Institute of Technology
Pasadena, CA, USA

J. J. Clark
Division of Applied Sciences
Harvard University
Boston, MA, USA

John Daugman
Cambridge University
Downing St.
Cambridge, UK, CB2 3EJ

Cathryn Downing
Cambridge University
Downing St.
Cambridge, UK, CB2 3EJ

Krishnan Ganapathy
Computer Science Department
Stetson University
North Woodland Blvd.
DeLand, FL, 32720, USA

Laurence Harris
Department of Psychology
York University
4700 Keele St.
North York, Ontario
Canada, M3J 1P3
harrisl@vm1.yorku.ca

David J. Heeger
NASA–Ames Research Center, and
Department of Psychology
Stanford University
Stanford, CA, 94305, USA

Geoffrey E. Hinton
Department of Computer Science
University of Toronto
Toronto, Ontario Canada
M5S 1A4

Ian P. Howard
Human Performance in Space
    Laboratory
Institute for Space and Terrestrial
    Science
York University, Toronto
Ontario, Canada, M3J 1P3
ihoward@ists.ists.ca

Frouke van Huet
Computer Science Department
State University of New York
    at Buffalo
Buffalo, NY, USA

Michael Jenkin
Department of Computer Science
York University
4700 Keele St.
North York, Ontario
Canada, M3J 1P3
jenkin@cs.yorku.ca

Bela Julesz
Laboratory of Vision Research
41 Gordon Road
Livingston Campus
Rutgers University
New Brunswick, NJ, 08903, USA

Allan D. Jepson
Department of Computer Science
University of Toronto
Toronto, Ontario, Canada
M5S 1A4
jepson@ai.toronto.edu

Stanley A. Klein
School of Optometry
University of California
Berkeley, CA, 94720, USA
klein@viewprint.berkeley.edu

Frank L. Kooi
TNO Institute for Perception
P. O. Box 23
3769 ZG Soesterberg
The Netherlands
kooi@izf.tno.nl

Alex Pentland
The Media Laboratory
Massachusetts Institute of
   Technology
Room E15-387, 20 Ames St.
Cambridge, MA, 02139, USA

Tomaso Poggio
Uncas and Helen Whitaker
   Professor
Department of Brain and
   Cognitive Sciences
Artificial Intelligence Laboratory
Massachusetts Institute of
   Technology
545 Technology Square
Cambridge, MA, 02139 USA
pottio@ai.mit.edu

D. Regan
Institute for Space and Terrestrial
   Science
Behavioural Sciences Building
York University
4700 Keele St.
North York, Ontario
Canada, M3J 1P3

Michael D. Revow
Department of Computer Science
University of Toronto
Toronto, Ontario, Canada
M5S 1A4
revow@ai.toronto.edu

Whitman Richards
Department of Brain and
   Cognitive Sciences
Massachusetts Institute of
   Technology
79 Amherst St.
Cambridge, MA, 02139, USA

Eero P. Simoncelli
The Media Laboratory, and
Department of Electrical
   Engineering and Computer
   Science
Massachusetts Institute of
   Technology
Cambridge, MA, 02139, USA

Richard Szeliski
Digital Equipment Corporation
Cambridge Research Lab
One Kendall Square
Bldg. 700
Cambridge, MA, 02139, USA
szeliski@crl.dec.com

John K. Tsotsos
Department of Computer Science
University of Toronto
Toronto, Ontario, Canada
M5S 1A4
tsotsos@ai.toronto.edu

Karen K. De Valois
Psychology Department and Vision
Science Group
Tolman Hall
The University of California
    at Berkeley
Berkeley, CA, 94720, USA
karen@kennedy.berkeley.edu

Deborah Walters
Cognitive Science Center
State University of New York
    at Buffalo
Buffalo, NY, USA

Christopher K. I. Williams
Department of Computer Science
University of Toronto
Toronto, Ontario, Canada
M5S 1A4
ckiw@ai.toronto.edu

Hugh R. Wilson
Visual Sciences Center
University of Chicago
939 Eash 57th St.
Chicago, IL, 60637, USA
hrw6@midway.uchicago.edu

A. L. Yuille
Division of Applied Sciences
Harvard University
Pierce Hall
Cambridge, MA, 02138, USA

Steven W. Zucker
Research Center for Intelligent
    Machines
McGill University, Montreal
Quebec, Canada
    and
Canadian Institute for Advanced
    Research

Spatial vision in humans and robots

Laurence Harris

Michael Jenkin

The purpose of this first chapter is to give a rather personal view of some of the issues that we consider are involved in studying spatial vision in humans and robots. On the face of it, the aims of people investigating spatial vision in humans would seem to be rather different from those of people developing robot visual systems. The former are biological and psychological scientists investigating Nature whereas the latter are computer scientists and engineers. But neither party feels that full understanding is in sight and each peeps into the other camp for hints. Each party is, of course, looking for different things. Biological researchers look to robotics for a theoretical framework within which to interpret their biological findings, whereas computer scientists and engineers hope, perhaps, to avoid the wasteful agony of re-inventing the visual system. Is this situation too circular to be useful?

There seems to be a great deal that robotic vision system designers can learn from biological vision. Many concepts and results from psychophysical and physiological research into human and animal vision have already been adapted to machine and robot vision (for example the motivation for center-surround like operators at the earliest stages of image processing, the use of low-level features as primitives in stereo matching algorithms, etc.). The study of biological vision has often lead to useful algorithms for machines (eg. Mayhew et. al's (1981) use of zero-crossings and peaks from bandpass channels in stereopsis algorithms). Is it possible for the biological community to take advantage of the results of the computational community? One potential area of fruitful transfer is to provide a testing ground for biological models. A robotic implementation of a biological model forces the modeller into specifying in absolute detail the limits and specifications of their model. Although it is not clear that passing such a test could ever validate a model, failing it can certainly demonstrate flaws!

Specifying *functional* task descriptions may be the best basis for useful interchange between the study of vision in humans and in robots. In this chapter we suggest a functional basis for dividing vision into spatial and temporal vision and consider that each of these divisions can be usefully further divided into proprioceptive and perceptual functions. We also divide "machine vision" into two separate (functional) classes: robot vision and seeing-machine vision based on these respective proprioceptive and perceptual uses of vision. Functional definitions also yield clarity to the problems that each study area faces. For example, why does this book claim to concern itself mainly with spatial vision and yet contain chapters on self motion (Chapter 4), motion perception (Chapters 9, and 19) and color vision (Chapter 8)?

A definition of spatial vision

The division of vision into spatial and temporal functions is a helpful simplification. Spatial vision is required by organisms to distinguish, identify and locate things. We define the field of study which can legitimately be called Spatial Vision as taking as its concern *the use of information to derive the spatial structure of the visual field*. Notice, interestingly, that this information is not, and cannot be, exclusively visual but must include motor and proprioceptive information about the position of the head and eyes. To be useful, the information must also include aspects of higher cognition (see Chapter 6). This also gives us a way of deciding whether color vision and some aspects of motion should be included in the study of spatial vision. These cues are included in as much as they contribute spatial information. Usually the role of color vision in this is relatively minor, however, except when conditions contrive to force the spatial system to rely on color, as happens, for example, under isoluminant conditions (see Chapters 8 and 20). But motion is often an important spatial cue (see Chapter 15).

Temporal Vision refers to the use of information to derive a description of changes in visual events over time. Notice that temporal vision too, requires extraretinal information such as copies of motor signals and signals about eye and head movements. It is also often dependent on higher cognitive processes such as prediction and intentions to perform motor acts.

Definitions in terms of spatial and temporal function might then be an acceptable way to divide up biological vision for investigation (or at least for discussion). There is even a possible anatomical substrate emerging further justifying this spatial/temporal division. The cortical projection of magnocellular cells in the lateral geniculate carry information more relevant to temporal vision whereas the parvocellular pathways form a substrate more suitable for spatial vision (see a recent review by Regan, 1989c; and Figure 7 in Chapter 15 of this book). Much discussion about the validity of this anatomical division of function has arisen from the fact that the two systems have many anatomical inter-connections. But once we admit that temporal information can have spatial function we have to expect or even require these inter-connections.

Vision is interactive with the world and requires non-visual information

The first task of seeing for humans or robots is to decide what to look at: vision is interactive. This almost-obvious truth has been largely overlooked by both schools of spatial-vision investigators.

The potential visual environment extends in all directions around a human or robot observer, with an infinite amount of detail in all parts of the visible electro-magnetic spectrum. Only limited samples of this environment can be taken at any one time (limited either by anatomy or processing capacity). And each sample (no matter of how large an extent) contains only poor spatial information and needs to be related to other samples taken from other view points to be useful. Having two eyes helps but, in order to see adequately, visually-guided translations of the organism or machine are required. Movements of the head and eyes take time and the successive images that result need to be integrated not only with each other but also with information about the movements that lead to them. As this required motion is not instantaneous, it follows that it is not possible to understand the world if vision is treated as an instantaneous spatial event.

The fact that vision is an active, interactive process has received relatively scant attention from both psychophysicists (but see for counter examples: Wolf et al., 1980; Yarbus, 1967 and, of course, Gibson, 1956) and physiologists (but see for counter examples: Adey and Noda, 1973; Bartlett et al., 1976; Duhamel et al., 1992; Fischer et al., 1981; Kimura et al., 1980; Schlag et al., 1980; Toyama et al., 1984) in part because it is methodologically so hard. Investigators generally go to extraordinary lengths to try to remove any interactive effects between their subjects and the stimuli by controlling fixation either by instructions (to humans) or by paralysis (of animal subjects). From the robot vision point of view, the desire to treat vision as "snapshot analysis" has partly resulted from limitations in the technology used to acquire digitized images. Digitizers obtain a single fixed snapshot of the world, and until very recently it was not possible to acquire temporal sequences of digitized images at anything near video rates, and even if the images could be acquired it was difficult or impossible to obtain hardware capable of processing the images in anything close to real time. Thus problems (such as edge detection, stereopsis, segmentation, etc.) have often been posed as tasks associated with a single image or image pair, rather than a problem that could be approached in a continuously sampled domain. Only in very recent years, as the technology has evolved, has the concept of actively controlling the image acquisition process come under study in the robot vision community (see Aloimonos et al., 1988; Ballard, 1991; Krotkov et al., 1992).

These methodological constraints on biologists as well as similar constraints on computer scientists and engineers might partially underlie why spatial visual tasks in robots and seeing machines (see below for definitions) have often worked with static, snapshot views. Indeed large sections of the machine vision literature deal with algorithms which operate on single images in isolation. For example, the collection of papers *Readings in Computer Vision* edited by Fischler and Firschein (1987) contains several hundred pages of computer vision papers, very few, if any, of which consider computer vision as an active process. Although it is possible to achieve some impressive results from sophisticated algorithms for machine-vision systems which operate on these purely spatial images, it may not be the most efficient or useful way of processing the images and certainly is less like a biological process. It may be that even purely spatial tasks such as extracting pattern information, may in fact be performed more effectively and efficiently if the context is used. This context, by definition, would include temporal information (describing what came before and maybe even after, the image in question) — even if all the machine has to go on is a sequence of snapshots.

Proprioceptive vision and perceptual vision

When it comes to spatial vision in machines, the question of what the machine is to be used for, and what information is therefore required by the machine is crucial. It is important to acknowledge that vision is used for two different functions in humans: for the reflex guidance of all aspects of self motion and for perception. A role of vision in reflex guidance is to provide information about the positions of parts of the body (for example the hands and, interestingly, the eyes) with respect to each other and with respect to reference points in the world. Another aspect of this function is to provide information about the whole body and its motion with respect to the world. We are terming this group of functions "proprioceptive vision". The concepts of proprioceptive and perceptual vision are so separate that it is almost confusing to call them both vision. Both have spatial and temporal aspects (although it is possible to argue that movement is more important for vision-as-proprioceptor, whereas spatial features are more important to perception). Thus we are proposing FOUR functional divisions of vision: proprioceptive spatial, proprioceptive temporal, perceptual spatial and perceptual temporal. And we wish to go further. We think it useful overtly to divide up machine vision itself into two categories corresponding to the proprioceptive and perceptual functions of vision.

We think it would be useful to distinguish between the different sort of machines that use vision-like processes. Using the proprioceptive and perceptual functions of vision as a guide, two groups fall out. We will call these *seeing machines* which are like perceptual machines and process images to extract what might be quite abstract information and *seeing robots* which use vision to achieve other aims.

A seeing machine is one whose primary task involves processing an image. Generally this is a single image taken in isolation, although it does not need to be. A camera or photocopying machine represents basic examples: image processing is the only function and, although there is a loose context for the images in the sense of the different frames of a film, this sequence information is not available and has no role in the processing of each individual image. More advanced examples of seeing machines are those that extract some higher-level information such as identifying patterns (see Chapter 5) or which make decisions based on such information. Seeing machines can be thought of as perfectly able to run off line, taking even a pre-stored image (or a pre-stored ensemble of images) and reporting on it.

Robot vision, on the other hand, in our definition, uses visual information proprioceptively to provide information about its interactions with the world. Robot vision (as opposed to seeing machine vision) is not designed to sense a single image in isolation, but rather to sense from the continuum. Robots can potentially interact with their environment by changing the way in which that sensing takes place for example by moving their cameras and camera mounts or by altering focus, or focal length, or wavelength of light they are receptive to, or by physically manipulating their environment so as to change the appearance or spatial relationships among the things that they sense. A robot has to operate in real time, responding as the world (including its own actions and inactions) unfolds. The primary function of a robot is not to process images any more than image processing is the primary function of a human (if we can be said to have a primary function at all!). Required information about the objects that the robot might be manipulating (shape, location, orientation, identity) as well as about parts of the robot itself (the position and orientation of the manipulators and of their component parts with respect to the manipulated items, with respect to other parts of the robot and with respect to reference points in the external world) might come from a teleceptor sense system using the visible part of the electro-magnetic spectrum but could come, perhaps beneficially, from other sources. Although robots can be built to exploit various types of sensors (such as sonar, laser range finders, shaft encoders, global positioning systems, infrared sensors, etc.), in order to simplify the task of operating in a particular environment, vision in the range of light to which humans are sensitive to is likely to be particularly important. Typically robots must operate in a world populated by humans, and objects in a human environment are colored or textured so that they are visible *for humans*. Thus the robot must be able to sense in the range of the spectrum which is visible *to humans*.

Building robots in a biological mould

If spatial vision in humans and robots is to be defined in terms of functional requirements, we must now ask what are these functional requirements? Robots are designed for specific tasks while human performance is generalized both in terms of the range of tasks that can be performed as well as the environments in which each task can be performed. As robotic development continues, however, robots will be applied to more varied tasks and it is the oft-stated goal that one day robots will replace humans in tedious and dangerous environments. If this corresponds to the required behavior of robots becoming more and more generalized, then the need for a more and more general-purpose visual system will become increasingly important.

Even if the "best" robot vision system is the one that performs tasks similar to the human visual system and which performs in environments which are similar to those that the human visual system expects, this still does not necessarily imply that robot and human visual systems should operate in similar ways. The late David Marr (1982) and others have proposed that machine systems should be built which model biological systems. Was Marr interested in building machines that see in order to model human behavior, or were biological models used only as a convenient source of inspiration? If a non-biological solution was found, would he and his followers have abandoned biological models in favor of the novel machine-based model? Even if the "biological solution" turns out to be the best solution for robot vision, there are many different ways in which the biological solution could be implemented. Should robots simulate biological vision to the neural level, for example? Should there be a one-to-one correspondence between neurons (or even smaller sub-systems or even molecules) in a particular robot and the particular biological system it is emulating? Or should there be correspondences between higher-level cognitive functions and robotic algorithms? Or between particular lower-level neural pathways and data flows? Whatever level is chosen, one thing is certain, we do not have enough understanding of the biological solution to carry out this kind of emulation. Also, there is never a single biological solution to any problem. Different species, by both convergent and divergent evolution, have arrived at myriad solutions to each aspect of the problem of extracting information from light. In using a biological system as a guide, which species should one choose for inspiration? The animal whose natural habitat most closely approximates the problem (e.g. bats or nocturnal animals for low-level vision)? Or humans, as a matter of principle?

If one can design a computational model of a particular biological process, even a complex one involving long range effects of neurotransmitters (for example), then a computational simulation of the model *can* be built although the model may be very slow when executed on a digital computer. But due to the difference between the underlying hardware in robots and the homologous biological anatomy, it seems unlikely that low-level biological solutions could ever be applied directly to robotic algorithms. Although concepts may be applicable, the biological engineering will not transfer as easily to robotic systems, and the underlying hardware may be so different as, in the end, to invalidate the applicability of biological results to robot vision. This problem can even emerge at higher levels. For example, there is considerable interest in the computational community in the construction of robotic stereo heads. As robots are limited only by the designers' imagination, material properties, and budget, many different solutions are possible. All of the head designs try to learn from the biological stereo vision, and to at least a limited extent try to model the biological solutions to varying levels of detail. For example, in one design (Jenkin et al., 1992) a large range of eye movements (including torsion) are modeled, but the eye movements are controlled by DC motors with optical shaft encoders. Are biological eye movement control strategies good models for these robot eye movements? Would it have been better to try and model the specific muscle groups in the eye? Until more is understood of biological systems, and more is understood about the limits of robotic vision hardware we must refrain from making definitive statements.

Conclusion

As the biological and computational communities continue to interact, it is important to recognize that there are inherent dangers in looking at results from a similar but different field. In the days of silk roads and sailing ships, European traders often sailed to the orient to obtain Chinese pottery and other artifacts which were highly prized at home. The first such items were truly Chinese in nature, as the Chinese artisans were selling goods which had been manufactured for "local" consumption. When the traders returned to Europe with the artifacts, local European artisans copied the patterns and styles of the Chinese pottery, introducing European themes into the scenes. Indeed the copies were often more highly prized than the originals as the detailing on the pieces contained European ideas, rendered in a Chinese-like style. The traders returned to China with the European copies, and had Chinese artisans make Chinese copies of European Copies of Chinese pottery. The results were highly prized in Europe (the Chinoiserie style), but had only a passing resemblance to the original work. The biological and computational communities run the danger of encountering a similar effect. Results published in the biological community are often used as models for computational processes. The computational machine models based on the biological models have then been cited as "solutions" to the biological problem, and then re-referenced in the biological community. The true limits of the original research can become lost in the transfer. By bringing the two communities together, through conferences, and books similar to this one, so that people are aware of the origins of the data and ideas they use, it should be possible to transfer results and concepts between the fields without encountering the Chinoiserie effect.

Spatial vision models:
problems and successes

Stanley A. Klein

1. Introduction

Computer vision has progressed slower than expected. Thus the existence of animal vision is comforting. At least we know that vision is not impossible. Human vision provides more than an existence proof since it is generally believed that insights from human vision are critical for progress in robot vision. A goal of this chapter is to point out aspects of human vision that may be of interest to workers in robotic vision. To that end, I will explore several classes of models of human suprathreshold visual discrimination. The models to be discussed are applicable to a wide range of tasks.

During the decade of the 70's a successful model of visual *detection* was developed, where detection means that the test pattern is presented on a *uniform* field. This model, to be called the "standard" model, will be described in Section 2. The standard model assumes that there are spatial filters at many positions and orientations and with many sizes. In the early days of the field there had been some confusion regarding the bandwidths of the underlying mechanisms because some data pointed to very narrow bandwidth (one quarter octave) mechanisms (Sachs et al., 1971) and other data pointed to medium bandwidth (one octave wide) mechanisms (Blakemore and Campbell, 1969). Stromeyer and Klein (1975) showed how medium bandwidth mechanisms with tuning functions similar to those found in cortical receptive fields could account for all the detection data as long as one allowed spatial probability summation. Norma Graham's excellent book (Graham, 1989) reviews all aspects of the "channel story" that are connected with detection (see Klein (1992) for an alternative, somewhat biased version). The review of Graham's book by Klein and Tyler (1992) points out that there are still a number of unanswered mysteries associated with detection. However, to a first approximation (accuracy up to factors of 2 or 3), the "channel" model proposed by Campbell and Robson (1968) does quite well. The story for suprathreshold discrimination is less clear, as will be discussed in the following sections.

Section 3 describes the bisection experiments of Klein and Levi (1985). The bisection thresholds are remarkably low and therefore provide a challenge to models of spatial vision. Two approaches for predicting these thresholds will be considered in Sections 4 and 5.

Section 4 presents the viewprint model of Klein and Levi (1985). It is of special interest for people interested in machine vision because it uses a very interesting representation of an image. It is a representation that throws away local phase information. The intent of this representation is to keep high quality information about relative position while degrading absolute position information. The discussion of the viewprint model is applicable to a wide class of filter models. The section ends with a discussion of the difficulties that confront filter models when applied to discrimination tasks. Work still needs to be done to learn how the local luminance distribution affects the mechanisms' gain control.

Section 4.1 goes back to the question of what is discrimination and introduces a model-free method that we call the Template Observer for calculating discrimination thresholds. Discrimination is similar to detection except that instead of presenting the test pattern on a uniform field it is presented on a suprathreshold pedestal. The Template Observer assumption is that as the pedestal strength is reduced the discrimination threshold gradually becomes equal to the detection threshold. The detection threshold of simple stimuli such as sinusoidal gratings or lines and edges can be taken as the raw input data specifying the sensitivity of the visual system. This model-free approach doesn't always work. The presence of the background can make a big difference in some tasks and very little difference in others. Texture discrimination, shape from shading, and face recognition can all be framed as discrimination tasks. It will be of interest to see which of these tasks can be predicted from the Template Observer approach.

Section 5 presents a Template Observer calculation of the very low bisection thresholds presented in Section 3. This model-free calculation is a striking success of the Template Observer approach.

In Section 6 the relative merits and deficiencies of different modeling approaches will be considered. I will argue that intermixing the approaches may be needed to obtain good predictions over a wide range of conditions.

2. The standard model

My first paper in vision (Stromeyer III and Klein, 1974) is one of my favorites. In it we did a calculation that set the stage for all my subsequent modeling. The experiment involved detection of a 9 c/deg test grating with four pedestals: a) a 9 c/deg pedestal, b) a 3 c/deg pedestal (the test is the third harmonic), c) a 1.8 c/deg pedestal (the test is the fifth harmonic) and d) no pedestal. We found that the 9 and 3 c/deg pedestals strongly *facilitated* the visibility of the test pattern over the no pedestal condition.

Nachmias and Sansbury (1974) found a similar facilitation when the pedestal and test had the same spatial frequency. The finding that a grating could facilitate the visibility of the third harmonic seemed inconsistent with the narrowly tuned channels that were in the air in the early 1970's. Stromeyer and Klein (1974) first had to argue that the presumed very narrow tuning was an artifact of spatial probability summation. Then we had to argue that medium bandwidth (1.5 octave full bandwidth) channels could do the facilitation. We showed that a mechanism with the medium bandwidth tuning demonstrated in adaptation studies (Blakemore and Campbell, 1969) did an excellent job of quantitatively predicting the magnitude of the first plus third harmonic facilitation and the lack of facilitation of a first plus fifth harmonic. The optimal mechanism that was able to achieve the facilitation was found to be a mechanism whose peak sensitivity was near the second harmonic. The lower tail of this mechanism was stimulated by the suprathreshold fundamental (1 octave below the peak) and the upper tail was sensitive to the test pattern (1/2 octave above the peak). The threshold nonlinearity that was demonstrated by the 9 on 9 c/deg facilitation was used to also produce the 9 on 3 c/deg facilitation. The same calculation showed that the medium bandwidth mechanisms were narrow enough that no interactions between a first and a fifth harmonic should be found, in agreement with the data.

The model used to calculate the discrimination threshold is the "standard model" mentioned earlier. It was the basis for subsequent spatial vision models (Wilson and Bergen, 1979; Wilson and Gelb, 1984; Klein and Levi, 1985). The model assumes a number of underlying filters at multiple positions and with multiple peak spatial frequencies. The important additional feature that the model had over earlier models is the presence of a threshold nonlinearity relating the output and input of the filters. The next step in the model is to search through all the filter outputs to find the mechanism with the greatest differential response. The differential response is the response to the test plus pedestal minus the response to just the pedestal. The search across space was easy in our first plus third harmonic stimulus because we were able to argue that the mechanisms located at the zero crossings of the pedestal would be most sensitive for our particular task. So the computer only had to do a one-dimensional search over mechanisms with different peak spatial frequencies.

This model is called a peak detection model since only the optimal mechanism contributes to the discrimination decision. Wilson's version of the standard model (Wilson and Bergen, 1979; Wilson and Gelb, 1984; Wilson, 1986) differs in two respects from the Stromeyer and Klein (1974) model. First, rather than assuming a continuum of mechanisms, Wilson's mechanisms are sparsely distributed in space and spatial frequency. They are separated by about an octave in spatial frequency and by about a quarter cycle in space. This sparse sampling has the advantage that calculations can be done more rapidly (a big deal a decade ago when personal computers were slow). Unfortunately, the sparse mechanism sampling has the disadvantage that it predicts a variety of cusps that are not compatible with the data (Wilson, 1986; Mayer and Kim, 1986). The second respect in which Wilson's version differs is that rather than looking at just the optimal mechanism he does a "line element" probability summation of the information contributed by all the mechanisms. As we argued (Stromeyer III and Klein, 1974; Stromeyer III and Klein, 1975) spatial probability summation is indeed needed to explain data when spatial beats are present. For most tasks, however, probability summation doesn't have a big effect on the results. Wilson has applied the standard model to a number of diverse discrimination tasks with fairly good success. I will, however, offer a critique (and a defense) of this model in Section 5. First, I would like to show how the standard model (with modifications) can explain the data that holds the Guinness record for best acuity.

3. The Guinness experiment

The main data to be discussed in this chapter comes from two bisection experiments done by Klein and Levi (1985). In the first experiment the stimulus was three bright lines on a computer monitor. A diagram of the stimulus is shown next to the "with overlap" legend in Figure 1. The observer's task was to indicate whether the central test line appeared above or below the midpoint of two outside reference lines. The angular separation between the test and reference lines is the independent variable. The solid triangles in Figure 1 show that when the separation is larger than 1.4 min, bisection thresholds are about 1/60 of the separation. For smaller separations the thresholds rise rapidly so that the best threshold is a displacement of 1.4 sec. In subsequent years we have come to realize that the bisection data shown by triangles in Figure 1, can not be explained by a unitary model. As will be shown in Figure 5 there are two regimes (Levi and Klein, 1990). Below separations of about 10 min is the filter regime, to be discussed in Section 4. At larger separations is the local sign regime, where thresholds are relatively independent of the characteristics of the lines such as their spatial frequency content (Levi and Klein, 1992b) or their contrast. The proportionality between threshold and separation in the local sign regime is explained by the increasing position uncertainty in peripheral vision. The data in Figure 1 represented by filled circles are for the case in which the test line does not overlap the pair of reference lines. For this nonoverlapping stimulus, filters are not able to operate effectively and so thresholds sharply increase in the filter regime.

In the second experiment, a pair of flanks was added 1.3 min outside the reference lines producing a 5-line bisection task. Thresholds decreased to .85 ± .04 sec (at 75% correct). This very small value was found consistently over about 10 runs. The angular threshold of .85 sec is remarkably small,

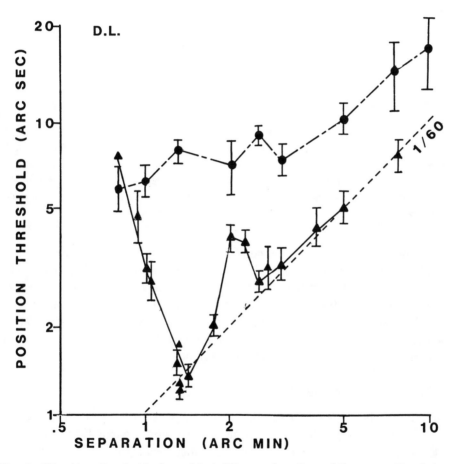

Fig. 1. *Bisection thresholds for subject DL as a function of the separation between the lines are shown by the filled triangles. The dashed line has a slope of 1, showing that threshold is a more-or-less constant fraction of the separation down to about 1.2 min. For still closer separations, thresholds increase rapidly. The filled circles show thresholds for bisection with the luminance cue removed by placing the test line adjacent to (see inset) the reference lines. At small separations this becomes a vernier task.*

SPACE

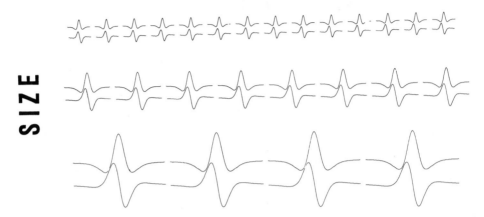

Fig. 2. *Schematic representation of the filter sampling for the viewprint calculation. Shown here are pairs of symmetric and antisymmetric receptive fields of different sizes and at different locations. In the standard models of discrimination only the symmetric mechanisms are usually considered. In the viewprint model, a Pythagorean sum is taken of the outputs of the pair of matched even and odd symmetric mechanisms to eliminate local phase information.*

corresponding to a linear distance of 1/4 inch at a distance of a mile, or to an eighth of the wavelength of yellow light when imaged on the retina. This bisection threshold presently holds the Guinness record for best position acuity (McFarlan, 1991). As a challenge for others to collect similar data, I will share my confidence that the record can be reduced to .6 sec without much trouble. I hope readers of this chapter will be inspired to run to the lab to try to claim the record for themselves.

4. The viewprint model

In modeling the bisection data described in Section 3, we decided to add one new ingredient to the standard model. To be more exact, we decided to subtract an ingredient, the local phase, which leads to a novel representation for spatial information. Since this representation will be of interest to researchers in computer vision we will first review the motivation for seeking a new image representation. The standard model looks at the output of a bank of filters such as shown in Figure 2. The filters can be assumed to be located at a continuum of positions and with a continuum of sizes. Figure 2 shows that at each position there is both a symmetric filter and an anti-symmetric filter. Many versions of the standard model only have symmetric filters (Wilson and Bergen, 1979; Wilson and Gelb, 1984; Malik and Perona, 1990; Bennett and Banks, 1991). There is a problem with representing the

Fig. 3. *This staff representation of music is presented as a vivid reminder of what is accomplished by the viewprint representation. In the case of music the abscissa is coarse time and the ordinate is coarse temporal frequency. A musician looking at this representation will be able to "hear" the sound of the music. This representation has lost the information about the absolute phase of each note. For the viewprint, time is replaced by space and temporal frequency is replaced by spatial frequency. Our hypothesis is that this representation of an image is less degraded by eye movements and by some uncertainty in the locations of the underlying mechanisms within a hypercolumn.*

image in terms of the output of symmetric mechanisms. The representation becomes too sensitive to the absolute position of the mechanism. A small uncertainty in position of the mechanism (e.g. due to an eye movement or simply due to a neural miscalibration) would drastically change the mechanism's expected output. Thus in the standard model the position of each mechanism must be known with great accuracy in order to make the filter outputs meaningful.

In order to develop a representation of the image that is less sensitive to the exact location of each mechanism we decided to look at a representation that is commonly used in audition, as shown in Figure 3. In the auditory version the horizontal axis is time with time increasing to the right and the vertical axis is temporal frequency with frequency increasing to the top. What is special about this representation is that local phase has been eliminated. Consider the sound represented by the upper-left most note in Figure 3. It is called an "E" note. Since it is a fifth above the standard "A" its frequency is 440 Hz $\times$ 3/2 = 660 Hz. This representation tells us the precise frequency of the waveform, corresponding to the distance between peaks of the wave, but it doesn't tell us anything about the phase of the wave. That is a good thing for the pianist, because if accurate phase had been needed the piano key would have had to be hit with a timing accuracy much better than a millisecond, well beyond human capability. A similar representation (a voiceprint) is used for analyzing human speech into formants and also for describing bird songs. We believe that this music representation is also useful for vision. When applied to vision we call this representation a "viewprint" because of its parallel to the voiceprint of audition.

Stromeyer and Klein (1975) first made use of this representation in order to show how probability summation would act differently on amplitude modulated and frequency modulated gratings. In order to produce a viewprint one must first assume a tuning function for the underlying mechanisms. Stromeyer and Klein assumed mechanisms with the spatial frequency tuning found by Blakemore and Campbell (1969) in adaptation studies. It is quite easy to produce a viewprint for a general tuning function when the stimulus is specified in the spatial frequency domain. See the Appendix of Stromeyer and Klein (1975) for details. The viewprint representation was used by Klein and Levi (1985) to account for the bisection data discussed in Section 3. In order to simplify the viewprint calculation for the spatial domain a new class of basis functions, called Cauchy functions, were introduced. The symmetric and antisymmetric Cauchy functions can be written as:

$$S_{n-1}(x) = \mathrm{Re}(1 + ix/\sigma)^{-n} = \cos^n(\theta)\cos(n\theta) \tag{1}$$

$$A_{n-1}(x) = -\mathrm{Im}(1 + ix/\sigma)^{-n} = \cos^n(\theta)\sin(n\theta) \tag{2}$$

with

$$\tan(\theta) = x/\sigma \tag{3}$$

where x is position, σ sets the scale or size of the mechanism and n sets the bandwidth or number of oscillations of the mechanism (the receptive field has about $.5\sqrt{n}$ cycles).

The Cauchy functions are special because the symmetric and antisymmetric functions are Hilbert pairs. That means that they have the same Fourier amplitude spectrum, which is given by:

$$C_n(f) = f^n \exp(-f\sigma) \tag{4}$$

The peak of the tuning function is at $f = n/\sigma$, its mean is at $f = (n+1)/\sigma$ and its variance is var $= (n+1)/\sigma^2$. One of the special attractions of the Cauchy functions is that because of the Cauchy contour integration theorem, it is easy to find analytic expression for the convolution of a Cauchy function with many standard functions.

The functions $S_2(x)$ and $A_2(x)$ corresponding to $n = 3$ are shown in Figure 2. These are broad bandwidth mechanisms with full bandwidths of about 2 octaves. Klein and Levi (1985) used the $n = 3$ and $n = 5$ Cauchy functions for predicting the bisection data.

When designing a filter model one must decide on the shape of the filter. One might decide to use filters with pretty orthogonality properties such as the wavelet basis functions. One might decide to use filters that have a pretty analytic structure in both space and spatial frequency such as the Cauchy functions. Or for good reasons one might want to use Hermite functions that Gabor (1946) thought minimized the joint space-spatial frequency uncertainty. Beware of the Hermites! Klein and Beutter (1992) showed that for the class of functions produced by an nth order polynomial times a Gaussian, the nth order Hermite function *maximized* rather than minimized the joint space-spatial frequency uncertainty.

In order to calculate a viewprint of an image, for each size, σ, one convolves the image with $S_n(x)$ and $A_n(x)$. For the bisection stimulus this convolution consists of a sum of three terms, one for each line of the stimulus.

$$S(x_m, \sigma) = S_n(x_1 - x_m) + S_n(x_2 - x_m) + S_n(x_3 - x_m) \tag{5}$$

$$A(x_m, \sigma) = A_n(x_1 - x_m) + A_n(x_2 - x_m) + A_n(x_3 - x_m) \tag{6}$$

where x_m is the location of the center of the mechanism and x_i are the locations of the three lines of the bisection stimulus. We are using the notation $S(x_m, \sigma)$ as the amount of stimulation of a symmetric mechanism centered at x_m and with a size σ.

So far everything is as it would have been in the standard model. Now comes the new step that eliminates the local phase. Phase is eliminated by simply taking the Pythagorean sum of the responses of the symmetric and the antisymmetric Cauchy functions.

$$P(x_m, \sigma) = \left[S(x_m, \sigma)^2 + A(x_m, \sigma)^2 \right]^{1/2} \tag{7}$$

In order to connect the filter output to psychophysical thresholds, the filter sensitivity must be normalized according to the contrast sensitivity function and one must introduce the nonlinear transducer function that produces facilitation at low contrasts (discussed in Section 2) and saturation at high contrasts. The intent of these nonlinearities is to convert the output of Eq. 7 into a measure of the signal to noise of the visual system, d'. Klein and Levi (1985) show that if the filters are normalized by the contrast sensitivity function, the signal to noise ratio of a mechanism is given by:

$$d' = 2.5\ln[1 + .5P(x_m, \sigma)^2] \tag{8}$$

Figure 4 shows what the viewprint of a three-line bisection stimulus looks like. The stimulus is three lines separated by 4 min. In the lower panel the middle line is given an offset of .08 min corresponding to a Weber fraction of 1/50. This value is chosen because it corresponds to the threshold for seeing the offset, as shown in Figure 1.In the upper panel the offset of the middle line is half-threshold (.04 min). The curved lines labelled 1, 6, 10, 14, and 18

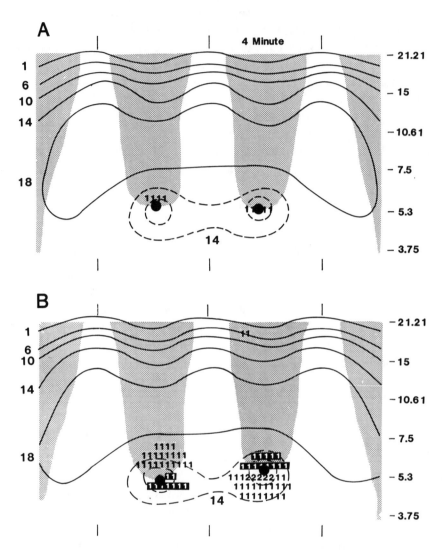

Fig. 4. *Viewprints for the three-line bisection stimulus using third order Cauchy functions as the underlying mechanisms. The interline separation was 4.0 arc min. The two panels correspond to two offsets of the test line. Lower panel: Threshold offset (0.08 min, corresponding to a 1/50 Weber fraction). Upper panel: A half-threshold (0.04 min) offset. The shading represents one bit of absolute phase (the sign bit). The contour lines are the iso-d' lines of the contrast-response function as indicated by the numbers by the lines. The clusters of slightly smaller numbers are the differential response and indicate the discriminability of the offset. Negative differential-response values are indicated by the reversed contrast numbers.*

are iso-d' contours. Thus a value of 10 means that that particular mechanism is 10 jnds (just noticeable differences) above threshold. The dotted contour lines are circling a region of the viewprint near a depression. The number 14 at the bottom of each plot indicates that the associated dotted contour line is at a level of $d' = 14$.

The two solid dots may be the most important features of the viewprint. They are a pair of null points. A null point corresponds to a mechanism whose spatial position, x_m, and size, σ, are such that neither the symmetric nor the antisymmetric mechanisms are stimulated. For a two-line stimulus the null point has a location, x_m, that is halfway between the two lines, so that the antisymmetric mechanism doesn't contribute. The size of the mechanism is determined by the condition that the stimulus lines fall on the zero crossings of the symmetric mechanism. The location of the zero crossing is given by Eq. 1:

$$\cos(n\theta) = 0 \qquad (9)$$

which implies

$$\theta = \pi/2n \qquad (10)$$

The angle θ is given by

$$\theta = x/\sigma = sep/2\sigma \qquad (11)$$

since the location of each line is a distance $sep/2$ from the center of the mechanism, where sep is the separation between the pair of stimulus lines. Combining Eqs. 10 and 11 shows that the mechanism size corresponding to the null point is:

$$\sigma = sep/(2\tan(\pi/2n)) \qquad (12)$$

For $n = 3$, $\sigma = sep\sqrt{3}/2 = .866sep$. For the three-line stimulus the location of the null points is close to where they would be for the two-line case.

The reason that the null points are so important is that they are the main features that significantly change when the middle line is shifted by a threshold amount. Notice that in the upper panel of Figure 4 the two null points are at about the same height (same σ). In the lower panel, the two null points are at visibly different values of σ. Other aspects of the viewprint are less sensitive to the shift of the test line. This shift in the vertical height of the nullpoints leads to a visible differential response of the mechanisms that are used to detect the offset.

The numbers printed near the null points are the differential responses in d' units. The differential response is simply the difference between the d' value of each mechanism after the middle line is given its offset and the d' value before the offset (when the middle line is exactly at the bisection point). A value of 1 means that that mechanism has a unity signal to noise ratio ($\Delta d' = 1$). The reversed contrast values in Figure 4 indicate that the mechanism activity with the displacement is less than the activity with no

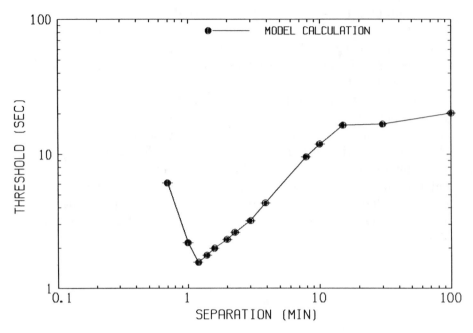

Fig. 5. *Viewprint predictions for a three-line bisection task. For separations less than 10 min, in the "filter" regime, the data agree remarkably well with the bisection data shown in Figure 1. For separations greater than 10 min the data are flat because a local sign cue, comparing the positions of each separate line as with a ruler, is most sensitive. The one place that the data and model diverge in the filter regime is at separations of about 2 min where the viewprint model fails to predict the sharp threshold elevation cusp that is seen in the data.*

displacement. If one would enlarge the region close to the null point one would find mechanisms whose differential response is larger than $\Delta d' = 2$. This is because the slope of the viewprint activity becomes extremely steep. Thus we have the unexpected problem that rather than having difficulty in predicting the very small bisection offsets, the model predicts offsets that are even smaller than what the human can see. Klein and Levi (1985) introduced a .5 min "final" blur to smooth out the null point. This final blur is a free parameter that can change the magnitude of the predicted threshold. Thresholds predicted by the viewprint model are shown in Figure 5. These predictions were originally shown by Klein and Levi (1987). For separations of less than 10 min the agreement with the data of Figure 1 is excellent (but remember that there was a free parameter that controls the final blurring). For separations greater than 10 min the viewprint predicts a constant threshold since thresholds are based on measuring the positions of each line separately. This is the local sign regime where as discussed by Klein and Levi (1987) and Levi and Klein (1990, 1992b) thresholds are degraded because of poorer spatial localization in peripheral vision. It would be nice to develop an approach for predicting the bisection threshold that is less sensitive to the many assumptions connected with the viewprint model. That is the topic of the next section.

A most serious question for computer vision is whether the viewprint representation can be inverted to reconstruct the original image. From what we have said so far the answer is clearly, NO! The process of taking the Pythagorean sum erased all the local phase information, so that it is not possible to tell whether a three line stimulus consists of light lines or dark lines. In order to recapture some of the phase information, we appended to the viewprint one bit of phase information. This phase information is indicated by the shading that is seen in Figure 4. The unshaded regions indicate the locations where the symmetric mechanisms receive positive stimulation. The shaded regions correspond to negative stimulation. Thus the viewprint representation is really a dual representation. The one bit of phase information is treated much the same as the color of the stimulus. There are clearly many tasks that depend on knowing the "color" or local phase. However, the "color" information might be coarser than the intensity information, in both spatial resolution and in intensity resolution. It is quite possible that the finest spatial discriminations, such as needed for the bisection task, are based on the Pythagorean sum where the local phase is eliminated. The advantage of using the Pythagorean sum is that it has greater spatial smoothness than does a representation that maintains local phase. Thus it is less degraded by eye movements and other factors contributing to spatial uncertainty, such as any uncertainty in the location of the mechanism.

I will end this section on filter models by pointing out some problems. The main trouble with filter models is that too many assumptions are needed. The typical filter model (Wilson, 1986) determines the sensitivity and nonlinearities of the mechanisms by using masking data involving small patches of sinusoids. One then assumes that these same mechanism properties are still valid when applied to a very different stimulus, such as three-line bisection on a dark background. There are so many ingredients that go into a model: the mechanism bandwidth, sensitivity, spatial sampling, spatial frequency sampling, nonlinearities, phase sampling, position uncertainty, orientation tuning, aspect ratio (length to width), type of probability summation. With so many ingredients it is difficult to know which aspects of the model are critical and which are irrelevant.

A second problem with present filter models, as stated earlier, is the lack of a good understanding of luminance gain control. This problem directly affects the viewprint prediction of the three-line and five-line bisection data. One needs to know the sensitivity of the mechanisms near the middle line. We showed (Klein and Levi, 1985) that bisection thresholds are not strongly affected by the line luminance. Further research on the spatial properties of the luminance gain control is needed.

4.1. The template observer

In this section we show how Geisler's photon based, "stimulus known exactly" Ideal Observer Model (1984, 1985, 1989) can be transformed to a contrast based model that has greater applicability to photopic vision. It works as follows. Suppose the observer's task is to discriminate between patterns A and B. Let $M_i(1 + E_{Ai})$ and $M_i(1 + E_{Bi})$ be the expected quantum catches in the ith cone for the two patterns, where M_i is the quantum catch due to the mean luminance background and E_{Ai} and E_{Bi} are fractional deviations from background. We have separated out the "mean luminance" M_i from the "contrast" $E_A i$ in order to develop an ideal observer model that only depends on contrast. In this "stimulus known exactly" case the ideal observer calculates the log of the likelihood ratio, which, from binomial statistics is simply given by

$$\text{LogLik} = \sum_i O_i \ln((1 + E_{Ai})/(1 + E_{Bi})) \tag{13}$$

where O_i is the observed number of photons absorbed in the ith cone and the summation is over all the cones. If the likelihood ratio exceeds a criterion level then one chooses pattern A. Geisler and Davila (1985) pointed out that for reasonably low contrasts, $E_i \ll 1$, the log likelihood becomes: $\text{LogLik} \approx \sum_i O_i(E_{Ai} - E_{Bi})$. This is a template match between the observed quantum catch and the expected catch of the *difference* in patterns to be discriminated. We will call this decision rule "The Template Observer". If one calls pattern E_{Bi} the "pedestal" pattern, then E_{Ai} becomes the "test plus pedestal" where the test pattern, the template, is $E_{Ti} = E_{Ai} - E_{Bi}$, and therefore:

$$\text{LogLik} \approx \sum_i O_i E_{Ti} \tag{14}$$

This equation is remarkably simple. It says that the most efficient way to detect a pattern is to overlap the stimulus with a matched template whose profile has the shape of the pattern to be detected. In this section we show how this matched filter approach can be used for predicting vernier acuity. In the next section the method is applied to the three-line bisection task discussed in Sections 3 and 4. As will be seen, this simple idea goes a long way towards explaining many features of spatial vision.

Geisler tested the ideal observer prediction with experiments on 2-dot contrast discrimination, 2-dot resolution and 2-dot separation discrimination. For all three tasks the human observer had an efficiency of between 10% and 20% of the ideal. That is, in order to make the discriminations the human needed to absorb about 5 to 10 times the number of photons than did the ideal observer. Averaged over three observers the efficiency for resolution and separation was 11% and 12% respectively. This result is exciting since it implies that hyperacuity is not "better" than resolution acuity. They are the same when measured with the proper metric! However, the ideal observer's predictions being about 3 times too small (square root of efficiency) implies that the noise limiting performance comes mainly from sources other than photon statistics. Thus one can not take the ideal observer predictions too seriously. One of the goals of my research in the last few years is to show how a modified ideal observer approach (based on the Template Observer) can be applied to the high luminance regime where factors due to photon noise can be replaced with the contrast based factors actually limiting performance.

Many experiments in spatial vision can be understood in terms of the Template Observer framework defined above (in our earlier publications we called it the "test-pedestal" framework). Theories similar to the Template Observer have been proposed before for vernier acuity. Watt's orthoaxial mechanism (Watt et al., 1983; Watt, 1984) calculates the amount of "error energy" produced by the vernier offset. Morgan and Aiba (1986) developed a theory to assess the "cone" activation produced by the offset. However, these researchers did not have a reliable way to calculate the absolute thresholds. Our new element is that we advocate *measuring* the visibility of the template in a detection task. This and the next section show how hyperacuity thresholds can be predicted from the individual's sensitivity to contrast.

Consider vernier acuity of an edge or a line. The edge offset is produced by adding a thin line to one half of the edge pedestal as shown in the top panel of Figure 6. The line offset is produced by adding a thin dipole to one half of the line pedestal as shown in the bottom panel. A dipole is a pair of equal strength, opposite polarity abutting lines. Klein, Casson and Carney (1990) proposed the shockingly simple idea that vernier thresholds could be understood in terms of the visibility of the test line (for edge vernier acuity) or the test dipole (for line vernier). Since the suprathreshold pedestal masks the test this prediction is not expected to hold at high pedestal contrasts. However, for low contrast pedestals, the masking should be reduced, so our hypothesis was that low contrast vernier acuity should be predicted by the detection threshold of a thin line or dipole. As shown by the data in Figure 7 for the case of line vernier acuity for two observers this hypothesis was correct! In the left panel the threshold units are minutes and in the right panel the data are replotted with thresholds in dipole strength units of %min^2 (see Klein, 1989 for details on multipole units). The dipole strength is given by the strength of the pedestal line (in units of %min, which is the % contrast of the line times its width in min) times the vernier offset (in min). Thus, the ordinate of Figure 7b is obtained by multiplying the ordinate of Figure 7a by the abscissa. The advantage of replotting the data as in Figure 7b is that the dipole detection thresholds can be directly plotted on the same graph as shown by the leftmost points connected by a dotted line. This new way of plotting the vernier data can be called a tvi curve (threshold vs. intensity). One might quibble about whether it should be

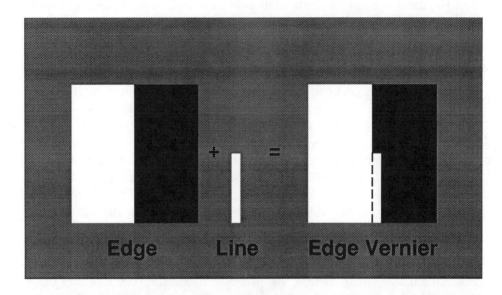

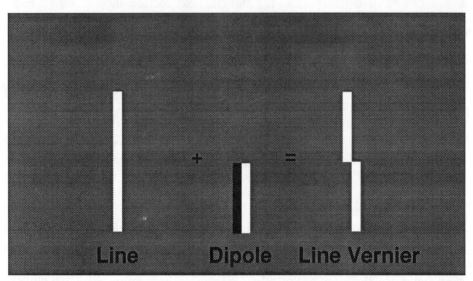

Fig. 6. *Illustration of how the Template Observer accounts for vernier acuity. The vernier offset of an edge is produced by adding a line to one half of the edge. Vernier offset of a line is produced by adding a dipole to one half of the line. When the line in (a) has the same contrast as the edge the edge will be shifted by the thickness of the line. Similarly for the dipole on a line pedestal in (b). If the test pattern had lower contrast then the centroid of the pedestal would shift by a smaller amount.*

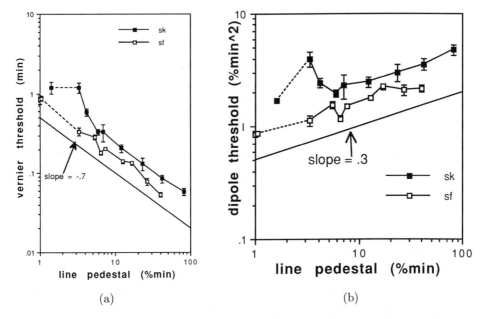

(a)   (b)

Fig. 7. *Panel (a) shows the vernier thresholds (in min) for a line for two observers as a function of line strength. Line strength has units of %min which is the % contrast of the line times its thickness in min. The solid line with a slope of −0.7 matches the slope of the data. The vertical location of the line has been shifted for ease of viewing. The error bars are 1 SE. Panel (b) shows the same data replotted using the same abscissa and with the vertical axis being the strength of the test dipole in units of %min² rather than vernier offset. This ordinate is the ordinate of panel (a) times the abscissa. The slope of the line is +0.3 since the slope is that of panel (a) plus one. The left-most data, connected by dotted lines, are the detection thresholds of a dipole on a uniform field background (zero pedestal strength). The ordinate for vernier acuity at low pedestal strength is close to the detection thresholds. The detection thresholds are also plotted in panel (a) by dividing the ordinate by the abscissa of panel (b). The resulting value corresponds to Ricco's diameter for detecting a dipole. These results provide a model-free prediction of vernier acuity of a line.*

called tvp (threshold vs. pedestal strength) rather than tvi, but tvi has a nice ring to it.

As discussed by Klein, Casson and Carney (1990) the dipole detection threshold can also be plotted on the left panel by dividing the dipole threshold (in %min²) by the line detection threshold (in %min) which is the abscissa value at which the detection datum is plotted. This quotient of the dipole and line detection thresholds are the counterparts of Ricco's summation area for dipole detection (see Klein et al., (1990) for details).

Figure 7b shows that when the dipole thresholds in the vernier task are extrapolated to the line detection threshold, the predicted detection threshold is in good agreement with the data. For observer SK Figure 7b shows that at the lowest two pedestal contrasts (below three times the line detection threshold) the vernier thresholds are elevated. This is not surprising since the target is barely visible. Geisler and Davila (1985) find that the ideal observer prediction of a two-dot hyperacuity task shows a similar degradation when the pedestal strength is close to its detection threshold and when the background luminance is not zero.

What have we accomplished so far? Sometimes when I look at Figure 7b I am impressed that an important result is shown. It looks like a model-free prediction of vernier acuity. No assumptions were needed about the linear and nonlinear properties of the underlying mechanisms. The only thing not explained is the shallow slope of the tvi curve whereby thresholds increase with masking contrast. However, sometimes when I look at Figure 7 it looks trivial. I say to myself, how could it be any other way. If the early stage of vision involves a linear filter then of course the visibility of the test pattern will not be masked at low pedestal contrasts. It seems like a tautology without content since Figure 7 shows that "of course" line vernier acuity must be based on the visibility of the dipole. However, in peripheral vision and for strabismic (but not anisometropic) amblyopes, vernier thresholds are 2–3 times worse than what the Template Observer would predict (Levi and Klein, 1992b). Thus, the extra 2–3 fold loss in peripheral vernier acuity shown in Figure 7b can not be explained by retinal factors such as poor quantum catch and early saturation of the peripheral cones since *all retinal factors are balanced* in our Template Observer (low contrast) approach. Levi, Klein and Aitsebaomo (1985) proposed that there might be a number of extra factors that are likely to be of cortical origin that account for the extra degradation found in peripheral vision and in strabismic amblyopes. We hypothesized that in peripheral vision undersampling or neural scrambling will affect a position task such as vernier acuity but have minimal effect on a detection task.

As was stated in the preceding paragraph one missing ingredient is an explanation of the tvi slope whereby a high contrast line pedestal masks the dipole detection. In order to account for the tvi slope, in a separate experiment we measured dipole contrast discrimination (Carney and Klein, 1989). The observer's task is to measure the visibility of a dipole test pattern, just as before, except now the masking pedestal is a suprathreshold dipole rather than a suprathreshold line. The data differ in two ways from that shown in Figure 7b. First, the tvi slope of the contrast discrimination is steeper than the vernier data, .6 vs. .3. Slopes of about .6 are commonly found in contrast discrimination studies (Legge and Foley, 1980). Second, when the abscissa is transformed to contrast threshold units (to be able to compare the line and dipole pedestals) the dipole detection thresholds are lower in the contrast discrimination task. This is not surprising since a pedestal facilitation effect is found in contrast discrimination but not in vernier acuity.

A detailed spatial vision model is needed to account for these discrepancies. I think it is clear why the tvi slope should be shallower for the vernier task. In a model with orientation tuned mechanisms, as the pedestal contrast increases the optimal mechanism for detecting the vernier offset changes. At higher contrasts one could use a mechanism tilted at a larger angle to avoid the masking. The consequence is that the masking effect would be smaller than if the same mechanism had been used at all contrasts. Exactly the same effect was found by Stromeyer and Klein (1974) in the task of detecting a 9 c/deg grating in the presence of a 3 c/deg pedestal as compared to a 9 c/deg pedestal, as a function of pedestal contrast.

Recently, we have applied the Template Observer to vernier acuity and contrast discrimination (jnd) of sinusoidal gratings (Hu et al., 1992). In the jnd stimulus the sinusoidal test grating was added in-phase to half of the pedestal whereas in the vernier stimulus the same test grating was added with a 90 deg phase shift to the pedestal (the phase was actually slightly greater than 90 deg in order to keep the contrast constant). Our use of sinusoids has an advantage over multipoles (edges, lines and dipoles) since both the test and pedestal have the same spatial frequency content for both the vernier task and the jnd task. This will simplify any future filter modeling.

Some of the results using sinusoids are shown in Figure 8: a) At low contrasts and for a mid-range of spatial frequencies (5–10 c/deg) the vernier and jnd thresholds are about equal. b) Vernier thresholds rise slower with increasing pedestal contrast than jnd thresholds (power exponents of .4 vs. .6). c) Vernier thresholds degrade with increasing spatial frequency whereas jnd thresholds are relatively unaffected. The Template Observer accounts for the success of the first-order effect of point a). The different tvi slopes of point b) are not bothersome because oriented mechanisms are able to avoid some of the masking at high contrasts and the facilitation at low contrasts as discussed earlier. What is somewhat bothersome is the sharp degradation of vernier thresholds at high spatial frequencies. In order to better understand this loss, further experiments were done varying the length of the gratings and the gap between the two halves. It was surprisingly found that at high spatial frequencies vernier thresholds were reduced when the grating length was shortened (holding the number of cycles constant). A small gap of about 2 min was used. Under these conditions the jnd thresholds were elevated. For short gratings as the gap increased the jnd thresholds were reduced but the vernier thresholds were elevated. The point of these results is that we found that one should compare the jnd and vernier data each under their optimal conditions. When this was done, the differences in spatial frequency tuning of the vernier and jnd configurations was much reduced. The Template Observer is not the final word, it is only the beginning. The Template Observer is used to predict discrimination thresholds under optimal conditions. It is clear that thresholds can be degraded by many

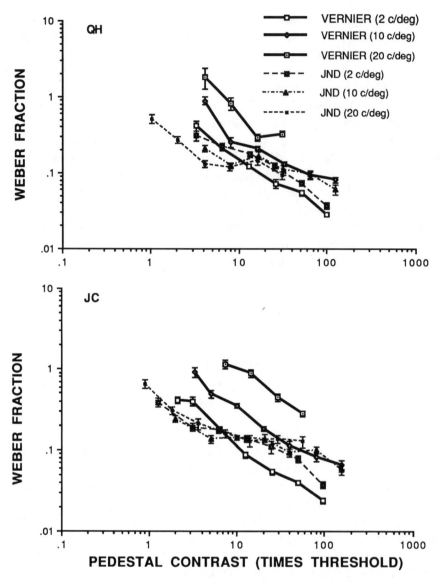

Fig. 8. *Data comparing vernier acuity and contrast discrimination (jnd) of sinusoidal gratings for two observers. Both thresholds are measured in contrast units. For the vernier task the shift of one half of the grating is thought of as being produced by adding a low contrast test grating with a 90 deg phase shift. The data show that to first order, vernier acuity is well predicted by contrast jnd. There are small differences in the dependence of the vernier and jnd data on pedestal contrast and on spatial frequency. The difference in spatial frequency dependence is lessened if an optimal stimulus length and optimal gap is used. The difference in contrast dependence can be understood if the vernier data is modeled using orientation tuned mechanisms that do not have full overlap with the pedestal grating.*

stimulus manipulations. For example, separating the features in a vernier task will sharply degrade vernier thresholds without affecting detection or jnd thresholds. Insight about the underlying mechanisms and their interactions is gained by looking at departures of the data from what is expected of the Template Observer.

5. Applying the template observer to the Guinness data

In order to develop one's intuition about how the Template Observer works it is instructive to apply the formalism to make a "model-free" calculation of the bisection data discussed in Section 3. This section will be the first time that this calculation has been published.

The stimulus that gave the best thresholds had 5 lines that were almost equally spaced. The task was to detect a shift of the middle line. As seen in Figure 6b a shift of a thin line is equivalent to adding a dipole to the line. The Template Observer model would say that under optimal conditions, the bisection threshold is equal to the dipole detection threshold. The dipole detection threshold is based on the visibility of a dipole on a uniform field. For our stimulus a uniform field corresponds to the case when the 5 lines are so close together that they become blurred, thus producing a uniform field. We will discuss later what happens when the separation between lines increases.

A dipole consists of a pair of opposite polarity, closely spaced thin lines. The strength of a dipole is equal to the strength of one of the constituent lines times the distance between the pair of lines. The strength of the line, in turn, equals the thickness of the line times its contrast. For the present case of closely spaced thin lines, the thickness of a line equals the line spacing and the contrast equals 100%. This method for calculating line strength can be justified by blurring each line so that the grating of thin lines becomes a uniform field. As discussed by Klein (1989) a blurring operation does not change the strength of a multipole (including a line). In that case the thickness of each line equals the line separation. The contrast produced by shifting the line can now be calculated as $c = \Delta L/L = -L/L = -100\%$.

We are now ready to proceed with the calculation. Suppose the line spacing in the bisection stimulus is s min, so the line strength is $100s$ %min, and suppose the bisection threshold is δ. The dipole strength, D, is then given by:

$$D = s\delta 100\%\text{min}^2. \tag{15}$$

The leftmost datum in Figure 6b shows each observer's dipole detection threshold. For one observer the threshold is slightly less than 1 %min^2 and for the other observer it is about 1.7 %min^2. The average gives a threshold of about $D = 1.3$ %min^2. Eq. 15 can be used to get an expression for the bisection threshold in terms of the line spacing:

$$\delta = D/100\%s = .013/s. \tag{16}$$

For a separation of 1.3 min which produced the best bisection thresholds (Klein and Levi, 1985) Eq. 16 leads to a predicted threshold of:

$$\delta = .013/1.3 = .01 \text{ min } = .6 \text{ sec} \tag{17}$$

This predicted value of .6 sec is very close to the experimental result of about 1.3 sec at $d' = 1$ (84% correct) or d=.85 sec at $d' = .68$ (75% correct). In more recent experiments (Carney and Klein, 1989) we have found bisection thresholds as low as .85 min ($d' = 1$). These experimental values are slightly higher than the Template Observer prediction. This may not be surprising since in actuality the stimulus was not a uniform field, but rather it was a very narrow stimulus field consisting of only 5 lines. Thus the edges of the stimulus could have masking effects. Also the background wasn't a uniform luminance. At a separation of 1.3 min there was a clear gap between lines. This could easily cause some elevation of threshold.

As seen in Eq. 16 if the separation between lines is halved, the bisection threshold should be doubled. Figure 1 shows that the bisection thresholds actually degrade faster than is predicted by Eq. 16. This extra degradation is undoubtedly due to the very small extent of the stimulus. When the line separation is 1 min the two reference lines are only 2 min apart. This is too small to provide the uniform background that is needed for optimal visibility of the dipole. The introduction of the two extra flanking lines in the 5 line bisection stimulus provided enough of a uniform field to allow thresholds close to that predicted by Eq. 17.

I consider the agreement of this crude calculation with the actual data to be most amazing. I would be very surprised if any filter model could come as close. As discussed in Section 4, the viewprint calculation involved a number of assumptions such as the mechanism bandwidth and a final blurring stage. Wilson (1986) also needed an assumption about the effective contrast of the stimulus to obtain the proper vertical scaling of the predicted bisection threshold. The calculation done in this section did not need any assumptions at all!

6. A comparison of three approaches

This last section compares three approaches for modeling spatial vision: 1) the "general framework" approach for texture discrimination, 2) the "multiparameter" detailed modeling approach, and 3) the model-free Template Observer approach discussed in Sections 4.1 and 5.

6.1. General framework, coarse models

The general framework approaches for texture discrimination of Malik and Perona (1990) and of Klein and Tyler (1986) will be discussed here. Malik and Perona (1990) seek to explain the data of the sort that Julesz used for developing his higher order statistics and later his texton model (Julesz, 1981). The model that they use is quite similar to the standard model discussed in Section 2. They assume symmetric filters of multiple sizes, orientations and positions. Since they are applying the filters to suprathreshold stimuli rather than to detection tasks they added some contrast gain control to the model in order to normalize the filter outputs. Their model is able to robustly predict the relative difficulty of texture discriminations for a wide range of different textures.

Klein and Tyler (1986) seek to predict texture discrimination of repetitive textures. Their formalism based on higher order correlation functions is an outgrowth of the Julesz "statistics" approach (Julesz, 1962). The goal of this approach is to classify the different types of phase discrimination. The model produces an ordering of which stimuli should produce easier phase discriminations.

In these "general framework" models no attempt is made to carefully measure the sensitivity or the tuning of the underlying mechanisms since the absolute magnitude of the discriminations are not predicted. Only the relative discriminability of different patterns are predicted. These models do not have sufficient structure to predict details such as the cusp shown in the bisection data of Figure 1 for separations of 2 min. The advantage of coarse "general framework" models is that they focus attention on what aspects of the model are essential and what are irrelevant. Thus for the texture discriminations considered by Malik and Perona the detailed assumptions going into the Wilson model are not relevant.

6.2. Multiparameter "exact" modeling

The filter models of Wilson and co-workers (Wilson and Bergen, 1979; Wilson and Gelb, 1984; Wilson, 1986; Wilson, 1991a) and of Klein and Levi (1985) have a quite different goal than the coarse models described in the preceding paragraphs. The goal here is to make precise predictions of the data. Wilson's multiparameter models are often misunderstood. It is thought by some that with so many parameters one could fit anything. That is unfair to Wilson. He actually has amazingly few free parameters. The shapes and sensitivities of his underlying filters are fixed by masking studies that were done years ago. Often one or two new parameters are needed for each different data set. For example, in amblyopic vision (Wilson, 1991a) some parameters are needed to characterize extra spatial losses that would not have shown up in the masking studies that set the filter characteristics. The hope is that these one or two extra parameters would be able to fit dozens of data points under a variety of different conditions.

If the structure of the underlying model is correct then the rich structure of the data should be able to be captured without detailed curve fitting. For example, let us consider the bisection data shown in Figure 1. Notice the dramatic cusp that appears at a separation of 2 min. As discussed in our article (Klein and Levi, 1985) this cusp has been replicated in independent experiments. A good filter model should produce the cusp naturally without needing a delicate cancellation of term. As seen in Figure 5 the simple viewprint model fails in this regard. Wilson's model is able to produce a cusp (Wilson, 1986) however, it produces too many cusps. The Wilson model cusps are produced by sparse sampling in space and spatial frequency.

It is easy to criticize a detailed model such as Wilson's. For example, the limited number of spatial frequency channels has been questioned by the smooth spatial frequency discrimination data of Mayer and Kim (1986). However, one must remember that it is exactly because detailed models are easy to criticize that they are valuable. Detailed models make very detailed predictions. Much can be learned from accurate predictions. Remember that Newton's theory of gravity is accurate to many, many decimal places. Extremely accurate measurements are needed to show that Newton's predictions are wrong and that Einstein's are correct. Coarse models such as those of Malik and Perona (1990) or Klein and Tyler (1986) might provide an excellent general structures for modeling, but since they don't make accurate predictions they may be hard to disprove. The subtle nuances of the data, such as the bisection cusp at 2 min separations, provide insight into the inner workings of the visual system. Detailed quantitative are needed to capture these details.

7. Template observer

The job of the Template Observer model discussed in Section 4.1 and 5 is to determine the overall sensitivity of discrimination tasks. This is exactly what filter models do poorly. It is difficult for filter models to predict the same hyperacuity thresholds for a wide variety of stimuli (Westheimer and McKee, 1977). In order to get the overall sensitivity correct, filter models typically must adjust one of the parameters of the model. Thus the Template Observer model is complementary to the models based on underlying mechanisms discussed previously. It is likely that successful predictions of discrimination tasks will require a combination of these approaches.

Acknowledgements

This research was supported by an Air Force Office of Sponsored Research grant AFOSR 89-0238. I thank Charles Stromeyer, Dennis Levi and Thom Carney for their collaborations over the past 20 years that made my research possible.

On cytochrome oxidase blobs in visual cortex

John Allman

Steven W. Zucker

How are the internal properties of objects in the visual world, e.g., color, contrast, and surface texture, represented? The physiological evidence suggests a separate system, starting in the visual cortex and based around so-called cytochrome oxidase blobs, which are collections of cells with higher metabolic activity than their neighbors. While the properties of these cells differ substantially from those involved in border detection, the current interpretation is that they are primarily involved in color processing. We question that interpretation, and propose an alternative, more encompassing hypothesis based both on what kind of information is represented in the blobs, and on how it is represented.

1. Introduction: functional specialization in cortex

The dominant abstraction in early vision is called functional specialization; to quote S. Zeki:

> "Detailed physiological recording from the different visual areas of the prestri-ate cortex have shown that each is specialized to process a different attribute of the visual scene, such as form, color, and motion, a finding which has led to the theory of functional specialization in the visual cortex."[1]

A similar position has been advocated by Livingstone and Hubel, (1984, 1987), and many others.

This separation of form and color has become almost dogmatic. It is based on a mixture of anatomical, cytochemical, and physiological evidence (summarized in Zeki, 1990), and it suggests why there are so many different visual areas in primate cortex: each supports a different, intuitively plausible function: V4 is the color area, MT the motion area, etc. Given his role in naming V4 the color area, I shall refer to this specific hypothesis as the Zeki-hypothesis.

---

[1] Zeki, 1990, p. 29.

Two questions arise. First, what organizational principles underlie the Zeki-hypothesis? Second, with function parceled according to it, the distinct anatomical connections that support it must be specified. Now, much of the input flows through the striate cortex, V1, so the task of separating data for each functional stream arises. In a serendipitous discovery, Margaret Wong-Riley (1979) discovered just such a candidate streaming system in striate cortex.

2. Cytochrome oxidase blobs

Arguing that highly active neurons will have high metabolic energy requirements, and hence will contain larger quantities of the enzyme cytochrome oxidase, Wong-Riley (1979) stained a section of the visual cortex for it. The result was a patchy distribution of cells, visually resembling "puffs", or "blobs" (Horton and Hubel, 1981; Horton, 1984). These blobs delimit neurons capable of sustaining higher metabolic levels of activity than the surrounding "interblob" neurons, and they exhibit different receptive field organizations. In particular, the blobs contain cells with circular-surround, opponent color receptive fields, while the interblob system contains orientationally-selective cells with little color selectivity. It was subsequently discovered by staining V2 for cytochrome oxidase that it, too, is differentially organized, with a "thin stripe", "thick stripe", and "interstripe" pattern. And most importantly for the Zeki-hypothesis, it was determined anatomically that the blob cells in V1 project to the "thin stripes" in V2 and then to V4. Zeki, Hubel and Livingstone, and many others, thus believed that they had found the anatomy in support of the "color system" hypothesis: blobs to thin stripes to V4. The interblob system handled form on the basis of contrast differences. The organizational principle was the explicit separation of color from contrast information. Thus, both questions posed above have proposed answers.

3. Concerns about the Zeki-hypothesis

Despite the attractive simplicity of the Zeki-hypothesis, there exist several fundamental problems. First, for the blob-thin-stripe-V4 system to be solely responsible for color processing, it follows that animals with little (if any) use for color should have little (or no) blobs. However, this is not the case. Galagos, lorises, and owl monkeys, all nocturnal primates, have well-developed blob systems (Horton and Hubel, 1981; Horton, 1984; Condo et al., 1987; Tootell et al., 1985; McGuinness et al., 1986). But because they live in dim lighting conditions, color vision is virtually impossible. Moreover, for blobs to be uniquely responsible for color, and no other aspects of vision, their functional evolution is questionable: after all, colorized films offer little survival value over the original black and white versions!

In general, the Zeki-hypothesis is questionable because there are both color activities that are known to take place outside of the blobs, and contrast activities within them (for a more technical review of the arguments against the Zeki-hypothesis, see Allman and Zucker, 1990).

In light of these concerns, we have formulated an alternative hypothesis. Before posing it, however, it is necessary to first review some of the architectural properties of the interblob system.

4. Border detection with orientationally selective neurons

Concentrate for a moment on the problem of inferring curves from images. Between the blobs are rich collections of orientationally-selective cells, whose receptive fields might be thought of as templates for particular pattern features such as short linear segments of curves, or more technically, tangents. Conceptually they amount to simple and complex cells (Hubel and Wiesel, 1977). Furthermore, such cells are organized into *hypercolumns*, which suggests that each position in the image is covered by a cell "with" each orientation. (For simplicity of presentation, we shall not consider ocular dominance, motion, and disparity selectivity in this paper.)

Now, the local description of the curve everywhere along it formally amounts to inferring the trace of the curve, or the set of points (in the image) through which the curve passes, its (approximate) tangent (or orientation) and curvature at those points, and their discontinuities (Zucker and Hummel, 1986). We call this the *tangent field*.

We have modeled the computation of the tangent field as a two step process, because a single evaluation of a simple cell's response is not sufficient to estimate orientation accurately near corners, junctions, and areas of the image where several curves approach one another. We have shown in addition that curvature is required, and that it can be computed from simple cell responses at multiple scales. This array of information can be considered as analogous to the distribution of activity in a cortical hypercolumn. Implicit is considerable information about the local distribution of light contrast. The rate of change of tangent direction or curvature is made explicit by taking differences of the responses of smaller and larger receptive fields. This model of endstopped simple cells thereby encodes both the orientation and curvature estimate (Dobbins et al., 1987). However, since this initial local measurement information is inherently inaccurate, we require a further interpretation into an explicit distributed representation of tangent and curvature at each point by establishing a consistent global interpretation of information gathered from the local measurements. Relaxation labeling (Hummel and Zucker, 1983) provides the formal framework for this, and the study of the resulting network has been reported in (Parent and Zucker, 1989; Zucker et al., 1989).

In summary, while the details of the boundary detection network and local circuitry are not important for the present proposal, it is important to observe that, at most points in the image, only one orientation will be present; at a selected few two might be present (e.g., crossing lines), but most of the cells in an orientation hypercolumn, signalling other orientations, will be relatively quiet. This stands in distinction to the blob system, and forms the basis for the Allman/Zucker hypothesis.

5. The Allman/Zucker hypothesis

We have shown that the boundary (hypercolumn) system codes geometric variables, and that, on average, only a small percentage will be responding fully. We stress that the firing rate of each neuron carries an indication of the strength of match between a cell's orientation preference and the underlying orientation indicated in the image. The signal is further confounded by contrast variations, so the neurons are designed to saturate rather rapidly in contrast (about one order of magnitude) and adapt to different scene conditions (Sclar et al., 1989).

Allman and Zucker hypothesized that the difference between the blob and the interblob systems is related to two different modes for representing visual information. In distinction to the geometric, hypercolumn system, Allman and Zucker specifically hypothesized that different *scalar* (or intensity) variables, such as color, contrast, and texture density, are carried by the blobs. Specifically, intensity is encoded explicitly over a very broad dynamic range, in which activity is proportional to the intensity variable (e.g., contrast). This difference in the encoding strategy requires much more metabolic machinery, and accounts for the cytochrome oxidase differences. No one else has applied these coding ideas to visual cortex (Ballard, 1986).

There is some indirect evidence in support of our hypothesis. The most direct data are from Maguire and Bazier (1982), who investigated the responses of neurons in monkey visual cortex to luminance differences. They found that orientation selective cells typically achieved maximum firing rates of less than 100 spikes/sec., and saturated within one order of magnitude contrast variation. Non-oriented cells were very different; they achieved firing rates approaching 300 spikes/s., and could often encode up to 4 log orders of magnitude in contrast variation. While this study was done before the blob system was discovered, it is likely that the oriented cells were in the interblob, hypercolumn system, while the non-oriented cells were in the blobs (or possibly layer 4C). Additional candidates for the blob cells, consistent with our hypothesis, are the "luxotonic" cells recorded in squirrel monkey (Bartlett and Doty, 1974) and macaque (Kayama et al., 1979).

6. Specific predictions

Although the support for our hypothesis is indirect, testable predictions do arise. The first of these relates to specific properties of the contrast response function for blob and interblob cells, and to their contrast adaptation (see Allman and Zucker, 1990, p. 980; cf. (Derrington and Lennie, 1984; Sclar et al., 1989)). The specific prediction is shown as Fig. 1 in Allman and Zucker, 1990.

The next two predictions arise as follows. First, given the apparent contrast, color, and other "material" properties associated with surfaces in the world, a fundamental theoretical question is: how can these properties be computed from the signals carried by blob cells. It follows, of course, that a negative result here would be devastating to our hypothesis. However, based on related work done a few years ago (Zucker and Hummel, 1986), we were able to show that a simple excitatory interaction between such cells was sufficient to recover contrast, if cells with a range of receptive field sizes were present. Current physiological evidence is supportive (Silverman et al., 1989), although this research was done before we were aware of the blob system. Much remains to connect them, and also to extend them to color. But the specific prediction that contrast and color signals can be extracted from the responses of blob cells via (predominantly) excitatory interactions is testable.

The second prediction involves texture. Although we have a wonderful facility at perceiving it, the physiology that carries it is only poorly understood. Textures can be broken into two categories, which we call texture flows and texture fields; texture flows are those patterns that exhibit an orientation (almost) everywhere, like fur, hair, or grass, while texture fields exhibit no orientation (e.g., salt-and-pepper mixtures, or stars in the sky) (Hel Or and Zucker, 1989). Since oriented texture flows can be naturally carried within the interblob system (Zucker, 1986), we predict that texture fields are carried within the blob system. We began to test this hypothesis psychophysically using apparent motion displays. There is already evidence that the blob system is separate from the motion systems, and that contrast and color (blob variables) act differently than borders (interblob variables) (Kolers and von Gruneau, 1976; Ramachandran, 1987). Furthermore, there is evidence that in un-oriented texture only density, not direct position, matters (Barlow, 1978); see also Livingstone and Hubel (1984). We have replicated these experiments involving contrast and color differences, and have extended them to texture field (density) differences. Specifically, we predict that texture density will appear identically to color and contrast, but different than borders and texture flows. Our preliminary investigations, reported at the Toronto meeting, support this prediction.

As a final comment, we mention that the implications of relating functional properties to metabolic activity extend far beyond information processing. In another study we have been able to relate the visual deficits reported in an individual who recovered from carbon monoxide poisoning to aerobic and anaerobic metabolic pathways via the blob/interblob systems

(Allman and Zucker, 1992). Connections between information processing, metabolism, and neuropsychology may well provide a new viewpoint toward understanding the visual cortex.

Acknowledgments

This research was supported by grants from NSERC, MRC, and the Hixon Professorship at Caltech.

Linear subspace methods for recovering translational direction

Allan D. Jepson

David J. Heeger

The image motion field for an observer moving through a static environment depends on the observer's translational and rotational velocities along with the distances to surface points. Given such a motion field as input we have recently introduced subspace methods for the recovery of the observer's motion and the depth structure of the scene. This class of methods involve splitting the equations describing the motion field into separate equations for the observer's translational direction, the rotational velocity, and the relative depths. The resulting equations can then be solved successively, beginning with the equations for the translational direction. Here we concentrate on this first step. In earlier work, a linear method was shown to provide a biased estimate of the translational direction. We discuss the source of this bias and show how it can be effectively removed. The consequence is that the observer's velocity and the relative depths to points in the scene can all be recovered by successively solving three **linear** problems.

1. Introduction

The basic problem we consider is how to obtain reliable information on the motion of a camera, along with distances to various points in its environment, from measurements of image motion (optical flow) alone. Here we pursue subspace methods which have been recently introduced for solving this problem (see Heeger and Jepson, 1990, 1992). The general approach involves splitting the problem into three subproblems, each of which can be solved in the following order. First, we obtain constraints which involve only the translational direction, $\vec{T}$, of the camera. These equations are independent of the camera's angular velocity, $\vec{\Omega}$, and do not involve knowing the distances to points in the scene. Secondly, given the resulting estimate for the translational direction, a set of linear equations can be obtained which involve only the rotational velocity as an unknown. Finally, given estimates of both the translational direction and rotational velocities of the camera, several methods are available for obtaining reliable information about the (relative) distances to various scene points (see Bolles et al., 1987; Matthies et al., 1989).

Unlike many previously proposed algorithms, our approach to motion analysis applies to the general case of arbitrary motion with respect to an arbitrary scene. There is no assumption of smooth or planar surfaces. The results in our previous work (Heeger and Jepson, 1990, 1992) demonstrate that our approach can be stable with respect to random errors in the flow field measurements, and that it performs quite favorably when compared with other proposed approaches. It is simple to compute and it is highly parallel, not requiring iteration and not requiring an initial guess. For a brief review of the existing literature see (Heeger and Jepson, 1992).

In this paper we are primarily concerned with simplifying the first step of the subspace methods in which the direction of translation is estimated independently of the rotational velocity and depths. The input data is taken to be a discrete set of optical flow vectors, say $\vec{u}(\vec{x}_k)$, for $k = 1, \ldots, K$, where $\vec{x}_k$ denotes the image position for the kth sample. It is convenient to collect these two-vectors into a single $2K$-dimensional vector, $\vec{\mathcal{O}}$. With this notation, the constraints on $\vec{T}$ take the simple form

$$\vec{\Psi}_i(\vec{T}) \cdot \vec{\mathcal{O}} = 0, \quad \text{for } i = 1, \ldots, K - 3, \tag{1}$$

where "·" denotes the usual vector inner-product. In previous work (Heeger and Jepson, 1990; Heeger and Jepson, 1992) we show how to compute the constraint vectors $\vec{\Psi}_i$, and show that these vectors are typically nonlinear functions of $\vec{T}$. We proposed that the nonlinear problem (1) can be solved for $\vec{T}$ simply by sampling the constraints on a mesh distributed over a hemisphere of possible orientations for $\vec{T}$, and then seeking points of least square error (Heeger and Jepson, 1990, 1992).

In Jepson and Heeger (1991) we introduced an alternative method for finding the camera's translational direction, which avoids sampling $\vec{T}$-space at many points, and results in a *linear* system for the translational direction. The key observation to make is that it is possible to redefine the constraint vectors $\vec{\Psi}_i(\vec{T})$ in equation (1) in such a way that the first $K - 6$ of them depend linearly on $\vec{T}$, while the remaining three constraint vectors are typically nonlinear functions of $\vec{T}$. From (1) we see that the first $K - 6$ vectors now lead to linear constraints on the translational direction. The step in our previous method which involved sampling constraints of the form (1) over $\vec{T}$-space can be replaced by the construction of these linear constraints, followed by a standard *linear* least squares solver. As a result this new method represents a huge savings in the computational resources required to obtain an estimate for $\vec{T}$.

There is, of course, a price to pay for this short cut. We are not using all of the available information to obtain this estimate of $\vec{T}$ (i.e. we are omitting the three nonlinear constraints). Therefore we can expect that the new approach will be more sensitive to errors in the input. Fortunately, we can show that for general scenes containing a rich depth structure this linear approach still does provide a robust estimate (Jepson and Heeger, 1991). However our preliminary experiments indicated that a straight forward implementation of the linear approach provides a biased estimate of the translational direction. This bias was observed to be more severe for images having smaller angular extents. In this paper we analyze the cause of this bias, and discuss a simple method for its removal. In related work Spetsakis (1991) discusses the bias observed in a completely different method for structure from motion, and comments on the possibility of the biases having a common cause. This is an important area of research, which we do not pursue here.

2. Basic algorithm

The basic situation we consider is an observer moving through a stationary environment. In the observer's coordinate frame this is equivalent to the scene undergoing a rigid motion, which is completely characterized by a translational velocity $\vec{T}$ and an angular velocity $\vec{\Omega}$. In particular, the instantaneous velocity of the point $\vec{X}(t)$ is

$$\frac{d\vec{X}}{dt} \equiv \vec{V} = \vec{T} + \vec{\Omega} \times \vec{X}. \tag{2}$$

Here we take $\vec{X} \equiv (X_1, X_2, X_3)$ to be a right-handed coordinate system fixed on the observer, with the nodal point of the imaging system at the origin. We set the focal length to f, and denote the image point at (X_1, X_2, f) by image coordinates $\vec{x} \equiv (x_1, x_2, 1) = (X_1/f, X_2/f, 1)$ (for vector operations later in this paper it is convenient to write $\vec{x}$ as a 3-vector). We put the transducer surface in front of the nodal point to avoid the need to reflect the image coordinates.

We assume that we are given the optical flow (image velocity) at a set of image positions, $\{\vec{x}_k\}$, for a single frame of the image sequence. From this information we wish to compute the direction of the translational velocity. As mentioned in the introduction, given this direction we are left with linear problems for each of the rotational velocity and the inverse relative depths. Here we consider only this first step, namely the computation of the translational direction.

For the algorithm proposed in Jepson and Heeger (1991), the optical flow data at each point is first expanded into the 3-vector

$$\vec{q}(\vec{x}_k) = Q(\vec{x}_k)\vec{u}(\vec{x}_k), \tag{3}$$

where

$$Q(\vec{x}) = \begin{pmatrix} 0 & 1 \\ -1 & 0 \\ x_2 & -x_1 \end{pmatrix}. \tag{4}$$

Notice that this preprocessing step is local; each image velocity is transformed separately.

The sample points $\{\vec{x}_k\}$ are subdivided into N (usually overlapping) patches. Let the nth image patch consist of sample points $\{\vec{x}_k\}_{k=1}^{K}$. Then for each patch we define a particular coefficient vector, $\vec{c}_n \equiv (c_{1n}, \ldots, c_{Kn})^T$. The details of the computation of a suitable coefficient vector are given in Appendix A. For our purposes here we only note that the coefficients have been normalized so that

$$\sum_{k=1}^{K} c_{kn}^2 = 1. \tag{5}$$

Given the transformed optical flow vectors $\vec{q}(\vec{x}_k)$, and the coefficient vector $\vec{c}_n$ for the nth image patch, we next build the *translation constraint vector*

$$\vec{\tau}_n \equiv \begin{pmatrix} \vec{c}_n \cdot (q_1(\vec{x}_1), \ldots, q_1(\vec{x}_K))^T \\ \vec{c}_n \cdot (q_2(\vec{x}_1), \ldots, q_2(\vec{x}_K))^T \\ \vec{c}_n \cdot (q_3(\vec{x}_1), \ldots, q_3(\vec{x}_K))^T \end{pmatrix}. \tag{6}$$

That is, the ith component of $\vec{\tau}_n$ is obtained by taking the inner-product of the coefficient vector $\vec{c}_n$ with the vector formed from the ith component of $\vec{q}(\vec{x})$ sampled over the image patch. The particular construction of the coefficient vectors $\vec{c}_n$ ensures that the resulting translation constraint vector, $\vec{\tau}_n$, is perpendicular to the true translational direction (see Appendix A).

Taken over all N image patches, each with its own $\vec{\tau}_n$, we now find that the translational direction $\vec{T}$ of the observer must satisfy the linear equation

$$\begin{pmatrix} \vec{\tau}_1^T \\ \vec{\tau}_2^T \\ \vdots \\ \vec{\tau}_N^T \end{pmatrix} \vec{T} = \vec{0}. \tag{7}$$

We can solve this in a least squares sense by accumulating the following 3×3 symmetric matrix

$$D \equiv \sum_{n=1}^{N} w_n \vec{\tau}_n \vec{\tau}_n^T. \tag{8}$$

Here we have included a weight, w_n, for each $\vec{\tau}$ vector, the choice of which is discussed further below. The least squares estimate for the translational direction is then given by the eigenvector for the smallest eigenvalue of this 3×3 matrix D. We have found it is also useful to look at the separation between the various eigenvalues of D, to detect situations for which one or more components of the translational direction are poorly determined by the linear constraints.

An important special case for the above computation is when the optical flow is sampled on a regularly spaced grid, and the image patches are all taken to have the same sampling pattern (eg. a $l \times l$ square grid). In such a case the coefficient vectors $\vec{c}_n$ can be precomputed and taken to be the same for each patch (see Appendix A). For a regular sampling pattern, then, the overall algorithm for the computation of the translational direction simplifies to the following. First the optical flow data $\vec{u}(\vec{x})$ at each sample point is transformed to a 3-vector, $\vec{q}(\vec{x})$, through a multiplication by the 3×2 matrix $Q(\vec{x})$. Three images, $q_i(\vec{x})$, are formed from each component of this vector. Each of these images is then convolved with the same precomputed mask made up of the coefficients of $\vec{c}_n$, and the three resulting images together provide an image of translation constraint vectors. That is, for each spatial position there is a translation constraint vector $\vec{\tau}_n$ known to be perpendicular to the observer's translational direction. These constraint vectors are finally compiled into the 3×3 matrix D, from which the translational direction can easily be obtained. It is also possible, of course, to avoid explicitly forming any of these intermediate images, and instead directly build the matrix D from the results of an equivalent linear transformation applied to the optical flow for each image patch. We choose to present the algorithm in the expanded form primarily to emphasize the simplicity of the computations involved.

3. Direct implementation

In this section we examine the performance of the basic algorithm on a simple test problem. Our previous work showed that the algorithm appears to be fairly robust, but suffers from a bias in the recovered translational direction. We review the observation of a bias here through a straight forward implementation. In subsequent sections we use these results for comparison with approaches designed to reduce or remove the bias.

Due to the ease in which we can obtain well controlled test data, we consider only computer generated data in this paper. Clearly for the results on such sequences to generalize to real sequences we need to model the noise properties of optical flow measurement techniques. Fleet and Jepson (1990), for example, report optical flow measurements with roughly Gaussianly distributed errors having a magnitude about 5% of the length of the optical flow vector. These error results were also obtained from simulated scenes, and therefore should be taken as a *lower* bound on the sorts of errors we can expect in practice (see also (Barron et al., 1992; Fleet, 1992)).

The optical flow data we use is generated from the depth map for the computer generated scene shown in Figure 1. The range of projected distances

Fig. 1. *(Left) Graphics image of an office* (128 × 128 *pixels). (Right) Image formed from the norm of the recovered $\vec{\tau}(\vec{x})$, with larger norms depicted by darker grey levels. Here the motion field is as in Figure 2 (left).*

along the optical axis (i.e. the range of values in the "Z-buffer") is roughly a factor of two for this scene. Since we expect the accuracy of the results to depend on the visual angle, we allow the focal distance to vary and keep the Z-buffer fixed. In Figure 2 we show a motion field generated using this Z-buffer, a 60 degree field of view, and a translational velocity of $(0, -1, 2)$ (image coordinate x_1 is to the right, x_2 is down, and the third component is forward along the optical axis). The rotational velocity was chosen so that the camera was fixating at the center of the image. Figure 2 (left) shows the flow field, while only the translational component is presented in Figure 2 (right). Note that there is a very significant contribution to the motion field from the rotational component. This is important since the algorithm is designed to project out the effects of the rotational motion.

The optical flow data was obtained by adding isotropic, Gaussianly distributed noise to the motion field. We used a noise amplitude such that each component of the error has a standard deviation equal to 10% of the length of the motion field vector (so the norm of the error is a factor of $\sqrt{2}$ larger than this). The actual amplitude of the noise is not particularly important. Indeed we have done some tests using up to 30% noise and observed a graceful degradation in performance. However, to deal with computed optical flow data we need to contend with noise that is correlated across nearby image locations, and with noise distributions which have longer tails signifying a higher probability of outliers. We do not deal with these issues here, although in Section 6 we do show the results of our algorithm given computed optical flow data.

Figure 1 (right) shows the norm of $\vec{\tau}$ generated by the algorithm. Here the patches for the optical flow data were chosen to be square 15 × 15

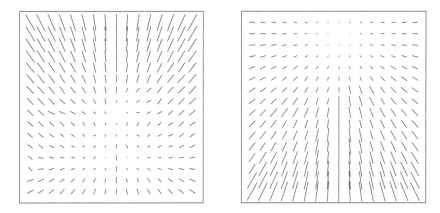

Fig. 2. *(Left) Flow field for the office scene, with translational velocity $\vec{T} = (0, -1, 2)$ (towards and up), and with a fixation point at the center of image. (Right) The component of the flow field due to only the translational motion. Note the focus of expansion, which is located at the true direction of translation.*

sampling patterns, with the samples each separated by a distance of two pixels. The coefficient vector was chosen to be the modified DOG mask discussed in Appendix A. The same mask was used for all patches and the translation constraint vectors $\vec{\tau}(\vec{x})$ were generated using the convolution algorithm described above. (Here we find it convenient to refer to the $\vec{\tau}$ generated for a particular patch as $\vec{\tau}(\vec{x})$, where $\vec{x}$ is the image coordinates for the center of the patch.) The norm of the resulting translation constraint vectors, $\vec{\tau}(\vec{x})$, is essentially the absolute value of the response of the DOG mask when applied to the inverse depth data with a general modulation by the length of $\vec{x} \times \vec{T}$ (see Jepson and Heeger, 1991). (No value was computed around the border of the image where the convolution mask would have extended beyond the edge of the image.) As we discussed in Jepson and Heeger (1991), the translation constraint vector $\vec{\tau}(\vec{x})$ has a large amplitude only where there is significant nonplanar variation in the depth structure. The amplitude response could clearly be useful for other operations such as image segmentation.

For a 60 degree field of view (measured along the horizontal center line), and 10% input error, the recovered translational direction was $(-0.007, -0.329, 0.944)$. The exact direction (after scaling) is $(0.0, -0.447, 0.894)$. The computed solution represents an error of about 13% in the recovered translational direction, or about 7 degrees of visual angle. Note that the vertical component of $\vec{T}$ (i.e. T_2) has the largest error, while the component of the error in the horizontal direction T_1 is only 0.4 degrees of visual angle. Thus the recovered translational direction is skewed about 7 degrees towards the optical axis. Twenty separate runs were done (each taking less than a minute on a Silicon Graphics 4D/340VGX), and the standard

Angular Extent (deg)	60	40	20	10	5
Error in Mean (deg)	7.0	12	19	24	26
Error T_1 (deg)	0.3 ± 0.1	0.2 ± 0.1	0.08 ± 0.04	0.03 ± 0.02	0.01 ± 0.01
Error T_2 (deg)	6.5 ± 0.6	11.4 ± 0.4	18.6 ± 0.2	23.6 ± 0.1	25.5 ± 0.01

Table 1. *Results from the basic algorithm*

deviation of the error measure (in degrees) was found to be less than a degree (see Table 1). In particular, we found that the method has a significant bias (roughly 7 degrees) in the recovered translational direction towards the orientation of the optical axis.

The same Z-buffer and 3D motion parameters were used for various other angular extents. The results of 20 runs for each extent are summarized in Table 1. For example, for a 20 degree field of view the recovered translational direction is strongly skewed towards the optical axis, with the average recovered translational direction having a a 19 degree error. The standard deviation in the radial direction (T_2) was only about 0.2 degrees of visual angle, which is negligible with respect to the mean error of 18.6 degrees in this component. As a result we can safely conclude that the error in the mean represents represents a strong bias in the method rather than random fluctuations. From Table 1 it is clear that the bias increases as the angular extent is reduced. A second important point is that the horizontal component of the translational direction (i.e. T_1) is recovered quite accurately even for a 20 degree angular extent. For significantly smaller extents, such as the 10 degree and 5 degree cases reported in Table 1, the recovered translational direction is skewed to within a few degrees of the optical axis, and thus an accurate horizontal component (nearly zero) may not be significant here.

4. Source of the bias

We have seen that the variance of the estimates for the direction of translation is small, but the basic method is seriously flawed by a significant bias. Note that in the absence of noise our method is exact, the various constraint vectors $\vec{\tau}(\vec{x})$ provide linear constraints on the translational direction. (Indeed, given the motion field to single precision floating point accuracy our program returns an estimate of the translational direction accurate to six digits.) The bias is clearly not a consequence of analytical errors. Moreover, only linear operations are used to construct the constraint vectors. Therefore we should expect that the bias can be understood through a simple linear analysis of the effects of noise in the optical flow on the resulting constraint vectors.

For our simulated optical flow it is relatively straight forward to compute the covariance of the constraint vectors $\vec{\tau}(\vec{x})$. In particular, since we are assuming the noise at different pixels is independent,

$$E[(\vec{\tau} - E[\vec{\tau}])(\vec{\tau} - E[\vec{\tau}])^T] = \sum_{i=1}^{K} c_i^2 E[(\vec{q}_i - E[\vec{q}_i])(\vec{q}_i - E[\vec{q}_i])^T].$$

Here $E[\vec{\tau}]$ and $E[\vec{q}_i]$ represent the expected values of the vectors $\vec{\tau}$ and $\vec{q}_i$. The last term in the above expression is the covariance of $\vec{q}_i$. By equation (3) this covariance can be rewritten in terms of the 3×2 matrix $Q(\vec{x}_i)$ and the covariance of the noise for the optical flow. Since the optical flow noise is assumed to be isotropic, its covariance is simply a constant, $\rho^2 ||u(\vec{x}_i)||^2$, times the 2×2 identity matrix. (For 10% noise in each component of the optical flow we use $\rho = 0.10$.) As a result, we can now rewrite the above equation as

$$E[(\vec{\tau} - E[\vec{\tau}])(\vec{\tau} - E[\vec{\tau}])^T] = \rho^2 \sum_{i=1}^{K} ||u(\vec{x}_i)||^2 c_i^2 Q(\vec{x}_i) Q^T(\vec{x}_i).$$

For our purposes here it is convenient to approximate this covariance matrix using the assumption that the norm of the optical flow is roughly constant over the sample points $\vec{x}_i$ used in any single patch. In particular, we replace the term $||\vec{u}(\vec{x}_i)||^2$ in the above sum with the weighted average

$$\sigma_u^2 = \sum_{i=1}^{K} c_i^2 ||u(\vec{x}_i)||^2 \tag{9}$$

(recall (5) which requires the coefficients c_i to be normalized such that the sum of their squares is one). This provides the approximate covariance matrix

$$C_n = \rho^2 \sigma_u^2 \sum_{i=1}^{K} c_i^2 Q(\vec{x}_i) Q^T(\vec{x}_i). \tag{10}$$

The sum in equation (10) is over terms which only depend on the particular sample points $\vec{x}_i$, and not on the optical flow.

Using equation (4), the sum in (10) can be shown to be

$$\sum_{i=1}^{K} c_i^2 Q(\vec{x}_i) Q^T(\vec{x}_i) = \begin{pmatrix} 1 & 0 & -x_1^n \\ 0 & 1 & -x_2^n \\ -x_1^n & -x_2^n & \alpha + \beta \end{pmatrix}. \tag{11}$$

Here x_1^n and x_2^n are the first and second components of the center $\vec{x}^n$ of the nth patch, which is defined in general by

$$\vec{x}^n = \sum_{i=1}^{K} c_{in}^2 \vec{x}_i.$$

(For the symmetric modified DOG masks used in this paper, $\vec{x}^n$ is just the position of the center pixel of the mask when applied to the nth patch.) Also

$\alpha = (x_1^n)^2 + (x_2^n)^2$ and the term β in (11) is given by

$$\beta = \sum_{i=1}^{K} c_i^2 [(x_{1i} - x_1^n)^2 + (x_{2i} - x_2^n)^2].$$

We see β is simply a measure of the variance of the sample points weighted by the coefficients c_i. For the case in which the $\vec{\tau}$ vectors are computed using convolution with the same set of coefficients, the value of β is simply a constant independent of $\vec{x}^n$.

The structure of the approximate covariance matrix C_n is best illustrated by its eigenvalues and eigenvectors, which provide the variances and principle directions. The eigenvalues for C_n are just $(\rho \sigma_u)^2$ times the eigenvalues of the matrix given in (11), and the eigenvectors of the two matrices are identical. The eigenvalues of the matrix in (11) are easily found to be $\lambda_1 = 1$, and

$$\begin{aligned} \lambda_+ &= (1 + \alpha + \beta)\gamma, \\ \lambda_- &= \beta / ((1 + \alpha + \beta)\gamma). \end{aligned} \tag{12}$$

Here

$$\gamma = \frac{1}{2} \left[1 + \sqrt{1 - 4\beta/(1 + \alpha + \beta)^2} \right].$$

The eigenvectors associated with these three eigenvalues are given (respectively) by the columns of the matrix

$$U = \begin{pmatrix} x_2^n & x_1^n & x_1^n \\ -x_1^n & x_2^n & x_2^n \\ 0 & \delta_+ & \delta_- \end{pmatrix}. \tag{13}$$

For simplicity, we have ignored the normalization factors for these column vectors. The constant δ_+ is given by $1 - \lambda_+$, and the second constant δ_- satisfies $\alpha = -\delta_+ \delta_-$.

The significance of these equations is most easily seen by considering sampling patterns having a small angular extent. In this case β, a weighted variance of the sampling pattern, is much smaller than one. To be specific, for the sampling pattern used here based on a 15×15 array of taps applied at every other pixel, β is 1.5×10^{-3} for the 60 degree field of view. This decreases to 6.0×10^{-4} for the 40 degree field of view, and to only 3.5×10^{-5} for the 10 degree field of view. As a consequence, we find δ_+ is roughly given by $-\alpha$, and δ_- is roughly 1. In particular, from (13) we see that the eigendirections can be simply determined from the position of the center of the image sampling pattern, $\vec{x}^n$. The eigenvalues for these three directions are 1, $\lambda_+ = 1 + \alpha + O(\beta)$, and $\lambda_- = \beta/(1+\alpha) + O(\beta^2)$. For an image having an angular extent of 60 degrees (side to side) α ranges from zero to a maximum of $2/3$, so the first two eigenvalues of C_n are roughly the same size. However, the third eigenvalue, corresponding to the sampling direction $\vec{x}^n$, is much smaller. The one standard deviation surface for the errors in $\vec{\tau}$ are

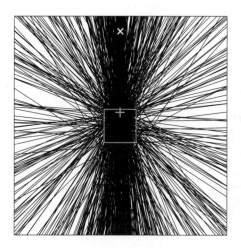

Fig. 3. *Translational constraint lines for $\vec{T}$, plotted in a 60 degree window centered on the optical axis (i.e. the same image coordinates as used for Figure 2). The true translational direction is indicated by the white "X". In order to accentuate the bias we used only a 10 degree field of view (grey box), and the recovered translational direction is indicated by the grey "+".*

ellipsoids having the shape of mildly elliptical "pancake", with the diameter along the minor axis of the ellipsoid much smaller than along the other two principal directions. (In fact the ratio of diameters is at least $1/\sqrt{\beta}$, which is 26 for a 60 degree field of view and 170 for 10 degrees.) In summary, we see the noise for the computed $\vec{\tau}$ vectors is far from isotropic, and the minor axis of each pancake is oriented along the direction of the center of the optical flow sampling pattern, $\vec{x}^{\,n}$.

To illustrate one effect of this non-isotropic error distribution we plot a large sample of the resulting constraints in Figure 3. Here the $\vec{\tau}$ vectors were computed given a 10 degree field of view (depicted by the grey box in Figure 3), and 10% image noise added to the flow field generated using the same 3D motion parameters as in Figure 2 (left). For each sampled $\vec{\tau}$ vector we plot the set of translational directions $\vec{T}$ which are perpendicular to $\vec{\tau}$, as projected onto an image having the same optical axis as the original but with a 60 degree angular extent. The set of translational directions perpendicular to a particular $\vec{\tau}$ forms a straight line in this image. One other property of the constraint vectors is needed to understand the distribution shown in Figure 3, namely that the exact $\vec{\tau}$ vectors tend to be nearly perpendicular to the mean sampling direction. In particular, the exact constraint lines tend to pass close to the sampling direction (Jepson and Heeger, 1991). Since the covariance of $\vec{\tau}$ is small in this direction, the noise does not perturb the position of the constraint lines very much near the sampling direction. As a result, in Figure 3 we see that almost all of the constraint lines pass through the ten degree field of view from which the optical flow data was sampled.

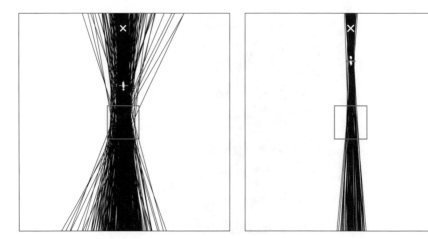

Fig. 4. *Translational constraint lines for the same case as in Figure 3, but for only those constraints having a signal noise ratio larger than 5 (left) or 30 (right). White "X"'s mark the true translational direction. A dot is used to indicate the result from each of 10 different noise samples, and they all lie on the vertical bars of the the grey "+"'s marking the mean recovered translational directions.*

The recovered direction is (roughly) the point that minimizes the sum of squared distances to all of these straight lines, with each distance weighted by the squared length of the particular $\vec{\tau}$. For this case the recovered direction is about 24 degrees away from the true translational direction. As can be seen from Figure 3, one source of this bias may be the significant portion of constraint lines that are extremely noisy. These arise from cases where the length of $\vec{\tau}$ is not much longer than the expected length of the noise. Due to the non-isotropic nature of the noise even these constraint line will also typically pass close to the sampling direction, and the result is a radial pattern of noisy constraints as depicted in Figure 3. For such a radial pattern, points near the center of the pattern will tend to have a smaller square distance to all of the lines, and hence these noisy constraints can be expected to provide some contribution to the bias.

Given the above estimate for the noise in a particular $\vec{\tau}$ vector it is a simple matter to implement a constraint on the signal to noise ratio of the constraint vectors used to estimate $\vec{\tau}$. For example, we use the standard deviation $\rho\sigma_u$ associated with the first eigenvalue of C_n, to define

$$SNR[\vec{\tau}(\vec{x})] = ||\vec{\tau}(\vec{x})||/[\rho\sigma_u]. \tag{14}$$

This estimate is used in two ways. First, we implement a simple threshold on the estimated SNR of each $\vec{\tau}$, if the estimate does not exceed a critical value then $\vec{\tau}$ is not used in the least squares problem. (In terms of equation (8) the weight w_n is set to zero.) For translation constraint vectors which exceed this threshold, we use the weight $w_n = (\rho\sigma_u)^{-2}$.

Angular Extent (deg)	60	40	20	10	5
Error in Mean (deg)	3.3	5.0	11	19	24
Error T_1 (deg)	0.08 ± 0.1	0.05 ± 0.1	0.03 ± 0.07	0.1 ± 0.03	0.1 ± 0.01
Error T_2 (deg)	3.0 ± 0.7	4.5 ± 0.7	10 ± 0.7	19 ± 0.5	24 ± 0.5

Table 2. *Results of using a threshold of 5.0 on the signal to noise ratio $SNR[\vec{\tau}]$, and using the scalar weights w_n.*

The rationale for this choice of weight is that, for a general translational velocity $\vec{T}$, the minimum distance between $\vec{T}$ and the plane perpendicular to $\vec{\tau}$ is $|\vec{\tau}\cdot\vec{T}|/\|\vec{\tau}\|$. The product of the square of this distance and the square of the SNR for $\vec{\tau}$ gives $(\vec{\tau}(\vec{x}^{\,n})\cdot\vec{T})^2/(\rho\sigma_u)^2$. This is precisely the contribution we obtain from the least squares objective function $\vec{T}^T D\vec{T}$ defined in Section 2, given that the weight w_n is chosen as above. Thus, we are weighting the distance between $\vec{T}$ and the plane perpendicular to $\vec{\tau}$ by the signal to noise ratio defined in (14).

The results of using this weighting scheme are shown in Figure 4. The input data were the same as for Figure 3. The threshold has successfully eliminated the wildly incorrect constraints, and clearly larger values of the threshold provide a tighter distribution of constraint lines near the true translational direction. However, the use of a threshold has reduced but not removed the bias. Indeed, the results of 10 runs are shown in each half of Figure 4. The scatter of the individual results is significantly less than the mean error (its about the size of the vertical bar of the "+" marking the mean recovered direction). Table 2 provides similar results from 20 runs using different random noise samples, for each of several given focal lengths. While there is a significant improvement in the performance over the basic algorithm (compare Table 1), the bias is still severe for smaller angular extents.

5. Removing the bias

In the previous section we noted the pancake shaped distribution for noise in the $\vec{\tau}$ vectors, and the property that the exact constraint vectors are nearly perpendicular to the sample direction. As we discussed above, these two properties contribute to the bias in the recovered translational direction, in part through the behavior of the constraint vectors having a low signal to noise ratio. However, even for relatively high signal to noise ratios the bias was still observed. In this section we briefly discuss the reason for this remaining bias, and demonstrate a simple method for its removal.

Consider a single constraint vector $\vec{\tau}(\vec{x}^{\,n})$ having a large signal to noise ratio, and assume it is nearly perpendicular to the sampling direction $\vec{x}^{\,n}$, as is typical. The plane perpendicular to this constraint vector forms the set of all translational velocities that are perfectly consistent with $\vec{\tau}(\vec{x}^{\,n})$. As discussed in the previous section, we are minimizing the objective function $\vec{T}^T D \vec{T}$, which is simply the sum of squared distances between the translational velocity $\vec{T}$ and the planes perpendicular to $\vec{\tau}(\vec{x}^n)$, for $n = 1, \ldots, N$, with each squared distance weighted by the square of the SNR for $\vec{\tau}(\vec{x}^n)$. The important point is that this term depends only on the relative angle between $\vec{T}$ and $\vec{\tau}(\vec{x}^n)$, and not on the orientation of $\vec{T}$ around the axis aligned with $\vec{\tau}(\vec{x}^n)$. The contribution of the nth patch to the overall objective function is therefore rotationally symmetric about the translation constraint vector $\vec{\tau}(\vec{x}^n)$. As we show below, it is precisely this symmetry which causes the significant bias.

Note that the rotational symmetry does not model the non-isotropic character of the noise in the recovered constraint vectors. In particular, the variance of $\vec{\tau}(\vec{x}^n)$ was seen to be much smaller in the direction of the mean sample point of the nth patch than in the perpendicular directions. The plane of translational directions $\vec{T}$ that are perpendicular to this constraint vector, therefore, will not wobble very much across the sampling direction for different noise samples. Instead the dominant effect of the noise will be to rotate the plane of translational velocities around the sampling direction. Roughly speaking we should expect the rotation around the sampling direction to have a variance that is $1/\beta$ times the variance across the viewing direction (i.e. the ratio of the eigenvalues of C_n). Recall that β is 1.5×10^{-3} for the 60 degree field of view and smaller for narrower fields. Thus an appropriate objective function should weight perturbations in $\vec{T}$ from the constraint plane much more heavily for translational directions nearly parallel to the sampling direction than for directions nearly perpendicular both the sampling direction and $\vec{\tau}(\vec{x}^n)$. The ratio of the weights on the same size error occurring at these two extremes should be $1/\sqrt{\beta}$, which for our current application increases from 26 for the 60 degree field of view, to 344 for the 5 degree field of view!

In terms of plots such as Figures 3 and 4, the appropriate cost function can be thought of in terms of the displacement between the translational direction $\vec{T}$ (in the image plane) and the depicted constraint line. The same perpendicular displacement should cost much more when it occurs near the sampling direction than when it occurs further away. By using a rotationally symmetric cost function we are in effect under-weighting perturbations near the sampling direction. Given a narrow aperture image we are consistently under-weighting the perturbations near the optical axis and, considering the magnitude of the appropriate weighting, we should expect a strongly biased estimate.

In order to correct this problem we need to use the non-isotropic character of the covariance matrix for the constraint vectors. A standard approach is to use the covariance matrix to generate a cost function in the following manner. Consider the space of all constraint vectors that are consistent with a given candidate translational direction $\vec{T}$. This is just the plane perpendicular to $\vec{T}$. If this was the true translational direction, then the exact $\vec{\tau}$ must be in this plane. A natural choice for the cost of such translational direction is the minimum squared distance between the measured constraint vector $\vec{\tau}(\vec{x}^{\,n})$ and this plane, where the distance metric is based on the covariance matrix C_n. That is, the cost is given by the minimum value

$$\min(\vec{\tau} - \vec{\tau}(\vec{x}^{\,n}))^T C_n^{-1}(\vec{\tau} - \vec{\tau}(\vec{x}^{\,n})), \quad \text{for } \vec{\tau} \cdot \vec{T} = 0.$$

This problem is easily solved, and we find the minimum value corresponds to

$$\frac{1}{(\vec{T}^T C_n \vec{T})}(\vec{\tau}(\vec{x}^{\,n}) \cdot \vec{T})^2.$$

That is, the appropriate cost function can be viewed in the same general form $\vec{T}^T D(\vec{T})\vec{T}$, but for $D(\vec{T})$ defined by

$$D(\vec{T}) = \sum_{n=1}^N w_n(\vec{T})\vec{\tau}(\vec{x}^{\,n})\vec{\tau}(\vec{x}^{\,n})^T, \tag{15}$$

with the weights

$$w_n(\vec{T}) = \frac{1}{(\vec{T}^T C_n \vec{T})} \tag{16}$$

Notice the weights depend on the translational velocity $\vec{T}$ itself, and thus in general the objective function $\vec{T}^T D(\vec{T})\vec{T}$ is no longer quadratic. We note in passing that by changing the sign of this objective function we obtain an approximation to the log likelihood of the translational direction $\vec{T}$, given all the constraint vectors $\vec{\tau}(\vec{x}^{\,n})$ which pass the condition on the signal to noise ratio. Thus we can view this approach as a maximum likelihood method, as has been suggested by Spetsakis (1988).

There are, of course, techniques for finding locally optimal values of non-quadratic objective functions. However, they require initial guesses and iterations, or alternatively, we might consider directly sampling the unit sphere of possible translational directions on a mesh to locate the minimum. The latter approach is similar to our earlier non-linear approach for finding the translational direction (Heeger and Jepson, 1990), and its use would largely eliminate the benefit of having linear constraints on the translational direction.

We would therefore like a quadratic objective function which effectively implements the one above. At first glance this seems like an impossibility. However, the key idea is that we are free to *add* noise to the constraint vectors $\vec{\tau}(\vec{x}^{\,n})$ in order to alter their covariance matrices; such a process is called dithering. If we can alter the covariance matrices C_n such that they are all scalar multiples of the same matrix, say C_0, then a simple (non-isotropic) rescaling of $\vec{T}$ will allow the nonquadratic objective function $\vec{T}^T D(\vec{T})\vec{T}$ to be written in an equivalent quadratic form. Note that we cannot do this rescaling trick with the original covariance matrices C_n since they are not all scalar multiples of each other. In particular, their one standard deviation surfaces were shown to be pancake shaped, with the minor axis of the pancake oriented along the mean sampling direction. As the mean sampling direction changes, the minor axis changes, and the various covariance matrices cannot be scalar multiples of each other. However, by dithering, we can pad the various pancakes so they all have the same shape.

In this paper we simply dither the constraint vectors to ensure that the resulting one standard deviation surfaces are all nearly spherical. For small angular extents this is rather crude, in that the minor axes of the various ellipsoids are nearly aligned to begin with, and a significantly smaller amount of dithering would suffice. However, for 90 degree fields of view we would be faced with dithering to spherical surfaces, as implemented here.

In particular, consider a computed constraint vector $\vec{\tau}(\vec{x}^{\,n})$ and the estimated covariance matrix C_n of the form described in Section 4. Two eigenvalues of C_n were shown to be roughly $\rho^2 \sigma_u^2$, while the third eigenvalue was a factor of λ_- smaller. The third eigendirection was shown to be roughly the mean sampling direction $\vec{x}^{\,n}$ for the nth patch. The dithering we use is simply to add a random component to each constraint vector, $\vec{\tau}(\vec{x}^{\,n})$, in the mean sampling direction $\vec{x}^{\,n}$, with an amplitude given by a mean zero Gaussian process having variance of $\sigma_{dith}^2 = \rho^2 \sigma_u^2 (1.0 - \lambda_-)$. That is,

$$\vec{d_n} = \vec{\tau}(\vec{x}^{\,n}) + N(0; \sigma_{dith}^2) \vec{x}^{\,n} / \|\vec{x}^{\,n}\|. \qquad (17)$$

The result of this dithering is that the covariance matrix of $\vec{d_n}$ has the minimum eigenvalue of $(\rho\sigma_u)^2$, which occurs twice, while the remaining eigenvalue is a factor of $(1 + \alpha)$ larger (see equation (12)). Since α is between 0 and 2/3 for all of the cases we are interested in here, we conclude that the covariance matrices of $\vec{d_n}$ are roughly isotropic. (We could of course dither in two directions to make the covariance perfectly isotropic, but remember that C_n is only an approximation of the true covariance. Also, our results below indicate that this extra dithering in not necessary in practice.)

Each constraint vector is used to generate a dithered vector $\vec{d_n}$, and these dithered constraint vectors are then used to generate

$$D = \sum_{n=1}^{N} w_n \vec{d_n} \vec{d_n}^T.$$

Here the weights are chosen exactly as in Section 4, namely w_n is zero if the signal to noise ratio of $\vec{\tau}(\vec{x}^{\,n})$ is below a threshold, and otherwise $w_n = (\rho\sigma_u)^{-2}$. Finally, the eigenvalues of D are found, and the eigenvector corresponding to the minimum eigenvalue provides the estimate for the translational direction. (We also check the ratio of the eigenvalues to detect cases in which only partial information on the translational direction is recovered.)

Fig. 5. *Translational constraint lines for the same case as in Figure 3, with a signal to noise threshold of 5 (left) and 30 (right). The dithering method was used on ten different runs for each threshold (dots), and the mean recovered translational direction is given by the grey "+".*

Angular Extent (deg)	60	40	20	10	5
Error in Mean (deg)	0.2	0.2	0.3	0.5	8.8
Error T_1 (deg)	0.08 ± 0.2	0.03 ± 0.14	0.01 ± 0.12	0.03 ± 0.09	0.03 ± 0.11
Error T_2 (deg)	0.2 ± 0.7	0.14 ± 0.8	0.3 ± 1.4	0.5 ± 5.4	8 ± 22

Table 3. *Results of the dithering method using a threshold of 5.0 on the signal to noise ratio, and the scalar weight w_n.*

The results of this process are shown in Figure 5 and Table 3. For all practical purposes, the bias is gone. The results in Table 3 show that the translation direction can be recovered quite accurately even down to a 10 degree angular extent. The standard deviation of the estimate in the radial direction increases as the angular extent is reduced, as is expected since the constraint lines become more parallel. However, the mean error in the method is consistently less than the standard deviation of the responses, indicating that the bias has virtually been eliminated. (There should be some bias left, since the dithered constraints do not have perfectly isotropic covariances, but it now appears to be negligible.) The horizontal component of the translational direction was recovered to within a fraction of a degree for all cases.

For the angular extent of 5 degrees we are approaching, or within, the domain of applicability of techniques which rely on an orthographic approximation, such as the factoring approach discussed by Tomasi and Kanade (1991). At this extreme we find that the eigenvalues values of the matrix D are in the proportion (300:1.2:1). The fact that the last two eigenvalues have nearly the same magnitude indicates that the translational direction is only weakly constrained within the plane spanned by the last two eigendirections. The first eigendirection of D provides a robust constraint that the true translational direction lies somewhere on the plane perpendicular to it, which is accurate to about a tenth of a degree. The separation of the smallest two eigenvalues increases as the angular extent increases, indicating that the translational direction becomes more strongly constrained in this plane. In particular, the proportions of the eigenvalues of D for the 10 degree extent are typically (300:1.6:1), for 20 degrees we have (250:3:1), and finally for the 60 degree case the proportions are (200:8:1). Thus, the proportions appear to be useful diagnostic of the nature of the information provided about the translational direction. We note in passing that the ratios of the eigenvalues of D, generated by the basic method and the weighted method discussed above, does not provide such a useful diagnostic. For example, in the 5 degree field of view the basic method produces the proportions $(5 \times 10^3 : 240 : 1)$, while the simple weighting produces $(1.2 \times 10^4 : 48 : 1)$. Both results indicate that the methods strongly constrain the translational direction to a unique line, as is verified by the small standard deviations of the observed responses (see Tables 1 and 2). The trouble is that a large part of this constraint is due entirely to the bias in the method. Therefore situations in which the true constraints are nearly defective are not identified by the eigenvalues of the matrix D generated by the biased methods. By destroying the bias, the dithering method avoids this problem.

6. Yosemite revisited

While the results of the dithering algorithm are an impressive improvement over the other methods reported here, they are based on the use of simulated optical flow data. As discussed above, there are several additional difficulties we might expect to be confronted with given real data. The two primary concerns are: 1) optical flow measurements are typically sparse; and 2) given an environment with occlusion boundaries the optical flow measurements will typically have numerous outliers (see Fleet, 1992).

There are two possible approaches to dealing with sparse data. In particular, the data values might be interpolated on a uniform grid. In this case we can apply our approach directly to the interpolated values, but we need to be concerned about correlations and structure introduced in the errors through the interpolation process itself. Alternatively, we might consider using only the sparse set of image points at which reliable estimates of optical flow can be obtained. In this case the coefficient vector $\vec{c}_n$ cannot be precomputed since it depends on the particular locations of the sample points. These coefficients must satisfy six linear equations (see Appendix A), and an efficient method for solving these equations is an important area for further research.

Fig. 6. *Results for frame 7 of the Yosemite sequence. The dithering method was used on ten different runs (dots). The error in the mean recovered translational direction is 1.5 degrees.*

There are also several possible approaches for dealing with the second problem, namely that optical flow methods must be expected to generate the occasional outlier. For example, given that some information about the 3D motion can be obtained with a crude method, we might consider using this information to identify outliers in the data. Methods from robust statistics could have an important application here.

For the purposes of this paper we simply demonstrate the existing algorithm on an optical flow field computed for the (synthetic) Yosemite image sequence. This sequence has been used with our non-linear algorithm, which produced an error in the translational direction of about 4 degrees (Heeger and Jepson, 1990). Here we use a different optical flow field, namely one provided by Eero Simoncelli generated using the method described in (Simoncelli et al., 1991). The field has been interpolated and sampled on a regular grid, so the convolution method can be directly applied. Due to errors in the interpolant near the borders of the image and near the horizon, we found it necessary to crop the flow field. In Figure 6 the outside frame represents our usual 60 degree field of view, the next largest rectangle represents the frame of the original Yosemite sequence, and the inside rectangle represents the field of view in which we kept the optical flow data.

The results of using 10 different noise samples in the dithering are shown in Figure 6. To get this quality of result we needed to use a large convolution mask. In particular we used a 31×31 square array formed by modifying a DOG mask with a center standard deviation of 3 pixels and 6 for the surround (see Appendix A). Successive taps for this mask were separated by 4 pixels, since it was found that smaller masks generated only a planar constraint on the translational direction. An additional 20 runs were performed (each run took 30 seconds on a SGI 4D/340VGX and computed about 1,000 translation constraint vectors), and they generated a mean translational direction with an error of 1.8 degrees. The standard deviation over these twenty runs was 1.3 degrees in the vertical direction and 0.5 degrees horizontally. These results compare favorably to those of our previous nonlinear method.

In summary, we have identified the cause of the bias in the basic linear subspace algorithm for the recovery of the translational direction. Moreover, we have demonstrated a simple method for its removal. The new method appears to be fairly robust and capable of generating useful diagnostics of its performance. Further work needs to be done before it can be generally applied to computed optical flow fields. However, the simplicity of the underlying approach, the absence of extraneous local minima, and no need for an initial guess or iterations, all provide strong motivating factors for pursuing this approach further.

Acknowledgements

Thanks to NSERC Canada, IRIS and NASA for financial support. Also thanks to Eero Simoncelli for providing the Yosemite flow, and to Alex Pentland and Brad Horowitz for providing the office scene.

Appendix A

Here we discuss the conditions on the coefficient vector $\vec{c}$ needed to ensure that the resulting translation constraint vectors $\vec{\tau}$ are orthogonal to the true translational direction. To do this we first need the basic equations for the motion field induced by a rigid motion. Image velocity, $\vec{u}(\vec{x})$, is defined as the derivatives, with respect to time, of the image coordinates of the projection of a scene point $\vec{X}(t)$. Using the rigid motion equation (2), and the perspective projection equation

$$\vec{x}(t) = \frac{1}{X_3(t)} \vec{X}(t),$$

we find that the image velocity is given by (see Heeger and Jepson, 1992)

$$\vec{u}(\vec{x}) = p(\vec{x})A(\vec{x})\vec{T} + B(\vec{x})\vec{\Omega}. \tag{18}$$

Here $p(\vec{x}) = 1/X_3$ is inverse depth, $\vec{T}$ is the translational velocity and $\vec{\Omega}$ is the rotational velocity. Also, the matrices A and B are given by

$$A(\vec{x}) = \begin{bmatrix} 1 & 0 & -x_1 \\ 0 & 1 & -x_2 \end{bmatrix}$$

$$B(\vec{x}) = \begin{bmatrix} -(x_1 x_2) & (1 + x_1^2) & -x_2 \\ -(1 + x_2^2) & (x_1 x_2) & x_1 \end{bmatrix}.$$

The $A(\vec{x})$ and $B(\vec{x})$ matrices depend only on the image position $\vec{x}$, not on any of the unknowns. (Note that the image position $\vec{x}$ is measured per unit focal length, so there is an implicit dependence on f.)

The first step of our algorithm involves the premultiplication of the image velocity samples by the matrix $Q(\vec{x})$ defined in (4). Using (18) above, the resulting vector $\vec{q}(\vec{x})$ is given by

$$\vec{q}(\vec{x}) = p(\vec{x})Q(\vec{x})A(\vec{x})\vec{T} + Q(\vec{x})B(\vec{x})\vec{\Omega}. \tag{19}$$

Here the product $Q(\vec{x})A(\vec{x})\vec{T}$ is easily seen to be

$$Q(\vec{x})A(\vec{x})\vec{T} = \begin{pmatrix} 0 & 1 & -x_2 \\ -1 & 0 & x_1 \\ x_2 & -x_1 & 0 \end{pmatrix} \vec{T} = \vec{T} \times \vec{x}, \tag{20}$$

where "$\times$" denotes the usual vector cross product. Similarly, a straight forward calculation shows that

$$Q(\vec{x})B(\vec{x})\vec{\Omega} = \begin{pmatrix} -(1+x_2^2) & x_1 x_2 & x_1 \\ x_1 x_2 & -(1+x_1^2) & x_2 \\ x_1 & x_2 & -(x_1^2+x_2^2) \end{pmatrix} \vec{\Omega} = \vec{x} \times (\vec{x} \times \vec{\Omega}). \tag{21}$$

Taken together, we find the simple expression for $\vec{q}(\vec{x})$

$$\vec{q}(\vec{x}) = (\vec{T} \times \vec{x})p(\vec{x}) + \vec{x} \times (\vec{x} \times \vec{\Omega}). \tag{22}$$

This form is sufficient to motivate the constraints on the coefficient vector $\vec{c}$.

In particular we seek coefficients which ensure that $\vec{\tau} \cdot \vec{T}$ vanishes, for the translation constraint vector defined by

$$\vec{\tau} = \sum_{i=1}^{K} c_i \vec{q}(\vec{x}_i). \tag{23}$$

It is useful to first consider only the component of $\vec{q}$ due to the translational velocity (i.e the first term on the right hand side of (22)). Notice that the inner product of this term with $\vec{T}$ must vanish, for all image positions $\vec{x}_i$, since the cross product $\vec{T} \times \vec{x}_i$ is perpendicular to $\vec{T}$. Thus, only the second term in (22) contributes, and we find

$$\vec{\tau} \cdot \vec{T} = \sum_{i=1}^{K} c_i \vec{T} \cdot [\vec{x}_i \times [\vec{x}_i \times \vec{\Omega}]]. \tag{24}$$

Here $\vec{T} \cdot [\vec{x}_i \times [\vec{x}_i \times \vec{\Omega}]]$, is simply a quadratic polynomial in terms of the image coordinates, whose coefficients depend on the particular values of $\vec{T}$

and $\vec{\Omega}$ (compare equation (21)). In fact, it can be shown that any quadratic polynomial can be represented by a particular choice of $\vec{T}$ and $\vec{\Omega}$. Therefore a sufficient condition for $\vec{\tau} \cdot \vec{T}$ to vanish is that the coefficients $\vec{c}$ must be orthogonal to the samples of any quadratic polynomial.

We can write this condition on the coefficients using a basis for the quadratic polynomials on the image plane, say $\{1, x_1, x_2, x_1^2, x_1 x_2, x_2^2\}$. This basis is evaluated at each image sample point, $\vec{x}_i$ for $i = 1, \ldots, N$, and the results are collected into the ith column of a $6 \times N$ matrix F. The condition that $\vec{c}$ is perpendicular to the samples of any quadratic polynomial is then equivalent to the condition that it is perpendicular to the samples of each of the basis polynomials, that is

$$F\vec{c} = \vec{0}. \tag{25}$$

Moreover, for generic sampling patterns, F is of full rank, so we can expect equation (25) to have a $K - 6$ dimensional space of solutions. Note that the 6-dimensional space of quadratic polynomials is invariant under affine deformations. Therefore the solution vectors of (25), namely $\vec{c}$, can also be taken to be invariant of affine deformations of the sampling pattern. As mentioned in Section 2, this invariance is important for the convolution form of our algorithm.

A couple of other methods can be understood from this formulation. In particular, the original nonlinear method described in (Heeger and Jepson, 1990, 1992) is equivalent to choosing the coefficients $\vec{c}$ such that they annihilate the samples of all polynomials of the same general form $\vec{T} \cdot [\vec{x} \times [\vec{x} \times \vec{\Omega}]]$. The difference is that we treated $\vec{T}$ as fixed (our candidate translational direction), and only varied the rotational velocity $\vec{\Omega}$. As a result, we required only three conditions on the coefficients instead of six. However the extra three conditions depend on the particular choice of $\vec{T}$, and thus the coefficients $\vec{c}$ also turn out, in general, to be functions of $\vec{T}$. In the notation of this paper, the consequence of this is that the translation constraint vectors $\vec{\tau}$ themselves depend on $\vec{T}$, and we obtain nonlinear constraints of the form $\vec{\tau}(\vec{T}) \cdot \vec{T} = 0$ on the translational direction. In general we note that a priori constraints on the translational or rotational velocities can be used to restrict the space of polynomials that the coefficients must be orthogonal to, thereby increasing the number of independent choices for the coefficients.

A second variant is due to da Vitorio Lobo and Tsotsos (1991). They consider only sampling patterns for which the sample points all lie on a line in the image plane passing through the projection of the true translational direction. That is, $\vec{x}_i = \vec{x}(s_i)$ where

$$\vec{x}(s) = (\vec{T} + s\vec{x}_0), \tag{26}$$

and the vector $\vec{x}_0$ is assumed to have a zero third component. Substitution of this expression for the sample points into (24) provides a polynomial that is quadratic in s, with the constant term

$$\vec{T} \cdot [\vec{T} \times [\vec{T} \times \Omega]] = 0.$$

Therefore, in this special case (24) takes the form

$$\vec{\tau} \cdot \vec{T} = \sum_{i=1}^{K} c_i s_i \left[a_0(\vec{T}, \vec{\Omega}) + a_1(\vec{T}, \vec{\Omega}) s_i \right],$$

for some coefficients a_0 and a_1. In particular the *product* $c_i s_i$ must be perpendicular to the samples of any *linear* polynomial in s (i.e. the above expression for $\vec{\tau} \cdot \vec{T}$ should vanish for any a_0 and a_1). This constraint can be satisfied given three or more distinct points $\{\vec{x}(s_i)\}_{i=1}^{3}$ that are collinear and have the true translational direction on the same line. In such a case, constant values for $c_i s_i$, $i = 1, \ldots, K$ can be computed for a particular sampling geometry. Finally, in order to eliminate the (unknown) terms s_i, it is convenient to first expand the Q matrix into the form

$$Q(\vec{x}(s)) = Q(\vec{T}) + s \begin{pmatrix} 0 & 0 \\ 0 & 0 \\ -x_{2,0} & x_{1,0} \end{pmatrix}.$$

Upon substitution of this expansion into $\vec{\tau} \cdot \vec{T}$ we find the terms depending on $Q(\vec{T})$ do not contribute to the inner product. Moreover, the remaining terms involve only the product $c_i s_i$, which are in fact the constant coefficients computed above. Therefore, we see the method of da Vitorio Lobo and Tsotsos reduces to a constant coefficient case in a novel way.

Returning to the method studied in this paper, we consider the constraint (25) on the coefficient vector. As we mentioned above this constraint is independent of any affine transformation of the sampling points, and depends only on the particular pattern of sample points in the patch. Therefore in situations where the patches are all chosen to be the same, such as the square $l \times l$ patches used in this paper, the *same* coefficient vector $\vec{c}$ can be precomputed and used for all the patches. Here we use a coefficient vector constructed by modifying a DOG (Difference of Gaussians) mask so that it satisfies (25). The center standard deviation of the original DOG was 1.5 pixels, and the surround was set to 3 pixels. A 15×15 set of filter taps was used. These DOG coefficients were modified by adding a quadratic polynomial which was windowed by the surround Gaussian (i.e. a Hermite function). The particular Hermite function added was uniquely determined by the constraint (25). The original DOG required only a small modification.

In addition, the result was normalized so that

$$\sum_{k=1}^{K} c_{kn}^2 = 1. \tag{27}$$

Finally, in Section 6 we used a DOG operator of twice the size (31×31), with twice the center and surround standard deviations listed above. This mask was modified in a similar way to satisfy (25).

Demodulation: A new approach to texture vision

John Daugman

Cathryn Downing

1. Introduction

The central argument of this chapter is that certain aspects of human texture vision can best be described in terms of a *demodulation* process of pattern analysis. We present evidence from psychophysical masking experiments as well as illustrations of perceptual organization, that suggest the existence of such underlying multiplicative representations. We also demonstrate a practical application of this demodulation process, in a system for automatic visual identification of persons based on the textural signature of the iris.

The notions of modulation and demodulation play important roles in communication theory (Gallager, 1968), coding and data compression, and information theory (Shannon and Weaver, 1949). A pattern or information-bearing signal can be encoded by modulating some parameter of a specified independent "carrier" signal, and subsequently decoded or recovered from it through a process of demodulation. Examples of carrier parameters that can be modulated and demodulated in such codes include amplitude (AM), phase (PM), and frequency (FM). These encoding operations can be information-preserving (invertible) while at the same time removing redundancies in the encoded signal, thus reducing the bandwidth required for its communication; moreover, many signals with overlapping spectra can be simultaneously communicated in a common medium by modulating them into separate "channels". The direct relationship between signal information content, or bit rate, and the modulation bandwidth required for its encoding, is made explicit in the theory of information.

These notions have currency in vision research, both because of the evidence for spatial frequency channels underlying early visual coding, and because some problems in perceptual organization require the extraction of embedded modulation patterns. A popular experimental paradigm in spatial vision began with seminal papers on beat frequencies by Burton (1973) and by Henning et al. (1975), which had their ultimate roots in the nineteenth-century work of Seebeck on the auditory "missing fundamental". Seebeck (1841) described the periodicity pitch heard in a complex waveform at its repetition frequency, despite an absence of spectral energy in the waveform at or anywhere near this frequency. For example, a tone generated by combining 8kHz, 10kHz, and 12kHz is heard as having a pitch of 2kHz, its missing fundamental, which challenges auditory theories of pitch perception based on frequency analysis. (Demodulation of the 3-tone complex would extract the perceived 2kHz envelope, modulating the amplitude of a 10kHz carrier.) Similarly, combining visual gratings whose spatial frequencies are 8, 10, and 12 cpd produces a substantial masking effect at the beat or repetition frequency of 2 cpd; Henning et al. (1975) interpreted this in terms of filter interaction, while others (following Burton, 1973) have favoured non-linear distortion products. Much subsequent work has pursued this AM experimental paradigm (e.g. Albrecht and De Valois, 1981; Nachmias and Rogowitz, 1983; Derrington and Badcock, 1986), but regrettably almost always with one-dimensional spatial frequency concepts and signals, thus greatly limiting both the richness and the relevance of the research for spatial vision. Moreover, this work has focused narrowly on evaluating the non-linear distortion hypothesis, ignoring larger and more interesting questions about the general role of demodulation in perception.

2. Analyzing patterns by amplitude- and phase-demodulation

It is informative and somewhat surprising to realize that any pattern can be described as the amplitude- and phase-modulation (AMPM) of a single carrier frequency. In the case of rather bandlimited patterns such as textures, the AMPM representation typically has much lower complexity than the original image itself, resulting in a very compact and efficient description. Intuitively, the reason this claim does not violate information theory is because the bandlimited character of textures is a form of redundancy, in that a particular scale and direction of undulation predominates. Once this "characteristic undulation" is extracted in the form of a carrier wave, the remaining structure of the texture is captured by much more slowly varying components specifying the amplitude and phase modulation of that carrier. Indeed, we propose that such compact, multiplicative representations seem to underlie some aspects of the human perceptual organization of texture.

An AMPM representation must not be confused with the familiar *amplitude spectrum* and *phase spectrum*, which are specified as functions of frequency in the Fourier domain and which comprise the Fourier transform. Rather, we are concerned here with deriving amplitude- and phase-specifying functions over the *space domain*, that modulate a derived carrier wave so as to represent some given pattern. We refer to the derivation of these three components as the process of *demodulating* the pattern.

Given some arbitrary spatial stimulus pattern of image intensities $S(x, y)$, our problem is to find a single carrier wave $C(x, y)$ together with its complex modulation phasor $Z(x,y)$, such that their modulation product reproduces the stimulus pattern:

$$S(x,y) = Z(x,y)C(x,y). \tag{1}$$

We show that such a decomposition exists and we claim that, particularly in the case of textures, such a representation is a very compact, redundancy-reducing form of image interpretation that also serves further goals in perceptual organization. The modulation phasor $Z(x,y)$ specifies in complex polar form over the image domain both the carrier wave's amplitude modulation $A(x,y)$ and its phase modulation $\phi(x,y)$:

$$Z(x,y) = A(x,y)e^{i\phi(x,y)} \tag{2}$$

Figure 1 illustrates these three derived modulation components $A(x,y)$, $\phi(x,y)$, and $C(x,y)$ in the case of a particular texture, together with its reconstruction from them. We now present the demodulation algorithm for finding these components of an AMPM representation for any given stimulus pattern.

2.1. Demodulation algorithm

1   Express the original pattern $S(x,y)$ in terms of a 2D Fourier series expansion:

$$S(x,y) = \sum_{k=-N}^{N} \alpha_k e^{i(\mu_k x + \nu_k y)} \tag{3}$$

having any required number $2N$ of paired conjugate 2D frequency components $(\mu_k, \nu_k) = (-\mu_{-k}, -\nu_{-k})$ and their associated complex coefficients $\alpha_k = a_k + b_k i$, with $\alpha_0 = 0$. Since $S(x,y)$ is an image and is therefore real, its expansion coefficients α_k are conjugate symmetric: $\alpha_k = \alpha_{-k}^*$. It is assumed for convenience that all values of the index k having the same sign $(+/-)$ always index components in the same half of the Fourier plane. It will be useful to denote the magnitude of each coefficient as $\|\alpha_k\| = \sqrt{a_k^2 + b_k^2}$ and its phase as $\theta_k = \tan^{-1}(b_k/a_k)$, so that $\alpha_k = \|\alpha_k\|e^{i\theta_k}$.

2   Use this expansion to compute the 2D coordinates of the spectral center-of-mass (μ_c, ν_c) of the stimulus pattern over the Fourier half-plane:

$$\mu_c = \frac{\displaystyle\sum_{k=1}^{N} \|\alpha_k\|\mu_k}{\displaystyle\sum_{k=1}^{N} \|\alpha_k\|} \tag{4}$$

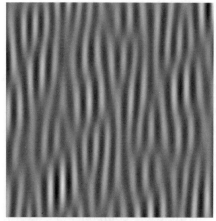

Original 6-component texture

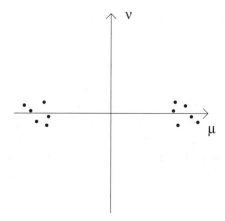

2D Fourier spectrum of texture

Derived phasor AM component

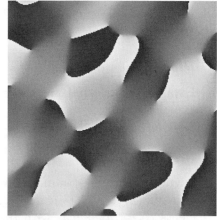

Derived phasor PM component

Derived carrier wave

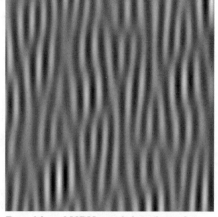

Resulting AMPM modulated carrier

Fig. 1.

$$\nu_c = \frac{\sum_{k=1}^{N} \|\alpha_k\| \nu_k}{\sum_{k=1}^{N} \|\alpha_k\|} \tag{5}$$

Such a spectral center-of-mass need not represent any frequency component actually present in the pattern, as is illustrated by the punctate spectral cluster in Figure 1.

3   Specify a single 2D Fourier component to be the carrier wave $C(x, y)$:

$$C(x, y) = e^{i(\mu_c x + \nu_c y)} \tag{6}$$

using the center-of-mass frequency (μ_c, ν_c) computed over the half-plane in Step 2. The simplest and most compact AMPM description is obtained by selecting a carrier frequency at, or near, the spectral center-of-mass.

4   Compute this carrier wave's associated AMPM complex modulation phasor $Z(x, y)$, by replacing each vector frequency (μ_k, ν_k) in the half-plane expansion of $S(x, y)$ by the vector difference frequency $(\Delta\mu_k, \Delta\nu_k)$ between itself and the carrier frequency (μ_c, ν_c):

$$Z(x, y) = \sum_{k=1}^{N} \alpha_k e^{i(\Delta\mu_k x + \Delta\nu_k y)} \tag{7}$$

where $\Delta\mu_k = \mu_k - \mu_c$ and $\Delta\nu_k = \nu_k - \nu_c$. Thus:

$$Z(x, y)C(x, y) = \left(\sum_{k=1}^{N} \alpha_k e^{i(\Delta\mu_k x + \Delta\nu_k y)} \right) e^{i(\mu_c x + \nu_c y)}$$

$$= \sum_{k=1}^{N} \alpha_k e^{i(\mu_k x + \nu_k y)} \tag{8}$$

and

$$Z^*(x, y)C^*(x, y) = \left(\sum_{k=1}^{N} \alpha_k^* e^{-i(\Delta\mu_k x + \Delta\nu_k y)} \right) e^{-i(\mu_c x + \nu_c y)}$$

$$= \sum_{k=1}^{N} \alpha_k^* e^{-i(\mu_k x + \nu_k y)}$$

$$= \sum_{k=-N}^{-1} \alpha_k e^{i(\mu_k x + \nu_k y)} \tag{9}$$

where the last step exploits the relations of conjugate symmetry among coefficients and 2D frequency components as noted under Step 1. It is clear by comparing (3), (8), and (9) that the original stimulus pattern $S(x,y)$ has been decomposed without loss into a carrier wave $C(x,y)$ and its modulation phasor $Z(x,y)$:

$$S(x,y) = Z(x,y)C(x,y) + Z^*(x,y)C^*(x,y) \qquad (10)$$

which may be further simplified to:

$$S(x,y) = 2\mathbf{Re}\{Z(x,y)C(x,y)\} \qquad (11)$$

It should be noted that the solution for $Z(x,y)$ specified in (7) is not equivalent to the trivial solution $Z(x,y) = \frac{1}{2}S(x,y)\exp[-i(\mu_c x + \nu_c y)]$, in which there would be no image code projection into carrier phase.

5   By expressing the modulation phasor $Z(x,y)$ in polar form, project out its amplitude modulation component $A(x,y)$ and its phase modulation component $\phi(x,y)$:

$$Z(x,y) = A(x,y)e^{i\phi(x,y)} \qquad (12)$$

where

$$A(x,y) = \left[\left(\sum_{k=1}^{N} \|\alpha_k\| \cos(\Delta\mu_k x + \Delta\nu_k y + \theta_k) \right)^2 \right.$$
$$\left. + \left(\sum_{k=1}^{N} \|\alpha_k\| \sin(\Delta\mu_k x + \Delta\nu_k y + \theta_k) \right)^2 \right]^{1/2} \qquad (13)$$

and

$$\phi(x,y) = \tan^{-1} \left(\frac{\displaystyle\sum_{k=1}^{N} \|\alpha_k\| \sin(\Delta\mu_k x + \Delta\nu_k y + \theta_k)}{\displaystyle\sum_{k=1}^{N} \|\alpha_k\| \cos(\Delta\mu_k x + \Delta\nu_k y + \theta_k)} \right) \qquad (14)$$

It is noteworthy that the amplitude modulation component $A(x,y)$ is actually independent of the chosen carrier frequency (μ_c, ν_c). By using trigonometric identities to combine terms in binomial expansions of the quantities within (13), it may be shown that $A(x,y)$ can also be expressed just in terms of all the vector difference frequencies among all of the components of $S(x,y)$ in the half-plane:

$$A(x,y) = \left[\sum_{m=1}^{N} \sum_{n=1}^{N} \|\alpha_m\|\|\alpha_n\| \cos((\mu_m - \mu_n)x \right.$$
$$\left. + (\nu_m - \nu_n)y + (\theta_m - \theta_n)) \right]^{1/2} \qquad (15)$$

This expression is computationally less useful than (13) since its complexity is quadratic rather than linear in the number of expansion terms (N^2 versus $2N$). However, it establishes the fact that the demodulation phasor AM component $A(x, y)$ depends only on the input image $S(x, y)$ and not on the choice of carrier frequency for demodulating it.

We have shown that the original stimulus pattern $S(x, y)$ can be represented completely in the form of a carrier wave $C(x, y)$ modulated in both amplitude and phase. The explicit computation of the carrier's AMPM phasor components $A(x, y)$ and $\phi(x, y)$ over the image, as defined in (13) and (14), comprise a demodulation representation of the original pattern.

2.2. Illustrations of texture demodulation phasors

It is informative to study the AMPM demodulation representation of various textures, both coherent and incoherent. Figures 1–5 illustrate several synthetic textures with their 2D spectra (top row), their derived phasor components $A(x, y)$ and $\phi(x, y)$ (middle row), and their derived carrier $C(x, y)$ together with the reconstruction of the original pattern from these components (bottom row). The mean luminance, or zero frequency, component of each texture has been omitted from the coordinate origin of the spectral plots. Figure 6 illustrates the demodulation of a natural textured scene, according to the same format.

3. Demodulation and perceptual organization

As suggested by Figures 1–6, perceptual organization for these kinds of textures seems to follow their AMPM description. The multi-component patterns are perceived as patchy, high contrast islands, partitioned by a meandering net of low contrast and phase reversal. Certainly perceptual organization does *not* correspond to the textures' 2D spectral description; for example, the original incoherent texture in Figure 1 is not perceived as six pure sinewaves. Even the fact that its spectrum is punctate rather than continuous is lost on the visual system. The Figure 1 texture is difficult to distinguish perceptually from 2D white noise that has been bandpass filtered in the same 2D frequency band, despite the fact that the noise has a continuous rather than punctate spectrum.

Perceptual organization for textures containing only two or three 2D frequency components is especially well described by the AM component of the AMPM phasor, as illustrated by Figures 4 and 5. For such patterns the dominating percept is generally the "beat" pattern, whose frequency and orientation are precisely those of the phasor AM component.

For textures containing only two components the beat pattern has a 2D frequency that can also be more simply computed as just the vector

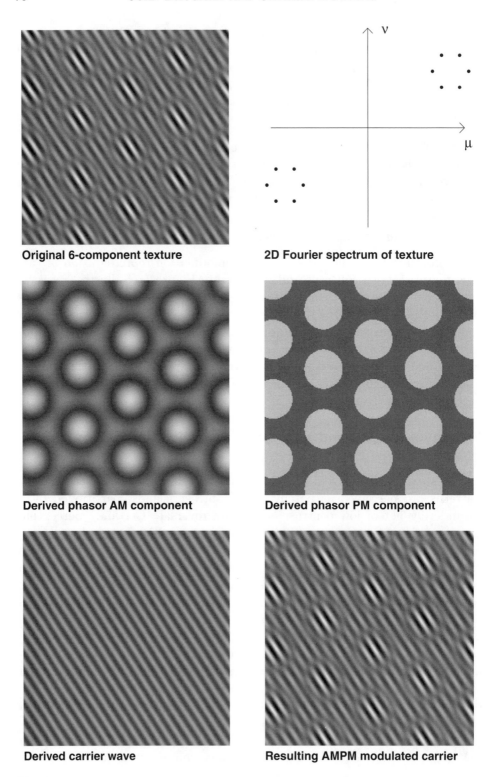

Fig. 2.

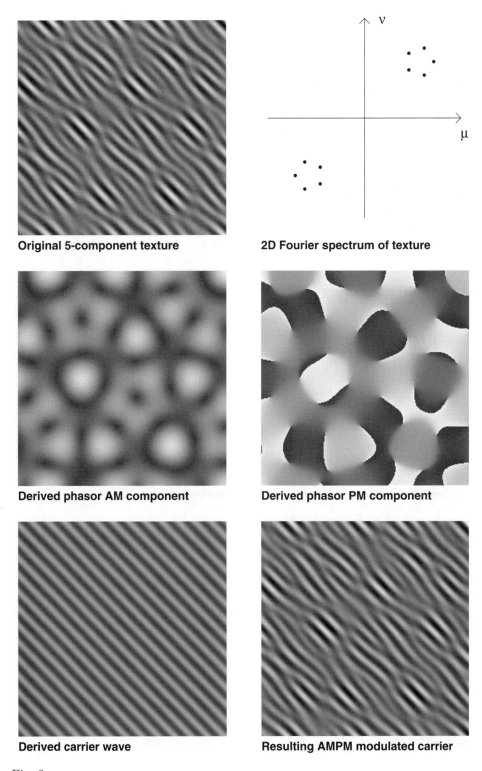

Original 5-component texture

2D Fourier spectrum of texture

Derived phasor AM component

Derived phasor PM component

Derived carrier wave

Resulting AMPM modulated carrier

Fig. 3.

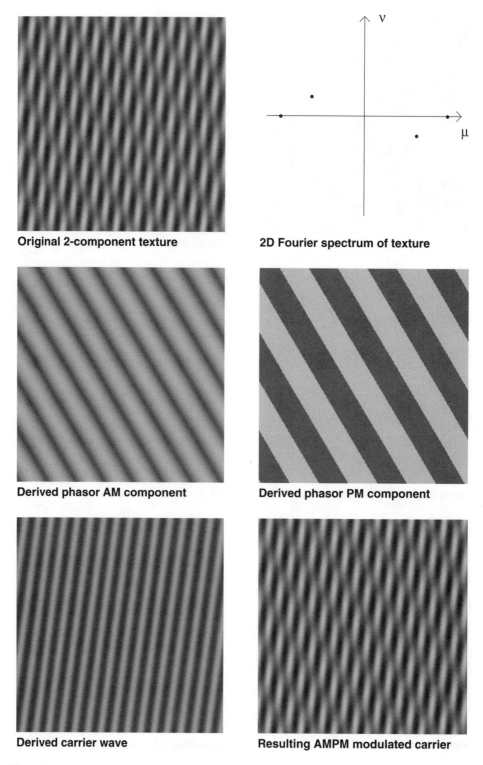

Original 2-component texture　　　　**2D Fourier spectrum of texture**

Derived phasor AM component　　　　**Derived phasor PM component**

Derived carrier wave　　　　**Resulting AMPM modulated carrier**

Fig. 4.

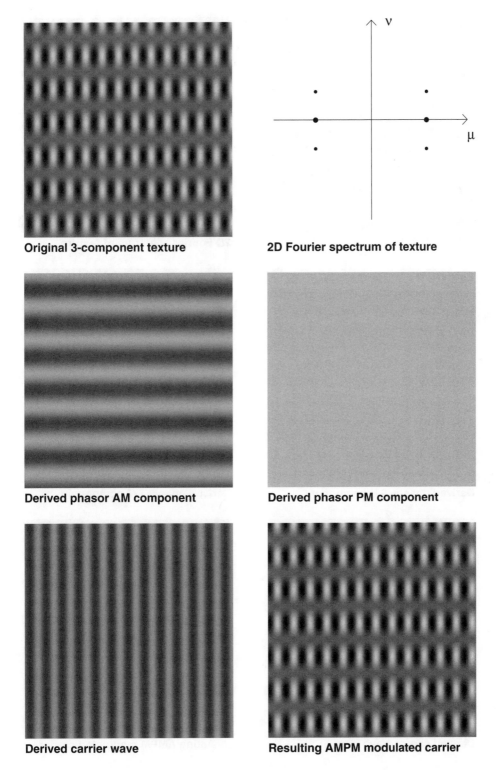

Original 3-component texture

2D Fourier spectrum of texture

Derived phasor AM component

Derived phasor PM component

Derived carrier wave

Resulting AMPM modulated carrier

Fig. 5.

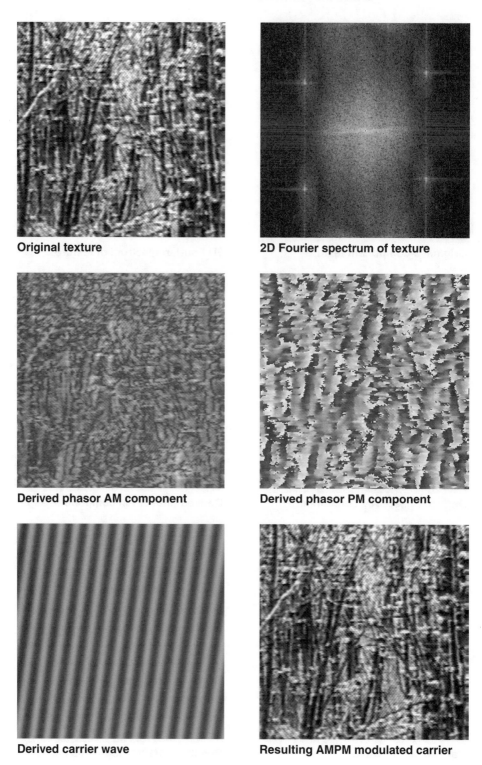

Original texture | 2D Fourier spectrum of texture

Derived phasor AM component | Derived phasor PM component

Derived carrier wave | Resulting AMPM modulated carrier

Fig. 6.

difference between the two frequency components present in the pattern. Figure 7 illustrates two examples of textures (left column) comprised of frequency pairs as indicated, together with their beat pattern frequencies (right column). The central schematic illustrates that the "parallelogram rule", famous from Newton's construction for the composition of forces, geometrically generates the vector difference beat frequency. Since there is no spectral energy at this vector difference frequency, it is labelled as the "nonspectral beat" to distinguish it from the true spectral components. The perceptual salience of the beat pattern is of some interest for this reason.

The AMPM phasor representation for arbitrary patterns can be regarded as based upon a generalization of this concept of difference frequency, since the spectral structure entering into the AM component $A(x, y)$ and the PM component $\phi(x, y)$ of the representation as defined in Equations (13) and (14) consists of the vector difference frequencies $(\Delta\mu_k, \Delta\nu_k)$ between the spectral components (μ_k, ν_k) and their center-of-mass (μ_c, ν_c).

3.1. Demodulation representation for two-component plaids

In the special case of textures comprising only two components (plaids), the AM component of their demodulation representation explicitly captures the perceived beat frequency. It is illuminating to derive the relationship between the periodicity of the phasor component $A(x, y)$, and the vector difference frequency generated by the parallelogram rule illustrated in Figure 7. If the two superimposed sinewave gratings that comprise the plaid pattern have 2D frequencies (μ_1, ν_1) and (μ_2, ν_2), so that $S(x, y) = \sin(\mu_1 x + \nu_1 y) + \sin(\mu_2 x + \nu_2 y)$, then the series expansion of the plaid stimulus as required for (3) in the Demodulation Algorithm is:

$$S(x, y) = \frac{i}{2}\left(e^{-i(\mu_1 x + \nu_1 y)} - e^{i(\mu_1 x + \nu_1 y)}\right) + \frac{i}{2}\left(e^{-i(\mu_2 x + \nu_2 y)} - e^{i(\mu_2 x + \nu_2 y)}\right). \tag{16}$$

The derived carrier wave $C(x, y)$ at the spectral center-of-mass of $S(x, y)$, as per (4) and (5), is:

$$C(x, y) = e^{i\left[\left(\frac{\mu_1 + \mu_2}{2}\right)x + \left(\frac{\nu_1 + \nu_2}{2}\right)y\right]} \tag{17}$$

The derived demodulation phasor $Z(x, y)$ as per (7) is:

$$Z(x, y) = -\frac{i}{2}e^{i\left[\left(\frac{\mu_1 - \mu_2}{2}\right)x + \left(\frac{\nu_1 - \nu_2}{2}\right)y\right]} - \frac{i}{2}e^{i\left[\left(\frac{\mu_2 - \mu_1}{2}\right)x + \left(\frac{\nu_2 - \nu_1}{2}\right)y\right]}$$

$$= -i\cos\left(\frac{(\mu_1 - \mu_2)}{2}x + \frac{(\nu_1 - \nu_2)}{2}y\right) \tag{18}$$

whose AM component, by definition, is:

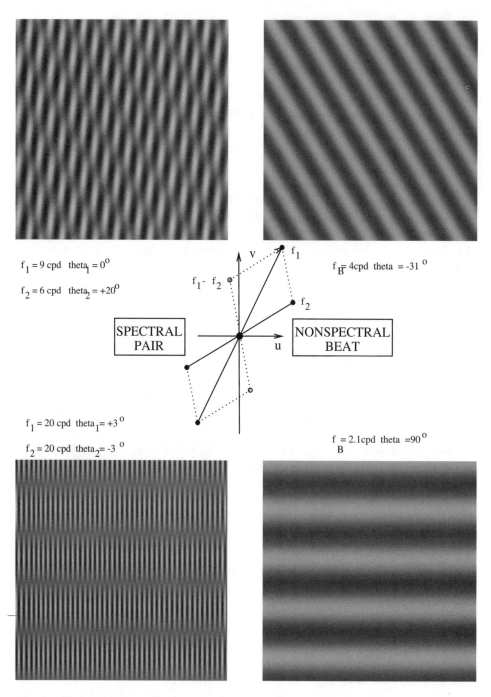

Fig. 7. *Parallelogram rule for calculating 2D beat frequencies in the simple case of textures containing only two Fourier components (plaids). The vector difference frequency for each two-component plaid on the left is shown on the right. Its wavelength matches the beat interval. Its repetition rate also corresponds to that of the phasor AM component $A(x,y)$ defined in (13) or (15) as illustrated in Figure 4.*

$$A(x,y) = \sqrt{\cos^2\left(\frac{(\mu_1 - \mu_2)}{2}x + \frac{(\nu_1 - \nu_2)}{2}y\right)}$$

$$= \sqrt{\frac{1}{2} + \frac{1}{2}\cos((\mu_1 - \mu_2)x + (\nu_1 - \nu_2)y)} \qquad (19)$$

(These expressions for $A(x,y)$ may also be gotten directly from (13) or (15), by recognizing that in this case, $\alpha_1 = \alpha_2 = -i/2$, so $\|\alpha_1\| = \|\alpha_2\| = \frac{1}{2}$ and $\theta_1 = \theta_2 = -\pi/2$.)

This function is periodic with vector frequency $(\mu, \nu) = ((\mu_1 - \mu_2), (\nu_1 - \nu_2))$, which is indeed the vector difference frequency between the two components of the plaid as was generated by the parallelogram rule in Figure 7. It should be recalled that $A(x,y)$ does not depend on the chosen carrier frequency, which for convenience we have placed at the spectral center-of-mass. The important point established here is that AMPM demodulation for the case of two-component textures always explicitly captures their beat vector frequency in its AM component. This derived component often dominates our perceptual organization of such stimuli, as was also demonstrated earlier for more complex patterns.

4. Demodulation and the perception of spatio-temporal beats

Psychophysical observations illustrated the human ability to extract 2D spatial and spatio-temporal beat frequencies from such patterns. The textures shown in Figures 1–5 were generated by a *Picasso C.R.T. Image Synthesizer* and displayed on a linearized Tektronix 608 monitor at a frame rate of 250 Hz. In general the textures also had temporal structure, since each Fourier component was given a temporal drift frequency ω_k as well. When all Fourier components in a given texture shared the same temporal frequency, the net-like structure was perceived to be stationary, while the underlying modulated carrier was perceived to be moving. Indeed, this is exactly the dynamic perceptual organization predicted by AMPM demodulation. Inspection of Equations (3) through (14) reveals that when the textures are generalized to include temporal frequency components ω_k, their derived carrier $C(x,y,t)$ is in motion unless the weighted average of all the ω_k temporal frequency components happens to be zero. But both $A(x,y)$ and $\phi(x,y)$ have no time-dependence if all the ω_k temporal frequencies are the same, since then all vector difference frequencies relative to the spectral center-of-mass in Equations (13) and (14) have zero as their temporal frequency component: $\Delta\omega_k = 0$. Thus the AMPM demodulation representation corresponds well to human perceptual organization of these dynamic textures, by decomposing them into a moving carrier multiplied by a stationary modulation phasor.

In further phenomenological experiments, using dynamic textures with only two components, Observers were asked to identify the moving beat frequency perceived in the patterns. Their task was to match the beat pattern's orientation, spatial frequency, and velocity, by manually setting these parameters for a third grating generated simultaneously by the *Picasso* on a second monitor. Observers' settings for these three parameters when presented with a variety of superimposed pairs of moving gratings are plotted in Figures 8, 9, and 10. Each observed setting is plotted against the predicted value for that AM parameter of the phasor that is derived by AMPM demodulation of the stimulus. The close agreement between predicted AM phasor parameters, and the Observers' settings for matching the perceived moving beat frequency, offers further support to the view that AMPM demodulation may underlie some aspects of human perception of textures.

Finally, it is worth noting that any such superimposed pair of drifting, oriented sinewave gratings with matched contrast is equivalent to the *product* of a different pair of sinewave gratings (apart from their mean luminance component). Since the observed beats occur wherever one of the equivalent product pair members has a zero-crossing, it might be argued that such a multiplicative representation may be a better and simpler description of the plaid than either its additive description or its AMPM description. Specifically, if the two gratings that are added together have spatial frequencies (f_1, f_2), orientations (θ_1, θ_2), and temporal drift frequencies (ω_1, ω_2), then their superposition is equivalent to the product of a different pair of gratings having spatial frequencies (f_3, f_4), orientations (θ_3, θ_4), and temporal drift frequencies (ω_3, ω_4), where:

$$f_3 = \frac{1}{2}\sqrt{f_1^2 + f_2^2 + 2f_1 f_2 \cos(\theta_1 - \theta_2)} \tag{20}$$

$$f_4 = \frac{1}{2}\sqrt{f_1^2 + f_2^2 - 2f_1 f_2 \cos(\theta_1 - \theta_2)} \tag{21}$$

$$\theta_3 = \tan^{-1}\left(\frac{f_1 \sin(\theta_1) + f_2 \sin(\theta_2)}{f_1 \cos(\theta_1) + f_2 \cos(\theta_2)}\right) \tag{22}$$

$$\theta_4 = \tan^{-1}\left(\frac{f_1 \sin(\theta_1) - f_2 \sin(\theta_2)}{f_1 \cos(\theta_1) - f_2 \cos(\theta_2)}\right) \tag{23}$$

$$\omega_3 = \frac{1}{2}(\omega_1 + \omega_2) \tag{24}$$

$$\omega_4 = \frac{1}{2}(\omega_1 - \omega_2) \tag{25}$$

However, this equivalent multiplicative representation for the two-component plaids fails, in two respects, to correspond to our perceptual organization of

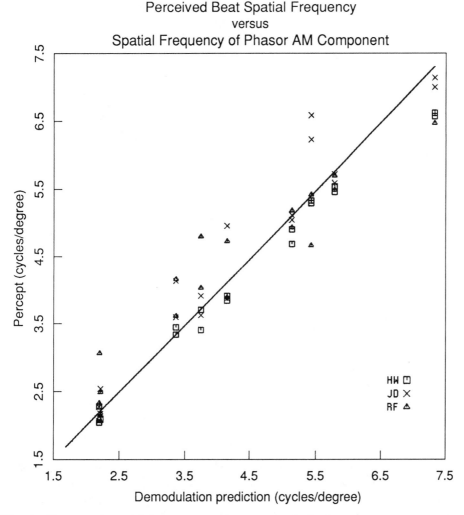

Fig. 8. *Observers' spatial frequency settings to match the beat component perceived in two-component moving textures, such as illustrated in Figure 4, plotted against the predicted spatial frequency of the phasor AM component as defined in (12).*

them. First, the equivalent multiplicative representation predicts not one, but two different sets of beat patterns, in different orientations (one for each of the component product sinewaves along their zero-crossing lines), yet we tend to perceive only the lower frequency beat pattern. The AMPM demodulation interpretation avoids this ambiguity by using the spectral center-of-mass to specify the carrier. Second, the morphology of the plaid pattern's contrast waveform has phenomenological cusps centered on the beat lines. These cusps are much narrower than the troughs of the equivalent product sinewave.

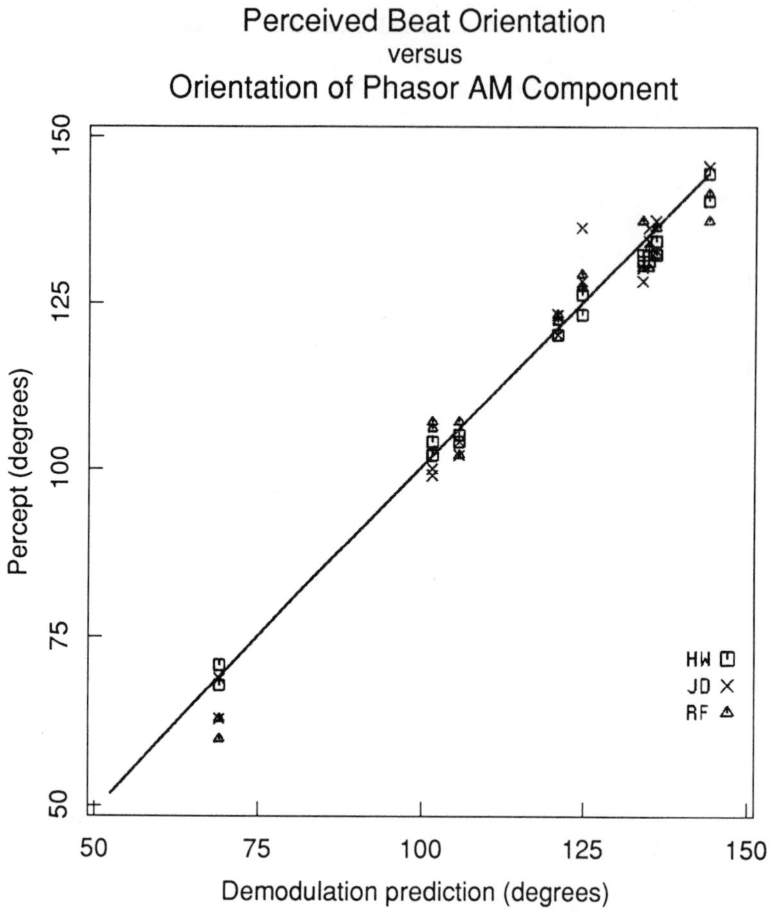

Fig. 9. *Observers' orientation settings to match the beat component perceived in two-component moving textures, such as illustrated in Figure 4, plotted against the predicted orientation of the phasor AM component as defined in (13).*

5. Masking at the demodulation phasor AM frequency

The preceding observations about perceptual organization of textures, and their perceived spatio-temporal beat structure, suggest further quantitative experiments involving psychophysical masking. The three component texture shown in Figure 5 has the spectral structure of a vertical carrier plus two sidebands, inclined at 26 degrees on either side of the vertical carrier and with half its contrast. Yet the pattern is perceived with predominantly horizontal structure, contrary to the theory of spatial frequency channels when specified in two dimensional form (Daugman, 1984). The panels of Figure 5 show that the AMPM representation decomposes this three component texture into just a vertical carrier multiplied by a horizontal raised sinusoidal AM component, with no phase modulation.

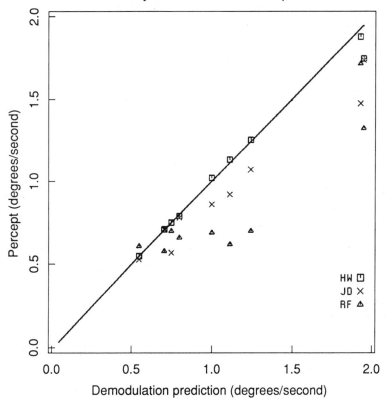

Fig. 10. *Observers' velocity settings to match the beat component perceived in two-component moving textures, such as illustrated in Figure 4, plotted against the predicted velocity of the phasor AM component as defined in (13).*

The purpose of the masking experiments using this texture was to investigate whether there is any threshold elevation corresponding to its horizontal AM component, despite the fact that the spectral structure of the mask only has components around vertical. The AMPM demodulation description of the texture predicts that there will be such an effect in the horizontal orientation, which accords also with our perceptual organization of the pattern. A further interest in this mask stimulus arises from the fact that, if convolved with the popular isotropic Laplacian-of-a-Gaussian $\nabla^2 G_\sigma(x, y)$ operator, at all scales of analysis σ specifying the scale constant of the Gaussian $G_\sigma(x, y)$, the only resulting zero-crossings are always in the vertical orientation. They are the zero-crossings of the vertical carrier, independent of the modulating sidebands that determine the horizontal structure in the pattern, as discussed in Daugman (1988b). Thus, a finding of a horizontal masking effect as predicted by the AMPM demodulation description of the pattern would be difficult to explain both for the $\nabla^2 G_\sigma(x, y)$ theory of early vision, and for the classical idea of spatial frequency and orientation tuned channels.

Two Observers (the authors) participated in two experiments investigating the masking produced by such three component textures. Stimuli were generated on a linearized Tektronix 608 monitor by a *Picasso*. We used a 2AFC paradigm, which required the Observers to indicate which of two successive trial intervals contained a horizontal sinewave test component. On half of the trials, a three component texture mask like that in Figure 5 was presented in one interval, which was chosen at random, while the same mask plus the horizontal test was presented in the other. On the remaining trials, no mask was presented: the test alone was presented in one of the two intervals, chosen at random. Over the course of each experiment, the horizontal test was presented at five different spatial frequencies, one of which corresponded to that of the demodulation phasor AM component of the mask. All of the tests matched this demodulation phasor component in orientation, but only in one case did they also match it in spatial frequency. In one experiment (Figure 11, top row) the two sidebands' ν spectral component matched the carrier's spatial frequency, and in the second experiment (Figure 11, bottom row) the sidebands' ν component was one-half of the carrier's spatial frequency. The sidebands' μ spectral component always equalled the carrier's frequency. These two different sideband configurations generate different demodulation phasor AM components, and hence different predictions about where masking should be greatest. In each of the panels of Figure 11, an arrow indicates the spatial frequency at which the demodulation representation predicts the greatest masking.

The experiments determined contrast threshold for test sinewave gratings at each of the five spatial frequencies, both with and without the three component mask. This was accomplished by randomly interleaving ten, 2-down 1-up staircase procedures (Wetherill and Levitt, 1965), one for each of the above conditions. Each Observer participated in four to eight sessions for each experiment. We computed threshold estimates for each staircase following Wetherill and Levitt's method. Figure 11 shows the threshold elevation factor (ratio of masked to unmasked detection thresholds) for horizontal test gratings presented with and without the three-component mask, at each of the five experimental spatial frequencies. Standard errors for these ratios have been calculated by Monte-Carlo simulation based on the sampled distribution of masked and unmasked thresholds. In each case, the masking is greatest at the frequency predicted by the demodulation AM component, as indicated by the arrows, and falls off as the test frequency departs from this predicted value. For both subjects and both experiments, t-tests confirm that the masking effect at the predicted frequency is significantly greater than the masking effects at test frequencies differing by a factor of two or more from the predicted frequency.

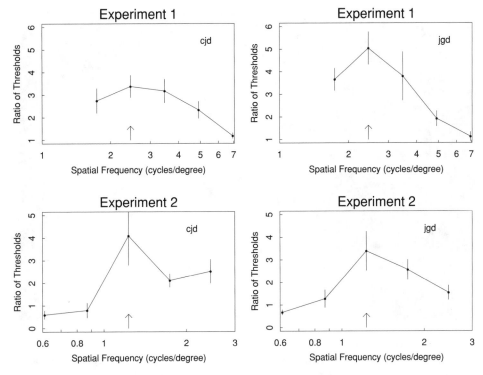

Fig. 11. *Threshold elevation factors for detection of horizontal test gratings of various spatial frequencies in the presence of a three-component AM mask. The mask was the generic three-component texture shown in Figure 5, comprising a vertical carrier plus two sidebands. In the upper row, both the μ and the ν components of the sidebands matched the carrier spatial frequency. In the bottom row, the sidebands' μ spectral components were equal to the carrier's spatial frequency while ν was half this spatial frequency. Arrows indicate the spatial frequency of the AM phasor component in the demodulation representation of the masking texture. Even though there is no horizontal spectral component present in the mask, this horizontal AM phasor component correctly predicts the location of peak masking effect for both Observers.*

These masking experiments confirm the predictions generated by the AMPM demodulation representation of the texture masks. The results further affirm that something like this representation may underlie some aspects of human texture vision, and they pose interesting challenges for alternative theories.

6. Application of texture demodulation in a practical system for biometric personal identification

We now describe a practical application of the AMPM demodulation representation in the field of automatic pattern recognition. The most unique, identifying feature of a person's face is the detailed texture of each eye's

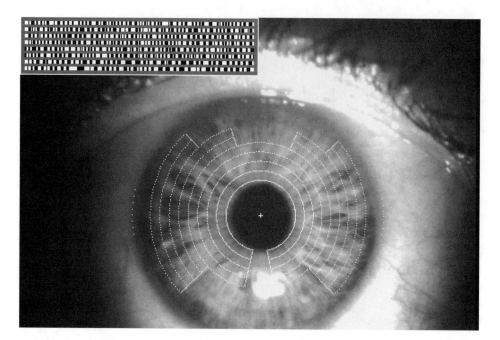

Fig. 12. *Application of AMPM texture demodulation for automatic visual personal identification, based on the texture of the iris. A multi-carrier, 256-byte "iris code" is shown inscribed in the corner of the Figure. Computing this code from a video image of the eye can establish or confirm its owner's identity with extremely high confidence.*

iris. This complex yet stable "biometric signature" can serve as the basis of a very rapid and high-confidence method of visually determining or confirming the identity of persons. A statistical estimate of the complexity (dimensionality) of monochromatically visible iris texture in a sample of the human population reveals variation corresponding to more than a hundred independent degrees-of-freedom. Designing automatic means for encoding and recognizing such a biometric signature, reliably and efficiently, is an interesting and challenging problem.

A multi-carrier 256-byte "iris code" has been developed using the AMPM demodulation concept described here and implemented in a practical device that uniquely identifies the iris texture of any person, in about a second, with astronomic confidence levels. An example of such an iris code is shown in the corner of Figure 12, together with the eye image from which it was computed; superimposed on the iris are certain mapping coordinates. The problem of pattern recognition is transformed essentially into a statistical test of independence on the phase reversals in the iris texture. Statistical decision theory provides a probabilistic basis for making identification decisions from rapid comparisons of iris codes, as well as for calculating the confidence

Hamming Distances for Authentics and Imposters

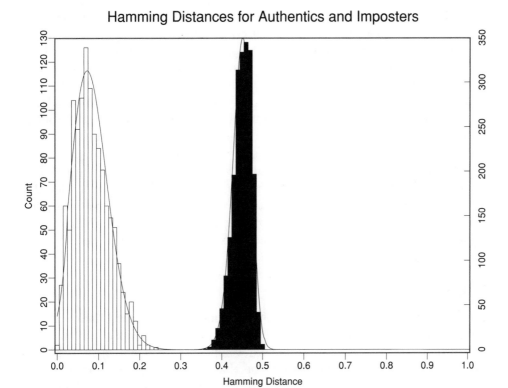

Fig. 13. *Performance histograms of the biometric personal identification system based on AMPM demodulation of visible iris texture. Measured Hamming distances between the multi-carrier "iris codes" as illustrated in Figure 12 are tallied both for images comparing different eyes (imposters, black histogram), and for different images of the same eye (authentics, white histogram). The non-overlapping separation between these two empirical histograms reflects the system's error-free identification performance on this database of several hundred images. This decision task has a $d'=8.41$ formal decidability.*

level associated with any identification decision. Figure 13 demonstrates the system's identification performance on a database of several hundred video images of persons' eyes. Texture dissimilarities, computed as Hamming distances between quantized demodulation phasor PM components, among all different (monochrome) images of same eyes are denoted "Authentics" and plotted in the white histogram, while computed dissimilarities between all images of different eyes, denoted "Imposters," are plotted in the black histogram. There is no overlap between these two empirical distributions. Exhaustive search for a match to any coded eye pattern has always produced the correct identity of the person if s/he has been enrolled in the database, and a correct rejection if not. The formal decidability of this decision task, analogous to detectability in a signal detection task, is measured at

d'=8.41. Fitting appropriate binomials to both distributions, the "cross-over point" between them (where the theoretical False Accept Rate equals the theoretical False Reject Rate, near a Hamming distance criterion of 0.321) corresponds to an error probability of 1 in 131,000 for both types of errors. For the typical Authentics match, near the mean of the white distribution (H.D. = 0.084), the theoretical probability of false recognition (Type II error) is 1 in 10^{31}; i.e. this is the theoretical area under the black probability distribution lying to the left of this Hamming distance criterion. For the typical correct rejection, i.e. near the mean of the Imposters distribution at H.D. = 0.45, the theoretical probability of a false accept (Type I error) is one in $10^{9.6}$. Some potential applications of this high-confidence identification technique based on biometric texture demodulation include passport control, bank cash machines, control over access to premises and assets, forensics, computer login control, security systems, financial authorization, licenses, and personal ID generally.

7. Discussion

Texture vision is a generic form of image analysis that raises many issues about perceptual organization, classification, data compression, and pattern recognition. In this chapter we have developed the concept of AMPM demodulation as a general coding scheme that can be used to represent any pattern, but which is particularly useful for textures. The scheme identifies the predominant or characteristic scale and direction of undulation within the pattern, specifying a 2D carrier frequency, and represents the whole pattern in terms of relative amplitude- and phase-modulations of such a carrier wave across the image. Because these AMPM modulation components are much more slowly varying over the image than the original texture is (given its bandlimited character), they generate a very efficient and compressive image code.

Our demodulation scheme is a form of predictive coding. It represents a pattern by its *departures* from a predicted 2D undulation. In this respect, AMPM demodulation can be regarded as an oriented, second-order variant of the isotropic first-order predictive coding that Srinivasan, Laughlin, and Dubs (1982) proposed as an interpretation of retinal ganglion cell center/surround structure. Such neurons are active only when the luminance in their receptive field surround fails to predict correctly the luminance in their center. They respond in proportion to this imbalance, in analogy with linear predictive coding of TV signals (Harrison, 1952; Oliver, 1952), and thus they create a relatively decorrelated "delta code" for the structure of the spatial image.

By embedding orientation within the idea of predictive coding, our scheme extends this concept in a way that may illuminate neural codes in the mammalian primary visual cortex. First, the use of oriented primitives rather than isotropic center/surround ones assigns to the "prediction" a certain correlation direction, or moment. Second, what is predicted is not luminance, but a scale and direction for its variation. The quadrature phase relationship discovered by Pollen and Ronner (1981) for adjacent oriented cortical simple cells would play an obvious role in the computation of the AMPM phasor components defined in Equations (13) and (14), which could be implemented in several ways. One such scheme is the model of image coding by oriented quadrature 2D Gabor filters originally proposed in Daugman (1980), which minimizes the conjoint 2D spatial/2D spectral uncertainty of the code primitives (Daugman, 1985) and which generates highly decorrelated image codes with large factors of entropy reduction (Daugman, 1989). Currently popular "energy models" for texture segregation (Landy and Bergen, 1991) are based on this idea of comparing the modulus of the output of oriented quadrature 2D Gabor filters (Daugman, 1987; Daugman, 1988a).

At a still more general level, the scheme discussed in the present work can be regarded as driven by redundancy reduction. This notion was anticipated in Mach's work on inhibition, but was first articulated as a general principle of sensory processing by Attneave (1954), and was independently given its strongest development in 1956 by Barlow (1961a). When the concept of lateral inhibition as a mechanism of redundancy reduction is reformulated to apply over the domains of orientation and spatial frequency rather than luminance, then the result is something like our scheme for AMPM demodulation coding. In this scheme the role of mean luminance is replaced by the derived carrier wave. The carrier itself could be extracted by winner-take-all competition among differently-tuned sets of oriented 2D Gabor simple cell quadrature modules, a competition implemented through the known cross-inhibitory interactions among neurons tuned for different orientations and spatial frequencies (Morrone et al., 1982). Then the modulation of complex cells receiving inputs from the prevailing subspace of such "carrier" simple cells would directly correspond to the AM component of the derived spatial modulation phasor $Z(x, y)$. Our observations about the perceptual organization of complex textures in relation to their AMPM demodulation components (Figures 1–6), together with the match between predicted phasor components and perceived spatio-temporal beats (Figures 8–10), and the psychophysical masking effects that correspond to the phasor AM component (Figure 11), are all compatible with the idea of such a cortical neural mechanism for AMPM demodulation coding.

What makes a good feature?

Allan D. Jepson

Whitman Richards

Perceptual information processing systems, both biological and non-biological, often consist of very elaborate algorithms designed to extract certain features or events from the input sensory array. Such features in vision range from simple "on-off" units to "hand" or "face" detectors, and are now almost countless, so many having already been discovered, or in use, with no obvious limit in sight. Here we attempt to place some bounds upon just what features are worth computing. Previously, others have proposed that useful features reflect "non-accidental" or "suspicious" configurations that are especially informative yet typical of the world (such as two parallel lines). Using a Bayesian framework, we show how these intuitions can be made more precise, and in the process show that useful feature-based inferences are highly dependent upon the context in which a feature is observed. For example, an inference supported by a feature at an early stage of processing when the context is relatively open may be nonsense in a more specific context provided by subsequent "higher-level" processing. Therefore, specification for a "good feature" requires a specification of the model class that sets the current context. We propose a general form for the structure of a model class, and use this structure as a basis for enumerating and evaluating appropriate "good features". Our conclusion is that one's cognitive capacities and goals are as important a part of "good features" as are the regularities of the world.

1. Introduction

In 1870 Lord Airy noted that human visual processing made special use of oriented line segments. His inference was based upon the fortification pattern observed during a migraine attack. Roughly one hundred years later Hubel & Wiesel (1959) confirmed this inference by direct recordings of neurons in the visual cortex of mammals. Since then, there has been a tremendous surge in the discovery of other neurons in all sensory modalities that are optimally sensitive to some specific feature of the sensory array (Rose and Dobson, 1985). In vision these range from the low-order space-time derivatives of intensity such as moving "edge" or "line" detectors, to more complicated patterns that include various symmetries, such as faces or hands (Barlow, 1953; Albright et al., 1984b; Gross et al., 1985; Lettvin et al., 1959; Perrett et al., 1982). To some extent, we expect these observed features to reflect the demands of survival imposed upon the species. Thus the high-level features found in primates are not expected to occur also in simpler animals, such as the fish or frog. Across species, therefore, we find an enormous spectrum of features, especially if we include those specialized trigger patterns or "innate releasing mechanisms" reported by the ethologists (Thorpe, 1963; Tinbergen, 1951). Given this vast collection, it might seem unlikely that one could abstract away some principles that define "what makes a good feature?" However, here we attempt to do just that.

Our guiding hypothesis is that "seeing" is the inference of world properties from image elements—i.e. the various patterns of intensities on the retina. A "feature" is typically viewed as a measurement of image structure, at the level for example of Marr's primal sketch (Marr, 1982). Clearly, many different kinds of measurements or "features" are possible. Intuitively, however, those most often sought after will point directly and reliably to a unique, *meaningful* event in the world. But the criterion that a feature be meaningful implies that the perceiver has some goal or context in mind. For example, for a baby gull the significance of a red spot in the image depends on whether it is seen in the context of a traffic light or as coloration on the beak of an adult gull (Figure 1). In the context of a beak, its salience is sufficient to trigger a feeding response. Somehow the gull is primed to immediately make the necessary inference. Hence we propose that "what makes a good feature" should include the property of having a ready explanation for its appearance (MacKay, 1978; MacKay, 1985).

Under this view, a simple intensity change, an oriented image-edge, or a "zero-crossing" segment analyzed in an open context is not a very good feature. Although we know that edges contain the bulk of information in an image (Barlow, 1961b; Curtis and Oppenheim, 1989; Zeevi and Shamai, 1989), many factors can create the intensity changes that trigger the "edge detector". These include shadows, material changes, scratches, occlusions, etc. Hence there is no unique structure that can be induced from a single intensity edge or line. Consequently, although line elements or edges may be our initial primitives, by themselves they do not exhibit structure over which useful inductions can immediately be made.

In contrast, consider configurations of features that exhibit very special relations to one another, such as two line segments which intersect to form a "T" or a "V", or two line segments that are collinear. As noted by many (Barlow, 1985; Binford, 1981; Lowe, 1985), intuitively, such coincidences imply very special "suspicious" and informative events. Surprisingly, however, in an unrestricted context, such as a world where sticks are positioned

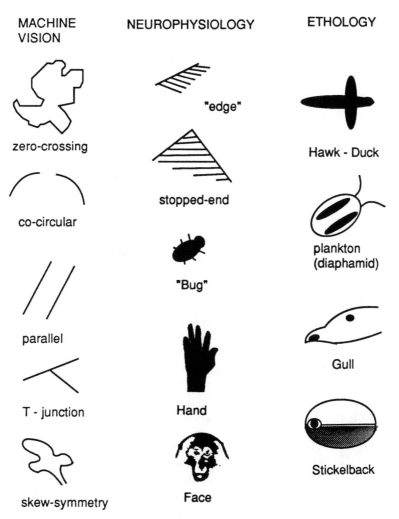

Fig. 1. *Typical features proposed by machine vision, neurophysiology, and ethology. What common properties do these features satisfy? What makes one feature better than another?*

arbitrarily, the observation of a "non-accidental" feature typically does *not* imply the intended world property. Again, context plays a crucial role, as illustrated in Figure 2 for the T-junction, which can arise in many different ways. To correct this situation, the corresponding world event must express a generic regularity in that context (Bennett et al., 1989; Marr, 1970; Reuman and Hoffman, 1986; Witkin and Tennenbaum, 1983). Our task here is to make note of such conditions needed to support our intuitive notions of what 'makes a good feature'. In the process, we will place a measure on just how "good" a particular feature is for inferencing, and show that such measures depend upon the current conceptualization of the world.

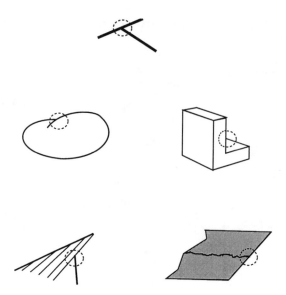

Fig. 2. *If the image primitives are contours (such as zero crossings), then features typically can be created in many ways. For example, the T-junction may arise either from an occlusion or from an actual T-vertex in 3D. Hence the interpretation associated with a feature depends strongly on the context. Alternate contexts can reverse the interpretation. For example, consider the peanut shape as a wire frame, or the bottom right figure as the view of a crack through a polygonal hole.*

2. Bayesian framework

To explore conditions that should be satisfied by a good feature, we use a probabilistic model as the analytical tool for modeling the perceiver's world and the reliability of its feature-based inferences. Our choice of a probabilistic model is *not* a claim that the perceiver necessarily has access to the various probability density functions we use in our analysis. Whether or not the perceiver itself needs to incorporate such a probabilistic model to distinguish between good and bad features, and whether the world needs to satisfy this particular model, are important issues addressed later in the second part of our proposal regarding the inference process itself. However, a Bayesian probabilistic formalism allows us to state clearly some conditions that a "good feature" should meet, and to explain why other, seemingly obvious proposals are inadequate.

The structure of the model is as follows. The external world consists of different classes of objects and events. We refer to each class as a context, C, within which are various properties that occur probabilistically. Our canonical property is denoted simply by P, and we assume it occurs in context C with the conditional probability $p(P|C)$. We denote the absence of property P by *notP*. Next, we consider that some measurements are taken of the objects and events in the world. We refer to a particular collection of such measurements as a feature F. Hence a feature will be identified with the set of all world events having measurements specified by F, and thus probabilities such as $p(F|C)$ are well defined. We wish to study the inference that property P occurs in the world, given both that the world context is C and that the measurements F are satisfied. Note that the probabilities $p(P|C)$ and $p(F|C)$ are considered to be objective facts about the world (or at least an idealization of the world), and are *not* statements about the perceiver's model of the world. In this section we keep the issue of whether or not a perceiver needs to use any probabilistic model of the world quite separate from our analysis of a good feature.

2.1. Reliable inferences

In the probabilistic formalism a measure of the success of inferring property P from F is the *a posteriori* probability of P given the feature F in the context C. A reliable inference makes this probability, namely $p(P|F\&C)$, nearly one, and the probability of an error, namely $p(notP|F\&C)$, nearly zero. It is convenient to consider the ratio of these two quantities, that is

$$R_{post} = \frac{p(P|F\&C)}{p(notP|F\&C)} \tag{1}$$

We consider the feature F to provide a reliable inference, in the context C, precisely when this probability ratio R_{post} is much larger than one. Below we consider how such a condition can be ensured.

Bayes' rule can be used to break down the probability ratio R_{post} into two components. The first component, L, is a likelihood ratio and relates to the measurement F of property P. The second component is another probability ratio, R_{prior}, and is related to the genericity of the world property P in context C. The decomposition of R_{post} has the simple form

$$R_{post} = L \cdot R_{prior} \tag{2}$$

Here the prior probability ratio R_{prior} is given by (compare equation (1))

$$R_{prior} = \frac{p(P|C)}{p(notP|C)} \tag{3}$$

and the likelihood ratio L is defined to be

$$L = \frac{p(F|P\&C)}{p(F|notP\&C)} \tag{4}$$

From equation (2) we see that the likelihood ratio L acts as an amplification factor on the prior probability ratio R_{prior}. Thus it makes sense that a good feature F have a large amplification factor:

Measurement Likelihood Condition: In context C, a good feature F for world property P provides a large likelihood ratio, that is

$$L = \frac{p(F|P\&C)}{p(F|not P\&C)} >> 1 \tag{5}$$

At first blush, a large likelihood value for L seems sufficient to capture the intuition that good features should point reliably to some property in the world. However, because L appears as a product with R_{prior} in equation (2), it is clear that we can not afford to let the prior probability ratio R_{prior} become too small. That is, we also require:

Genericity Condition: Given a context C and a constant $\delta > 0$, the property P occurs with probability $p(P|C) > \delta$ or, equivalently

$$R_{prior} = \frac{p(P|C)}{p(not P|C)} > \frac{\delta}{1-\delta} > 0 \tag{6}$$

By "generic" we mean that P occurs with a probability greater than zero within context C. The Genericity Condition puts a lower bound of δ on this probability. Given that L and R_{prior} satisfy the likelihood and genericity conditions, it follows from equation (2) that $R_{post} > L\delta/(1-\delta)$. Hence, when $L >> (1-\delta)/\delta$, the two conditions together ensure a reliable inference.

2.2. The importance of significant priors

To illustrate how the reliability of an inference depends on both a large likelihood ratio and a generic world property, consider a context consisting of a random 3D arrangement of two sticks. In this context consider the *non-generic* property that two sticks form a "V" intersection in 3D. For our analysis it is more convenient to let property P include both perfect and nearly perfect "V"'s (see Figure 3). That is, for some tolerance ϵ, property P means the endpoints of two sticks come within the distance ϵ of each other in 3D. The measurement provided in the feature F is simply that the projected distance (with respect to some specified ray) between the two endpoints is less than ϵ. This feature formally consists of all stick configurations in which both endpoints lie somewhere within the depicted cylinder. (Informally F consists of two endpoints lying within a disc of radius ϵ in an "image" plane formed by orthographic projection). The measurement F holds when the sticks have property P, and therefore $p(F|P\&C) = 1$. On the other hand, if the two sticks do not satisfy property P then the probability of F is simply proportional to the area of the disc of size ϵ. The likelihood ratio L is therefore proportional to $1/\epsilon^2$, which is much larger than one for small values of ϵ. Hence this situation satisfies the measurement likelihood ratio condition.

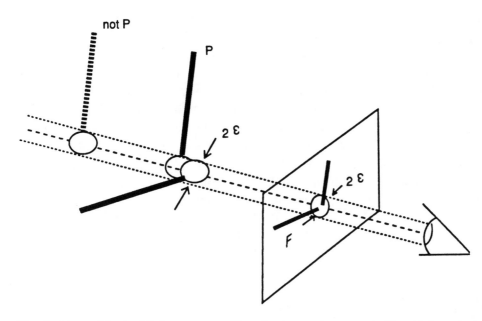

Fig. 3. *Two sticks in 3D form a near-V vertex to create property P, which projects into the V-junction image feature F. The resolution for the sticks forming a V is taken as a disc of radius ε in the image (assuming orthographic projection) and, for the 3D tolerance, the sphere of similar radius. Although the measurement likelihood ratio condition is satisfied, the conditional probability of P, given the observation F and a random world context, favors notP — i.e. that the endpoints of the two sticks lie at separate locations within the cylinder of radius ε.*

Given that $L \gg 1$, should we then infer the 3D property "V", given the measurement F of such a V-junction feature? Surprisingly, in our chosen random world such a conclusion is almost always guaranteed to be *WRONG*. Hence, in this model context, the feature F could hardly be a worse indication of the intended world property P. The probability of an endpoint lying within the sphere to form a "V" is much lower than the probability that the endpoint lies anywhere in the cylinder. More specifically, the joint probability of property P and having feature F, in our model world, is proportional to the volume of the ball of radius ϵ around the endpoint of a stick. That is, $p(P\&F)$ is proportional to ϵ^3. However, feature F is satisfied whenever the endpoint of the second stick lies anywhere within a cylinder of radius ϵ about the ray passing through the endpoint of the first stick and hence $p(F)$ is proportional to ϵ^2. Consequently the conditional probability of property P, given the feature F and a random world context will be $O(\epsilon^3/\epsilon^2) = O(\epsilon)$. Thus for small ϵ we are almost guaranteed to be wrong if we infer P. The appropriate inference would be to infer "$notP$", that is, the endpoints do not actually come close in 3D.[1]

Referring again to the decomposition of R_{post} (equation (2)), we see that the problem with our "V" example is that even though the likelihood ratio L provided by F is proportional to $1/\epsilon^2$ and is thus much larger than one, it is not large enough to amplify the prior probability ratio $R_{prior} = 0(\epsilon^3)$ to a reasonable level. To correct this, we need a significant prior probability that an endpoint lies within a particular sphere, i.e. $R_{prior} > \delta$. In that case $R_{post} = \delta/\epsilon^2 >> 1$. But this is simply the genericity condition, which requires a context in which the 3D "V" structures are fairly common. In other words they are a regularity in that context (Bennett et al., 1989; Marr, 1970; Witkin and Tennenbaum, 1983), such as if we are in a blocks world where edges form V's, or perhaps another where "victory signs" are created by finger arrangements. Once again, then, the context plays a major role in the inferences that features support.

2.3. Informativeness

By requiring that both the genericity condition be satisfied as well as $L >> 1$, we now can be assured that the feature F in context C will be a reliable predictor of world property P. However, a third condition is needed to ensure that the inference of P is actually informative. For example, in a context of randomly placed sticks (e.g. C_{open}) consider a world property P such as two skewed sticks. For simplicity we assume an orthographic image mapping and let the feature F correspond to two skewed lines in the image. Then the probability of this feature is $p(F|P\&C) = 1$. However, since the orthographic image of two parallel lines must also be parallel, it follows that $p(F|notP\&C) = 0$. Therefore the image feature F consisting of two skewed lines provides an infinite likelihood ratio for L. Also the genericity condition is satisfied since the sticks have both a random position and orientation. Therefore it follows that the probability of such a skewed arrangement in the random world is one and R_{prior} is infinite. Hence R_{post} must also be infinite, and the inference is certain. Nevertheless, such a feature is simply confirming the obvious and should not be included in our definition of a good feature. This can be corrected by adding a condition that the a priori probability $p(P|C)$ is not too close to one. (An analogous situation also occurs when a property P is so overwhelmingly unlikely that, even after the observation of F, the a posteriori probabilities favor $notP$. This case is caught by the requirement of significant priors discussed above.)

---

[1] This problem was discussed at length some years ago at a workshop on Perceptual Organization arranged in 1984 by A. Pentland and A. Witkin. See also Knill and Kersten (1991) for another example.

Hence to insure that a feature not confirm the obvious, we add the following condition:

Informativeness Condition: Given a context C and a constant $\delta > 0$, the property P occurs with probability $p(P|C) < (1 - \delta)$, or, equivalently,

$$R_{prior} = \frac{p(P|C)}{p(notP|C)} < \frac{1 - \delta}{\delta} \qquad (7)$$

Collecting our conditions together, we now arrive at the following proposal for a good feature:

Bayesian Proposal: Given a constant δ, a good image feature F for world property P in (world) context C satisfies

1   Likelihood ratio condition:

$$L >> 1/\delta;$$

2   Genericity condition:

$$R_{prior} = p(P|C)/p(notP|C) > \delta/(1 - \delta)$$

3   Informativeness condition:

$$R_{prior} = p(P|C)/p(notP|C) < (1 - \delta)/\delta,$$

and $p(F|P\&C)$ and $p(C)$ are significantly bigger than zero.

Here we have written the conditions using the probability ratios appearing in the Bayesian formula (2). The constant δ should be chosen such that we consider probabilities larger than $1 - \delta$ as virtually certain in order that the information condition rules out features that simply confirm virtually certain events. Also, in terms of δ, the genericity condition requires that the property P have a probability larger than δ and thus P is not virtually impossible. The particular choice of δ and a quantitative threshold for L are left open in the above proposal. We expect that the choice of these quantities would depend on the utility or risk involved in making, or failing to make, the appropriate inferences, which we do not pursue here. Finally, note the desirability that the inference can be made reasonably often. That is, the context C should not be too rare, and given the generic property P, the measurements F should also be common. This new requirement has been incorporated as part of the informativeness condition.

2.4. Non-monotonicity of inferences

We close this section with one final example of the role context plays in our proposal. Most people see Figure 4 as depicting three blocks: one block resting on top of another, and a third twisted block that lies behind. Note

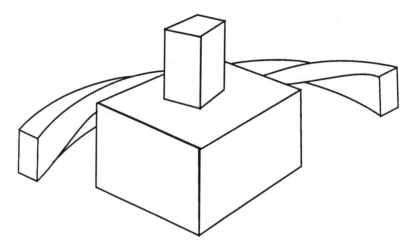

Fig. 4. *A blocks-world example where the non-accidental property "collinear" is ignored (see text for discussion).*

that two of the vertical lines associated with the Y-junctions are actually collinear in the image, creating the useful (non-accidental) collinear feature suggested by Lowe (1985). This feature certainly satisfies our likelihood ratio condition. So why don't we see the two blocks as having collinear edges in 3D with one block floating above the other? (A similar example having an accidental view of a "Y" vertex, due to Steve Draper, is given by Hinton (1977).)

To understand the use of collinearity as a feature, we consider inferences appropriate for three different contexts. Each of these contexts is simply a statement about regularities in the scene generating process, and are not meant to imply different stages in the perceiver's visual information processing system. The first context is an "open context", C_{open}, which consists of randomly placed line segments. In particular, collinear, coterminating, or parallel lines in the world are non-generic (i.e. probability zero) in this context. However, although the likelihood ratios for all these properties are easily seen to be large, as was the case for the "V" feature discussed earlier, the *a priori* probabilities for these "non-accidental" properties are too small to warrant their inference. Hence in the context C_{open} the overwhelmingly probable conclusion is that the collinear, coterminating, and parallel lines in the image simply arise due to some cause other than being the projections of their corresponding 3D properties. (An obvious possibility is measurement noise and a special view of the scene.)

Now consider a second context, C_{group}, similar to the first, but with regularities added that make, say, collinear lines or parallel edges much more probable than they would be in the unstructured context C_{open}. For example, such a context would result if there are processes in the world that cause the 3D line segments or edges to form structures having particular regularities such as textured flow fields (Stevens, 1978; Kass and Witkin, 1988) or blocks with parallel faces (Lowe, 1985). Now the significant prior probability of these specific structures in that context and the large likelihood ratio provided by the non-accidental feature, together ensure that the inference of the corresponding 3D structure is reliable. Given Figure 4 in this context then, and given the alignments and parallel edges, one might infer that these image elements arose from a related group of 3D objects (as indeed they did!).

The third context involves a collection of blocks, C_{block}, where the blocks can rest on one another or float about freely. If blocks float freely then their position and orientation with respect to the other blocks is assumed to be random, with vanishing *a priori* probabilities R_{prior} for collinear or parallel edges. So again the situation is analogous to the case of the V-junctions presented earlier (Figure 3). Hence, although the likelihood ratio L is high in context C_{block}, the prior probability that the two blocks would be floating in just such a way to make a pair of edges collinear is vanishingly small, and the resultant *a posteriori* probabilities R_{post} rule against the interpretation that the two edges happen to be collinear. Instead, we favor some other cause, such as an accidental viewpoint. Finally, we note in passing that the occluded twisted block in Figure 4 is seen as just that — a single block but not as two, although none of the edges are collinear. However, in the context C_{block}, it is reasonable to expect that the implicit axes of the right and left portions of the twisted block could be extracted. Such features satisfy a cocircularity regularity (Parent and Zucker, 1989), which is also a "non-accidental" property, and hence the "one block" inference is justified.

Our point then is that the context in which the scene configuration arose is crucial to the interpretation of a feature, since a change in context can reverse the appropriate inference. In our example, the 3D collinearity conclusion is justified only in the middle context C_{group}; in the less structured context C_{open} and in the most structured context C_{block} the 3D collinear regularity for these lines is not viable. Hence the appropriate inference is non-monotonic with the degree of structure or specification within the context (McCarthy, 1980; McDermott and Doyle, 1980; Reiter, 1980; Salmon, 1967).

3. Model classes

A major point of our analysis of "what makes a good feature" is that supportable inferences are context-sensitive. Features must be evaluated in terms of generic properties or regularities in a specialized context or model class, as contrasted with an open context like a "random-world" model. Implicit in this treatment is that the external world indeed has some non-arbitrary structure, and that our own internal models can express this structure in terms of certain regularities explicitly stated as part of the model.

How are these regularities expressed in the Bayesian formalism, and how can they be mirrored in the perceiver's conceptualization of the world?

In an attempt to capture the notion of a regularity, within a probabilistic representational system of a perceiver, Barlow (1985) proposed "good features" should satisfy the "suspicious coincidence" condition $p(A\&B) >> p(A)p(B)$, where A and B are two observations.[2] The intent of the condition is to notice special situations that are not expected by an independence assumption of the occurrence of A and B. Although "suspicious" implies to us that there is a current context, this is not an explicit part of Barlow's proposal, which requires the very controversial computation of estimating context-free probability distribution functions (i.e. $p(A) = \Sigma p(A|C)p(C)$ summed over all possible contexts). Barlow (1990) discusses at length elsewhere how a neural system might learn the appropriate distribution functions (see also Clark and Yuille, 1990).

One way to capture the intent of Barlow's proposal within the Bayesian framework is to consider the feature observation in the context C_p where the associated property is generic, as contrasted with the current, less specialized context C_o where the property (or properties) are non-generic. More specifically:

Suspicious Coincidence: The observation of a feature F represents a suspicious coincidence in the context C_o if there is a more specialized (i.e. detailed) context C_p such that,

1   the likelihood ratio involving feature F and property P is large in both contexts, and

2   the probability of P in the specialized context C_p is much larger than in the current context C_o, that is

$$p(P|C_p) >> p(P|C_o).$$

For example, in our discussion of the blocks in of Figure 4 we first considered the open context C_{open} of random lines. The collinearity feature F has a large likelihood in context C_{open}, but the prior probability of 3D collinear lines is negligible. However, in the grouping context C_{group}, the prior probability is significant and the likelihood ratio is still large. Hence, we would consider the observation of collinear lines in context C_{open} as a suspicious coincidence with respect to the more structured context such as C_{group}. Note that this conclusion is not to be considered a reliable inference that context C_{group} actually occurs in the world. (An analysis similar to the one presented in Section 2 could derive suitable additional conditions to ensure a reliable inference of the new context.) Rather, Barlow's notion

---

[2] Based on the text, we assume that the intended inequality is as appears here. However, note that for the independent event hypothesis, the inequality can be applied in either direction.

of suspicious coincidences simply provides an approach for chaining through to more detailed contexts as further regularities are uncovered and assimilated. We do not pursue this chaining process here, and instead concentrate on how a specific context might be represented.

Clearly an internal model can not be expected to match exactly the behavior of external events. In terms of our Bayesian proposal, the internally represented probability density functions $p(P|C_i)$ can not be identical to their external world counterparts, $p(P|C_w)$, say. In particular, as the contexts become more and more specialized (and hence the measures on the probability density functions become more and more biased), the world model and the perceiver's conceptualizations may diverge. We would like to minimize the effects of this divergence. In other words, we seek model contexts, properties, and features that are robust under errors in our estimates of the conditional probability measures. This is a different type of robustness than was considered in earlier, where the appropriate probability distributions and the particular context were given as facts.

One class of properties in which robustness is (nearly) ensured in the face of modeling errors are those that are "non-accidental", such as the collinearity of two sticks. First we consider such properties as idealizations where our resolution ability is unlimited; later we return to the issue of dealing with finite resolution. More specifically, we assume here that the likelihood ratio for the collinearity feature, for example, goes to infinity as the measurement error, ϵ, decreases to zero. If we consider a world context, C_w, which has a positive probability mass for situations in which two 3D sticks are precisely collinear, then the prior probability ratio R_{prior} is also at least as large as this positive constant. Equation (2) then shows that the *a posteriori* probability ratio R_{post}, and thus the reliability of the inference of collinear lines in the world, can be made arbitrarily large by taking ϵ sufficiently small. For our earlier non-accidental feature the "V", a similar idealization is to put a point mass of probability (i.e. a Dirac distribution) at the occurrence of the 3D "V" intersection (see Figure 3). Then, as we make ϵ smaller the contribution of this point mass stays fixed, while the probability of the remainder of the cylinder reduces to zero. As a result, the *a posteriori* probability ratio of a "V" intersection goes to infinity as ϵ decreases, and the correct inference is virtually assured. Note that this is a constraint on the shape of the probability density function, rather than on its detailed value. The following describes a sub-class of regularities that meets this condition.

3.1. Two kinds of regularities

Given any model for objects or properties in a world, the structural regularities associated with that model can be divided simply into two classes: those configurations or relations that arise when the elements of the model are positioned arbitrarily with respect to one another, and those that require special placements (Poston and Stewart, 1981). For example, let our objects be a line and a plane, and let our assumed model of structural relations to be nil — in other words there are no specialized arrangements in the world. Then if the line and plane are each thrown out haphazardly in 3-space, we expect the line to intersect the plane at some arbitrary angle (Figure 5). An alternate configuration, such as the line lying exactly in the plane, is impossible, unless someone placed it there. These two configurations depict respectively transversal and non-transversal intersections of two objects. Intuitively, the notion of transversality is one of event stability between objects: slight perturbations of the arrangement do not affect the topology. For example, a knife plunged into an apple would create a transversal cut (unless precisely radial), whereas the cut would be non-transversal if the knife were tangent to the apple as if peeling its skin. In the latter case, proper peeling requires precise alignment with the tangent plane of the apple. Such events which are not stable to slight perturbations of the elements that create it are called "non-transversal". Thus, given an assumed context of random stick-world, the "V" vertex formed by the two lines in 3D is a non-transverse event, but two lines skewed and non-intersecting in 3-space would be a transverse arrangement.

Non-transversality, then, appears at first blush to be the "non-accidental" proposal of Lowe (1985). However, here we use the terminology "transversal and non-transversal" because these terms are context-sensitive and can be applied to world models with arbitrary statistical properties. Thus, in a non-random world model, say one describing body parts, the arrangement such as the V-vertex which we previously considered non-transverse can become transverse (because this is the configuration of an arm). However, in this same model class, the T-junction or parallel line configuration would continue to be non-transverse. Still another example would be an assumed model context where objects are taken to obey two-fold reflectional symmetry. Then a line perpendicular to a plane will be a transversal arrangement, whereas in the absence of such a symmetry constraint, such a 90 degree intersection is non-transverse. Hence the notion of transversality also involves categorical properties considered special in the current model class. An important type of world regularity can be specified by adding on top of this categorical structure an indication of whether or not a particular non-transversal category has a non-zero prior probability of occurring.

3.2. Key features

Let us define a model space $\mathcal{M}$ simply as a manifold constructed by parameterizing some modeling domain. The parameters could be involved in descriptions of (3D) position, attitude and shape of various parts, or reflectance properties of surfaces, or higher order structures such as the

TWO KINDS OF REGULARITIES

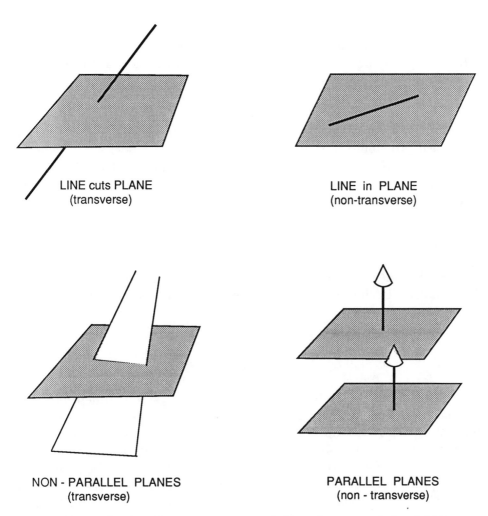

Fig. 5. *Two kinds of regularities, transverse (left) and non-transverse (right).*

sounds of a babbling brook. Also various categories P are represented as subsets of the model space, some of which form non-transversal submanifolds within $\mathcal{M}$. For example, our two sticks "V" example corresponds to a model space R^{10}, where the ten parameters describe the position and orientation of the sticks. Consider the category P for which the two sticks form a V-junction (for simplicity, with a particular pair of endpoints). This is a 7-dimensional hyperplane in our model space. We note in passing that this 7-dimensional space has other "special" configurations within it, such as the 5-dimensional hyperplane representing the situations when the two sticks are also collinear.

Next we need to specify how $\mathcal{M}$ and the various categories are meant to represent (or "mirror") structure and events in the world. In particular, we assume a fixed mapping between events in the world and categories within $\mathcal{M}$. The stick example suffices to illustrate the mapping between coterminating sticks in the world, and the representation of this event in $\mathcal{M}$. To avoid unnecessary details we simply identify a world property as P_w, and use P_m to refer to the corresponding category within $\mathcal{M}$. Given this correspondence, we can take a world context C_w (which the reader may assume is simply an index to an appropriate probability density function) along with the associated probability distribution $p(P_w|C_w)$, and consider the "ideal probability distribution" induced on the model space, namely $p(P_m|C_m) = p(P_w|C_w)$. Of course, this ideal probability measure in NOT to be considered part of the perceiver's conceptualization. However, we need to make an assumption about its general structure, namely:

Mode Hypothesis: Given a model space $\mathcal{M}$ and a context C_w then the probability measure $p(m|C_w)$ can be decomposed into the sum $\sum_{i=0}^{n} p_i(m|C_w)$ for $m \in \mathcal{M}$. Here p_0 is the background measure and p_i for $i > 0$ is a measure having support only on the non-transversal category P_i within $\mathcal{M}$. Each of these measures is assumed to have density functions of the form

$$p_i(m|C_w) = \mu_i(m)\beta_i exp(-H_i(m|C_w)), i = 0, \ldots, n \qquad (8)$$

for $m \in \mathcal{M}$ (see Skilling, 1991). Here μ_0 is the Lebesgue measure on $\mathcal{M}$ and μ_i for $i > 0$ are Lebesgue measures on the property spaces P_i (i.e. delta distributions). The terms β_i can be taken to be 0 or 1, depending on whether the ith mode is a regularity in context C_w. Finally, the remaining terms involving H_i provide a reweighting of the uniform Lebesgue measures; they are exponentiated simply to insure the weights are positive.

The Mode Hypothesis can be seen to be a hypothesis about the form of the "ideal" probability density, for properties within a model class (Bobick, 1987; Marr, 1970). The basic idea is that robust features should supply reliable inferences over a wide range of possible choices for the specific background probability density and for the non-transverse probability densities. In other words, the robustness of the inferences should follow from the structure of the probability density, which in the ideal case will be a collection of delta functions. Ideally, all the perceiver needs to maintain is the locations of these delta functions, but not knowledge of their probability distributions $p(P_w|C_w)$ because typically this information will not be available. Instead we take the (perhaps, extreme) position that an assumed context, C_m, is simply a specification of which categories P_i have a non-zero probability mass. In terms of equation (8), C_m specifies which normalization constants β_i are nonzero, but says nothing about the details of the actual density functions in terms of the weight functions $H_i(m|C_w)$. Different modes can be selected in different contexts, and that is the only control of (assumed) context the perceiver has. For convenience we will abuse the notation, and take $p(m|C_m)$ to mean *any* one of the set density functions which satisfy equation (8), and is non-zero only on the selected modes specified by the model context C_m.

The stick example provides a concrete case, where the world context consisted of two randomly placed sticks. The particular probability density p_0 is assumed to be a smooth function of both the location and orientation of the two sticks. Such a distribution can be written in the form presented for a background measure. Many different choices for H_0 are possible, describing for example a uniform distribution within a cube, or a Gaussian distribution, etc. The important property of p_0 is that, *independent* of the choice of H_0, it assigns zero probability to all non-transversal manifolds such as the P_i of $\mathcal{M}$. Suppose there are two regularities in this particular world context. One causes the two sticks to form a V-junction with a non-zero probability, and the other causes these V-junctions to form the degenerate case of collinear sticks. Such a world satisfies the Mode Hypothesis, with the V-junctions and the collinear V-junctions forming the only non-transversal sets which have positive probability mass. Within this particular context, such regularities will support robust inferences from their measurements, even though the (unavailable) density functions associated with the perceiver's internal model space C_m do not match exactly the associated objective density functions in the world, namely $p(P_w|C_w)$.

To support this claim, we now proceed to develop the relation between the special class of non-transverse properties $P_i \in \mathcal{M}$ and their associated features F_i. Hence, in addition to a model space $\mathcal{M}$, we now require a measurement space $\mathcal{I}$ and an imaging mapping, π, from $\mathcal{M}$ onto $\mathcal{I}$. (This basic set up is similar to that used in Observer Mechanics (Bennett et al., 1989) with the exception that for us the various spaces and mappings are all part of the perceiver's representational framework. For Observer Mechanics these entities *are* the world.) Features F_i are identified with subsets or submanifolds within the measurement space $\mathcal{I}$. To illustrate this mapping, consider again the two stick case. Then, given orthographic imaging, the 10-dimensional configuration space for two sticks will be imaged to a 6-dimensional feature space. Within this feature space, is the 4-dimensional hyperplane (a non-transversal set) consisting of all possible images containing V-intersections. We assume that the imaging map π correctly models the qualitative structure of the transduction and subsequent measurement processes of the perceiver (again, detailed noise models are not assumed). Finally, we define the probability of a feature F, say $p(F|P\&C_w)$ to be the probability induced by the image map and the measure on $\mathcal{M}$. That is, $p(F|P\&C_w)$ is given by the probability of the set of all models m which image to F, namely $\pi^{-1}(F)$. Similarly, given a model context, $p(F|P\&C_m)$

is taken to mean any one of the induced measures consistent with the model context C_m.

A model class is defined to be a pair of spaces $\mathcal{M}$, $\mathcal{I}$, along with the imaging map π. In addition to these spaces a model class includes two lists of categories, one a list of model properties (or categories) P_i within $\mathcal{M}$, the other a list of features F_i within $\mathcal{I}$. Finally, a particular model context C_m for a perceiver is simply a selection, from the list of categories P_i, of those which are assumed to have a non-zero mass in the "ideal" probability measure. Given this framework, we obtain our robust feature:

Key Feature Definition: Given a model class and a model context C_m, then F is a Key Feature for a world property P in context C_m if

1   P is non-transverse within $\mathcal{M}$, yet generic in C_m (i.e. $p(P|C_m) > 0$);

2   the probability of the feature in the absence of property P is zero,

$$\text{(i.e. } p(F|notP\&C_m) = 0); \tag{9}$$

3    $p(F|P\&C_m)$ is greater than zero.

More simply put, F is a key feature for a property P if P is a generic nontransverse mode in the model space, and F occurs in the presence of P, but never in its absence. (Hence in the special case where F is non-transverse and generic, F will be a key feature provided that the conditions for P are satisfied.) Notice that we only refer to zero and positive probabilities in the Key Feature Definition, which is appropriate because no particular positive values are specified by the model context C_m. The fact that F is a key feature is independent of the detailed quantitative structure of the "ideal" probability measure $p(P_w|C_w)$. Rather, as desired, it depends only on the proper selection of active modes. Hence what becomes critical is not just the types of measurements used to construct a model space, but rather the types of submanifolds within this space that the perceiver can recognize or build (see Feldman, 1991, 1992, and Sober, 1975, for additional constraints on such submanifolds). For example, in Figure 6 on the left we see three configurations projected onto an image plane, which can be directly viewed as key-feature arrangements for a "point" and "line" in a random world, or for two planes. On Figure 6 (right) however, we envision a model space having parameters α, β, γ, which contains various property categories, e.g. P_1 and P_2. The features involve measurements that result in constraint surfaces within the model space (e.g. F_1 and F_2 for the full space, or f_1 and f_2 for the reduced space). Concrete examples of such constraint surfaces for observer motion or the inference of surface reflectance are given in Section 5. For now, we simply point out that the structure of the intersection of two such constraint surfaces can provide a "key feature" for a world property.

By using the earlier formalism provided in Section 2 one can easily check that key features provide a robust inference of world property P_w.

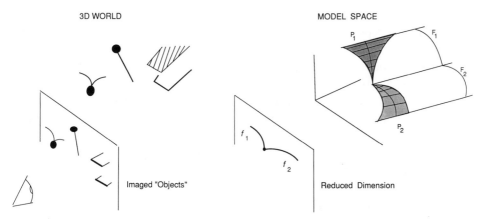

Fig. 6. *Two different event spaces to which our proposal (9) applies: Left, 3D "objects" projected into the image plane; Right, a high order space parameterized by α, β, γ with features F_1 and F_2 that provide constraint surfaces for these parameters (or constraint lines, f_1 and f_2 in the case of the reduced dimension).*

Specifically, referring to the definition (9), the last two requirements ensure that the likelihood ratio is infinite, while the first ensures that the *a priori* probability must be positive. Therefore the *a posteriori* probability ratio for property P is infinite, that is, P is certain to occur. Clearly, a key-feature must be an idealization to have such strong properties. Indeed we have assumed that there is no resolution limit on the measurement process, and that the modes themselves have no *transverse* structural variability (i.e. our ideal modes are non-transverse, whereas noise can be expected to make them transverse). Shortly we will deal with these issues. First, however, we show how, given any model space, the special class "Key Features" can be identified, and how a measure can be placed on the "informativeness" of each feature in that class.

3.3. A simplified internal model

To begin, we assume that the perceiver has the ability to parse events in any given model space into configurations consisting of points, line segments, edges and corners (Figure 7). In this first example, we also assume that the events in the 3D world are similarly points, lines, edges and corners, which are imaged onto a 2D space. (Later, we will consider world events that are not these simple geometric primitives and more general types of features.) In order to recognize non-transversal arrangements of these primitives, the perceiver must also have available concepts that help define the "interesting" relations between them. These concepts act like Peano's axioms in geometry. They dictate the fundamental nature of the world as we see it. Here, we choose notions of coincidence, parallelness, perpendicular, collinear and coplanarity.[3] It is understood that the perceiver understands that coincidence applies to points, end-points of lines, planes, etc. and recognizes the distinctions between these types of coincidences. Similarly, intrinsic to the concept of parallelness is the knowledge that this relation applies only to lines or planes, etc. (These conditions can be formalized, but the formalization adds little to the understanding of our proposal.) Finally, we allow knowledge of "special" concepts that may be defined outside the particular model space, but can be mapped into it. The gravity vector for a "blocks" world model space would be an example. These concepts, then, define the perceiver's internal model for the property space under consideration.

3.4. Key feature enumeration

Given a well-formulated internal model, it is a relatively straightforward task to enumerate the form that the different key features will take. In particular, we seek non-transversal properties which image to non-transversal features. The non-transversality of the feature is sufficient to ensure that the feature occurs with probability zero in the absence of all regularities. We begin with point-to-line arrangements, then consider line-to-line, and finally line-to-virtual line, namely the gravity vector. Along the way, a measure of the inferential power of any given feature will also be specified. From these examples, it should be clear how additional key features can be enumerated for any well-specified model class. We consider only the case where our given object relations are generic in our model class, which is taken to be a specialization of an open class. Moreover, we consider measurements consisting of the position and orientation of points and line segments in an orthographic image. In terms of our formalization the features arising from such measurements are constraint sets in the model space. However, since the mapping from these image measurements to the constraint set is fairly intuitive, we ignore this step and consider "features" to be the usual image measurements of position and orientation.

Point to line Consider first the possible non-transverse relations between a point and a line. Let the line be taken as a reference in the 3-space in which the point and line appear. The positioning of the point then has three degrees of freedom, say α, β, γ (corresponding to x, y, z in some coordinate frame built upon the line). For our given internal model, we can entertain only four ways of positioning the point with respect to the line: it can be either coincident (with an end point), collinear (on the line), perpendicular or coplanar — parallel is undefined for this pair. These relations are given in the left column of Figure 8.

---

[3] Clearly there are other choices, such as cocircularity, special tesselations, etc. Just which concepts are selected is of course a critical issue, but beyond the scope of this paper.

SIMPLIFIED INTERNAL MODEL

A. **OBJECTS** in the model space are constructed from Points, Lines (Segments) and Planes (Facets).

B. **OBJECT ELEMENTS**

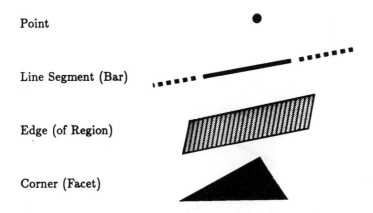

Point

Line Segment (Bar)

Edge (of Region)

Corner (Facet)

C. **CONCEPTS** (innately) available to the perceiver.

1. "Object" Type: point, line, segment, etc.

2. "Object Relations: parallel, coincident, perpendicular, collinear, co-planar (symmetry).

3. "Special" Property: gravity.

D. **CONTEXT** (or model class)

Variable over contexts.

Fig. 7. *The basic ingredients of the observer's internal model.*

POINT TO LINE SEGMENT

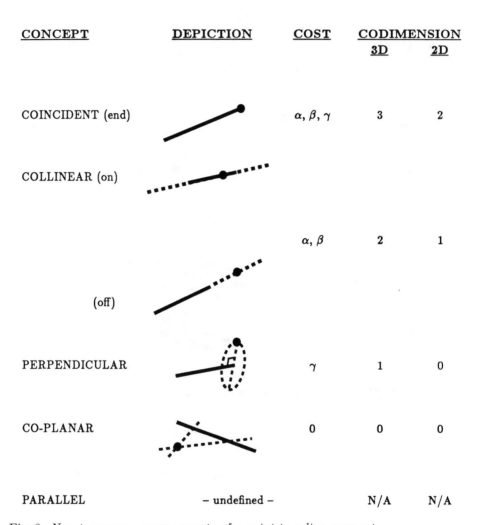

CONCEPT	DEPICTION	COST	CODIMENSION 3D	2D
COINCIDENT (end)		α, β, γ	3	2
COLLINEAR (on)				
		α, β	2	1
(off)				
PERPENDICULAR		γ	1	0
CO-PLANAR		0	0	0
PARALLEL	– undefined –		N/A	N/A

Fig. 8. *Non-transverse arrangements of a point to a line segment.*

For *coincidence*, there is only one relation, namely with the point positioned at the end of the line segment. In 3-space, such positioning costs us three degrees of freedom (DOF) as indicated in the third column: namely, α, β and γ all are now fixed. We call this cost the "codimension" of the arrangement (see Poston and Stewart, 1981), which in this case is *three*. Similarly, in the 2D image the coincidence relation requires that both image coordinates of the point are fixed, giving a codimension of *two*.

The next relation is *collinear*, with the point lying on the line itself or on its extension. Only one degree of freedom (DOF) of positioning remains,

LINE TO LINE SEGMENT

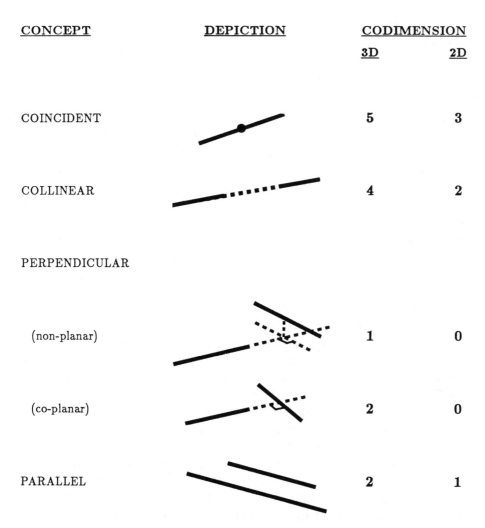

CONCEPT	DEPICTION	CODIMENSION	
		3D	**2D**
COINCIDENT		5	3
COLLINEAR		4	2
PERPENDICULAR			
(non-planar)		1	0
(co-planar)		2	0
PARALLEL		2	1

Fig. 9. *Non-transverse arrangements of one line segment to another, again in a "random world" context.*

hence the 3D codimension for this non-transverse arrangement is two (or one in the image plane because the point must lie on an infinite 2D line).

The relation of *perpendicular* between a point and a line occurs when the point lies in the plane of the end point of the line — as if the line were the normal vector to the plane. Because the point can be placed anywhere in this plane and still satisfy the relation, the codimension of this configuration is one. In the image, however, the point can lie anywhere with respect to the line. Thus the special arrangement is lost and the codimension of this set of images is zero. Finally, the point may be placed arbitrarily in space, creating the single transverse arrangement in 3D. Then a plane is defined, but because the configuration is transverse, the codimension is zero.

The possible key-features given these concepts are limited to just those situations in which the configuration has a positive codimension in both 3D and 2D. That is, for a point and a line only the coincident and collinear configurations qualify.

Line to line In a similar manner we can enumerate all non-transverse arrangements between two line segments, given this particular "model world" (Figure 9). Now, however, we have increased the degrees of freedom for the positioning and pose from three to five. The extra two provide the orientation of one line relative to the other. Hence when two lines are coincident (i.e. collinear with coincident endpoints) there are no remaining degrees of freedom and the codimension is five. Similarly, a *collinear* arrangement between two lines in 3-space will have codimension 4, because one translation remains allowable. For the *perpendicular* configuration we have two cases, one where the two lines are coplanar (codimension 2) and the other when they are not (codimension 1). Finally, two lines can be *parallel*, and this arrangement has codimension 2 because only the orientation (two DOF) of one line to the other is restricted.

The above codimensions were specified for the configurations in a 3-space. However often the observer has available only a projection of the property space. In this case, just as when the three-dimensional world is imaged onto our retina, the specialness of a configuration may be lost. The most obvious instance is when the non-transverse arrangement is specified by an angle, such as "perpendicular". Unless the viewpoint is special, angular relationships are not preserved on projection. In our line-to-line example, the two perpendicular configurations in 3-space will project into arbitrary, transverse relations in the lower dimensional "image" space. Hence these arrangements have codimension zero in 2D, as indicated in the last column of Figure 9. Similarly, we note that coincident lines now have codimension 3 in a plane, collinearity 2 and parallelness 1. Hence only these three latter configurations have the chance of meeting the criteria for a Key Feature.[4]

In our "modal" world where properties are configured to satisfy point, line or planar constructions in a property space, clearly many non-transversal arrangements are possible. The point-to-point and line-to-line examples only

---

[4] All projections into a lower subspace need not reduce the codimension of the arrangement. For example, a point at the end of a line segment, in the context that the dot must be on the line, is codimension one both in the 3D world as well as in the 2D image. Symmetry constraints are also often preserved in the projection without reducing the codimension.

illustrate the simplest. If we were to continue to complete the pairwise cases, four more pairs would have to be considered (point-to-point, point-to-face, line-to-face, face-to-face), for five possible relations, not including the two-fold pairing of relations. Multiplying these thirty pairwise cases by the number of added elements for triples, quadruples, etc., rapidly explodes the possibilities. Hence even for our simple model world the space of key features is very rich. Nevertheless, in principle all the non-transversal cases in both the model and image spaces can be identified.

Line to gravity Often, factors extrinsic to the feature space may impose special frames within the space, as part of the internal model. Such frames create special categories and alter the codimension of events in that feature space. The gravity vector G is a typical example. Because this particular vector defines a virtual line, having no ends nor specific position, the conceptual relations "coincident and collinear" are undefined, and only the parallel relation can be used with this vector. The codimension of a line parallel to the gravity vector is two. Given this special frame vector G, we now have the key feature "vertical line", of codimension one in the 2D image plane, assuming again that lines can be placed arbitrarily.

One final point. Note that if an extrinsic frame such as gravity is imposed upon a feature space, then additional natural concepts such as "vertical" or "horizontal" may be defined within the model class. Further examples are given in the enumeration of point to line segment in a gravity frame (Figure 10, lower).

4. Statistical variability

Although the intuitions behind our notion of a key feature seem compelling, it is useful to consider how our proposal can be extended to natural environments that include both structural variations within a particular world category as well as imaging and measurement noise. As presented, the important notion of non-transversality is an idealization. In practice, the red spot on the gull's beak (or the stickleback's eye) will not lie precisely at a vertex. Or, the process creating a line may leave only point traces (such as a texture flow field). And, finally, the measurements on the image will be noisy. Hence, we can expect to see distributions of points in the event spaces, not well-marked trajectories. Clearly a random cluster of points, such as Figure 11a can not support a key feature, whereas Figure 11b looks promising. How then do we proceed to test whether the observed distribution of points in the event space supports a key feature? Fortunately, a good part of the necessary machinery is available, provided that one knows in advance the possible model types that apply (Kendall, 1989). But this is indeed the case because all the "low-order" types of Key Features have been enumerated. The procedure, then, is simply to test the hypothesis that the

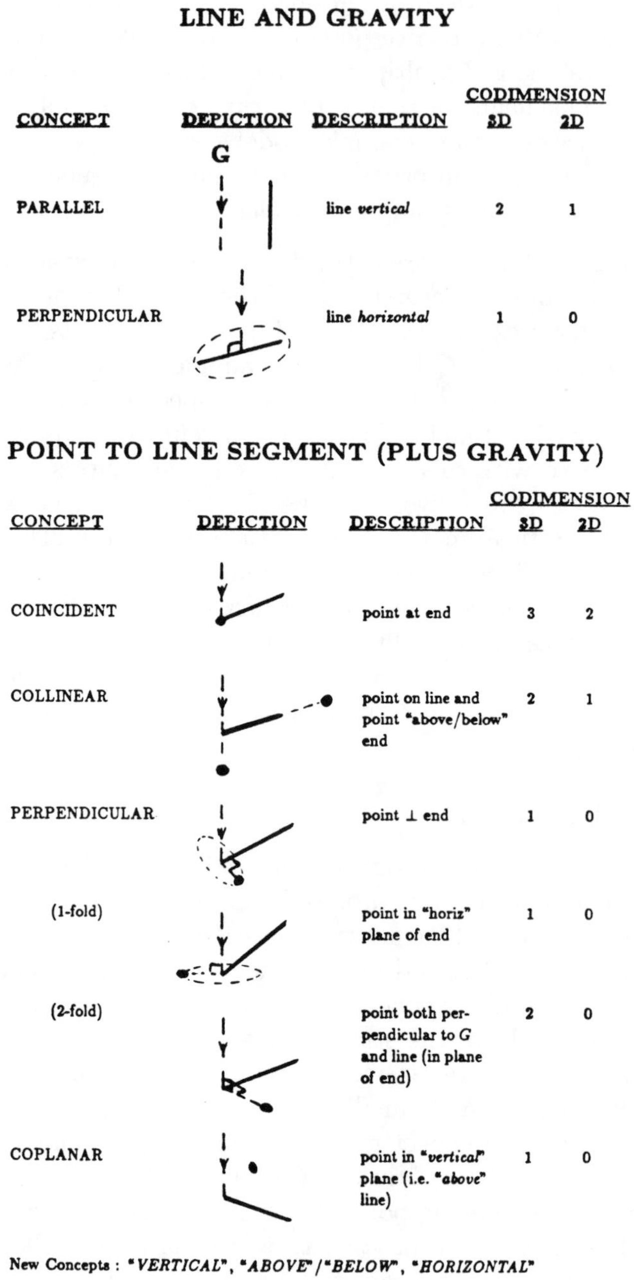

LINE AND GRAVITY

CONCEPT	DEPICTION	DESCRIPTION	CODIMENSION 3D	2D
PARALLEL		line *vertical*	2	1
PERPENDICULAR		line *horizontal*	1	0

POINT TO LINE SEGMENT (PLUS GRAVITY)

CONCEPT	DEPICTION	DESCRIPTION	CODIMENSION 3D	2D
COINCIDENT		point at end	3	2
COLLINEAR		point on line and point "above/below" end	2	1
PERPENDICULAR		point ⊥ end	1	0
(1-fold)		point in "horiz" plane of end	1	0
(2-fold)		point both perpendicular to G and line (in plane of end)	2	0
COPLANAR		point in "*vertical*" plane (i.e. "*above*" line)	1	0

New Concepts : "*VERTICAL*", "*ABOVE*"/"*BELOW*", "*HORIZONTAL*"

Fig. 10. *The addition of a coordinate frame, such as the gravity vector, expands the Key Feature possibilities.*

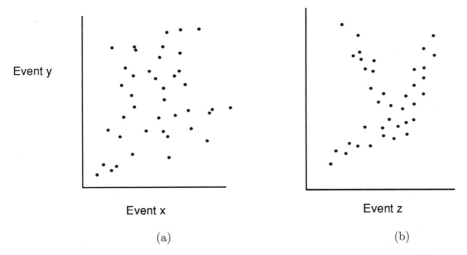

Event y

Event x

Event z

(a)

(b)

Fig. 11. *(a): A cluster (or perhaps two!) of points whose specialness is difficult to demonstrate statistically. (b): A pattern of points that is much simpler to show is non-arbitrary, not only because the subspace is more coherent, but especially because the arrangement is non-transversal for a simple line-segment model.*

points in the feature space support one of the Key Feature configurations known to the perceiver.[5]

4.1. Data description

To illustrate a version of Shape Statistics, consider the configuration in Figure 11b. We know that the coincidence of three lines is a special configuration of codimension 2 in the event space. The task is then to obtain a probability density function (*pdf*) for each line and separately for their intersection. To estimate each line (and hence its trajectory), we can create a density function concentrated along a 1D curve or spine, following the methods of Leclerc (1989) or Hinton et al. (1992). Denote this spine together with its associated *pdf* as a "caterpillar". An important property of these approaches is that such caterpillars provide an appropriate form of description for each "image". In particular, for Figure 11b we might expect that a process similar to Leclerc's would extract a description in terms of three straight caterpillars. Their width would be determined from the scatter of the data points perpendicular to the spine. In addition, the endpoints of the linear segments would also be provided only to within the same resolution. Similarly, for 11a, the same process might be expected to choose a description involving only one or two blobs.

---

[5] Note that Kendall and Kendall (1980) provide a very detailed analysis of the collinear Key Feature applied to the data of Stonehenge in order to test the hypothesis that the alignments marked some interesting astronomical event.

Given these descriptions it is now clear how to deal with images such as Figure 11b. Presumably we have recovered precisely three line segments along with an estimate for possible errors in the positions of the endpoints. This provides a "stick image", to which we can apply our usual repertoire of Key Feature models (i.e. candidate configurations). The only difference is that we have an explicit estimate for the noise variability, so we could expect to get more detailed estimates of the basic probabilities and likelihoods in our Bayesian proposal.

It is interesting to note the similarity in our proposal for good model descriptions and good features. For example, the "three stick" configuration is a specialization of a description including polynomial spines, suggesting that lower dimensional descriptive models can be found on particular *nontransversal* submanifolds in higher dimensional descriptive spaces. The observation that an interpretation is close to one of these non-transversal sets suggests that we collapse the description to the smaller space. This is analogous to observing a non-transversal feature in our model class.

4.2. Decision rules

The extraction of a good description for Figure 11b, followed by the inference of a triple junction, is clear in principle but it raises some difficult issues. Both Figures 11a and 11b are fairly clear cut in terms of their structure, with only one model fitting very well in either situation. However, consider adding more noise to Figure 11b to obtain some intermediate cases. Presumably the parse into three separate lines becomes less certain, as does the quantitative data on the parameters for the lines. In an abstract feature space the picture is of a noise estimate associated with each feature which covers a larger region as the input noise is increased. A final point is that, in terms of our Bayesian proposal, the likelihood ratio L for observing particular regularity will decrease (basically, by adjusting the width of the caterpillar we are keeping $p(F|P\&C)$ roughly constant, but this increased width will also cause the probability of false targets, $p(F|notP\&C)$ to increase). As a result the inferences will become less certain or, once the Informativeness Condition fails, uninformative.

We discussed the problem of choosing a good description of the data in the previous section. Given a description we are now faced with choosing an appropriate inference from our model class. How can such a decision be made? Simple structural rules, such as choosing the most singular model (highest codimension) consistent with the data description, or the least singular model, can easily be shown to be inappropriate. Similarly, the maximum likelihood description will generically be a transversal point in the feature space, and thus the regularities will almost never be inferred. Recall that the regularities only support strong inferences if their *a posteriori* probabilities are sufficiently large, and the likelihood ratio L for features associated with properties serves as the amplification factor from *a priori* probabilities to *a posteriori* probability ratios. A decision rule based on maximum *a posteriori* probability (MAP) estimates is possible, given estimates for the prior probabilities (Clark and Yuille, 1990). However, it is not clear that such useful estimates on the priors are possible to simply memorize, especially when we need these priors for each of a wide range of contexts. Thus for MAP estimation to work we need to estimate the priors on the fly from the model class, with the one glimmer of hope here being that the estimates may only need to be accurate to within an order of magnitude, or so. A different approach involves placing a partial order on various possible interpretations (see Jepson and Richards, 1991, 1992). This partial order could be made on the basis of probability estimates, or some other form of preference relation. For example, for the blocks in Figure 4 we may estimate that a floating collinear interpretation (codimension 4) is significantly less probable than an accidental view interpretation (codimension 1 or 2 depending on whether or not the blocks are assumed to be right angled), especially since we have no way of explaining this codimension 4 event. Difficult research issues remain for the resolution of these problems.

4.3. Ideal observers

Recently, Bennett et al. (1989) have constructed a probabilistic framework called "Observer Mechanics" which provides an alternative model for both the world and the perceiver. The major component of this model is an "observer" which is the 6-tuple (X, Y, E, S, π, η) where (loosely speaking) X is a configuration space of quantities being observed, and Y is the imaging space formed by the many-to-one mapping $\pi : X \to Y$. Within X lies a set E of "distinguished configurations" that play the role of our non-transversal categories. The images of configurations within E form the set of features S observed in Y. Hence S corresponds to our non-transversal image features. Finally, for each $s \in S$, $\eta(s, \cdot)$ is a probability measure on $\pi^{-1}(s)$.

An ideal observer is defined in terms of an unbiased measure μ_x on the configuration space X. We take this measure to be the probability of a particular configuration in X, but in the absence of any structuring influence producing the distinguished configurations captured in E. That is, μ_x is analogous to our background probability distribution p_0. Within this framework, an observer is then said to be ideal if

$$\mu_x[\pi^{-1}(s) - E] = 0. \tag{10}$$

In other words, when there is no regularity or structure in E, there is a zero probability of observing an element of S that does not result from an element of E (i.e. the probability of a false target, is zero). In terms of our earlier example, the probability of a "V" image feature is just the probability of the set of all configurations in X which project to S, namely $\mu_x(\pi^{-1}(S))$.

In a random stick world this probability is zero, and this implies that the previous equation must be satisfied (see the discussion around equation (3.3) in *Observer Mechanics*). Therefore, there exists an "ideal observer" for 3D "V"'s in a random stick world. In fact, if we identify the set E with world property P and identify the set $S = \pi(E)$ with image feature F, then $F = \pi(P)$ using our terminology an ideal observer can be constructed precisely when:

Ideal Observer Proposal: The image feature F is non-generic in the absence of world property P, and occurs with probability 1 in the presence of world property P.

Besides the condition that F occurs with probability one in the presence of P (which may be regarded as a consequence of our definition of $F = \pi(P)$), the only condition on an ideal observer is that the false target rate must be zero. Hence the measurement likelihood ratio must be infinite. Thus ideal observers are similar to our key features, in that both require an infinite likelihood ratio L. However, unlike key features, ideal observers include situations such as the "V" observer in a random stick world, even in the absence of a world regularity for "V"'s. In addition, ideal observers include the case of two randomly placed sticks, where the world property P is simply the occurrence of non-parallel sticks. This property occurs with probability one, yet there is still a feature having an infinite likelihood ratio. In our Bayesian proposal we include conditions that eliminate cases such as these. In particular, the V-observer is eliminated by the requirement that the world property is generic, and the skewed-sticks observer is eliminated by the informativeness condition.

Observer mechanics recognizes this problem but deals with these degenerate cases in a rather different manner. Both the V-observer and the skewed-sticks observer are essentially "no-op" observers. The V-observer in a random stick world detects a feature with probability zero, so it never reports a V observation. On the other hand, the skewed-stick observer detects its feature with probability one, and always responds. In both cases, the performance has zero probability of being wrong, which justifies the term "ideal". The conclusions of these "no-op" observers can reliably be used as input to other observers, and that is the primary requirement on an ideal observer. The problem we posed in this paper is different, we actually want useful, robust, and informative features. As a result, our definition of a key feature is (roughly) a subset of the situations for which there is an ideal observer, and to specify this subset we require structure both in the regularities of the world and in the conceptualization of the perceiver.

A second difference between our formulation and observer theory is that given a feature, we attempt to make categorical statements about world properties within a model context, whereas observer theory strives to place probability measures on world properties that are supported by observing a particular feature. Given a feature s, the conclusion of the observer is provided by a probability measure $\eta(s, e)$, with e in the distinguished space E (corresponding to P). This measure $\eta(s, \cdot)$ is called the interpretation kernel. In our framework this distribution is the *a posteriori* probability distribution $p(m|F \& P)$, conditional on both the feature F and the property P. For example, given the skewed-stick observer, the interpretation kernel would provide the *a posteriori* probability for the 3D position and orientation of the two sticks. In contrast, our approach provides only the categorical response that the two sticks are indeed skewed in 3D. The computation of such a interpretation kernel clearly involves detailed *a priori* probability distributions, which we have attempted to avoid. However we note that, in situations where the priors can be computed, the incorporation of analogs to the interpretation kernel could play a role in extending our "categorical" good feature formulation. For our purposes in this paper, we only point out that the most plausible approaches for the computation of these priors involve the manipulation of assumed regularities in the world, which again ties in with our notion of a model class.

5. Examples

Our treatment of Key Features within a feature space has been limited to configurations built from points, lines, edges, and facets. Although we have tried to stress that these elemental object types are not the only primitives that one might use, it is easy to regard our treatment as applying only to a "blocks world". The essential point, however, is that it really doesn't matter what sensory attributes or dimensions we consider, nor the particular object types chosen as "observable" primitives in that space of features. For example, we could explore non-transverse configurations in time rather than space, or frequency-time as in an acoustic feature space (Bregman, 1990). Here, however, we will present three further examples taken from vision.

5.1. Innate releasing mechanisms

Lorentz, Tinbergen and other ethologists (Thorpe, 1963) have noted that certain species-specific stimuli will trigger patterns of behavior in animals. Several examples were illustrated earlier in Figure 1. For example, a red spot near the tip of the beak of an adult gull will elicit feeding behavior from the young chick. Indeed, any such red spot located near the apex of a cone suffices. Clearly this can be idealized as a very non-transverse arrangement. In a 3D world, a spot at the vertex of a cone would have a minimum codimension 3 — even if the cone were given in the class of feature elements. Depending upon the sophistication of the gull's color system, we could easily add another 2 for the codimension of the specific color "red".

Furthermore, this releasing stimulus is generic (all gull parents have the spot) and is modal (there is no sea of red spots near the ends of cones visible to the chick). A similar analysis applies to the red belly of the stickleback, with the eye lying at the vertex formed by the color contour and the front face of the fish (see bottom illustration in Figure 1). The other patterns in Figure 1 also are idealized non-transverse and generic for species. A "stick version " of the hawk-duck configuration in 3-space has codimension 3 when stationary, but codimension 5 when moving along the long axis — the latter projecting into an image event of codimension 3 even if the symmetric relation is ignored. Similarly, the symmetries of the plankton eaten by perch have a high codimension in a world where line elements would otherwise be arbitrary or "fish-like". All of these "events" satisfy the key-feature constraints, and project into significant non-transversal, yet generic configurations with a robust codimension.

5.2. Ego motion

When we move in the world, we effortlessly compute our direction of translation. Only in the case where our fixation direction is aligned with the direction of body motion is the computation relatively simple, for then the optic array has two-fold symmetry as noted by Gibson (1950). However when we look to the side as we move forward, then the optical flow field is complex with gross asymmetries (Koenderink and van Doorn, 1981; Regan and Beverley, 1982; Richards, 1975). Nevertheless, a simple Key Feature can be derived from this flow field (see Chapter 4 and Jepson and Heeger, 1990 and see relevant neurophysiology by Frost, 1985).

Its form is as illustrated in Figure 12. The depiction places the observer at the center of a unit sphere. The flow pattern is on the surface of this field. For each local patch of flow (assuming an arbitrary angle between the direction of translation and the line of regard) there will be a residual, net flow vector. This vector defines a great circle on the unit sphere. The direction of body translation lies on this circle. Because two great circles always intersect (at two points), we need to inspect a third patch of flow to create a triple intersection. This is equivalent to three lines intersecting in a plane and hence has codimension one, which can be potentially increased as more patches are examined. In addition, the power of the key feature might be further augmented if we also have extrinsic frame vectors that act like the gravity vector in Figure 12, such as those derived from vestibular inputs. This space housing the key feature for Ego Motion is thus much like that shown earlier in Figure 11b where events in the feature space lie on loci that radiated from a single vertex. Here, then, we have a specific instance where noise and resolution will affect the robustness of the key feature (see Chapter 4).

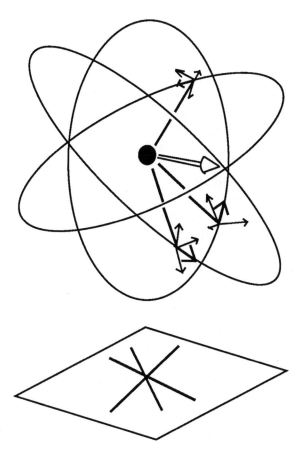

Fig. 12. *A Key Feature for the translation direction for ego motion has the same type of non-transversal configuration as that for finding the spectral quality of the illuminant!*

5.3. Color: finding the spectral content of the illuminant

Our previous examples stressed geometric relations in the world. To make the point that the relevant geometry is not in the world, but rather in the perceiver's representation of the world property, we provide one final example of a key feature.

A classical problem in vision is computing the spectral content of the scene illuminant. This computation is needed in order that this component of the reflectance function can be "discounted" when recovering the spectral reflectance of a surface. Shafer (1984) and Lee (1986) independently proposed a simple model for reflecting surfaces that solves this problem (see also Gershon et al., 1987). The image intensities arising from light reflected off a surface is broken into a matte (diffuse) and specular (mirror) component. These components add, with weights depending upon the surface orientation, the viewer's position and the reflectance properties of the surface. However, because the model is linear, for any given patch of surface, the locus of observed image intensities in the three color channels must lie on a plane containing the perfect diffuser, the perfect mirror, and the origin (see Figure 13). (We are assuming the ambient light has the same spectral density as the illuminant.) Any two such planes intersect along a line passing through the origin. A third plane that intersects the other two along the same line provides a key feature for the illuminant direction having codimension one. In Figure 13 we have shown a projection of these planes along the intersection line and see that a "Y" vertex is created. Obviously, the strength of the feature can be increased by examining more patches, with each additional patch adding another unit to the codimension.[6]

5.4. Abstract model spaces

Note that both the color and motion Key Features have the same form in their separate spaces. This similarity is important, because it illustrates that the "models" used in any event space can be quite simple, yet still have very significant inductive power, across a range of world properties. Also, in these particular model spaces, the chosen parameterizations seem compelling — matching our intuitions as to which properties might be represented. However, the representation of events within the model space need not be simple lines or planes. Indeed, for complex objects like an animal's face or a tree we should expect that the properties and relations might appear in the form of more complex, curved surfaces which themselves may be "viewed" or projected onto several different lower dimensional spaces to facilitate indexing, for example, as illustrated earlier in Figure 6. Such model spaces and their projections are quite consistent with our proposal, and would appear to be physiologically plausible. However, note that in such mappings that mirror particular "real world" properties, the co-dimension of a key feature becomes ambiguous and, as mentioned earlier, it is the inferred property that is assigned the codimension associated with the particular key feature configuration observed internally.

6. Summary

Previously, others such as Binford (1981), Lowe (1985), and Witkin and Tennenbaum (1983), have noted that good features should reflect

---

[6] The Key Feature may have more structure than that described. For example, if the projection plane is chosen properly, then the lines will be straight. This requires a check on collinearity between samples taken from the same patch. In addition, we have knowledge about where "natural" illuminants should lie in our color space, namely along the black body locus. (This locus acts like the "gravity" vector.) (Jepson et al., 1987; Lee, 1989)

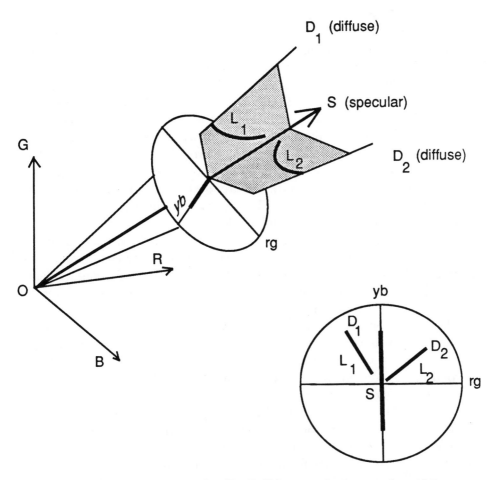

Fig. 13. Top: *Representation in the (R, G, B) space of responses L_1 and L_2 to two surface patches, lit by the same source S, that have different diffuse components of reflectance (D_1 and D_2). The two planes described by L_1 and L_2 intersect along the axis S, which describes the chromaticity of the illuminant, because the specular component of reflectance is common to both objects. The responses from two or more objects that define distinct planes can thus be used to find the axis S that describes the chromaticity of the illuminant.* Bottom: *Projection of L_1 and L_2 onto the chromaticity plane rg − yb. The lines described by the responses intersect at the point S marking the chromaticity of the illuminant. If the perceiver's model incorporates the knowledge that most daylight illuminants lie on a segment of the yb axis, as indicated, then two patches suffice to define a "crow's foot" key feature configuration. (Adapted from D'Zmura and Lennie, 1986.)*

"non-accidental" configurations that are specially informative yet typical of the world (such as two parallel lines). However, we note that the intuitively robust character of an inference based on a non-accidental feature is not simply due to the fact that they have a large likelihood ratio (i.e. the feature is expected when the world property is present, but very rare in the absence of the property). In the discussion of our Bayesian Proposal we have shown that a large likelihood ratio is clearly not sufficient to ensure robust inferences (see also Knill and Kersten, 1991). Rather, the likelihood ratio simply serves as a lever for raising the *a priori* probability of the particular world property. Given too low an *a priori* probability this lever is insufficient to provide a high *a posteriori* probability and hence a robust inference. This notion of a reasonably large prior probability is implicit in the discussion of a non-accidental feature, and explicit in the presentation of the intuition behind Observer Theory, yet the full impact it has on the definition of a good feature was not made explicit.

The analysis of the two block example in Figure 4 shows that the definition of a good feature must include a specification of the cognitive context in which it is being used. The collinearity feature, a classic non-accidental feature, is reliable in some contexts but nonsense in others. The difference hinges on what the perceiver is willing to assume are regularities in the world. Thus good features are necessarily bound to the current context of analysis, to conceptual models, and to the regularities that a perceiver expects to be operative (MacKay, 1978, 1985). The fact that a feature can be good in one context, but nonsense in a more specialized context, reflects a common phenomena in inductive inference known as non-monotonicity (Salmon, 1967). Whether your bias is for perceivers who maintain a detailed probabilistic model of their world, or for those which use a logical framework, this non-monotonic behavior must be dealt with by the explicit use of contextual information (McDermott and Doyle, 1980; Reiter, 1980).

Given that the specification of "good features" requires the specification of the current context, we suggest a model class as an appropriate form for representing contextual information. Basically a model class is an abstract space of models about the world, which has been carved up into various categories. Some of the categories are transversal, representing open subsets of the space. Other categories exist on subsets (submanifolds) of the parameter space and have a smaller dimension than that of the embedding space. These latter categories are non-transversal, and their degree of specialization can be roughly measured by their codimension, that is, the difference in dimension between the embedding space and the particular category. In addition, the model space can be projected to the image, where a similar categorization in terms of transversal and non-transversal image features can be made. Our canonical example is of a non-accidental property or feature such as collinear lines, which is non-transversal in both the world and image spaces. Indeed we pursue our proposal in some detail for such geometric features, but we also show it has applications to other domains such as motion or color interpretation.

So far this conceptualization is independent of whether or not certain categories support robust inferences in that it does not specify whether any non-transversal category reflects a regularity in our world. There is no notion of probabilities in this categorization. To fully specify a model class we need to select particular categories as corresponding to regularities that are considered possible within the current context, thus entertaining Bayesian-like propositions (Pearl, 1988). However, we prefer to keep the categorical conceptualization itself independent of the notion of regularities, or of probabilities in the world, to allow for the same set of categories to be used in a host of different contexts. Given the regularities, a Key Feature supports the inference of a particular non-transversal but generic world category (i.e. one expected or selected by the perceiver). Hence such a feature carries within itself its appropriate interpretation, in that the regularity has already been specified in the world, and this step of the inference process becomes rather trivial. Finally, given the appropriate qualifications provided by the Bayesian Proposal, such a key feature can be expected to provide a reliable inference for that particular regularity in the world.

For a structured, non-arbitrary world and for a defined set of (internal) concepts about primitive object types and their possible relations, the set of Key Features can be enumerated. All such features are not equally powerful with respect to their inference strength. As a measure of this power, we suggest the codimension of the Key Feature configuration, with respect to the class of models computable in the feature space. Our proposal requires a slightly different view of "feature detectors" than that customarily taken. Rather than simply providing a "measurement" as an oriented bar mask might do, our "feature detector" recognizes a non-transverse configuration in an event space constructed from such measurements. The class of configurations recognizable are only those non-transverse arrangements that can be computed for the types of object primitives and relations specified. The principal task, then, is to discover the object types used to construct the event spaces, for these will generate the model classes. We suspect that the relations computed within the different event spaces will be similar, and relatively trivial. Their reliability, of course, will depend upon how well the conceptual relations and primitives match the actual building blocks and constraints imposed by Nature on constructions in the real world.

Acknowledgments

WR is supported by AFOSR 89-504 and AJ by NSERC Canada, IRIS Canada, and CIAR. We appreciate the helpful comments and issues raised by Jacob Feldman, Horace Barlow, Richard Mann and Donald Hoffman.

Hand-printed digit recognition using deformable models[*]

Christopher K. I. Williams

Michael D. Revow

Geoffrey E. Hinton

Hand-printed digits can be modeled as splines that are governed by a small number of control points. For each known digit, the control points have preferred home locations, and deformations of the digit are generated by moving the control points away from their home locations. Images of digits can be produced by placing Gaussian ink generators uniformly along the spline. Real images can be classified by separately fitting each digit model to the image, and picking the model that fits best. We use an elastic matching algorithm to minimize an energy function that includes both the deformation energy of the digit model and the log probability that the model would generate the inked pixels in the image. The model with the lowest total energy wins. If a uniform noise process is included in the model of image generation, some of the inked pixels can be rejected as noise as a digit model is fitting a poorly segmented image. The digit models learn by modifying the home locations of the control points.

1. Introduction

Hand-printed characters can take on a great variety of shapes, especially when they are produced by a diverse population of writers. This variability makes the use of rigid templates impractical for hand-printed character recognition. It has long been realized (e.g. Ullmann, 1972; Burr, 1981b) that this limitation can be overcome by using elastically deformable models, and recent work (e.g. Yuille, 1990; Grenander et al., 1990) has provided a general framework for the problem. For images of single digits this framework implies that the best interpretation of an image is the model that minimizes an energy function that includes both the deformation energy of the digit model and the data misfit between the model and the image.

An alternative approach to digit recognition is based on statistical pattern recognition techniques; an example is the use of a feedforward neural network for ZIP code digit recognition by le Cun et al. (1990). This method

[*] This chapter is a revised and expanded version of Hinton, Williams and Revow (1992)

requires the segmentation and normalization of the digit image before the recognition stage. However, in some cases, it is not possible to correctly segment and normalize the digits without using knowledge of their shapes, so to achieve close to human performance on images of whole ZIP codes we believe it will be necessary to use models of shapes to influence the segmentation and normalization of the digits. One way of doing this is to use a large cooperative network that simultaneously segments, normalizes and recognizes all of the digits in a ZIP code. A first step in this direction is to take a poorly segmented image of a single digit and explain the image properly in terms of an appropriately normalized, deformed digit model plus noise. The ability of the model to reject some parts of the image as noise is the first step towards model-driven segmentation.

2. Elastic models

Ideas on the use of deformable models for pattern recognition go back at least as far as the early 1970's (Ullmann, 1972; Widrow, 1973; Fischler and Elschlager, 1973). Burr (1981a, 1981b) investigated several types of elastic matching procedures for character recognition problems, using dot and line models, and showed how a model could be progressively deformed to fit data. However, his methods were not designed to optimize an objective function trading off data-fit and model deformation energies. More recent work (e.g. Terzopoulos and Fleischer, 1988; Yuille, 1990; Mjolsness, 1990; Grenander et al., 1990) has emphasized the concept of a model deformation energy and a probability distribution over shapes. The deformation energy has a very physical interpretation as being the amount of energy required to elastically deform the fundamental shape into the distorted shape. By using the Gibbs distribution from statistical physics it is possible to relate the probability of a configuration to the deformation energy by $P_{def} \propto e^{-E_{def}}$. This means that shapes that are distorted further away from the fundamental shape will have a lower probability. By using this probability distribution a single deformable template can model a great variety of instances of an object.

Our elastic models are based on splines. Each model contains parameters that define an ideal shape and also define a deformation energy for departures from this ideal. These parameters are initially set by hand but can be improved by learning. They are an efficient way to represent the many possible instances of a given digit.

Each digit is modeled by a deformable spline whose shape is determined by the positions of about 8 control points. Every point on the spline is a weighted average of four control points, with the weighting coefficients changing smoothly as we move along the spline.[1] To generate an ideal

---

[1] In computing the weighting coefficients we use a cubic B-spline and treat the first and last control points as if they were doubled. Bartels et al. (1987) is a useful reference on the use of splines for geometric modeling.

example of a digit we put the 8 control points at their home locations for that model. To deform the digit we move the control points away from their home locations. With a spline model it is easy to model topological variants of a digit by small changes in the locations of the control points. For example, small changes in control point locations can deform the loop of a 2 into a cusp and then an open bend (see Figure 1). This advantage of spline models is pointed out by Edelman et al. (1990) who use a different kind of spline that they fit to character data by directly locating candidate control points in the image.

Currently we assume that, for each model, the control points have independent, radial Gaussian distributions about their home locations. Thus the probability of finding the control points within a small hypervolume δV of control point space is

$$P_{def} = \delta V \prod_c \frac{1}{2\pi\sigma_c^2} \exp\{-\frac{(\mathbf{x}_c - \mathbf{x}_c^h)^2}{2\sigma_c^2}\} \tag{1}$$

$$-\log P_{def} = -\log \delta V + N_c \log 2\pi\sigma_c^2 + \sum_c \frac{(\mathbf{x}_c - \mathbf{x}_c^h)^2}{2\sigma_c^2} \tag{2}$$

where $\mathbf{x}_c$ is the position of a control point, $\mathbf{x}_c^h$ is the *home* position of a control point, N_c is the number of control points and σ_c^2 is the variance of a control point. The last term in equation 2, which is proportional to the sum of the squares of the departures of the control points from their home locations, is the deformation energy (E_{def}).

The deformation energy function only penalizes shape *deformations*. Translation, rotation, dilation, elongation, and shear do not change the shape of an object so we want the deformation energy to be invariant under these affine transformations.[2] We achieve this by computing the deformation energy of each model its own "object-based frame". When we fit the model to data, we repeatedly recompute the best affine transformation between the object-based frame and the image (see section 4). The repeated recomputation of the affine transform during the model fit means that the shape of the digit is influencing the normalization.

Although we will use our digit models for recognizing images, it helps to start by considering how we would use them for generating images. The generative model is an elaboration of the probabilistic interpretation of the elastic net given by Durbin, Szeliski and Yuille (1989). Given a particular spline curve in the image, we space a number of "beads" uniformly along the spline. Each bead defines the center of a Gaussian ink generator. The number of beads on the spline and the variance of the ink generators can easily be changed without changing the spline itself.

---

[2] Currently we do not impose any penalty on extremely sheared or elongated affine transformations, though this might improve performance (see section 7).

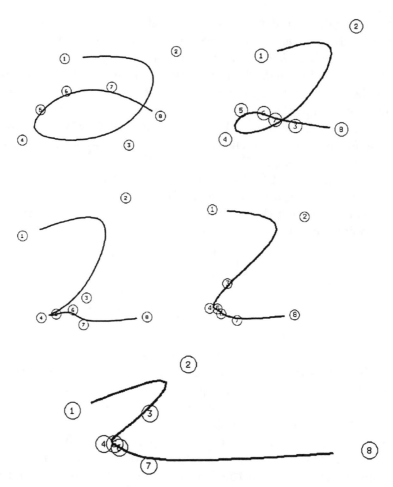

Fig. 1. *A cubic B-spline model of a 2 using eight control points. By varying the positions of the control points it is possible to change the loop of a 2 into a cusp and then an open bend. In the bottom example, control point number 8 has been moved to the right creating a long "tail".*

The generative model

To generate a noisy image of a digit we would run the following procedure:

- Pick one of the digit models

- Pick a deformation of the model, in object-based coordinates, by choosing a location for each control point from under the Gaussian distribution defined by the model. The probability of picking a deformation is proportional to $e^{-E_{def}}$

- Pick an affine transformation from the model's intrinsic reference frame to the image frame (i.e. pick a size, position, orientation, slant and elongation for the digit). Map the object-based locations selected for the control points into image-based locations

- Compute the spline curve in image coordinates and space Gaussian generators uniformly along the spline

- Repeat many times:

  Either (with probability π_{noise}) add a randomly positioned noise pixel
  Or pick a bead at random and generate a pixel from the Gaussian distribution defined by the bead.

3. Recognizing isolated digits

We recognize an image by finding which model is most likely to have generated it. Each possible model is fitted to the image and the one that has the highest posterior probability $P(D|X)$ is the winner.

$$P(D|X) = \frac{P(D)}{P(X)} \int P(X|D,m)P(m|D)dm \tag{3}$$

where X is the data, m is a vector of instantiation parameters which includes the affine transform variables and the control point locations, and D indexes a model. $P(D)$, the prior probability on model D and $P(X)$ are assumed to be the same for all models. We can approximate this integral by just considering the best fitting model instance, which has parameters m^*.[3] Letting E denote the negative logarithm of this approximate probability, we have

$$E_D = -\log P(m^*|D) - \log P(X|m^*, D) \tag{4}$$

The first term factorizes into the sum of the deformation energies for each separate control point, because they have independent probability distributions (see equation 2). The second term can also be factorized into a sum of separate log probabilities for each inked pixel provided we assume that each inked pixel is generated by an independent sample from a probability density function defined by the Gaussian beads and a uniform noise field. The probability of a point sample landing within a particular pixel is the product of the probability density at the centre of the pixel and the area of the pixel.[4] The probability is the sum of the probabilities of all the possible

---

[3] In effect, we are assuming that the integral in equation 3 can be approximated by the height of the highest peak, and so we are ignoring variations between models in the width of the peak or the number of peaks. Using this approximation means that we are in fact finding the maximum a posteriori (MAP) estimator.

[4] We assume that the probability density function varies linearly across the pixel.

ways of generating the point sample from the mixture of Gaussian beads or the uniform noise field.

$$P(i) = \frac{\pi_n}{N} + \frac{1 - \pi_n}{B} \sum_{beads} P_b(i) \tag{5}$$

where N is the total number of pixels, B is the number of beads, π_n is the mixing proportion of the uniform noise field, and $P_b(i)$ is the probability of the pixel i under Gaussian bead b.

4. The search procedure for fitting a model to an image

The objective for each model is to find a set of instantiation parameters m^* which minimize the total energy E. We search for this maximum by starting from an initial guess and then using a continuation method to home in on a good solution. The continuation method solves a sequence of progressively harder tasks with the solution to one task providing a good starting point for the solution to the next task in the sequence (Blake and Zisserman, 1987).

The initial position for a digit model is determined by calculating a minimal vertical rectangle around the data, and adjusting the offset and the x and y scale factors of the affine transformation so that the character model just fills that box. We start by finding a near optimal fit of the model to the data when the Gaussian beads all have a large variance. This involves only a few iterations of moving the control points and recomputing the affine transformation. At high variance, only a few beads are required to form a smooth ridge of higher probability along the spline, so the fit is very fast. After fitting at the highest variance, we slightly increase the number and reduce the variance of the beads according to a predetermined schedule and adjust the fit of the model to the data. The final fit of the model to the data is achieved after increasing the number of beads and reducing their variance four times, with several iterations at each variance. This fitting technique resembles the elastic net algorithm of Durbin and Willshaw (1987), except that our elastic energy function is much more complex and we are also fitting an affine transformation.

We have used conjugate gradient methods for optimizing the objective function E, but our preferred technique for the elastic matching is based on the Expectation and Maximization (EM) algorithm of Dempster, Laird and Rubin (1977). The algorithm is guaranteed to not increase E as it adjusts the instantiation parameters.[5]

---

[5] When the variance of the Gaussians is decreased, it is quite possible that the objective function will be increased. However, if the variance is adaptively adjusted by the EM algorithm rather than being externally imposed, the objective function will not increase.

The expectation step

Given the current locations of the Gaussian beads, compute the responsibility that each Gaussian has for each inked pixel. This is just the posterior probability of generating the pixel from that Gaussian given that it must be generated from one of the Gaussians or from the uniform noise field. The responsibility of bead b for pixel i is given by

$$r_b(i) = \frac{P_b(i)}{\sum_g P_g(i) + \frac{B\pi_n}{N(1-\pi_n)}} \tag{6}$$

We can think of each inked pixel as attached to each Gaussian bead by a spring whose stiffness is proportional to the responsibility of the bead for the pixel.[6] This mechanical analogy results from the fact that the log probability under a Gaussian is proportional to the squared distance from the mean, so it acts just like the energy of a spring.

The maximization step

The M step of the EM algorithm requires the adjustment of the instantiation parameters to maximize the posterior probability (or equivalently minimize E), assuming that the responsibilities remain fixed. For our problem this would require solving a set of simultaneous cubic equations for the affine transformation and deformation parameters. This is too difficult, so we use a two stage procedure which decreases (or at least does not increase) the objective function at each stage. First, holding the affine transformation constant, we invert a 16×16 matrix to find the image locations for the 8 control points at which the forces pulling the control points towards their home locations are balanced by the forces exerted on the control points by the inked pixels.[7] These forces come via the forces that the inked pixels exert on the Gaussian beads. The 16 linear equations for the control point positions are derived by taking $\partial E / \partial \mathbf{x}_c = 0$ for each control point.

The second stage involves adjusting the affine transformation and deformations by holding the new *image* locations of the control points fixed. This is also a non-linear problem, but we have found that choosing the affine transformation that minimizes the sum of the squared distances, in image-based coordinates, between the control points and their home locations gives satisfactory results. The second step is guaranteed not to alter

---

[6] The stiffness of the spring is also inversely proportional to the variance of the Gaussian.

[7] In the generative model presented above, the deformation occurs in object-based coordinates. For fitting the model to data it is more convenient to work entirely in image coordinates. We can achieve this by mapping the radial Gaussian prior distribution for each control point through the affine transformation to get an appropriately scaled elliptical Gaussian distribution in the image. This elliptical Gaussian defines the cost of deformations in image coordinates.

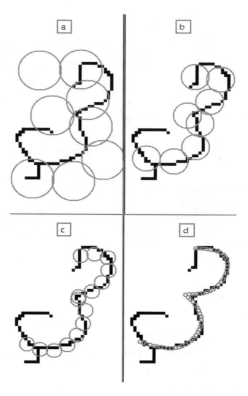

Fig. 2. *The sequence (a) to (d) shows some stages of fitting a model 3 to data. The grey circles represent the beads on the spline, and the radius of the circle represents the standard deviation of the Gaussian. (a) shows the initial configuration, with eight beads equally spaced along the spline. In (b) and (c) the variance is progressively decreased and the number of beads is increased. The final fit using 60 beads is shown in (d). The initial variance was about 65 times the final variance. We use about three iterations at each of five variances on our "annealing schedule". In this example, we used $\pi_{noise} = 0.3$ which makes it cheaper to explain the extraneous noise pixels and the flourishes on the ends of the 3 as noise rather than deforming the model to bring Gaussian beads close to these pixels.*

the data-fit term because the data-fit depends only on the image positions and variances of the Gaussian beads, and these are uniquely determined by the image positions of the control points.

Some stages in the fitting of a model to data are shown in Figure 2. The search technique usually avoids local minima when fitting models to isolated digits, but if we detect an unsatisfactory fit, we try alternative starting configurations for the models. We use four other positions, translated right, above, left and below the original one. These are tried in turn, and the retry process stops when a fit is found that is not rejected. If all five possible starting positions are rejected, then the case is rejected.

There are three situations in which we reject a fit and try the search from a different initial position.

- We reject a fit when the posterior probabilities of both models are similar, i.e. if the absolute difference between the energies E_D (equation 4) of the models is small.[8]

- A fit is rejected when the "winning" model accounts for the data by becoming excessively deformed, i.e. if the deformation energy is large. See Figure 3a and b.

- A model can find an incorrect fit while remaining relatively undeformed (Figure 3c and d. In many cases this problem can be related to an inadequacy in our definition of the data-fit energy. There is no explicit penalty for beads that generate pixels where there are none in the image. For example, the obviously incorrect fit in figure 3c should be rejected. One simple solution is to penalize beads that are far from any inked pixels. We used the penalty term

$$C = - \sum_{b \,\in\, beads} \log \sum_{\substack{i \,\in\, inked \\ pixels}} P_b(i) \tag{7}$$

A bead only makes a large contribution to this cost when all the inked pixels are far from the bead.[9] We reject cases where C is large for the winning model.

5. Learning the digit models

We have investigated two different learning techniques for adjusting the home positions and variances of the control points. In maximum likelihood (ML) learning each digit model is trained only on the images of that digit in the training set.[10] The objective is to adjust the model parameters (θ^D) so as to maximize the likelihood of generating those images from the model.

$$L_{ML} = \sum_{\substack{training \ images \\ of \ class \ D}} [\log P(X^D | \theta^D, m^*) + \log(m^* | \theta^D)] \tag{8}$$

where X^D is a training data image containing a digit of class D. This maximization is done iteratively, using EM updates given by $\partial L / \partial \theta_j^D = 0$. For example, the updated home location of each control point (in the object-based frame) is the average location of the control point in the final fits of the model of the digit to the instances of the digit, as illustrated in Figure 4.

---

[8] We can do this if we make energies insensitive to scale, see section 7.

[9] A more correct approach is discussed in section 7 under the heading "Explaining the white pixels".

[10] Actually, learning only occurs on those training cases where the correct model wins, because the model will tend to be excessively distorted when it has fitted wrongly.

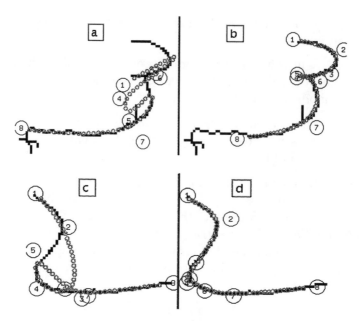

Fig. 3. *The final model configurations shown in (a) and (c) are rejected. In (a) the deformation energy exceeds the threshold, and the search is restarted from a different initial position, leading to the fit shown in (b). (c) is rejected because the the value of C is large, but an alternative starting position leads to the configuration shown in (d).*

There is a potential difficulty with the calculation of $\partial L_{ML}/\partial \theta_j^D$. Changing a parameter of an elastic model causes a simple change in the energy of the configuration that the model previously settled to, but the model no longer settles to that configuration. So it appears that we need to consider how the energy is affected by the change in the configuration. Fortunately, derivatives are simple at an energy minimum because small changes in the configuration make no change in the energy (to first order). Thus the inner loop settling leads to simple derivatives for the outer loop learning, as in the Boltzmann machine (Hinton, 1989).

An alternative to maximizing the likelihood of the image given the digit is to maximize the mutual information between the correct digit class and the probabilities assigned to the various classes by the digit models. The maximum mutual information (MMI) criterion emphasizes correct discrimination rather than correct modeling of the image data, and it generally leads to better discriminative performance. We do discriminative learning by maximizing

$$L_{MMI} = \sum_{\substack{all \\ images}} \log P(C|X) \tag{9}$$

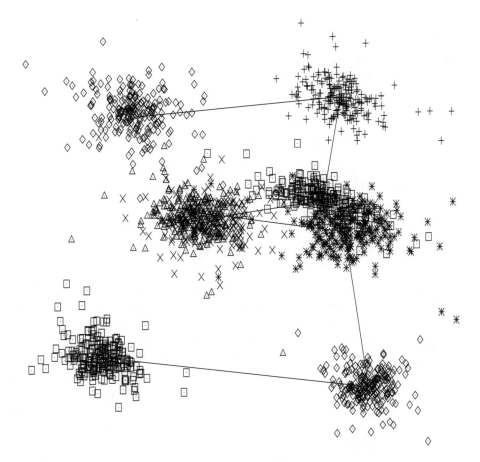

Fig. 4. *The figure illustrates the maximum likelihood learning procedure for the control point home locations of a 3 model. Each symbol cluster shows the final positions of a control point (in the object based frame) on each of the training cases. The solid lines connect the new control point home locations.*

where

$$P(C|X) = \frac{e^{-E_C}}{\sum_D e^{-E_D}} \tag{10}$$

is the probability of the correct digit C.

We have tried both of these learning techniques, and have obtained similar results with each one. Discriminative learning requires that we fit each model to each image; in contrast, with maximum likelihood training we only have to fit the correct digit model to each image, so it is much faster. If the distribution of images really can be modeled by choosing the appropriate parameters for our set of digit models, and if the fitting and learning processes do not get trapped at local optima, then maximum likelihood learning does just as well as discriminative learning at discrimination (Brown, 1987). If, however, the distribution of images is not well modeled by any set of parameters for our digit models, discriminative learning will generally yield better discrimination, since it will not waste parameters trying to model aspects of the images that are irrelevant to discrimination. The fact that MMI was no better than ML is weak evidence that the type of generative model we are using may be fairly good.

6. Results on the hand-filtered dataset

We are trying out the scheme out on a relatively simple task — we have a model of a two and a model of a three, and we want the two model to win on "two" images, and the three model to win on "three" images.

We have tried many variations of the character models, the preprocessing, the initial affine transformations of the models, the annealing schedule for the variances, the mixing proportion of the noise and the control point variances.

We took images of five digit ZIP codes from the training portion of the United States Postal Service Handwritten ZIP Code Database (1987)[11]. The images were preprocessed to eliminate variations due to stroke-width and paper and ink intensities. First, a standard local thresholding algorithm (White and Rohrer, 1983) is used to make a binary decision for each pixel. We then segment the image by cutting out five boxes, each of which contains one of the five largest connected components. The connected components are thinned, leaving an image with a spine one pixel thick.[12] We manually checked all images produced, removing those in which this procedure failed (e.g. touching digits).

Clearly, the dataset is not comparable to sets used by other researchers. Since our initial goal was to find a way of accurately characterizing the shapes of digits, we decided to restrict our initial experiments to two's and three's that are clearly discriminable by humans. Our system now achieves very good discrimination on these examples. Of course, our results give very little indication of how well our method would perform on data that includes examples of all of the digits and examples that people cannot reliably discriminate.[13]

The performance of the system using the hand-crafted models was 18 errors and 1 reject on a test set of 304 two's and 304 three's. This improved to 4 errors and 2 rejects after learning. The four errors are shown in Figure 5. The training set has 418 cases, and we have a validation set of 200 cases to tell us when to stop learning. Most of the improvement in performance

[11] Made available by the Office of Advanced Technology, USPS

[12] Thinning allows us to reduce the variability in the data-fit term due to thin or thick pen strokes.

[13] The US Postal Service will soon be releasing a segmented database which will allow us to make better comparisons with other methods.

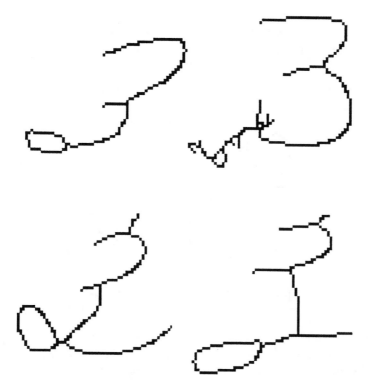

Fig. 5. *The four cases in the test set which were wrongly classified. The bottom two cases have "flourishes" (see section 7)*

occurred after the first pass of learning. Figure 6 shows the effect of maximum likelihood learning on the home positions of the control points. Similar results were obtained with discriminative training. It would also be possible to adapt the variances of each control point, although we did not do this for the simulations reported.

7. Discussion

Spacing the beads

In determining where on the spline to place the Gaussian beads, we initially used a fixed set of blending coefficients for each bead. These coefficients are the weights used to specify the bead location as a weighted centre of gravity of the locations of 4 control points. Unfortunately this yields too few beads in portions of a deformed digit that have been greatly stretched but are still governed by just a few control points (like the elongated tail of the bottom 2 in Figure 1). So these portions are expensive to explain even though the spline fits them well. Performance was much improved by spacing the beads uniformly along the spline. However, using this uniform spacing of

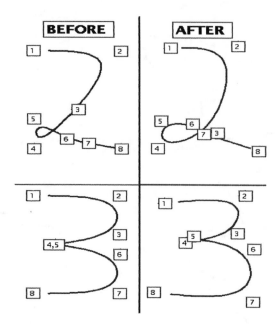

Fig. 6. *The two and three models before and after learning. The control points are labeled 1 through 8. We used maximum likelihood learning in which each digit model is trained only on instances of that digit.*

beads does mean that the search procedure (see section 4) could conceivably increase the objective function, as the repositioning of the beads is not taken into account when the new control point positions are calculated.

Penalizing affine transformations

In the research reported here we do not penalize extreme elongations, shears, or rotations. In effect we have assumed that all affine transformations of a digit are equiprobable. It would be better to penalize unlikely affine transformations by associating an additional deformation energy with the affine transformation itself. This energy, which could be learned, would represent the negative log of the prior probability of the affine transformation.

Having an explicit representation of the affine transformation of each digit should, in the future, prove very helpful for recognizing multiple digits, since it will allow us to impose a penalty on differences in the affine transformations of neighboring digits.

Invariance of recognition under affine transformations

There is an obvious way to ensure that the classification of a digit is invariant under affine transformations of the original image. We simply define the deformation energy and the data-fit energy in such a way that they are invariant under affine transformations. This ensures that the equilibrium configuration at which the deformation forces balance the data-fit forces will remain invariant, and also the energy differences between the fits of the different digit models will remain the same.[14]

It is easy to make the deformation energy invariant: We simply define the deformation in the object-based coordinate system. Affine transformations of the original image are then balanced by the affine transformation from the object-based to the image coordinate system, thus leaving the positions of the control points unchanged in the object-based system. It is also fairly easy to make the data-fit energy invariant if we assume that when an affine transformation is applied to the original image, it is also applied to the grid that is used to turn a continuous intensity field into discrete pixels. So when the image of the digit gets bigger, each pixel gets bigger and the number of pixels remains the same. We must also apply the same affine transformation to the Gaussian beads so that they scale up appropriately.[15]

Unfortunately, the digitization process has its own scale, orientation, shear and elongation and these do not change when affine transformations are applied to the original intensities. Given that the digitization process defines a natural scale, we could simply give up on the idea of achieving invariant recognition. Consider, for example, a digit that is so small that it only occupies a few pixels. There is not enough data to justify a highly improbable deformation so it is not clear that we want the same balance between data-fit and deformation terms when a digit is very small. Alternatively, we can try to compensate for the fact that the digitization process does not undergo the appropriate affine transformation. The major difficulty is that the number of pixels in a digit increases as it gets larger and this increases the number of data-fit forces. We can compensate for this by simply treating each inked pixel as some fraction of an "ideal" pixel. We could try to calculate this fraction by using the determinant of the affine transform from object-based to image coordinates, but then models with very different determinants would weight the inked pixels very differently. We have found that it is better to

---

[14] Actually, since the fitting process may get trapped at local energy minima, it is not sufficient to make the energy function invariant. It is also necessary to ensure that the whole fitting process, including the starting configuration of the model, is appropriately transformed.

[15] The obvious way to do this is by defining the Gaussian beads in object-based coordinates and then mapping them into the image through the affine transformation. One problem with doing this is that different digit models may use very different affine transformations leading to very different variances for their Gaussian beads. We therefore scale the variances of the circular beads in the image by the determinant of the initial affine transformation (found by fitting a rectangular box around the data). Using the mechanical view, it may seem strange that the energies can remain unchanged even when distances, and hence the extensions of the springs, increase by a factor of s. Spring stiffnesses decrease by a factor of s^2 and forces therefore *decrease* by a factor of s. The work done in getting from one configuration to another remains invariant because it is the product of the force and the distance.

simply down-weight each pixel in proportion to the number of pixels in the image.[16]

One more correction is necessary in order to make the data-fit energy independent of scale. The cost of explaining a pixel as noise must remain constant, and this cost involves the total number of pixels in the image (see equation 5). Scale invariance requires that we use the number of ideal pixels, so in addition to down-weighting each actual inked pixel in proportion to the number of inked pixels, we should also treat N in equation 5 as a constant that does not change as the size of the image increases.

More elaborate spline models

By using spline models, we build in a lot of prior knowledge about what characters look like, so we can describe the shape of a character using only a small number of parameters (16 coordinates and 8 variances). This means that the learning is exploring a much smaller space than a conventional feed-forward network. Also, because the parameters are easy to interpret, we can start with fairly good initial models of the characters. So learning only requires a few updates of the parameters. We can probably afford to use more parameters in the digit models. Obvious extensions of the deformation energy function include using elliptical Gaussians for the distributions of the control points (5 parameters instead of the current 3), or using full covariance matrices for neighboring pairs of control points.

More elaborate ways of generating ink from splines

One obvious generalization is to use elliptical rather than circular Gaussians for the beads. If strokes curve gently relative to their thickness, the distribution of ink can be modeled much better using elliptical Gaussians. However, an ellipse takes about twice as many operations to fit and is not helpful in regions of sharp curvature. Our simulations suggest that, on average, two circular beads are more flexible than one elliptical bead.

At high variance, our generative model is obviously inadequate because the inked pixels that it produces will be very scattered and will have no tendency to cohere into sharp strokes. Our only way of achieving coherence is to lower the variance. At the beginning of the fitting process, however, we know that our estimates of the position of the pieces of the stroke are unreliable but we also know that the inked pixels should cohere into a sharp stroke. No single variance can capture both these kinds of knowledge.

---

[16] This has the desired effect when an image is scaled up. However, if an image only contains a few inked pixels, it can deform a model just a strongly as an image of the same size containing many more pixels. Also, if there are a lot of noise pixels in the image they can reduce the ability of the other pixels to deform a model.

There is an interesting way of allowing the generative model to assign much higher probability to more coherent images, even when the Gaussians have high variance. Instead of generating ink directly from the Gaussians, we use the Gaussians to generate probabilities that individual pixels are inked. Then, we treat these probabilities as bias terms in a Markov Random Field (MRF) that stochastically assigns one of the two labels "figure" or "noise" to each inked pixel. The MRF uses a locally defined energy function that penalizes label assignments in which nearby inked pixels have different labels. A mean field approximation of this MRF can easily be combined with the elastic fitting of a digit model. On each iteration of the elastic fit, the digit model provides new bias terms for each inked pixel in the MRF, and a few iterations of the mean field MRF are then used to update the label probabilities on the inked pixels. The data-fit term in the cost function is modified to reflect the probability of generating the inked pixels with a particular figure/noise labeling.

As a consequence of its preference for coherent images, the MRF method makes it much cheaper to explain noise that forms continuous lines or blobs than it is to explain the same number of randomly scattered noise pixels. Also, it assigns heavier penalties to places where the labeling switches within a continuous line of inked pixels than it does to places where the figure and the noise are not connected. We are currently investigating this technique.

Throughout this paper we have assumed that the data that must be fitted consists of inked pixels. But there is nothing to prevent a similar approach being applied to preprocessed images that contain short oriented stroke segments or stroke-edge segments. Each Gaussian bead can represent a probability distribution over oriented features. We simply add an orientation distribution whose mean is defined by the orientation of the spline at that bead and whose variance is influenced by the curvature of the spline. Unfortunately, our current implementation of this approach is prone to get trapped at local optima when a section of the spline (typically in the loop of a 2) gets fitted to the bar segment data with an orientation error of 180 degrees.

Structured noise and flourishes

Presegmented images of single digits contain many different kinds of noise that cannot be eliminated by simple bottom-up operations. These include descenders from the line above, deliberate underlines, bits of other digits, corrections, dirt in recycled paper, smudges, and misplaced postal franks. To really understand the image we probably need to model a wide variety of structured noise. We are currently experimenting with one simple way of incorporating noise models. We first fit a mixture of a digit model and a uniform noise field to a poorly segmented image of a digit. Then we try to fit more complicated noise models to the residual noise. A good fit greatly

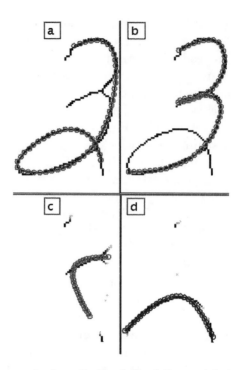

Fig. 7. *The top two panels show the final fit of the models to an image of a three which has a flourish at the bottom; (a) 2 model (b) 3 model. In (a), the 2 model accounts for most of the flourish data and hence has a lower data-fit energy. The lower panels illustrate the residual images obtained by subtracting off the portion of the image accounted for by the basic model. The fit of flourish models is also shown.*

decreases the cost of that noise and hence improves this interpretation of the image.

The idea of trying to find better explanations of the residual noise image can also be used to deal with the flourishes that frequently appear on the ends of digits. The basic model of a digit does not include these flourishes and at least half the errors in our test set are caused by the excessive cost of explaining large flourishes using the uniform independent noise model. Figure 7 shows an example of this type of error which occurred in the training set. The 3 model made a reasonably good fit to the data, but was unable to account for the flourish on the bottom end of the data and was forced to explain each of those pixels as an independent piece of noise. The 2 model used the flexibility of its loop to model the flourish, leaving only the cusp region of the data to be explained as noise.

We have briefly experimented with a way of handling flourishes. Figure 7 shows the residual image obtained by subtracting out the portion of the image accounted for by the digit model. Top and bottom flourish models are then initialized. Each flourish is allowed three control points (so it can easily model a curved stroke). One control point is strongly tied to its "home location" which is coincident with the end control point of the digit model. The other two control points can easily be moved by the data-fit forces. Hence flourishes have much weaker priors on their shapes as compared to digit models. This makes good initialization even more critical than for digit models. A separate affine transformation for the flourish models is unnecessary as they only have deformation energy associated with a single control point.

Ultimately, of course, we want to use a less greedy algorithm in which the flourish and structured noise models are fitted *during* the fitting of each digit model, but we currently have no efficient way of doing this because it is hard to choose sensible initial configurations for the flourish and noise models before we know which bits of the image are noise and which bits are the digit. This objection does not apply to the very primitive uniform noise model in which noise pixels are generated independently, which is why we *can* use this noise model during the fitting of the digit. Nor does it apply to the Markov Random Field model of noise described above.

Explaining the white pixels

A significant drawback of our generative model is that it does not treat the white pixels as evidence. It maximizes the likelihood of generating the inked pixels, but it does not pay a sufficiently severe penalty for assigning high probabilities of ink to white pixels. As a result, a model can fit the data well even if some of its Gaussian beads are a long way from the nearest inked pixel. Some of the classification errors seem to be caused by this weakness of the generative model. We have therefore formulated an alternative generative model in which the white pixels must also be generated.

We assume that the image is generated from the spline by a two-stage stochastic process. The first stage computes the probability $\hat{P}(i)$ that each pixel in the image would be inked if *multiple* samples were taken from the probability distribution defined by the Gaussian beads and the uniform noise process (see equation 5). We imagine taking N_B samples from this distribution, where N_B is the number of inked pixels in the image[17] and we compute the probability that none of these samples landed within a particular pixel. This gives the predicted probability that the pixel is not inked, and its complement $\hat{P}(i)$ is the predicted probability that the pixel is inked.

$$\hat{P}(i) = 1 - (1 - P(i))^{N_B} \tag{11}$$

---

[17] To maximize the likelihood of generating the image we should, ideally, take more samples than there are inked pixels because several samples may fall on the same pixel. However, the penalty incurred by using the wrong number of samples is unlikely to affect the relative goodness of fit of different models.

The second stage of the image generation process then uses these predicted probabilities to independently decide whether to ink each pixel. Given the predicted probabilities, $\hat{P}(i)$, the log probability of generating exactly the correct image is

$$\log P(X|m, D) = \sum_{\substack{i \in inked \\ pixels}} \log \hat{P}(i) + \sum_{\substack{j \in uninked \\ pixels}} \log(1 - \hat{P}(j)) \qquad (12)$$

This can also be viewed as the cost of encoding the image data using the predicted probabilities to do the encoding.

When the Gaussians have high variance, each sample only has a very small probability of landing on a particular pixel, and the chance of two samples landing on the same pixel is negligible. So there is a simple approximation for the probability of inking a pixel; $\hat{P}(i) \simeq N_B P(i)$. Also, when the Gaussians are large, all of the pixels have a low predicted probability of being inked and in this case the log probability of generating the image given the predicted pixel probabilities is dominated by the cost of generating the inked pixels:

$$\log P(X|m, D) \simeq \sum_{\substack{i \in inked \\ pixels}} \log P(i) + N_B \log N_B \qquad (13)$$

Note that the term involving N_B will be the same for all models, and can therefore be ignored. So at high variance, this generative model is almost the same as the one we are already using. At low variance, the two generative models are very different in the way they penalize different fits. In particular, the second generative model makes it more expensive for parts of an instantiated digit model to lie in white space. We are currently experimenting to see whether this improves discrimination.

Because there are so many more white pixels, the second generative model appears to require much more computation, but this is an illusion. At high variance, where many white pixels fall under each Gaussian bead, we simply use the other generative model since it is almost equivalent. At low variance, each Gaussian bead only has a significant effect on a small number of white pixels, because the estimated probabilities for pixels far from any bead are dominated by the noise term. So we never have to deal with the product of all the beads with all the pixels.

A completely different elastic model

Before we tried using splines to model digits, we used models that consisted of a fixed number of Gaussian beads with elastic energy constraints operating between neighboring beads. The deformation energy was described by three kinds of terms—displacements of the beads away from their home positions, changes in the distance between pairs of beads and changes in the curvature of triples of beads. With this type of energy function, we had great difficulty using a single model to capture topologically different instances of a digit. For example, in Figure 1 the sign of the curvature reverses as the loop of the 2 changes to a cusp and then to an open bend.

Spline models also make it easy to increase the number of Gaussian beads as their variance is decreased. This coarse-to-fine strategy is much more efficient than using a large number of beads at all variances, but it is much harder to implement if the deformation energy explicitly depends on particular bead locations, since changing the number of beads then requires a new function for the deformation energy.

8. Conclusion

One of our main motivations in developing elastic models is the belief that a strong prior model should make learning easier, should reduce confident errors, and should allow top-down segmentation. Although we have shown that elastic spline models can be quite effective, we have not yet demonstrated that they are superior to feedforward nets and there is a serious weakness of our approach: Elastic matching is slow. Fitting the models to the data takes *much* more computation than a feedforward net. So in the same number of cycles, a feedforward net can try many alternative bottom-up segmentations and normalizations and select the overall segmentation that leads to the most recognizable digit string. In the long run, however, we expect that it will be more efficient to use shape knowledge to guide segmentation, rather than just using it to filter out poor segmentations.

Acknowledgements

This research was funded by Apple and by the Ontario Information Technology Research Centre. We thank Peter Brown for advice on Gaussian mixture models, Allan Jepson and Richard Durbin for suggesting splines, David MacKay for insights on Bayesian methods and the members of the Toronto Connectionist Research Group for many helpful discussions. Geoffrey Hinton is the Noranda fellow of the Canadian Institute for Advanced Research.

The role of color in spatial vision

Karen K. De Valois

Frank L. Kooi

1. Introduction

Color vision is a remarkable adaptation that allows the viewer to detect changes in the spectral distribution of light largely independently of effective intensity. This impressive ability carries significant associated costs, both in terms of the large neural investment required and in the accompanying loss of spatial resolution. Color vision is not necessary for survival, nor does its absence produce an obvious and severe degradation in the ability of a human, for example, to navigate through its environment, find an appropriate food source or mate, or escape predators. Although the aesthetic power of color is often mentioned, it is clearly not required for the production of works of art and beauty, as the continuing popularity of black-and-white photography and cinematography attests. Why, then, should we have devoted such a massive amount of our visual systems to the processing of color? Some 80–90% of the geniculo-striate pathway appears to be involved in color vision, and this pathway is certainly that most responsible for our conscious visual perception. What do we gain from this enormous investment?

Consider first the nature of the world our visual system evolved to detect and analyze. Virtually all natural scenes contain variations in both the intensity of light and its spectral distribution. It is rare indeed to find a substantial area of the world in which light intensity varies but chromaticity does not, or, conversely, in which chromaticity varies but intensity does not. Variations in both intensity and spectral distribution are associated with reflectance borders, marking the boundaries between objects. Either should thus provide a good source of information about the structure of the world. However, the maps of color variation and luminance (or effective intensity) variation are usually not identical for any given visual scene. Since both are typically associated with reflectance borders, why are they nonisomorphic? The differences arise primarily because the world, which is three-dimensional, is not uniformly illuminated. Rather, most illuminants, particularly those of nature such as the sun, are directional. The light they shed upon a scene originates from a relatively small area and illuminates a large region. Thus, some objects lie between the light source and other parts of the scene, creating shadows.

The part of a scene that is in shadow is typically illuminated by light of much lower intensity than a corresponding unshaded part, and it thus reflects much less light. The shadow can create a border of quite high luminance contrast. The spectral distribution of the light falling on the shaded area is also usually somewhat different than the light that comes directly from the illuminant. If the target area is outside and is illuminated by the sun, for example, the spectral distribution of the light falling on the shaded region will be shifted slightly toward the short wavelengths, due to Rayleigh scattering by the atmosphere. If the scene is indoors, the spectral distribution of the light falling on any particular area may be affected by the reflectance characteristics of nearby surfaces. In either case, however, it is the exception, not the rule, for the spectral difference across a shadow border to be pronounced, or indeed even noticeable. Although in principle neither the intensity nor the spectral distribution of the light reflected from various parts of a complex scene should be perfectly correlated with the presence of object borders, the differences in spectral distribution that do not directly signal borders are effectively minimal, while the differences in intensity are large and obvious. Thus there are pronounced luminance borders that do not directly indicate object borders. Although such shading information can be used to help determine the three-dimensional structure of the world and can be used even when the spectral distribution of the light from the shaded area is inappropriate or different from that that would normally occur (Cavanagh and Leclerc, 1989), this is a complex task that requires a great deal of processing. A naïve approach to the problem would suggest that luminance shadows might be at least as disruptive in terms of object segregation and differentiation as they are potentially helpful in the analysis of three-dimensional shape.

The obvious chromatic borders within a scene are much more likely to be associated unambiguously with reflectance borders than are luminance borders. They might thus be expected to provide a straightforward, less problematic source of information about the spatial structure of the environment — in particular, about the differentiation of the visual scene into discrete objects. In other words, color vision should potentially be quite helpful in solving many of the problems of spatial vision, and for certain problems such as object segregation it could provide more reliable information than luminance vision. Clearly quantitative differences between color and luminance processing exist in contrast sensitivity, resolution, temporal processing and motion, which are all somewhat degraded at isoluminance (see below). Is the spatial analysis of color-defined patterns also degraded? By spatial analysis we mean low level tasks such as orientation and spatial frequency discrimination as well as perceptual tasks such as object segregation.

To determine whether chromatic information can play a significant role in spatial vision, one must address several basic questions. First, what fundamental visual tasks can be done with only color information? If a visual pattern contains chromatic variation without correlated luminance variation, can an observer successfully carry out a variety of visual spatial tasks? This question is most commonly approached by testing for various abilities when the stimulus is at isoluminance, and we shall briefly review several such studies. This is not the only way to ask this question, however, nor is it perhaps the best. An alternate (though rarely used) method is to encode the relevant information by chromatic variations, but to embed the chromatic stimulus within a pattern of uninformative luminance variations. The pseudoisochromatic plates that are widely used to assess color vision in a clinical setting are examples of the use of chromatic information embedded within an uninformative luminance pattern.

When spatial judgments can be successfully based on chromatic information alone, it is important to determine how performance on spatial tasks at isoluminance compares to performance on the same tasks when the stimuli are defined by luminance variations. It is well known that spatial acuity at isoluminance is poorer than comparable measures made with luminance contrast, for example, but a relevant question is whether it is so much poorer that it is useless. If performance on all spatial tasks were very much worse with color than with luminance, one might justifiably question the usefulness of color for the processing of spatial information. A very crude, rudimentary ability may not be worth the investment required to support it, so it is important to make quantitative comparisons of performance on similar tasks under each condition, that is, with only luminance information available and with only chromatic information available.

We shall also consider briefly the question of what happens to perception at equiluminance. Several reports during the last few years have suggested that not only do performance measures differ at isoluminance, but many less-quantifiable but ultimately perhaps more interesting aspects of perception also differ dramatically when luminance contrast is not present but chromatic contrast is. The world looks very different at isoluminance. Does this imply that the underlying organization is also very different?

This raises the final question of interest — namely, what is the structure underlying chromatic spatial vision? We would like to know how this structure compares to that underlying luminance vision. Our understanding of the mechanisms of luminance spatial vision derives in part from psychophysical investigation and in part from physiology, but we have much less physiological data on which to draw when we consider the mechanisms of chromatic spatial vision. We may, however, be able to come to some reasonable conclusions if comparable psychophysical tasks reveal comparable kinds of behavior when the spatial patterns are defined solely by color variations and when they are defined by luminance variations.

2. Experimental results

Contrast sensitivity The first and simplest task of spatial vision is that of pattern detection, or contrast sensitivity. The spatial contrast sensitivity function for luminance-varying patterns shows a rapid attenuation at high spatial frequencies, with a gentler but still pronounced fall-off at spatial frequencies lower than the peak (see De Valois and De Valois, 1988, for examples), when plotted on log-log coordinates. The entire function is band-pass, with a peak at some intermediate spatial frequency (in the range of about 2–5 c/deg at photopic luminance levels). Under optimal conditions, the high-spatial-frequency cut-off point will be about 60 c/deg, a value which is predictable either from the geometry of the foveal cone mosaic or from the characteristics of the eye's optical system.

The spatial contrast sensitivity function for isoluminant, color-varying gratings is markedly different. There is a rapid loss of sensitivity at high frequencies, but no low-frequency attenuation is seen (van der Horst et al., 1967; van der Horst and Bouman, 1969; Granger and Heurtley, 1973; Mullen, 1985). The color contrast sensitivity function, then, is low-pass, not band-pass. Geisler (1989) has shown, however, that essentially all of the difference can be accounted for by receptoral and pre-receptoral factors, implying that the neural substrates for color and luminance are equally efficient. This does not imply that the machinery is the same, of course, but it does suggest that color is not processed by a fundamentally inferior system. Below we shall consider some data that specifically allow us to compare the ways in which different kinds of spatial information are encoded when defined by color or by luminance variations. The more rapid fall-off in sensitivity at high spatial frequencies for color as compared to luminance is sometimes taken as evidence that color is not a very useful substrate for spatial vision. This is based upon the assumption that it is the high-frequency information that is particularly important in determining spatial structure, a view that is reinforced by reliance upon models using edge detection as a first step in object recognition. The very high spatial frequencies that define a sharp edge are not detectable if they exist solely in the chromatic domain. However, it is instructive to note that even in the luminance domain, high spatial frequencies are not visible outside the small region restricted to the foveal representation in or near the plane of fixation. Traditional assumptions about the significance of high frequency information may be in error. To the extent that crucial spatial information is carried in the low spatial frequencies, the color vision system is well-designed to participate in its analysis.

Spatial frequency discrimination Good spatial vision requires not only that the visual system be able to detect objects of interest; it must also be capable of discriminating between patterns that are detected. One dimension of interest is that of size or spatial frequency. At suprathreshold contrasts, a normal observer can discriminate between two luminance sinusoidal gratings that differ in spatial frequency by a factor of about 2–4% of the base frequency (Caelli et al., 1983; Skottun et al., 1987; Regan et al., 1982; Thomas, 1983; Webster et al., 1990). For example, a high-contrast grating of 2 c/deg can be reliably differentiated from another grating of 2.04 c/deg, even when the two gratings are matched for apparent contrast (Webster et al., 1990).

Can two gratings that are defined solely by chromatic differences be discriminated as readily? Webster (1988) and Webster, De Valois and Switkes (1990) compared spatial frequency discrimination for the same subjects using either gratings formed by luminance variation or gratings formed by isoluminant chromatic variations along two axes of particular theoretical interest (Krauskopf et al., 1982). Along one axis, as the chromaticity of the pattern changed, absorption by the L and M cones changed in equal and opposite ways, while absorption by the S cones remained constant. The other was a tritanopic confusion axis, along which the ratio of L to M cone absorption remained constant while S-cone absorption varied. They found that a spatial frequency increment of only about 4–5% of the base frequency could be reliably discriminated. For example, a reference grating of 2.0 c/deg could be distinguished from a test grating of 2.08 c/deg when contrast differences were not useful cues. The difference between the spatial frequency discrimination thresholds for luminance and chromatic gratings averaged 35–40%. These results show that spatial information based solely upon chromatic differences can be used to make sensitive and reliable discriminations about spatial frequency and presumably, thus, size, even though performance is quantitatively poorer than when the same judgment is based on luminance differences.

This study illustrates one interesting and important problem in the study of chromatic spatial vision. It is well known that many characteristics of luminance vision are determined in part by the pattern contrast. For example, the apparent spatial frequency of a grating can be affected by contrast (Davis et al., 1986), as can the minimum discriminable difference in spatial frequency (Skottun et al., 1987). Although luminance contrast can be readily specified using a standard metric such as the Michelson contrast, there is no comparable, agreed-upon metric for defining chromatic contrast. Further, no definition based upon the stimulus (like Michelson contrast) would allow a simple and direct comparison between chromatic and luminance contrasts. Thus, if color spatial vision, like that based upon luminance differences, can be affected by contrast, then it is important to have some method for equating the effective contrasts of the stimuli of interest. Webster, et al. (1990)

chose to equate their luminance- and chrominance-varying patterns on the
basis of multiples of their respective detection threshold contrasts. Thus, a
luminance grating of 16 times its threshold contrast was compared with a
chromatic grating of 16 times its threshold contrast. When luminance and
chromatic contrasts are equated in this manner, it can be seen that for a
given high-multiple-of-threshold contrast (here 20 times threshold), the minimum discriminable spatial frequency difference for isoluminant chromatic
gratings (4–7%) is somewhat greater than that for the same subjects for
luminance gratings 2–5%). Thus, on this task using patterns that are well
above threshold contrast, performance at isoluminance is poorer than performance with luminance differences alone even when patterns are equated
in terms of multiples of threshold contrast. The significant result, however,
is not just that there is a difference, but also that discrimination with only
chromatic information is quite good. A very small frequency difference is
readily discriminated, showing that on this task, at least, color is a potentially useful stimulus for spatial vision.

Orientation selectivity The question of whether orientation can be reliably
discriminated based solely upon chromatic information is particularly interesting because it has been reported that neurons in V1 (the cortical area that
demonstrates the first and most precise orientation selectivity for luminance
patterns) do not have orientation tuning for isoluminant stimuli. Livingstone and Hubel (1984), for example, report that V1 neurons that respond
to purely chromatic stimuli typically have little or no selectivity for stimulus
orientation. Although there have been brief reports of orientation-selectivity
for isoluminant chromatic gratings (Elfar and De Valois, 1991), it is widely
assumed that chromatic information alone cannot support good discrimination of orientation (see, for example, Livingstone and Hubel, 1987). If this
were so, it would be a devastating criticism of the proposition that color
vision can be used to perform many of the basic tasks of general spatial
vision. Orientation is obviously of prime importance.

Webster (1988) and Webster et al.(1990) examined the ability of subjects
to make orientation discriminations for both luminance-varying gratings and
isoluminant chromatic gratings, using the same subjects and comparable
experimental protocols. They found that at high contrasts, orientation discrimination thresholds for two subjects averaged 0.65 deg for luminance and
0.99 deg for isoluminant chromatic gratings. Although these threshold values for luminance orientation discrimination are slightly higher than those
reported in other studies (e.g., Bradley et al., 1987; Eisner and MacLeod,
1980; Cavanagh et al., 1987; Regan et al., 1982), they show that orientation
discrimination based upon luminance cues is very good indeed. However,
the more significant finding for the present discussion is that color alone,
even in the absence of luminance cues, can subserve excellent discrimination
of orientation. It is particularly noteworthy that similar threshold values

were obtained for both chromatic axes used. Even two patterns defined by chromatic variations along a tritanopic confusion axis can be reliably discriminated when their orientations differ by only a degree or so. Further, even at detection threshold, subjects could reliably discriminate whether a particular stimulus was a chromatic grating or a luminance grating and, in the case of chromatic gratings, along which color axis it lay. Thus despite the contrary hints from physiology, color vision again has proven to be an adequate substrate for good spatial vision.

Contrast coding When a luminance contrast increment is detected in the presence of a suprathreshold masking contrast (and both mask and test are equated for spatial frequency), the increment threshold is a function of the mask contrast (Legge and Foley, 1980). When mask contrasts are very low (in fact, near detection threshold), sensitivity to a contrast increment is increased. Detection of the pattern requires less added contrast in the presence of the mask than in its absence. As mask contrast rises, the increment threshold increases proportionately, with the entire function being approximately fit by a power function (Legge and Foley, 1980; Swift and Smith, 1983). When the same procedure is carried out using gratings that vary solely in chromaticity, a similar contrast dependence is found (Switkes et al., 1988). Facilitation occurs at near-threshold mask contrasts, and sensitivity falls progressively as mask contrasts climb to high suprathreshold levels. The best-fitting power function is similar to that found for luminance-varying patterns.

Similarly, when a subject adapts for a prolonged period to a high-contrast luminance grating of some spatial frequency, f, then measures the spatial contrast sensitivity function, a band-limited loss in contrast sensitivity peaking at the adaptation frequency is found (Blakemore and Campbell, 1969). The amplitude of the contrast sensitivity reduction is a function of the contrast of the adaptation grating. When the same experiment is repeated using isoluminant chromatic gratings, a similar contrast dependence of adaptation is seen (Bradley et al., 1988).

Spatial frequency tuning The spatial frequency selectivity of luminance channels has been shown by masking studies in which the masking effect was defined as a function of the spatial frequency difference between mask and test. Such studies reveal spatial frequency band-limited mechanisms operating in the luminance domain. With very low contrast masks (when one operates in a summation regime), bandwidths are quite narrow (well below one octave—Sachs et al., 1971; Legge and Foley, 1980). With high contrast masks, bandwidths are typically substantially broader, although still band-limited (see, for example, Legge and Foley, 1980). When both mask and test patterns are isoluminant, chromatically-varying gratings, very similar selectivity is found (Switkes et al., 1988). If mask contrasts are equated for masking effectiveness (i.e., chosen to give approximately equivalent amounts of masking), masking bandwidths for color and for luminance do not differ significantly.

Pattern adaptation studies also reveal the spatial frequency selectivity of color-analyzing mechanisms. Adaptation to a high-contrast sinusoidal luminance grating produces a temporary, band-limited reduction in contrast sensitivity (Blakemore and Campbell, 1969). Similarly, adaptation to a suprathreshold chromatic grating also produces a transient, band-limited reduction in chromatic contrast sensitivity (Bradley et al., 1988). In both cases, the loss in contrast sensitivity peaks at the spatial frequency of the adaptation pattern.

Orientation tuning The orientation tuning of the mechanisms underlying orientation discrimination of chromatic patterns, like spatial frequency tuning, has been studied using an adaptation paradigm. As with luminance (Blakemore and Campbell, 1969), adaptation to an isoluminant grating of a particular orientation selectively reduces contrast sensitivity for the detection of another grating of identical of similar orientation (Bradley et al., 1988). The adaptation effect for color, however, differs in that the measured orientation bandwidth is significantly greater than that found for luminance patterns. In fact, when the adaptation pattern is greatly suprathreshold in contrast, the orientation of the test pattern may have to deviate from the orientation of the adaptation pattern by 90° before the effect completely disappears, as opposed to the much smaller orientation difference required for luminance. Thus, although there clearly is orientation selectivity in the mechanisms underlying chromatic discrimination, it appears to be less marked than that in mechanisms underlying luminance discrimination.

Depth perception Another important spatial visual task is to determine the distance of an object from the viewer. There are both monocular and binocular mechanisms that subserve depth perception. Although the binocular mechanism (stereopsis) has probably been more widely studied — and is certainly more beloved of visual theorists — the monocular cues to depth may be of greater practical significance. Few rigorous studies of depth perception at isoluminance with only monocular cues present have been carried out, and the reports from the existing experiments are contradictory. Livingstone and Hubel (1987) fail to see depth in isoluminant patterns that would otherwise produce a strong appearance of depth. Troscianko et al. (1991), on the other hand, find that depth from perspective cues is maintained at isoluminance.

There have been rigorous, quantitative studies looking at stereoscopic depth at isoluminance. The results of these studies are contradictory, however. In the initial report, Lu and Fender (1972) found that the ability to see depth in a random-dot stereogram disappeared at isoluminance. De Weert and Sadza (1983), in an exhaustive and well-controlled study of the phenomenon, found that although stereopsis based on luminance cues was compromised at contrasts lower than about 10%, no luminance ratio (presumably including isoluminance) eliminated the perception when there was significant chromatic contrast in the pattern. Livingstone and Hubel (1987) later failed to find stereopsis for random-dot patterns at isoluminance, however. Tyler and Cavanagh (1991) report that stereomotion at isoluminance is quite robust, though its dependence upon temporal frequency is different from that of luminance stereomotion. Thus, it is difficult to draw any firm conclusions about the encoding of depth at isoluminance, although it appears to be at least somewhat poorer than with luminance variations.

The role of color in object segregation Although this is probably the most important of the questions we raise, it is the one on which we have the least information. The role of color is most often addressed by studying vision at isoluminance, a very unnatural condition. Informal observations suggest that the presence of large color differences can profoundly affect the ability to perform other simple tasks that do not depend directly on color contrast. For example, the subjective difficulty of making heterochromatic brightness matches is well known and can be readily appreciated by an attempt to compare the relative brightnesses of differently colored objects in a normal visual environment. We have studied a related phenomenon quantitatively by asking subjects to detect the presence of a luminance grating alone or when masked by either another luminance grating or an isoluminant chromatic grating (De Valois and Switkes, 1983; Switkes et al., 1988). We found that the presence of chromatic contrast at a nearby spatial frequency and orientation can greatly increase the luminance contrast required for the detection of the test grating. Similar and related observations have been reported by Cole et al. (1990).

It is clear that in the case of pattern detection, color can have a powerful detrimental effect on performance on a luminance task. The suggestion we made in the beginning, however, was that color could potentially have a beneficial influence, that by using color variations one should be able to segment a scene more easily and reliably. The usefulness of color variations in such tasks has been demonstrated for machine vision systems (Swain and Ballard, 1990). In order to see whether color does in fact play an important role in scene segmentation and object segregation in human vision, we (Kooi, 1990; Kooi et al., 1992) have studied the perception of plaid patterns. A moving plaid, composed of two superimposed and (in our case) orthogonal sine wave gratings, can appear either as a single structure moving coherently or as two transparent surfaces sliding past one another. Adelson and Movshon (1982) showed that the degree of sliding or transparency increases as the similarity between the components decreases. They reported that contrast, spatial frequency and depth all influence the appearance of coherence versus transparency. Note that this perceptual judgment is really a reflection of how the scene is segmented. If both component gratings are seen as belonging to the same object, the entire pattern appears to be a single surface moving coherently. When the two gratings are seen as being separate objects, perceptual transparency occurs and sliding is seen, with two concomitant directions of motion. This is exactly the kind of situation in which one might expect color to play a profound role, and indeed it does. We (Kooi, 1990; Kooi et al., 1992) found that adding color symmetrically to a moving luminance plaid (that is, adding the same amount of color contrast to both gratings in an identical manner) increases pattern coherence. However, adding color asymmetrically to the two components will increase sliding. These effects can be quite large and dramatic. A plaid pattern that is normally seen as being quite coherent will break apart dramatically when color is added asymmetrically to the two gratings. The crucial factor is not the amount of color contrast added, but whether or not it is added to the two components in the same way. Identical chromatic patterns (e.g., red-green gratings) can be added to each component, but if the phase at which they are added differs, the effect will still be to produce perceptual fracturing of the plaid.

Color therefore influences object segregation (in this case, based on motion) in a manner consistent with what one might expect from logical considerations. Regions of the same color are more likely to belong to the same object, while regions of different color are more likely to belong to different objects, and our perceptual systems seem to take those probabilities into account. This suggests that not only does one have the ability to make spatial judgments based in whole or in part upon chromatic information, but that ability is normally used in making perceptual decisions.

Perception at isoluminance We have briefly considered some of the quantitative psychophysical comparisons between performance based upon luminance variations and that based solely upon chromatic variations. Here we wish to raise the subject of the perceptual appearance of the world in the absence of luminance variations. Isoluminance is a condition that does not exist in the natural visual world, at least not over any extended spatial region. It should not be surprising, then, that visual scenes appear strange under such an unnatural condition. Gregory (1977) has discussed some of the unusual appearances associated with isoluminant stimuli.

One kind of perceptual observation that has historically been of great interest to students of the visual system is the set of geometrical illusions. Livingstone and Hubel (1987) report that geometrical illusions are absent at isoluminance. Another interesting observation is that the apparent speed of a moving isoluminant grating is significantly slower than the apparent speed of a luminance grating moving at the same real speed (Cavanagh et al., 1984). A third oddity of isoluminance is that under that condition the accommodative response is absent (Wolfe and Owens, 1981; Switkes et al., 1990). It would be of interest to determine whether, or to what extent, the failure of the accommodative mechanism could be responsible for some of the strange perceptions.

3. Underlying mechanisms — spatial channels

A wealth of evidence accumulated over the last three decades has suggested that the specificity for spatial frequency and orientation seen for luminance vision reflects the tuning of aggregates of physiological mechanisms loosely operating together. These mechanisms are referred to by the rather non-specific term channels. Although the precise definition of channel varies (see De Valois and De Valois, 1988; Graham, 1989 for examples), those who find the concept useful have based their analysis of channel characteristics on similar kinds of experimental studies. The most widely used of these have been adaptation, masking and subthreshold summation, which, in procedure, is identical to a masking experiment using a very low-contrast mask. Although spatially tuned mechanisms that analyze chromatic variations have not been as widely studied, some similar experiments have been carried out. Several of these have been briefly reviewed above.

Analysis of surface reflectances and shadows argues that it would be advantageous for the visual system to create a spatial map based on color differences that is separate from that based upon luminance differences. Both masking and adaptation results suggest that such a spatial map exists and that the mechanisms responsible for contrast coding of spatial color patterns are very much like those underlying luminance contrast coding. As with contrast coding, the mechanisms underlying spatial frequency tuning in chromatic and luminance domains appear to be similar, as evidenced by detection and discrimination studies and by pattern adaptation. The observations on object segregation using moving plaid patterns demonstrate the influence of chromatic information on a spatial perception task. However, the peculiarities associated with perception of depth and motion at isoluminance, the failure of visual accommodation, and the generally strange appearance of the visual world at isoluminance all suggest that there are some fundamental differences between the way space is analyzed through luminance and the way it is mapped based upon color variations. The nature of those differences remains, at least in part, a mystery.

Nonlinear processes in pattern discrimination and motion perception

Hugh R. Wilson

1. Introduction

One of the most dramatic discoveries of the past 15 years is the existence of multiple visual areas in the cortex, each apparently optimized for the processing of different visual attributes (Zeki, 1978; Mishkin et al., 1983; Van Essen, 1985; Maunsell, 1987; Maunsell and Newsome, 1987). As illustrated in Figure 1, two primary pathways emerge from striate cortex (V1): a form vision pathway reaching inferior temporal cortex (IT) via areas V3 and V4, and a motion and optic flow analysis pathway to middle temporal cortex (MT) and beyond (Mishkin et al., 1983; De Voe and Van Essen, 1988). It seems natural to think that such disparate visual tasks as shape and motion analysis would require specialized visual machinery, and there is indeed psychophysical evidence in support of this (Treisman, 1982; Treisman, 1983; Nakayama and Silverman, 1986). Even granted this, however, Figure 1 reveals a puzzle: why do both the form and motion pathways receive input directly from V1 and also indirectly via V2? To put it otherwise, what additional processing occurs in V2 (highlighted in gray) that makes its parallel projection to both the form and motion pathways advantageous?

Although the question just posed is based on anatomical observations, I shall argue in this chapter that recent results in visual psychophysics suggest an answer. Psychophysical studies of pattern discrimination indicate that additional processing is necessary to determine the shape of texture boundaries (Bergen and Landy, 1991; Landy and Bergen, 1991; Graham, 1991; Sutter et al., 1989; Wilson and Richards, 1992). This suggests that simple luminance contours and contours defined by texture boundaries or discontinuities are processed in parallel. In a like vein, it has recently been shown that visual motion analysis involves both the processing of the Fourier components of the stimulus and independent processing of non-Fourier components generated by a rectifying or squaring operation (Chubb and Sperling, 1988; Chubb and Sperling, 1989; Turano and Pantle, 1989). Experiments

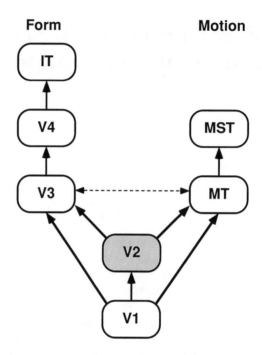

Fig. 1. *Anatomy of primate visual cortical areas (after Van Essen, 1985). Among other connections, primary visual cortex (V1) projects in parallel to V2, V3, and MT (middle temporal cortex). V2, in turn, projects to both V3 and MT. The pathway from MT to MST and beyond has been associated with visual motion analysis, while the pathway including V3, V4, and IT (inferior temporal cortex) is involved in shape or form perception. This article raises a key question: why do both form and motion pathways (eg. V3 and MT) receive projections both directly from V1 and indirectly from V1 via V2 (gray)? The answer is suggested by a comparison between this diagram and Figure 11. This diagram is greatly simplified by the omission of many other visual areas and connections, although one of these is shown (dashed line). Finally, note that all connections shown are reciprocal.*

on the perceived direction of moving two-dimensional patterns (Ferrera and Wilson, 1990; Yo and Wilson, 1992) have led to the conclusion that these two motion pathways combine to produce a final estimate of the direction of stimulus movement. It will be shown below that the extraction of texture boundaries and the processing of non-Fourier motion involve common elements that are inherently nonlinear. A comparison of the nonlinearities emerging from these psychophysical studies with responses of single cells in primate V2 (von der Heydt et al., 1984; von der Heydt and Peterhans, 1989) suggests that primate V2 performs a nonlinear filtering operation on the output of V1 in order to detect the location and motion of texture boundaries.

This chapter will first summarize evidence for parallel linear and nonlinear analyses in pattern discrimination. Next, evidence for the combination of linear (Fourier) and nonlinear (non-Fourier) motion pathways will be discussed. Finally, the results will be related to the parallel V1 and V2 projections to both the cortical form and motion pathways.

2. Pattern discrimination

Extensive psychophysical evidence indicates that the retinal image is first processed in parallel by a number of filters selective for orientation and spatial frequency (Wilson and Bergen, 1979; Wilson et al., 1983; Phillips and Wilson, 1984; Graham, 1989; De Valois and De Valois, 1988; Wilson et al., 1990). Measurements of the orientation (Phillips and Wilson, 1984) and spatial frequency bandwidths (Wilson et al., 1983) derived from psychophysical masking studies are in good quantitative agreement with physiological results from single neurons in macaque striate cortex (De Valois et al., 1982). In the fovea, the psychophysical data are consistent with the existence of mechanisms tuned to six different spatial frequencies ranging from 0.8 to 16.0 cycles per degree (cpd), each having a bandwidth in the 1.25–2.0 octave range[1]. Orientation bandwidths were found to decrease from $\pm 30°$ at 0.8 cpd to $\pm 15°$ at 16.0 cpd.

As these psychophysical measurements apparently reflect the characteristics of various classes of cells in human striate cortex, it should be possible to use them to calculate the cortical response to an arbitrary visual stimulus. Such calculated responses to pairs of stimuli should therefore permit us to predict just how accurately the two may be discriminated. Such predictions of pattern discrimination thresholds have proven accurate for a wide range of discrimination tasks including spatial frequency discrimination, vernier acuity, two line separation acuity, and curvature discrimination (Wilson and Gelb, 1984; Wilson and Regan, 1985; Wilson, 1986; Wilson and Richards, 1989; Wilson, 1991b). Here I shall first briefly discuss vernier acuity and then focus on curvature discrimination, which leads directly to evidence for nonlinear processing.

As psychophysical pattern discrimination thresholds represent the smallest difference between patterns that can be accurately detected, it follows that thresholds should be predictable from the difference in mechanism response to a pattern pair. Let the two-dimensional spatial filter or receptive field of a visual unit be designated by $RF(x, y)$. Masking studies have shown that $RF(x, y)$ for a vertically oriented unit may be described by the equation (Wilson et al., 1983; Phillips and Wilson, 1984):

$$RF(x, y) = A \left[e^{-x^2/\sigma_1^2} - B e^{-x^2/\sigma_2^2} + C e^{-x^2/\sigma_3^2} \right] e^{-y^2/\sigma_y^2} \qquad (1)$$

---

[1] Spatial frequency and orientation bandwidths are defined as full bandwidth at half amplitude. Although the existence of just six distinct spatial frequency tunings in the fovea is controversial, these six do provide a complete representation of all stimulus information, and additional mechanisms are thus redundant.

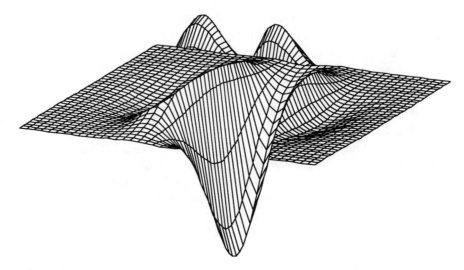

Fig. 2. *Perspective plot of a visual filter measured psychophysically (Wilson et al., 1983). The filter, described by Equation (1), has a central excitatory zone flanked by inhibitory zones and weak secondary excitatory zones. Note the excellent agreement with characteristics of simple cell receptive fields measured physiologically (Movshon et al. 1978). The overall dimensions of this plot, which represents the smallest filter measured psychophysically, are 0.2° by 0.2°. These small filters, with a peak spatial frequency of about 16.0 cpd, are primarily responsible for fine spatial discrimination tasks like vernier acuity.*

This filter consists of a narrow excitatory center with space constant σ_1 flanked by an inhibitory region with gain B and space constant σ_2, which is flanked in turn by a weak secondary excitatory zone with gain C and space constant σ_3. This profile is multiplied by a single Gaussian in the orthogonal direction. A perspective plot of this function is shown in Figure 2. Formulas for units with other orientations are obtained through rotation of coordinates, and parameter values for all filters have been tabulated elsewhere (Wilson, 1991b).

Single units in striate cortex generate a highly nonlinear response as stimulus contrast increases. Simple cells, for example, show a true threshold characterized by half-wave rectification (i.e. zero response to negative inputs) followed by a monotonic increase with contrast leading to a compressive nonlinearity and saturation (Albrecht and Hamilton, 1982; Sclar et al., 1990). Psychophysical evidence indicates the presence of a very similar nonlinearity, which may be described mathematically as (Nachmias and Sansbury, 1974; Legge and Foley, 1980; Legge, 1981; Wilson, 1980; Wilson and Gelb, 1984):

$$R = \frac{S^{3-\epsilon}}{1 + S^2} \qquad (2)$$

where

$$S = \int_{-\infty}^{\infty} \int_{-\infty}^{\infty} RF(x - x', y - y')P(x', y')dx'dy' \qquad (3)$$

is the response of the linear filter to pattern $P(x, y)$. Thus, a model psychophysical unit behaves much like a cortical simple cell, and this description will therefore be referred to as the simple cell model.

The simple cell model predicts that pattern discrimination thresholds may be calculated from the differential responses of a collection of units tuned for different orientations (θ), spatial frequencies (ω), and neighboring retinal locations (Δx). If we let $\Delta R(\omega, \theta, \Delta x)$ designate the difference in response of a model simple cell to a pair of patterns, P1 and P2, the discriminability of these patterns will then be a monotonic function of the distance between pattern representations in a multi-dimensional neural response space:

$$\Delta R = \left(\sum_{\omega} \sum_{\theta} \sum_{\Delta x} |\Delta R(\omega, \theta, \Delta x)|^2 \right)^{1/2} \qquad (4)$$

By convention, the model has been normalized so that $\Delta R = 1.0$ at the 75% correct threshold in a two alternative forced choice experiment. Complete details of this model have been published elsewhere (Wilson, 1991b).

Let us examine how this simple cell model operates in predicting vernier acuity (Wilson, 1986). A vernier stimulus is shown superimposed on several simple cell receptive fields in Figure 3A–D. Relative to 3A it is apparent that a slight offset of one of the vernier bars will partially shift it into an inhibitory zone (gray) of the receptive field at the point marked by the arrow in 3B. Thus, a shift of one bar by a fraction of the width of the excitatory central zone (white, +) can produce a significant change in neural response. Panels 3C and 3D show the comparable situation for a receptive field oriented at 15° to the axis of the vernier stimulus. Here the same small offset also moves one of the bars partially into the inhibitory region (arrow in 3D). Thus, a very small vernier offset may be expected to produce a significant change in the computed neural response. Although the stimuli in Figure 3 have been shown optimally positioned in the receptive field for illustrative purposes, it must be emphasized that neighboring cortical units overlap so extensively that there will always be a unit close to optimally located[2].

Vernier thresholds predicted using the equations above bear out this qualitative picture. The graph in Figure 3E compares the simple cell model predictions (solid line) with data from Westheimer and McKee (1977) plotting vernier thresholds as a function of bar separation. The theory correctly

---

[2] To optimally sample the image at the Nyquist frequency, adjacent receptive fields must be spaced no further that 40% of the receptive field center width apart. This follows from the observation that filters described by equation (1) respond to spatial frequencies up to about 2.5 times the peak frequency.

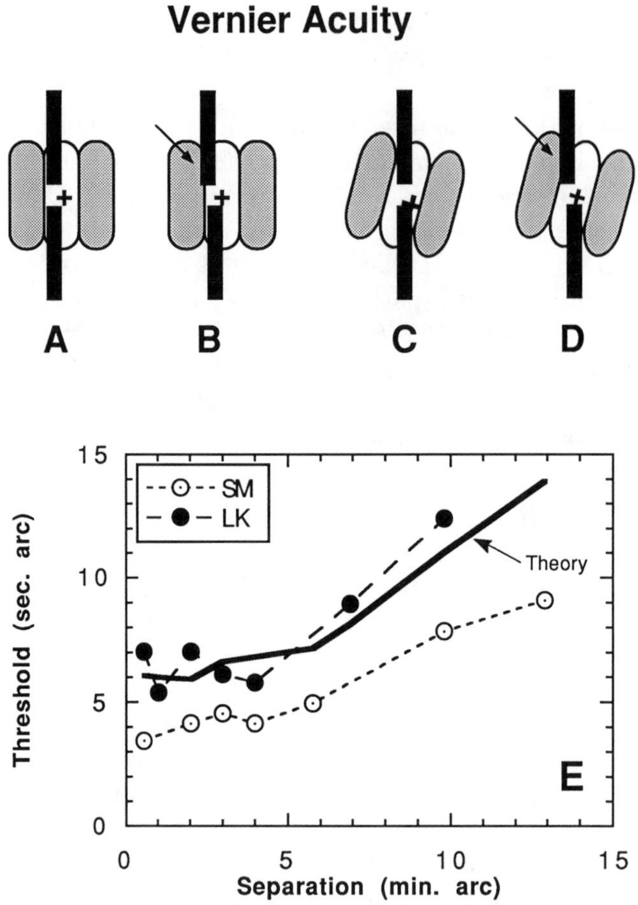

Vernier Acuity

Fig. 3. *Theoretical prediction of vernier thresholds. A and B compare the response of a visual filter like that in the last figure to aligned bars (A) and bars with a small vernier offset (B). Note that a very small offset of the top bar in B displaces it partially into the inhibitory zone (gray) at the point indicated by the arrow. Thus, a small offset will produce a significant change in the filter response. The same holds true for a filter oriented at 15° to the stimulus axis, as shown in C and D. A small offset again displaces the top bar into the inhibitory zone in D at the point marked by the arrow. The bottom panel plots two data sets from a study by Westheimer and McKee (1977). The experiment measured vernier thresholds as a function of the separation between the adjacent ends of the vernier bars. The solid line plots the theoretical prediction of the model described in the text.*

predicts a graceful rise in threshold as the separation between the ends of the bars increases. As the bars are progressively separated, they become too widely separated to jointly stimulate the smallest receptive fields. At this point the thresholds are determined by the next larger receptive fields, which produce proportionately larger vernier thresholds. Note that the simple cell model also correctly predicts that the smallest vernier thresholds will be about 5.0 sec. arc, even though the smallest receptive fields have a center width of 1.9 min. arc. It should be emphasized that these predictions are made with no free parameters[3].

Curvature discrimination provides a second informative application of the model (Wilson, 1985; Wilson et al., 1990; Wilson and Richards, 1989; Wilson and Richards, 1992). Curved contours are shown superimposed on model receptive fields in Figure 4A and 4B. The sharper curve in A clearly invades the inhibitory surround at the points indicated by the arrows, while the gentler curve in B does not. Thus, differences in curvature will produce differences in neural response, and these may be used to predict curvature increment thresholds. The same observations obtain for responses to curved black-white edges, so Figure 5 compares experimental increment thresholds for edge curvature discrimination (open circles, Wilson et al., 1992) with theory (dash-dot line). The simple cell model clearly provides a good fit to the data over the range of edge curvatures tested[4].

Several recent studies have provided definitive evidence for more complex, non-linear processing in texture segregation (Bergen and Landy, 1991; Landy and Bergen, 1991; Sutter et al., 1989; Graham, 1991), and our research has led to the same conclusion through an analysis of curvature discrimination at texture boundaries (Wilson and Richards, 1992). Consider the stimulus in Figure 4C. Here the curved boundary is defined not by a simple luminance edge but rather by the locus of a 180° phase shift in a square-wave grating. When the square-wave is of high spatial frequency (16 cpd in these studies), the information concerning curve shape is largely orthogonal to the orientation of the grating bars. Can the simple cell model predict curvature discrimination at these curved texture boundaries? The solid circles in Figure 5 plot average curvature increment thresholds measured at a 16 cpd texture boundary (Wilson and Richards, 1992). Relative to discrimination at a simple luminance edge (open circles), discrimination at the texture edge is uniformly worse by a modest factor averaging 2.4. The simple cell model, however, predicts thresholds that are about ten times higher for the texture edges (thin dashed line in Figure 5). The reason for this is illustrated in Figure 4C. Even the smallest psychophysically measured receptive fields, which are tuned to about 16 cpd (Wilson et al., 1983), are long enough to integrate over several cycles of the square-wave grating when they are oriented along

---

[3] There are a number of constants required to specify the six filters described by equation (1) and the nonlinearity in equation (2). However, all of these constants were independently measured in masking experiments (Wilson et al., 1983; Phillips and Wilson, 1984), and they retained these fixed values for all model predictions.

[4] Wilson and Richards (1989) discovered that line curvature discrimination utilized a comparison of curve orientation at two points for low curvatures. This minor modification of the simple cell model is also incorporated in the edge curvature predictions of Figure 4. See Wilson and Richards (1989) for further details on this point.

Curvature Discrimination

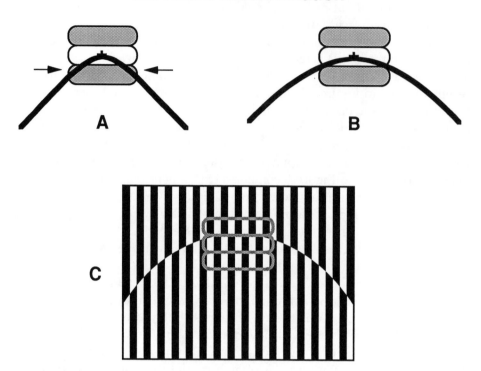

Fig. 4. *Curvature discrimination experiments. The contour in A is curved more sharply than that in B. As a result, note that the contour in A impinges on the inhibitory zone (gray) of the visual filter at the points indicated by arrows, while the more gentle curve in B does not. Thus, visual units with simple cell characteristics will respond differentially to contours of differing curvature. Although not shown, the same is true for units at other orientations relative to the curve. Note that the principles illustrated in A and B will also obtain for a curved black-white edge. A curved texture boundary, defined by the locus of a 180° phase shift in a 16 cpd square wave grating, is illustrated in C. Note that simple cell type filters, such as that outlined in gray, will integrate the black and white regions of the texture and thus fail to generate a significant response to the curved contour.*

the texture boundary. Thus, these cells provide a very weak response and correspondingly poor discrimination.

An explanation of curvature discrimination at texture boundaries can be provided by adopting a nonlinear processing model (Bergen and Landy, 1991; Landy and Bergen, 1991; Sutter et al., 1989; Graham, 1991). The version of these models developed here is the simplest that can successfully predict curvature discrimination at texture boundaries. As schematized in Figure 6, the extraction of texture boundaries requires three stages. First, the image is processed by the simple cell filters that have already been dis-

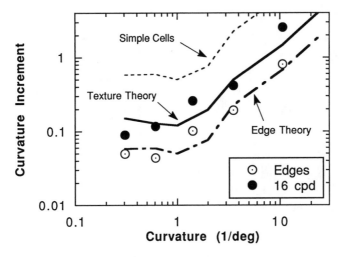

Fig. 5. *Data and predictions of curvature discrimination thresholds. The open circles plot mean thresholds for discrimination of the curvature of a black/white edge, while the solid symbols are mean thresholds for discrimination of texture boundary curvature (see Figure 4C, data from Wilson and Richards, 1992). Calculations utilizing simple cell type filters, including that in Figure 2, produced the accurate edge theory predictions plotted by the dash-dot line. However, this simple cell model predicts that discrimination of texture boundary curvature should be about four times worse than is measured (thin dashed curve labeled "Simple Cells"). The texture model described in the text accurately predicts discrimination at curved texture boundaries, as shown by the solid line.*

cussed. The results of this filtering are shown in Figure 6A for the stimulus shown in Figure 4C. Note that the filtered response vanishes along the texture boundary, because the levels of excitation and inhibition are balanced at these points. The next processing stage requires full-wave rectification of the stimulus[5]. As responses to the black and white bars of the square-wave grating are respectively conveyed by off-center and on-center simple cells, full-wave rectification can easily be implemented by summing on-center and off-center responses over an appropriate region. The final processing stage involves orientation selective filtering of the rectified image. As shown in Figure 6B, this filtering extracts the locus of the curved texture boundary.

Two points must be made concerning this second stage filtering. First, the filters must be at a lower spatial frequency (larger) to eliminate responses to the individual bars of the square-wave grating. In the model for texture

[5] Wilson and Richards (1992) employed a squaring operation for mathematical convenience. As the squared term is the lowest non-vanishing term in the Taylor series expansion of a full-wave rectifier, the differences between the two operations are not significant. The visual system clearly implements full-wave rectification by pooling on- and off-center units as described in the text.

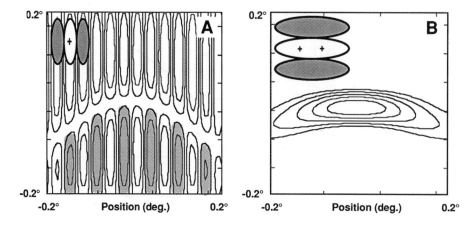

Fig. 6. *Application of the texture model to boundary curvature extraction. Panel A provides a contour plot of responses generated by the oriented filter illustrated in the upper left when applied to the texture pattern in Figure 4C. Note that these simple cell filters respond well to the bars defining the texture but fail to respond at all along the curved boundary. In the lower half of A responses to the black bars are plotted in gray to emphasize that these linear filters give alternate positive and negative responses. The model response in B was generated by full-wave rectification of A followed by filtering using the larger, horizontally oriented filter shown as an inset. As shown by the contour plot in B, this sequence of oriented filtering, rectification, and second stage filtering generates a response along the curved texture boundary. This texture model predicts the texture discrimination thresholds plotted with a solid line in Figure 5.*

curvature discrimination (Wilson and Richards, 1992), these filters were chosen to be a factor of two larger (i.e. one octave lower in frequency). This is sufficient, as the rectified responses to the grating bars are at twice the grating frequency, so that the second stage filters fall two octaves below them. Second, the final filter in Figure 6B is orthogonal to the simple cell filters in the first stage, but several different second-stage orientations would generally be used to filter the image.

This texture boundary model analyzes curvature in exactly the same manner as the simple cell model encapsulated in Equations (1) to (4), except that the response in Equation (3) is computed using the first-stage filtered and rectified neural image rather than the retinal luminance distribution. For texture boundaries defined by the locus of a 180° phase shift in a square-wave grating, the effect of first-stage filtering and rectification is to transform the texture boundary into a Gaussian blurred line, with the blur function being determined by the vertical Gaussian of the simple cell filter in Equation (1) (Wilson and Richards, 1992). Curvature discrimination thresholds computed using the texture boundary model are plotted as the solid curve in Figure 5. In agreement with the data, predicted discrimination of texture boundary curvature is only modestly poorer than is discrimination of simple edge curvature. In the model this modest degradation results from the Gaussian blurring produced by simple cell filtering followed by rectification and from the use of filters that are two times (one octave) larger for the second stage processing. Note that the texture boundary model both fits the data and produces an improvement in discrimination over simple cell processing alone (dashed curve) by a factor of almost five! This model also predicts two line separation discrimination accurately for lines defined by texture boundaries (Wilson and Richards, 1992). The relationship of texture boundary processing to cortical anatomy will be developed in the discussion.

3. Two-dimensional motion

Our discussion of pattern discrimination has led to the postulation of a pathway that employs a sequence of filtering, full-wave rectification, and filtering at a lower frequency to extract texture boundary locations. A number of studies suggest that a similar processing sequence may be involved in motion perception. Chubb and Sperling (1988, 1989) have analyzed perception of drift balanced stimuli, and they have concluded that the visual system must employ full-wave rectification in order to extract a motion signal from these stimuli. Similarly, Turano and Pantle (1989) have studied moving patterns in which the amplitude of a stationary cosine grating is modulated by a moving cosine. All of these stimuli are instances of non-Fourier motions because the Fourier components of the stimulus move in opposite directions, thus canceling responses in simple direction selective mechanisms, and the sum of the Fourier motions does not agree with the motion percept. Clearly, non-linear processing is involved in the analysis of non-Fourier motion, but just how does non-Fourier motion relate to more basic forms of motion analysis? To rephrase, what is the relevance of non-Fourier motion, which is not common in nature, to visual motion processing in general? A lead to this question has been provided by Turano (1991), who provided evidence that non-Fourier motion signals combine with other motion signals at a subsequent processing stage.

A series of psychophysical studies (Ferrera and Wilson, 1987; 1990; 1991; Yo and Wilson, 1992) have led to a model that integrates non-Fourier motion into the general analysis of two-dimensional motion (Wilson et al., 1992). These studies have all been based on an analysis of patterns composed to two cosine gratings at different orientations moving in different directions, patterns termed "plaids". Adelson and Movshon (1982) first introduced these stimuli to psychophysics, although a line grating version was previously analyzed by Wallach (1935). Two examples of these stimuli are depicted in Figure 7. One might at first conjecture that the direction of motion

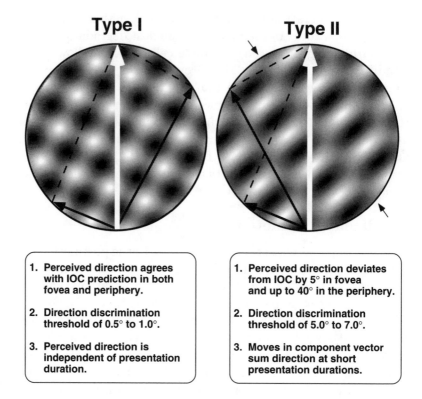

Type I

Type II

1. Perceived direction agrees with IOC prediction in both fovea and periphery.

2. Direction discrimination threshold of 0.5° to 1.0°.

3. Perceived direction is independent of presentation duration.

1. Perceived direction deviates from IOC by 5° in fovea and up to 40° in the periphery.

2. Direction discrimination threshold of 5.0° to 7.0°.

3. Moves in component vector sum direction at short presentation durations.

Fig. 7. *Grating plaid patterns employed in motion experiments. Each pattern is the sum of two cosine gratings that move in the directions and with the speeds indicated by the two black vectors in each panel. For each pattern, the intersection of constraints (IOC) direction is directly upward, as indicated by the solid white vector in each panel that points to the intersection of the dashed constraint lines. In a Type I plaid (left) the velocity vectors for the two component gratings fall on opposite sides of the IOC resultant (at +30° and −70° in the example), while in a Type II plaid (right), both component vectors fall on the same side of the IOC resultant (at −30° and −70° in this case). The two dimensional motion model extracts the direction of motion of texture boundaries, such as that falling between the small arrows on the circumference of the circle at the right, using non-Fourier motion analysis. This is combined with the component vectors to compute the final pattern direction. Key psychophysical results are listed below each pattern.*

would be given by the vector sum of the component grating velocities, but this is not so. If the assumption is made that the two moving gratings form part of a rigidly moving pattern, the direction of pattern motion is determined by the intersection of constraints (IOC) construction (Fennema and Thompson, 1979; Adelson and Movshon, 1982). The results of the IOC construction are illustrated in Figure 7 for two different plaids. In both cases the velocities of the component cosine gratings (black arrows) are given for the case in which the plaid is rigidly moving upwards (white arrows). The key observation behind the IOC construction is that each component grating, which is one-dimensional, can only provide information about the velocity vector orthogonal to the orientation of its bars. Thus, each component grating only constrains two-dimensional pattern motion to lie along a constraint line indicated by the thin dashed lines in the figure. The intersection of two constraint lines determines the unique direction of rigid, two-dimensional plaid motion.

Granted that the IOC construction provides a geometrically exact solution to the problem of two-dimensional plaid motion, one must ask: does the visual system actually implement the IOC construction? This empirical question has been answered by studying the perceived motion of two classes of plaids. As shown in Figure 7, the component grating velocity vectors (black arrows) in Type I plaids fall on opposite sides of the IOC resultant vector (white arrow). Type II plaids, on the other hand, have both component velocity vectors lying on the same side of the IOC resultant. Note that the component vector sum direction will always lie fairly close to the IOC direction for Type I plaids, while this will not be true for Type II plaids. The conceptually important point is that Type I plaids seldom provide a very critical test of the IOC construction, while Type II plaids do provide that test.

Several major points have emerged from measurements of the perceived motion of Type I and II plaids:

1   Type I plaids always move in the IOC direction. Type II plaids deviate from the IOC direction by about $5.0°$ in the fovea (Ferrera and Wilson, 1990) and by up to $40°$ in the visual periphery (Yo and Wilson, 1992).

2   In the fovea, direction discrimination thresholds for Type I plaids are $0.5° - 1.0°$, but thresholds for Type II plaids are $5.0° - 7.0°$ (Ferrera and Wilson, 1990).

3   For brief presentations (60 ms) in the fovea, Type II plaids are perceived to move in the vector sum direction, and they only attain a perceived direction within $5.0°$ of the IOC direction after 150 ms (Yo and Wilson, 1992).

4   Type I plaids produce powerful, non-linear masking effects in which thresholds are elevated up to four times more by the plaid than by one of its components at twice the contrast (Ferrera and Wilson, 1987). Type II plaids, on the other hand, produce no more masking than the nearer component.

These results clearly demonstrate that the visual system does not implement the IOC construction for analyzing the motion of Type II plaids. As

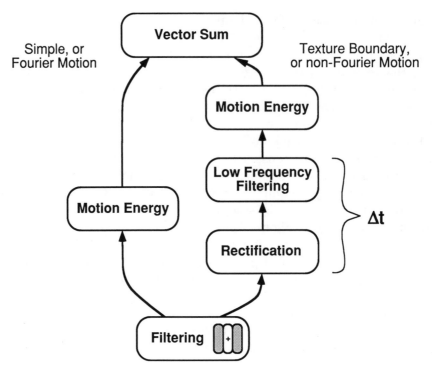

Fig. 8. *Diagram of two-dimensional motion model. Following a common first stage using simple oriented filters (bottom), the stimulus is processed in parallel by a simple (Fourier) motion energy pathway (left) and a texture boundary (non-Fourier) motion pathway (right). Responses of the two motion pathways are finally combined through neural computation of the vector sum direction. The texture boundary motion pathway requires two additional processing stages — full-wave rectification and oriented filtering at a lower spatial frequency — before the extraction of motion energy. The model hypothesizes that these additional stages require the additional processing time Δt, and thus responses from the non-Fourier motion pathway will be delayed in arriving at the vector sum stage. Psychophysical measurements put the value of Δt at about 60 ms (Yo and Wilson, 1992). ©Pergamon Press, 1992.*

the only special significance of Type II patterns is that they provide the most critical test of IOC predictions, it therefore appears that the visual system has evolved a different strategy for two-dimensional motion analysis. We have developed a quantitative model that predicts the psychophysical data above and that is consistent with known cortical anatomy and physiology (Wilson et al., 1992). The basic computations in the model are outlined in Figure 8. Consider first the pathway on the left. An initial stage of simple cell filtering, which will extract the orientations of the component gratings, is followed by a motion energy computation that computes the direction of motion of each component and generates a signal that is a monotonic function of component velocity. The exact nature of the motion energy computation is not critical: either the Reichardt motion detector (Reichardt, 1961) or the Adelson and Bergen (Adelson and Bergen, 1985) motion energy model will suffice. As recent physiological measurements on direction selective complex cells in the cat support the motion energy model (Emerson et al., 1992), this model may be preferred. This pathway extracts the motion of the Fourier grating components of the stimulus.

The pathway on the right of Figure 8 is more complex. Following simple cell filtering, there is rectification and a second stage of orientation selective filtering one octave lower in spatial frequency – exactly the sequence of operations that were employed to explain pattern discrimination at texture boundaries. Following this, motion energy is extracted, but this is now the motion of texture boundaries. Note that this processing pathway includes the rectification operation that is characteristic of non-Fourier motion analysis (Chubb and Sperling, 1988; 1989).

The final stage of the model combines both the simple (Fourier) and texture (non-Fourier) motion pathways by computing a direction equivalent to the vector sum of these inputs. Although computation of the vector sum direction might seem to be a difficult operation for nerve cells, we have shown that it can be implemented by a simple neural network (Wilson et al., 1992). Let us assume that direction selective neurons have their preferred directions spaced at $15°$ intervals[6]. Each response neuron at the final model stage will now receive a weighted sum of the activity in both the Fourier and non-Fourier pathways. As suggested by Perrone (1990), let us assume that these inputs are weighted by the cosine of the angle between each input and the direction signalled by the response neuron. Designating the response unit for direction Ω by $R(\Omega)$ and the Fourier and non-Fourier inputs for direction θ respectively by $F(\theta)$ and $NF(\theta)$, the equation is:

$$R(\Omega) = \sum_{\theta=15°}^{360°} \cos(\Omega - \theta)F(\theta) + \sum_{\theta=15°}^{360°} \cos(\Omega - \theta)NF(\theta) \qquad (5)$$

The angle Ω for which $R(\Omega)$ obtains its maximum value can be proven to be the vector sum direction (Wilson et al., 1992, Appendix I). Extraction of the maximum response among a group of neurons is readily accomplished by mutual inhibition: if each neuron strongly inhibits all others except itself, the strongest response will pass through uninhibited while suppressing all others. The properties of such networks have been well studied and are sometimes metaphorically dubbed "winner take all networks" (Feldman and Ballard, 1982).

It is worth mentioning here that Equation (5) makes it unnecessary for the Fourier and non-Fourier inputs to the final stage to be perfectly direction

---

[6] This figure is not crucial, and the model has also been implemented with a 22.5 deg spacing.

selective as Reichardt (1961) units are. The reason is that small responses in the non-preferred direction will be subtracted out by the $\cos(\Omega - \theta)$ weighting function, thus effectively generating opponent motion inputs from simple motion energy units (Emerson et al., 1992). In fact, the model produces identical predictions even with inputs having a direction selectivity index of 0.55, which is the average for motion units in V1 (Rodman and Albright, 1987)[7].

Given the structure of the model, let us consider how it analyzes plaid motion and how it accounts for the psychophysical findings listed above. The most important conceptual point is that the vector sum operation does not calculate the vector sum of the component grating velocities. Rather, it computes the vector sum of the component velocities plus the non-Fourier components generated by full-wave rectification. In the case of Type I plaids, the vector sum of the Fourier plus non-Fourier components generally falls near the vector sum of the Fourier components alone (Wilson et al., 1992), so these patterns will not be discussed here. The situation is very different for Type II patterns, where the perceived direction deviates substantially from the component vector sum direction. I shall therefore focus discussion here on Type II patterns and the theoretical explanation of the surprising psychophysical results associated with them (see above).

Let us consider the Type II pattern illustrated in Figure 7B. The polar coordinate plot in Figure 9 shows the responses of the Fourier (gray) and non-Fourier (outlined white) pathways to the final stage where the vector sum is computed. It should be noted that the breadth of the response ranges results from the direction bandwidths of the motion energy units. As is apparent from the pattern illustration in Figure 7B, the neural responses to the individual grating components fall well to the left of vertical. Thus, a vector sum over these alone would lead to a predicted direction of motion far from the true direction of rigid translation, which is vertically upward. The non-Fourier motion responses (white), however, fall on the opposite side of the polar plot and thus provide a countervailing set of vector directions. The explanation for this may be understood from an examination of the pattern in Figure 7B. The rectification and lower frequency filtering operations on this pattern detect texture boundaries such as that lying between the two arrows on the circumference of the circle. The direction of motion of this texture boundary is orthogonal to its orientation and thus to the upper right. This explains the distribution of non-Fourier component vectors in Figure 9. The vector sum direction, computed by the final stage of the neural network, is indicated by the black arrow. While it falls close to the IOC direction (vertically upwards), which is the geometrically correct

---

[7] A direction selectivity index of 0.55 occurs when the response to motion in the non-preferred direction is 45% of the response in the preferred direction.

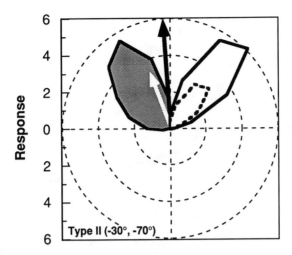

Fig. 9. *Polar coordinate plot of model responses to the Type II plaid in Figure 7. The component units in the simple or Fourier motion pathway respond to the grating components moving at −30° and −70° (relative to the IOC direction) with the activity pattern shown by the gray lobe on the left. The non-Fourier motion pathway responds to the moving texture boundaries in the image, thus generating the activity pattern plotted as a solid white region enclosed by the solid black line. The subsequent vector sum operation on these responses (see previous figure) predicts the perceived direction shown by the solid black arrow. The prediction agrees with psychophysical data by indicating a deviation from the IOC direction (directly upwards) by about 4.0° towards the component grating directions (Ferrera and Wilson, 1990). In peripheral vision the strength of the non-Fourier pathway is reduced by 50% (small dashed white lobe on right), and this results in the much greater deviation of predicted direction (white arrow) toward the component directions. Psychophysical data also support this prediction (Yo and Wilson, 1992). ©Pergamon Press, 1992.*

direction for rigid translation, it deviates by 3.5° towards the direction of the component gratings, which agrees with the psychophysical data (Ferrera and Wilson, 1990). Model calculations for the direction of Type II patterns were averaged over 22 representative plaids and produced an average bias in the direction of the component gratings by 5.0° (Wilson et al., 1992).

Several other aspects of Type II motion perception are readily explained by further consideration of this example. Let us first consider Type II motion in the periphery. Previous studies have indicated that non-Fourier motion processing is weaker in the periphery than in the fovea (Turano and Pantle, 1989; Chubb and Sperling, 1988; Chubb and Sperling, 1989). The large deviations in the perceived direction of Type II plaids in the periphery can be quantitatively explained simply by reducing the strength of the non-Fourier inputs by a factor of 2.0. In consequence, the vector sum becomes strongly biased towards the component grating directions. For the

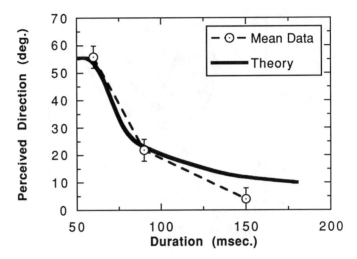

Fig. 10. *Perceived direction of motion of a Type II plaid as a function of presentation duration. Average data for several subjects indicate that the perceived direction agrees with the component vector sum direction (55°) at 60 ms duration but rapidly moves towards the IOC direction (0°) until the perceived deviation is only about 5° after 150 ms (Yo and Wilson, 1992). The theoretical prediction of perceived direction is plotted as a solid line. The model prediction results from the delayed arrival of the non-Fourier motion signal at the vector sum stage (see Figure 8). Thus, the vector sum calculation is dominated initially by the component directions (gray lobe in Figure 9).*

Type II plaid illustrated in Figure 7B, this leads to a predicted direction of 18.6°. Data collected at 15° in the visual periphery show that Type II patterns are perceived to move in a direction up to 40° away from the IOC prediction, yet the direction is never quite as extreme as the direction of the component gratings (Yo and Wilson, 1992). This results from the fact that the non-Fourier signal still contributes to the computation, albeit to a much lesser degree. It should be noted here that the relative strength of the non-Fourier signal doubtless changes continuously with retinal eccentricity, as is suggested by studies of another peripheral motion illusion (Cormack et al., 1992).

The most striking evidence for the motion model schematized in Figure 8 is doubtless the change in perceived direction of foveal Type II plaids at short duration. As shown by the solid circles and dashed line in Figure 10, these patterns appear to move in the vector sum direction at a duration of 60 ms and do not approximate the IOC direction until durations of about 150 ms (Yo and Wilson, 1992). In other words, at a 60 ms duration Type II plaids move in the component vector sum direction, and additional processing is necessary to correct this. A very simple interpretation of this phenomenon is provided by the model. As the texture boundary or non-Fourier pathway requires two additional operations, namely rectification and a second filtering stage, it is natural to suppose that these will consume additional time. Thus, the non-Fourier signal will arrive at the vector sum stage after the arrival of the Fourier motion signal. Model simulations in which non-Fourier processing was assumed to require an additional 60 ms produced the theoretical result shown by the solid curve in Figure 10 (Wilson et al., 1992). Thus, the obvious assumption that additional neural processing requires additional time leads to a natural explanation of the dependence of Type II plaid direction on duration.

This model for two-dimensional motion also predicts aspects of plaid masking (Ferrera and Wilson, 1987), direction discrimination thresholds for plaids (Ferrera and Wilson, 1990), and the dependence of plaid direction on relative component contrast (Stone et al., 1990). Finally, although the model has only been applied to moving plaids, it performs well with arbitrarily complex patterns undergoing rigid translation. This follows from the observation that such patterns are sums of many moving cosine gratings at different orientations. Detailed discussion of these points would lead us too far from the central focus of this chapter, however, and the interested reader is referred to the original article (Wilson et al., 1992).

4. A proposed synthesis

Discussions of both pattern discrimination and two-dimensional motion perception have led to the introduction of parallel processing pathways. In both cases the simpler pathway employs oriented filters with simple cell characteristics to extract individual components of the image. The more complex pathway employs a sequence of filtering, full-wave rectification (or squaring), and second stage filtering an octave lower in spatial frequency to compute the locus of texture boundaries. Recent studies of texture discrimination have converged towards a model incorporating filtering, rectification, and subsequent filtering to explain a wide range of results (Bergen and Landy, 1991; Landy and Bergen, 1991; Graham, 1991; Sutter et al., 1989; Wilson and Richards, 1992). In motion processing, however, the connection between non-Fourier motion and texture boundary motion has not been made previously. This is probably because previous non-Fourier motion studies used one-dimensional stimuli, such as stationary cosine gratings with a moving amplitude modulation envelope (Turano and Pantle, 1989). It is only when one examines non-Fourier processing in two dimensions that the connection between non-Fourier and texture boundary motion becomes apparent. The major innovation of the motion model in Figure 8 is that it combines Fourier and non-Fourier motion analysis via a vector sum operation, thereby making non-Fourier motion an integral part of virtually all two-dimensional motion analysis.

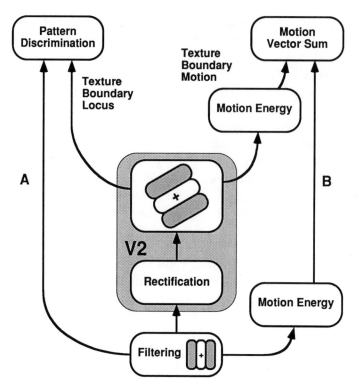

Fig. 11. *Integrated model for visual pattern discrimination and two-dimensional motion. Starting with the initial oriented filtering stage at the bottom, one pathway (A) leads directly to the pattern discrimination stage, while a second pathway (B) provides input to the motion vector sum operation following extraction of Fourier motion energy. Correlations with cortical anatomy and physiology suggest that A reflects properties of the V1→V3→V4→IT pathway, while B reflects properties of the V1→MT projection. The third pathway from the initial filtering operation leads to the full-wave rectification and subsequent oriented filtering operations depicted in the gray box. (Note that the second filter is larger than the first and generally has a different orientation.) Physiological studies (von der Heydt et al. 1984; von der Heydt and Peterhans, 1989) suggest that these rectification and filtering operations occur in V2. The operations in the gray box extract the positions of texture boundaries and provide a direct input to the pattern discrimination stage. In addition, they provide a texture boundary (non-Fourier) motion stimulus to the motion vector sum stage. Identification of the motion vector sum stage with MT suggests that the non-Fourier motion pathway should be identified with the V1→V2→MT projection.*

How might the processing stages necessary for both pattern discrimination and motion analysis be parsimoniously integrated? The schematic in Figure 11 illustrates the most compact manner in which this might be done. As all image processing sequences begin with oriented, simple cell type filtering, this operation forms a common first stage for all processing. The results of this filtering are sent directly to a pattern discrimination stage on the one hand (pathway A), and they are sent in parallel to the site of the motion vector sum operation following extraction of motion energy signals (pathway B).

The texture analysis pathways also receive their input from the initial filtering stage. This is next full-wave rectified and filtered at a lower spatial frequency, as illustrated in the gray box in Figure 11. The resultant signals are sent directly to the pattern discrimination apparatus to provide information about the location of texture boundaries, and they are sent in parallel to the motion vector sum stage following extraction of texture boundary (non-Fourier) motion energy.

The scheme in Figure 11 incorporates all of the computational stages that have been found necessary to date for both pattern discrimination and two-dimensional motion, but is this scheme anatomically and physiologically plausible? A comparison between Figures 1 and 11 suggests that it is. In particular, cortical area V1 projects to areas V2, V3, and MT in parallel. As both oriented simple cells and cells with direction selectivity for motion are common in V1, the first filtering stage and the extraction of Fourier motion energy in the model are assumed to occur in V1. Pathway A in the model thus corresponds to the V1→V3 projection, while pathway B corresponds to the V1→MT projection.

Identification of rectification and second stage filtering with processing in V2 is based on physiological data reported by von der Heydt, Peterhans, and Baumgartner (1984) and von der Heydt and Peterhans (1989). They discovered a class of neurons in primate V2 that respond to the orientation and position of texture boundaries in patterns very similar to that shown in Figure 4C. For example, these V2 cells gave orientation dependent responses to the pattern discontinuity or illusory contour in Figure 12A. However, no cells were found in V1 that could detect this texture boundary. As shown by the simulation in Figure 12B, the texture model employing rectification followed by orientation selective filtering mimics responses of these V2 cells to such texture boundaries. Although von der Heydt and Peterhans (1989) have developed a somewhat different model to explain their single unit results, the psychophysically derived texture model produces the same responses as V2 cells to the patterns under consideration here.

Given the association of rectification and second stage filtering with V2 processing, the remaining two pathways in the model are readily related to cortical anatomy. The V2→V3 projection is associated with the model pathway that extracts texture boundary location, and the V2→MT pathway is associated with the extraction of texture boundary (non-Fourier) motion. There is one ambiguity regarding identification of the V2→MT projection with the model texture boundary motion pathway: motion energy extraction in this pathway might occur either in V2 or else among a subset of MT neurons. This ambiguity can be resolved physiologically by comparing the responses of V2 and MT cells to non-Fourier motion stimuli.

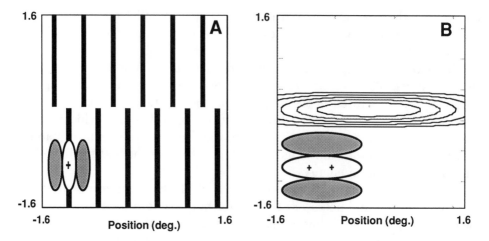

Fig. 12. *Extraction of illusory contours by the texture boundary pathway. The stimulus in A is first filtered by the vertical, simple cell filter shown on the lower left. Following full-wave rectification, filtering by a larger, horizontally oriented filter (lower left in B) provides an accurate estimate of the texture boundary location, as shown by the contour plot of neural activity in B. The model response to the texture boundary in A is thus similar to the responses of V2 neurons (but not V1 neurons) to the same stimulus (von der Heydt, Peterhans and Baumgartner, 1984 ©AAAS 1984; von der Heydt and Peterhans, 1989 ©Oxford University Press 1989).*

These correlations of model computations with aspects of cortical anatomy and physiology lead to an identification of the motion vector sum operation as residing in cortical area MT. In support of this, the model units that compute the vector sum direction have response properties identical to those reported physiologically for MT neurons. Thus, they have the same preferred direction of motion for a single grating and for a moving plaid (Movshon et al., 1986; Rodman and Albright, 1989). Furthermore, the inhibitory interactions postulated by the model to compute the maximum response (see Equation 5) would be extremely easy to implement in MT. MT has been reported to have a columnar organization in which cells with the same preferred direction of motion are grouped within a column, while adjacent columns have smoothly varying direction preferences (Albright et al., 1984a). Recurrent lateral inhibition among these direction selective columns would result in computation of the maximum response direction as required by the model. Inhibition between different preferred directions of motion has recently been reported in MT neurons (Snowden et al., 1991).

There are a number of limitations in the proposed relationship between the model and cortical anatomy. First among these is the observation that all of the model pathways project centrally, yet V1 also receives feedback projections from V2, V3, and MT. The best that can be said at this point is that we have little evidence, physiological or otherwise, concerning the role of these reciprocal connections. A second point is that there are many more interconnections among cortical areas than are shown in Figure 1. To cite but one, V3 and MT are interconnected. As the visual system is capable of discriminating shapes defined only by motion discontinuities (Regan, 1989b), one might tentatively assign this role to the MT→V3 pathway. Such conjectures should form a useful framework for further research.

Cavanagh and Mather (1990) have suggested a qualitative model for low level visual processing that shares a number of elements with the quantitative model presented here. For example, they agree with the current model in suggesting that Fourier and non-Fourier motion both involve the same type of motion energy computation stage. However, they do not regard non-Fourier motion as forming an integral part of two-dimensional motion analysis, and they refrain from associating their processing stages with cortical anatomy. Grossberg (1991) has also suggested a role for the V2→MT pathway in motion processing. In his view this pathway is responsible for motion in depth as well as long range motion of illusory contours. Again, the key element missing here is an appreciation of non-Fourier motion as integral to virtually all two-dimensional motion analysis.

The purpose of this chapter has been to develop a unified framework for pattern discrimination and motion perception and to relate this to cortical anatomy and physiology. The model sketched in Figure 11 accounts for a large body of psychophysical data on pattern discrimination and motion perception, and it appears to be consistent with cortical anatomy and physiology as currently understood. Doubtless many details of this model will be found to be incorrect, but the success with which it integrates a wide range of current knowledge suggests that it will provide a useful conceptual framework for generating novel experimental questions.

Acknowledgments

This research was supported in part by NIH grant #EY02158 and a Chicago Brain Research Foundation Grant to the author.

Will robots see?

Stanley A. Klein

Will robots ever *really* see? Imagine a robot 10,000 years in the future. At that time we should finally understand the visual system and be able to build robots whose visual performance surpasses humans'. We will then ask: when a robot claims to be seeing, are its sensations the same as mine? The problem is to connect the first person "feel" of an event (qualia) to the third person performance or explanation of the same event. Neuroscience is gradually making progress in connecting third person behavior (including your consciousness) to the simpler activity and interactions of neurons and molecules. The question to be discussed in this chapter is different. It is how subjective, first person, qualia (my consciousness) fits into the structure of objective science.

This chapter has three parts. First, I examine what it will take to convince me that robots can truly see or feel. I will argue that passing a performance test, such as the Turing test (Turing, 1950), is not sufficient since a performance test does not tell me what the robot is actually *feeling*. I do believe, however, that a robot from 10,000 years in the future should be able to convince me that it really does have the same raw sensations (e.g. the color qualia) as those that I feel. However, even though robotic qualia may someday exist, I claim that there will still be a barrier to reducing the qualia to the robot's circuitry. The preceding sentence with its denial of reductionism would sound quite weird were it not for the existence of another nonreductionistic theory: quantum mechanics. Quantum mechanics, the central theory and framework for all of chemistry (and therefore biology) and almost all of physics, is a dualistic theory with a split between the observer and the observed. The second part of the chapter discusses the nature of the quantum duality. The main thesis of this chapter is that the existence of a consistent duality for specifying the role of the observer provides new grounding for exploring how the mind might be related to the body. Knowing that a self-consistent duality is possible gives one courage to explore the possible connection between the duality of quantum mechanics and the duality of the mind-body problem. The third part of this chapter connects the quantum duality to the qualia duality and the role of the homunculus. The present chapter clarifies and emphasizes points that were made in my more detailed paper (Klein, 1991) on the nature of quantum mechanics and its connection to the mind-body problem.

1. What will it take to convince me that a robot's feeling of redness is similar to mine?

I will be asking whether robots could be given the *human* sensation of redness. This issue is a strong version of the philosophical problem of qualia (qualia are the "raw feelings" of a sensation) and is the essence of the mind-body problem. It is a strong version of the qualia question because I am not merely asking whether robots will feel, but I am asking whether their feelings can be similar to those of humans. Later in this section I will point out that this "strong" version of qualia is in fact easier to establish than the question of can robots have qualia of any sort, not necessarily human.

Asking whether robots will see is equivalent to asking whether they will feel or think. This chapter will at times focus on feeling rather than seeing since, for me, the feel of a throbbing headache is more vivid than seeing red.

Turing (1950) proposed a method to test whether computers can think. His method will be adapted to help us determine whether computers have qualia. In the original Turing test, a human must decide whether his computer terminal is hooked up to a computer or to a human. Let us update the Turing test to the year 12,000 A.D. when futuristic robots look and act like humans (such as the robot "Mr. DATA" in *Star Trek: The New Generation* television series). The amount of knowledge of human experience and human physiology that the robot will require for passing the Turing test is so enormous as to be incomprehensible (Dennett, 1985; French, 1990). However, when we remember that in less than 100 years we have gone from the horse and buggy to massively parallel, *analog*, neural network computers, it is incomprehensible to imagine what technology will be like in 10,000 years. A recent Turing test contest at the Boston Computer Museum showed that for restricted topics of conversation present computers do well (Scientific American, January, 1992), so with an additional 10,000 years, successful robots are quite plausible.

Before deciding whether a robot has feelings it is useful to first ask the same question about humans (other than myself) and animals. There is no way to *prove* that your feeling of redness is the same as mine since a first person experience (qualia) is a private matter (several entertaining stories in Hofstadter and Dennett, 1981 make this quite clear). Most of us do believe, however, that we humans are built pretty much the same, and by empathy we believe that red looks the same to you as it does to me. There is also no doubt in my mind that dogs feel and see. I believe that the pain a dog feels when its paw is stepped on feels similar to my pain when my foot is stepped on. The reason for this belief of mine is that the dog's response to pain is similar to how I would respond. I can easily empathize with the dog's yowl. The question "can robots have feelings" is being asked in the same spirit as the question "do dogs have feelings". I can't prove that a dog's feelings are similar to mine, but somehow a dog can convince me that they are indeed similar. It might be possible for a robot to do the same.

One might think that a robot whose external appearance is indistinguishable from that of a human might have an easier time convincing me it had feelings than it would be for a dog to convince me. That is not true, at least for me. I would constantly worry that the robot was programmed to be a good actor able to "fake" feelings. Let us suppose that I am engaged in a futuristic Turing test in which my task is to determine whether an individual is a human or a robot; and whether or not it has feelings. Suppose that after ten days of living with it, I would have developed sufficient empathy to believe that its seeing and feeling is similar to mine. Imagine my shock when on the eleventh day I would ask it (or him) how it operates, and it opens up its front panel to reveal wires instead of meat. Suppose that when asked how it was able to respond in such a human-like fashion it tells me that it has an enormous look-up table with facts about how humans would respond. There is little doubt in my mind that even though this robot could pass the Turing test, I would not believe that it had feelings similar to mine, even though from the outside they looked similar. I would think that if the robot did have feelings they would surely be different from my feelings. The situation is similar to the sonar of a bat (Nagel, 1974). Even if I understood the sonar circuitry perfectly I would still have no idea what the sonar feels like to the bat. Thus qualia provide information beyond knowledge of the sonar circuitry. The sonar qualia can not be communicated objectively. That qualia provide something extra is central to the arguments of this paper.

The dog's pain is different from the bat's sonar. Although I don't know the feel of sonar I do believe that a dog's feeling of pain isn't very different from my own pain. The reason is that I have a strong belief that dog's pain circuits are wired up similar to those of humans. Searle (1980) would say that the "meat" of dogs is similar to the "meat" of humans. (In fact much of this argument about whether computers can see is similar to Searle's discussion of whether computers can understand). Since I know that I have feelings and since dogs and I are made of similar meat, I presume that dogs have similar feelings. This is not meant to be a syllogism but rather my attempt to explain why I do indeed think that dogs and I have similar feelings. The sonar of bats, on the other hand, involves a neural system that has no parallel for humans so I have no basis to empathize about that system. Note that the way I have come to these conclusions by using empathy is very different from the type of logical reasoning that I use in the rest of science. This point about different modes of knowledge is compatible with my forthcoming argument for why a dualistic science is needed to handle qualia.

The robot could reconvince me that it had true human feelings if it would sit down with me and give me the following long lecture on human and

robot anatomy and physiology. It would tell me to not be put off by all
the wires and silicon. It would say that its lookup tables are not at all
like the lookup tables of 20th century computers but rather more like the
synaptic lookup tables governing human responses. It would show me its
circuit diagrams pointing out the structures that mimic my limbic system,
hippocampus, amygdala, frontal lobes, neocortex, etc. It would remind
me of how these human neural structures are involved in perceptions and
consciousness. Even though the robot's structures were made of silicon, I
would gradually become convinced that its brain operated just the same as
my brain. It is quite likely that I would again, through empathy, become
convinced that the robot had the same feelings and sight as I have.

Let us look at what we have accomplished. I have argued that it should
be possible for a robot to someday have the same qualia as mine. Why did
I restrict the robot's qualia to be just like mine? The surprising answer is
that it is easier to convince me that the robot has my qualia than that it has
general qualia. French (1990) has giving a provocative analysis of the Turing
test and comes to a similar conclusion. He discusses a set of questions whose
answers depend intimately on human experience. French concludes:

> "Turing invented the imitation game only as a novel way of looking at the
> question 'Can machines think?' But it turns out to be so powerful that it
> is really asking: 'Can machines think exactly like human beings?' As a real
> test for intelligence, the latter question is significantly less interesting than
> the former"[1].

The same criticism might be leveled at the present analysis since we are
asking whether the robot sees like me rather than whether the robot sees in
general. This was done since all that I have to do is become convinced that
the robot's circuitry and sensors are isomorphic to mine. I don't have to ask
about the general nature of what it means to see. Knowing that I see, and
knowing that the robot's visual system works just like mine is enough. I do
not believe that this narrower question is "less interesting".

The foregoing argument based on empathy has a critical flaw. Just because I empathize with a dog or robot or other human and believe they
feel and see like me, does that make it so? Isn't the situation similar to
that of the people I see on the streets near campus who truly believe in the
magical power of crystals (remember I live in Berkeley)? Does that mean
crystals do indeed have power? (Before answering with a quick NO, one
should remember the possible placebo effect whereby crystals woven into
one's pants can give one the self-confidence to achieve feats that one would
otherwise have avoided. See addendum #2 at the end of this chapter for
a comment on the connection between science and religion.) In any case
I could be wrong about the robot. The robot might have tricked me, and

---

[1] French, 1990, p. 64.

my belief that it has feelings does not mean it actually does have feelings. Rather than being a humanoid (a robot with human feelings) the robot might be a zimbo. A zimbo, created by philosophers, is a zombie (a creature with no qualia) that has been upgraded to have access to its internal states. Dennett (1991) argues (not convincingly) that a zimbo's access to its internal states is indistinguishable from consciousness. Let us suppose that the crucial difference between a zimbo and a humanoid is that the zimbo is missing a connection between its frontal lobes and its amygdala. When the robot had the conversation with me about its physiology it neglected to point out its missing critical connections, and in my naivete, I didn't notice. My point is that there is a solid test for whether the robot is a humanoid (establish the equivalence of its anatomy and physiology to a human's). A zimbo may have tricked me into thinking that it is a humanoid, but a more careful investigator would have noticed the missing links and realized that the robot was a zimbo devoid of human qualia.

Notice that in the preceding paragraph I postulated that the critical difference between a humanoid and a zimbo is a particular physiological connection. I did this to be very clear that the presence or absence of qualia is linked to physiology. Past versions of duality had the mental realm decoupled from the physical, mechanistic realm. I want to be very clear that my notions of qualia are solidly grounded in neural activity. Thus, the robot's statement "I have a throbbing headache" could be replaced with no loss by the sentence "My 'throbbing headache neurons' are active". From this identity theory one might conclude that there is nothing special about qualia. A satisfactory theory of qualia must have a place for the "outsider's" third-person point of view that the robot's feeling of redness is identical to its "neural" activity.

In order to provide further clarification on the connection between qualia and physiology it is useful to ask which neurons are hooked up to our visual awareness. A popular guess is that one's visual consciousness must partly reside in primary visual cortex (area V1 of monkey or area 17 of humans and cats). This guess is made because only in V1 does one find the very finest receptive fields and the most detailed retinotopic mapping that seems characteristic of our conscious awareness. Later areas lose the nice retinotopic organization and high resolution of V1. When I say the homunculus partly resides in V1 or that the homunculus is aware of the neural activity in V1, what I really mean is that the human observer can sense the activity of the V1 neurons through introspection (more about the homunculus will come later). A surprising result is associated with this claim. It turns out that one of the clearest structures of V1 anatomy are the ocular dominance columns. The inputs to V1 from the two eyes are not randomly intermixed. One region of cortex gets input mainly from the left eye and an adjacent region gets input mainly from the right eye. The regions alternate approximately every

.5 mm. One would think that if consciousness had access to the activity of V1 neurons one would have awareness of eye of origin. Amazingly enough, most humans do not have conscious access to this information. Thus, if you were looking at a scene and a brief light were flashed to just one eye, you would not be able to tell which eye received the flash. One must be very careful in doing these experiments to be sure that all extraneous cues are removed (such as some light reflected from your nose) since humans are very clever at using subtle cues. Blake and Cormack (1979) claimed that certain humans, called amblyopes, who have lost their binocularity of vision do have access to eye-of-origin information. One might think that by studying the different circuitry of amblyopes one might learn where eye-of-origin aware-ness resides. However, we showed (Barbeito et al., 1985) that when careful controls were taken with amblyopes they were not able to discriminate eye of origin. We were careful to minimize the sensory cues produced by the distortions that are typically found in the amblyopic eye.

It turns out that the ocular dominance structures are not present in all layers of visual area V1. Although they are easily visible in the input layers of V1, in the output layers there is no distinct segregation of right and left eye selective neurons. Our awareness, therefore, seems to be focussed on these output neurons.This story of our lack of eye-of-origin qualia in spite of clear anatomical structures signalling eye-of-origin information shows how psychophysics and anatomy can be used to pin down the neural substrate of qualia. Few doubt that with continued progress in vision research we will someday have a very pretty story connecting visual qualia with particular neural activity patterns. However, there still remains the problem of the feel of the feeling from an insider's (first person) point of view.

To sharpen the issue of whether qualia are something special it is useful to look at the writings of one of the strongest foes of qualia. Two chapters by Dennett ("Qualia Disqualified", (Dennett, 1991); and "Quining Qualia", (Dennett, 1988)) provide the strongest attacks on the notion of qualia that I have come across. I read the chapters with trepidation, fearing that he would produce devastating arguments showing that qualia made no sense. He provides numerous clever gedanken experiments about how subjective sensations can get mixed up and how they do not contain information be-yond what the neurons already know. One of Dennett's most interesting thought experiments is the story of the color scientist, Mary, first proposed by Jackson (1982) to demonstrate the existence of qualia.

> "Mary is a brilliant scientist who is, for whatever reason, forced to investi-
> gate the world from a black-and-white room via a black-and-white television
> monitor. She specializes in neurophysiology of vision and acquires, let us sup-
> pose, all the physical information there is to obtain about what goes on when
> we see . . . What will happen when Mary is released from her black-and-white
> room or is given a color television monitor? Will she learn anything or not?

It seems just obvious that she will learn something about the world and our visual experience of it. But then it is inescapable that her previous knowledge was incomplete."[2]

Jackson uses this story to show that there is something extra besides the physical information of associated with knowledge of wavelengths, intensities, and color theory. But Dennett (1991) adds a cute twist to the story:

"And so, one day, Mary's captors decided it was time for her to see colors. As a trick, they prepared a bright blue banana to present her as her first color experience ever. Mary took one look at it and said "Hey! You tried to trick me! Bananas are yellow, but this one is blue!"[3]

Dennett goes on to say how Mary was able to figure out the true color. He reminds us that she has access to all the physical information that is available. She presumably has some device that can measure the ratios of stimulation of her different cones, enabling her to calculate that her "blue" cones are receiving more than expected stimulation from the banana. By this calculation she figures out that her captors are tricking her. Dennett's purpose in this addendum to the Mary story is to point out that for a clever Mary, the subjective percept does not contain more objective information than what is already in the neural activity. I would agree. Qualia are not necessary for making a decision about whether a banana is blue or yellow. The neural firing rates contain that information. Dennett seems to be missing a crucial point, however. From Mary's point of view there is a big difference between her figuring out that the banana was blue based on her calculation of the relative cone catches and her subjective impression of blue. Simply calculating the relative cone catches would not inform her of the *feel* of blue. Churchland (1986) does, however, remind us of an important caveat. In the original Mary story we are told that she has *unlimited* knowledge of human physiology. Churchland presumes that part of her unlimited knowledge is an ability to imagine or hallucinate any desired brain state. In that case Mary would know the feel of the desired color qualia since she embodies human physiology. However, if Mary didn't have the ability to hallucinate new brain states (or to selectively stimulate particular neurons), then even though she knew all about the physiology of the color system she would not know the feel of red if the only stimuli available were black and white. To my relief, all of Dennett's arguments against qualia are similar to the Mary story: that qualia add no measurable information. My point is that although the qualia information is not measurable, it does add a subjective *feel*.

Philosophers have gone in many circles around this question of how to integrate raw subjective feelings with objective neural activity. Is qualia

---

[2] Jackson, 1982, p. 128.
[3] Dennett, 1991, p. 399.

nothing other than the neural activity or is it something extra? I suspect that I, too, would have continued to flip-flop on this topic for the rest of my life if I hadn't been aware of that most peculiar scientific theory called quantum mechanics. As will be discussed in the last part of this chapter, quantum mechanics has legitimatized the role of the observer, the homunculus, as being outside the normal reductionistic laws of nature. Quantum mechanics provides a language for having reductionism at the same time as having an observer outside the reductionist framework. It is the natural language for discussing the mind-body problem.

Quantum mechanics is the theory underlying all of chemistry and biology. It is the theory that tells us how solids and liquids and molecules are reduced to atoms, how atoms are reduced to electrons, protons and neutrons and how protons and neutrons are reduced to quarks, gluons and possibly strings. What is surprising about quantum mechanics is that it is a dualistic theory. Quantum mechanics provides an existence proof that an elegant, consistent duality is possible between the observer and the observed. The rest of this chapter is devoted to describing quantum mechanics and pointing out its relevance to the problem of connecting qualia to neurophysiology.

2. The dualistic nature of quantum mechanics

This chapter is not the place to give an introduction to quantum mechanics. I will only point out some aspects of quantum mechanics that are relevant to the mind-body duality. Feynman's book, QED, on the interactions of electrons and light (Feynman, 1985) provides an excellent discussion of the laws of quantum mechanics. Herbert's Quantum Reality (Herbert, 1985) is a well-written book on the interpretations of quantum mechanics written for the layman and Wheeler and Zurek (1983) have collected the most important original articles on the topic of quantum measurement. Further details and references can be found in Klein (1991).

The mind-body duality of Descartes has fallen into disrepute because of the difficulty that philosophers have had in developing a consistent theory of the mind-body split. It is rare to find a respectable book on the mind-body problem that will defend the dualistic nature of mind and body. Rather, philosophers work hard to show that any apparent duality is inconsistent. As an example consider Dennett's treatment of duality in his recent book (Dennett, 1991), in the chapter titled "Why dualism is forlorn". He first claims it violates the law of conservation of energy and is thus in conflict with physics. Then he says:

"This fundamentally anti-scientific stance of dualism is, to my mind, the most disqualifying feature, and is the reason why in this book I adopt the apparently dogmatic rule that dualism is to be avoided at all costs. It is not that I think I can give a knock-down proof that dualism, in all its forms, is false or incoherent, but that, given the way dualism wallows in mystery, accepting dualism is giving up."[4]

I include this selection from Dennett because it typifies the attitude of most neurophilosophers. The bashing of dualism is based on the ill-formed dualism of Descartes. Before one attacks dualistic theories in general one had better read up on the dualistic Copenhagen interpretation of quantum mechanics. Dualism is not antiscientific. It is the foundation of the most profound theory in all of science. As will be emphasized in the present chapter the quantum duality is the theory of how the observer and the observed interact. That is exactly what philosophers since Descartes have been seeking. My goal is to clarify the connection between the quantum mechanics duality and the duality relevant to qualia. The main message from quantum mechanics is that it is not necessary to fight duality. Rather one should embrace it. I suspect Descartes would have loved it.

The dualistic nature of quantum mechanics was developed by Niels Bohr and is called the Copenhagen interpretation. Although the Copenhagen interpretation may appear mystical, it is in fact a very pragmatic worldview (Stapp, 1972). The Copenhagen interpretation of quantum mechanics says that the universe must be split into two parts, each of which is governed by very different laws. Above the split is the real world with which we are familiar. Experiments are set up, observations are made, feelings are felt. The observer lives above the split. The world looks almost like the classical world of Newton in which matter exists as particles with definite locations. Below the split the laws are different. No observations are allowed. An amplitude (a complex number) is associated with every path the universe can take. Feynman (1985) provides rules for calculating the amplitude for each possible path (including paths with particles going backwards in time in a manner that doesn't violate causality above the split). The total amplitude is obtained by adding up all the individual amplitudes, one for each possible path. The connection between the two halves of the duality is deceptively simple: the probability of any event above the split is given by the square of the total amplitude that was calculated below the split. Several characteristics above and below the split are summarized in Table 1.

The connection that I am making between the mind-body problem and quantum mechanics is not complicated. I am merely pointing out that in quantum mechanics the observer has the very special role of being on the other side of the duality from the underlying laws of nature. I, quite naturally, want to identify the mind, or homunculus, with the observer of quantum mechanics. Other investigators who are exploring the connection between quantum mechanics and the mind have a much more ambitious program. They often identify the mind with the waves beneath the split.

---

[4] Dennett, 1991, p. 37.

Below split	Above split
to be observed	observer
exact laws (no probabilities)	probabilistic laws
Feynman rules	Classical rules (with some nonlocality)
behaves like waves	behaves like particles
local interactions	some nonlocality
body (neurons causing throbbing headache)	mind (feel of throbbing headache)
determinism	free will

Table 1. *Characteristics above and below the split*

Penrose (1989), for example, believes that consciousness must be understood in terms of a quantum state with quantum transitions. My approach is much more modest. It merely makes legitimate the dualistic language that many previous authors have found convenient to use in describing the mind and brain (Descartes, 1664).

The free will–determinism duality in the above list should not be misunderstood. By free will I do not mean the amount of "freedom" that quantum mechanics allows due to its probabilistic structure. Rather I mean the notion of freedom that comes from having an improved language and status for the homunculus that is provided by physics. An excellent discussion of these issues was presented by Searle (1984). However, since Searle is unhappy with dualisms he acknowledges that

> "when it comes to the question of freedom and determinism, I am — like a lot of other philosophers — unable to reconcile the two."[5]

The quantum duality provides a framework for reconciling these seemingly incompatible ideas.

In order to fully appreciate the Copenhagen Interpretation one must have an understanding of the famous debates between Bohr and Einstein (Bohr, 1949). Their discussions on this topic occurred from 1926, when Heisenberg and Schroedinger developed the quantum rules, until 1935, when Einstein published the paradox (Einstein et al., 1935) that was the precursor to Bell's Theorem. In the Einstein-Bohr debates, Einstein would propose a clever experimental method by which the state of the system could be measured without disturbing the system. Bohr would then think for a few hours or days and then show how Einstein's measuring instruments would disturb the system by exactly the right amount to produce the quantum mechanical uncertainty. Bohr showed that the laws above the split were not deterministic, but rather were probabilistic (see second row of above table). Einstein believed in a "real" universe that existed independent of observers. Bohr believed that an outside observer was needed to make the observed system real since before the observation, the system's properties were not

---

[5] Searle, 1984, p. 86.

yet decided. With quantum mechanics the act of observation produces a transition converting the wave-like world below the split to the particle- like material world above the split. This transition from the spread-out wave to the localized particle is often called "the collapse of the wave-packet".

Although Bohr "won" the debates, Einstein's cause has not died. There have been many attempts by physicists to develop theories with no need for an outside observer. These theories have the wave-packet collapse at an early well-defined point, well before the human observer. Penrose (1989), for example, believes that quantum gravity (a theory that does not yet exist) will cause the collapse whenever a subsystem has 10^{-5} grams of mass or energy. Most physicists, however, doubt that the duality of quantum mechanics will be changed by gravity. The majority of physicists grudgingly accept the dualistic Copenhagen interpretation.

The modern version of the Bohr-Einstein debate is based on Bell's theorem (Bell, 1965; see Klein, 1991 for details). Bell examined a simple system consisting of two particles with correlated polarizations. We will consider the two particles to be photons (Bell used electrons). He showed that the following three principles can not all be true: reality, locality, and quantum mechanical predictions. By reality one means that each photon had a definite polarization before the measurement was made. Reality means the state of each photon is independent of the observer. Locality means that well-separated particles can not interact simultaneously. For the Bell scenario it means that after the two photons have been separated they can not interact. Bell showed that any theory that is real and local will produce correlated polarizations that disagree with the predictions of quantum mechanics. Bell's theorem with pairs of photons has recently been tested (Aspect et al., 1982) and the quantum predictions were verified. This means that either reality or locality is wrong. My preference is to say that below the split reality is not present and above the split some locality is not present (while causality is maintained).

The substantive issue in the Bohr-Einstein debates and Bell's theorem has an amazing parallel to the debates on whether qualia could be reduced to the activity of underlying neurons. Einstein abhorred a dualistic system. Similarly, most neuroscientists and philosophers consider duality to be ugly, unnecessary and inconsistent. Einstein wanted to show that the phenomenology of what we see in our macroscopic experiments is nothing other than the activity of underlying deterministic particles and fields. Similarly neurophilosophers want to show that our throbbing headaches are nothing other than the activity of our underlying neurons.

An important outcome of the Bohr-Einstein debates was the realization that the new quantum mechanics was the first theory of modern science in which the role of the observer could not be ignored. In a sense, quantum mechanics brings the Copernican revolution full circle and restores the observer to the "center of the universe". In all previous theories the interaction of the observer could be made arbitrarily small so there was no question about a world "out there" existing independent of observation.

It is thought by some that the collapse of the wave packet is not a real change in the state of the system but rather a change of our *knowledge* of the system. Bell's theorem and Aspect's experiment have eliminated this possibility. Bell showed that it wasn't just knowledge that changed when an observation was made, but rather the state of the system changed. In fancy words, an observation produces an ontological change in the state of the world rather than merely an epistemological change.

In neurophilosophy one also argues about whether the difference between qualia and neural mechanisms is an ontological difference or merely an epistemological difference. Is the feel of my throbbing headache and the neural causes of my throbbing headache merely a difference in how we gather knowledge about the same event? Bell's theorem doesn't often get applied to the mind-body problem, so it is not surprising that neurophilosophers and neuroscientists have been able to argue against a dualistic framework. However, since all agree that the brain is based on quantum mechanics, the observer-observed duality will not be able to be avoided for long.

The big problem and its solution: where is the split? The biggest challenge to any dualistic system is to specify the exact placement of the split and to describe precisely the nature of the interaction between the two halves of the split. Neurophilosophers have not succeeded in developing a clean mind-body duality and for that reason have abandoned the quest. Physicists, von Neumann (1932) in particular, figured out how to do it, in a most elegant manner. On the critical question of where must the split be placed, Von Neumann came up with a most amazing answer: **IT CAN BE PLACED ANYWHERE** (Herbert, 1985). The split is movable. It wasn't easy for nature to make the split movable. The laws of nature below the split (Feynman rules) and the laws above the split (classical mechanics with some nonlocality that doesn't violate causality) must be very special. Also the connection between the two halves (the square of the amplitude below the split equals the probability above the split) is very specific. If any of the laws are changed there is a good chance that the split could no longer move freely. It is not surprising that the vague duality of Descartes didn't succeed. Only the most precise, carefully crafted duality has a chance of being self-consistent.

Physicists usually place the split just below their measuring instruments (bubble chambers and geiger counters). Thus in the physicist's placement, almost everything encountered by humans is above the split. Only microscopic entities are below the split. To the physicist a fancy geiger counter is not needed to make an observation. When a cosmic ray leaves a track in a rock, the rock can be considered to make the observation. When a tree falls in Siberia without a human witness, the tree can be considered to be real because the tree and the ground can act as the observer. Although a rock can be an observer, it doesn't have feelings since its behavior and inner workings doesn't produce empathy in me. Thus most placements of the split are inappropriate for discussions of the mind-body problem.

3. The quantum duality and the homunculus

For the qualia-neuron (mind-body) duality the split would be placed within my brain. Eugene Wigner is a highly respected physicist who gave a clear discussion of this placement (Wigner, 1961). Since he uses a visual detection task as his gedanken experiment, his article is of interest to psychophysicists. When I talk about placing the split inside my brain, I do not necessarily mean that the split has a spatial location, e.g. placing the limbic neurons on one side and cortical neurons on the other side. The split can be between modes of activity of the brain. Consider, for example, how physicists place the split within a geiger counter that has a needle pointer as the readout device. Only the center of mass mode of the needle is typically placed above the split. If the needle consists of 10^{23} atoms then one mode (just the center of mass mode of motion) would be above the split and $10^{23} - 1$ modes of oscillation would be below the split. For the case of a redness qualia, one would place the redness firing pattern together with the relevant attention and consciousness activity above the split (once they are figured out) and all other neural activity below.

The flexibility of the movable split avoids the paradoxes of previous dualities. If the split is placed within my brain then I am the observer and my qualia are not reducible to neural activity. Other humans would be beneath the split, so from my standpoint, their subjective experiences would be fully reducible to the activity of their neurons. Previous mind-body dualities treated all brains alike so there would have been a problem with reductionism. The quantum mechanical duality, on the other hand, allows me to fully reduce your brain to its neurons, while not reducing my brain.

There is a vast history of physicists writing about the role of human consciousness in quantum mechanics (Wigner, 1961). The main problem with this past research is that the articles by physicists tend to be too technical and are therefore inaccessible to neurophilosophers (Stapp, 1990, is an exception). The evidence that the quantum duality has not had much impact on neurophilosophy is glaring. Consider, for example, the recent books by Patricia Churchland (1986), Paul Churchland (1988) and Dennett (1991) on the mind/brain problem. These books are clear, witty, and intelligent and yet they attack a very old version of duality rather than dealing with the improved quantum duality. The wonderful collection of articles and commentaries by Hofstadter and Dennett (1981) does have some comments on the quantum duality but they do not seem to appreciate how well the quantum observer can serve as the mind-body homunculus. It is because neurophilosophers do not seem to have caught on to the relevance of the quantum duality that the present article is being written.

Let us now reestablish contact with the discussion at the beginning of this chapter concerning whether robots can have qualia and examine how the quantum duality might fit in. An excellent framework to explore the computational theory of the mind has recently been developed by Searle (1990a). He distinguishes between three positions: Weak AI, Strong AI and Cognitivism.

1   **Weak AI: brain processes (and mental processes) can be simulated on a digital computer**
Searle has no problem accepting the Weak AI position, and I presume neither do most people reading this book on robotic vision. In terms of the duality split, the Weak AI position merely claims that if the split is placed high, then everything below the split, including other people's brains, can be understood in terms of the laws of biology, chemistry and physics. Since few disagree with the Weak AI position, nothing more will be said about it.

2   **Strong AI: the mind is a computer program**
Searle disagrees with this Strong AI position that is held by many neurophilosophers (Searle, 1980; Searle, 1990b) and computer scientists. Based on his definitions of mind (as dealing with meaningful entities) and computer programs (formal manipulations of meaningless symbols), Searle (1984, 1990b) logically deduces that the Strong AI position is false. A similar conclusion comes from considerations of the quantum duality. A computer program is a logical construct so there is no place for the quantum split. The split can only be placed in the real physical world not in an idea or formal program. Thus Strong AI does not allow for an outside observer to provide meaning or to feel qualia. Therefore the mind can not be a computer program. Rather than quibble about whether Searle is being fair in using an abstract computer program rather than a program plus computer it is best to shift the debate from Strong AI to Cognitivism (Searle, 1990a) where the real action is located.

3   **Cognitivism: the brain is a digital computer**
Cognitivism, which claims that the brain operates as a computer (I would include deterministic, analog, neural networks as a form of computer), is the main topic of Searle's recent paper (Searle, 1990a). He argues that the central question "Is the brain a digital computer" is ill-defined because of a tacit assumption requiring a homunculus to be the observer. I believe that the quantum duality provides a framework that removes the problems of Cognitivism related to the homunculus.

Searle's main task in his recent article (Searle, 1990a) is to point out the fallacies of Cognitivism. From my point of view, Searle's main accomplishment in his article is to unintentionally provide a strong argument for the quantum duality approach to the connection between brains and computation. I say unintentionally because Searle would never consider himself a dualist. Searle makes the point that computation is in the eye of the beholder. All the 0's and 1's being manipulated by the computer, the syntax, would be meaningless fluctuations of voltages rather than computations were it not for an outside observer providing the computational interpretation. Searle goes on to show how all of Cognitivism makes a tacit assumption of an outside homunculus. The homunculus can not be reduced to simplified structures within the system without having it disappear with nothing remaining to provide the needed interpretation of symbols.

The Cognitivist need for a homunculus is used by Searle to show that Cognitivism is not meaningful since the tacit need for an outside agent violates the "closed system" basis of Cognitivism. The quantum duality is exactly what is needed to rescue Cognitivism. It allows one to invoke a homunculus that is outside the reductionist laws and yet is compatible with these laws. The beauty of the quantum duality is that the placement of the split is maximally slippery. It can be placed wherever it is needed. As I emphasized before (Klein, 1991) the power of the quantum duality is that it legitimizes a multiplicity of seemingly incompatible worldviews. Only one worldview at a time is allowed, but they can take turns being true. The uniqueness of the placement has the advantage that it avoids the infinite regress that is often associated with mental models involving the homunculus. By providing a self-consistent framework for the outside observer (the homunculus), quantum duality legitimizes Cognitivism. The quantum duality allows the subjective feel to have its legitimate place in the description of nature.

Is the homunculus we have been discussing active or passive? The quantum homunculus is often thought of as merely a passive observer. However, in quantum theory the observer does play the most important role of collapsing the wave packet to "determine" which of the many possibilities are to be actualized. Stapp (1990) emphasizes this role as a vital aspect of consciousness. When the quantum split is placed low, near the geiger counters, there is no connection to the mind. However, when it is placed high, near my consciousness machinery, my homunculus becomes the "chooser" of different alternatives. This role of the observer has the flavor of some "freedom" of choice.

Suppose the robot says: "I see red". The meaning of this sentence depends on where the split is placed. If the split is placed between me and the robot (with me as the observer) then the sentence can be totally understood in terms of algorithmic computations by the robot's visual and vocal machinery connecting the visual stimulation to the sound output. With this placement of the split the robot is not an observer and it would be devoid of qualia, since I am choosing to define "see" as requiring a conscious homunculus as observer. If, however, the split is placed between the robot's consciousness module (or whatever the neural substrate of consciousness will turn out to be) and the rest of its circuitry, then the sentence "I see red" will mean that the *robot* observer is having an experience of red. As discussed in the first part of this paper, if the robot's circuitry was closely matched to my own anatomy and physiology, then I might well come to believe that the robot's percept of red is similar to my own percept. Thus the answer to the question of whether the robot senses the qualia of redness depends on my placement of the split. Some readers will undoubtedly be bothered that a single question can be answered either yes or no. This ambiguity produces a relativistic ontology (Klein, 1991) that may be disturbing at first. For each new placement of the split there are new observers and a new ontology. Quantum physicists are gradually getting accustomed to this strange view of reality. It is time that neurophilosophers also learned about the quantum reality.

It is not easy to get used to the quantum mechanical duality. The different placements of the split can produce bizarre ontologies. I can put the split in Bishop Berkeley's position, just below my own homunculus. This produces the solipsist position in which I am the only observer and the rest of the world exists only if I look. The flexible quantum duality allows the validity of even this most bizarre solipsist position. If the quantum duality can tolerate solipsism it should not be surprising that a lower split placement allows humans (and dogs and robots) to be observers with qualia.

Addendum #1

After most of the above was written, I had a discussion with Searle about some of the issues brought up in this paper. He had one major problem and I had one major surprise. His problem was that he wasn't yet convinced that the duality of quantum mechanics was the same as the duality of the mind-body problem. I believe that he is both right and wrong. For most placements of the quantum split he is correct. When the split is placed low, so that a stone acts as the observer, there is no connection with the mind-body problem. However, I believe the situation is different when the split is placed between the mode of activity of my brain corresponding to what we call "the homunculus" and the rest of my brain and body. In that case I claim that the quantum duality is identical to the mind-body duality. I will continue these discussions with Searle and maybe within a few years he will change his mind.

My big surprise was that Searle felt that when the neural circuitry of consciousness becomes understood (which we both agree is likely in the next 200 years) the mind-body problem will be resolved. I was surprised because I believe that discovering the neural circuitry is part of third person explanations and is not equivalent to having a framework that has a place for subjective feelings and qualia. Maybe I shouldn't have been surprised since in his excellent chapter on the mind-body problem (Searle, 1984) he is clear that "pains and other mental phenomena just are features of the brain". So it seems that Searle, like most scientists, doesn't believe that there is a mind-body problem. I would, of course, agree that for third person explanations there is no problem in connecting someone's mind to his brain, but I still believe a framework with an observer outside the system is useful for interpreting first person experience. This difference of opinion is directly connected with Searle's rejection of dualism. Our further discussions may help to clear up these misunderstandings. Stay tuned.

Addendum #2

Gerald Edelman has just published (Edelman, 1992) one of the most interesting books on the connection of the mind to biology (I always believe that the most recent book I read is the best one). His viewpoint, like Searle's as just discussed, is that the mind can be understood from biology. Even though Edelman has a brief discussion of quantum physics he does not want to connect the quantum duality to the mind-body duality. Edelman, like most scientists and philosophers, rejects any notion of duality as applied to the mind-body problem. What I think is going on is that there are two types of homunculus that are getting confused. I will call them the biology homunculus and the physics homunculus. Edelman provides an excellent framework for the biology homunculus. It is likely that within 200 years the neural circuitry of consciousness will be understood and the biology homunculus will take its place along with DNA as a "simple" solution to what had been thought to be an "impossible" problem. At that point, most people may well believe that the mind-body problem has been "solved". Indeed, I would agree that the most interesting aspect of the mind-body problem will then be solved. The quest to understand the biology homunculus is in fact, an important reason why I am studying visual perception. However, I say again that gaining an understanding of the biology homunculus will not provide a framework or a language for discussing qualia. What is needed is the physics homunculus, that can act as an observer "outside" of the biological reductionistic brain. The clever quantum duality allows the physics homunculus to be present and observing without disturbing the workings of the biological machinery.

It is worth emphasizing a point made in my earlier paper (Klein, 1991). In one sense the role of the physics homunculus is negligible. It doesn't explain anything about how the brain works. All it does is allow us to not be embarrassed to say that the my raw feel of an experience is outside the realm of science. Thus, not much meat has been left for the mental half of Descartes' duality. On the other hand, the raw feels of my subjective states are the most important part of my experience. Furthermore, for many people on this planet the physics homunculus has an added attraction. It legitimatizes a spiritual (meaning subjective) realm. Descartes' original duality provided a framework for the coexistence of science and religion. The quantum duality has shown how Descartes' vision can be fleshed out to be a consistent, powerful, and flexible framework for understanding our place in the universe.

Acknowledgements

This work was partially supported by AFOSR grant 89-0238.

3D object recognition and matching: on a result of Basri and Ullman[*]

Tomaso Poggio

The main point of this note is to characterize the algebraic structure of the views of one 3D object under orthographic projection. Consider the linear vector space $\mathcal{R}^{3N}$ of 3D views of all objects, with a 3D view being the vector of the x, y and z coordinates of each of N feature points. Consider the subspace $V_{ob_i}^{3N}$ generated by one view of a specific object and by the action on it of the group of *uniform* linear transformations $\mathcal{L}$ (i.e. the same linear transformation is applied to each feature point). $\mathcal{L}$ is an algebra of order 9, and therefore a linear vector space isomorphic to $\mathcal{M}_3$ (that is the space of the 3×3 matrices with real elements). Thus, $V_{ob_i}^{3N}$ is a linear vector space isomorphic to $\mathcal{R}^9$. The projection operator (orthographic projection) that deletes the z components from the 3D views, maps $V_{ob_i}^{3N}$ into a linear vector subspace $V_{ob_i}^{2N}$, isomorphic to $\mathcal{R}^6$. $V_{ob_i}^{2N}$ consist of vector with x and y components and can be written as the direct sum $V_{ob_i}^{2N} = V_x^N \oplus V_y^N$, where V_x^N and V_y^N are non-intersecting linear subspaces, each isomorphic to $\mathcal{R}^3$. In addition, I have proved (Basri has obtained this result independently) that $V_x^N = V_y^N$, which implies that 1.5 snapshots are sufficient for "learning" an object (generically). If 3D translations are included, a linear subspace, isomorphic to $\mathcal{R}^2$ must be added to the linear space spanned by the 2D views of one object. The 1.5 views theorem implies that the x and the y vectors obtained from the 2 frames are linearly dependent. This in turn implies that 4 matched points across two views are sufficient (generically) to determine 1-D epipolar lines for matching all other points. This is a very useful result (first obtained in a different context by Huang and Lee (1989)) in correspondence problems involving 2 frames and affine, uniform transformations in $3D$.

1. Introduction

Basri and Ullman (1990) have recently discovered the striking fact that under orthographic projection a view of a 3D object is the linear combination of a small number of views of the same object. In this note, we reformulate

---

[*] Most of the content of this paper has appeared as IRST Technical Report 9005–03, 1990.

their results in the more abstract setting of linear algebra. This framework makes the result very transparent: the constraint of linear transformation (the same linear transformation for each vertex) implies immediately that the set of views of an object spans a 9-dimensional space, independently of the number of vertices; orthographic projection preserves linearity while reducing the number of dimensions to 6. Simple considerations show that the linear spaces of the x and y coordinates are nonintersecting and that each has dimension 3. Furthermore I prove that they are equivalent, implying that 1.5 snapshots are sufficient to learn the model of one object.

2. Any view of a 3D object is a linear combination of a small, fixed number of views

This section provides the main result of Basri and Ullman (in the second subsection).

2.1. Any 3D-view of an object is a linear combination of 9 views

Let us define a *3D-view* of a 3D object as:

$$\mathbf{X}^{obj} = \begin{pmatrix} x_1 \\ y_1 \\ z_1 \\ x_2 \\ y_2 \\ z_2 \\ . \\ . \\ . \\ x_n \\ y_n \\ z_n \end{pmatrix}$$

with $X \in \mathcal{R}^{3n}$, which is a vector space in the usual way.

I consider the set of *uniform* (my definition) linear operators on $\mathcal{R}^{3n}$, defined by the $3n \times 3n$ matrices $\mathbf{L}^{3n}$, where $\mathbf{L}^{3n} = \mathbf{I}_n \otimes L$ is the tensor product of $\mathbf{I}_n$ and L:

$$\mathbf{L}^{3n} = \begin{pmatrix} L & 0 & . & 0 \\ 0 & L & . & 0 \\ . & . & . & . \\ 0 & 0 & . & L \end{pmatrix}$$

where

$$L = \begin{pmatrix} l_{11} & l_{12} & l_{13} \\ l_{21} & l_{22} & l_{23} \\ l_{31} & l_{32} & l_{33} \end{pmatrix}$$

is an affine transformation on $\mathcal{R}^3$. Translation in $3D$ space is taken care of separately (see later).

The space of the $\mathbf{L}^{3n}$ operators is a vector space which is *isomorphic* to the vector space of the L matrices. It therefore has a basis of 9 elements independently of n.

I can express

$$\mathbf{L}^{3n} = \sum_{i=1}^{9} a_i \mathbf{L}_i^{3n}$$

where a_i can be identified with the appropriate $l_{i,j}$ and L_i^{3n} with the usual basis for L^{3n}, i.e. with the elementary matrices E, and thus

$$\mathbf{X} = \mathbf{L}^{3n}\mathbf{X}_0 = \sum_{i=1}^{9} a_i \mathbf{L}_i^{3n}\mathbf{X}_0 = \sum_{i=1}^{9} a_i \mathbf{X}_i$$

where $\mathbf{X}_i$ are 9 independent 3D views of the specific object, needed to span the 9 elements of L, 3 for each coordinate, and X_0 is a particular view chosen as the "initial" view. Thus:

Theorem 2.1 *The vector space V_{Ob}^{3D} generated by the action of uniform linear transformations on a 3D view of a specific object is a 9-dimensional subspace of $\mathcal{R}^{3n}$, 3 dimensions for x, 3 for y and 3 for z.*

Thus any object ob_i generates a corresponding low dimensional subspace $V_{ob_i}^{3D}$ of all possible views of all objects ($\mathcal{R}^{3n}$). Of course, $V_{ob_i}^{3D} \not\equiv \mathcal{R}^{3n}$, *iff* $n > 3$. In other words, to have object specificity, i.e., for this result to be *nontrivial*, it is necessary that $n > 3$. Notice that $\mathcal{R}^{3n} = V_{ob_i} + V_{ob_2} + \dots$.

2.2. Any 2D-view of a 3D object is a linear combination of 6 2D-views

Now consider the orthographic projection $P : \mathcal{R}^{3n} \to \mathcal{R}^{2n}$, defined by $P\mathbf{X} = \mathbf{x}$, that is

$$P\begin{pmatrix} x_1 \\ y_1 \\ z_1 \\ x_2 \\ y_2 \\ z_2 \\ . \\ . \\ . \\ x_n \\ y_n \\ z_n \end{pmatrix} = \begin{pmatrix} x_1 \\ y_1 \\ x_2 \\ y_2 \\ x_3 \\ y_3 \\ . \\ . \\ . \\ x_n \\ y_n \end{pmatrix}$$

with P being a linear operator with the matrix representation

$$P = \begin{pmatrix} 1 & 0 & . & . & . & . & . & . & . & 0 \\ 0 & 1 & 0 & . & . & . & . & . & . & 0 \\ 0 & 0 & 0 & 1 & 0 & . & . & . & . & 0 \\ . & . & . & . & . & . & . & . & . & . \\ . & . & . & 0 & 0 & . & 1 & 0 & 0 \\ 0 & 0 & . & . & . & . & . & 0 & 1 & 0 \end{pmatrix}$$

We define $\mathbf{x}$ as the *2D-view* of a 3D object.

The result below follows immediately (6 views span the elements of L in the first 2 rows) and is the main result of Basri and Ullman (in a different formulation):

Theorem 2.2   *The vector space V_{ob_i} given by $V_{ob_i} = PV_{ob_i}^{3D}$ is a six-dimensional subspace of $\mathcal{R}^{2n}$ (the space of all 2D orthographic views of all 3D objects), i.e. $\mathbf{x_{ob}} = \sum_{i=1}^{6} a_i \mathbf{x}_{ob}^i$.*

Remark: The inclusion of rigid translations is equivalent to the addition of a two-dimensional linear subspace (the same for all objects), spanned by the vectors

$$\mathbf{t_x} = \begin{pmatrix} 1 \\ 0 \\ 1 \\ 0 \\ . \\ . \\ . \end{pmatrix}$$

and

$$\mathbf{t_y} = \begin{pmatrix} 0 \\ 1 \\ 0 \\ 1 \\ . \\ . \\ . \end{pmatrix}$$

3. The x and the y coordinates of a view are each a separate linear combination of 3 views

In the previous section we have seen that any *2D-view* of a 3D object under orthographic projection is the linear combination of 6 *2D-views*. This section reformulates another observation of Basri and Ullman: the x coordinates of a *2D-view* are a linear combination of the x coordinates of 3 *2D-views* and the y coordinates are a linear combination of the y coordinates of 3 *2D-views*, the two combinations being independent of each other.

Let us consider a similarity transformation of **x**:

$$TX = \begin{pmatrix} x_1 \\ x_2 \\ x_3 \\ \cdot \\ \cdot \\ \cdot \\ x_n \\ y_1 \\ y_2 \\ \cdot \\ \cdot \\ \cdot \\ y_n \\ z_1 \\ \cdot \\ \cdot \\ \cdot \\ z_n \end{pmatrix}$$

Under this similarity transformation, $\mathbf{L}^{3n}$ becomes a 3×3 matrix of 9 (that is 3×3) blocks. Each block is a multiple of $I \in \mathcal{R}^{n,n}$ (notice the "isomorphism" to L!).

$$T^T L T = \begin{pmatrix} I_{11} & I_{12} & I_{13} \\ I_{21} & I_{22} & I_{23} \\ I_{31} & I_{32} & I_{33} \end{pmatrix}$$

where

$$I_{11} = \begin{pmatrix} l_{11} & 0 & 0 & \cdot & \cdot & \cdot \\ 0 & l_{11} & 0 & \cdot & \cdot & \cdot \\ 0 & 0 & l_{11} & \cdot & \cdot & \cdot \\ \cdot & \cdot & \cdot & \cdot & \cdot & \cdot \end{pmatrix}$$

and so on for the other blocks.

The same argument of the previous section makes it clear that defining

$$\xi = \begin{pmatrix} x_1 \\ \cdot \\ \cdot \\ \cdot \\ x_n \end{pmatrix}$$

$$\eta = \begin{pmatrix} y_1 \\ \cdot \\ \cdot \\ \cdot \\ y_n \end{pmatrix}$$

the following holds:

$$\xi = \sum_{i=1}^{3} l_{1i}\xi_i$$

$$\eta = \sum_{i=1}^{3} l_{2i}\eta_i.$$

Thus we have proved:

Theorem 3.1 *The subspace spanned by the vectors ξ — the x components of $\mathbf{x}$ — which is a n−dimensional subspace of V_{ob}^{2D} (which is 2n-dimensional), is spanned by three views of the x coordinates of the object undergoing uniform transformations, i.e., each ξ can be represented as the linear combination of 3 independent ξ_i. The same is true for the η: each η is an independent linear combination of 3 independent η_i. Again, $n > 3$ in order for this to be non-trivial (since $\xi \equiv \mathcal{R}^n$ for $n \leq 3$).*

Remark: The basis of ξ and the basis of η depend on the specific object.

4. V_x and V_y have the same basis, i.e. 1.5 snapshots suffice

We know from the previous sections that $V_{ob_i}^{2N} = V_x^N \oplus V_y^N$, where $dimV_x = dimV_y = 3$. A stronger property holds:

Theorem 4.1 $V_x = V_y$ *(in the sense of Furlanello)*

Proof. Assume that V_x and V_y are not identical (I consider the projections of the x and y components expressed originally in the same base in V) restrictions: then there is a vector $\mathbf{y}$ which is in V_y and not in V_x (or viceversa). Then I can take the 3D view that originated $\mathbf{y}$ (through orthogonal projection) and apply to it a legal transformation consisting of a rigid rotation of 90 degrees in the image plane (such a transformation is in L and therefore is legal). The x view of that 3D vector is the $\mathbf{y}$, contradicting the assumption. It follows that $V_x = V_y$.

Remarks

1   The same argument shows that $V_x = V_y = V_z$

2   The same basis of three vectors spans V_x and V_y (separately).

3   The property that the x views and the y views of the same 3D object from the same snapshot are independent is generic, since if they were dependent, a very slightly different object, differing only in the y coordinate of one vertex would have independent views (Bruno Caprile, pers. com.).

4   In general, 1.5 snapshots are sufficient to provide a basis

5   Any 4 vectors from V_x and V_y are linearly dependent.

5. A corollary of the 1.5 views theorem: given four matched points, correspondence for motion or recognition is easy

A direct consequence of the above 1.5 views theorem is that the 4 vectors (from 2 orthographic views) of the $\mathbf{x}$ and $\mathbf{y}$ components of an object undergoing an uniform affine transformation in 3D (in particular a rigid transformation in 3D) are linearly dependent, that is

$$\alpha_1\mathbf{x}_1 + \beta_1\mathbf{y}_1 + \alpha_2\mathbf{x}_2 + \beta_2\mathbf{y}_2 = 0$$

This implies that the correspondence of at least 4 points (including translations) in two frames determines epipolar lines for the matching of all other points (the observation is due to Ronen Basri; see also Amnon Sha'shua; a similar result—but not this proof—was first obtained by Lee and Huang, 1988). This means that for each point (x_1, y_1) in frame 1 the corresponding point in frame 2 satisfies the equation

$$y = mx + A$$

with $m = \alpha_2^*$ and $A = -(\alpha_1^* x_1 + \beta_1^* y_1)$ and $\alpha_1^* = \alpha_1/\beta_2$ and so on. Translations are taken care of by matching one point in the two frames. Three additional "generic" points are needed to solve for α_1^*, α_2^* and β_1^*.

Therefore in problems of matching between 2 frames—in motion or recognition—four points are sufficient to determine epipolar lines along which the matching of the other points can be more easily found.

6. The case of rigid transformations, i.e., rotations in 3D

The previous two section have considered the case of *uniform linear transformations* in 3D of a 3D object. The space of such transformations is a vector space that contains as a nonlinear subspace the group of the rigid rotations in 3D (which is easily seen not to be a vector space). Can we characterize what the restriction to rigid rotations means? This section addresses this question.

Consider the restriction $L = R$ with $R^T R = I$. Then:

$$\begin{cases} l_{11}^2 + l_{12}^2 + l_{13}^2 = 1 \\ l_{11}l_{21} + l_{12}l_{22} + l_{13}l_{23} = 0 \\ l_{21}^2 + l_{22}^2 + l_{23}^2 = 1 \end{cases}$$

The equations define a nonlinear subspace of the space $\xi = \{l_{11}, l_{12}, l_{13}\}$ isomorphic to $\mathcal{R}^3$, and of $\eta = \{l_{21}, l_{22}, l_{23}\}$, also isomorphic to $\mathcal{R}^3$. Of course, ξ is a linear subspace of $\mathcal{R}^n$, the *space of all views of the x coordinates of all objects.* Rotations are the intersection of ξ with the conics defined by the previous equations.

The 2D views of one object defined by uniform affine transformations span $\{l_{11}, l_{12}, l_{13}\} = \mathcal{R}^3$. The 2D views of one object defined by rigid transformations, i.e., rotations, span a nonlinear subspace of $\mathcal{R}^3$, namely, the surface of the unit sphere in $\mathcal{R}^3$. All points on the *unit* sphere are allowed for $\{l_{11}, l_{12}, l_{13}\}$ (thus we "use up" two parameters). The triplet $(l_{21}l_{22}l_{23})$ is determined as one parameter family. Geometrically, once the vector l_{11}, l_{12}, l_{13} is fixed on the unit sphere, an orthogonal circle is determined on which the vector (l_{21}, l_{22}, l_{23}) must lie.

Acknowledgements

Daphna Weinshall explained to me that Basri and Ullman's result was not restricted to rigid rotations despite what I had read in their original Weizman Technical Report. Bruno Caprile and Federico Girosi provided several useful suggestions. Shimon Ullman told me about the futility of trying to extend the last section because of Huang's recent results on structure from motion. Cesare Furlanello was the only person to read it carefully and to explain to me what the little mathematics in it really means.

Surface interpolation networks

Alex P. Pentland

Good solutions to spatial interpolation problems, using either a regularization or a 2-D Kalman filtering formulation, can be obtained in only a few iterations using a simple feedback network with orthogonal wavelet receptive fields.

1. Introduction

Surface interpolation is a common problem in both human and computer vision. Perhaps the most well-known interpolation theory is regularization (Poggio et al., 1985; Terzopoulos, 1988). However this theory has the drawback that the interpolation network requires hundreds or even thousands of iterations to produce a smoothly interpolated surface. Thus in computer vision applications surface interpolation is often the single most expensive processing step. In biological vision, timing data from neurophysiology makes it unlikely that many iterations of cell firing are involved in the interpolation process, so that interpolation theories have been forced to assume some sort of analog processing. Unfortunately, there is little experimental evidence supporting such processing outside of the retina.

Moreover, the technique of regularization is applicable only to single images or, at most, to image sequences from statically-viewed fixed environments. To integrate information across multiple views of a changing environment, the optimal estimation technique of Kalman filtering is required (Broida and Chellappa, 1986; Faugeras et al., 1986). Filters that estimate range at every point have been built (Matthies et al., 1989; Heel, 1990; Singh, 1990), and have demonstrated their accuracy and robust behavior. However many researchers (especially those interested in biological vision) have remained skeptical because of the great computational cost and the complex, non-biological nature of the existing algorithms for Kalman filtering at every image point.

In this paper I will show how efficient, biologically-plausible solutions to these problems can be obtained by using orthogonal wavelet bases. The plan of this paper is to briefly review both the regularization and Kalman filter approaches to surface interpolation, and then to describe how a careful choice of receptive field or *basis* can be used to obtain more efficient solutions. I will then describe a mathematical solution and corresponding network, and show numerical examples.

1.1. *Background: regularization*

In computer vision the surface interpolation problem typically involves constructing a smooth surface, sometimes allowing a small number of discontinuities, given a sparse set of noisy range or orientation measurements. Mathematically, the problem may be defined as finding a function $\mathcal{U}$ within a linear space $\mathcal{H}$ that minimizes an energy functional $\mathcal{E}(\mathcal{U})$,

$$\mathcal{E}(\mathcal{U}) = \inf_{\mathcal{V} \in \mathcal{H}} \mathcal{E}(\mathcal{V}) = \inf_{\mathcal{V} \in \mathcal{H}} (\mathcal{K}(\mathcal{V}) + \mathcal{R}(\mathcal{V})) \tag{1}$$

where $\mathcal{K}(\mathcal{V})$ is an energy functional that is typically proportional to the curvature of the surface, and $\mathcal{R}(\mathcal{V})$ is an energy functional that is proportional to the residual difference between $\mathcal{V}$ and the sensor measurements. When the solution exists, the variational derivative $\delta_{\mathcal{U}}$ of the energy functional vanishes,

$$\delta_{\mathcal{U}} \mathcal{E}(\mathcal{U}) = \delta_{\mathcal{U}} \mathcal{K}(\mathcal{U}) + \delta_{\mathcal{U}} \mathcal{R}(\mathcal{U}) = 0 \tag{2}$$

The linear operators $\delta_{\mathcal{U}}\mathcal{E}$, $\delta_{\mathcal{U}}\mathcal{K}$, and $\delta_{\mathcal{U}}\mathcal{R}$ are infinite dimensional and normally dense. To solve Equation 2, therefore, it must first be projected onto a discretization S of $\mathcal{R}$ containing n nodes. The resulting matrix equation is written

$$\lambda \mathbf{K} \mathbf{U} + \mathbf{R} = 0 \tag{3}$$

where λ is a scalar constant, $\mathbf{U}$, $\mathbf{R}$ are $n \times 1$ vectors and $\mathbf{K}$ an $n \times n$ matrix; these are the discretization of $\mathcal{U}$, $\delta_{\mathcal{U}}\mathcal{R}(\mathcal{U})$, and $\delta_{\mathcal{U}}\mathcal{K}(\mathcal{U})$, respectively. To make explicit the dependence of $\mathbf{R}$ on $\mathbf{U}$, I will write the regularization equation as follows:

$$\lambda \mathbf{K} \mathbf{U} + \mathbf{S} \mathbf{U} - \mathbf{D} = 0 \tag{4}$$

i.e., $\mathbf{R} = \mathbf{S}\mathbf{U} - \mathbf{D}$, where $\mathbf{D}$ is a $n \times 1$ vector whose entries are the measured coordinates d_i where sensor measurements exist and zero elsewhere, and $\mathbf{S}$ is a diagonal "selection matrix" with ones for nodes with sensor measurements and zeros elsewhere.

2. Choice of basis

When $\mathcal{K}$ is chosen to be the stress within a bending thin plate (as is standard), then $\mathbf{K}$ is the *stiffness matrix* familiar from physical simulation. One interesting consequence of this choice is that the rows of $\mathbf{K}$ are similar to the familiar difference-of-Gaussians receptive fields found in biological systems, so that an interpolated surface (i.e., a solution $\mathbf{U}$ to Equation 4) can be obtained by iterating a two-layer network of "neurons" with biologically-plausible receptive fields (Terzopoulos, 1988). Unfortunately, several thousand iterations are often required to obtain such an interpolated surface. Although sophisticated multiresolution techniques can improve performance, the best reported algorithms still require several hundred iterations.

The cost of surface interpolation is proportional to both the bandwidth and condition number of $\mathbf{K}$. Both of these quantities can be greatly reduced by choosing the correct *basis* (a set of n orthogonal vectors) and associated coordinate system in which to solve the problem. In neural systems, transformation to a new basis or coordinate system can be accomplished by passing a data vector through a set of receptive fields; the shapes of the receptive fields are the new basis vectors, and the resulting neural activities are the coordinates of the data vector in the coordinate system defined by these basis vectors. If the receptive fields are orthonormal, then we can convert back to the original coordinate system by adding up the same receptive fields in amounts proportional to the associated neurons activity.

For the class of physically-motivated smoothness functionals, the ideal basis would be both spatially and spectrally localized, and (important for computer applications) very fast to compute. The desire for spectral localization stems from the fact that, in the absence of boundary conditions, discontinuities, etc., these sort of physical equilibrium problems can usually be solved in closed form in the frequency domain. In similar fashion, a spectrally-localized basis will tend to produce a banded stiffness matrix $\mathbf{K}$. The requirement for spatial localization stems from the need to account for local variations in $\mathbf{K}$'s band structure due to, for instance, boundary conditions, discontinuities, or other inhomogeneities.

2.1. Orthogonal wavelet bases

A class of bases that provide the desired properties are generated by functions known as *orthogonal wavelets* (Mallat, 1987; Daubechies, 1988). Orthogonal wavelet functions and receptive fields are different from the wavelets previously used in biological and computational modeling because *all* of the functions or receptive fields within a family, rather than only the functions or receptive fields of one size, are orthogonal to one another. A family of orthogonal wavelets $h_{a,b}$ is constructed from a single function h by dilation of a and translation of b

$$h_{a,b} = |a|^{-1/2}\, h\left(\frac{x-b}{a}\right), \qquad a \neq 0 \tag{5}$$

Typically $a = 2^j$ and $b = 1, ..., n = 2^j$ for $j = 1, 2, 3....$ The critical properties of wavelet families that make them well suited to this application are that:

- For appropriate choice of h they can provide an orthonormal basis of $\mathbf{L}^2(R)$, i.e., *all* members of the family are orthogonal to one another.

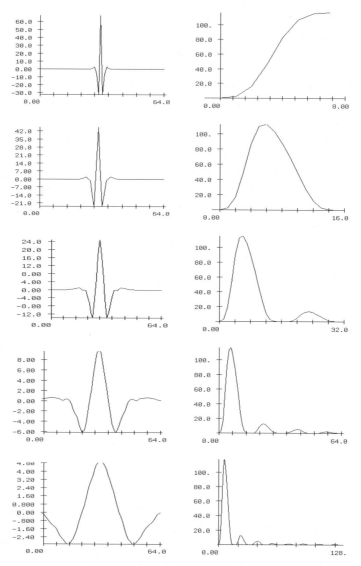

Fig. 1. *Five elements of the wavelet basis set "closest" to the Wilson-Gelb psychophysical model of human spatial vision. Left column: Wavelet filter family "closest" to Wilson-Gelb model (filters have been arbitrarily scaled for display). Right column: The power spectra of these filters on a linear scale.*

- They can be simultaneously localized in both space and frequency.

- Digital transformations using wavelet bases can be *recursively* computed, and so require only $O(n)$ operations.

Such families of wavelets may be used to define a set of multiscale orthonormal basis vectors. I will call such a basis Φ_w, where the columns of the $n \times n$ matrix $\mathbf{\Phi}_w$ are the basis vectors. Because $\mathbf{\Phi}_w$ forms an orthonormal basis, $\mathbf{\Phi}_w^T \mathbf{\Phi}_w = \mathbf{\Phi}_w \mathbf{\Phi}_w^T = \mathbf{I}$. That is, like the Fourier transform, the wavelet transform is self-inverting. The left-hand column of Figure 1 shows a subset of $\mathbf{\Phi}_w$; from top to bottom are the basis vectors corresponding to $a = 1, 2, 4, 8, 16$ and $b = n/2$. The right-hand column shows the Fourier power spectrum of each of these bases; it can be seen that they display good joint spatial-spectral localization. All of the examples presented in this paper will all be based on the wavelet basis illustrated in this figure.[1]

The shapes shown in the left-hand column of Figure 1 are the receptive field profiles that transform an input signal into, or out of, the wavelet coordinate system. I developed this particular set of wavelets to match as closely as possible the human psychophysical receptive field model of Wilson and Gelb (1984); there is only a 7.5% MSE difference between this set of wavelet receptive fields and the Wilson-Gelb model (Pentland, 1991).[2] *This set of wavelets, therefore, provides a good model of human spatial frequency sensitivity, and of human sensitivity to changes in spatial frequency.*

On digital computers, transformation to the wavelet coordinate system is normally computed recursively using separable filters. A two-dimensional example is illustrated in Figure 2. At the first level of recursion, the input image (a) is split into low-pass, horizontal high-pass, vertical high-pass, and diagonal high-pass sub-bands, as shown in (b). This is accomplished by convolving the input image with filters whose coefficients come from the highest-frequency wavelet basis, shown at the top left of Figure 1, and then subsampling by taking every other value. The high-pass sub-bands that result from these three convolutions are the product of the first $\frac{3}{4}n$ rows of $\mathbf{\Phi}_w^T$ (the highest-frequency basis vectors) and the input image $\mathbf{D}$.

At each successive level of recursion the low-pass image is split into four more bands, in the limit producing $\mathbf{\Phi}_w^T \mathbf{D}$, the complete wavelet transform of $\mathbf{D}$, shown in (c). Note that at each iteration the *same* filters are used to split the image; it is the process of recursive application that generates the entire family of filters shown in Figure 1. To go from the wavelet coordinate system to the original coordinate system, one simply reverses the process, recursively summing these same basis vectors by first inserting extra zeros

---

[1] Note: Because these filters are orthogonal to only one part in ten thousand, they are perhaps best described as quadrature mirror filter approximations to a true wavelet. I will continue to refer to them as wavelets, because the mathematics presented here depends on the properties of wavelets, and because the differences are not significant in this context.

[2] This set of wavelets was developed by applying the gradient-descent QMF design procedure of Simoncelli and Adelson (1990). using the Wilson-Gelb filters as the initial "guess" at an orthogonal basis. Wavelet receptive fields from only five octaves are shown, although the Wilson-Gelb model has six channels. Wilson, in a personal communication, has advised us that the Wilson-Gelb "b" and "c" channels are sufficiently similar that it is reasonable to group them into a single channel.

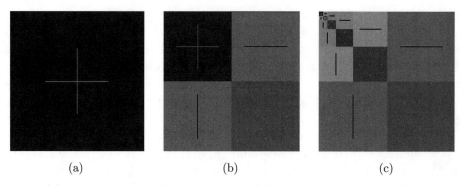

Fig. 2. *(a) A* 128×128 *node input image* **D**, *(b) sub-bands comprising the first level of the wavelet transform, which are the product of the highest frequency members of* $\boldsymbol{\Phi}_w^T$ *and the input image* **D**, *(c) the complete transform* $\boldsymbol{\Phi}_w^T\mathbf{D}$. *Total execution time: approximately 2.0 seconds on a Sun 4/330.*

between each transform value and then convolving with the same filters. For further information see Simoncelli and Adelson (1990).

3. Surface interpolation using wavelet bases

It has been proven that by using wavelet bases linear operators such as $\delta_\sqcap\mathcal{K}$ can be represented extremely compactly (Albert et al., 1990). This suggests that $\boldsymbol{\Phi}_w$ is an effective preconditioning transform, and thus may be used to obtain very fast approximate solutions. The simplest method is to transform a previously-defined $\mathbf{K}$ to the wavelet basis,

$$\tilde{\mathbf{K}} = \boldsymbol{\Phi}_w^T\mathbf{K}\boldsymbol{\Phi}_w \tag{6}$$

then to discard off-diagonal elements,

$$\boldsymbol{\Omega}_w^2 = \operatorname{diag}\left(\boldsymbol{\Phi}_w^T\mathbf{K}\boldsymbol{\Phi}_w\right) \tag{7}$$

and then to solve. Note that for each choice of $\mathbf{K}$ the diagonal matrix $\boldsymbol{\Omega}_w^2$ is calculated only once and then stored; further, its calculation requires only $O(n)$ operations. In numerical experiments I have found that for a typical $\mathbf{K}$ the summed magnitude of the off-diagonals of $\tilde{\mathbf{K}}$ is approximately 5% of the diagonal's magnitude, so that we expect to incur only small errors by discarding off-diagonals.

Case 1. The simplest case of surface interpolation is when sensor measurements exist for every node so that the sampling matrix $\mathbf{S} = \mathbf{I}$. Substituting $\boldsymbol{\Phi}_w\tilde{\mathbf{U}} = \mathbf{U}$ and premultiplying by $\boldsymbol{\Phi}_w^T$ converts Equation 4 to

$$\lambda\boldsymbol{\Phi}_w^T\mathbf{K}\boldsymbol{\Phi}_w\tilde{\mathbf{U}} + \boldsymbol{\Phi}_w^T\boldsymbol{\Phi}_w\tilde{\mathbf{U}} = \boldsymbol{\Phi}_w^T\mathbf{D} \tag{8}$$

By employing Equation 7, we then obtain

$$(\lambda\mathbf{\Omega}_w^2 + \mathbf{I})\tilde{\mathbf{U}} = \mathbf{\Phi}_w^T\mathbf{D} \tag{9}$$

The approximate interpolation solution $\mathbf{U}$ is therefore

$$\mathbf{U} = \mathbf{\Phi}_w(\lambda\mathbf{\Omega}_w^2 + \mathbf{I})^{-1}\mathbf{\Phi}_w^T\mathbf{D} \tag{10}$$

Note that this computation is accomplished by simply transforming $\mathbf{D}$ to the wavelet basis, scaling the convolution filters (receptive fields) appropriately at each level of recursion, and then transforming back to the original coordinate system. To obtain an approximate regularized solution for an $\sqrt{n} \times \sqrt{n}$ image using a wavelet of width w therefore requires approximately $8wn + n$ add and multiply operations.

Case 2. In the more usual case where not all nodes have sensor measurements, the interpolation solution may require iteration. In this case the sampling matrix $\mathbf{S}$ is diagonal with ones for nodes that have sensor measurements, and zeros elsewhere. Again substituting $\mathbf{\Phi}_w\tilde{\mathbf{U}} = \mathbf{U}$ and premultiplying by $\mathbf{\Phi}_w^T$ converts Equation 4 to

$$\lambda\mathbf{\Phi}_w^T\mathbf{K}\mathbf{\Phi}_w\tilde{\mathbf{U}} + \mathbf{\Phi}_w^T\mathbf{S}\mathbf{\Phi}_w\tilde{\mathbf{U}} = \mathbf{\Phi}_w^T\mathbf{D} \tag{11}$$

The matrix $\mathbf{\Phi}_w^T\mathbf{S}\mathbf{\Phi}_w$ is diagonally dominant so that the interpolation solution $\mathbf{U}$ may be obtained by iterating

$$\mathbf{U}^{t+1} = \mathbf{\Phi}_w(\lambda\mathbf{\Omega}_w^2 + \tilde{\mathbf{S}})^{-1}\mathbf{\Phi}_w^T\mathbf{D}^t + \mathbf{U}^t \tag{12}$$

where $\tilde{\mathbf{S}} = \text{diag}(\mathbf{\Phi}_w^T\mathbf{S}\mathbf{\Phi}_w)$ and $\mathbf{D}^t = \mathbf{D} - (\mathbf{K} + \mathbf{S})\mathbf{U}^t$ is the residual at iteration t. I have found that normally no more than three to five iterations of Equation 12 are required to obtain an accurate estimate of the interpolated surface; often a single iteration will suffice.

Note that for this procedure to succeed, the largest gaps in the data sampling must be significantly smaller than the largest filters in the wavelet transform. Further, when λ is small and the data sampling is sparse and irregular, it can happen that the off-diagonal terms of $\mathbf{\Phi}_w^T\mathbf{S}\mathbf{\Phi}_w$ introduce significant error. Therefore when using small λ I have found that it is best to perform one initial iteration with a large λ, and then reduce λ to the desired value in further iterations.

Discontinuities. The matrix $\mathbf{K}$ describes the connectivity between adjacent points on a continuous surface; thus whenever a discontinuity occurs $\mathbf{K}$ must be altered. Following Terzopoulos (1988), we can accomplish this by disabling receptive fields that cross discontinuities. In a computer implementation, the simplest method is to locally halt the recursive construction of the wavelet transform whenever one of the resulting bases would cross a discontinuity.

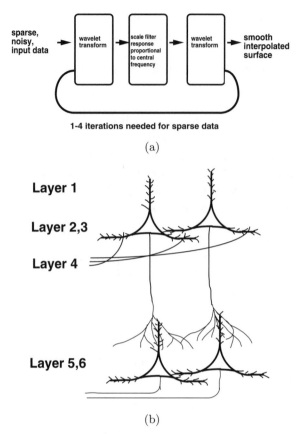

(a)

(b)

Fig. 3. *(a) A biological mechanism for surface interpolation, (b) one possible neural implementation.*

3.1. A biological implementation

Figure 3(a) illustrates the process of surface interpolation using wavelet receptive fields. This example is for the case where $\mathbf{S} = \mathbf{I}$, more generally a second such mechanism is required in order to also compute $\tilde{\mathbf{S}} = \boldsymbol{\Phi}_w^T \mathbf{S} \boldsymbol{\Phi}_w$. The input data $\mathbf{D}$ is passed through a layer of neurons with receptive fields such as are shown in Figure 1 at each location. This computes $\boldsymbol{\Phi}_w^T \mathbf{D}$, the wavelet transform of $\mathbf{D}$. The activity of each neuron is then scaled by a factor dependent upon its central frequency, thus computing $(\lambda \boldsymbol{\Omega}_w^2 + \mathbf{I})^{-1} \boldsymbol{\Phi}_w^T \mathbf{D}$. Finally, each neuron's output is summed with a spatial distribution equal to its receptive field, thus computing the inverse wavelet transform and obtaining the interpolated surface $\mathbf{U} = \boldsymbol{\Phi}_w (\lambda \boldsymbol{\Omega}_w^2 + \mathbf{I})^{-1} \boldsymbol{\Phi}_w^T \mathbf{D}$.

Figure 3(b) illustrates one way this computation can be mapped onto neurons. In this figure the input layer arborizes very locally, with the pyramidal cell's basal dendrites producing receptive fields shaped as in Figure 1. It is important to note that wavelet receptive fields can be produced from an initial unspecific center-surround receptive field structure by, for instance, either Kohonen's or Linsker's "learning" mechanisms (Kohonen, 1982; Linsker, 1986).

This transforms the input to the wavelet basis. The sensitivity of these neurons is presumed inversely proportional to their central frequency. The output axons then arborize with the spatial distribution of Figure 1 among the apical dendrites of a second layer of neurons, producing receptive fields similar to those of the basal dendrites. This produces the inverse wavelet transform, so that the output of the second layer of neurons is an interpolated surface.

3.2. Examples

Figure 4(a) shows the height measurements input to a 64×64 node interpolation problem (zero-valued nodes have no data); the vertical axis is height. These data were generated using a sparse (10%) random sampling of the function $z = 100[\sin(kx) + \sin(ky)]$. Figure 4(b) shows the resulting interpolated surface. In this example, Equation 12 converged to within 1% of its true equilibrium state with a single iteration. Execution time was approximately 1 second on a Sun 4/330.

Figure 5 illustrates a second example that uses real image data and incorporates discontinuities. Shown in the top row are two 128×128 images of the same scene taken with different apertures, thus varying the depth of field. By comparing the amount of blur present in these two images depth estimates can be extracted, as first described by Pentland (1987). The resulting depth estimates are shown in Figure 5(c). Figure 5(d) shows the first iteration of the wavelet-based surface interpolation process. Point and line breaks were introduced into the estimated surface based on examination of the local strain energy, and the estimation process repeated for two additional iterations. The final estimated surface (after a total of three iterations) is shown in Figure 5(f). Execution time is approximately 15 seconds on a Sun 4/330 computer.

4. Surface interpolation by Kalman filtering

The technique of regularization is applicable only to single images or, at most, to image sequences from statically-viewed fixed environments. To integrate information across multiple views of a changing environment, the optimal estimation technique of Kalman filtering is required (Friedland, 1986).

Kalman filtering was first applied in computer vision in the mid-1980's, in order to track specific visual features across multiple images and to estimate 3-D distances (Broida and Chellappa, 1986; Faugeras et al., 1986). Recently some machine vision researchers have extended this approach to estimating

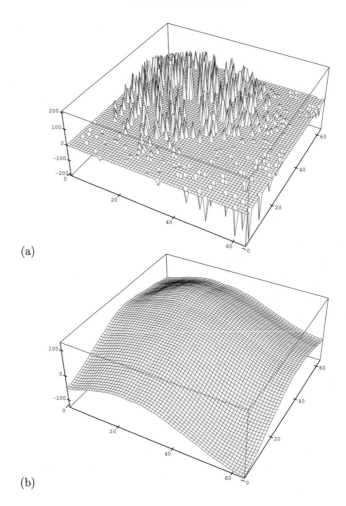

(a)

(b)

Fig. 4. *A typical surface interpolation problem. (a) Height data for a 64 × 64 node surface; these data were generated by a 10 % density random sampling of the function $z = 100[\sin(kx) + \sin(ky)]$, vertical axis is height. (b) Interpolated surface. After one iteration (approximately 1 second on a Sun 4/330) the algorithm converged to within 1% of the true equilibrium state.*

depth, optical flow, and other quantities at every image pixel (Matthies et al., 1989; Heel, 1990; Singh, 1990). However despite demonstrated accuracy and robust behavior, many researchers have remained skeptical because of the great computational cost and the complex, non-biological nature of the algorithms. Just as in the case of regularization, however, use of the wavelet transform allows construction of efficient, biologically-plausible 2-D Kalman filter mechanisms.

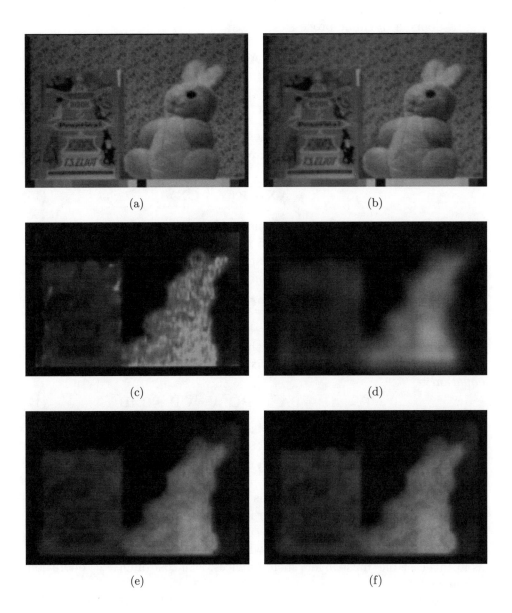

Fig. 5. *Two 128 × 128 images of a scene taken with (a) long and (b) short depth of field (data from Bove, 1989) (c) Range extracted by comparing the amount of blurring in the two images, as described in Pentland (1987) (d) first iteration of estimation, (e) second iteration, and (f) third iteration of estimation with breaking. Total time: approximately 15 seconds on a Sun 4/330 computer.*

4.1. Background: the Kalman filter

Let us define a dynamic process

$$\frac{d}{dt}\mathbf{X} = \mathbf{AX} + \mathbf{B}a \tag{13}$$

and observations

$$\mathbf{Y} = \mathbf{CX} + n \tag{14}$$

where a and n are white noise processes having known autocorrelation matrices. Then the optimal estimate $\hat{\mathbf{X}}$ of $\mathbf{X}$ is given by the following continuous *Kalman filter*

$$\frac{d}{dt}\hat{\mathbf{X}} = \mathbf{A}\hat{\mathbf{X}} + \mathbf{K}(\mathbf{Y} - \mathbf{C}\hat{\mathbf{X}}) \tag{15}$$

with correctly chosen Kalman gain matrix $\mathbf{K}$.

The gain matrix $\mathbf{K}$ in Equation 15 minimizes the covariance matrix $\mathbf{P}$ of the error $\mathbf{e} = \mathbf{X} - \hat{\mathbf{X}}$. Assuming that the cross-variance between the system excitation noise a and the observation noise n is zero, then

$$\mathbf{K} = \mathbf{PC}^T\mathcal{N}^{-1} \tag{16}$$

where the observation noise autocorrelation matrix $\mathcal{N}$ must be non-singular (Friedland, 1986). Assuming that the noise characteristics are constant, then the optimizing covariance matrix $\mathbf{P}$ is obtained by solving the *Riccati equation*

$$0 = \dot{\mathbf{P}} = \mathbf{AP} + \mathbf{PA}^T - \mathbf{PC}^T\mathcal{N}^{-1}\mathbf{CP} + \mathbf{B}\mathcal{A}\mathbf{B}^T \tag{17}$$

where $\mathcal{A}$ is the autocorrelation matrix of the acceleration noise a.

This case, where the noise characteristics are constant, is the simplest type of Kalman filter. It provides an efficient, robust method of estimating the state variables of non-stationary processes. However if this technique is applied to (for instance) estimate distance at every point in a $n \times n$ pixel image sequence with significant correlations over a distance d, it requires multiplying $n^2 \times n^2$ matrices at a cost of $O(n^2 d)$ operations per image. Even worse is the more normal case where noise characteristics are variable, as in this case one must *invert* such matrices, at a cost of $O(n^4 d)$ operations per image!

The central problem is that image pixels are correlated with one another, so that the matrices $\mathcal{N}$ and $\mathbf{K}$ have many non-zero bands. If the image pixels were independent, then $\mathcal{N}$ and $\mathbf{K}$ would typically be diagonal, allowing separate estimates to be made at each pixel. Thus if we could find a transformation that decorrelated the image pixels, then we could decouple the Kalman filter equations by posing them in the transformed space. Describing such a transform, and the resulting decoupling, is a key result of this paper.

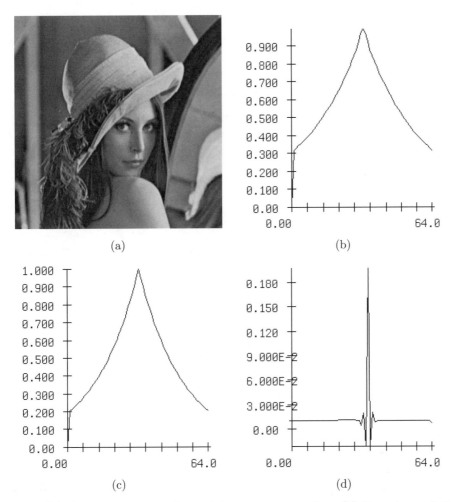

Fig. 6. *(a) An image commonly used in image processing, (b) its autocorrelation function, (c) A second-order Gauss-Markov process autocorrelation with $\rho = 0.95$, (d) Gauss-Markov autocorrelation after transformation to the wavelet coordinate system.*

4.2. *Decorrelating the image*

Figure 6 illustrates the performance of the wavelet transform at decorrelating image structure. Figure 6(a) shows an image commonly used in image processing, and Figure 6(b) shows one row from its autocorrelation matrix. Figure 6(c) shows one row from the autocorrelation matrix of a second-order Gauss-Markov process; it can be seen that the second-order Gauss-Markov process with $\rho = 0.95$ provides a good model of the image's autocorrelation structure. Figure 6(d) shows this autocorrelation function after transformation to the wavelet coordinate system. As can be seen, in the wavelet coordinate system the autocorrelation matrix is very nearly diagonal. It is this decorrelating property that has made wavelets quite useful in image compression, and will prove crucial to our Kalman filtering application.

5. Constructing a Kalman filter: an example

As an example I will show how to construct a simple Kalman filter for an observable point-by-point quantity $\mathbf{U}$ (e.g., range) and its time derivative $\dot{\mathbf{U}}$ (e.g., velocity) at each point in an $\sqrt{n} \times \sqrt{n}$ image. In state-space notation our system of equations is

$$\frac{d}{dt}\begin{bmatrix} \mathbf{U} \\ \dot{\mathbf{U}} \end{bmatrix} = \begin{bmatrix} \mathbf{0} & \mathbf{I} \\ \mathbf{0} & \mathbf{0} \end{bmatrix}\begin{bmatrix} \mathbf{U} \\ \dot{\mathbf{U}} \end{bmatrix} + \begin{bmatrix} \mathbf{0} \\ \mathbf{I} \end{bmatrix} a \tag{18}$$

where $\mathbf{U}$ and $\dot{\mathbf{U}}$ are $n \times 1$ vectors containing each point's range and velocity, $\mathbf{I}$ is the $n \times n$ identity matrix, and a is an $n \times 1$ noise vector due to the unknown accelerations of the observed points. The observed variable will be estimated point-by-point ranges $\mathbf{U_o}$:

$$\mathbf{U}_o = \mathbf{U} + n \tag{19}$$

where n is an $n \times 1$ vector of observation noise. The Kalman filter is therefore

$$\frac{d}{dt}\begin{bmatrix} \mathbf{U} \\ \dot{\mathbf{U}} \end{bmatrix} = \begin{bmatrix} \dot{\mathbf{U}} \\ \mathbf{0} \end{bmatrix} + \begin{bmatrix} \mathbf{K}_1 \\ \mathbf{K}_2 \end{bmatrix}\left(\mathbf{U}_o - \begin{bmatrix} \mathbf{I} & \mathbf{0} \end{bmatrix}\begin{bmatrix} \hat{\mathbf{U}} \\ \hat{\dot{\mathbf{U}}} \end{bmatrix}\right) \tag{20}$$

where $\mathbf{K}_1$ and $\mathbf{K}_2$ are the $n \times n$ Kalman gain matrices for velocity and acceleration, respectively.

We will assume that n and a originate from independent second-order Gauss-Markov noise processes. As shown in Figure 6, such processes are nearly completely decorrelated in a wavelet-defined coordinate system, so that they their autocorrelation matrices become nearly diagonal. Thus we have that

$$\mathcal{N} \approx \mathbf{\Phi}_w \mathbf{N} \mathbf{\Phi}_w^T \qquad \mathcal{A} \approx \mathbf{\Phi}_w \mathbf{A} \mathbf{\Phi}_w^T \tag{21}$$

where $\mathbf{N}$ and $\mathbf{A}$ are *diagonal* matrices. Given this approximation to $\mathcal{N}$ and $\mathcal{A}$ we may then use Equations 17 and 16 to determine the Kalman gain matrices, which are

$$\mathbf{K}_1 = \mathbf{\Phi}_w(2\mathbf{A}\mathbf{N}^{-1})^{1/2}\mathbf{\Phi}_w^T \qquad \mathbf{K}_2 = \mathbf{\Phi}_w(\mathbf{A}\mathbf{N}^{-1})\mathbf{\Phi}_w^T \tag{22}$$

Substituting this result into Equation 20 we obtain

$$\frac{d}{dt}\begin{bmatrix} \hat{\mathbf{U}} \\ \hat{\dot{\mathbf{U}}} \end{bmatrix} = \begin{bmatrix} \hat{\dot{\mathbf{U}}} + \mathbf{\Phi}_w(2\mathbf{A}\mathbf{N}^{-1})^{1/2}\mathbf{\Phi}_w^T\left(\mathbf{U}_o - \hat{\mathbf{U}}\right) \\ \mathbf{\Phi}_w(\mathbf{A}\mathbf{N}^{-1})\mathbf{\Phi}_w^T\left(\mathbf{U}_o - \hat{\mathbf{U}}\right) \end{bmatrix} \tag{23}$$

Letting $\tilde{\mathbf{U}} = \mathbf{\Phi}_w^T \mathbf{U}$, and premultiplying by $\mathbf{\Phi}_w^T$, we obtain

$$
\frac{d}{dt} \begin{bmatrix} \hat{\tilde{\mathbf{U}}} \\ \hat{\tilde{\mathbf{U}}} \end{bmatrix} = \begin{bmatrix} \hat{\dot{\tilde{\mathbf{U}}}} + (2\mathbf{A}\mathbf{N}^{-1})^{1/2} \left(\tilde{\mathbf{U}}_o - \hat{\tilde{\mathbf{U}}} \right) \\ (\mathbf{A}\mathbf{N}^{-1}) \left(\tilde{\mathbf{U}}_o - \hat{\tilde{\mathbf{U}}} \right) \end{bmatrix} \tag{24}
$$

as $\mathbf{\Phi}_w^T \mathbf{\Phi}_w = \mathbf{I}$.

That is, in the wavelet coordinate system defined by $\mathbf{\Phi}_w$, the Kalman filter equations are decoupled into n independent two-variable Kalman filters. The major consequence of this decoupling is that only $O(n)$ computations and $O(n)$ storage locations are required. Even in the variable-noise case (not discussed here due to space limitations) only $O(n)$ computations are required, as even space-varying Markov $\mathcal{N}$ are approximately diagonal in the wavelet coordinate system (Simoncelli and Adelson, 1990).

Because the equations are decoupled, we may write the Kalman filter separately for each point in the wavelet coordinate system. We can now formulate a finite-difference position prediction for time $t + \Delta t$:

$$
\hat{\tilde{u}}_i^{t+\Delta t} = \hat{\tilde{u}}_i^t + \hat{\dot{\tilde{u}}}_i^t \Delta t + k_i \left(\tilde{u}_{o,i}^t - \hat{\tilde{u}}_i^t \right) \tag{25}
$$

where $\hat{\tilde{u}}_i$ is the ith element of $\hat{\tilde{\mathbf{U}}}$, and $k_i = (a_i/n_i)\Delta t^2 + (2a_i/n_i)^{1/2}\Delta t$.

5.1. A possible neural mechanism

Equation 25 is exactly the central-difference update rule for direct time integration of the second order differential equation

$$
\tilde{m}_i \ddot{\tilde{u}}_i + \tilde{u}_i = \tilde{u}_{o,i} \tag{26}
$$

which describes the time behavior of a spring with unit stiffness, mass $\tilde{m}_i$, and loads $\tilde{u}_{o,i}$. Thus the Kalman filter equations may be interpreted as hysteresis that integrates data over time by giving a certain amount of mass or inertia to the previous estimates.

This suggests the neural mechanism illustrated in Figure 7(a). The input measurements $\mathbf{U}_o^t$ are passed through a layer of neurons with receptive fields such as are shown in Figure 1 at each location. This computes $\tilde{\mathbf{U}}_o^t = \mathbf{\Phi}_w^T \mathbf{U}_o^t$, the wavelet transform of $\mathbf{U}_o^t$. The activity of each neuron is then averaged with predictions based on the previous estimates, using a weighting that reflects the relative confidence of the old estimates and new measurements, thus computing new estimates $\tilde{\mathbf{U}}^t$ in the wavelet coordinate system. Finally, each neuron's output is summed with a spatial distribution equal to its receptive field, thus computing the inverse wavelet transform and obtaining the estimated values in the original coordinate system $\hat{\mathbf{U}}^t = \mathbf{\Phi}_w \hat{\tilde{\mathbf{U}}}^t$.

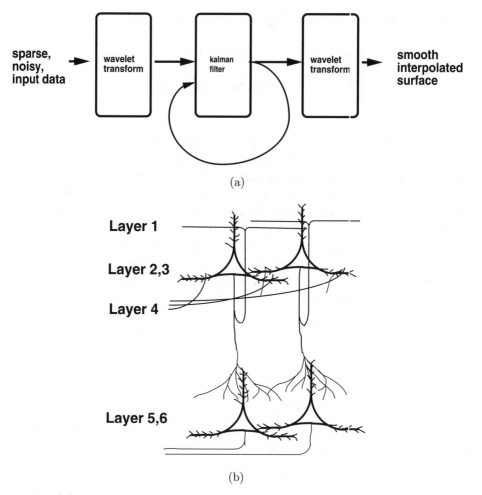

Fig. 7. *(a) A biological mechanism for Kalman filtering, (b) one possible neural implementation.*

Figure 7(b) illustrates one way this computation can be mapped onto neurons; it is identical to the mechanism of Figure 3 except for the addition of a feedback loop.

As in Figure 3, the input layer arborizes very locally, with the pyramidal cell's basal dendrites producing receptive fields shaped as in Figure 1. This transforms the input to the wavelet basis.

Recurrent axons from these neurons form the core of the Kalman feedback loop, by allowing predictions based on the previous instant's activity to be averaged with new inputs. Such prediction might be accomplished by hysteresis, however the details of such a neural mechanism are far from clear. Finally, the output axons then arborize with the spatial distribution of Figure 1 among the apical dendrites of a second layer of neurons, producing

Fig. 8. *(a) The sixth frame of a fly-though of Yosemite valley, (b) the true range map associated with frame 6, (c) range plus additive correlated noise with a signal-to-noise ration of 1:1, (d) Kalman filter range estimates at frame 6.*

receptive fields similar to those of the basal dendrites. This produces the inverse wavelet transform, so that the output of the second layer of neurons is the new estimated surface.

5.2. Estimation examples

Figure 8(a) shows the sixth frame from a synthetic image sequence of Yosemite valley from the vantage point of a small plane flying down the center of the valley floor. A sequence of corresponding range images, the sixth of which is shown in Figure 8(b), were generated by reprojecting a digital terrain map of the area from the same set of viewpoints. In these range images brighter points are closer to the camera, and darker points are further away. These 128×128 range images were then corrupted by the addition of uniformly distributed *correlated* noise ($Power(\omega) = \omega^{-0.2}$ where ω is spatial frequency) resulting in a sequence of range images with a signal-to-noise ratio of 1:1, as is illustrated by Figure 8(c).

Accurate estimates of pixel-by-pixel range cannot be obtained by averaging successive frames of the noisy range images, as the range values vary as a nonlinear function of both space and time. This nonlinear variation is caused by the curved camera path, and by the resulting perspective distortion. Similarly, regularization of individual frames does not produce accurate estimates of range due to the large amount of correlated noise.

Therefore a Kalman filter was constructed as described above. Both range and velocity were estimated, with breaks introduced into the surface based on internal strain energy. The computation time was approximately 5 seconds per frame on a Sun 4/330.

The estimated range after frame 6 is shown in Figure 8(d). By comparing the estimated range shown in (d) to the true range shown in (b), it can be seen that a good estimate of surface shape is obtained. At frame 6 the mean per-pixel error in the position estimate was 8.5% of the initial error, an improvement of 21 db. The mean per-pixel error in the velocity estimate was 5.5% of the initial error, an improvement of 25 db.

6. Summary

I have described a method for surface interpolation by regularization that uses orthogonal wavelets to obtain good interpolations with only a very few iterations. The method has a simple biological implementation, and its performance was illustrated with wavelets that accurately model human spatial frequency sensitivity.

For non-stationary input, however, it is necessary to use a Kalman filter formulation to integrate information across time. Normally the technique is computationally expensive, as it requires large matrix multiplications or inversions. By decorrelating the image using a wavelet transform, however, the Kalman filter equations can be decoupled, greatly decreasing the cost of solution. As in the case of regularization, this wavelet transform technique leads to a simple and biologically-plausible implementation.

Uncertainty models for $2\frac{1}{2}$-D and 3-D surfaces

Richard Szeliski

Computer vision relies heavily on building $2\frac{1}{2}$-D and 3-D models of surfaces as an intermediate representation. These surfaces are used to integrate information from multiple visual cues and to accumulate information over time. To make the best use of such information, it is important to model the uncertainty associated with each measurement and the resulting uncertainty in surface shape. This paper discusses how to model and estimate this uncertainty and how to make use of this information in sequential estimation algorithms. The formulation is developed first for $2\frac{1}{2}$-D depth or distance maps, and later extended to true 3-D surfaces. A new coupled depth-intensity model is developed to improve the accuracy of these algorithms. The paper also compares surface-based and feature-based representations of depth, and proposes a unified representation which encompasses both.

1. Introduction

Surfaces are widely used in computer vision as an intermediate representation for modeling the shape of the observer's environment. When combined with other attributes such as color and reflectivity, the geometric description provided by surfaces is sufficient to account for most of the optical phenomena seen in real-world images. Surface descriptions can be used directly in a number of vision-based tasks such as navigation (obstacle avoidance), manipulation (choice of grasp points), and automatic 3-D model acquisition. They can also be used as an intermediate stage in object recognition algorithms, since they provide a more stable and useful description than the original intensity images.

In human and animate vision, multiple retinotopic maps are used to extract higher-level features and to remove or attenuate the effects of environmental conditions such as illumination. Recent psychophysical experiments suggest that the perception of coherent surfaces is an essential component of the disambiguation of rivalrous stereograms and the perception of depth from motion. It is thus quite probable that mechanisms for accurately estimating surface properties such as depth and orientation are embedded into animate visual systems.

Models of visible surface perception are usually selected either on the basis of a computational theory or through fitting to empirical neurophysiological or psychophysical data. An alternative approach is to use probabilistic models, which are well suited for dealing with the noisy nature of real-world sensors and for incorporating external (*a priori*) knowledge about problem domains. Probabilistic models are particularly useful when we aggregate information from multiple modalities (multisensor fusion) and/or incorporate information over time (sequential estimation). They not only allow the computation of optimal estimates, but also give a quantitative measure of the *uncertainty* in these estimates.

The application of probabilistic models to surface descriptions is a fairly recent development (Geman and Geman, 1984; Szeliski, 1989). This is because the probabilistic modeling of surfaces poses a number of fundamental difficulties. First, the high dimensionality of surface-based descriptions makes it expensive to model higher order statistics such as covariances. Fortunately, Markov Random Field models (Geman and Geman, 1984) can help us here. Second, while parametric models of surfaces have attractive properties such as viewpoint invariance, the automatic selection of parameterizations remains an open problem. Third, while researchers have developed optimal sequential estimation algorithms for pure geometric entities such as points, lines, and planes (Ayache, 1991), surfaces cannot yet be estimated with comparable accuracy.

This paper surveys the modeling of uncertainty in two and three-dimensional surfaces and provides novel solutions to some of these outstanding problems. We begin with a review of visible surface modeling and Bayesian uncertainty modeling applied to $2^1/_2$-D surfaces. We show how these probabilistic models can be used to incrementally estimate surfaces from sequences of optic flow measurements. We introduce a new coupled depth and intensity model and show how it improves the convergence rate of incremental surface estimation. Turning to 3-D surfaces, we review parametric surfaces and discuss the difficulty of determining good parameterizations for complex objects. We propose a solution which involves sequentially estimating surface elements and then postprocessing them with a particle-based surface interpolator. We present a comparison of surface-based and feature-based representations, and close with a proposal for unifying the two representations.

2. Regularized surface estimation

The traditional approach to modeling visible surfaces in low-level and intermediate-level vision is to use a collection of two-dimensional piecewise continuous functions computed directly from input images. Such representations were first suggested by Marr (1978), whose $2\frac{1}{2}$-*dimensional* ($2\frac{1}{2}$-*D) sketch* encodes local surface orientation and distance to the viewer as well as discontinuities in the orientation and distance maps, and by Barrow and Tenenbaum (1978), whose *intrinsic images* represent scene characteristics such as distance, orientation, reflectance, and illumination in multiple retinotopic maps.

The computational theory of visible surface reconstruction has been formalized using a number of techniques, including variational principles (Grimson, 1983), regularization (Poggio et al., 1985; Terzopoulos, 1988), and physically-based modeling (Terzopoulos et al., 1987). In regularization, a visible surface is computed from a set of constraints d (such as those provided by stereo matches) by finding the function u which minimizes the weighted sum of two energy functionals

$$\mathcal{E}(u) = \mathcal{E}_{\mathrm{d}}(u, d) + \lambda \mathcal{E}_{\mathrm{s}}(u). \tag{1}$$

The *data compatibility* functional $\mathcal{E}_{\mathrm{d}}(u, d)$ measures the distance between the solution and the sampled data d, and the *stabilizing* functional $\mathcal{E}_{\mathrm{s}}(u)$ measures the smoothness of the solution. The regularization parameter λ controls the amount of smoothing performed.

An example of regularization applied to visible surface modeling is the interpolation of a piecewise continuous surface $u(x, y)$ through a sparse set of data points $\{(x_i, y_i, d_i)\}$. The data compatibility term in this case is a weighted sum of squares

$$\mathcal{E}_{\mathrm{d}}(u, d) = \frac{1}{2} \sum_i c_i [u(x_i, y_i) - d_i]^2, \tag{2}$$

where the confidence c_i is inversely related to the variance of the measurement d_i, i.e., $c_i = \sigma_i^{-2}$. The smoothness functional is

$$\mathcal{E}_{\mathrm{s}}(u) = \frac{1}{2} \iint \rho(x, y)\{[1 - \tau(x, y)][u_x^2 + u_y^2] + \tau(x, y)[u_{xx}^2 + 2u_{xy}^2 + u_{yy}^2]\}\, dx\, dy, \tag{3}$$

where $\rho(x, y)$ is a *rigidity* function, and $\tau(x, y)$ is a *tension* function (Terzopoulos, 1986b). The rigidity and tension functions are used to introduce depth ($\rho(x, y) = 0$) and orientation ($\tau(x, y) = 0$) discontinuities (Figures 1a and 1b). The minimum energy solution of the above system is a *thin plate surface under tension* (Terzopoulos, 1986b).

To compute a numerical solution to a regularized problem, we first convert the functionals $\mathcal{E}_{\mathrm{d}}(u, d)$ and $\mathcal{E}_{\mathrm{s}}(u)$ to discrete energy functions using finite element analysis (Terzopoulos, 1988; Szeliski, 1989). If we fix the continuity control functions $\rho(x, y)$ and $\tau(x, y)$ and discretize the surface using a fine rectangular mesh, these energy functions are quadratic with a simple regular structure. The data compatibility function becomes

$$E_{\mathrm{d}}(\vec{u}, \vec{d}) = \frac{1}{2}(\vec{u} - \vec{d})^T \mathbf{A}_{\mathrm{d}}(\vec{u} - \vec{d}), \tag{4}$$

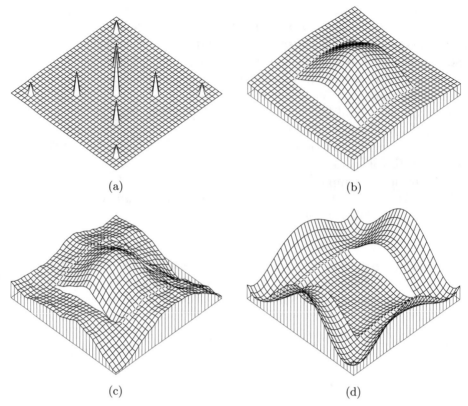

(a)   (b)

(c)   (d)

Fig. 1. *Sample data and interpolated surface: (a) data points, (b) thin plate solution with two depth and two orientation discontinuities, (c) random fractal sample from posterior distribution, (d) uncertainty (variance) field (see Section 3). The depth discontinuities are shown as missing line segments, while the orientation discontinuities appear as white dots at the nodes.*

where $\vec{u}$ is the discretized surface, $\vec{d}$ are the data points, and $\mathbf{A}_d$ is a diagonal matrix (for uncorrelated sensor noise). The discrete smoothness energy is

$$E_s(\vec{u}) = \frac{1}{2}\vec{u}^T \mathbf{A}_s \vec{u}, \tag{5}$$

where the *stiffness matrix* $\mathbf{A}_s$ is sparse and banded, with a bandwidth equal to one of the image dimensions. The rows of $\mathbf{A}_s$ can be described in terms of computational molecules (Terzopoulos, 1988).

The resulting total energy function $E(\vec{u})$ is quadratic in $\vec{u}$

$$E(\vec{u}) = \frac{1}{2}\vec{u}^T \mathbf{A}\vec{u} - \vec{u}^T \vec{b} + c, \tag{6}$$

with

$$\mathbf{A} = \mathbf{A}_d + \lambda \mathbf{A}_s \quad \text{and} \quad \mathbf{b} = \mathbf{A}_d \vec{d}. \tag{7}$$

The energy function has a minimum at $\vec{u}^*$, the solution to the linear system of algebraic equations

$$\mathbf{A}\vec{u} = \vec{b}. \tag{8}$$

The energy can thus be rewritten as

$$E(\vec{u}) = \frac{1}{2}(\vec{u} - \vec{u}^*)^T \mathbf{A}(\vec{u} - \vec{u}^*) + k. \tag{9}$$

Once we have derived the discrete energy function, we can use a variety of techniques to find the minimum energy solution $\vec{u}^*$. For large sparse systems such as the ones obtained with our fine discretization, the most efficient and parallelizable techniques are iterative relaxation algorithms such as successive overrelaxation (Blake and Zisserman, 1987), multigrid relaxation (Terzopoulos, 1986a), and hierarchical basis conjugate gradient descent (Szeliski, 1990a). Alternative multiresolution representations of the surface can also be used (Szeliski and Terzopoulos, 1989b; Szeliski, 1989). The design of efficient and robust algorithms for computing visible surface representations, which includes the important problem of discontinuity detection, has been the subject of a great deal of research in computer vision (see Blake and Zisserman, 1987; Terzopoulos, 1988; Szeliski, 1989 for reviews).

3. Bayesian surface estimation

A Bayesian model is a statistical formulation of an estimation problem that consists of two separate components. The first component, the *prior model*, $p(\vec{u})$, describes the probability distribution of our state $\vec{u}$ (in this case, a surface) in the absence of any sensed data. The second component, the *sensor model*, $p(\vec{d}|\vec{u})$, describes the probability of sensing values $\vec{d}$ if the surface $\vec{u}$ is viewed. These two probabilistic models can be combined to obtain a *posterior model*, $p(\vec{u}|\vec{d})$, which allows us to draw the backward inference, describing the probability that the surface $\vec{u}$ has been viewed given that data values $\vec{d}$ have been sensed. To compute this posterior model we use Bayes' Rule

$$p(\vec{u}|\vec{d}) = \frac{p(\vec{d}|\vec{u})\, p(\vec{u})}{p(\vec{d})}, \tag{10}$$

with the normalizing denominator

$$p(\vec{d}) = \sum_{\vec{u}} p(\vec{d}|\vec{u}).$$

When applied to surface representations, the prior model is used to bias the solutions towards smooth surfaces, i.e., to encode the smoothness constraint (Szeliski, 1987; Szeliski, 1989). This can be done conveniently by using a Gibbs (or Boltzmann) distribution of the form

$$p(\vec{u}) = \frac{1}{Z_\mathrm{s}} \exp(-E_\mathrm{s}(\vec{u})), \tag{11}$$

where $E_\mathrm{s}(\vec{u})$ is the discrete smoothness energy defined in (5), and Z_s (called the *partition function*) is a normalizing constant. Because the energy function $E_\mathrm{s}(\vec{u})$ can be written as a sum of local clique energies, the prior distribution (11) is a Markov Random Field (Geman and Geman, 1984).

For surface interpolation, the sensor model is a discrete sampling of the surface $\vec{u}$ with white (independent) Gaussian noise added to each measurement. This multivariate Gaussian distribution can be written as

$$p(\vec{d}|\vec{u}) = \frac{1}{Z_\mathrm{d}} \exp(-E_\mathrm{d}(\vec{u}, \vec{d})), \tag{12}$$

where $E_\mathrm{d}(\vec{u}, \vec{d})$ is given by (4). More sophisticated sensors models can easily be developed and used within this Bayesian framework (Szeliski, 1989; Szeliski and Terzopoulos, 1991).

We are now in a position to derive the posterior distribution $p(\vec{u}|\vec{d})$ using Bayes' Rule. From (10), (11) and (12) we have

$$p(\vec{u}|\vec{d}) = \frac{p(\vec{d}|\vec{u})\, p(\vec{u})}{p(\vec{d})} = \frac{1}{Z} \exp(-E(\vec{u})), \tag{13}$$

where

$$E(\vec{u}) = E_\mathrm{d}(\vec{u}, \vec{d}) + E_\mathrm{s}(\vec{u}). \tag{14}$$

The *maximum a posteriori* (MAP) estimate $\hat{\vec{u}}$, i.e., the value of $\vec{u}$ that maximizes the conditional probability $p(\vec{u}|\vec{d})$, is the same as the surface $\vec{u}^*$ which minimizes the discrete energy $E(\vec{u})$ obtained from regularization.

While energy-based and Bayesian modeling may ultimately yield the same estimate, there are several advantages to the probabilistic formulation. First, the statistical assumptions corresponding to a smoothness constraint can be explored by randomly generating samples from the prior model (Szeliski, 1987). This also gives us a powerful method for generating stochastic surfaces such as fractals (Figure 1c) (Szeliski and Terzopoulos, 1989a). Second, the data constraint energies can be derived in a principled fashion from the known noise characteristics of the sensors (Szeliski, 1989; Szeliski and Terzopoulos, 1991). Third, Bayesian modeling can be used to integrate multiple measurements (Matthies et al., 1989), as we show in Section 4. Fourth, the uncertainty in the posterior model can be quantified, as we show below. Additional uses and advantages of the probabilistic modeling of visual primitives can be found in (Szeliski, 1989; Ayache, 1991; Szeliski and Terzopoulos, 1991).

To compute the uncertainty in our posterior estimate, we note that the posterior distribution $p(\vec{u}|\vec{d})$ given by (13) is a Gibbs distribution with a quadratic energy given by (9). This distribution is a multivariate Gaussian with mean $\vec{u}^*$ and covariance $\mathbf{A}^{-1}$. Thus, to characterize the uncertainty, we need only invert the matrix $\mathbf{A}$.

In practice, computing and storing $\mathbf{A}^{-1}$ is not feasible for surfaces, because while $\mathbf{A}$ is sparse and banded, $\mathbf{A}^{-1}$ is not. We can obtain a reduced description of the uncertainty if we compute only the diagonal elements of $\mathbf{A}^{-1}$, i.e., the variance at each point on the surface (Szeliski, 1989). We have developed two methods to compute this variance. The first involves computing the values sequentially by replacing the right hand side of (8) with unit vectors. Each solution $\vec{u}_i$ to the system

$$\mathbf{A}\vec{u}_i = \vec{e}_i, \qquad e_{ij} = \delta_{ij}$$

is a row of $\mathbf{A}^{-1}$ and indicates the covariance between the ith surface point and all others. By keeping only the ith element of $\vec{u}_i$, we obtain the variance field, which measures local uncertainty, as shown in Figure 1(d). The second method uses a Monte-Carlo approach which generates random samples from the posterior distribution by adding a controlled amount of Gaussian noise to the relaxation step of an iterative solver for (8) and then accumulates the desired statistics (Szeliski, 1989).

The uncertainty modeling method we have developed is just one of several possible approaches. Spatial likelihood maps have been developed for surfaces represented in spherical coordinates (Christ, 1987). Occupancy maps (Elfes and Matthies, 1987) indicate the likelihood of a surface being present in a two- or three-dimensional array. The advantage of our energy-based formulation is that it explicitly models the correlation between adjacent points on the surface.

Uncertainty maps can be used to grow a "confidence region" around the surface estimate, indicating an envelope within which the surface is likely to lie. This can be useful in navigation and manipulation applications, and can also be used to determine where additional sensing would be helpful (active vision) (Waithe and Ferrie, 1991). However, the most useful application of uncertainty modeling is in the sequential estimation of surface shape, as we discuss next.

4. Sequential surface estimation

Bayesian models of surfaces are particularly well suited to integrating information from multiple measurements (multisensor fusion) or estimating surface shapes over time (sequential estimation). When the surfaces or observer are moving or changing over time, our problem becomes one of dynamic system estimation. Such problems can be solved using either batch processing techniques such as epipolar plane image analysis (Bolles et al., 1987) or by sequential estimation algorithms such as the Kalman filter (Gelb,

1974). The advantage of the Kalman filter is that estimates are available immediately and that the storage costs are reduced.

The Kalman filter extends the Bayesian model by adding a *system model* to the prior and sensor models. In the Kalman filter, the prior model is a multivariate Gaussian with mean $\vec{\hat{u}}_0$ and covariance $\mathbf{P}_0$ denoted by

$$\vec{u} \sim N(\vec{\hat{u}}_0, \mathbf{P}_0). \tag{15}$$

For surface estimation problems, we set $\vec{\hat{u}}_0 = \mathbf{0}$ and $\mathbf{P}_0^{-1} = \mathbf{A}_s$. The sensor model relates each new measurement vector $\vec{d}_k$ to the current state $\vec{u}_k$ through a measurement matrix $\mathbf{H}_k$ and the addition of Gaussian noise $\vec{r}_k$,

$$\vec{d}_k = \mathbf{H}_k \vec{u}_k + \vec{r}_k, \quad \vec{r}_k \sim N(0, \mathbf{R}_k). \tag{16}$$

For surface interpolation, we let $\mathbf{H}_k = \mathbf{I}$ and $\mathbf{R}_k^{-1} = \mathbf{A}_d$. The system model describes the evolution of the current state vector $\vec{u}_k$ over time using a known transition matrix $\mathbf{F}_k$ and the addition of Gaussian noise $\vec{q}_k$,

$$\vec{u}_k = \mathbf{F}_k \vec{u}_{k-1} + \vec{q}_k, \quad \vec{q}_k \sim N(0, \mathbf{Q}_k). \tag{17}$$

To compute the current state estimate $\vec{\hat{u}}_k$, we first *predict* or *extrapolate* the old estimate $\vec{\hat{u}}_{k-1}$ and its covariance $\mathbf{P}_{k-1}$

$$\vec{\hat{u}}_k = \mathbf{F}_k \vec{\hat{u}}_{k-1} \tag{18}$$

$$\vec{\hat{P}}_k = \mathbf{F}_k \mathbf{P}_{k-1} \mathbf{F}_k^T + \mathbf{Q}_k. \tag{19}$$

We then *correct* or *update* the estimate and its covariance

$$\vec{\hat{u}}_k = \vec{\hat{u}}_k + \mathbf{P}_k \mathbf{H}_k^T \mathbf{R}_k^{-1} (\vec{d}_k - \mathbf{H}_k \vec{\hat{u}}_k) \tag{20}$$

$$\mathbf{P}_k^{-1} = \vec{\hat{P}}_k^{-1} + \mathbf{H}_k^T \mathbf{R}_k^{-1} \mathbf{H}_k. \tag{21}$$

Of the above four equations, the first three are expressed in terms of the covariance matrices $\mathbf{P}_k$, while the fourth uses the inverse covariance (or *information*) matrices (which we can denote by $\mathbf{A}_k$). For surface modeling, we observed in Section 3 that the information matrices are sparse, while the covariance matrices are not. Our implementation of the Kalman filter for surfaces therefore uses information matrices to model the uncertainty. This involves performing a linear system solution of

$$\mathbf{A}_k \Delta \vec{\hat{u}}_k = \mathbf{H}_k^T \mathbf{R}_k^{-1} (\vec{d}_k - \mathbf{H}_k \vec{\hat{u}}_k)$$

in (20), and finding a way to implement (19) using inverse covariances. This can be achieved by partitioning the information matrices into a diagonal matrix arising from the measurements ($\mathbf{H}_k^T \mathbf{R}_k^{-1} \mathbf{H}_k^T$ in (21)), and a banded matrix encoding the smoothness constraint ($\mathbf{P}_0^{-1}$) which is assumed not to vary over time (Szeliski, 1989). Similar ideas can be applied to other physically-based models in computer vision (Szeliski and Terzopoulos, 1991).

To demonstrate the utility of the sequential estimation of surfaces, we have developed an algorithm that builds a dense depth map from a sequence of

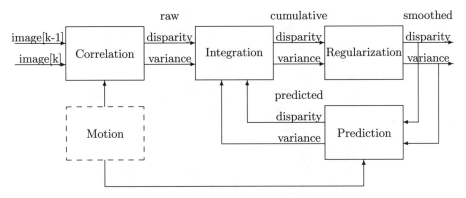

Fig. 2. *Block diagram of the sequential depth estimation algorithm*

images where the motion of the observer is known (Matthies et al., 1989). The input to this algorithm consists of optic flow fields computed from successive pairs of images. These flow fields are converted into *disparity* (inverse depth) maps, which are then aggregated over time using the 2-D Kalman filter (Figure 2). Regularization-based smoothing is used to reduce the noise in the flow measurements and to fill in areas where flow was not reliably estimated. A key feature of this method is that the variance of each flow measurement is estimated locally from the shape of the correlation surface, and this variance is propagated through the Kalman filter (Matthies et al., 1989). To keep the representation *iconic* (2-D image-based), the disparity and uncertainty maps are warped (re-sampled) between frames using the current disparity estimates to predict the amount of inter-frame motion. The result of applying this algorithm to a sequence of 10 images is shown in Figure 3.

5. Joint estimation of depth and intensity

While the incremental computation of visible surfaces based on probabilistic surface modeling has produced impressive results, its theoretical convergence rate is poorer than that of feature-based approaches (Matthies et al., 1989). An intuitive way to see why is to consider disparity estimation as line fitting in a spatio-temporal cube of image data. An edge-based estimator which estimates both the disparity (slope) and sub-pixel location (intercept) of these lines has a variance of $\sigma_F^2(n) \propto 1/n^3$, where n is the number of images (Matthies et al., 1989). An iconic algorithm which averages successive displacements is equivalent to a stereo match between the first and last image, and therefore has $\sigma_I^2(n) \propto 1/n^2$.

The reduced rate of convergence occurs because we ignore the temporal correlations between successive flow measurement (Matthies et al., 1989). One way of compensating for such correlated measurements is to introduce additional state variables (Gelb, 1974). In our case, the most natural choice

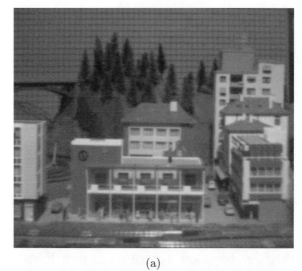

(a)

(b)

Fig. 3. *Depth map computed from image sequence: (a) first frame of image sequence, (b) intensity-coded depth map computed from combined sequence of horizontal and vertical motions*

of variable is the intensity distribution over the surface. To achieve the optimal rate of convergence, we estimate both the disparity and intensity fields and model the correlation between these two fields.

In our new formulation, it is no longer necessary to use a separate flow computation module (although we may wish to use one initially to provide more robust disparity estimates). Instead, we use a single measurement equation which relates new images to the underlying disparity and intensity fields. The equations defining the temporal evolution of the intensity f and disparity d fields (assuming no occlusions) for a camera translating horizontally are

$$f(x + \Delta t\, d(x, y, t), y, t + \Delta t) = f(x, y, t) \tag{22}$$
$$d(x + \Delta t\, d(x, y, t), y, t + \Delta t) = d(x, y, t). \tag{23}$$

Given a sequence of noisy sampled images

$$g(x, y, t) = f(x, y, t) + n(x, y, t), \tag{24}$$

we could solve for the intensity and disparity at time T using a batch minimization algorithm. With the addition of appropriate smoothness constraints on f and d, this would be *regularized depth from motion*.

If we wish to estimate the current intensity and disparity images in an incremental fashion, we can use the *extended Kalman filter* (Gelb, 1974, p. 188). In this model, we replace (17) and (16) with

$$\vec{u}_k = \vec{f}_k(\vec{u}_{k-1}) + \vec{q}_k, \quad \vec{q}_k \sim N(0, \mathbf{Q}_k) \tag{25}$$
$$\vec{d}_k = \vec{h}_k(\vec{u}_k) + \vec{r}_k, \quad \vec{r}_k \sim N(0, \mathbf{R}_k). \tag{26}$$

We then use the same updating equations as before with

$$\mathbf{F}_k = \frac{\partial \vec{f}_k}{\partial \vec{u}}(\vec{\hat{u}}_{k-1}) \tag{27}$$

$$\mathbf{H}_k = \frac{\partial \vec{h}_k}{\partial \vec{u}}(\vec{\hat{u}}_k) \tag{28}$$

To apply the extended Kalman filter to (22) and (23), we must discretize the f and d functions in both space and time. This leads to a set of warping equations

$$f_k(i, j) = \text{interpolate}(\{i + d_{k-1}(i, j), j, f_{k-1}(i, j)\})(i, j) \tag{29}$$
$$d_k(i, j) = \text{interpolate}(\{i + d_{k-1}(i, j), j, d_{k-1}(i, j)\})(i, j), \tag{30}$$

i.e., the new intensity and disparity fields are obtained by interpolating through the collection of shifted intensity and disparity estimates and then re-sampling (Matthies et al., 1989). The system transition matrix $\mathbf{F}_k$, which is the Jacobian of the above set of non-linear equations, models the dependence of the new states on the old states. In particular, $\mathbf{F}_k$ contains entries which link the new intensities to the old disparities through an approximation to the intensity gradient.

Because the covariance matrix of the predicted fields models the correlations between the intensity and disparity estimates, a simple discrete measurement equation based on (24) is sufficient to update both fields. A disadvantage of the above formulation is that if the previous estimate $\vec{\hat{u}}_{k-1}$ of $f(x, y)$ and $d(x, y)$ was not accurate, then the value of $\mathbf{F}_k$ will not be very good. A better solution is to use (29) itself as the measurement equation. We can then use the *iterated extended Kalman filter* (Gelb, 1974, p. 190) to repeatedly calculate $\vec{\bar{u}}_k$ and $\mathbf{H}_k$ until good convergence is obtained.

While it has yet to be tested empirically, the joint modeling of intensity and disparity has the potential for improving the accuracy of depth from motion algorithms and for simplifying their implementation.

6. 3-D surface reconstruction

The computation of visible surface representations (2-D depth or elevation maps) is a useful step in the construction of higher-level shape descriptions, and can also be used directly in a number of applications such as obstacle avoidance. For many vision applications, however, we need a representation that can integrate surface descriptions from widely disparate views. Such applications require the use of full 3-D surface models, which are generally viewpoint invariant and can represent parts of the surface that are not currently visible. For example, we may wish to reconstruct the 3-D shape of an object as it rotates in front of a camera (Szeliski, 1991). Such 3-D models could be used to "learn" new objects in a recognition system, or to "reverse engineer" computer-aided design (CAD) models from real-world objects. Alternatively, we may wish to model the portion of the environment behind a mobile robot which was previously seen but is not currently visible.

Choosing an appropriate representation for a 3-D surface is not as straightforward as it was for visible surfaces, where scalar functions defined over two-dimensional domains provided a natural and convenient representation. The simplest way to extend visible surfaces to 3-D is to use *parametric surfaces*, where the 3-D coordinates of a surface $\vec{x} = [X\ Y\ Z]$ are functions of the underlying parameters $(u, v) \in [0, 1]^2$. The elastic properties of the surface can be specified by applying the same smoothness energies as were used for the piecewise continuous spline under tension (3) to each component of $\vec{x}$ independently. The resulting patch behaves somewhat like a deformable sheet of paper or a thin stretchable membrane.

To obtain a 3-D surface more suited to modeling true 3-D objects, we can "seam" together the two opposite edges of the parametric sheet $u = 0$ and $u = 1$ to obtain a deformable tube model. The *symmetry-seeking models* of Terzopoulos, Witkin, and Kass (Terzopoulos et al., 1987), couple this tube model $\vec{x}_T(u, v)$ with a deformable spine $\vec{x}_S(v)$ to obtain a physically-based model that responds to image forces. A simpler, though less flexible, version of this model is a cylindrical representation, where the radius is a function of angle and height $r(\theta, z)$. Other primitives that may be suitable for modeling 3-D surfaces include *generalized cylinders* (Brooks et al., 1979), where an arbitrary cross section is swept along a spine curve, and *superquadrics* (Pentland, 1986).

Probabilistic surface modeling can be applied to 3-D parametric surfaces just as easily as it was to $2^1/_2$-D surfaces. Because surface modeling is always a combination of internal smoothness constraints and external data fitting constraints, we can still build prior and sensor models to reflect these two components, using the Gibbs distribution to link energies with probabilities. As the energies become more complicated, we may no longer be able to model the surface as a correlated Gaussian field (because the energies are not quadratic), but we can still develop appropriate Bayesian models. Sequential estimation algorithms based on the extended Kalman filter can still be developed, although they will no longer be optimal compared to batch algorithms. Nevertheless, the same advantages originally obtained using probabilistic models, which include the ability to sensibly weight new measurements and to model the uncertainty in our estimates, are still available (Terzopoulos and Metaxas, 1991).

A potential disadvantage of a parametric representation is that many different parameterizations can be used to represent the same surface, which can complicate the matching of surfaces in recognition tasks. A solution to this problem is to reparameterize the sheet using canonical parameters based on local curvature (Vemuri et al., 1989). A more serious disadvantage is that the topology of the parametric surface (and sometimes even its rough shape) must be known in advance before it can be fitted to data. In computer graphics, where the emphasis is on modeling, this problem has attracted a fair deal of attention (Loop and DeRose, 1990). In computer vision, the application of parametric surfaces has been limited to simple topologies such as sheets (Vemuri et al., 1989) or cylinders (Terzopoulos et al., 1987). A more general solution, based on systems of interacting particles, will be presented at the end of the next section.

7. Incremental 3-D patch/point estimation

To investigate the feasibility of incremental 3-D surface modeling, we have been studying the construction of such models from image sequences of objects rotating in front of a camera (Szeliski, 1990a). In our setup, a single object rotates on a turntable which has been marked so that the current angle of rotation can easily be determined (Figure 4a). Because the camera parameters have already been determined in a pre-calibration phase, we know for each image the exact 3-D transformation relating the turntable (object) coordinates to the camera coordinates. Our problem is thus the standard depth from known motion problem, except that we wish to recover a full 3-D shape description. We call this problem *shape from rotation*, to emphasize that we wish to integrate and represent shape information from a full 360° range of views.

Many different techniques could be used to extract 3-D information from this sequence of images. One of the simplest is to compute a bounding

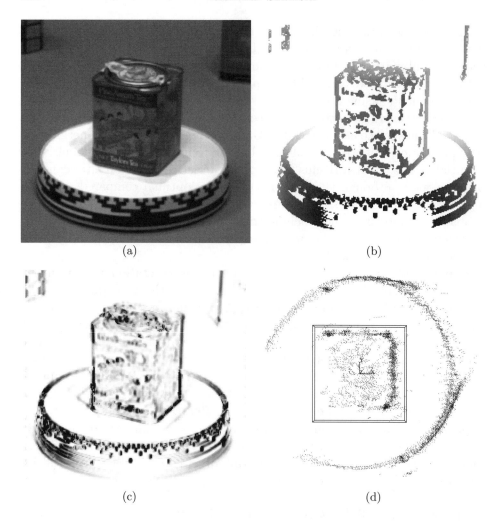

(a)   (b)

(c)   (d)

Fig. 4. *Flow computed from* assam *image sequence: (a) first image in sequence (b) depth map from flow (darker is nearer) (c) certainty in depth estimates σ_z^{-2} (darker is higher certainty) (d) top view of 3-D point cloud*

volume for the object by intersecting the volumes formed by the binary object silhouettes and the camera centers (Szeliski, 1990b). Other approaches involve tracking curves on the object's silhouette and surface (Giblin and Weiss, 1987; Cipolla and Blake, 1990). The technique which we describe here uses optic flow measurements to compute a dense and detailed surface model (Szeliski, 1991). It is thus similar to incremental iconic depth from motion estimation (Matthies et al., 1989), except that the surface shape is not represented as a 2-D map.

Ideally, we would like to represent our 3-D surface in parametric form. However, constructing such a representation before a rough surface shape

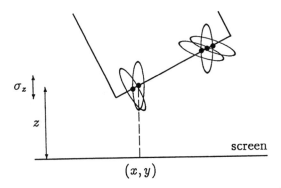

Fig. 5. *Merging uncertainty ellipses*

is known, is not possible. We therefore adopt a different approach, where each optic flow measurement is converted to a 3-D point with an associated 3-D covariance matrix (Figure 5). Each of these points represents a small patch of the surface. Alternative methods for estimating and tracking such patches can be found in Hung et al., citeyearHung88 and Rehg and Witkin (1991). Even though these points are not explicitly connected into a surface (since it may be difficult to reliably segregate points on different surfaces), they form a dense model of shape.

As successive image pairs are processed, we wish to integrate and merge our 3-D measurements in order to reduce positional errors and to build a full 3-D model. Instead of warping our description to keep it iconic, we keep a list of 3-D points, where each point has both a position and a 3×3 covariance matrix that reflects the confidence in that measurement. This allows us to represent points that are not currently visible, and avoids reducing resolution as the surface slants away from the camera. To avoid an excessive buildup of points and to increase the accuracy of point locations, we merge points from adjacent viewpoints if their projected centers lie within a $1/2$ pixel in the image plane, and if their difference in depth (weighted by their joint uncertainty) is below a threshold (Figure 5) (Szeliski, 1991). The resulting algorithm incrementally builds a surface description represented as a cloud of points whose accuracy improves over time (Figure 6).

The next step in building our 3-D surface model is to take this collection of 3-D points and to interpolate a surface through them. If we do not know the desired parametric form or a rough shape for the surface, this problem can be quite difficult. To solve this dilemma, we have developed a new 3-D surface interpolation model based on interacting *oriented particles* (Szeliski and Tonnesen, 1992). These particles, which represent local surface patches, have energy functions which favor the alignment of normals of neighboring particles, thus endowing the surface with an elastic resistance to bending. The particles also have a preferred inter-particle spacing distance, which encourages a uniform sampling density over the surface. We can think

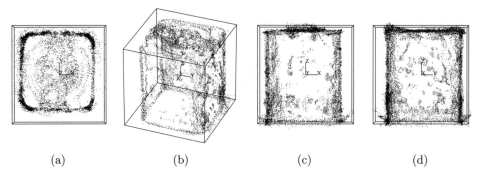

(a)   (b)   (c)   (d)

Fig. 6. *Final merged data from* assam *image sequence: (a) top view (b) oblique view (c) front view (d) side view. The wireframe cube represents the object coordinate system.*

Fig. 7. *Surface interpolation through a collection of 3-D points. The surface extends outward from the seed points until it fills in the gaps and forms a complete surface.*

of these particle as being a mesh-based (finite element) description of the surface, and the inter-particle energies as discrete approximations to some smoothness metric computed over the surface. To interpolate across gaps in the surface where there are no data points, we add new particles where it is energetically favorable (Figure 7). We can also delete points in areas where the sampling density is too high. Once the particles cover the whole object in a uniform manner, we derive the explicit surface model by triangulating the point locations.

8. Feature-based vs. surface-based models

An alternative to directly modeling and estimating surfaces is to compute a visual description based on simpler geometric entities such as points, lines, and planes (Ayache, 1991) or 3-D space curves (Kass et al., 1988). These simpler primitives have several potential advantages when compared to full surface descriptions. First, because the reduced description completely describes the primitive (e.g, the 5 parameters for a 3-D line) we can obtain better accuracy in the estimation of these parameters. Second, matching features may be less computationally expensive than computing quantities such as optic flow. Third, the parameters describing each feature can be updated independently, which can be much faster than the iterative smoothing required when using correlated fields. Fourth, because the description does not have to be re-sampled, the implementation is much simpler and there is no potential loss of accuracy. Fifth, features such as edges may be more stable under changes of illumination or viewing directions than raw intensities. Finally, edges or other features may be a sufficient representation for many vision-based tasks such as recognition and positioning (Lowe, 1985).

On the other hand, feature-based descriptions have a number of limitations and potential disadvantages. It may not always be easy to find features such as lines or curves reliably in images, especially in smoothly varying or in highly textured areas. In particular, methods based on line segments may only work in restricted man-made environments. Features may also shift position depending on the local structure of the image or may disappear and reappear under small changes in viewpoint. The correspondence problem of matching features may sometimes be more difficult or expensive than image-based correlation, especially when the local intensity structure around the feature is ignored. Perhaps the most serious drawback is that if a surface-based description is to be computed from a collection of 3-D geometric primitives, this process may be more difficult and error-prone than estimating the surface from the beginning.

How do we determine which of these representations is more suitable for vision applications? While the answer will often be task-dependent, we could build a representation which simultaneously models both surfaces and discrete features lying on these surfaces. Features such as edges are then represented as discontinuities in the intensity distribution, and their subpixel 3-D location are explicitly modeled. Intensity edges serve as potential candidates for depth discontinuities or creases (Gamble and Poggio, 1987). The position of intensity edges is updated by matching their projection to the output of image-based edge detectors. Edges also locally modify the smoothness constraints on the intensity and shape fields (Terzopoulos, 1988). Note that representing information only at the edges is also a possibility, since edges (zero-crossings) capture the relevant information in a signal if they are computed at multiple resolutions (Yuille and Poggio, 1986).

A possible discrete implementation of such a representation would consist of a collection of 3-D points which define a mesh (triangulation) lying on the surface. Each 3-D point has a position, an intensity, possibly a normal, and a covariance matrix characterizing the uncertainty in these parameters. Each point also has a list of neighbors in the mesh, which may vary over time. Certain points are tagged as edge points, and these are linked together to form 3-D curves. Edge points modify the smoothness in their neighborhood. In the case of depth (shape) discontinuities, edge points are only linked to surface points on the upper side of the discontinuity. Free-floating curves, and even isolated points, are also possible.

Higher level primitives such as line segments or planes can also be added to this representation. A line segment has a list of edge points which belong to it, and its representation is updated by doing a weighted least squares fit to the positions of the individual points. Another way to implement this is to add additional forces coupling the constituent points to the line. A probabilistic formulation is also possible, where the likelihood of a point belonging to a line moderates its interactions with the line (for example, using robust statistics (Huber, 1981)).

This generalized surface representation can be built up incrementally from a sequence of images. As certain areas become more visible, additional mesh points are added to keep the resolution fairly uniform (weak inter-node forces can also be used to keep the spacing uniform). As it becomes evident that surfaces are separate, their meshes can break apart. Free-floating edges can attach themselves to surfaces if they are sufficiently close. Measurements inconsistent with the rest of the model can be thrown out. Of necessity, the behavior of this system is built on a heuristically chosen physically-based model. As the description becomes more stable, however, probabilistically-based updating rules can be used to ensure good convergence for the surface model parameters.

The implementation of a complete modeling system based on this new representation will obviously be quite challenging. However, the potential for accurately modeling both surface shape and sparse geometric features makes this a promising approach to robust and accurate shape recovery.

9. Conclusions

The modeling of visible and 3-D surfaces is an essential component of many computer vision tasks. Associating spatially-varying uncertainty estimates with such surfaces allows us to obtain robust estimates, to integrate information from different sensors and vision modules, and to accumulate information over time. For visible surfaces ($2^1/_2$-D depth maps), we can develop uncertainty models using the Gibbs distribution to relate energies (such as smoothness) to probabilities. This in turn allows us to develop sequential estimation algorithms based on the Kalman filter which incrementally build surface descriptions from image sequences. To improve the convergence rate of these algorithm, we have suggested jointly estimating depth and intensity.

Our ultimate goal is to develop estimation algorithms for full 3-D surface models. Such models are viewpoint independent and allow us to model parts of the visual world that are not currently visible. Building such models is difficult if we do not know the parameterization or topology ahead of time. Our current solution to this problem is to estimate local surface patches, and to later sew these patches into complete surfaces using a mesh-based representation. Our long-term goal is to build complete 3-D surfaces models directly from images, using a representation which models both continuous functions such as shape and intensity and sparse features such as edges and points, and using explicit uncertainty modeling to integrate the information in a statistically optimal fashion.

An orientation based representation for contour analysis

Deborah Walters

Krishnan Ganapathy

Frouke van Huet

The ρ-space representation for contour images is presented in this chapter. It is an orientation based representation useful for the computer interpretation of line drawings and other types of contour images. Human psychophysical experiments have found a class of image features which are important in the human perception of contour images, but which are hard to detect using computer vision algorithms. The rho-space representation enables the detection of that class of features through the incorporation of a definition of connectivity which agrees with human perception.

Rho-space algorithms for early visual processing which utilize the ρ-space representation enable portions of a contour image to be automatically selected which have the highest probability of containing the most perceptually significant information. In addition the algorithms allow easy segmentation and grouping of image contours into sets which have the highest probability of being single objects or object parts.

Just as visual processing in the mammalian brain uses a special purpose highly parallel architecture (the visual cortex and associated structures), a highly parallel special purpose architecture (the ρ-space machine) is presented for the implementation of the ρ-space algorithms.

1. Why study contour images?

The study of contour image analysis is important for both practical and theoretical reasons. Contour images such as technical drawings, maps and even cartoons are often used as a means of visual communication between humans. In an attempt to improve human/computer communication through the use of such images, computer vision algorithms have been designed which attempt to analyze and understand contour images (Chakravarty, 1979; Nevatia and Babu, 1980; Ejiri et al., 1984; Lee et al., 1985; Malik, 1987; Mansouri et al., 1987).

1.1. Theoretical considerations

Some of the earliest work in computer vision dealt with the analysis of contour images (Roberts, 1965; Guzman, 1969; Waltz, 1975), but the inability to extend the early techniques to deal with natural images led to the demise of contour image research. Thus the study of contour images may appear to be a return to the dark-ages of computer vision, but with the current practical applications of contour image analysis we see the opposite problem: the computer vision algorithms developed to deal with natural scenes often do not extend to the analysis of contour images. For example, the recent interest in Active Vision (Bajcsy, 1988; Aloimonos et al., 1988; Ballard, 1991) is both exciting and stimulating, but is not applicable to 2-dimensional static contour images. Similarly, the extremely important work in the integration of information from different sources for computer vision (Poggio et al., 1988; Poggio et al., 1990) is not applicable to contour image analysis, as there is no motion, no color, no depth information available in contour images. Only the edge information and the texture created by edges is available. Thus the techniques that deal with the uncertainly and poor results of individual computer vision modules by integrating information from several sources is not possible for contour images. In some senses the analysis of contour images may even be harder than the analysis of natural scenes, since the paucity of different types of information means that the edge algorithms used must produce results superior to those required for natural images. We can't compensate for the poor results of edge detection and segmentation with motion and other information, therefore we need to have improved edge detection and segmentation algorithms.

While the increase in the required accuracy of the edge detection and segmentation algorithms means contour image analysis may be more difficult than natural scene analysis, contour image analysis may be more tractable because of the simplifying constraints that arise due to the nature of contour images. The realization that contour images are used in communication between humans suggests that a communication model be used to uncover some of the constraints. In this model a contour image is generated by a human, and then acts as a channel of communication, and finally is perceived by a human. Because there is a human perceiver we know that all information in the contour image must be in a form readily perceivable by humans. Thus psychophysical studies of the human perception of contour images can suggest which aspects of contours could possibly convey information and thus suggest useful constraints for contour image analysis. In addition, the fact that the images are generated by humans means that the information conveying aspects of the images must also be readily generated by humans. For example, if humans cannot reliably draw a contour containing a curvature extrema and a contour lacking a curvature extrema, then this provides evidence against the use of curvature extrema as necessary image features. Thus the study of human motor control may suggest additional constraints.

A third means of uncovering useful constraints is the study of the 'physics' of contour image generation. Just as in the analysis of natural images it is useful to consider the physics of the interaction of light and objects in the scene with the imaging system (Horn, 1986), in contour images an understanding of the image formation process can yield useful constraints. One result of the study of contour image generation is the model of contour images discussed below.

1.2. Practical applications

There are many practical applications for contour image analysis algorithms. Even before the entire problem of contour understanding is solved there are several applications which would benefit from partial solutions, yet cannot be solved by existing algorithms (Chakravarty, 1979; Nevatia and Babu, 1980; Ejiri et al., 1984; Lee et al., 1985; Malik, 1987; Mansouri et al., 1987). For example, with the widespread use of Computer Aided Design (CAD) systems to generate contour images such as architectural drawings and utility company maps, there is a need to transfer many of the older hand produced drawings and maps into the same format used by the CAD systems in order to allow easy update of the older drawings and maps. Although digitizing the images is easily done, extracting the graphical information from the digitized images is more difficult. There are automated systems designed for this purpose, but the current models have problems with intersecting lines and corners and thus require significant retouching by human operators which is both tedious and expensive. An improvement in the computer vision algorithms used in such systems which would remove the necessity for human touch-up would be beneficial.

Another example comes from the pre-press printing industry, where computer graphics systems are used to generate the color screens used in printing such contour images as the Sunday comics. The line drawing comics are first digitized and then color filled on computer graphics workstations. However there are several limitations in the system which require a manual touch-up of the artwork before digitization. Figure 1a illustrates some of these problems, for example there is a gap in the contour defining the left half of the roof. In cartoons there are often gaps in the lines which define a region, which cause problems when filling algorithms are used as the fill color will spread out of the region through the gaps and produce undesirable filling of surrounding regions. Yet the gaps are not a problem for human perception as we appear to have mechanisms which enable us to infer a closed region even when there exist gaps in the contours defining the region. In fact, artists often take advantage of such mechanisms and intentionally create

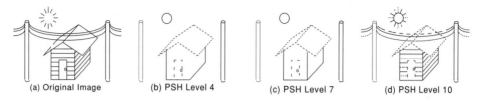

Fig. 1. *Illustration of color-filling problems and their solution using the PSH. The different line styles indicate the results of the segmentation algorithm.*

images with gaps. A related problem is that artists sometimes use illusory contours to define regions. For example, in Figure 1a the sun is defined by an illusory contour, and thus no actual contours exist which would allow the sun to be color filled. The current solution to both problems is to manually ink in the gaps and the illusory contours before the image is digitized.

The third problem illustrated in Figure 1a is the division of a single perceptual region into separate parts by overlapping contours. The telephone wires divide the roof into multiple sections, each of which would have to be individually color filled. The fourth problem is similar: a single perceptual region can be divided into many separate regions by texture or pattern contours. For example, the house walls are divided into many separate regions by the lines representing the clapboards which again causes problems if it is desired to color the walls a single color. The current solution is to manually erase portions of the texture and pattern lines and the overlapping contours to allow the color to spread across the entire perceptual region. The fifth problem occurs when the contours used to define different surfaces of the object divide a single perceptual region into separate parts. For example, in Figure 1a the roof would be divided by its center line, even if the telephone wires were not there. Again it would be necessary to manually erase a portion of such dividing contours. The pre-press industry has found that the cheapest manner for handling all of these problems is to manually retouch the contour images before they are digitized for color-filling. But the manual retouching process could be eliminated entirely with the use of effective computer vision algorithms for contour images which would result in a significant savings in time and labor.

2. Contour image analysis

Three of the important tasks for contour image analysis are: the determination of which contours are perceptually significant; the segmentation of contours in sets likely to correspond to object parts; and, the grouping of contours into sets likely to have arisen from a single object. This chapter will present algorithms have been designed to accomplish these three tasks (Walters, 1987; Krishnan and Walters, 1988; Krishnan, 1988). The algorithms are based on psychophysical experiments which show that the orientation

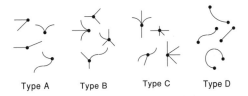

Type A   Type B   Type C   Type D

Fig. 2. *Examples of each of the four types of orientation discontinuity. The dots indicate the location of the orientation discontinuity in each example.*

discontinuities of contour images convey much of the perceptually significant information in human perception of contours (Walters and Weisstein, 1982). Orientation discontinuities occur at image points where there is a discontinuity in the tangent (or local orientation) of a contour; for example at a contour corner.

Assumption 1 *Orientation discontinuity information is perceptually important and must be preserved during the analysis of contour images.*

It has been shown that all possible orientation discontinuities can be classed as one of just four perceptual types (Walters, 1987). These types can be expressed in terms of 'contour segments' which can be informally defined as the smooth sections of a contour which lie inclusively between the end points and/or orientation discontinuities of a contour (see below for a formal definition).

1   Type A discontinuities consist of just two contour segments which coterminate at an orientation discontinuity.

2   Type B discontinuities consist of three or more contour segments which all terminate at an orientation discontinuity.

3   Type C discontinuities consist of at least one contour segment which terminates as it abuts at least one other contour segment which does not terminate at the abutment.

4   Type D discontinuities are the terminations of a single contour segment which does not abut or coterminate with another contour segment.

Figure 2 shows four examples of each type of orientation discontinuity. Perceptually, the four types of discontinuities form a hierarchy such that contour segments having the Type A discontinuities are the most salient and those having the Type D discontinuities are the least salient (Walters, 1987). An individual contour segment which has no orientation discontinuities (i.e. a closed contour) has perceptual salience equivalent to a contour segment which has two Type A discontinuities. Thus a circle and the sides of a square have equal perceptual salience.

Why should such differences in perceptual salience exist? What possible use could the human organism have for such distinctions? It has been shown that the perceptual salience correlates with perceptual significance (Walters, 1987). This can be understood by making two basic assumptions.

Assumption 2   *Viewing position is representative (Binford, 1981; Barrow and Tennenbaum, 1981; Cowie, 1983; Lowe, 1985).*

Assumption 3   *Object position is representative.*

These assumptions allow certain inferences to be made relative to the probable interpretation of the different types of contour segments relative to the contours in the depicted scene. Contour segments can correspond to nonoccluding contours of objects, to occluding contours of objects, to occluded contours, to surface marking contours, to wire object contours, or to noise. From the Assumption 2 it is possible to infer that contour segments which terminate at a Type A discontinuity have the highest probability of corresponding to the occluding contours of objects, and that contour segments terminating at Type B discontinuities have highest probability of corresponding to non-occluding object contours. From Assumptions 2 and 3 it is possible to infer that a contour segment which terminates at a Type C discontinuity has the highest probability of corresponding to an occluded contour. Similarly a contour segment which terminates at a Type D discontinuity has the highest probability of corresponding to noise or to the end of a wire object.

Since object recognition is generally possible from viewing just the occluding contours of an object, but not from viewing the other object contours alone, and since object recognition is one of the most important parts of contour image perception, it can be inferred that the contour segments which terminate at Type A discontinuities should be the most perceptually significant in an image. Similarly, the contours segments which terminate at the Type B discontinuities should be the next most significant. Since occluded contours are less significant than other object contours, it can be inferred that contour segments which terminate at the Type C discontinuities are the next most significant, which leaves the contours which terminate at the Type D discontinuities as being the least significant.

Each nonclosed contour segment is defined to have exactly two ends and thus terminates at two orientation discontinuities. In terms of the types of discontinuities at which a contour segment terminates there are thus ten possible types of contour segments, and the ten types form the ten levels of the Perceptual Significance Hierarchy (PSH). At the top level of the PSH are only those contour segments which have either no discontinuities or terminate at two Type A discontinuities. At the second level are the contour segments from the first level and any contour segments which terminate at a Type A and a Type B discontinuity. At the third level of the PSH are the contour segments from the second level as well as those contour segments which terminate at a Type A and a Type C discontinuity. And so on, until

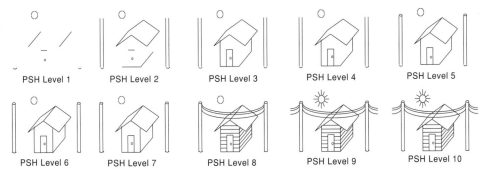

Fig. 3. *An example of the Perceptual Significance Hierarchy (PSH) as applied to a simple image.*

at the tenth level are all the contour segments present in the original image. Figure 3 shows the ten levels of the PSH for the image from Figure 1a.

The contour segments at the top the PSH have the highest probability of being perceptually significant, while those that appear only at the bottom of the hierarchy have the least (Walters and Krishnan, 1987). The PSH representation of a contour image can be utilized to aid in solving several problems in contour image analysis as discussed in the next sections.

2.1. Uses of the perceptual significance hierarchy (PSH)

One potential use of the the PSH is as a means of directing visual attention in a biological organism. The retina is constantly bombarded with immense amounts of information, and some means of selecting out which information is likely to be most useful and thus should be processed either first or most quickly is necessary. As the contour segments at the top of the PSH have the highest probability of being perceptually significant, it may be useful for an organism to concentrate any limited visual processing to those image regions which contain such contour segments. Thus if the PSH were one result of the earliest stages of visual processing, it could be used to direct visual attention to those regions of the image which would have the highest probability of providing useful information. Under the assumption that the earliest visual processing is both parallel and rapid, it would be useful to limit the later more serial and slower processing to those regions of the image which are the most likely to contain information useful to the organism.

The PSH can be used to solve several of the problems described in the color filling problem by allowing the user to interactively select the appropriate levels of the PSH representation of the image. To solve the problem of the roof being divided by the telephone wires the user could select Levels 2, 3, or 4 of the PSH (Figure 3) as the roof is one undivided region at those levels and thus could be colored with a single color fill operation. Also, the house walls are one region at those levels and could be filled in one step. If instead

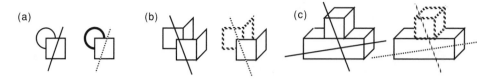

Fig. 4. *Segmentation of planar, origami and three-dimensional objects. The different line styles indicate the different segments.*

the user wanted to color the two halves of the roof or the two walls of the house different shades, then the selection of the Levels 5, 6, or 7 of the PSH (Figure 3) would provide the appropriate image. If the user wanted to color each clapboard of the house a different shade, then Levels 8, 9 or 10 of the PSH could be selected (Figure 3) where each clapboard is a separate region. (The problems of gaps in the contours and most illusory contours are solved by the ρ-space algorithms discussed below. Note that the gap in the roof has been filled in and that the illusory contour which represents the sun has been formed.)

2.2. Segmentation and grouping

From Assumptions 2 and 3, it is also possible to make inferences useful for the segmentation of the image contours into sets which have a high probability of having arisen from a single object, and to group the contours into sets which have high probability of having arisen from a single object surface (Walters, 1987). The Segmentation Algorithm (SA) (Appendix A) is based on the following inferences: contour segments which coterminate at a Type A or Type B discontinuity have a high probability of having arisen from the same object; and, contour segments which terminate at a Type C discontinuity have a high probability of having arisen from different objects than the contour segments which pass through a Type C discontinuity. The SA uses the PSH to segment the image, starting at a given level of the PSH and working down as far as desired. The Figure 1b–d shows the results of the segmentation algorithm at several levels of the PSH when processing is begun at the top level of the PSH for the contour image shown in Figure 1a. The different line styles are used to represent the many different segments. Note that the segmentation doesn't change as new contours from the the lower levels of the PSH are added. Also note that the segments correspond to readily named objects or object parts: roof, house walls, door, telephone pole, etc. The segmentation appears to agree with human perception. Figure 4 shows the segmentation of simple planar, origami and three-dimensional images. Note that the extra 'noise' line does not interfere with the segmentation of the underlying objects. Also note that even though the two blocks in part c are accidentally aligned, the image is correctly segmented.

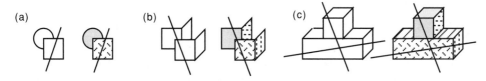

Fig. 5. *Grouping of planar, origami and three-dimensional objects. The different filling patterns indicate the regions defined by the different groups of contour
segments.*

The Grouping Algorithm (GA) (Appendix B) is closely related to the SA
and differs only in that the sets of contours are grouped based on object
surfaces, and thus the GA is similar to region based segmentation. Thus
a single contour segment which is part of a single object may be divided
into different groups which correspond to the different surfaces of the object.
Another difference is that the GA groups adjacent pairs of contour segments
which are each occluded by another contour segment or group. Figure 5
shows the results of the GA applied to simple scenes containing planar,
origami and three-dimensional objects. The different filling patterns indicate
the regions defined by the different groups of contour segments. Note that
the 'noise' lines which intersect regions do not have an effect on the grouping.
Also note that even though the three-dimensional objects are accidentally
aligned, the grouping results are correct in the sense that what is perceived
by a human as a single surface is interpreted as a single surface by the
algorithm. Also note that the top surface of the bottom block is represented
as a single surface, even though it is depicted by two non-adjacent regions
in the image plane.

2.3. How far can we go without knowledge-based processing?

The PSH, SA and GA algorithms produce results which are generally in
agreement with human perception. This may be surprising since the algorithms use no domain-specific knowledge (Brooks, 1984). Only the most
general type of knowledge that can be applicable to all stylus generated images is used in the PSH, SA and GA algorithms. It is interesting to note
just how much can be accomplished without resorting to knowledge-based
processing. However the algorithm results will not always be correct, in
which case, the subsequent application of domain-specific knowledge can be
useful for correcting the results. The PSH, SA and GA are meant to be fast,
simple algorithms which can reduce the amount of processing that must be
done by more complex knowledge-based algorithms by providing a generally
correct first-pass result. The applications discussed at the beginning of the
chapter are examples of the many problems where the PSH, SA and GA
may provide all the processing required for solutions to the problems.

2.4. How can orientation discontinuities be detected?

In order to use the Perceptual Significance Hierarchy, the Segmentation Algorithm and the Grouping Algorithm the orientation discontinuities of contours must be detected. Although the orientation discontinuities have been discussed thus far in terms of continuous Euclidean geometry, a practical implementation must detect the discontinuities in digitized images which have a discrete geometry. A major obstacle for the detection of such features is that even the definition of a contour is non-obvious in the discrete geometry domain. Rosenfeld has one of the best discrete definitions of a contour (or arc): a set of connected points, such that all but two points have exactly two neighbors and the two points have exactly one neighbor each (Rosenfeld, 1979). The connectivity here is the standard image-based 8-connectivity. This definition works well for a single contour, but if two contours intersect then neither satisfies the definition of a contour although both are still perceived by humans as contours. The problem arises because the connectivity used in Rosenfeld's definition is based on spatial position alone, while the human perception is based on a connectivity which includes local contour orientation.

Another problem is that many of the preprocessing algorithms commonly used for contour images have the unfortunate effect of removing or attenuating information at orientation discontinuities (Canny, 1983; Hildreth, 1987). Since it was not known that orientation discontinuities play an important role in human vision and thus may be important for machine vision, computer vision algorithms were not designed to preserve orientation discontinuity information. In fact, the opposite design constraint was sometimes used: algorithms should remove orientation discontinuities as their presence complicates the mathematics. For example, many edge detectors have the effect of smoothing out edges at orientation discontinuities such as corners and thus remove the discontinuities (Marr and Hildreth, 1980). In addition, intersecting contours are also a problem for edge detection algorithms. Marshall refers to this as the 'cross problem' (Marshall, 1990) and points out that most systems cannot detect or even represent the multiple edges occurring at an intersection. Thinning algorithms are also problematical since they do not preserve the orientation discontinuity information at the ends and intersections of contours (Rosenfeld and Kak, 1982; Ballard and Brown, 1982).

The solution to these problems is three-fold and involves the use of an orientation based representation for contour images (Walters, 1987; see Chapter 3), the use of appropriate definitions of connectivity and contours, and the use of a model of contour images. The solutions will be discussed in more detail after the orientation based ρ-space representation and the contour image model are described.

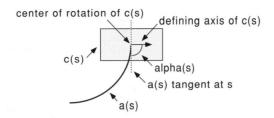

Fig. 6. *Cross-section and axis used in defining modified ribbons.*

3. Modified ribbon model of stylus generated images

Most contour images are generated by some type of stylus mechanism. Traditional examples of stylus's are pens, pencils, brushes, chalks and crayons. More modern examples would include the light pens, mice and trackballs used in computer drawing programs. What these devices have in common can be understood in terms of a model of stylus generated images. Just as the shape of certain types of three-dimensional objects can be understood as generalized cylinders (Binford, 1971) which have an axis in three-dimensional space and a two-dimensional cross-section which is moved along the axis to sweep out the shape, stylus generated images can be understood in terms of ribbons which are generated when a line or a disk is swept along a coplanar axis (Rosenfeld, 1986). Contour images which are generated by stylus mechanisms can be modeled as modified ribbons which allow the possibility of any shape cross-section.

Definition 1 *A modified ribbon is the planar surface swept out by a one-dimensional or two-dimensional cross-section, $c(s) = [\alpha(s), \beta(s), \gamma(s), \delta]$, moving along a coplanar axis, $a(s)$, such that the center of rotation of $c(s)$ lies at s, where s is the arclength along the axis, δ is the defining axis of $c(s)$ and originates at its center of rotation, $\alpha(s)$ is the angle between δ and the tangent of $a(s)$ at s, $\beta(s)$ is the shape of the cross-section at s, and $\gamma(s)$ is the size of the cross-section at s.*

Figure 6 illustrates the cross-section and axis used in defining the modified ribbon. A discrete modified ribbon is an exact model of contour images generated with computer drawing programs. The shape and size of the the cross-section are fixed and correspond to the shape and size of the program pen or brush, while the axis corresponds to the path swept out by the user. Figure 7 shows two examples of such ribbons. The angle, $\alpha(s)$, may be fixed or may vary with the direction of the axis. For example in many calligraphy contour images the angle, $\alpha(s)$, varies such that the cross-section remains at a fixed angle in relation to the image vertical (as in Figure 7b).

In human generated stylus images the modified ribbon model may be more complex. For example, when drawn with a pencil, the thickness of contours and thus the cross-section size, $\gamma(s)$, may vary as a function of the pressure

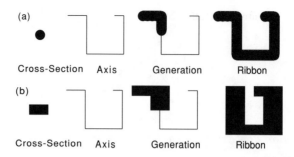

Fig. 7. *Examples of modified ribbons with constant cross-sections showing: the cross-sections, c(s); the axes, a(s); one step in the generation process; and, the final ribbons.*

applied by the artist. When a brush is used, the model becomes even more complex, as the shape of the cross-section, $\beta(s)$, will vary as the portion of the pigmented brush that is in contact with the drawing surface varies.

One motivation for defining the ribbon model of contour images is because it in turn can be used to define the desired result of thinning or skeletonization algorithms. Generally thinning algorithms are defined in terms of the computation, and require a subjective opinion to evaluate the results. This subjectivity is removed when the modified ribbon model of the contour image is used.

When a person drawing the contour image desires to indicate an orientation discontinuity, it is accomplished by placing an orientation discontinuity in the axis. It is not done by altering the shape or size of the cross-section. It is the ribbon axis that generally contains the most information, while the shape and size of the cross-section generally contains only peripheral information. For example, in a technical drawing it is the ribbon axis which gives the information about the shape, size and location of the object being depicted, while the types of information that may be represented in terms of line style (i.e. cross-section size and shape) may concern the class of object (for example, thick lines may represent walls, while thinner lines may represent windows in an architectural drawing). It is not surprising then, that when humans perceive stylus generated contour images the contour axis appears to compose a major portion of the percept. Thus it may be important for computational vision algorithms to extract the contour axes from contour images.

Assumption 4   *When stylus-generated contour images are input to a thinning algorithm, the desired output is the modified ribbon axes, a(s), of the contours.*

When a thinning algorithm satisfies Assumption 4 it will have the property of preserving the local orientation discontinuity information which is important for contour perception. For example, consider the simple case shown in Figure 7a where the cross-section of the stylus is a fixed radius circle. Note that there are six orientation discontinuities in the axis, four corners (Type A discontinuities) and two end points (Type D discontinuities). However neither the outer nor the inner edges of the ribbon contour contain all the orientation discontinuities. Thus if just the contour edges were used in the analysis of this image, extracting the orientation discontinuity information would be more difficult than using the ribbon axis. Thus the use of thinning algorithms to extract the modified ribbon axes will facilitate contour analysis.

For the theoretical analysis of the contour algorithms presented here it will be assumed that contour images can be adequately modeled by the modified ribbon model and that a thinning algorithm satisfying Assumption 4 has been applied to the contour images. Although most thinning algorithms do not in fact satisfy this assumption, useful results can still be obtained from the contour algorithms as shown below. A thinning algorithm which does satisfy the assumption is discussed in (Walters and Fang, 1992).

4. Rho-space representation

The use of an appropriate representation can greatly simplify many computations, and this is true for contour image analysis. The ρ-space representation was designed to enable both connectivity and contours to be defined in a manner which agrees with human perception (Walters, 1987). The ρ-space representation also allows multiple orientations to be represented at a single image point and thus is useful in solving the 'cross problem' and in detecting the four types of perceptually relevant orientation discontinuities (Walters, 1987). In addition the ρ-space representation will be used by a set of ρ-space algorithms which preserve orientation discontinuity information during the initial stages of visual processing.

A geometric model is useful for visualizing the ρ-space representation for contour images. First, consider the continuous case, where the image plane is assumed to be finite, rectangular and nondiscretized: in this case ρ-space can be visualized as a toroidal space (Figure 8a). The local orientation axis, ρ, is circular and runs along the central circular axis of the toroid. The spatial position axes, x_ρ and y_ρ, are all orthogonal to the ρ axis, and for each value of ρ, they are orthogonal to each other. The horizontal spatial position axes, x_ρ, lie within the plane formed by the circular ρ axis, while the vertical spatial position axes, y_ρ, are all orthogonal to the plane of the ρ axis. Each cross-section of the space which is orthogonal to the ρ axis represents an image plane and contains those image points whose local orientation corresponds to a value of ρ where the image plane intersects the ρ axis. (Figure 8a shows eight of the infinitely many possible cross-sections.)

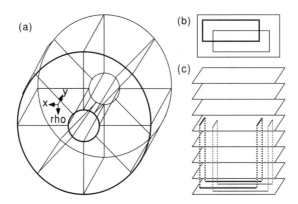

Fig. 8. *Graphical Depiction of the Rho-Space Representation. (a) Continuous ρ-space toroid. (b) Simple image. (c) Discrete ρ-space representation of the simple image.*

The ρ-space representation of a continuous contour image can be visualized in the continuous ρ-space model. For example, the outer contours of a vertically oriented square in image space would appear as two vertical contours in the cross-section with a corresponding orientation of $\pi/2$, and two horizontal contours in the cross-section corresponding to an orientation of pi. A circular contour would appear as a double helix whose long axis is wrapped into a circle along the orientation axis of the toroid.

For discretized, rectangular contour images, the discrete geometric model of the ρ-space representation is a rectangular columnar space as illustrated in Figure 8c. The ρ axis runs along the vertical axis of the space. The spatial position axes, x_ρ and y_ρ, lie within each horizontal plane, $P(\rho)$, of the space. The number, n, of such planes is determined by the number of discrete orientations to be represented in rho-space. Figure 8c shows the case where $n = 8$: eight discrete orientations are represented in this version of ρ-space. Each discrete point is $p(x, y, \rho)$, where x and y are indexed over the spatial coordinates of the image and ρ is indexed from 0 to $n-1$. Ordinarily the orientations range from 0 to π, but when the contours are signed and thus contain not only local orientation information but also information as to the direction of the contour, then the range is from 0 to 2π. It is assumed that the top plane is connected to the bottom plane, so the discrete ρ-space is also topologically a toroid. For the remainder of this chapter only the discrete ρ-space representation will be considered.

The discrete ρ-space can also be modeled as a three-dimensional binary array, where $p(x, y, \rho)$ represents an element of the array. When $p(x, y, \rho) = 1$, a contour point of orientation, ρ, located at image location (x, y) is being represented. When no contour point is present at image location (x, y), $p(x, y, \rho) = 0$.

4.1. Transforming images into the rho-space Representation

How are contour images represented in ρ-space? Contours in an image are represented by their ribbon axes in the ρ-space representation, while blob regions are represented by their edges. Each axis or edge point has an (x, y) image location, and a local orientation, and is translated into the ρ-space point, (x, y, ρ), where ρ is the plane whose orientation is closest to that of the axis or edge point.

The ρ-space representation allows multiple orientations to be represented for a single image location and thus overcomes one limitation of other edge representation systems. This ability is important for the representation of the perceptually important orientation discontinuities.

The following sections describe how connectivity and contours are defined in the ρ-space representation.

4.2. Inhibitory and excitatory neighborhoods

Connectivity and contours in ρ-space are defined in terms of local neighborhoods. The neighborhoods are based on the following assumption concerning contour images.

Assumption 5   *Only a single contour segment can exist within a small region of the ρ-space representation of a contour image.*

From this assumption it is possible to generate a small neighborhood for each point, $p(x, y, \rho)$, in ρ-space which is comprised of two parts: an excitatory neighborhood which consists of those points which could lie on the same smooth contour segment as $p(x, y, \rho)$; and an inhibitory neighborhood which consists of those points which could not lie on the same smooth contour as $p(x, y, \rho)$.

The inhibitory neighborhoods are defined using $2s+1$ by $2s+1$ inhibitory neighborhood arrays, $I_{\rho,s}$. (For the set of 16 edge operators used in the examples in this chapter, $I_{\rho,s}$ has the dimensions 7 by 7, and is specified in Appendix C.) The array indices are established such that $i_{\rho,s}(0,0)$ refers to the central location of the array, thus the indices range from $-s$ to $+s$.

Definition 2   *The ρ-space point $p'(x', y', \rho')$ is in the* inhibitory neighborhood of span s *of the ρ-space point $p(x, y, \rho)$ if and only if $|x - x'| <= s$, and $|y - y'| <= s$, and $(|\rho - \rho'| <= k$ or $|\rho - \rho'| = n-1)$ and $i_{\rho',s}(x - x', y - y') = 1$.*

The excitatory neighborhoods are defined in a similar manner with the addition of each excitatory neighborhood being divided into two regions, side 0 and side 1. The excitatory neighborhood arrays, $E_{\rho,j,s}$ are used to define both parts of the excitatory neighborhoods. The indices have the same ranges as in the inhibitory arrays, $I_{s}ub\rho, s$, with the addition that j ranges from 0 to 1. Appendix D gives the values of $E_{\rho,j,s}$ for the edge operators used in this chapter.

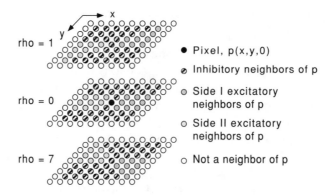

Fig. 9. *Graphical Depiction of Rho-Space Excitatory and Inhibitory Neighborhoods.*

Definition 3   *The ρ-space point $p(x', y', \rho')$ is in the side j excitatory neighborhood of span s of the ρ-space point $p(x, y, \rho)$ if and only if $|x-x'| <= s$, and $|y - y'| <= s$, and $((|\rho - \rho'| <= k$ and $e_{\rho', j, s}(x - x'', y - y'') = 1)$ or $(|\rho - \rho'| = n - 1$ and $e_{\rho', |j-1|, s}(x - x'', y - y'') = 1))$.*

Figure 9 shows a graphical representation of the excitatory and inhibitory neighborhoods for a point $p(x, y, 0)$. Only those portions of each plane which contain any neighborhood points are displayed. All undisplayed points are not part of p's neighborhood.

4.3. Connectivity in rho-space

Connectivity is defined in ρ-space using neighborhoods: the excitatory neighborhoods just defined, and a cylindrical neighborhood. Many of the advantages of the ρ-space representation are a function of these neighborhood based definitions. There are two types of connectivity in ρ-space: *image independent connectivity* and *image dependent connectivity*. When an 'L' shaped figure is observed, there are two possible interpretations. One is that it is formed of two lines which coterminate. The *image-independent connectivity* captures this percept.

Definition 4   *The point, $p'(x', y', \rho')$, is connected in the image-independent sense to the point, $p(x, y, \rho)$, if and only if p' lies in the excitatory neighborhood of p.*

The other possible interpretation of an 'L' shaped figure is that of a single line that contains an orientation discontinuity. The second type of connectivity is *image dependent connectivity* and is required for the second percept. An image point that corresponds to a Type A orientation discontinuity will project to two separate points in the ρ-space representation. However the two points will be assumed to be connected via the *image-dependent connectivity*. To define this it is necessary to first define a cylindrical neighborhood.

Definition 5 $p'(x', y', \rho')$ *is a* cylindrical neighbor of span g *of point,* $p(x, y, \rho)$, *if and only if* $|x - x'| <= g$, *and* $|y - y'| <= g$ *and* $c_g(x - x', y - y') = 1$.

C_g is an array which specifies which points in each plane of ρ-space are in the cylindrical neighborhood and is given in Appendix E. The cylindrical neighborhood is simply a ρ-space cylinder of radius, g, whose long axis lies parallel to the ρ-axis. Actually, as the discrete ρ-space is topologically a toroid, the cylindrical neighborhood is also topologically a toroid.

Definition 6   *Two points,* $p(x, y, \rho)$ *and* $p'(x', y', \rho')$, *are* connected in the image-dependent sense *for a span of* g, *if and only if* p' *is a cylindrical neighbor of* p, *and* p *and* p' *are both contour end points in a single Type A discontinuity.*

Thus along each vertical line through the space, there is the potential of connectivity between any two points on the line, and the potential is realized for two points if a Type A discontinuity is present at each. For example, Figure 8c shows the ρ-space representation of the image consisting of two intersecting rectangles depicted in Figure 8b. The dotted lines represent the *image-dependent connectivity*, while the solid lines represent the *image-independent connectivity*.

4.4. The definition of contours in rho-space

By using the ρ-space representation for contour images and its neighborhood based definitions of connectivity, it is possible to define a contour in a manner that does agrees with the human perceptual idea of a contour or line.

Definition 7   *A contour segment* is a set of ρ-space points which are connected in the image independent sense, such that exactly two points in the set are connected to other points in the set on only one side of their excitatory neighborhoods, and the remaining points are connected to other points in the set on both sides of their excitatory neighborhoods.

This definition is identical to Rosenfeld's definition of a digital arc (Rosenfeld, 1979) with two exceptions. First, the contour is defined in the ρ-space representation, instead of in the image plane. Second, a ρ-space definition of connectivity is used instead of the image based connectivity. The ρ-space definition solves the cross problem, as two contour segments which intersect in the image plane both still satisfy the definition of contour segments and can be easily represented in ρ-space. However, two contour segments whose angle of intersection is less than the difference between the orientations represented in adjacent ρ-space planes, then the cross problem is not solved by the representation alone. Marshall (1990) and Freeman and Adelson (1990) have proposed solutions to the cross problem which are also unable to handle acutely intersecting contours. Although the ρ-space representation alone is unable to handle such intersections, the ρ-space algorithms can be used to solve the problem.

The following definitions will be useful for further describing contour segments.

Definition 8   *An* end point *is a contour segment point which is connected to other points of the contour segment only on one side of its excitatory neighborhood.*

Definition 9   *An* interjacent point *is a contour segment point which is connected to other points of the contour segment on both sides of its excitatory neighborhood.*

Thus the L-shaped figure could be described as two separate coterminating contour segments, and this would agree with the one possible percept of the figure. For the other percept it would be desirable to define the L-shaped figure as a single entity, and thus the following definition of a 'contour' is necessary.

Definition 10   *A* contour *is a set of contour segments whose contour end points are connected in the image-dependent sense.*

With these two definitions and the definitions of connectivity, contours in ρ-space can now be interpreted in either manner, and each agrees with one of the two possible human percepts. Figure 8c illustrates one of the advantages of the ρ-space definitions. The lines in Figure 8b are perceived by humans as being two separate rectangles. If the lines were to be grouped according to this percept, then the dark lines would form one group and the light lines would form another. Note that while the dark rectangle and light rectangle are connected in the image, they are not connected in the ρ-space representation. Thus the grouping formed automatically in ρ-space agrees with the human percept. It is the definitions of connectivity used in ρ-space that cause this to happen, which is not surprising since the definitions used were based on the human perception of contour images.

4.5. Definitions of orientation discontinuities in the rho-space representation

One of the benefits of the ρ-space representation of contour images is that it allows the easy definition of all four perceptually significant classes of orientation discontinuities. This is accomplished using the cylindrical neighborhoods.

1   The point, $p(x, y, \rho)$ is part of a Type A discontinuity if and only if: p is a contour end point; there is exactly one other contour end point,

p', in p's cylindrical neighborhood; and, there are no interjacent contour points belonging to additional contour segments in p's cylindrical neighborhood.

2   The point, $p(x, y, \rho)$ is part of a Type B discontinuity if and only if: p is a contour end point; there are at least two other contour end points, p' and p'', in p's cylindrical neighborhood; and, there are no interjacent contour points belonging to additional contour segments with do not terminate in p's cylindrical neighborhood.

3   The point, $p(x, y, \rho)$ is part of a Type C discontinuity if and only if: p is a contour end point; and, there is at least one interjacent contour point belonging to an additional contour segments in p's cylindrical neighborhood.

4   The point, $p(x, y, \rho)$ is part of a Type D discontinuity if and only if: p is a contour end point; there are no other contour end points in p's cylindrical neighborhood; and, there are no interjacent contour points belonging to additional contour segments in p's cylindrical neighborhood.

Thus the detection of the four different types of orientation discontinuities is a simple counting task in the cylindrical neighborhoods. Again the ρ-space representation makes it easy to represent the perceptually important image information.

5. The rho-space machine

Just as visual processing in the mammalian brain uses a special purpose highly parallel architecture (the visual cortex and associated structures), a highly parallel special purpose architecture (the ρ-space machine) is useful for the implementation of the ρ-space algorithms. The ρ-space machine even has several similarities to the array of cells in Area V1 of the visual cortex which have oriented receptive fields: both consist of a large number of very simple processors which have both input and output connections to a large number of other processors; and both may be involved in the analysis of the local orientation of contours.

Just as the geometric model of the ρ-space representation makes it easier to visualize the representation's connectivity, the ρ-space machine will make it easier to visualize the algorithms which operate on the ρ-space representation.

The ρ-space machine is a fine-grain parallel architecture consisting of a very simple processor for each point in the discrete ρ-space representation. Thus the ρ-space machine can be visualized as an h by w by n array of processors, where h is the height of the image, w is the image width and n

is the number of discrete orientations being represented. For example, with $h = 512$, $w = 512$, and $n = 8$ the number of required processors is 2,097,152.

Each processor receives input from and can send output to the other processors to which it is connected. Each processor requires connections to the processors in its inhibitory neighborhood, in both sides of its excitatory neighborhood, and in its cylindrical neighborhood. Each processor thus requires connections to $(2(2s+1)(2k+1) + (\pi/2)(2c+1)(n(2k+1))) - 1$ other processors, where $2k+1$ is the height of the excitatory and inhibitory neighborhoods, s is their span, and c is the span of the cylindrical neighborhoods. For the small neighborhoods used in the example images presented in this chapter, $s = 3$, $n = 8$, $k = 1$, and $g = 3$, thus each processor needs connections to 331 other processors. These connections could be implemented as direct connections, however to decrease the fan-in and fan-out it would be possible to use only six direct connections for each processor and have the other connections implemented by passing information through directly connected processors.

The required processing and memory capabilities of each processor are limited. All arithmetic is integer and only summation, subtraction and conditional logic are required. Only four bytes of memory are required for the direct connection implementation, although additional memory is required for the indirect connection implementation. In addition there needs to be access to a global 'black-board', which again could be done through indirect connections. The ρ-space machine could be easily implemented by designing special purpose chips.

6. The rho-space algorithms

A set of ρ-space algorithms have been designed to transform a contour image into the ρ-space representation. The ρ-space algorithms are simple neighborhood based computations and use the same neighborhoods used in defining contours and connectivity in the ρ-space representation. The following sections give the background information necessary to understand the ρ-space algorithms.

Assumption 6 *Contour images are binary and contain one pixel wide contours and multiple pixel wide blobs.*

Most digitized contour images would not initially satisfy all of Assumption 6, and thus would require binarization and thinning preprocessing. In addition, any contour images which contained non-contour or blob regions would have to be preprocessed so that only the contours were thinned while the blob regions remain unthinned. By Assumption 1 both the binarization and thinning algorithms need to preserve the orientation discontinuity information. Although the Assumptions 1 and 6 are theoretically necessary, in actual practice many images that do not conform to the assumptions can be adequately processed using the ρ-space algorithms. Thus even when inadequate thinning algorithms are used, the results of the ρ-space algorithms may still be adequate for contour image analysis.

To transform an image into the ρ-space representation it is necessary to know both which image points are contour points and the local orientation (contour tangent) of each contour point. There are various ways that this information could be determined: some type of edge detection could be used to locate the contour points, and then the contour point locations could be differentiated to compute the local orientation (Asada and Brady, 1986). However there are several problems with such an approach. First, as mentioned before, most edge detection algorithms do not have the necessary property of preserving orientation discontinuity information, thus both the position and the orientation information at corners and intersections will be wrong. Second, it would be nice to have a method which computed both the presence of contour points and their local orientation in a single process. This is possible using a set of local, oriented, convolution style edge operators which yield both edge location and edge orientation information.

Assumption 7   *The input to ρ-space consists of the responses of a set of oriented edge operators applied to a contour image.*

The operators used for the example images are elongated discrete first derivative operators with a width of 2 pixels, a length of seven pixels and a magnitude such that the range of possible responses from each operator is -100 to 100. The width of the operators was chosen to be the smallest possible as the image contours are defined to be only one pixel wide. The aspect ratio of these operators was chosen to approximate the aspect ratio of what Hubel and Wiesel referred to as 'simple cells' in the mammalian visual cortex (Hubel and Weisel, 1968).

Convolution style edge operators yield non-zero responses not only at edges, but also in an area surrounding each edge, and around any noise pixels that may be in the original image. Some means of postprocessing must be used to extract the responses that correspond to edges from the multiplicity of responses. The basic hypothesis underlying the following algorithms is that the local patterns of responses of oriented edge operators contain sufficient information to extract the relevant responses. The ρ-space algorithms will utilize simple neighborhood computations to take advantage of the information in the local pattern of responses, and will transform a contour image into its ρ-space representation.

For the first algorithm, the ρ-space points are treated as integers, but for all the rest of the algorithms the ρ-space points contain only cardinal labels. The computations necessary for each stage of processing are very simple. To illustrate this the first and second algorithms are described in detail. The rest of the ρ-space algorithms are described briefly. More detailed descriptions of the remaining algorithms can be found in (Walters and Fang, 1992) and (Krishnan, 1988).

6.1. Lateral inhibition

The Lateral Inhibition (LI) algorithm removes many of the edge operator responses which could not be part of image contours based on the following constraint.

Assumption 8 *Rho-space points associated with large magnitude responses of the oriented edge operators have a higher probability of being contour points than ρ-space points associated with smaller magnitude responses.*

This assumption is possible because the edge operators have uniform magnitude and the contrast between the image contours and the image background is constant. The following constraint is based on this assumption and Assumption 5, recalling that the inhibitory neighborhood of a point includes all those points which could not be part of the same smooth contour.

Constraint 1 *A point, p, is a potential contour segment point if and only if its magnitude is greater than or equal to the magnitude of each point in its inhibitory neighborhood of span s.*

This constraint is implemented in the following parallel algorithm.

LATERAL INHIBITION ALGORITHM:
    PARALLEL FOR (all $p \neq 0$) DO
        IF ($p <$ every neighbor in p's Inhibitory Neighborhood
           of Span s) THEN
           ($p := 0$);
        END;
    END;

6.2. Short range linear excitation algorithm

The Short Range Linear Excitation (SRLE) algorithm removes additional points which have a low probability of corresponding to contour points, based on the following constraint.

Constraint 2 *Potential contour segment points which do not have collinear neighboring points are not potential contour segment points.*

The (SRLE) algorithm removes isolated points: those which do not have a neighbor on at least one side of their excitatory neighborhoods. At the same time, as the information contained in the magnitude of the edge operator responses is no longer necessary, the SRLE algorithm removes the magnitude information and labels the points as either 'end points' or 'interjacent points'.

SHORT RANGE LINEAR EXCITATION ALGORITHM:
  PARALLEL FOR (all $p \neq 0$) DO
    IF (p has nonzero neighbors on both sides of its
      excitatory neighborhood)THEN
      (p's Type Label is set to 'interjacent point');
    ELSIF (p has nonzero neighbors on only one side of its
      excitatory neighborhood) THEN
      (p's Type Label is set to 'end point');
    END;
  END;

6.3. Spur removal

The discrete nature of both the pixel locations and the oriented operator responses can cause discretization problems, several of which appear as short spurs on the extracted contours. This stage of processing removes the unnecessary spurs using the excitatory and inhibitory neighborhoods.

6.4. Contour labeling

The next stage of processing provides a unique label for each image contour segment in the ρ-space representation by using connected connected component labeling. Any parallel three-dimensional connected component labeling algorithm can be used (Miller and Stout, 1992). After the labeling each potential contour point now has two labels: the Type Label which indicates whether the point is an interjacent point or an end point; and, the Contour Label which indicates on which contour the point lies.

6.5. Orientation discontinuity detection

In this stage of processing the four types of orientation discontinuities are detected using the cylindrical neighborhoods. Each ρ-space end point now has an additional label indicating the type of discontinuity present.

6.6. Short gap filling

Any short gaps in the contour segments of length less than or equal to the $2s + 1$ are filled at this stage using the excitatory neighborhoods.

6.7. Long range linear inhibition

Short, unconnected contour segments of length less than $2s + 1$ are removed at this stage.

6.8. Long gap filling

Long gaps are filled in contours at this stage using long oriented neighborhoods (Krishnan, 1988). This stage is only necessary if image contours intersect at shallow angles.

6.9. The final result of the rho-space algorithms

After the edge detection and the ρ-space algorithms have been applied, the original contour image is in its final ρ-space representation form. At this stage the Perceptual Significance Hierarchy Algorithm, the Segmentation Algorithm and/or the Grouping Algorithms can be applied.

6.10. Illusory contours

It was initially a surprise to find that if illusory contours were present in the original image, they were turned into actual contours in the ρ-space representation of the image. It was surprising because the ρ-space algorithms were not designed to generate illusory contours. The illusory contours are created by an interaction between edge detection and lateral inhibition which produces a short orthogonal line at the free ends of contours, and the gap filling which joins together short linear contour segments. The short orthogonal lines produced by edge detectors are generally thought to be an unfortunate side effect of the operators, thus it is interesting to see how they may play a useful role in machine perception.

Grossberg and Mingolla (1985) have an interesting model of illusory contour formation which utilizes the end-stopping of lines. Their system is different in that it is actually an attempt to model the low-level physiology of neurons, and thus uses a continuous mathematical model to simulate their behavior. However in spite of the very different type of implementation, the similarity in both the mechanism and the results of illusory contour formation between the their system and ours suggests that both may capture some basic property of illusory contours.

6.11. Scale

The PSH, SA, GA and ρ-space algorithms have been presented for a single image scale. While in many cases this is all that is required for the analysis of contour images, there are some cases where individual contours contain useful information at more than one scale (Witkin, 1986). In such cases it would be necessary to implement the ρ-space algorithms at a number of different scales. This would be readily accomplished through the use of different scale edge operators. Since the sizes of the ρ-space neighborhoods are a function of the scale of the edge operator used, a different set of neighborhoods would be required at each scale. The edge operators used for the example image shown in this chapter would correspond to the smallest scale operators.

7. Algorithm implementation

There are two different ways that the ρ-space algorithms can be run on a ρ-space machine.

One way would be to have a pipeline of ρ-space machines with each performing just one stage of the computations. The output of one ρ-space machine would serve as the input to the next. No clocking would be necessary as long as the input data were to remain present throughout the entire computation time. The other way would be to use a single ρ-space machine and run each algorithm on the machine consecutively. This would require either clocking or reprogramming of the ρ-space machine for each algorithm.

Although all of the algorithms presented assume a parallel architecture, such as the ρ-space machine, they are all easily implemented on a pipe-lined image processing system, or on a general-purpose serial computer. The images shown in this chapter were processed on a Sun workstation with an attached image processing system.

Since the computations involved are all simple, the processing time is minimal. However, because of the large amount of data that is generated, the time required for reading in and out images may be long unless an image processor with adequate image memory is used.

7.1. Example image from edge detection

One way in which the ρ-space algorithms were tested was on an image consisting of a noisy grey-scale checkerboard. This is a test image that has been used to compare edge detection algorithms (Grimson and Hildreth, 1985). Although the ρ-space algorithms were designed for use with stylus generated contour images, they also perform well on grey scale images such as the one seen in Figure 10a.

In Figure 10b we see the nonzero responses of the edge detection. In Figures 10b and c the results of the ρ-space processing are displayed as the image that one would see by looking down on top of ρ-space and placing the largest positive value which occurs in any plane at position (x, y) in the pixel $p(x, y)$. Figure 10c shows the results after lateral inhibition. Note that many of the edge responses have been removed at this stage. Figure 10d shows the results after short-range linear excitation. In Figure 10d through f the results are displayed by treating each ρ-space plane as a binary image where a zero indicates no contour point is present and a one indicates a contour point. The binary images are ANDed together and the result displayed with the zero's as white and the one's as black. The short range linear excitation

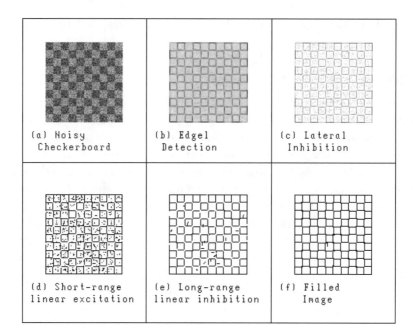

Fig. 10. *Example Image from Edge Detection. (a) Original image with added noise. (b) Composite results after edge detection. (c) Composite results after lateral inhibition. (d) Composite results after short range linear excitation. (e) Composite results after long range linear inhibition. (f) Composite results after filling.*

has removed the isolated contour points. Figure 10e shows the results after long-range linear inhibition has removed more of the noise induced contour points. The final version after filling is seen in Figure 10f. Note that all of the edge pixels in the original image are labeled as contour pixels, thus the conditional probability of an assigned edge, given a true edge is 1.0 (Grimson and Hildreth, 1985). The one short segment caused by noise remaining in Figure 10f results in a non-zero value (0.0006) for the conditional probability of an actual edge. It is interesting to note that the performance of the ρ-space algorithms is superior to other edge detection algorithms on this type of image (Grimson and Hildreth, 1985; Haralick, 1984).

7.2. Example image from character recognition

Figure 11a shows another test image. This one comes from the field of character recognition and shows three overlapping hand-printed characters with added uniform noise. This is a difficult image for a character recognition system not just because of the added noise, but because the characters overlap and most character recognition systems require segmented characters as input. The ρ-space algorithms can provide useful preprocessing in such cases, as they can allow the characters to be easily segmented. Figure 11b

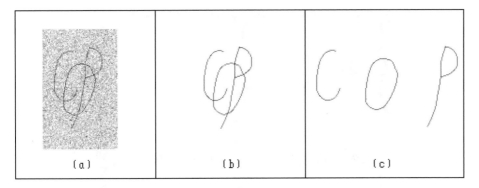

Fig. 11. *Example Image from Character Recognition Field. (a) Original image of overlapping characters with added noise. (b) Composite image of contours that could be potential characters. (c) Contours segmented into the three sets likely to be single characters.*

shows the contour segments which were long enough to be potential characters and Figure 11c shows the three separate groups or segments found in the image. Note that each group or segment corresponds to a single character which could then be input to a character recognition system. Not all alphanumeric characters would be segmented into a single segment: some characters would produce multiple segments in the ρ-space algorithms. Multiple segments would occur for characters where the stylus is lifted during the generation phase. Each segment would correspond to a physical event in the image generation; an individual stroke of the stylus. Thus the segmentation captures information important in image generation which could then be useful for character recognition. Recall that the ρ-space algorithms do not have any information about characters incorporated into them. They are based instead on generic information about stylus generated images, which thus applies to images of characters.

7.3. Example cartoon image

The final example comes from the pre-press industry: the color filling problem described earlier. A cartoon was scanned to produce a digitized image, which was then thresholded. The edges of blob regions were detected and the contours thinned using a standard thinning algorithm. The resulting image was convolved with the set of oriented edge operators and the ρ-space algorithms were applied. The thinned image is displayed in Figure 12a.

The rest of the images in Figures 12 and 13 show results of the Segmentation Algorithm as composite images. In Figure 12b the segment of the image corresponding to the coat and chair is highlighted. This is a case where a segment does not correspond to a single object or object part. The artist has intentionally drawn both objects with a continuous stroke or with

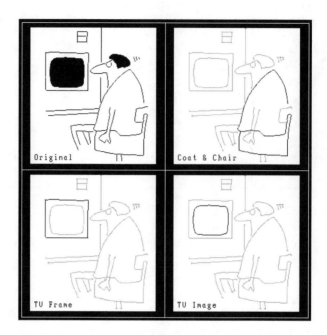

Fig. 12. *Example Cartoon Image. (a) Processed input image. (b)–(d) Composite images showing some of the individual segments produced by the ρ-space algorithms.*

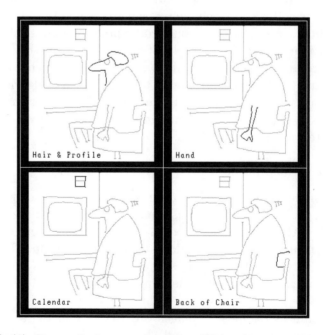

Fig. 13. *(a)–(d) Composite images showing additional segments produced by the ρ-space algorithms.*

adjoining strokes. As this cartoon was not meant to be color-filled this would not be perceived as a problem. However if it were to be color-filled, the chair portion could be readily filled, while the coat portion would require an extension of the line at the back of the coat which would have to be done by hand. Note that the portion of the coat which is occluded by the hand has been generated by the ρ-space algorithms. Parts c and d of Figure 12 show the segments which correspond to the TV frame and TV image respectively, and are correct. Figure 13a shows a segment corresponding to the hair and profile. Again the segment does not correspond to a single object. This time the problem was caused by the thinning algorithm. The new thinning algorithm based on the stylus generated image model would not have produced this problem. Figure 13b shows the hand segment, while parts c and d show the calendar and chair back segments respectively.

From our analysis of cartoon images it appears that the ρ-space algorithms solve at least eight percent of the problems that require hand retouching in the color-filling application. As the color-filling process requires a human to operate the computer graphics system and manually perform the color-filling it is possible to have the operator correct the remaining problems using the computer graphics system. Thus while it was found that correcting the original number of problems on the computer graphics system was more expensive than having the images manually retouched with ink and white-out before digitization, the reduction in the number of problems after the ρ-space processing now makes it more cost effective to correct the remaining problems on the computer graphics system and thus dispense with the entire manual retouching process. This is an example of a computer vision application where perfect performance is not required, as there is still a human in the loop who can correct any remaining problems. Given the current level of performance of most computer vision systems, it would be useful to uncover more applications such as this one in which a vision system can be useful without first having to achieve one hundred percent correct performance.

Acknowledgements

This research was supported in part by the National Science Foundation Grants IST-8409827 and IRI-8705553 awarded to the first author.

Appendices

A. Parallel Segmentation Algorithm for Level x (SA)

FOR (PSH Level $= x$ to 10) DO
    WHILE (segment connected to labeled segments of single label) DO

    (attach label to adjacent segment);
  END;
  WHILE (segment unlabeled and connected to multiple labels) DO
    (attach multiple labels);
  END;
   IF (any segment unlabeled) THEN
    (attach labels via connected component analysis);
  END;
END;

B. Parallel Grouping Algorithm (GA)

FOR (all segments) DO
  (attach unique $label_1$ to each side of segment);
END;
FOR (all Type A, B and C discontinuities) DO
  (equivalance adjacent $label_1$'s of terminating segments);
END;
FOR (all segments) DO
  (replace $label_1$ with lowest equivalent $label_1$);
  (set value of $label_2$ to value of $label_1$);
END;
FOR (all Type C discontinuities and segment intersections) DO
  (break nonterminating segments into two segments);
  (assign unique $label_2$ to each new segment);
END;
FOR (all Type A, B and C discontinuities and intersections) DO
  (equivalance adjacent $label_2$'s of terminating segments);
END;
FOR (all segments) DO
  (replace $label_2$ with lowest equivalent $label_2$);
END;

C. Inhibitory Neighborhood Arrays of Span $s = 3$

$$I_{0,3} = \begin{pmatrix} 1 & 1 & 1 & 1 & 1 & 1 & 1 \\ 1 & 1 & 1 & 1 & 1 & 1 & 1 \\ 0 & 0 & 0 & 1 & 0 & 0 & 0 \\ 0 & 0 & 0 & 0 & 0 & 0 & 0 \\ 0 & 0 & 0 & 1 & 0 & 0 & 0 \\ 1 & 1 & 1 & 1 & 1 & 1 & 1 \\ 1 & 1 & 1 & 1 & 1 & 1 & 1 \end{pmatrix} \quad I_{1,3} = \begin{pmatrix} 1 & 1 & 1 & 1 & 1 & 1 & 0 \\ 1 & 1 & 1 & 1 & 1 & 0 & 0 \\ 1 & 1 & 1 & 1 & 0 & 0 & 0 \\ 0 & 0 & 0 & 0 & 0 & 0 & 0 \\ 0 & 0 & 0 & 1 & 1 & 1 & 1 \\ 0 & 0 & 1 & 1 & 1 & 1 & 1 \\ 0 & 1 & 1 & 1 & 1 & 1 & 1 \end{pmatrix}$$

$$I_{2,3} = \begin{pmatrix} 1 & 1 & 1 & 1 & 1 & 0 & 0 \\ 1 & 1 & 1 & 1 & 0 & 0 & 0 \\ 1 & 1 & 1 & 0 & 0 & 0 & 1 \\ 1 & 1 & 0 & 0 & 0 & 1 & 1 \\ 1 & 0 & 0 & 0 & 1 & 1 & 1 \\ 0 & 0 & 0 & 1 & 1 & 1 & 1 \\ 0 & 0 & 1 & 1 & 1 & 1 & 1 \end{pmatrix}$$

$$I_{3,3} = I_{1,3}^T$$

$$I_{4,3} = I_{0,3}^T$$

$$I_{5,3} = \text{the reflection about the } y \text{ axis of } I_{3,3}$$

$$I_{6,3} = I_{2,3}^T$$

$$I_{7,3} = I_{5,3}^T$$

D. Excitatory Neighborhood Arrays of Span $s = 3$

$$E_{0,0,3} = \begin{pmatrix} 0 & 0 & 0 & 0 & 0 & 0 & 0 \\ 0 & 0 & 0 & 0 & 0 & 0 & 0 \\ 0 & 0 & 0 & 0 & 1 & 1 & 1 \\ 0 & 0 & 0 & 1 & 1 & 1 & 1 \\ 0 & 0 & 0 & 0 & 1 & 1 & 1 \\ 0 & 0 & 0 & 0 & 0 & 0 & 0 \\ 0 & 0 & 0 & 0 & 0 & 0 & 0 \end{pmatrix} \quad E_{1,0,3} = \begin{pmatrix} 0 & 0 & 0 & 0 & 0 & 0 & 1 \\ 0 & 0 & 0 & 0 & 0 & 1 & 1 \\ 0 & 0 & 0 & 0 & 1 & 1 & 1 \\ 0 & 0 & 0 & 1 & 1 & 1 & 1 \\ 0 & 0 & 0 & 0 & 0 & 0 & 0 \\ 0 & 0 & 0 & 0 & 0 & 0 & 0 \\ 0 & 0 & 0 & 0 & 0 & 0 & 0 \end{pmatrix}$$

$$E_{2,0,3} = \begin{pmatrix} 0 & 0 & 0 & 0 & 0 & 1 & 1 \\ 0 & 0 & 0 & 0 & 1 & 1 & 1 \\ 0 & 0 & 0 & 1 & 1 & 1 & 0 \\ 0 & 0 & 0 & 1 & 1 & 0 & 0 \\ 0 & 0 & 0 & 0 & 0 & 0 & 0 \\ 0 & 0 & 0 & 0 & 0 & 0 & 0 \\ 0 & 0 & 0 & 0 & 0 & 0 & 0 \end{pmatrix}$$

$$E_{0,1,3} = \text{the reflection about the } y \text{ axis of} E_{0,0,3}$$

$$E_{1,1,3} = \text{the reflection about the } x \text{ axis of the reflection}$$
$$\text{about the } y \text{ axis of } E_{1,0,3}$$

$$E_{2,1,3} = E_{2,0,3}^T$$

$$E_{3,0,3} = E_{1,1,3}^T$$

$$E_{3,1,3} = E_{1,0,3}^T$$

$$E_{4,0,3} = E_{0,1,3}^T$$

$$E_{4,1,3} = E_{0,0,3}^T$$

$E_{5,0,3} =$ the reflection about the y axis of $E_{3,0,3}$

$E_{5,1,3} =$ the reflection about the y axis of $E_{3,1,3}$

$E_{6,0,3} =$ the reflection about the y axis of $E_{2,1,3}$

$E_{6,1,3} =$ the reflection about the y axis of $E_{2,0,3}$

$$E_{7,0,3} = E_{5,1,3}^T$$

$$E_{7,1,3} = E_{5,0,3}^T$$

E. Cylindrical Neighborhood Array of Span $g = 3$

$$C_g = \begin{pmatrix} 0 & 0 & 1 & 1 & 1 & 0 & 0 \\ 0 & 1 & 1 & 1 & 1 & 1 & 0 \\ 1 & 1 & 1 & 1 & 1 & 1 & 1 \\ 1 & 1 & 1 & 1 & 1 & 1 & 1 \\ 1 & 1 & 1 & 1 & 1 & 1 & 1 \\ 0 & 1 & 1 & 1 & 1 & 1 & 0 \\ 0 & 0 & 1 & 1 & 1 & 0 & 0 \end{pmatrix}$$

Detection and discrimination of motion-defined and luminance-defined two-dimensional form

David Regan

1. Camouflage and the breaking of camouflage by relative motion

A major function of the human visual pathway is to provide a neural basis for recognizing external objects, and for judging their different locations, speeds and directions of motion in the outside world. It is widely assumed that, to perform this function, retinal images features are first partitioned into discrete packages, each package corresponding to a different external object. Because of the effortless ease and accuracy with which the visual pathway usually carries out retinal image partition, the formidable difficulty of the task was not fully recognized until recently, when scientists attempted to instruct machines to recover the external objects in rather simple scenes from TV camera images of those scenes.

Clearly, in order to segregate the retinal image of an object from the retinal image of that object's surroundings, the object's retinal image must differ visually in some way from the retinal image of its surroundings. The great majority of empirical studies on the detection and discrimination of spatial attributes of objects have been restricted to objects defined by differences in luminance (LD objects)—such as, for example, luminance gratings and bright lines—and theoretical efforts to define the necessary and sufficient conditions for figure-ground segregation have been largely restricted to this case (Marr, 1982). However, it is well known that the human visual pathway can distinguish an object from its surroundings (i.e., achieve figure-ground segregation) when the object and surroundings are identical in luminance. For example, Helmholtz (1909) noted that relative motion alone can not only support the visual detection of a camouflaged object, but can also support some degree of spatial discrimination in that the shapes of motion-defined (MD) objects can be recognized and their relative positions perceived.

> "Suppose, for instance that a person is standing still in a thick woods, where it is impossible for him to distinguish, except vaguely and roughly, in the mass of foliage and branches all around him what belongs to one tree and what to

another, or how far apart the separate trees are, etc. But the moment he begins to move forward, everything disentangles itself, and immediately he gets an appreciation of the material contents of the woods and their relations to each other in space, just as if he were looking at a good stereoscopic view of it."[1]

This point is brought out by a Victorian magic lantern entertainment depicted in Figure 1. If Figures 1A and 1B are enlarged, photocopied onto transparent sheets, and placed one on top of the other, the flying bird is virtually invisible. But when sheet B is moved over sheet A, the flying bird is immediately revealed, and remains visible as long as it is moving.

Before going on, we should distinguish between two types of two-dimensional (2D) figure-ground segregation by motion alone.

1.1. Type A: moving figure

A perfectly-camouflaged textured figure is rendered visible by its bodily translation relative to its identically-textured surroundings. When texture motion is continuous, case A includes Helmholtz' everyday situation of camouflaged form that is revealed by motion parallax. Case A also includes the finding that a camouflaged textured form can be revealed by a single abrupt bodily displacement of the form relative to its surroundings, provided that the displacement is not too large (Regan and Spekreijse, 1970; Anstis, 1970; Julesz, 1971; Braddick, 1974).

1.2. Type B: stationary figure

A perfectly-camouflaged textured figure remains stationary relative to its identically-textured surroundings, and is rendered visible by motion of the texture within the form relative to the texture surrounding the form (MacKay, 1976).

2. Issues to be discussed

For our present purpose, the relevant point brought out by the informal Figure 1 demonstration is that the shape of the flying bird can be recognized. This implies that humans can do more than merely detect the presence of a motion-defined form: shape discrimination is possible, in rudimentary degree at least. But this informal demonstration provides no quantitative information on how the acuity of shape and other spatial discriminations compare for motion-defined and luminance-defined form. I discuss this question below while describing the effects of dot contrast, dot speed, dot lifetime, presentation duration, target area and retinal eccentricity on detection and

---

[1] Taken from the 1962 edition of Helmholtz (1909, Southall's translation 1962), pp. 295–296.

A

B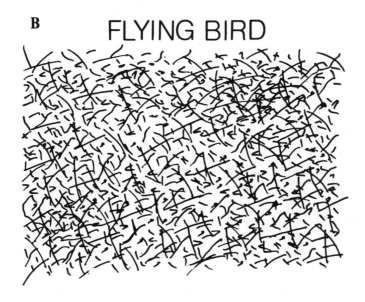

Fig. 1. *Form from motion. If a transparency of (b) is superimposed on a transparency of (a), the bird is virtually invisible, but when (a) is moved across (b) the bird is not only immediately seen, but its shape is recognized. This demonstration can also be achieved by projecting slides of (a) and (b). The principle was described in a children's book published in the late 1930s, but the basic idea dates from Victorian times at least. The effectiveness of camouflage in this particular example was achieved as follows: The bird is defined by 21 penstrokes in ordered array; the background is composed of the same 21 penstrokes drawn at random. From Regan (1986a). ©VNU Science Press, 1986. Reprinted with permission.*

discrimination for MD and LD form. The following two theoretical issues are then discussed in the context of visual abnormalities in patients with neurological disorders: (1) is the detection of MD and LD form determined by the same neural mechanism?; (2) does the same neural mechanism determine any given spatial discrimination for MD and LD form? This chapter ends with an attempt to relate psychophysical findings in human to current knowledge of functional neuroanatomy in monkey.

3. Apparatus

In Sections 5 through 9 below, the display was not generated by a computer. The significance of this point is described below.

In Sections 5 through 9, a pseudo-random pattern of bright dots subtending 2.2 × 2.2 deg was generated by laboratory-built hardware electronics, displayed on a CRT (Tektronix model 608 with green P31 phosphor) and viewed from a distance of 207 cm. There were 100 complete frames per sec. Dots subtended about 2.0 min arc, and mean dot separation was 6 min arc (approx. 1000 dots in all). A new dot pattern could be generated every frame. Dots could be moved in any direction by applying an analog voltage to the monitor's x and/or y plates. The motion of dots within a rectangular sub-area of the entire 2.2 × 2.2 deg pattern could be controlled independently of the motion of dots outside this area, and the orientation, x-y dimensions and location of the area were controlled by external voltages independently of dot motion. This rectangular sub-area could not be demarcated visually from the rest of the dot pattern if the dot velocity inside and outside the sub-area were the same. By means of a beamsplitter, the dot pattern was optically superimposed on a circular, uniformly-illuminated green area of diameter 3.7 deg and luminance 2.1 cd m^{-2}. Dot contrast could be varied by placing neutral density filters immediately in front of the CRT that generated the dot pattern so as to reduce the intensity of the dots without affecting the 2.1 cd m^{-1} luminance of the 3.7 deg superimposed light. Dots were switched off except during the pattern presentations. A new pseudo-random dot pattern was generated for each trial.

In contrast with a computer-generated display, dots could be moved by an indefinitely small distance and their direction of motion could be altered by an indefinitely small angle. Dot speed could be made indefinitely slow while maintaining a jump rate of 100 per sec. The dimensions of the camouflaged rectangle could be altered by indefinitely small amounts, and indefinitely slowly while maintaining a jump rate of 100 per sec.

In order to measure thresholds of about 0.3 deg, it was necessary to present orientation differences as small as 0.1 deg. A pixel-based system has the disadvantage that the long edges of an inclined bar are stepped rather than being straight, and this limits the smallest change in orientation. For example, a bar 600 pixels in length oriented at 0.1 deg to the vertical would have only a single one-pixel step along its length—whatever the viewing distance. Our display has the advantage that indefinitely small changes in orientation can be generated.

In section 10 below, the motion-defined letters were generated by a computer.[2] The dot pattern in Figure 2A contained a camouflaged letter that could not be detected when the dots were either all stationary or all moving in the same direction at the same speed. Figure 2A illustrates the effectiveness with which the letter was camouflaged when all dots were stationary.

---

[2] Software to generate motion-defined letters is available gratis to researchers. Send a blank 5.25 or 3.25-in. disc in a returnable cardboard disc envelope. The program will run *only* on an IBM PC type 386 or clone with a VGA "Wonder Plus" graphics card.

4. Unconfounding the multiple cues to motion-defined form

At first sight, the observation that motion parallax can enhance or even create an object's visibility might be taken to imply that figure-ground segregation can be supported entirely by the action of velocity-sensitive neural mechanisms. However, this conclusion does not necessarily follow. In point of fact, it is not self-evident that figure-ground segregation caused by motion parallax can be wholly or even partially attributed to motion.

Real-world motion parallax confounds several cues to figure-ground segregation, even when the object has exactly the same luminance, color, texture and depth as its surroundings. These cues include the following:

1   Retinal image velocity is different on either side of the object's boundaries.

2   During any given time interval, different distances are moved by points within and outside the boundaries of the object's retinal image.

3   The third cue is that texture continuously appears or disappears along the object's boundaries (except for those parts that are oriented parallel to the object's direction of motion). Therefore, in principle, local flicker sensors could detect and localize the object's boundaries.

In order to study the role of relative velocity in the visual extraction of form from motion, it is necessary to deconfound the three cues to form listed above. The reason for using equal and opposite speeds rather than different speeds or different directions of motion, and for choosing type B motion-defined form rather than type A motion-defined form is brought out in Figure 2 for the case of the motion-defined letters used in Section 10 (the argument is exactly the same for the motion-defined rectangles used in Sections 5 through 9). In Figure 2B the letter, camouflaged in Figure 2A, was made visible to the eye by moving the dots within the letter rightwards at V deg/s while moving the dots outside the letter leftwards at V deg/s, so that relative velocity was 2V deg/s. Note that the letter itself was stationary. Figure 2B illustrates that, although the letter was clearly visible to the eye, the letter was almost invisible in a photograph. This was because the human visual pathway is sensitive to the direction of motion, but a camera is not. Figure 2E–G illustrates the reason why we chose to move dots within the camouflaged form at the same speed as dots outside the camouflaged form, but in the opposite direction (Regan, 1986a). To aid explanation, the dot density in Figure 2D–G was 2% rather than the 25% used in the experiment. Figure 2E confirms that, just as in Figure 2B, the letter, though visible to the eye, was almost invisible to a camera when dots inside and outside the letter moved at equal and opposite speeds. However, when dots outside the letter moved at a different speed

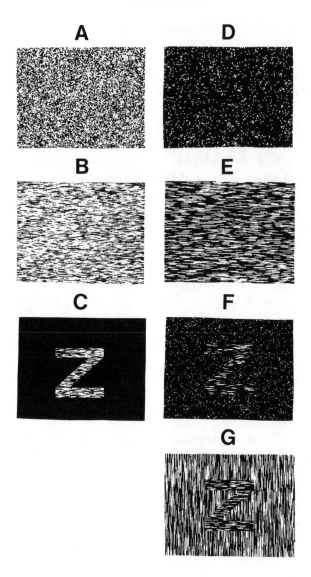

Fig. 2. *(A) A letter was perfectly camouflaged within this pattern of dots. Dot density was 25%. (B) Dots within the letter moved rightwards at speed V while dots outside the letter moved leftwards at the same speed V. This motion rendered the letter visible to the eye but, as illustrated here, the letter was almost invisible to the camera, because the edges of the letter were defined only by an abrupt change in the direction of motion. (C) A contrast-defined letter was created by switching off all the dots outside the letter. (D) As for (A), but dot density was 2%. (E). As for (B), but dot density was 2%. (F) As for (E) except that all dots outside the letter were stationary. (G) As for (E) except that dots outside the letter moved vertically while dots inside the letter moved horizontally. From Regan et al. (1992). ©Oxford University Press, 1992. Reprinted with permission.*

to dots inside the letter (Figure 2F) the letter was not only visible to the eye, but was also evident in a photograph. This was also the case when the letter itself was moving (type A motion-defined form) whether it was surrounded by stationary dots or by dynamic random noise. Again, when dots inside and outside the letter moved in different directions, the letter was evident in a photograph (Figure 2G). Clearly, the letters in Figures 2F and G could not have been rendered visible by differences in the direction of dot motion — a camera is not sensitive to the direction of motion. Rather, they were rendered visible by texture contrast. Therefore, if a form is rendered visible to the eye by a difference in either speed or the direction of motion, we cannot necessarily assume that the visibility is created entirely or even partly by the neural processing of motion information. *In principle, the letter could be seen and recognized by a subject who was totally blind to motion per se.* For example, temporal integration in cortical neurons that were sensitive to the length and orientation of a line might cause them to respond to a moving dot as though the moving dot were a line of some specific length and orientation — much as the camera responded in Figures 2F and G.

However, we cannot assume that the retinal image was identical to the camera image in Figure 2B. In particular, we cannot assume that the eye remained stationary rather than tracking one or other set of dots. For example, if the eye tracked the dots within the bar, the retinal image would approximate Figure 2F rather than Figure 2B. By measuring eye movements using an SRI double Purkinje eye tracker, we showed that, for our small (2 to 3 deg subtense) displays, tracking eye movements were not appreciable. But to resolve the uncertainty directly we stabilized the retinal image (Regan, 1986a). We could then assume that texture contrast had been removed as a cue to figure-ground segregation.

We should add that careful inspection of the 2% dot density photograph (Figure 2E) reveals the camouflaged letter and (with a little imagination) one might also read the letter in the Figure 2B photograph of the stimulus we used in this study. This is logically unavoidable, because dots are created and destroyed only along the non-horizontal boundaries of the concealed letter. Therefore, trajectories that are shorter than average occur only near the letter's boundaries. This weak cue to the shape of the letter can be masked by creating a new random dot pattern many times per second, and we have shown that spatial discriminations are little degraded by the manoeuvre (Hamstra and Regan, 1991; Regan, 1986a; Regan and Hamstra, 1991) so that, in practice, the accretion and deletion of texture at the letter's boundaries seems to make little contribution to visibility. Having eliminated both the blur line length and the texture creation/destruction cues, we can attribute the bar's detection exclusively to velocity-sensitive neural mechanisms.

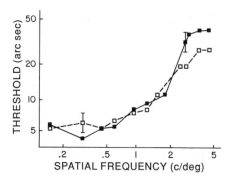

Fig. 3. *Grating detection threshold as a function of grating spatial frequency for a motion-defined sinewave grating. Ordinates plot threshold amplitudes of oscillation of the dots. Each dot in the pattern oscillated at a temporal frequency of 2 Hz. Note that sensitivity did not fall off at the lowest spatial frequencies tested. Nakayama and Tyler (1981). ©Pergamon Press, 1981. Reprinted with permission.*

5. Detection of motion-defined form in the central and peripheral visual field

5.1. Spatial frequency filtering characteristic for motion-defined grating detection

The detection of motion-defined form has been studied using both spatially-periodic targets (gratings) and non-periodic targets (isolated rectangles and isolated letters).

Nakayama and Tyler (1981) created motion-defined sinewave gratings by imposing a sinusoidal variation of dot velocity across a pseudo-random pattern of dots. Their spatial frequency filtering function for gratings defined by relative motion, shown in Figure 3, brings out the point that detection sensitivity for motion-defined gratings falls off more rapidly at high spatial frequencies than does detection sensitivity for luminance-defined gratings. In Figure 3, sensitivity falls off above about 0.7 cpd, and grating acuity can be estimated at 5 to 10 cpd. Nakayama and Tyler concluded that the spatial summation field size for detecting motion-defined form is larger than for detecting luminance-defined form. They estimated summation field size to be about 2° in their experimental conditions. Using a different approach, Richards (1971) arrived at a similar estimate.

5.2. Spatial summation for detecting a discrete motion-defined area

Detection thresholds for a motion-defined square fell as the square's area was increased, but the curve levelled out for areas above 1–2 deg^2 (Figure 4A). For comparison, Figure 4B shows the corresponding threshold curve for a solid, bright, luminance-defined square. The two curves have approximately the same shape, but the upper curve is shifted a considerable distance

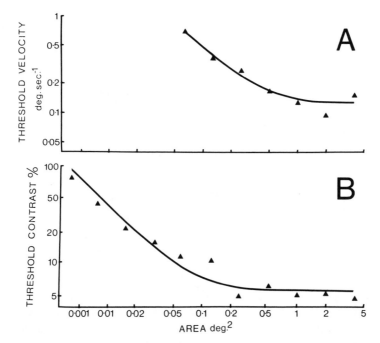

Fig. 4. *Spatial summation for detecting a motion-defined and a luminance-defined square. (a) Dot velocity threshold versus area of the camouflaged motion-defined dotted square. (b) Contrast threshold versus area of the bright solid luminance-defined square. The presentation duration was 0.15 s. From Regan and Beverley (1984). © Optical Society of America, 1984. Reprinted with permission.*

along the abscissa, indicating that the summation field area for the dotted motion-defined target was about five times greater than for a luminance-defined target when both fell on the same para-foveal retinal location at 1.5° eccentricity (Regan and Beverley, 1984).

5.3. Temporal summation for detecting a discrete motion-defined area

Detection threshold for a 1.0 deg^2 motion-defined square progressively falls as presentation duration is increased, asymptoting towards a value of 1–2 min arc/sec. for durations over 2–5 sec (Regan and Beverley, 1984). Detection thresholds for a solid, bright, luminance-defined square level off at much briefer presentation times. For parafoveal viewing the summation time constant is about 750 ms for a 1.0 deg^2 motion-defined square compared with about 60 ms for a luminance-defined square.

5.4. Effect of retinal eccentricity on the spatiotemporal characteristics of motion-defined target detection

Figure 5 shows that log detection threshold for a motion-defined dotted square is closely proportional to eccentricity. The slope of the line grows

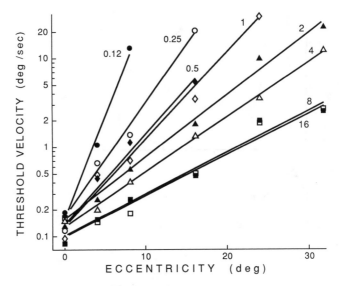

Fig. 5. *Log detection threshold for a motion-defined square is proportional to retinal eccentricity. The effect of eccentricity is less for larger rectangles. The number at the end of each plot is the area of the square in deg². The presentation duration was 0.15 s. From Regan and Beverley (1984). ©Optical Society of America, 1984. Reprinted with permission.*

progressively less as target size increases. In other words, eccentricity has less effect on detection threshold for lager targets. For a target of constant area a we can write:

$$\log V_\theta = \log V_o + K_a\theta \tag{1}$$

where velocity V_θ is the detection threshold at eccentricity θ, V_o is the detection threshold for central viewing $(\theta = 0)$ and K_a is a constant that depends on the area of the motion-defined target. Figure 5 shows that this equation is valid over a 130-fold range of target areas ranging from 0.12 to 16 deg², corresponding to a 200:1 range of speed thresholds.

The effect of eccentricity on temporal summation is quite different from the effect on spatial summation. The integration time constant differs by only 40% at eccentricities of 0 and 16°, contrasting with the roughly 100-fold difference in summation field area at these two locations in the visual field (Regan and Beverley, 1984).

5.5. Dissociation of (a) detection of local motion from (b) detection of motion-defined form.

A theoretical model for figure-ground segregations of MD objects was proposed by Reichardt and his colleagues (Reichardt et al., 1983a, b; Reichardt, 1986). Detectors sensitive to the direction of *local motion* feed a *spatially-integrative* stage which achieves figure-ground segregation for MD form. It

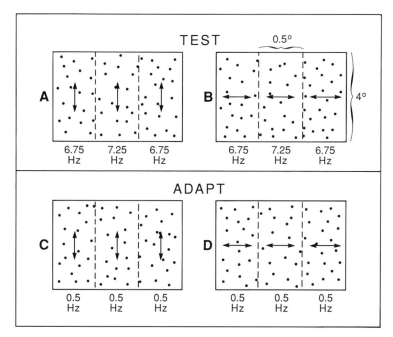

Fig. 6. *Unconfounding the detection of local motion from figure-ground segregation for MD form. See text for details. From Regan (1986b).* ©*Pergamon Press, 1986.*

is relevant to our discussion that this model is also capable of figure-ground segregation for LD form and that, in accord with section 5.3 above, temporal summation for form detection is considerably longer for MD form than for LD form (Reichardt, personal communication, 1986).

Figure 6 illustrates a beat frequency technique for pychophysically dissecting apart the first-stage local motion detectors from the second-stage MD form detectors. Figure 6 C&D show adapting stimuli. All dots oscillated at 0.5 Hz, but there was a phase difference of 180 deg. between the oscillation of dots in the central bar and the two outer bars so that the visibility of the bar pattern fluctuated at 0.5 Hz. In C the adapting pattern was defined by shearing (S) motion and in D by perpendicular compressive/expanding (P) motion. The test stimuli were quite different. Dots oscillated at F=6.75 Hz outside the central bar and at $(F + \Delta F) = 7.25$ Hz inside the central bar. The visibility of the bar pattern fluctuated at the same frequency as for the adapting stimulus, but the test frequency for local motion detectors was either 6.75 or 7.25 Hz, much higher than the 0.5 Hz adapting frequency for local motion detectors. In (a) the test pattern was defined by S motion and in (b) by P motion. The value of ΔF could be manipulated independently of F, thus enabling the effect of dot oscillation frequency to be dissociated from the frequency of figure-ground or boundary processing (frequency ΔF bypassed the first stage local motion detectors and was seen only by the spatially-integrative form detection stage).

6. Subjective observations

6.1. Illusory displacement and motion of a stationary motion-defined form

A striking illusion was observed when a rectangular aperture within a random dot pattern was rendered visible by causing the dots within the area to move with a ramping waveform, while the surrounding dots remained stationary. Subjects reported that the aperture as-a-whole appeared to be in motion when the dots moved even though the aperture itself was, in fact, stationary. There was a second illusory effect: the aperture appeared to change its location as much as several degrees[3] (Regan & Beverley, 1984, pp. 437 & 440). This illusory motion and translation was greater in peripheral than in foveal vision. When the motion of the dots within the aperture was oscillatory rather than unidirectional, the stationary aperture appeared to oscillate from side to side, and again the illusory translation was greater in peripheral than in foveal vision. Similar observations have since been reported by Anstis (1989), Ramachandran and Anstis (1990) and De Valois and DeValois (1991).

6.2. Edge sharpness

At high speeds, subjects reported that a motion-defined rectangle appeared to have sharp edges and had the same shape, size and location on each of several successive presentations. Edge sharpness was much better than would be expected from the 6 min arc inter-dot separation. The appearance of motion-defined edges was quite different at low than at high dot speeds. Subjects reported the impression of an irregularly-shaped and diffuse-edged area rather than a sharp-edged rectangle, and stated that the irregular area appeared to have a different shape and size on each presentation of the same stimulus (Regan and Beverley, 1984).

This change in subjective appearance of the camouflaged bar might be understood in terms of neural "sharpening" caused by interactions between velocity-sensitive neurons with rather large receptive fields. At high dot velocities many neurons are excited, and lateral interactions give rise to the impression of a sharp-edged bar. At low dot velocities only few (the most sensitive) neurons are excited so that lateral interactions are less effective and the sharpness and shape of the bar are determined more by the receptive field size of the most excited neurons than by lateral interactions (Regan, 1989b). An analogous explanation has been offered for the rise of orientation discrimination threshold, spatial frequency discrimination threshold

---

[3] The reason why these two illusions are specified separately is that, although a real object necessarily changes its location when it undergoes translational motion, illusory motion is not necessarily associated with a change of location—as, for example, in the Waterfall illusion.

and line separation threshold at low contrasts (Regan and Beverley, 1983, 1985; Morgan and Regan, 1987).

At first sight the subjective sharpness of a high speed motion-defined edge might seem to conflict with Nakayama & Tyler's finding that visual sensitivity to a motion-defined grating is restricted to low spatial frequencies (see Figure 3), because if a linear system faithfully signals sharp edges it will also respond to high spatial frequencies.On the other hand,this conflict may indicate merely that the neural processing of a motion-defined edge involves nonlinear lateral interactions such that linear systems theory does not predict correctly the response to an isolated edge (i.e. a spatial transient) from the response to an extended repetitive grating pattern (Regan, 1991a).

7. Vernier acuity for motion-defined and luminance-defined form

The illusory displacement of a stationary MD aperture and the apparent sharpness of high-speed MD edges raised the question whether, even though the absolute location of an MD aperture is signalled inaccurately, sensitivity to the precise *relative* locations of MD objects might remain acute. I addressed this question by measuring psychometric functions for the vernier task using both MD and LD targets (Regan, 1986a).

Vernier acuity for a motion-defined bar was measured by introducing a vernier step.For purpose of illustration the dots within the bar were rendered stationary when taking the photographs in Figure 6B & C. During the experiment, however, to ensure that figure-ground segregation was supported exclusively by velocity-sensitive neural mechanisms, dots within and outside the bar were moved at equal and opposite speeds, the retinal image was stabilized, and an entirely new dot pattern was created very 0.125 sec (Regan et al., 1986a). Thus, during the experiment,the camouflaged bar was clearly evident to the eye, but was almost invisible to a camera (Figure 6A). Dot density was about 200 dots deg^{-2}, and contrast was near 100%.

The main finding was that, in our conditions, vernier acuity for a motion-defined dotted bar was not significantly different from vernier acuity for an uncamouflaged luminance-defined dotted bar that was created by removing all dots outside the bar's boundaries. Vernier acuity was 27 sec arc for the best subject and 45 sec arc for the worst. With a solid bright-bar LD vernier target, our subjects had vernier acuities of 5 to 8 sec arc that approximated classical values in the literature. (A solid bright bar is the limiting case of high dot density.) It has been reported that, as dot density is progressively raised above about 200 dot deg^{-2}, vernier acuity for an LD bar grows progressively better than vernier acuity for an MD bar (Banton and Levi, 1990), just as visual acuity for an LD letter grows progressively better than visual acuity for an MD letter (Figure 15 below).

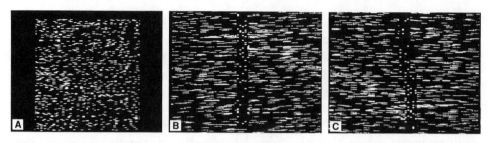

Fig. 7. *(A) This pseudo-random pattern of dots contains a camouflaged bar. As illustrated, the bar is almost invisible to a camera when the dots inside and outside the bar move in opposite directions at the same speed. (B,C) The bar is visible to a camera when the dots inside and outside the bar move at different speeds. From Regan (1986a). ©VNU Science Press, 1986. Reprinted with permission.*

Although vernier acuities of 25–45 sec arc might seem poor compared with the best values in the literature (2–5 sec arc), they are considerably smaller than the 120 sec arc dot size and 360 sec arc mean dot separation of the stimulus, and the 7200 sec arc estimated summation field diameter for the detection of motion-defined targets. In an attempt to explain this discrepancy between vernier acuity and receptive field size, Regan (1986a) pointed out that some authors have suggested that vernier acuity for conventional bright-line targets can be explained in terms of contrast sensitivity and the luminance distribution in the retinal image, but that this cannot be the case for the motion-defined bar of Figure 7A because there was no luminance cue to the bar's presence. An intriguing clue is that subjects reported that the stationary (type B) MD bar did not appear to have a vernier step. Rather, the bar-as-a-whole appeared to be tilted. Subjects performed the vernier task as though it were an orientation discrimination task. According to this idea, the 27 sec arc vernier threshold was equivalent to an orientation discrimination threshold of about 0.2 deg. Subsequent research showed this threshold to be closely equivalent to threshold in a genuine orientation discrimination task (see Figure 10). On this basis, I proposed that vernier acuity for a type B MD bar is determined by the relative activity of orientation-tuned neural mechanisms, perhaps by opponent processing as illustrated in Figure 9 (Regan et al., 1986a).

When the vernier target was presented as type A MD form (i.e. the whole bar moved), subjects reported that it looked quite different than when presented as type B MD form. The bar appeared to be vertical with a clear vernier step. Rather than using illusory orientation as the principal cue, subjects reported that the principal cue to the task was the sharp vernier step. But the thresholds obtained were the same as for the type B bar, even though the task was subjectively so different. I suggested that, for a type B MD bar, vernier acuity is determined by the relative activity of local motion detectors whose receptive fields are not spatially coincident, a suggestion that echoes the spirit of Westheimer's (1975, 1979) hypothesis of vernier discrimination for luminance-defined bright lines.

8. Orientation discrimination for motion-defined and luminance-defined form

8.1. Orientation discrimination for luminance-defined form and an opponent-process model of discrimination

The importance of orientation in visual processing was brought out by Hubel and Wiesel's discovery that the primate visual pathway is organized at the anatomical level in terms of orientation columns for LD form. Whether this same columnar organization holds for responses to MD form remains to be established.

Considering first the processing of orientation for LD form, there is a problem in reconciling the finding that orientation discrimination for bars or gratings (0.15 to 0.5 deg) is far less than the estimated orientation turning bandwidths of psychophysical channels (10 to 20 deg) or the 14 to 26 deg bandwidths of the most sharply-tuned neurons in monkey striate cortex (Westheimer et al., 1976; Andrews, 1965; Andrews, 1967; Andrews et al., 1973; Burbeck and Regan, 1983; Campbell and Kulikowski, 1966; Blakemore and Nachmias, 1971; De Valois et al., 1982). Because the bandwidth estimations cited are based on detection data, this problem can be seen as one of reconciling detection and discrimination data.

Two findings that also call for explanation are that a subject's ability to discriminate the orientations of two successively-presented gratings was not significantly affected when the contrast of successive presentations was randomly varied (Regan and Beverley, 1985) nor when the spatial frequency of successive presentations was randomly varied (Burbeck and Regan, 1983). Here we have an important problem: how to reconcile (a) the finding that subjects effortlessly unconfound changes of grating orientation from simultaneous changes of grating contrast and spatial frequency with (b) physiological evidence that, in general, the firing of any given single neuron in monkey striate cortex confounds changes in orientation, contrast and spatial frequency.

One proposed explanation for these findings is that, for a LD bar or grating of any given orientation, detection is chiefly determined by the cells that are most sensitive at that orientation, while discrimination is chiefly mediated by the relative activity of comparatively weakly-excited cells. This hypothesis has been framed in two formats: an opponent-process format (Westheimer et al., 1976; Regan, 1982; Regan and Beverley, 1985), and a line-element format (Wilson and Regan, 1985; Wilson, 1991b). In principle, opponent-process and line-element models are equivalent when both are linear. However, they are not necessarily equivalent when they are nonlinear

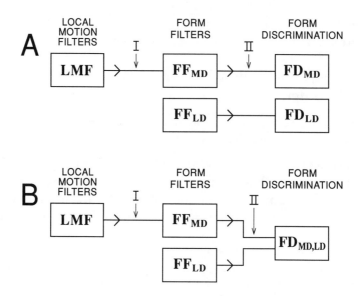

Fig. 8. *Form detection and form discrimination for motion-defined form and luminance-defined form. (A) Filters for luminance-defined form (FF$_{LD}$) that determine detection threshold for LD form feed a form discrimination stage (FD$_{LD}$) that determines discrimination threshold for LD form. Filters sensitive to the direction of local motion (LMF) determine thresholds for detecting and discriminating the direction of coherent motion. This LMF stage feeds filters for motion-defined form (FF$_{MD}$) that determines detection thresholds for MD form. The FF$_{MD}$ stage feeds a form discrimination stage (FD$_{MD}$) that determines discrimination threshold for MD form. (B) Discrimination for both MD and LD form is determined by a common discrimination stage, FD$_{MD,LD}$.*

(Wyszecki and Stiles, 1967). But in the present context a more important difference is that opponent-process models assert that there exists in the brain a physical mechanism that carries out the opponent computation, whereas this physical mechanism is not explicit in line element models (Wyszecki and Stiles, 1967).

A proposed hierarchical opponent-process model is illustrated in Figure 8. Retinal image information passes first through orientation-tuned filters that achieve figure-ground segregation by responding to bars or gratings defined by luminance contrast (stage FF$_{LD}$), and this first stage feeds a second, opponent-orientation, stage (FD$_{LD}$) that determines orientation discrimination (Regan and Beverley, 1985; Regan and Price, 1986). The basic idea is that orientation information may be encoded by neurons that are broadly tuned to orientation without losing information about small differences in orientation—provided that the tuning properties of the neurons are stable and that their noise levels are low (Regan, 1982, 1985). The information is stored in the population activity of the neurons. Figure 9A explains how the most sensitive neuron (b) detects the grating but responds hardly at all when the grating's orientation changes from θ_1 to θ_2. On the other hand, there is a substantial change in the relative activity of comparatively weakly-excited neurons (a) and (c). The two most important neurons for discrimination will be those with the largest difference in sensitivity profile slope. We proposed that these neurons provide the strongest input to an opponent-orientation mechanism whose sensitivity is jointly determined by (1) the relative slopes and (2) the noise that is not common to neurons (a) and (c) (Regan and Beverley, 1985). Note that it is the slope of the tuning curve rather than the bandwidth that determines discrimination.

An opponent (or line element) hypothesis can also explain why subjects effortlessly unconfound a change in orientation from simultaneous changes in contrast and spatial frequency. This is possible if the opponent-orientation stage is fed by neurons that prefer different orientations, but whose dynamics and dependencies on contrast and spatial frequency are identical (Regan and Beverley, 1985; Regan and Price, 1986).

Figure 9A illustrates a testable prediction of the opponent-process model. If the sensitivity of neuron (b) is reduced there will be the following consequences: (1) although contrast detection threshold will rise near orientations θ_1 and θ_2, orientation discrimination threshold will not; (2) discrimination threshold will rise where the slope of sensitivity profile (b) is greatest, i.e. about 15–20 deg on either side of the peak sensitivity of neuron (b). This predicted dissociation between post-adaptation changes in detection and discrimination was tested experimentally and, as shown in Figure 9B, the data were closely in accord with the predictions.

8.2. Orientation discrimination for motion-defined form and an opponent-process model of discrimination

Now we turn from orientation discrimination for LD form to orientation discrimination for MD form. Filled and open symbols in Figures 10 and 11 show that, at high dot speeds and high contrasts, orientation discrimination can be as good for an MD bar as for an LD bar. Furthermore, the absolute value of discrimination threshold (0.3 to 0.6 deg) compares well with the best values in the literature for a bright line or luminance grating. To account for these findings, I proposed that detection and orientation discrimination for MD bars can be described in terms of the sequence of processing stages illustrated in Figure 8. **First stage:** *Local motion filters* (LMF) sensitive to the directions of local motion. This first stage determines thresholds for detecting the presence of coherent motion and discriminating its direction (see Section 11 below). **Second stage:** An array of *orientation-tuned filters* (FF$_{MD}$) sensitive to MD form and to MD (i.e. kinetic) edges. These filters achieve figure-ground segregation and determine detection thresholds for MD form. We suppose that the orientation tuning bandwidths are considerably broader than 0.6 deg, and that all orientations are represented.

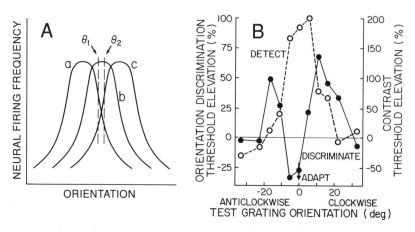

Fig. 9. (A) The continuous lines represent tuning curves of three neurons that are driven from the same retinal location. When the orientation of a stimulus grating changes slightly from θ_1 to θ_2 (marked by arrows), the response of the most active of the orientation-tuned neurons (b) changes negligibly, but there is a substantial change in the relative activations of neurons a and c. (B) Post-adaptation changes in orientation discrimination threshold (continuous line) and contrast detection threshold (dashed line) caused by inspecting a vertical grating (at 0 on abscissa). Modified from Regan and Beverley (1985). Reprinted with permission.

Third stage: A form-discriminating opponent-orientation stage that receives input from stage FF_{MD} and that determines orientation discrimination threshold. We suppose that discrimination threshold is determined by the pattern of activity within the set of orientation-tuned-filters.

A procedure for dissociating local motion detection from form detection (stages LMF and FF_{MD} in Figure 8) has already been described (Section 5.5 and Figure 6). As will be described, this dissociation is also observed in neurological patients with white matter lesions (Section 10 below).

A procedure for dissociating the form detection and orientation discrimination stages is as follows. Figure 12 shows the effect of presentation duration on orientation discrimination for a MD bar (filled circles) and for a LD bar (open circles) of fixed dot speed. Discrimination threshold was evidently much more affected by presentation duration for the MD bar than for the LD bar. However, because dot speed was fixed in Figure 12, the MD bar was less visible at short than at long presentation durations. Figure 13 shows the result of repeating the Figure 12 experiment at constant visibility. Each symbol in Figure 13 represents discrimination data collected for dot speeds that were some fixed multiple of bar detection threshold. The large elevation of orientation discrimination threshold at short presentation durations that was so evident in Figure 12 (filled circles) was almost abolished in Figure 13. Similar results were obtained when dot lifetime rather than presentation duration was varied (Regan and Hamstra, 1990, 1992).

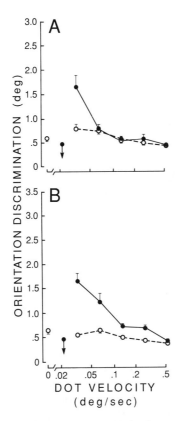

Fig. 10. *Orientation discrimination threshold (ordinates) versus dot speed (abscissae) for a dotted bar defined by relative motion (filled symbols) and for the same bar defined by luminance contrast (open symbols) Dot contrast in (B) was 0.7 log units lower than in (A). Bar detection thresholds are arrowed. The random pattern of 2 min arc bright dots subtended $2.2 \times 2.2°$ and mean dot separation was 6 min arc. The camouflaged bar subtended $1.5 \times 0.22°$. The dot pattern was superimposed on a uniformly-illuminated area of diameter $3.7°$ and luminance 2.1 cd m^{-2}. Presentation duration was 1.0 s. From Regan (1989b). ©Pergamon Press, 1989. Reprinted with permission.*

Our proposed explanation for the difference between the data of Figure 12 and 13 was that normalizing dot speed with respect to detection threshold caused the output of stage FF_{MD} to be constant for every value of presentation duration, i.e. the output of stage FF_{MD} was constant for any given symbol in Figure 13. Following this line of thought, the data of Figures 12 and 13 can be taken to imply that the form detection and form discrimination stages can be dissociated by manipulating presentation duration — on the grounds that stage FF_{MD} is strongly affected by presentation duration but the discrimination stage is not (Regan and Hamstra, 1992). Detection and spatial discrimination for MD form can also be dissociated by brain lesions, as discussed below in Section 10.

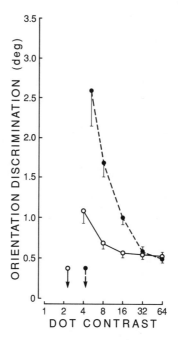

Fig. 11. *Orientation discrimination threshold (ordinates) versus dot contrast (abscissae) for a dotted bar defined by relative motion (filled symbols) and for the same bar defined by luminance contrast (open symbols). Dot speed was 0.5 deg/sec throughout. Bar detection thresholds are arrowed. Other details as in Figure 10. From Regan (1989b). ©Pergamon Press, 1989. Reprinted with permission.*

9. Shape discrimination for motion-defined and luminance-defined form

First we should define what, for our present purpose, we mean by 'shape discrimination' for two-dimensional form. By definition, the shape of a 2D form is independent both of the area of the form and of any given linear dimension. If we consider 2D forms that lie entirely within the xy reference plane, we can define the shape of a form with any required precision in terms of its relative linear dimensions along N fixed azimuths in the xy plane, where $N > 2$. According to this definition, two forms differ in shape if, for any given value of N, their relative dimensions cannot be equated by a relative rotation and translation of the two forms within the xy reference plane. Thus, a necessary requirement of a shape discrimination mechanism is that it should respond to relative dimensions along different azimuths. Our present purpose is served most simply by rectangular forms in a fixed orientation. For convenience we chose a fixed horizontal/vertical orientation. By randomly interleaving rectangles of different areas and different aspect ratios, we forced subjects to base their judgements on a comparison of two or more linear dimensions in different azimuths. This procedure ensured

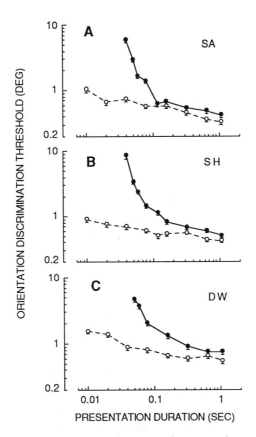

Fig. 12. *Orientation discrimination threshold (ordinates) versus presentation duration (abscissae) for a dotted bar defined by relative motion (•) and for the same
dotted bar defined by luminance contrast (○). The vertical bars mark one standard
error. Dot lifetime was equal to presentation duration. Dot speed was 0.68 deg/sec,
so the relative dot speed was 1.4 deg/sec. A, subject 1. B, subject 2. C, subject
3. From Regan and Hamstra (1992). ©Pergamon Press, 1992. Reprinted with
permission.*

that the only cue to shape was the aspect ratio (a/b), and that no reliable
cue to shape was provided by a alone, nor by b alone, nor by any other
single linear dimension, nor by $a - b$, nor by area (ab). (Dimensions a and
b were, respectively, the height and width of the test rectangle).

The main findings, shown in Figure 14, were as follows: (1) at high dot
speeds and high dot contrasts the best value of the just-discriminable change
in aspect ratio was about 2%; (2) this aspect ratio threshold was approximately the same as for LD rectangles created by switching off all dots
outside the MD rectangle (Regan and Beverley, 1984; Regan, 1989a; Regan
and Hamstra, 1990; 1991).

Let us first suppose that the visual system encodes the shape of the rectangle in a way that is equivalent to the following sequence of processes:

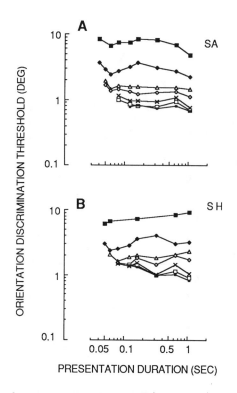

Fig. 13. *Orientation discrimination threshold (ordinates) versus presentation duration (abscissae) for a dotted bar defined by relative motion. Along any given curve, every point was recorded at a dot speed that was the same fixed multiple (N) of the relevant bar detection threshold. Thus, along any given curve, every point was recorded at a different dot speed. Key:* ■, $N = 2$; ◆, $N = 4$; △, $N = 8$; ◇, $N = 10$; ×, $N = 15$; □, $N = 20$; ●, $N = 25$. *Dot lifetime was equal to presentation duration. A, subject 1. B, subject 2. From Regan and Hamstra (1992). ©Pergamon Press, 1992. Reprinted with permission.*

(1) encode of the locations of each of the four edges; (2) calculate of the separation of opposite edges to obtain the side lengths a and b of the rectangle; (3) compare a and b. Thus a shape-discrimination threshold of 2% implies that the location of each of the four edges is encoded with a precision and accuracy of approximately 12 sec. arc for rectangles of area 0.47 deg^2. This transcends the 25 sec arc separation of cones at the foveal center and is considerably less than the separation of cones at about 0.4 deg eccentricity, which is where each edge would be located if the subject fixated the center of the rectangle (Osterberg, 1935; Miller, 1979), thus putting our subjects' performance in the 'hyperacuity' range (Westheimer, 1979). A 12 sec arc precision and accuracy is difficult to reconcile with the 360 sec arc mean separation of stimulus dots and with a diameter of summation fields of roughly 7200 sec arc for the detection of MD targets (Richards, 1971; Nakayama and Tyler, 1981; Regan and Beverley, 1984).

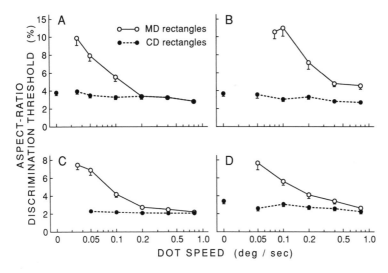

Fig. 14. *Aspect-ratio discrimination threshold (ordinate) versus dot speed (abscissa) for a motion-defined rectangle (open circles) and for a luminance-defined rectangle (filled circles). Threshold was defined as the smallest discriminable change in the ratio a/b, where a and b were, respectively the height and width of the stimulus rectangle.Dot contrast in panels B and C was 0.6 log units less than in panels A and B. The leftmost filled circle in each panel corresponds to zero dot speed. Results for one subject are shown in A & B and for a second subject in C & D. Viewing was monocular. From Regan and Hamstra (1991). ©Pion Press, 1991. Reprinted with permission.*

One possible solution is to assume that the separation of opposite edges (i.e., a and b) is encoded directly rather than via stage (1) above. A similar suggestion has been made previously in the context of line-interval discrimination (Morgan and Regan, 1987). In particular, it was proposed that the visual pathway contains 'coincidence detectors' that signal with high precision the separation of parallel lines. The precision of approximately 24 sec arc in the encoding of a and b required by the data above might be explained by opponent processing. We propose here that the value of a is represented by the distribution of excitation in one population of coincidence detectors, and the value of b by the distribution of excitation in a second population. If this is the case, the precision with which dimensions a and b could be encoded would be limited, not by the width of the receptive field profile of a coincidence detector, but rather by the following three factors: (1) the maximum slope of the relevant receptive field profile; (2) the component of receptive field noise that is not common to the receptive fields being compared; (3) the noise at the opponent processing stage (Regan, 1982; Regan and Beverley, 1983, 1985, Wilson and Gelb, 1984). Evidence has been reported previously for a physiological mechanism that compares orthogonal dimensions, is sensitive to the aspect ratio of rectangles, and selectively responds to rigid objects (Beverley and Regan, 1980).

10. Detection and recognition of motion-defined letters in patients with ophthalmological and neurological disorders

The procedures used for obtaining the data in Figures 4 to 7 and 10 to 14 are not convenient for studies of patients. This was the reason for developing a method for measuring detection and spatial discrimination of MD form along the lines of the familiar Snellen letter reading test that can be implemented with an IBM PC (Regan and Hong, 1990). The stimulus is illustrated in Figure 2.

Visual acuity for recognizing MD letters was estimated from psychometric functions in control subjects. Figure 15 (open circles) shows that visual acuity for recognizing MD letters was approximately independent of dot density over a wide range of dot densities (approximately 1000:1). On the other hand, filled circles in Figure 15 show that visual acuity for recognizing LD letters (see Figure 2C) improved with dot density. Consequently, visual acuities for MD and LD letters were similar only at low dot densities. This distinction suggested that visual acuities for MD and LD letters are not determined entirely by the same neural mechanism.

In a study on patients with multiple sclerosis and optic neuritis, speed thresholds for recognizing and for detecting MD letters were estimated from psychometric functions. Speed thresholds for detecting the presence of coherent dot motion and for discriminating leftward from rightward motion were also measured. Visual acuity for recognizing MD letters was measured. Finally, luminance-defined letters were created by switching off all dots outside the letters (Figure 2C), and contrast thresholds for recognizing these MD letters were measured.

Visual acuity for recognizing MD letters was less affected by disease than was speed threshold for recognizing MD letters. Some patients with multiple sclerosis showed elevated speed thresholds for recognizing MD letters — even a complete failure of recognition — though speed thresholds for detecting MD letters were normal, as were coherent motion thresholds and contrast thresholds for recognizing LD letters (Regan et al., 1991; Giaschi et al., 1991, 1992). Conclusions were as follows. (1) Because the failure to recognize MD letters spared recognition of LD letters, the selective loss could not be attributed to a general failure of form recognition. (2) Furthermore, the recognition of MD and LD form is not entirely determined by the same neural mechanism. (3) The hypothesis that motion information is processed hierarchically (Section 8 above) is supported by the finding that white matter disease can dissociate (a) the recognition of MD form, (b) the detection

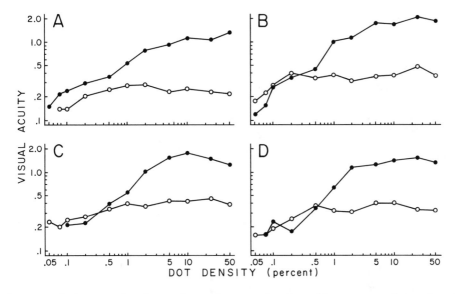

Fig. 15. *Ordinates plot decimal visual acuity for dotted letters on a log scale. Abscissae plot dot density on a log scale. Open symbols, letters rendered visible by impressing equal and opposite speeds of 0.3 deg/sec on dots inside and outside the letters. Filled symbols, uncamouflaged letters, as illustrated in Figure 2C with a dot speed of 0.3 deg/sec. Presentation duration was 4 sec. Dot contrast was 1.0. Viewing distance was 9 m and dot diameter approximately 3 sec arc. A–D show data for four subjects. From Hong and Regan (1990). ©Williams and Witkins, 1990. Reprinted with permission.*

of MD form and (c) the detection and discrimination of coherent motion.

Because multiple sclerosis is associated with the presence of multiple, widely-distributed plaques in white matter we were left with the questions whether this selective pattern of loss can be caused by a single discrete white matter lesion and, if so, whether this lesion must have some unique cerebral location and extent. We therefore studied 13 patients with unilateral cerebral hemispheric lesions following neurosurgery. The extent of the lesions was verified by CT scan. Visual acuity was between 6/6 and 6/3 for all patients. Speed thresholds for recognizing MD letters were abnormal in seven patients whose lesions are shown in Figure 16. All seven patients who failed to recognize motion-defined letters had extensive lesions in parieto-temporal white matter underlying Brodmann cortical areas 18, 19, 37, 39, 21 and 22. The hatched areas are the regions of overlap of three or more lesions. The black areas indicated by arrows in B and C are the regions of overlap of five lesions. The lesion was located in the left hemisphere for three of the seven, and in the right hemisphere for the other four. Four patients showed a selective loss of ability to recognize motion-defined letters, while the ability to detect those same letters was spared, as was the ability to detect coherent

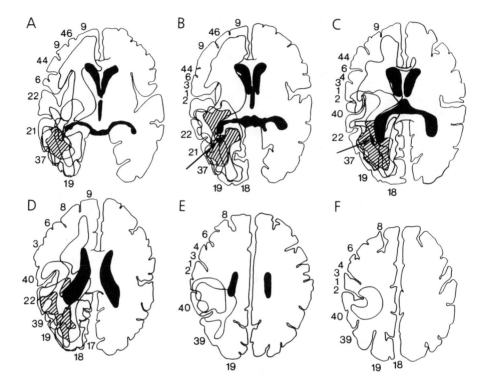

Fig. 16. *The outlines mark the lesion boundaries delineated by CT in seven patients with unilateral cerebral hemisphere damage who had abnormal speed thresholds for recognizing motion-defined letters. Lesions are plotted onto six templates of axial brain anatomy. The templates represent slices approximately 8 mm apart, oriented 15 deg above the orbitomeatal line. The right hemisphere is on the left side of each slice. Ventricles are marked in solid black. Brodmann numbers of adjacent cortical areas are marked. For explanatory purposes, all lesions are plotted onto the right hemisphere. Hatching shows regions of overlap of three or more lesions. The black areas indicated by arrows in B and C indicate overlap between the lesions in five patients. From Regan et al. (1992). ©Oxford University Press, 1992. Reprinted with permission.*

motion and discriminate its direction (type I loss). Three patients showed a loss of ability to both recognize and detect motion-defined letters, while the ability to detect coherent motion and discriminate its direction was spared (type II loss). Speed thresholds for recognizing MD letters were normal in the other six patients. In none of these six patients did the lesion extend into the area of overlap shown in Figure 16.

This study added the following conclusion to the three listed above: (4) a specific loss of ability to detect and/or recognize MD form that spares the ability to detect and discriminate coherent motion was produced by lesions that involved the localized cerebral region specified above, but not by lesions outside that localized region.

11. Psychophysical implications

The clinical findings just described reject the hypothesis that the detection of MD and LD form is determined by the same neural mechanism.

These clinical findings provide further support for the psychophysical hypothesis proposed in Section 8.2 above that motion information is processed hierarchically. In particular, the clinical data are consistent with the processing sequence proposed in Section 8.2, namely, (local motion filters) → (filters for MD form) → (form discrimination). The clinical data, however, do not discriminate between the two alternative hypotheses outlined in Figures 8 A & B. Hypothesis 1 is that not only the detection of MD and LD form, but also the discrimination of MD and LD form is determined by independent neural processes (Figure 8A). Hypothesis 2 is that a single common neural process determines the discrimination of MD and LD form, although the detection of MD and LD form is still determined by independent neural processes (Figure 8B). In terms of hypothesis 1,the type I pattern of visual loss described in section 10 is explained by interruption of the visual signals at I, arrowed in Figure 8A. According to hypothesis 2, this type I pattern of visual loss is caused by interruption of signals at I, arrowed in Figure 8B. In terms of hypothesis 1, the type II pattern of visual loss described in section 10 is explained by interruption of motion signals at II, arrowed in Figure 8A. According to hypothesis 2 this type II visual loss is caused by interruption of motion signals at II, arrowed in Figure 8B.

12. Physiological implications

Before discussing the physiological implications of our findings we should define the difference between coherent motion stimuli and non-coherent motion stimuli. Until recently, almost the only kinds of motion stimuli used to investigate vision in clinical and basic research alike were (A) motion of an isolated object, and (B) bodily flow of a texture or dot pattern within a stationary frame. These two kinds of stimuli are examples of coherent motion stimuli. Clinical studies were almost entirely restricted to measuring a patient's ability to detect (as distinct from discriminate) the motion of such stimuli. Although, even in normally-sighted subjects, selective blindness to coherent *motion in depth* is common (Richards and Regan, 1973; Regan et al., 1986b; Hong and Regan, 1989), a selective loss of the ability to detect coherent *frontal plane motion* seems to be rare, and confirmed cases are reported only occasionally (Zihl et al., 1983).

During the last decade, the study of psychophysical responses to coherent motion have been extended to include measurements of speed discrimination and direction discrimination (McKee, 1981), and several new tests of visual motion processing have been introduced. One of these new tests measures the ability to detect and spatially-discriminate camouflaged, motion-defined, two-dimensional form (Regan and Beverley, 1984; Regan, 1986a,

1986b, 1989b, Vaina, 1989; Banton and Levi, 1990; Regan and Hamstra, 1990, 1991). Another new test measures the ability to detect the presence of global motion and to discriminate its direction for a dot pattern that contains dots moving in different directions (Morgan and Ward, 1980; Williams and Sekuler, 1984; Zucker, 1984; Newsome and Pare, 1988; Siegel and Andersen, 1988; Downing and Movshon, 1989; Baker et al., 1991). One-dimensional or two-dimensional expansion or contraction is a third kind of non-coherent motion, and there is psychophysical evidence that the human visual pathway contains neurons selectively sensitive to this kind of non-coherent motion (Regan and Beverley, 1978, 1980) as well as microelectrode evidence that such neurons exist in cat (Regan and Cynader, 1979) and monkey (Zeki, 1974; Tanaka and Saito, 1989; Saito et al., 1986) visual cortex.

All these new kinds of stimuli differ from the older kind of coherent-motion stimuli in a single common respect. Suppose that each point in the visual field is analyzed by a separate "local motion detector" (Reichardt et al., 1983a; Reichardt et al., 1983b; Reichardt, 1986; van Santen and Sperling, 1984; van Santen and Sperling, 1985) and that the response of any given local motion detector is not affected by the activity of any other local motion detector. In principle, the presence of motion and the direction of motion of a coherently-moving texture could be signalled correctly by a single one of these local motion detectors. But this is not the case for any of the newer kinds of stimuli mentioned above. For example, the overall direction of motion of a dot pattern whose motion is non-coherent cannot be estimated from the motion of any single dot because the speeds and/or directions of motion of different dots may be quite different: correct psychophysical judgements require that the motion of many dots be taken into account. Therefore, spatially-integrative (i.e., global) processing is necessary for consistently correct psychophysical responses (Morgan and Ward, 1980; Vaina, 1989). The same situation obtains when we consider motion-defined form. Even the *detection* of a camouflaged shape that is revealed by motion contrast requires the visual system to compare the speed and direction of motion at different locations in the visual field. In other words, figure-ground segregation cannot be achieved entirely on the basis of local processing of motion: spatially-integrative (i.e., global) processing is required also (Regan and Beverley, 1984). And the correct performance of tasks such as letter recognition, shape discrimination and orientation discrimination for motion-defined form require still further spatially-integrative processing: detection is not enough for the correct performance of these tasks (Regan, 1982, 1986a, Regan1986b, Regan et al., 1982; Regan and Beverley, 1983, 1984, 1985).

Many caveats attend any attempt to associate a lesion at location L with a loss of some visual function X (Glassman, 1978). To support the assertion that the lesion caused the loss of function, one would need to deny that

visual function X was determined by the pattern of activity at several locations, one of which was location L. Furthermore, if several locations were
interconnected so as to form a system, the function X might be a property
of the system as a whole. And if this distributed system were nonlinear,
the system property X may not be evidenced by any of the component elements of the system alone, including the component located at L (Blaquiere,
1966; Marmarelis and Marmarelis, 1978; Mountcastle, 1979; Regan, 1991b).
Therefore, we conclude that integrity of the areas of overlap in Figure 16
"is necessary" for recognizing MD form. We note that our present evidence
falls well short of what would be required to conclude that the overlap area
is the physiological substrate for recognition of MD form. For example, because they involved white matter, the lesions may have interrupted signals
passing through the overlap region to more central location(s) whose neural activity was the physiological basis for recognition. A second caveat is
that in no patient was the lesion restricted entirely to the region of overlap.
Therefore, we cannot be sure that a lesion to the overlap area alone would
have produced a selective loss of ability to recognize motion-defined form.
In particular, we cannot deny that to produce this selective loss it is necessary that an extensive volume of parieto-occipital white matter must be
damaged. (Bear in mind though that the selective loss was not observed in
any of the six patients whose extensive lesions did not include the areas of
overlap shown in Figure 16.)

Turning to the experimentally-demonstrated properties of visual pathway
neurons in nonhuman primate, the detection of the motion-defined letters
used in this study requires neurons that respond to the coincidence of texture moving rightward at one location in the visual field and texture moving
leftward at a different location in the visual field. Neurons sensitive to opponent motion exist in monkey visual cortex, in area MT (Allman et al.,
1985a, 1985b, Van Essen, 1985), in the more central medial superior temporal (MST) area that receives input from MT, and also in parietal area
7a that receives input from MST (Maunsell and Van Essen, 1983; Motter
and Mountcastle, 1981; Saito et al., 1986; Tanaka and Saito, 1989; Tanaka
et al., 1989). Neurons that respond to a motion-defined bar (i.e. that can
detect a motion-defined bar) have been found in areas MT as well as in areas
MST and 7a (Allman et al., 1985a, 1985b, Saito et al., 1986; Tanaka et al.,
1989). These neurons might provide a physiological basis for the *detection*
of motion-defined letters. However the *recognition* of motion-defined letters
requires still further neural processing. Little can be said about a possible
physiological basis for recognition, because no studies have yet been reported
on correlations between an alert, behaving monkey's performance in a shape
recognition task for motion-defined form and the simultaneously-recorded
firing of single cells.

It has been proposed that, in monkey, a predominantly M (magnocellular)-
stream pathway that passes into the parietal lobe through cortical area V1

and then through areas MT and MST to area 7a is important for the perception of motion, while a parallel predominantly P (parvocellular)-stream pathway that passes into the temporal lobe through cortical areas V1 and V4 is important for the perception of color and form (Van Essen and Maunsell, 1983; Van Essen, 1985; Desimone et al., 1985; Maunsell and Newsome, 1987; De Voe and Van Essen, 1988; Merigan and Maunsell, 1990; Merigan et al., 1991a, 1991b). There are several analogies between this hypothesis and the hypothesis that the human visual pathway contains two parallel pathways passing through striate cortex, one of which (the dorsal pathway) processes the "where" while the other (the ventral pathway) processes the "what" of stimulus attributes (Ungerleider and Mishkin, 1982). Figure 17A, B illustrates this parallel pathway concept. Evidence that, in monkey, the magnocellular stream is relatively important for the detection of motion-defined form was reported by Schiller, Logothetis and Charles (1990) who investigated the differential effects of lesions restricted to the magnocellular or to the parvocellular layers of the lateral geniculate nucleus on the behavioral responses of monkeys to a variety of visual stimuli.

One way of linking our present findings to animal evidence for the parallel processing of motion and form rests on the evidence that there are many interconnections between cortical areas in the so-called motion and form pathways, some of which descend from prestriate areas in the motion pathway to striate cortex (Van Essen, 1985; Van Essen et al., 1990). In particular, we suggest that interconnections between the two pathways may be important for the detection and recognition of motion-defined form. In all seven brain-lesioned patients who lost ability to recognize motion-defined letters, the responsible lesions involved white matter, and may have interrupted interconnections between the homologues of areas in the V1/MT/MST/7a pathway and of areas in the V1/V4/IT pathway. But these suggestions can only be tentative because part of the animal evidence is lacking. The monkey data just cited are restricted to neural properties in areas of monkey visual *cortex*, and with the interconnections between cortical areas. It is known, however, that at least 20 subcortical structures project directly to visual cortex, and that in some cases (e.g., the connections between claustrum and cortex), the connections are reciprocal and organized in a precise point-to-point fashion, thus preserving the retinotopic projection (Tigges and Tigges, 1985; Sherk, 1986). In view of these facts, it seems unlikely that a complete understanding of the relation between structure and function in primate visual pathway will be achieved without taking into account the reciprocal interconnections between cortex and subcortical structures. In particular, the (at least) nine visual areas and (at least) 20 subcortical structures constitute a distributed system, whose system properties presumably underlie visual perception (Mountcastle, 1979). A glance at Figure 16 brings out the point that the lesions shown quite probably interrupted some of the

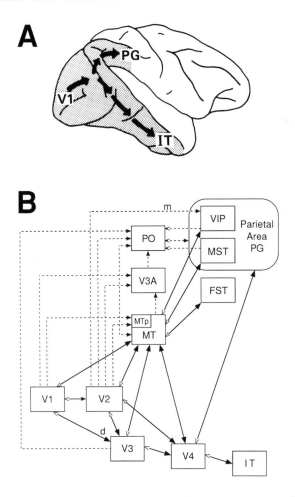

Fig. 17. *This figure illustrates the hypothesis that striate cortex (V1) is the source of two pathways. One, directed dorsally into the parietal lobe, is important for the processing of motion information and for the comprehension of spatial relationships and for visual guidance of movement. The second, directed ventrally into the temporal lobe, is important for the processing of color and spatial form and for object recognition. From Desimone et al. (1985). ©Pergamon Press, 1985. Reprinted with permission.*

interconnections between cortex and subcortical structures. Therefore, although it has been possible to discuss the results of some other studies (Vaina, 1989; Baker et al., 1991) entirely in terms of the properties of cortical areas and the connections within cortex, it would not be appropriate to do so here. The relevance of this point is that, with the possible exceptions of the interconnections between cortex and the lateral geniculate nucleus and superior colliculus, our current knowledge of the role of cortical-subcortical visual connections in visual perception is sparse (Tigges and Tigges, 1985;

Regan, 1989a). Finally we note that, in the context of distributed systems, it is intriguing that a parieto-temporal lesion in *either left or right hemisphere* produced a selective loss of ability to recognize motion-defined letters. This implies that the distributed system whose properties underlie the recognition of foveally-viewed motion-defined form involves structures in both hemispheres.

Acknowledgements

The research on which this chapter is based was carried out in collaboration with K.I. Beverley, D. Giaschi, S. Hamstra, X.H. Hong, A. Kothe and J.A. Sharpe. Parts of the work were supported by grants from the Natural Sciences and Engineering Research Council of Canada, the U.S. National Eye Institute, and the Medical Research Council of Canada. This research was sponsored by the U.S. Air Force Office of Scientific Research.

An inhibitory beam for attentional selection

John K. Tsotsos

A scheme to solve the problem of selective visual attention using hierarchical winner-take-all circuits was proposed by Koch and Ullman (1985). Their idea has played a prominent role in many current theories of visual attention. However, their scheme imposes unreasonable computational restrictions and leads to an architecture that is not as biologically plausible as once believed. This presentation will propose a new version of winner-take-all networks that solves the problem of locating and localizing items in the visual field and shows how to implement the idea of an inhibitory attentional beam. The scheme is based on the foundation laid by Koch and Ullman, but incorporates several novel changes and additions which permit a proof of convergence with constant time convergence properties, address the issue of saliency maps and the binding across representations, and includes much tighter comparisons to the biology. The results are directly applicable to any sensory field and are not restricted to vision.

1. Introduction

The space of neural responses may be considered as a huge, multi-dimensional search space, where each point represents the strength of response of one hypothesis existing in space and in time. More than one hypothesis exists at each point in space and time, each one competing with the rest to describe the perceptual objects or events at that point. The goal of visual processing then could be to find the set of strongest hypotheses such that they are most consistent with the input and the reasons for considering this particular input in the first place. The identification of this maximal hypothesis set is the goal of the search task. The simplest, parallel method of maximum selection is perhaps the winner-take-all (WTA) scheme proposed by Feldman and Ballard (1982). WTA is an iterative, neurally-plausible, and very simple mechanism to find a unique maximum, which is based on mutual inhibition among units that are all connected to one another[1]. However, it must be emphasized that the space is not small and the search problem is potentially intractable (Tsotsos, 1989). A WTA on its own does not offer a plausible solution simply because it would have to operate over too large a search space; connectivity requirements could not be realized nor could convergence be guaranteed if arbitrary weights are permitted. Further, since the maximal hypothesis set is the target of the search, a unique hypothesis does necessarily exist.

Koch and Ullman (1985) proposed a particular form of the winner-take-all process for shifts in selective visual attention. The key points of their proposal are: 1) a number of features are computed and represented in parallel in different topographical maps; 2) a selective mapping exists from these representations into a central non-topographic representation such that this central representation contains the properties of only a single location in the visual scene at any time; 3) conspicuity of locations in the topographic maps is the major determinant of selection and selection is realized by a winner-take-all network; 4) inhibition of the selected item will cause an automatic shift towards the next most conspicuous location. Additional rules for the computation in step 3 are proximity and similarity preferences; they are not detailed nor implemented however. The Koch and Ullman WTA idea has played a role in many views and theories of attention and explanations of attentional phenomena, including those of Anderson and Van Essen (1987), Nakayama and Mackeben (1989), and Fuster (1990).

Koch and Ullman reject a general WTA process based on mutual inhibition: they point out that the connectivity requirements make the scheme biologically implausible (each unit must be connected to all others, thus for an n-unit field, n^2 connections are required for the WTA process). Further, they argue, the scheme is not guaranteed to converge if arbitrary weights and initial configurations are permitted. These problems led them to a proposal for implementation of the method that involved a new inhibition rule and a tree of intermediate nodes. They are correct on both arguments; however, they may have tried to solve far too general a task. There are number of problems with the Koch and Ullman scheme:

(a) Winner-take-all networks possess a troublesome feature: because they are based on mutual inhibition, the winning unit has a final response strength that is attenuated. Thus, although the location of the winner may be known, its value is not meaningful. If the value is to be passed on to a central representation as they suggest, some additional mechanism is then required to recover that value. Further, the winning value is not representative of the items selected in visual space because

---

[1] It is a special case of general relaxation labeling procedures (Hummel and Zucker, 1983) as is the new version of the updating rule to be presented later in this paper.

it was initially computed using the non-attended receptive field. A re-computation is required for this and such a re-computation was not included.

(b) The proposal requires the WTA to act as a gating function on the saliency map; however, the saliency map combines features into a conspicuity measure and thus does not represent any feature explicitly. No other mechanism is proposed to achieve the proper gating action.

(c) Koch and Ullman separate selection from input processing, that is, the input is first processed in whatever manner is appropriate by individual units (such as line detectors) and then selection takes place. It seems that this separation may be artificial and inappropriate given recent results from single-cell recordings in awake and behaving primates (such as (Moran and Desimone, 1985)), where the behavior of a single cell makes it appear as if the receptive field changes properties as a result of attentive selection. Thus, a scheme that integrates attentive selection with interpretive processing may be more biologically plausible.

(d) Conspicuous locations need not be single locations, but may be regions. Koch and Ullman do not permit multiple winners in their algorithm.

(e) The intermediate tree of computations of very small branching factor which is necessitated by the connectivity and convergence properties of the WTA rule does not seem to have an immediate biological counterpart. There is no evidence for a tree in the strict computational sense; however, the computations do seem to be hierarchical in nature.

(f) A side-effect of using a tree of intermediate WTA computations over very small networks is that a shift of attention requires time proportional to the number of branches of the tree that must be traversed upwards from the previous focus and then downwards to the new focus of attention and this traversal distance is related to topographic distance. Koch and Ullman use the results of Shulman, Remington and McLean (1979) and of Tsal (1983) as part of the justification for their shifts of attention requiring time proportional to topographic distance. Those authors found that attention shifts with constant velocity passing through and processing intermediate locations as it moves. However, Remington and Pierce (1984) show that distance has no effect on attention shifts; there is no attentional gradient. They further point out a very important constraint: Efficient coordination with the saccadic eye movement system in reading or visual search tasks would dictate rapid, time-invariant movements to match saccade dynamics. To complicate the matter even more, Ericksen and Murphy (1987) claim that prior experimental evidence is conflicting, with assumptions dubious and data interpretation problematic. They say that attention shifts pose an "open problem". More recently, Kröse and Julesz (1989) found no proximity effect and conclude that a parallel scheme is needed to find prospective locations which are then checked by a slow serial process.

Further analysis and a new approach seem to be required.

2. An inhibitory attentional beam

Complexity analysis of the problem of visual search has led to several constraints that are important for the design of a vision system (Tsotsos, 1990; Tsotsos, 1988; Tsotsos, 1989). Note that the collection of constraints below form a sufficient but not necessary set:

1   parallelism of sufficiently high degree;

2   hierarchical organization through the abstraction of prototypical visual knowledge in order to cut search time at least logarithmically;

3   localization of receptive fields, noting that the physical world is spatio-temporally localized and that objects and events, and their physical characteristics, are not arbitrarily spread over time and space;

4   using the observation that not all visual stimuli require all possible parameter types for interpretation, separable, logical maps permit selection of individual maps as required;

5   hierarchical abstraction of the input token arrays so as to maintain semantic content yet reduce the number of elements;

6   tokens of visual parameters at high resolution cannot be directly accessed, but must be obtained by the tuning of computing units and through the input abstraction hierarchy;

7   predictions for the overall configuration of the visual system in terms of lower bounds on the size and number of maps and upper bounds on the required degree of parallelism;

8   an inhibitory attentional beam.

Most of these constraints are consistent with the increasing literature on single-cell recordings in striate and extrastriate visual cortex from awake and behaving primates (Bushnell et al., 1991; Fuster and Jervey, 1981; Braitman, 1984; Moran and Desimone, 1985; Mountcastle et al., 1987; Haenny and Schiller, 1988; Haenny et al., 1988; Spitzer et al., 1988; Maunsell et al., 1988; Motter, 1988; Fuster, 1988, 1990; Andersen et al., 1990). Also, the constraints on structure are consistent with primate visual cortex neuroanatomy (Felleman and Van Essen, 1991). Most importantly however, complexity analysis quantitatively confirms what has been widely believed for a long time: selective attention is a major contributor to reducing the amount of computation. The nature of attention is to inhibit the portions of a sensory field that are not selected.

Constraints (5) through (8) require some elaboration. The beam concept is a result of a connectivity argument: low spatial resolution at the highest levels of the visual hierarchy and fixed connectivity suggests attentive access of visual information through the input abstraction hierarchy. If it is true that the sizes of visual maps are small, then complete connectivity across a higher level map is not biologically infeasible as Koch and Ullman claimed. In humans, it is known that V1 has on average 2100 hypercolumns per hemisphere (Stensaas et al., 1974) and it is known from primate studies that the higher areas are smaller yet. If a hypercolumn represents processing units of all types and all constrained to the same visual space[2], and adjacent hypercolumns represent processing in physically adjacent visual space, then it is not unreasonable to consider the spatial resolution of a visual map in the cortex to be determined by the number of hypercolumns it contains. Thus, across a visual map, each column in the map would require only a small number of additional connections in order to implement a completely connected network for a winner-take-all process.

Finally, the common idea of an attentional spotlight does not permit any way for the message of selection to reach the input items that are in fact selected. This, and the previously described considerations led to the concept of an inhibitory attentional beam, introduced in (Tsotsos, 1990). This beam is rooted at the top of an abstraction pyramid so that at the top level there is a spotlight selecting a single item (or items). The beam illuminates the sub-pyramid whose apex is defined by the spotlight at the top and has a simple internal structure consisting of a "pass zone" and an "inhibit zone". The pass zone of the beam is required for obvious reasons: this is the pathway through the pyramid that is selected for further processing. The inhibit zone is needed because if a single unit is selected at the top level of the hierarchy, then it has a receptive field which is potentially very large, much larger than the selected item (it would correspond exactly to the sub-pyramid of the beam). The sensory stimuli within the receptive field but which are not selected may be regarded as noise interfering with the processing of the selected items. The "signal-to-noise" ratio is greatly enhanced if the unwanted stimuli are attenuated or eliminated. Selection leads to processing of the selected input as if it were the only stimulus in the sensory field. Desimone et al. (1990) have concluded that attention may not be necessary if there is only one item in the visual field. Within the beam explanation, the reason why they and others observe no attentional effect in their experiments with single items is clear. Although the beam mechanism

---

[2] This is known to be true at least for V1 and MT in primates (see Albright and Desimone, 1987).

may always be active, its effect on a field of only one stimulus cannot be observed since the beam seeks to achieve a single stimulus visual field.

It is important to distinguish the beam concept in this paper from that of Posner (1980) and from the feature integration theory of Treisman and colleagues (1988). Posner proposes an attentional system that enhances performance in a spatially restricted region. Treisman on the other hand, believes that attention is required to integrate features. The experimental paradigms within which each of these ideas was developed differ from one another (see Briand and Klein, 1987 for detailed discussion on this). More to the point, neither concept has been detailed sufficiently so as to offer a mathematical framework and an implementation or circuit model. The beam in this paper refers in principle to the fact that attention must operate in the three-dimensional structure of the brain and in practice to the circuits that provide downward flowing information within the visual processing hierarchy, and not simply the two-dimensional region of visual space on which the spotlight shines as Posner defines it[3] and as Treisman uses it.

3. Realization of the inhibitory beam

As described earlier, the basic idea proposed by Koch and Ullman is useful and the new scheme in this paper borrows much from it. It motivated the basic processing algorithm shown below as Algorithm 1. However, it has been modified so that multiple items in the input and time-varying input can be handled. Also, the final stage of the algorithm is not simply the routing of information as Koch and Ullman claim, but rather a recomputation using only the stimuli that were found as "winners" at the input level of the hierarchy.

```
1.   receive stimulus at input layer (continuously over time)
2.   receive task guidance at top layer (asynchronously, as it
        is available)
3.   do  4 through 8 forever
4.       compute output representation with task guidance if
            available or without if unavailable
5.       apply inhibitory beam using the WTA hierarchy and
            task guidance
6.       re-compute output representation
7.       extract selected output item
8.       inhibit item(s) at input that represented the
            selected item if unchanged
```

---

[3] "Attention can be likened to a spotlight that enhances the efficiency of detection of events within its beam"(Posner, 1980).

Algorithm 1.

The sequence of actions in the above algorithm leads to a timing of process-ing actions that is consistent with the observations and hypotheses of Fuster (1990) and of Desimone (1991, personal communication). The major steps of this algorithm will be described in more detail in several stages, beginning with the presentation of a new winner-take-all updating rule plus proof of convergence.

3.1. WTA updating rule

The updating rule presented by Koch and Ullman must be replaced so that the updating function does not suffer from the problems described earlier. The new winner-take-all process is non-destructive for the winner. That is, the winning units will maintain its actual response strength while the other units decay in strength. It is accomplished using a simple obser-vation: if the inhibitory signal is based on the response differences, then an implicit but global ordering of response strengths is imposed on the entire network on the basis of pair-wise local information. The largest item will thus not be inhibited at all, but will participate in inhibiting all other units. The smallest unit will not inhibit any other units but will be inhibited by all. The new function which controls the WTA process for a given unit is:

$$s_i' = R\left[s_i - \frac{1}{\sum_{j \in M, j \neq i} w_{ij}} \left(\sum_{j \in M, j \neq i} w_{ij} R\left[s_j - s_i\right]\right)\right] \qquad (1)$$

where R is a rectifying function ($R[x] = x$ if $x > 0$, otherwise $R[x] = 0$), $0 < w_{ij} \leq 1$, $0 \leq s_i \leq 1$, and M is the set of locations on the sensory map with non-zero strength. This can be enhanced to include a "variance" threshold and a scale parameter as follows:

$$s_i' = R\left[s_i - \frac{1}{\sum_{j \in M, j \neq i} w_{ij}} \left(\sum_{j \in M, j \neq i} w_{ij} \Delta_{ij}\right)\right] \qquad (2)$$

if $0 < \Theta_i < s_j - s_i$ and $((x_i - x_j)^2 + (y_i - y_j)^2)^{\frac{1}{2}} < C$, then $\Delta_{ij} = s_j - s_i$

else $\Delta_{ij} = 0$

where C specifies a priori scale, Θ is the variance threshold, x_k, y_k is the location in the sensory field represented by unit s_k. The variance threshold could reflect the acceptable variation across an item. That is, responses could vary from one another within this threshold and still be considered as arising from the same physical stimulus. The scale parameter could place a bound on the sphere of influence of a given unit; units that are farther than C units from s_i would not affect s_i in any way.

Proposition: *The WTA updating rule of Equation (1) is guaranteed to converge for all inputs provided* $0 < w_{ij} \leq 1, 0 \leq s_i \leq 1$.

Proof: Let $\dfrac{1}{\sum_{j \in M, j \neq i} w_{ij}} \left(\sum_{j \in M, j \neq i} w_{ij} R[s_j - s_i] \right)$ be termed the contribution to a unit.

1   Since the contribution to unit i depends on a difference function, an ordering of units is implicitly imposed depending on their response magnitude.

2   Unit j will inhibit unit i only if s_j is larger than s_i. Thus, the largest units (a unique maximum is not required) will have a contribution of 0 and will remain unaffected by the iterative process.

3   All other units will have strictly positive contributions and thus will decay in magnitude or remain at zero.

4   The rectifying function guarantees that no unit receives an updated value that is negative and thus oscillations cannot occur.

5   The iterations are terminated when a stable state is reached (no units change in magnitude).

It is thus trivially shown that the process is guaranteed to converge and locate the largest items in the sensory field.

It is important that the convergence properties of this scheme be investigated. From the updating function, it is clear that the time to convergence depends only on three values: the magnitude of the largest unit, the magnitude of the second largest unit and the parameter Θ. The largest unit, recall, is not affected by the updating process at all. The largest unit, however, is the only unit to inhibit the second largest unit. The contribution term for all other units would be larger than for the second largest because those units would be inhibited by all larger units. This, along with the fact that they are smaller initially, means that they would reach the lower threshold faster than the second largest unit. Convergence is achieved when all units but one decay in value to Θ; therefore the time to convergence is determined by the time it takes the second largest element to reach this value. This makes the convergence time independent of the number of units in the WTA process. The amount of inhibition per iteration of the updating rule for the second largest unit s_2 where the largest unit is s_1 is given by equation 2 which simplifies for this situation to :

$$s_2' = 2s_2 - s_1$$

s_1 is constant. Convergence is achieved when $s_2' \leq \Theta$. At the kth iteration, $s_2^k = 2^k s_2^0 - (2^k - 1)s_1$. Convergence will thus require $\log_2((s_1 - \Theta)/(s_1 - s_2^0))$ iterations. A bound on this number of iterations is desirable. Arbitrarily small differences between values are not allowed; the differences must be at least Θ, so the denominator of the logarithm can be no smaller than Θ. s_1 can be no larger than 1.0. Thus, the upper bound on the number of iterations is given by:

$$\log_2 \left(\frac{1.0 - \Theta}{\Theta} \right)$$

If convergence is required within K iterations, then the following expression gives the appropriate value of Θ that will guarantee the convergence:

$$\Theta = \frac{1}{2^K + 1}$$

This tacitly assumes that $s_1 > \Theta$. If $K = 1, \Theta = 0.333$ and s_1 may not be large enough in some situations; moreover such a large theta may not be sensible given that it is a variance threshold for responses caused by the same physical stimulus. A "gain" parameter will solve this problem. Re-define the contribution to include a gain parameter $A, A \geq 1$, so that:

$$s_i' = R \left[s_i - \frac{A}{\sum_{j \in M, j \neq i} w_{ij}} \left(\sum_{j \in M, j \neq i} w_{ij} \Delta_{ij} \right) \right]$$

In this case, at the kth iteration, $s_2^k = (1 + A)^k s_2^0 - ((1 + A)^k - 1)s_1$ Convergence will require $\log_{1+A}((s_1 + \Theta)/(s_1 - s_2^0))$ iterations. Using the same argument as above, if convergence is required within K iterations, then the following expression gives the appropriate value of Θ that will guarantee the convergence:

$$\Theta = \frac{1}{(1 + A)^K + 1}$$

Knowledge of the magnitudes of values with which the WTA process works will help determine appropriate values of A. Large gain amplifiers may be more expensive to realize in neural circuitry, as they are in silicon, and this may be an important constraint on the acceptable gain magnitudes. Of course, no gain is needed at all if the expense of more iterations is permissible. If 5 iterations are possible given the time constraints, Θ can be set to 0.03, for example, and gain control may not be necessary. In general, if the allowable variance is known and the maximum number of permissible iterations is given, then the gain may be set as:

$$A = \left(\frac{1 - \Theta}{\Theta} \right)^{\frac{1}{K}} - 1$$

Constant time convergence of all WTA processes no matter their size can be guaranteed throughout the hierarchy. This is possible only because the iterative update is based on differences of units and thus only the largest and second largest values need be considered; a two-unit network is thus easy to characterize.

3.2. Pruning a hierarchy of winner-take-all processes

Next, assume a hierarchical representation where units are represented by their response strength. Connectivity from layer to layer need not be fixed and each layer (indeed, each unit) may have different connectivity patterns including overlap. WTA processes are set up for the top layer as a whole, and for each set of inputs for each unit everywhere else in the hierarchy as follows.

Suppose that the top layer of the visual processing hierarchy is completely connected in such a fashion so that a winner-take-all process operates across the entire visual field: it could compute the global winner. It could be autonomous and could accept guidance for areas or stimulus qualities to favor if that guidance were available but would operate independently of such guidance otherwise. This global winner would be represented by a receptive field that is necessarily very large since it is at the top of the visual processing hierarchy. In order to then localize the global winner in the sensory field, a hierarchy of WTA processes are activated as a result of the global winner. The global winner activates a WTA that operates only over its direct inputs. This would select the winner within the global receptive field. In this way, all of the branches of the hierarchy that do not contribute to the winner would be pruned from the search space. This pruning idea is then applied recursively to as many successively lower layers as is reasonable. The end result is that from a globally strongest response, the cause of that largest response is localized in the sensory field at the earliest levels.

Complete connectivity required for the top level is biologically feasible for representations of the size predicted by the complexity level analysis and for the visual areas where hypercolumn counts have been done as described earlier. Complete connectivity only within a receptive field for all other levels also does not violate connectivity constraints if each receptive field has a small number of thousands of inputs. This structure may be realized by inserting a layer of independent WTA gating networks in between each pair of layers as shown in Figure 1. There are two types of units in this hierarchy at each layer k (layers denoted by subscripts):

interpretive units (I_k) which receive visual input from below and perform processing related directly to the interpretation of that input (color, edges, motion for example); and,

gating units (G_k) which compute the winner-take-all result for a particular interpretive unit and gate input through to the next higher interpretive units.

It is hypothesized that these units exist as appropriate assemblies of neurons rather than as single neurons.

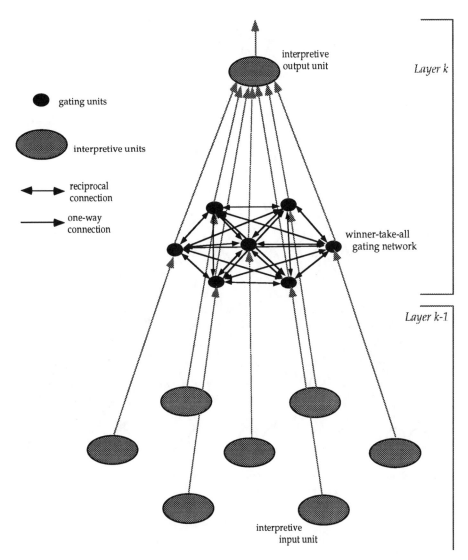

Fig. 1. *The interpretive input hierarchy with WTA processes across the inputs to each interpretive unit. In this example, the function of the gating units is to inhibit "non-winning" signals at each level, effectively pruning the hierarchy and implementing the inhibitory beam.*

An example of the implemented beam process in operation will be shown. Response strength of each node is computed in the same manner. Response equals the sum of all inputs: the examples shown thus code unweighted luminance. This simple demonstration generalizes easily to the case where response of a unit is given by any weighted-sum function of its inputs; these need not be uniform throughout the hierarchy but may be different at each

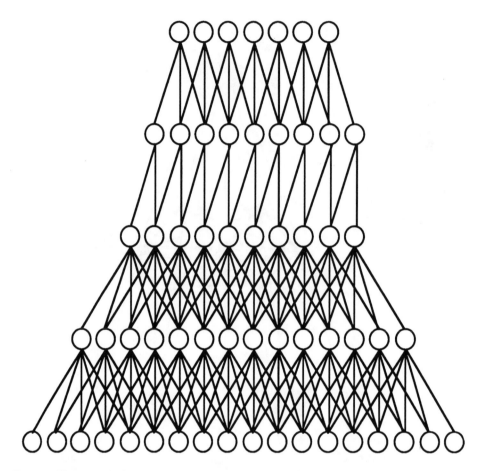

Fig. 2. *The sample hierarchy of interpretive units (the gating units are not shown) with an input layer, 3 intermediate layers and an output layer. This and following diagrams are coded as follows: solid circles are units which are active; solid lines are connections which are active; gray circles are inactive units and dashed lines are connections that are inhibited by the beam. Missing lines show pathways which are "don't cares".*

level. Although one dimensional sensory fields are shown, the extension to two or higher dimensional fields is trivial.

Figure 2 gives the basic hierarchy on which the process is demonstrated with only the interpretive units displayed (gating networks are omitted to clarify the figure). Connectivity may vary between levels and the number of levels may vary. The first figure shows the representation after the first application of step 4 of Algorithm 1 without task guidance, the next figure shows the representations after step 5 of Algorithm 1, and the last two figures show the representation after the second and third iterations through step 5.

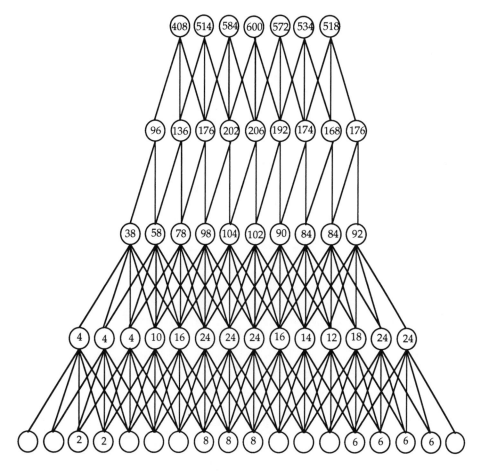

Fig. 3. *This is the initial configuration for the first example. If there is no attentional selectivity, the input, consisting of three items (a pair of '2's, a trio of '8's, and a quartet of '6's) would lead to the given output layer with the simple computation proposed for this example.*

If a simple stimulus pattern is applied to the input layer, as is shown in the input layer, the remaining nodes of the hierarchy will compute their responses based on a summation of their inputs resulting in the configuration of Figure 3. The first pass of the WTA scheme is shown in Figure 4. It is clear that the largest item is found and that the overall action is precisely the inhibitory beam that was proposed in (Tsotsos, 1990). It must be emphasized that this form of selection permits the response at the top of the hierarchy to be determined using only the data selected at the early stages of the hierarchy: it is as if only the selected data were present in the sensory field and any other conflicting stimuli did not exist. Once this first stimulus item is processed, it is inhibited as Koch and Ullman proposed and the next is selected (Figure 5 and then Figure 6 for the third item).

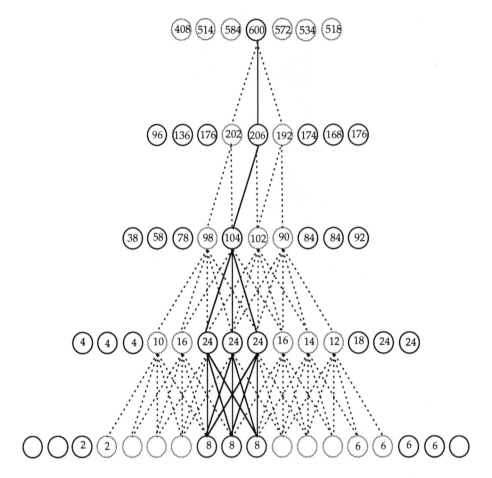

Fig. 4. *The first ("brightest") item is selected and any pathways leading to the same receptive fields in which the item is found are inhibited. The beam's pass and inhibit zones are clear. This, and successive examples showing the beam are snapshots taken during the computation at the point just after the beam is applied but before re-computations are performed on the selected items within the beam's pass zone.*

Culhane and Tsotsos (1992) show many more examples of the implemented process for real images, using both brightness and edge computations in the interpretive units.

3.3. Propagation of inhibitory effects and of task guidance

The hierarchy as shown in Figure 1 is now augmented by a parallel, interlaced hierarchy of beam units (B_k) which provide top-down guidance for visual selection, whether the selection be for regions in space or sub-ranges of visual feature to attend to (see Figure 7). As well, the beam hierarchy

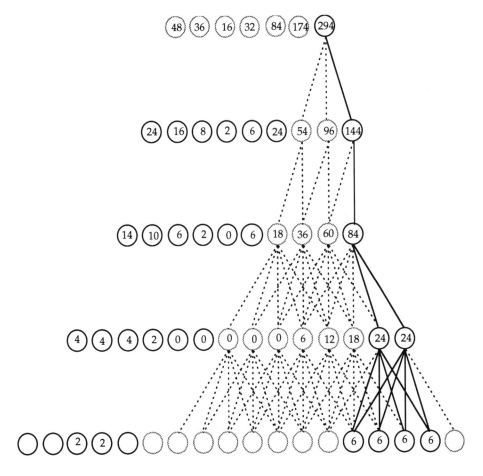

Fig. 5. *The first selected item is inhibited, the hierarchy is re-computed and the second brightest item is selected.*

provides an important conduit for upward-flowing information not directly associated with the interpretive computations, such as location information. Gating units may be directed by beam units and also provide output to the next layer of beam units downward. A brief overview of the function of the gating and beam units will be presented here and details can be found in (Tsotsos, 1991).

The top-down guidance can take several forms. It may simply select the type of computation that is permitted to pass through, for example, 45-degree oriented lines versus all orientations of lines. Or, it may both select and enhance responses from the selected feature type. In tests with the winner-take-all algorithm, it has been observed that the latter leads to enhancement of responses as observed in Spitzer, Desimone and Moran (1988) for attended units. Much more experimentation is required to discover the nature of such task-specific guidance signals.

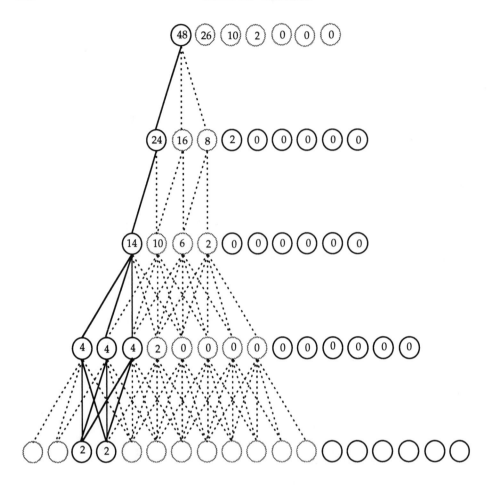

Fig. 6. *The second selected item is inhibited, the hierarchy is re-computed and the final item is selected.*

Each beam unit receives signals from many gating units as well as top-down task selection information. The algorithm which controls the selection process is presented in (Tsotsos, 1991). The important actions of the algorithm can be illustrated by considering what effect overlapping receptive fields have on the function of the beam hierarchy. Figure 8 shows an example of overlap.

Here, several problems must be considered. There is potential for ambiguity in three ways, each related to a different signal that is propagated along the hierarchy. Beam units receive three signals: task specific directions, inhibitory signals from the the gating units and location information from winning units below, and propagate these signals to higher or lower parts of the beam hierarchy as appropriate. The confluence of inhibitory magnitudes is handled by imposing a "min" function, that is the inhibition that is

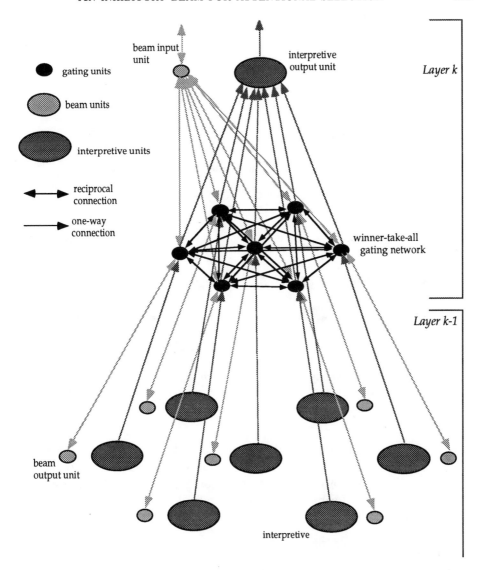

Fig. 7. *Two adjacent layers in the interpretive visual hierarchy. The inhibitory beam hierarchy is added to the structure in Figure 1.*

passed on downwards is the strongest of that received from all sources. This is perhaps the simplest resolution to the problem of confluence of inhibitory signals. Simple sums, weighted sums, products of differences would not lead to meaningful results or would not ensure that the inhibitory value is between 0 and 1.0. The top-down task guidance signals are passed through an "AND" function. That is, all task-specific signals must be satisfied by gating units below their point of confluence in order for the signal to pass. In this way, it is ensured that any pathways above the point of confluence

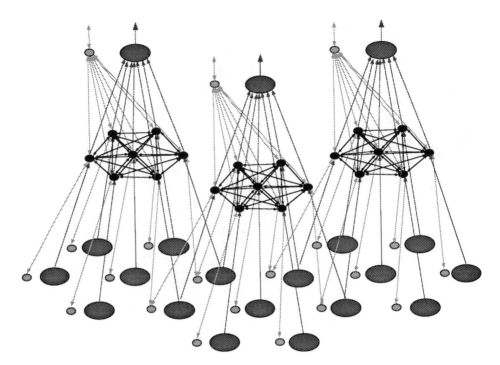

Fig. 8. *The downward flowing information from the beam units at the higher level have more than one target beam unit at the next lower level due to the fact that interpretive units have overlapping receptive fields.*

have their task requirements satisfied. Finally, the location signals are put together into a list creating a list of signals which can be decoded as described in (Tsotsos, 1991). This strategy for dealing with the confluence of downward flowing information is equally valid for confluence from multiple beams as for confluence within a beam.

4. Summary

The implementation of the inhibitory attentional beam has a number of important properties that make it preferable to the Koch and Ullman scheme both as a hypothesis of biological attentional mechanisms and also as a computational tool for attention in machine sensing systems:

- the scheme integrates attentive selection with interpretive processing resulting in behavior that is consistent with single-cell recordings in tasks requiring attention both with respect to changes in receptive field structure and temporal response changes;

- WTA process is provably convergent and requires constant time irrespective of the locations or numbers of the sensory items, consistent with current views on the scanpath of attentional fixations;

- the method permits multiple winners within a single representation;

- the intermediate layers of computations can be mapped directly onto the hierarchy of areas in the visual cortex;

- no single saliency map that combines features into a conspicuity measure is required;

- multiple beams are permitted across different representations of visual information;

- receptive fields of many sizes are permitted at each level with overlap and algorithms are provided to deal with the potential ambiguities;

- task knowledge can provide scale selection plus feature salience.

The result is a very fast, automatic, independent, continuous and reactive system.

In Felleman and Van Essen (1991) the pathways in the macaque visual cortex are described in great detail, including the fact that among the 32 visual areas there are 121 reciprocal-pair connections[4]. What could the functional significance for these paired connections be? The proposal in this paper requires such paired connections (see Figure 7). The layers of computation described in this proposal may be likened to visual areas. Thus, the question can be re-phrased as: could the implementation of an inhibitory attentional beam across visual areas be one of the functionalities of some of these reciprocal connections?

Acknowledgements

Allan Jepson and Sean Culhane provided useful discussion. The author is the CP-Unitel Fellow of the Canadian Institute for Advanced Research. This research was funded by the Information Technology Research Center, one of the Province of Ontario Centers of Excellence, the Institute for Robotics and Intelligent Systems, a Network of Centers of Excellence of the Government of Canada, and the Natural Sciences and Engineering Research Council of Canada.

---

[4] There are 32 areas with 305 known pathways connecting them. Of these pathways, 121 are known to be reciprocal pairs (one for each of top-down and bottom-up directions), 5 are known to be singlets (one direction only), and 58 pathways are not being critically tested.

Bayesian models, deformable templates and competitive priors

Allan L. Yuille

J. J. Clark

1. Introduction

This chapter will discuss some theories of machine vision with relevance to psychophysics. In honor of recent events in Eastern Europe this chapter will be written in terms of the Marxist dialectic of thesis, antithesis and synthesis.

The *thesis* consists of the standard general Bayesian model for early vision — our specific example is the motion coherence theory (Yuille and Grzywacz, 1988; 1989).

The *antithesis* is a special purpose Bayesian theory based on parametric priors — we describe as an example of this type of theory the use of deformable templates for facial feature recognition (Yuille et al., 1989; Hallinan, 1991).

These two types of theory are essentially the opposites of each other. To unify them into a *synthesis* we propose the idea of competitive priors, which is a form of strongly coupled data fusion (Clark and Yuille, 1990).

2. Bayesian models of early vision

Bayes and priors The starting point of Bayesian theories of vision is the observation that vision is ill-posed (Bertero et al., 1987) in the sense that there is too little information reaching the retina to determine the visual scene uniquely.

The visual system, therefore, must make assumptions about the world in order to ensure a unique interpretation. These assumptions can be thought of as natural constraints on the solutions (Marr, 1982). A classic example of such a constraint is the rigidity assumption used in determining structure from motion (Ullman, 1979).

Methods for solving the vision problem through the application of constraints on the solution can be formulated nicely within a Bayesian framework. This formalism subsumes approaches based on energy functions or regularization theory.

To illustrate the Bayesian approach to vision, let us assume that we measure some data d from which we wish to obtain an interpretation f. Bayes' theorem (Bayes, 1783) states that

$$P(f|d) = \frac{P(d|f)P(f)}{P(d)}, \tag{1}$$

where: (i) $P(d|f)$ is the probability of the data d given f, (ii) $P(f)$ is the *a priori* probability of f corresponding to the natural constraints, and (iii) $P(d)$ is the prior probability of the data, expressable as $\sum_f P(d|f)P(f)$. Observe that since $P(d)$ is independent of f it does not affect the relative probabilities of different f's, hence it can be considered a normalization constant.

The Bayesian theory of vision says that we should choose the interpretation f^* that maximizes $P(f|d)$. In other words the most probable interpretation given our prior assumptions $P(f)$ and the visual sense data d.

Clearly the prior $P(f)$ will affect f^* and hence lead to a perceptual bias. The more the problem is unconstrained, i.e. the less information there is in $P(d|f)$, then the stronger the bias. Since the priors bias perception one can try to explain psychophysical experiments in terms of such priors (Bülthoff and Yuille, 1991). This follows Marr's claim that the search for natural constraints "is in a deep sense what makes this field of investigation into a science"[1].

2.1. Motion coherence theory

We now give an explicit example of these ideas based on work on motion perception (Yuille and Grzywacz, 1988; Yuille and Grzywacz, 1989).

The psychophysical evidence shows that for a large class of motion stimuli the perceived motion is more coherent than the true motion, this is related to Gestalt theories of perception (Koffka, 1935). Examples are:

1   Motion cooperativity (Williams et al., 1986; Williams and Sekuler, 1984).

2   Motion capture (Ramachandran and Anstis, 1983).

3   Variations on the Aperture Problem (Nakayama and Silverman, 1988).

The motion coherence theory was developed in an attempt to explain these phenomena. The theory assumes that there is an initial motion measurement stage, perhaps using motion energy filters (Adelson and Bergen, 1985; Heeger, 1987; Grzywacz and Yuille, 1990), which gives a local measurement of velocity and which is then followed by a spatial integration stage using

---

[1] Marr 1982, p. 104.

a smoothness assumption. The precise nature of the velocity measurement depends on the stimuli. For isolated random dots we assume that it supplies the true dot velocity. For a moving contour, because of the aperture problem, we assume that the measurement stage provides only the component of velocity normal to the contour.

The theory suggests that for, isolated random dots, the perceived velocity $\vec{v}(\vec{x})$ minimizes the cost function

$$E[\vec{v} : d] = \sum_{i=1}^{N} \left| \vec{v}(\vec{x}_i) - \vec{d}_i \right|^2 + E_S[\vec{v}], \tag{2}$$

where $\{\vec{d}_i\}$ for $i = 1, ..., N$ are the outputs of the measurement stage.

The key assumption is in the choice of the smoothness constraints. It is argued (Yuille and Grzywacz, 1989) that the motion smoothness priors suggested for related problems (Horn and Schunk, 1981; Hildreth, 1984) are inappropriate. One specific reason is because they impose smoothness too globally. It is suggested that the smoothness requirement should fall off with distance. This can be imposed by using a smoothing prior of form

$$E_S[\vec{v}] = \lambda \sum_{n=0}^{\infty} \frac{\sigma^{2n}}{2^n n!} \int \left| \frac{D^n \vec{v}}{D^n \vec{x}} \right|^2 d\vec{x}. \tag{3}$$

It can then be shown that the velocity field that minimizes the energy is a linear combination of Gaussian functions centered on the data points. More precisely

$$\vec{v}(\vec{x})^* = \sum_{i=1}^{N} \vec{\alpha}_i G(\vec{x} - \vec{x}_i), \tag{4}$$

where the α_i are the solutions to the linear equations $\sum_{j=1}^{N} \{\lambda \delta_{ij} + G(\vec{x}_i - \vec{x}_j)\} \vec{\alpha}_j = \vec{d}_i$.

Like all energy function or regularization theories this can be re-interpreted in terms of probabilities. A standard way is to define a Gibbs distribution $P[\vec{v}] = e^{-\beta E[\vec{v}]}/Z$, where β is a constant and Z is a normalization constant (Parisi, 1988). Observe that quadratic terms in the energy function correspond to Gaussian distributions. By comparing with equation (1) we see that $E_S[\vec{v}]$ can be re-interpreted as a prior. Minimizing the energy function is equivalent to maximizing the probability distribution. The probabilistic formulation is attractive since it is more general and since it provides an optimal estimator (assuming the probability distributions are correct).

It was shown by computer simulations that the motion coherence theory gave similar results to human perceptions in the experiments described earlier. Further experiments (Watamaniuk et al., 1992) also gave support for predictions of the theory.

2.2. Motion coherence for long range motion

Since Braddick (1980) it has been standard to divide vision up into short-range and long-range motion (though, as we will discuss later, this distinction has been questioned by psychophysicists — Cavanagh, 1991). Yuille and Grzywacz (1989) argued that, at the theoretical level, the distinction may be due mainly to the different form of the measurements while the prior assumptions about the motions may be similar. For short-range motion, motion either continuous or closely sampled in time, this could be modeled by assuming that the motion energy filters could be used to give initial velocity estimates. For long range motion we assume that the system sees two snapshots of the image at different times and hence has a correspondence problem between features in the image (Ullman, 1979).

To make this more precise we assume N indistinguishable features which are at positions $\{\vec{x}_i\}$ in the first frame and $\{\vec{x}_a\}$ in the second frame. We define a binary matching field $\{V_{ia}\}$ such that $V_{ia} = 1$ if the feature at $\vec{x}_i$ is matched to the feature $\vec{x}_a$, and $V_{ia} = 0$ otherwise. If $V_{ia} = 1$ then the feature at $\vec{x}_i$ has traveled a distance $\vec{x}_a - \vec{x}_i$ and hence corresponds to a velocity $\vec{x}_a - \vec{x}_i$ (where we have normalized the distance between time frames to be one unit). The constraints on the velocity field can then be constrained by a matching field

$$E_M[V, \vec{v}] = \sum_{ia} V_{ia} \, |\vec{v}(\vec{x}_i) - (\vec{x}_a - \vec{x}_i)|^2 \,, \tag{5}$$

where we impose a constraint that $\forall a$ there exists a unique i such that $V_{ia} = 1$ and vice-versa. This ensures that there is a one-to-one correspondence between features in the image frame. It is straightforward to relax the constraint by allowing features to avoid being matched by paying a penalty (Yuille and Grzywacz, 1989).

We can combine this into a full energy function by using the same smoothness prior as before. Hence we are assuming that the prior assumptions on motion are similar for both long-range and short-range motions. This yields

$$E[V, \vec{v}] = E_M[V, \vec{v}] + E_S[\vec{v}]. \tag{6}$$

$E[V, \vec{v}]$ is minimized over all $\{V_{ia}\}$ and $\{\vec{v}(\vec{x})\}$ simultaneously. The intuition is that we match features in such a way that the resulting interpolated velocity field is as smooth as possible.

This theory can be contrasted with Ullman's minimal mapping theory (Ullman, 1979) which is able to explain a number of psychophysical experiments. It can be shown that in the limit as $\sigma \to 0$ then the motion coherence theory becomes equivalent to minimal mapping. For non-zero values of σ the motion coherence theory gives a smoother velocity field (observe that σ gives a measure of the scale of spatial interactions). Hence we argue that the motion coherence theory is likely to give a better description of motion capture experiments for long-range motion. Some experiments which give support to this claim were performed (Grzywacz et al., 1989).

Since we can give a possible explanation for motion coherence for both short-range and long-range motion using the same prior assumption on the velocity field we argue that the distinction between these class of motions may be due more to the measurement stage rather than to the natural constraints used for global integration.

This argument seems consistent with the results of Cavanagh and Mather (1990) and Cavanagh (1991). These authors argue that the short-range/long-range dichotomy is not a valid distinction and is "a direct consequence of the stimuli used in the two paradigms" (Cavanagh, 1991). Since the choice of stimuli would mainly affect the measurement stage it is plausible that the global integration is similar for the two paradigms.

2.3. Critique of the motion coherence theory

Despite these successes the motion coherence theory is only designed to describe a limited class of motion phenomena. It has, for example, no mechanism for detecting motion boundaries (though such a mechanism would be straightforward to add). Nor will it yield the correct result for expanding motion where the precise form of smoothness assumptions used by the theory are invalid.

One can contrast explanations of this type based on a single "generic" prior with the "bag of tricks" theory developed by Ramachandran and Anstis (1986). We argue that Ramachandran gives no method for deciding what trick to use and that several of his tricks would appear as manifestations of a generic smoothing prior. Nevertheless there are situations where a generic motion smoothness is clearly inappropriate and the bag of trick idea is attractive. We will return to this in the final section.

3. Deformable templates

Template matching is one of the classic approaches to feature detection. In its most basic form it involves convolving an image with a mask corresponding to the feature to be detected. Large values of the convolved image, imply good matches between the template and the image, and can be interpreted as detected features.

This approach is very effective in certain domains but it has a number of drawbacks. It will fail if the object in the image is slightly deformed (possibly due to foreshortening) or if the lighting in the scene is very different from that used to generate the template. Thus one needs a template that is relatively invariant to geometric distortions and lighting variations. In addition one would like to have a confidence measure of detection that is also relatively invariant.

The deformable template approach (Yuille et al., 1989; Grenander et al., 1990; Hallinan, 1991) attempts to solve these problems. The approach is related to elastic matching (Fischler and Elschlager, 1973; Burr, 1981b; Kass et al., 1987; Durbin and Willshaw, 1987; Durbin et al., 1989).

The deformable template approach consists of three basic elements:

1   A parameterized *Geometrical Model* for the feature including prior probabilities for the parameters. This model allows one to specify a geometric measure of fitness that quantifies how well the geometrical aspects of the solution fit to the specified model.

2   An *Imaging Model* to specify how a deformable template of specific geometry will give rise to specific intensities in the image. This can be expressed in terms of an imaging measure of fitness, which captures how closely the measured image values match those predicted by the imaging model.

3   An algorithm using the geometrical and imaging measures of fitness to match, through adaptation of the free parameters of the model, the template to the image.

It is attractive to formalize this definition of the deformable template approach in terms of the Bayesian formulation. Suppose $T(\vec{g})$ specifies the geometrical model of the template with a prior probability $P(\vec{g})$ on the template parameters $\vec{g}$. The imaging model $P(I|T(\vec{g}))$ gives the probability of producing an image I from a template $T(\vec{g})$. Thus $P(I|T(\vec{g}))P(\vec{g})$ can be used to synthesize features.

Bayes' theorem can be used to obtain a measure of fitness that expresses how well our deformable template matches the imaging and geometrical models. We write

$$P(T(\vec{g})|I) = \frac{P(I|T(\vec{g}))P(T(\vec{g}))}{P(I)}. \tag{7}$$

This gives us a probability of detection of a template, $P(T(\vec{g})|I)$, in terms of the imaging model and the prior probabilities. By maximizing $P(T(\vec{g})|I)$ with respect to $\vec{g}$ we can find locally optimal candidate matches. We can also use the precise value of $P(T(\vec{g})|I)$ as a confidence criterion for the matches.

3.1. Facial feature extraction by deformable templates

The following section is based on work described in (Yuille et al., 1989). It gives the basic intuition for the deformable template approach. It uses

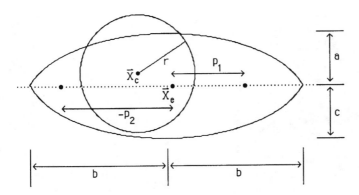

Fig. 1. *The eye template. The geometry, see text, is specified by the parameters $\vec{x}_e$, $\vec{x}_c$, p_1, p_2, r, a, b, c with an additional parameter θ specifying the orientation. The iris, R_b is represented by the circle centered on $\vec{x}_c$ and the whites, R_w by the region outside the circle but inside the two parabolae.*

the notation of energy function minimization, but is still clearly a Bayesian approach.

This work is aimed at extracting facial features such as the eyes and mouth. It is motivated by the following factors: (i) the edges of these features are rarely step edges in the intensity and so standard edge detectors are poor at detecting them, (ii) valleys and peaks in the image intensity seem more salient than edges as cues for facial features.

This suggests: (i) building in as much prior knowledge as possible about the geometry of the feature to be detected, (ii) representing the feature by a parameterized model with as few parameters as possible, (iii) making the template interact with intensity peaks and valleys.

We first specify the eye template geometry — see Figure 1. It is represented by eleven parameters $\vec{g} = (\vec{x}_t, \vec{x}_c, r, a, b, c, \theta, p_1, p_2)$. The iris is modeled as a circle with center $\vec{x}_c$ and radius r. The template as a whole has center $\vec{x}_t$ and orientation θ which defines two directions $\vec{e}_1 = (\cos\theta, \sin\theta)$ and $\vec{e}_2 = (-\sin\theta, \cos\theta)$ It is bounded by two parabolae specified by parameters a, b, c: they correspond to $\vec{x}(\alpha) = \vec{x}_t + \alpha\vec{e}_1 + \{a - \frac{a}{b^2}\alpha^2\}\vec{e}_2$ and $\vec{x}(\alpha) = \vec{x}_t + \alpha\vec{e}_1 - \{c - \frac{c}{b^2}\alpha^2\}\vec{e}_2$ for $|\alpha| \leq b$. In addition two parameters p_1 and p_2 are given to determine the positions of the centers of the peaks $\vec{x}_e + p_1\vec{e}_1$ and $\vec{x}_e + p_2\vec{e}_1$ (p_2 will be a negative number).

An energy term is used to impose relations between different parameters, such that the center of the eye is close to the center of the iris. It can be seen that, by using the Gibbs distribution (Parisi, 1988), we can transform this into prior probabilities on the parameter values.

$$E_{prior} = \frac{k_1}{2}\,||\vec{x}_e - \vec{x}_c||^2 + \frac{k_2}{2}(p_1 - p_2 - \{r + b\})^2 + \frac{k_3}{2}(b - 2r)^2. \quad (8)$$

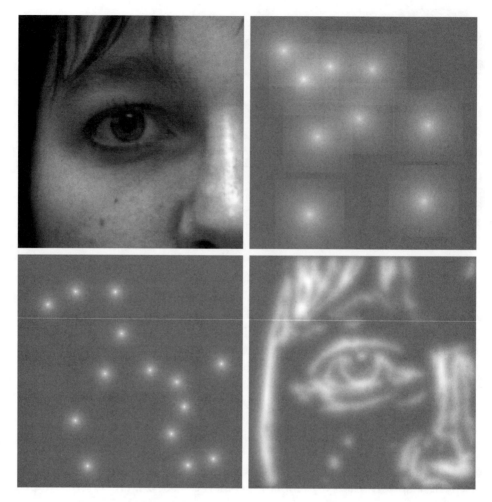

Fig. 2. *The potential fields for a typical eye, top left. The valley (top right), peak (bottom left) and edge (bottom right) fields extracted by the method described in (Hallinan, 1991).*

The imaging model assumes that the iris corresponds to a valley in the image intensity, the whites to peaks and the boundaries to edges, so we must extract edge, valley and peak fields from the intensity data. In (Yuille et al., 1989) these fields are computed by using morphological filters (Maragos, 1987; Serra, 1982). These filter responses are then smoothed by convolving with a filter, $e^{-\rho(x^2+y^2)^{1/2}}$, to give edge, valley and peak fields $\Psi_e(x,y)$, $\Psi_v(x,y)$ and $\Psi_p(x,y)$. Figure 2 shows potential fields for an "archetypal" eye. Hallinan (1991) describes an alternative way to compute these fields.

The potential fields are designed for coarse-scale matching. They will select salient regions of the image and guide the template towards them.

The imaging model will also include intensity terms which are useful for fine scale matching.

We now define the interaction energy between the deformable template and the image. This has contributions from the valley (the iris), peaks (the whites of the eyes) and edges (boundaries of the iris and the eyes). More specifically

$$E_v = -\frac{c_1}{|R_c|} \int_{R_c} \Psi_v(\vec{x})dA. \tag{9}$$

$$E_e = -\frac{c_2}{|\partial R_c|} \int_{\partial R_c} \Psi_e(\vec{x})ds - \frac{c_3}{|\partial R_w|} \int_{\partial R_w} \Psi_e(\vec{x})ds. \tag{10}$$

$$E_p = -c_4\{\Psi_p(\vec{x}_e + p_1\vec{e}_1) + \Psi_p(\vec{x}_e + p_2\vec{e}_1)\}. \tag{11}$$

$$E_I = \frac{c_5}{|R_c|} \int_{R_c} I(\vec{x})dA - \frac{c_6}{|R_w|} \int_{R_w} I(\vec{x})dA. \tag{12}$$

Here R_b, R_w, ∂R_b and ∂R_w correspond to the iris, the whites of the eye, and their boundaries—see Figure 1. Their areas, or lengths, are given by $|R_w|$, $|R_b|$, $|\partial R_w|$, and $|\partial R_b|$. A and s correspond to area and arc-length respectively.

The algorithm uses a search strategy based on steepest descent that attempts to find the most salient parts of the eye in order. It first uses the valley potential to find the iris, then the peaks to orient the template, and so on.

To implement this strategy we divide the search into a number of epochs with different values of the parameters $\{c_i\}$ and $\{k_i\}$. The updating in each epoch is done by steepest descent in the total energy

$$E = E_v + E_p + E_e + E_I + E_{prior} \tag{13}$$

i.e. $\frac{dr}{dt} = -\frac{\partial E}{\partial r}$.

In the first epoch c_1 is the only non-zero parameter and hence only the valley forces act on the template. The center of the eye $\vec{x}_t$ is set equal to the center of the iris $\vec{x}_c$. During this epoch the iris drags the eye-template towards the eye. In the next epoch the parameters c_2 and c_5 are switched on to tune the position and size of the iris. After this stage the position and size of the iris are considered fixed and an inertia term

$$E_{inertia} = \frac{k_4}{2}(r - r_{old})^2 + \frac{k_5}{2}\left\|\vec{x}_t^{old} - \vec{x}_t\right\|^2 \tag{14}$$

is added to the energy. This destroys the symmetry in the E_{prior} to ensure that the parameter values of the iris can influence the parameter values of the remainder of the template, but not *vice-versa*. Finally, the remainder of the

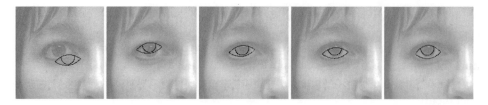

Fig. 3. *An action sequence of an eye-template. The sequence left to right, top to bottom, corresponds to the epochs in the minimization process.*

template is activated. c_4 is turned on to enable the peak fields to orient the template and c_3 and c_6 are switched on to make fine scale adjustments. The system changes epoch automatically when the rate of change of variables appropriate to that epoch remain below a cutoff for a sufficient number of iterations. Further details of the implementation can be found in (Yuille et al., 1989). Results from this template are shown in Figure 3.

This result can be interpreted in terms of probability by defining the Gibbs distribution $P(\vec{g}) = e^{-\beta E(\vec{g})}/Z$ where β is a positive constant, corresponding to the inverse temperature, and Z is a normalization factor. Maximizing P, with respect to $(\vec{g})$, is equivalent to minimizing E.

4. Competitive priors

There are several clear differences between the two approaches described in the previous sections. We can summarize these differences as follows.

Standard energy function or regularization models tend: (i) to be general purpose, (ii) have one generic prior assumption, and (iii) use no top-down information.

In contrast deformable templates are: (i) special purpose, (ii) use different prior assumptions for different features, and (iii) top-down information.

The question naturally arises whether models of early vision should have one generic prior. It is clear that when designing a visual system for performing a specific visual task the prior assumptions should be geared towards the task. Hence a set of different systems geared towards different tasks and competing with each other would seem preferable to a single generic prior (Clark and Yuille, 1990).

Such a viewpoint has strong support from psychophysical experiments. In addition to Ramachandran's bag of tricks there is also the work of Nakayama and Shimojo (1990) that argues that early vision is more similar to making inferences rather than the type of smoothing imposed by regularization theory. Jepson and Richards (1992), and Chapter 6, have also developed a theoretical approach along these lines.

In this chapter we develop an approach based on competitive priors. We assume that we have a set of different prior assumptions $P_1(f), P_2(f), \ldots,$

$P_N(f)$. This leads to a set of different modules, each trying to find the solution that maximizes their associated conditional probability:

$$P_1(f|d) = \frac{P_1(d|f)P_1(f)}{P_1(d)},$$

$$\vdots$$

$$P_N(f|d) = \frac{P_N(d|f)P_N(f)}{P_N(d)}. \tag{15}$$

Each module would find its best interpretation, given its prior assumptions, and then the overall system allows these modules to compete to determine the most probable interpretation. This is a form of data fusion, as the output of multiple sources of information is being combined. Unlike standard data fusion techniques, the above method does not simply do a weighted average or optimal estimation based on the data, but rather selects the solution from the module which is most appropriate. In (Clark and Yuille, 1990) this type of data fusion was referred to as an example of strongly coupled data fusion, wherein data fusion occurs through the interaction of distinct modules rather than through post-hoc combination of the outputs of the modules.

Nakayama has argued (personal communication) that this competitive approach stresses the importance of the $P_i(d|f)$ terms (i.e. what was referred to in Clark and Yuille (1990) as the image formation model) over the prior terms $P_i(f)$. The idea here is that one not only can change the prior model for the solutions, but one can also change the prior model of how candidate solutions generate the data.

To make this more precise consider the specific example of shape from shading. Energy function based methods, such as Horn and Brooks (1986), assume a specific form of smoothness for the surface. The algorithm is therefore biased towards the class of minimal surface defined by the exact form of the smoothness constraint. This prevents it from correctly finding the shape of surfaces such as spheres, cylinders and cones.

On the other hand there already exist algorithms that are guaranteed to work for specific types of surfaces. Pentland (1989) designed a local shape from shading algorithm that, by the nature of its prior assumptions, is ensured to work for spherical surfaces. Similarly Woodham (1981) has designed a set of algorithms that are guaranteed to work on developable surfaces, a class of surfaces which includes cones and cylinders.

Thus instead of a single generic prior it would seem more sensible to use different theories, in this case Horn and Brooks, Pentland and Woodham's, in parallel. A goodness of fitness criterion is required for each theory to determine how well it fits the data. These fitness criteria can then be used to determine which theory should be applied.

Each of the above examples of the shape from shading problem can be differentiated by their choice of prior surface model. One can also distinguish shape from shading algorithms by the assumed image formation model (i.e. the $P_i(d|f)$ terms). Some approaches assume Lambertian surfaces, others can handle specular surfaces, and so on. The competitive prior approach suggests that we allow algorithms that use different image formation models to compete and use the results of the one that has the maximum value of some fitness criterion. In Clark and Yuille (1990) a strongly coupled data fusion algorithm for doing shape from shading was proposed which used the competitive approach. In this algorithm two different image formation models were used: a Lambertian reflectance model and a specular reflectance model. These two models were used to provide shape measurements which were allowed to compete. A fitness criterion based on probabilistic likelihood ratios was used to determine which measurement would be taken as the most appropriate.

Work on transparency (Bülthoff and Kersten, 1989) also supports the competitive prior approach. In this application depth data must be fit to a number of different surfaces. A single generic smoothness prior is inappropriate in this case. The situation seems more similar to minimal description length ideas (Risannen, 1983) where one searches for the simplest explanation for a set of data, in terms of a previously specified "vocabulary" of descriptions, that is consistent with the observations.

4.1. Determining the fitness of prior models

A key aspect of the competitive prior approach is how one determines that one prior is more appropriate in a given situation than another. There are a number of approaches that could be used in determining the fitness of a prior model. We describe some of these below.

As the first example of computing the fitness of image formation models, we describe the approach of Clark and Yuille (1990) for determining the image formation model to use in shape from shading. In this application the two competing image formation models were that of Lambertian reflectance and specular reflectance. The problem of deciding whether the Lambertian model or the specular model is most appropriate is considered as one of deciding, in the presence of noise, whether we have one signal or another (the binary decision problem of statistical communication theory). The optimal Bayesian decision rule, $\delta(\gamma|\vec{d})$ for this problem is that which minimizes the "average risk", where the average risk is defined as (Middleton, 1987)

$$R(p(S), \delta) = \int_\Omega dS p(S) \int_\Gamma d\vec{d} p(\vec{d}|S) \int_\Delta d\gamma C(S, \gamma) \delta(\gamma|\vec{d}) \qquad (16)$$

In equation 16 S is the "signal" (i.e. either Lambertian or specular), $p(S)$ is the *a priori* probability of the signal, $\vec{d}$ is the (noisy) data, γ is the decision (e.g. $\gamma = 1$ for specular, -1 for Lambertian), $p(\vec{d}|S)$ is the "image formation model" relating how a signal (either specular or Lambertian) gives rise to the data (and hence depends on $\hat{n}(\vec{x})$), and $C(S, \gamma)$ is the cost associated with making the decision γ when the signal is actually S. For the binary case we can replace the integration over the signal space (Ω) by a sum of two terms corresponding to the two elements in the signal space. The *a priori* density on S is now a sum of two delta functions, $p(S) = q\delta(S - S_{specular}) + p\delta(S - S_{Lambertian})$. Similarly, the decision space Δ contains only two possible decisions $(\gamma = +1, \gamma = -1)$, and so the integral over the decision space can also be reduced to a sum of two terms. There are four possible combinations of arguments to the cost function and we define $C_{1-\alpha} = C(S_{specular}, \gamma = +1)$, $C_\alpha = C(S_{specular}, \gamma = -1)$, $C_{1-\beta} = C(S_{Lambertian}, \gamma = -1)$, and $C_\beta = C(S_{Lambertian}, \gamma = +1)$. We now can write the average risk as (Middleton, 1987)

$$R(p, q, \delta) = qC_{1-\alpha} + pC_{1-\beta} + q\alpha(C_\alpha - C_{1-\alpha}) + p\beta(C_\beta - C_{1-\beta}) \qquad (17)$$

where

$$\alpha = \int_\Gamma p(\vec{d}|S = S_{specular})\delta(\gamma = -1|\vec{d})d\vec{d} \qquad (18)$$

and

$$\beta = \int_\Gamma p(\vec{d}|S = S_{Lambertian})\delta(\gamma = +1|\vec{d})d\vec{d} \qquad (19)$$

The α and β are related to the probability of making an error in the decision process.

The optimum Bayes decision rule can be shown to be (Middleton, 1987): Decide specular when $\Lambda < \mathcal{K}$, and Lambertian otherwise. Λ is the *generalized likelihood ratio,* and is given by

$$\Lambda = \left(\frac{p}{q}\right)\left(\frac{p(\vec{d}|S = Lambertian)}{p(\vec{d}|S = specular)}\right) \qquad (20)$$

Note that Λ is always non-negative. K is a decision threshold, and is related to the costs as follows,

$$\mathrm{K} = \frac{C_\alpha - C_{1-\alpha}}{C_\beta - C_{1-\beta}} \qquad (21)$$

We can determine the form of Λ once we have specified the two image formation models, $p(\vec{d}|S = S_{specular})$ and $p(\vec{d}|S = S_{Lambertian})$. The determination of the threshold K requires the specification of the cost of making a mis-classification. Typically we will want to use these costs to embed our constraint concerning the suppression of small regions in the segmentation of the image into Lambertian and specular regions. This will require that the costs be dependent on the spatial structure of the solution, and hence implies that an iterative procedure is required to embed this constraint through the specification of the costs. In the absence of this constraint we could set $C_{1-\alpha}$ and $C_{1-\beta}$ to be zero (i.e. no cost assessed for correct segmentation) and set $C_\alpha = C_\beta$. Then K=1. We can then rephrase the decision process as: decide specular when $\log \Lambda < 0$ and decide Lambertian otherwise. The quantity $\log \Lambda$ is seen to be

$$\log \Lambda = [(E - \hat{n} \cdot \hat{s})^2 - \log p] - [(E - (\hat{h} \cdot \hat{k})^m)^2 - \log q] \qquad (22)$$

This corresponds to the difference in the energies between the two possible solutions in the energy function formulation. The terms $- \log p$ and $- \log q$ represent the *a priori* constraint of the energy function formulation (i.e. the *a priori* expectation of a piece of surface being either specular or Lambertian — the minimum area constraint could possibly be embedded here by making p and q be dependent on the surface normal field $\hat{n}(\vec{x})$). We can see the relationship between the energy function formulation and the optimal binary decision making formulation of the segmentation process. If the energy corresponding to the assumption of specular image formation model is less than the energy for the assumption of the Lambertian image formation model then $\log \Lambda$ will be less than zero, and we would decide on the specular solution.

The binary decision method described here can be extended to the case where there are a multiple number of possible image formation models (each corresponding to a different surface shading law). A more complex decision rule would need to be used in place of the simple threshold, but the general approach would be the same.

For a single image of a scene it may be hard to identify the appropriate prior. If several viewpoints are available then additional evidence becomes available. In particular, we could use consistency between views to determine which prior is appropriate. For example, the Horn and Brooks (1986) shape from shading algorithm uses a prior smoothness assumption that will tend to bias objects towards the fronto-parallel plane. As one moves the camera about in space and repeats the shape from shading process the fronto-parallel plane moves as well. For highly curved objects this will lead to inconsistency between different viewpoints, resulting in a perception of non-rigidity. One can use this inconsistency as evidence that this prior can be rejected. If shape from shading algorithms using different prior models (models of the image formation process as well as of the surface) are operating in parallel, one can use the viewpoint consistency as a way of determining which prior models are most appropriate.

Sheinberg, Bülthoff and Blake (1990) have developed a theory for texture perception where the accuracy of the assumptions about the texture distribution can be evaluated by the magnitude of the $P(d|f)$ term. This provides a mechanism for allowing various texture priors to compete. Obviously this approach as it stands can only work for a single assumed image formation model $P(d|f)$, but it may be possible to extend it to multiple competing image formation models by evaluating the magnitude of $P(d|f)$ over a set of different $P(d|f)$s.

Finally, one aspect of the competitive prior approach is that priors can use the competitive pressure as a stimulus for adaption. One can alter the prior models in various ways that depend on the fitness criteria so that the fitness criteria increase in value after the adaption. It is an interesting research problem to determine how to do the adaption. One requires knowledge of what aspects of a prior model can be altered (e.g. changing of some free parameters of the model), as well as some scheme for actually altering the values (e.g. gradient descent of some kind).

5. Conclusion

As Marr (1982) argued the search for natural constraints, or priors, is what turns vision into a science. In the past computational vision theorists have tended to concentrate of general purpose generic priors, as illustrated in section 2. One can argue, however, that, as in section 3, it may be better to use more specific priors geared towards different tasks. The concept of competitive priors, described in section 4, gives a possible way of reconciling these two approaches.

There is some similarity here to ideas in Active Vision where images are examined in order to extract information for performing certain tasks. The competitive priors might correspond to the tasks the system is interested in.

Acknowledgements

We would like to acknowledge support from the Brown/Harvard/MIT Center for Intelligent Control Systems with US Army Research Office grant DAAL03-86-K-0171. One of us, JJC, would like to acknowledge NSF grant: number IRI-9003306. One of us, ALY would like to thank the Systems Research Center with National Science Foundation grant CDR-85-00108.

Cycloversion, cyclovergence and perceived slant

Ian P. Howard

1. Introduction

Rotation of an eye about the visual axis is known as ocular torsion. Conjugate torsion of the two eyes is known as cycloversion. Optokinetic cycloversional movements of the eyes are evoked by rotation of a frontal plane display around the fixation point (Brecher, 1934; Howard and Templeton, 1964; Petrov and Zenkin, 1973; Crone, 1975; Cheung and Howard, 1991). A small cycloversional movement is evoked by visual inspection of a large static display of lines tilted from the vertical in the frontal plane (Goodenough et al., 1979). Rotation of the head about the roll axis in the dark induces an opposed cycloversional rotation of the eyes, known as counter-rolling, with a velocity gain of about 0.6 up to a limiting amplitude of about 8° (Collewijn et al., 1985; Ferman et al., 1987a). When the head is tilted with eyes open the optokinetic and vestibular signals combine to increase the velocity gain of counterrolling up to about 0.7 (Leigh et al., 1989). Some degree of torsion occurs as the eyes move into a tertiary position of gaze, although the extent to which this is labeled torsion depends on the chosen system of coordinates (Fry, 1968; Ferman et al., 1987b). Disjunctive torsion, or cyclovergence, is evoked by cyclodisparities in the images in the two eyes (Kertesz and Sullivan, 1978) and as a component of horizontal vergence (Allen and Carter, 1967). Cyclophoria, or torsional misalignment of the two eyes, may occur in the absence of cyclofusional stimuli. Although torsion is normally neither produced nor inhibited by voluntary effort, it can be evoked voluntarily after an extended period of practice (Balliet and Nakayama, 1978).

The terminology for torsion has been confused and we offer the following definitions. Cyclorotation refers to the rotation of a visual object about the visual axis of an eye with respect to head coordinates. It is signed positive if the top of the object rotates towards the median plane of the head (incyclorotation) and negative if it rotates in the other direction (excyclorotation). A common rotation of two dichoptic stimuli is conjunctive cyclorotation and any difference in their rotations is disjunctive cyclorotation. The term 'declination' refers to the total signed angle of disjunctive cyclorotation of a pair of dichoptic stimuli (Ogle and Ellerbrock, 1946) and the term 'inclination' refers to the slant of an object in the median plane of the head with respect to the horizontal, signed positive top away. If a is the interpupillary distance and d the observation distance, then a line with an inclination i projects as a pair of retinal images with a declination angle ϕ. The angle of declination is related to the angle of inclination by the following expression:

$$\phi = 2\tan^{-1}\left(\frac{a}{2d\tan i}\right) \qquad (1)$$

The cyclodisparity of a specified pair of dichoptic images is their relative orientation in retinal coordinates, designated positive or negative according to whether the images are rotated top towards or top away from each other. Two dichoptic line images have zero cyclodisparity if they appear parallel. Dichoptic line images fall on corresponding retinal meridia if each lies on a retinal meridian passing through the fovea and if they appear parallel. Cycloduction is the torsional state of a single eye indicated by the dihedral angle between the median plane of the head and the plane containing an arbitrarily specified meridian of the eye and the visual axis. Cycloduction is designated incycloduction or excycloduction according to whether the eye is rotated top towards or top away from the median plane. Cycloversion is the equal component of the eyes cycloductions, designated levocycloversion when the eyes rotate top to the subject's left and dextrocycloversion when they rotate top to the subject's right. Cyclovergence is the difference between the eyes' cycloductions, designated incyclovergence or excyclovergence according to whether there is a net top-in or top-out relative rotation. Cyclovergence is zero when two horizontal nonius lines on opposite radii of a dichoptic display in the frontal plane appear parallel. It is best to use horizontal nonius lines as reference because, when corresponding horizontal meridia are parallel, corresponding vertical meridia may have a slight positive declination (von Helmholtz, 1909). Any such declination of vertical corresponding meridia causes the vertical horopter (the locus of points in space that stimulate corresponding vertical retinal meridia) to be inclined, top away, out of the frontal plane (Nakayama, 1977). The inclination of the vertical horopter may also be affected by cyclovergence which accompanies a change in horizontal vergence (Amigo, 1974). It follows from these definitions that, for horizontal lines, cyclodisparity equals disjunctive cyclorotation minus cyclovergence.

Various investigators over the last 100 years, including Hering (see Ogle and Ellerbrock, 1946), Verhoeff (1934), Kertesz (1972) and Krekling (1973), denied that cyclovergence occurs and in most textbooks the response is not mentioned. In some cases investigators changed their minds when they used more effective stimuli, in particular stimuli which subtended a visual angle in excess of 25° and which contained many horizontal and vertical elements.

Methods such as the corneal reflex method, electrooculography and the use of Purkinje images do not record eye torsion. Methods which rely on photographing the iris landmarks or episcleral blood vessels do not provide a continuous record. The photographs must be analyzed frame by frame which is time consuming (Howard and Evans, 1963). Kertesz (1972) used the photographic method but failed to find cyclovergence. It is now known that his stimulus was too small. Crone and Everhard-Halm (1975) and Hooten et al. (1979) used the photographic procedure with a more adequate stimulus and obtained clear evidence of cyclovergence.

A scleral search-coil mounted on an annular contact lens has been developed (Collewijn et al., 1985) which is now available from Skalar Medical in Delft. When the coil is placed on an eye within an oscillating magnetic field a voltage proportional to the sine of the torsional position of the eye is generated (Robinson, 1963; Collewijn et al., 1975). With this method a virtually noise-free signal is obtained that continuously registers the torsional position of an eye to within a few minutes of arc. The only drawback of the method is that the contact lenses may be worn for only about 30 minutes at one time. Kertesz and Sullivan (1978) used the scleral-coil procedure and obtained a cyclovergence response of 3.5° to a plus or minus 5° step of cyclodisparity in dichoptically presented patterned displays subtending 50°. We have used the scleral-coil method in a series of experiments on cyclovergence which will be described in the following sections.

2. The dynamics of cyclovergence

We used the search-coil procedure to measure, for the first time, the dynamics of cyclovergence (Howard and Zacher, 1991). The display and apparatus are shown in Figure 1. The stimulus subtended 80° and was chosen because it contains a broad range of spatial frequencies, has both vertical and horizontal elements to act as cyclofusional stimuli and as good stimuli for keeping horizontal and vertical vergence constant. A regular grid pattern is best avoided because the eyes have a tendency to misconverge on such stimuli and a random-dot pattern is not a good choice for a stimulus designed to excite orientation detectors. Since the display was round and the surroundings black, there were no stationary lines to provide a cyclofusional anchor. Identical left and right displays were rear projected onto screens and combined by mirrors into a single fused display in the subject's frontal plane at a distance of 50 cm. The dichoptic displays were rotated in counterphase about the fixation point to give peak-to-peak amplitudes of disjunctive cyclorotation of 2, 6 or 12°, at frequencies of between 0.05 and 2 Hz. The gain of cyclovergence was defined as the mean peak-to-peak

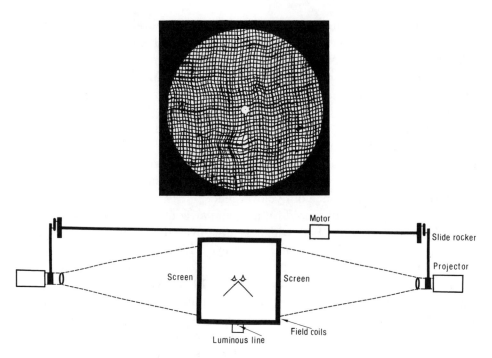

Fig. 1. *Diagrammatic top view of the apparatus. The magnetic field coils were contained in the 1m cubic framework surrounding the subject. The dichoptic displays, shown in the insert, were projected onto Mylar screens and combined by the half-silvered mirrors into a dichoptic image, 80° in diameter at a distance of 50 cm. A servo motor and rocker arms rotated slides in antiphase to the two eyes at various frequencies and amplitudes (From Howard and Zacher, 1991). ©Springer-Verlag, 1991.*

amplitude of cyclovergence over the peak-to-peak amplitude of disjunctive cyclorotation of the stimulus. A set of records is shown in Figure 2 and the gain and phase-lag of the mean responses of three subjects are shown in Figure 3. The amplitude and gain of the response decreased with increasing stimulus frequency. As stimulus amplitude increased, response amplitude also increased but gain was highest for low-amplitude cyclorotations. For an amplitude of 2° and a frequency of 0.05 Hz the gain reached 0.87 for one subject. The phase lag increased from a few degrees at a frequency of 0.05 Hz to over 100° at a frequency of 2 Hz.

The dependence of cyclovergence gain on the amplitude of cyclorotation demonstrates that the cyclovergence system is non-linear. The function relating gain in decibels to frequency for 6 amplitude, has a slope of 20 db/decade for the five highest frequencies. This is the value one would expect of a first-order system. However, the phase lag at the corner frequency corresponding to a gain of −3db is much smaller than would be expected from a first-order or a second-order system.

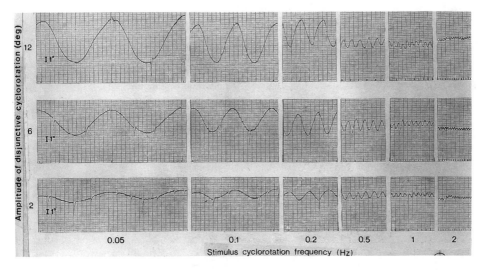

Fig. 2. *A set of cyclovergence records of one subject for five frequencies and three amplitudes of disjunctive cyclorotation of the stimulus. The sharp impulses are blinks (From Howard and Zacher, 1991).*

When there are no corresponding stimuli the eyes of many people drift into a state of torsional misalignment, or cyclophoria. The cyclovergence mechanism is well designed to prevent this from happening when corresponding images are present. Thus, human cyclovergence is not the ineffective, vestigial response that many investigators have supposed and it may be concluded that perturbations in the torsional alignment of binocular images of a few degrees and up to a frequency of about 0.2 Hz, will be largely corrected by the cyclovergence of the eyes.

3. The dynamics of cycloversion

A display rotating about the line of sight in the same direction for both eyes induces optokinetic torsion in the direction of stimulus motion. Brecher (1934) and was the first to observe this response by looking at the conjunctival blood vessels as the subject fixated the centre of a rotating sectored disc and it has since been measured objectively (Howard and Templeton, 1964; Crone, 1975; Collewijn et al., 1985). Kertesz and Jones (1969) reported that the amplitude of optokinetic torsion is a function of the angular velocity and spatial frequency of the rotating pattern. In none of these studies was the gain or phase lag of the response measured.

We used the search-coil procedure to obtain a continuous record of optokinetic torsion evoked by a full-field display of random black dots on the inside of a white sphere into which subjects looked as it rotated at a constant velocity of 30, 45 or 60°/s or rotated back and forth sinusoidally at various frequencies up to 2Hz and through various amplitudes up to 80°

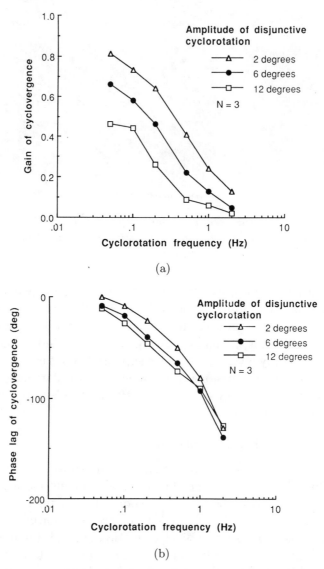

(a)

(b)

Fig. 3. *The mean gain (a) and phase lag (b) of cyclovergence for three subjects as a function of cyclorotation frequency for three amplitudes of disjunctive cyclorotation (From Howard and Zacher, 1991).* ©*Springer-Verlag, 1991.*

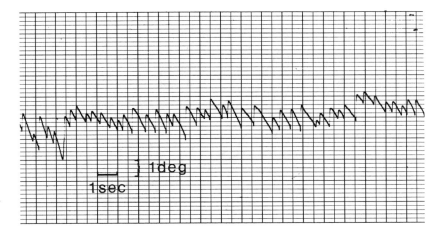

Fig. 4. *A set of cycloversion records of one subject made in response to a large patterned display rotating about the visual axis.*

(Cheung and Howard, 1991). A sample of the records is shown in Figure 4. The gain and phase lag of the response as a function of the frequency and amplitude of sinusoidal stimulus rotation are shown in Figure 5. The mean gain of cycloversion is less than the mean gain of cyclovergence but this is not surprising because cycloversion is normally produced by head tilt and is then supplemented by inputs from the utricles.

4. The stimulus for cyclovergence

The cyclovergence system is complicated by the fact that not all cyclodisparities signify that the eyes are misaligned. Consider a surface covered with vertical and horizontal lines which is inclined in depth about a horizontal axis. The cyclodisparity in the images of the vertical lines provides a stereoscopic cue to the orientation of the surface in depth. However, any misalignment of the images of the horizontal lines can be due only to torsional misalignment of the eyes. Now consider a similar surface slanting in depth about a vertical axis. The images of the vertical lines remain parallel and so do the images of horizontal lines close to the point of fixation. The images of horizontal lines above the point of fixation acquire a cyclodisparity proportional to their eccentricity and so do the images of lines below this point, but with opposite sign. This pattern of differential disparities provides a cue to surface slant but any mean cyclodisparity in the set of horizontal lines across the visual field as a whole can be due only to torsional misalignment of the eyes. One would predict therefore that cyclovergence is not evoked by cyclodisparities in vertical lines because these are used to register depth but is evoked by cyclodisparities in horizontals averaged over the visual field.

When we change our convergence to different depth planes, horizontal disparities in the plane of convergence are nulled and those arising from objects

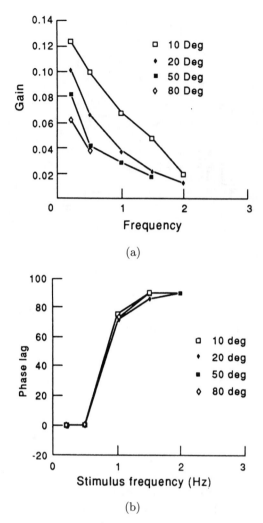

Fig. 5. *The gain (a) and phase lag (b) of cycloversion as a function of the frequency of sinusoidal stimulus rotation for four amplitudes of rotation (from Cheung and Howard, 1991).* ©*Pergamon Press, 1991.*

at other distances remain. In other words, horizontal vergence is controlled only by disparities in the plane to which we are attending. Cyclovergence, on the other hand, is designed to correct torsional misalignment of the eyes and, since the effects of torsional misalignment do not vary with distance, cyclovergence does not involve any process of attentional selection. The following two hypotheses may be constructed from these arguments:

1   cyclovergence is evoked most effectively by disparities in horizontals.

2   the disparity detectors which evoke cyclovergence have large receptive fields and respond preferentially to cyclodisparities distributed over large areas.

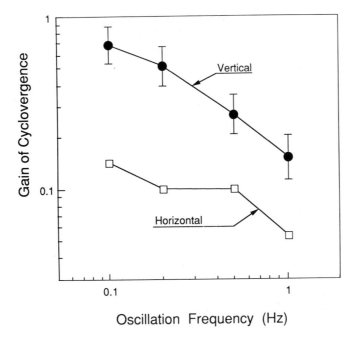

Fig. 6. *The mean gain of cyclovergence evoked by disjunctive cyclorotation of vertical lines and of horizontal lines.*

In order to test hypothesis 1 we compared the gain of cyclovergence evoked by disjunctive cyclorotation of a pattern of vertical lines with that evoked by disjunctive cyclorotation of a pattern of horizontal lines (Rogers and Howard, 1991). The results are shown in Figure 6. They confirm earlier psychophysical evidence that cyclorotation of horizontal lines induces more cyclovergence than cyclorotation of vertical lines (Nagel, 1868; Verhoeff, 1934; Crone and Everhard-Halm, 1975).

If one wished to design a robotic system in which the torsional alignment of stereoscopic images was automatically adjusted, it would be wise to base the adjustment on the cross correlation between horizontal elements in the two images. Residual cyclodisparities in non-horizontal elements could then be used to extract information about the slant of surfaces and objects in depth.

In conformity with hypothesis 2 Kertesz and Sullivan (1978) found that cyclovergence is evoked more strongly by large visual displays and in particular that the response is weak for displays subtending less than 20°. This is probably the main reason why many investigators denied the existence of cyclovergence; they used displays which were too small. We investigated this question in more detail by measuring the gain of cyclovergence for stimuli confined to the central 5, 20 and 40° of the visual field and then for a 75° diameter stimulus in which the central 5, 20 and 40° were occluded by a black disc (Shen and Howard, 1991). Since there was no interaction

Normalized cyclovergence gain as a function of stimulus size

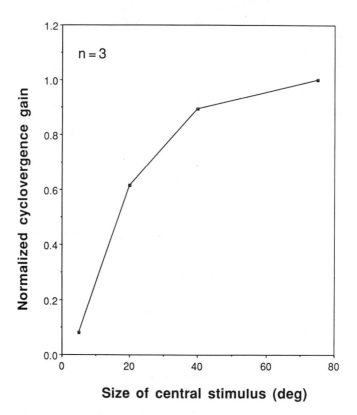

Fig. 7. *Cyclovergence as a function of the angular subtense of a central cyclorotating display.*

between stimulus frequency and the area of stimulation we averaged the results across stimulus frequency. From Figure 7 it can be seen that the response was virtually zero with a stimulus confined to the central 5° and increased with increasing diameter of the central display. On the other hand, it can be seen from Figure 8 that the response did not vary as a function of how much of the central retina was occluded. Even a 40° central mask did not reduce the response below the value obtained with a 75° stimulus.

It may be concluded that cyclovergence requires a large stimulus, but this does not have to be on the central retina. If cyclovergence is driven by point disparities then this might explain the need for a large stimulus since point disparities in a rotating display increase linearly with stimulus eccentricity. Otherwise one would have to assume that cyclovergence is driven by orientation disparity detectors with large receptive fields. This would make sense since the only purpose of cyclovergence is to keep the images of the main horizontal features of the visual field in orientational

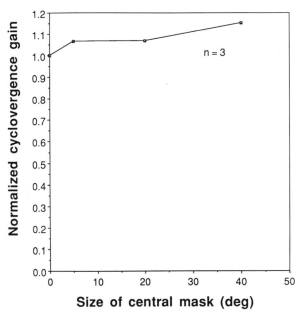

Fig. 8.   *Cyclovergence as a function of the angular subtense of a central black occluder.*

alignment so that residual disparities in vertical elements can be used to code differential slants of particular objects, especially those in the centre of the visual field.

5. The stimulus for cycloversion

The effects of increasing the area of the centrally placed display are shown in Figure 9. It can be seen that there is a sizeable response from a 5° stimulus. The effects of increasing the area of a central occluding disc are shown in Figure 10, from which it can be seen that the gain of cycloversion, unlike that of cyclovergence, is significantly reduced by occlusion of the central retina. In these respects cycloversion resembles horizontal OKN, which is not surprising since both responses are evoked by stimulation of retinal motion detectors which are more numerous in the central visual field.

6. Cyclovergence and the nonius procedure

The nonius procedure is a psychophysical method used to measure cyclover-gence. In this method, cyclovergence is indicated by the angle through which a line presented to one side of the fixation point in one eye has to be ro-tated to appear parallel to a line presented in the opposite field of the other

Normalized cycloversion gain as a function of stimulus size

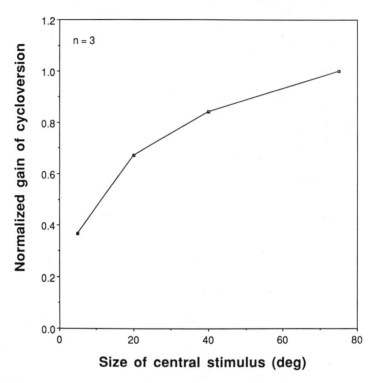

Fig. 9. *Cycloversion as a function of the angular subtense of a central cyclorotating display.*

eye. Dichoptic stimuli of this sort are known as Volkmann discs and are the torsional equivalent of nonius stimuli used to measure horizontal and vertical vergence. Hofmann and Bielschowsky (1900) were the first to use this method systematically. With it they recorded cyclovergence of about 5° induced by disjunctive cyclorotation of a textured display through 8°. Verhoeff (1934) used the nonius method and found cyclovergence to be a slow response induced more by horizontal lines than by vertical lines, a finding in line with objective measurements reported by Crone and Everhard-Halm (1975) and with our own results.

We used the display shown in Figure 11 to measure cyclovergence by the nonius method. The textured dichoptic display was cyclorotated disjunctively to a fixed amplitude of 12° and at frequencies between 0.05 and 2 Hz through an amplitude of 12°. The apparent relative tilting motion of the two nonius lines in the small insert at the center of the display was nulled by an opposed physical oscillation which the subject controlled by turning a knob. The resulting nonius settings were then compared with objective

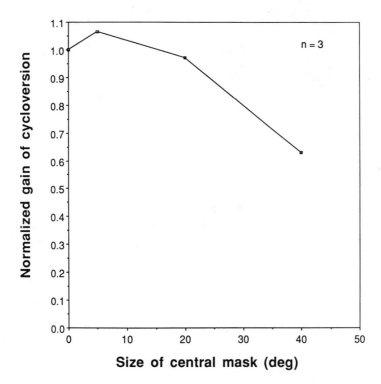

Fig. 10. *Cycloversion as a function of the angular subtense of a central black occluder.*

measures of cyclovergence obtained under the same conditions. Figure 12 shows that the two measures agreed but only when there was a very low-frequency of stimulus cyclorotation, demonstrating that the nonius method is a valid measure of static or slowly changing cyclovergence. However, the nonius settings were too high when the stimulus was oscillating. We believe that this is due to motion contrast between the moving display in each eye and the test line in each eye. We agree with Shipley and Rawlings (1970) that a nonius method is the only satisfactory psychophysical method for measuring vergence, horizontal, vertical or torsional, but the method is valid only for stationary or near stationary stimuli.

7. Cyclovergence and perceived slant

We next looked at the relationship between an objective measure of cyclovergence and judgements of the visual vertical. Several investigators have assumed that any error in the vertical setting of a test line in the median plane is due to cyclodisparity induced into the line by cyclovergence. Using

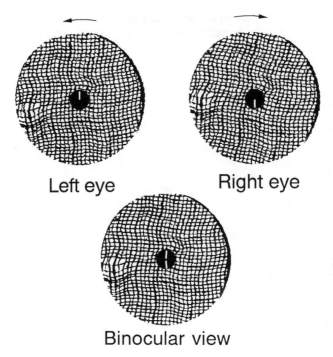

Fig. 11. *The display used to measure cyclovergence by the nonius method. The textured dichoptic display was cyclorotated disjunctively at frequencies between 0.05 and 2 Hz and amplitudes of 12, 6 and 2°. The apparent relative tilting motion of the two nonius lines in the small insert at the center of the display was nulled by an opposed oscillation which the subject controlled by turning a knob.*

this assumption, Ogle and Ellerbrock (1946) reported that vertical displays evoke more cyclovergence than do horizontal displays. We believe that this contradiction with our own results arises because the assumption is false. One problem is that the test line may contaminate the results. This problem is at least partially overcome by presenting the test stimulus briefly after the stimulus for cyclovergence has been removed (Ellerbrock, 1954). But even with this precaution the perceived slant of the test line has been found not to correspond to the cyclodisparity in the line (Hampton and Kertesz, 1982). I shall discuss the possible reasons for this and related phenomena.

The textured display used in our experiments appeared to remain in the frontal plane even when disjunctively cyclorotated through 12°, corresponding to a slant of about 60°. This could be due to the the fact that cyclodisparities are nulled by cyclovergence. However, cyclodisparities were not fully nulled since the gain of cyclovergence was not one. The other possibility is that depth is signalled by disparity discontinuities rather than by constant gradients of disparity within the visual field. There is considerable evidence that this is so for horizontal disparity (Tyler, 1974; Anstis et al., 1978; Brookes and Stevens, 1989; Gillam et al., 1984). Further-

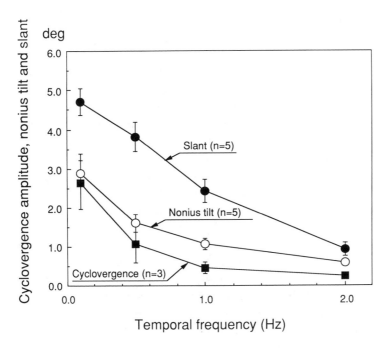

Fig. 12. *The nonius settings, line slant settings and objective amplitudes of cyclovergence for various frequencies of disjunctive stimulus cyclorotation through an amplitude of* 12°.

more, temporal changes in horizontal disparity applied evenly over the visual field are not interpreted as changes in distance (Gogel, 1963; Erkelens and Collewijn, 1985; Regan et al., 1986b). The same principle is also evident with cyclodisparities. Slanted surfaces or lines appear less slanted than they are, an effect known as the equidistance tendency (Gogel, 1956; 1963). Random-dot stereograms differing in orientation by as much as 7°, although binocularly fused, do not appear to slant in depth (Julesz, 1964). The fact that the corresponding vertical meridia are extorted with respect to each other by about 2° when the horizontal meridia are parallel causes the vertical horopter to be inclined top away according to the formula mentioned in the Introduction. However, this has been found not to cause vertical lines to appear inclined (Cogan, 1979).

A vertical test line superimposed on our cyclorotated textured display appeared to slant in a direction opposite that corresponding to the disparity in the display. Similar slant contrast effects in vertical lines have been known for some time. For instance, a line slanted in the median plane appears to slant only a fraction of its actual slant until a vertical comparison line is placed next to it (Ogle, 1946) and a vertical line appears to slant in a direction opposite to the real slant of two flanking lines (Werner, 1938). Ogle (1946) explained depth contrast by stating that cyclovergence transfers some of the cyclodisparity from the images of the inducing stimulus into the images of the test line and that this causes a corresponding decrease in the perceived slant of the inducing stimulus and an increase in the perceived slant of the test line. Ogle did not subject his theory of depth contrast to direct test. The other view is that cyclodisparities which occur evenly over a large display are not registered by the visual system for the purpose of making depth judgements. Displays containing such disparities are perceived to lie in the frontal plane; they are said to normalize to the frontal plane. A small object which actually lies in the frontal plane generates relative disparities between it and the normalized background. Relative disparities are registered and give rise to the impression that the object is slanted or inclined with respect to the background. This is the effect known as depth contrast. Since relative disparities are not affected by vergence, depth contrast is also not affected by vergence.

We measured the perceived change in slant of a vertical test line superimposed on a black disc at the center of a disjunctively cyclorotating background. The line was the fused image of two dichoptic lines which could be cyclorotated in antiphase to produce the impression of a single line oscillating in depth through an angle determined by the amplitude of cyclorotation. By controlling the actual slant of the test line, subjects could null the apparent change in slant of the line induced by the disjunctive cyclorotation of the textured background. This was done over the same set of frequencies and amplitudes used in our other experiments. Objective measurements of cyclovergence were also obtained. The results are shown in Figure 12.

In all conditions the test line appeared to slant and the textured display appeared vertical even though it was undergoing disjunctive cyclorotation. I believe this depth normalization of the background is due to the perceptual system using the major part of the visual scene as a frame of reference for perceived slant. It can be seen from Figure 12 that at all frequencies the perceived slant of the test line was greater than the cyclodisparity induced into it by cyclovergence. If the line appeared to slant by an amount equal to the relative cyclodisparity between the images of the line and the images of the background its perceived slant would be independent of the degree of cyclovergence. It can be seen in Figure 6 that for low frequencies of stimulus oscillation, the perceived slant was almost as large as the relative cyclodisparity between line and background. At higher frequencies it fell below this value which I believe is due to the inability of the perceptual system to keep pace with rapid changes in cyclodisparity.

It may be concluded that for a large stationary display and low frequencies of cyclorotation the perceived slant of a vertical test line reflects the total cyclodisparity between line and background, that is, it is a measure of the relative cyclorotation of the images of the scene, and is independent of the amount of cyclovergence. The angular displacement of nonius lines depends only on the cyclodisparity induced into the test lines and is therefore a measure of the cyclovergence of the eyes.

The visual system can tolerate some orientational misalignment of images in stereoscopic viewing systems because the eyes cyclorotate to compensate for the misalignment. Furthermore, even if the images are not perfectly aligned they will appear fused because of a neural mechanism that fuses disparate images within the limits of Panum's fusional areas. If a stereoscopic system has an oscillating misalignment of the images above about 0.5 Hz, the capacity of the cyclovergence system to make compensations is severely limited.

The following conclusions are relevant to the use of stereoscopic display systems such as are used in helmet-mounted flight simulators or remote control devices. 1) Torsional misalignment of binocular images of a few degrees and up to a frequency of about 0.2 Hz, will be largely corrected by the cyclovergence of the eyes. 2) Uncorrected torsional misalignments of images will not cause large textured scenes to appear slanted but may cause vertical lines or objects to appear slanted. 3) If a torsionally misaligned display is set within surroundings which are in normal torsional alignment, and especially if the surroundings contain horizontals, then the perceived slant of surfaces and objects in the display will be severely distorted relative to the surroundings. 4) Operators could easily be trained to read the torsional misalignment of images in a stereoscopic display from a calibrated pair of nonius test lines superimposed, on demand, on the center of the display. 5) The perceived slant of a vertical test line is a valid measure, not of absolute cyclodisparity in the test line, but of the relative cyclodisparity between test line and cyclorotated background. Torsionally misaligned images can be most precisely brought into orientational alignment by rotating them until a vertical line viewed binocularly through semi-silvered mirrors has zero slant.

Model of visual motion sensing

David J. Heeger

Eero P. Simoncelli

A number of researchers have proposed models of early motion sensing based on direction-selective, spatiotemporal linear operators. Others have formalized the problem of measuring optical flow in terms of the spatial and temporal derivatives of stimulus intensity. Recently, the spatiotemporal filter models and the gradient-based methods have been placed into a common framework. In this chapter, we review that framework and we extend it to develop a new model for the computation and representation of velocity information in the visual system. We use the model to simulate psychophysical data on perceived velocity of sine-grating plaid patterns, and to simulate physiological data on responses of simple cells in primary (striate) visual cortex.

1. Introduction

More than forty years ago, Gibson (1950; 1957) noted that visual motion perception is essential for an observer's ability to explore and interact with his/her environment. As an observer moves and explores the environment, the visual stimulation in his/her eye is constantly changing. Somehow he/she is able to perceive the spatial layout of the scene, and to discern his/her movement through space. Imagine, for example, that you are watching a scene from a movie that was shot with the camera in motion. The visual stimulation in your eye is an array of light that changes over time, yet you experience a sense of moving through a three dimensional space.

Since Gibson's initial work, perception of motion has been studied extensively by researchers in the fields of visual psychophysics, visual neurophysiology, and computational vision. It is now well-known that the visual system has mechanisms that are specifically suited for analyzing motion (see Nakayama, 1985, for review), and that human observers are capable of recovering accurate information about the world (e.g., three-dimensional trajectory, relative distance, shape) from visual motion (e.g., Wallach and O'Connell, 1953; Johansson, 1975; Warren and Hannon, 1988; 1990).

The first stage of motion perception is generally believed to be the measurement of optical flow. Optical flow is a field of two-dimensional velocity vectors, indicating the speed and direction of motion for each small region of the visual field.

A number of machine vision algorithms have been developed for measuring optical flow fields from sequences of (e.g., video) images. At the same time, psychophysicists and neurophysiologists have performed experiments to study the manner by which people and animals sense velocity. Little effort, however, has gone into integrating the results from the three disciplines of computational vision, visual psychophysics, and visual neurophysiology.

In this chapter, we describe a model for the computation and representation of velocity information in the primate visual system that accounts for a variety of psychophysical and physiological observations. We use the model to simulate psychophysical data on perceived velocity of sine-grating plaid patterns, and to simulate physiological data on responses of simple cells in primary (striate) visual cortex.

2. The model

In this section, we review two algorithms for measuring flow fields, the gradient-based methods and the spatiotemporal filtering methods. Following Adelson and Bergen (1986), and Simoncelli and Adelson (1991b, 1991a), we show that these two methods can be expressed in a common mathematical framework. Finally, we introduce some extensions to this framework to develop our new model of biological motion sensing.

2.1. Gradient-based methods

Researchers (Horn and Schunk, 1981; Lucas and Kanade, 1981; Nagel, 1987) and others have proposed algorithms that compute flow from the spatial and temporal derivatives of intensity. Following the standard gradient formulation, we assume that the stimulus is shifted (locally translated) over time, and that the shifted intensity values are conserved. This intensity conservation assumption is expressed as follows:

$$f(x, y, t) = f(x + v_1, y + v_2, t + 1), \tag{1}$$

where $f(x, y, t)$ is stimulus intensity as a function of space and time, and $\vec{v} = (v_1, v_2)$ is velocity. Note that this intensity conservation assumption is only approximately true in practice. For example, it ignores possible changes in intensity due to lighting changes.

We further assume that the time-varying stimulus intensity is well approximated by a first-order Taylor series expansion:

$$f(x + v_1, y + v_2, t + 1) \approx f(x, y, t) + v_1 f_x(x, y, t) + v_2 f_y(x, y, t) + f_t(x, y, t),$$

where f_x, f_y, and f_t are the spatial and temporal derivatives of stimulus intensity. Substituting this approximation into equation (1) gives:

$$v_1 f_x(x, y, t) + v_2 f_y(x, y, t) + f_t(x, y, t) = 0. \tag{2}$$

This equation relates the velocity, at one point in the visual field, to the spatial and temporal derivatives of stimulus intensity. We refer to equation (2) as the *gradient constraint*.

Combining constraints It is impossible to recover velocity, given the gradient constraint at only a single position, since equation (2) offers only one linear constraint to solve for the two unknown components of velocity. Gradient-based methods solve for velocity by combining information over a spatial region. The different gradient-based methods use different combination rules. A particularly simple rule for combining constraints from two nearby spatial positions is:

$$\begin{bmatrix} f_x(x_1, y_1, t) & f_y(x_1, y_1, t) \\ f_x(x_2, y_2, t) & f_y(x_2, y_2, t) \end{bmatrix} \begin{bmatrix} v_1 \\ v_2 \end{bmatrix} + \begin{bmatrix} f_t(x_1, y_1, t) \\ f_t(x_2, y_2, t) \end{bmatrix} = \vec{0}, \tag{3}$$

where the two coordinate pairs (x_i, y_i) correspond to the two spatial positions. Each row of equation (3) is the gradient constraint for one spatial position. Solving this equation simultaneously for both positions gives the velocity that is consistent with both constraints.

Lucas and Kanade (1981) suggested combining constraints from more than just two spatial positions, by squaring and summing:

$$R(v_1, v_2) = \sum_{x,y} [v_1 f_x(x, y, t) + v_2 f_y(x, y, t) + f_t(x, y, t)]^2. \tag{4}$$

Each squared term in the summation is a constraint on the flow from a different (nearby) position. The summation is taken over a local spatial region, e.g., in a Gaussian weighted window. Since there are now more constraints than unknowns, there may not be a solution that satisfies all of the constraints simultaneously. In other words, $R(v_1, v_2)$ will typically be non-zero for all (v_1, v_2). The choice of (v_1, v_2) that minimizes $R(v_1, v_2)$ is the least squares estimate of velocity.

Least squares estimate One way to find the minimum of $R(v_1, v_2)$ is to evaluate the function at a number of points (say, on a fixed square grid) and to pick the smallest result. Figure 1 shows some examples. Figures 1(a) and (b) depict sine-grating plaid stimuli. The component gratings in the two stimuli have different orientations and spatial frequencies, but the speeds of the component gratings were chosen so that both plaids moved rightward with the same velocity. Figures 1(c) and (d) show $R(v_1, v_2)$ for (a) and (b), respectively. Each point in (c) and (d) corresponds to a different velocity, with the center of each image corresponding to zero velocity. Brightness

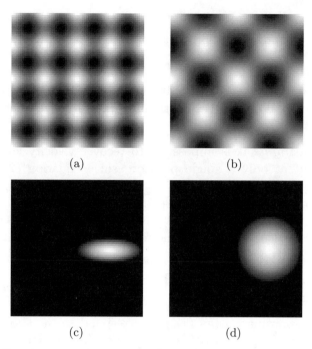

(a)   (b)

(c)   (d)

Fig. 1. *Distributed representations of velocity for rightward moving plaid stimuli. (a) and (b) Plaid stimuli made from pairs of gratings. Both plaids moved rightward with the same velocity. (c) and (d) Distributed representations corresponding to stimuli in (a) and (b), respectively. Each point corresponds to a different velocity (center corresponds to zero velocity). Brightness at each point is inversely proportional to $R(v_1, v_2)$ in equation (4). Locations of the peaks correspond to the correctly perceived velocities.*

at each point is inversely proportional to $R(v_1, v_2)$, and the locations of the peaks correspond to the velocity estimates. The peaks correspond to the correct velocity in both cases, despite of the difference in the spatial structures of the two stimuli[1].

Since equation (4) is a quadratic expression, there is a simple analytical expression for the velocity estimate. The solution is derived by taking derivatives of equation (4) with respect to v_1 and v_2, and setting them equal to zero:

$$\frac{\partial R(v_1, v_2)}{\partial v_1} = \sum_{xy} [v_1(f_x)^2 + v_2(f_x f_y) + (f_x f_t)] = 0$$

[1] Some algorithms do not always compute the correct velocity for sine grating plaid patterns. In particular, models proposed by Watson and Ahumada (1985), by Heeger (1987), and by Grzywacz and Yuille (1990) give the wrong solution unless the spatial frequencies of the gratings equal the preferred spatial frequency of the filters. Grzywacz and Yuille (1990) claim that their method does not depend on the spatial frequency content of the stimulus, but in fact that claim is not true for sine grating stimuli.

$$\frac{\partial R(v_1, v_2)}{\partial v_2} = \sum_{xy} [v_2 (f_y)^2 + v_1 (f_x f_y) + (f_y f_t)] = 0$$

These equations may be rewritten as a single equation in matrix notation:

$$\mathbf{M} \cdot \vec{v} + \vec{b} = \vec{0},$$

where

$$\mathbf{M} = \begin{pmatrix} m_{11} & m_{12} \\ m_{12} & m_{22} \end{pmatrix}, \qquad \vec{b} = \begin{pmatrix} b_1 \\ b_2 \end{pmatrix},$$

and where

$$m_{11} = \sum (f_x)^2$$
$$m_{22} = \sum (f_y)^2$$
$$m_{12} = \sum (f_x f_y)$$
$$b_1 = \sum (f_x f_t)$$
$$b_2 = \sum (f_y f_t).$$

The least-squares solution is then given by

$$\hat{\mathbf{v}} = -\mathbf{M}^{-1} \vec{b}, \tag{5}$$

presuming that $\mathbf{M}$ is invertible.

Aperture problem When the matrix $\mathbf{M}$ in equation (5) is singular (or ill-conditioned), there are not enough constraints to solve for both unknowns. This situation corresponds to what has been called the aperture problem. For some patterns (e.g., a very gradual curve) there is not enough information in a local region (small aperture) to disambiguate the true direction of motion. For other patterns (e.g., an extended grating or edge) the information is insufficient regardless of the aperture size.

The latter case is illustrated in Figure 2(a). The diagonal line indicates the locus of velocities compatible with the motion of the grating. At best, we may extract only one of the two velocity components. Figure 2(b) shows how the motion is disambiguated when there is more spatial structure. The plaid pattern illustrated in Figure 2(b) is composed of two moving gratings. The lines give the possible motion of each grating alone. Their intersection is the only shared motion.

Combining the gradient constraints according to the summation in equation (3) is related to the intersection of constraints rule depicted in Figure 2. The gradient constraint, equation (2), is linear in both v_1 and v_2. Given measurements of the derivatives, (f_x, f_y, f_t), there is a line of possible solutions for (v_1, v_2), analogous to the constraint line illustrated in Figure 2(a). For each different position, there will generally be a different constraint line. Equation (3) gives the intersection of these constraint lines, analogous to Figure 2(b).

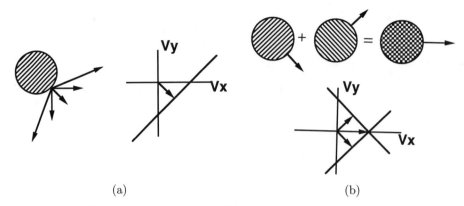

(a)   (b)

Fig. 2. *(a) Single moving grating. The diagonal line indicates the locus of velocities compatible with the motion of the grating. (b) Plaid composed of two moving gratings. The lines give the possible motion of each grating alone. Their intersection is the only shared motion.*

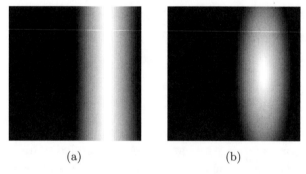

(a)   (b)

Fig. 3. *Distributed representations of velocity for a vertical grating stimulus moving to the right. (a) Since the velocity is ambiguous, there is no peak in the distribution. (b) Responses are biased slightly by adding a small offset to the diagonal elements of* M. *This corresponds to a slight prior preference for slower speeds. Including the prior gives a broad peak in the distribution.*

Prior bias To deal with the aperture problem, we could consider combining constraints over a larger spatial area (e.g., Horn and Schunk, 1981). Instead, we add a slight prior preference for slower speeds. The resulting velocity estimate is approximately equal to the *normal flow*, the component of motion parallel to the spatial intensity gradient.

The prior preference is implemented by adding a small offset to each of the diagonal entries of **M**. Elsewhere (Simoncelli et al., 1991), we formally prove that adding this offset gives a Bayesian estimate for velocity. The Bayesian estimator incorporates a prior likelihood for each possible velocity. The offset is the (inverse) variance of this prior probability distribution. Adding the offset yields a slight bias toward lower speeds. The bias is greater for low contrast stimuli, i.e., when the entries of **M** are small.

Figure 3 illustrates the effect of the prior. Figure 3(a) shows $-R(v_1, v_2)$, from equation (4), for a drifting sine grating stimulus. Since the velocity of the grating is ambiguous (due to the aperture problem), there is no peak in the distribution. Rather the distribution is shaped like a ridge. Any velocity along this ridge is an equally good interpretation of the stimulus' motion. Figure 3(b) shows that including the prior gives a distribution with a broad peak. The location of the peak corresponds approximately to the normal flow, but at a very slightly slower speed.

2.2. Space-time filtering methods

In this section, we reformulate the gradient-based flow algorithm, this time in terms of biological mechanisms. We first review the spatiotemporal linear model of biological motion sensing. Then we relate that model to the gradient method.

Space-time orientation A number of authors have proposed models of biological motion sensing based on direction selective, spatiotemporal linear operators (Fahle and Poggio, 1981; Watson and Ahumada, 1983; Watson and Ahumada, 1985; Adelson and Bergen, 1985; van Santen and Sperling, 1985; Heeger, 1987; Heeger, 1988; Grzywacz and Yuille, 1990). These authors have explained that visual motion is like orientation in space-time, and that spatiotemporally-oriented, linear operators can be used to detect and measure it.

Figure 4 shows a simple example. Figure 4(a) depicts a vertical bar moving to the right over time. Imagine that we film a movie of this stimulus and stack the consecutive frames one after the next. We end up with a three-dimensional volume (space-time cube) of intensity data like that shown in Figure 4(b). Figure 4(c) shows an *x-t* slice through this space-time cube. The slope of the edges in the *x-t* slice equals the horizontal component of the bar's velocity (change in position over time). Different speeds correspond to different slopes.

Spatiotemporal linear operators The response of a linear operator is expressed as a weighted sum, over local space and recently past time, of the stimulus intensities. Specifically, the response, $L(t)$, is the inner product in space and the convolution in time of a stimulus, $f(x, y, t)$, with the spatiotemporal weighting function of the operator, $g(x, y, t)$:

$$L(t) = \iiint_{-\infty}^{\infty} g(x, y, \tau) f(x, y, \tau - t) \, dx \, dy \, d\tau. \tag{6}$$

The triple integral in the above equation is simply a weighted sum of the stimulus intensities over space and time.

The linear operators that we consider in this chapter have weighting functions with positive and negative subregions. The positive and negative

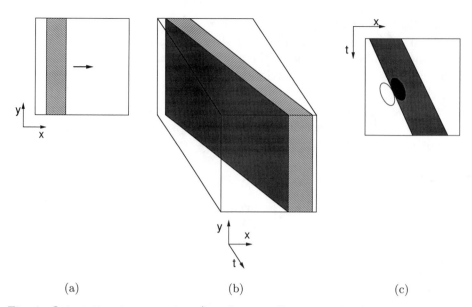

(a)   (b)   (c)

Fig. 4. *Orientation in space-time (based on an illustration by Adelson and Bergen, 1985). (a) A vertical bar translating to the right. (b) The space-time cube of stimulus intensities corresponding to motion of the vertical bar. (c) An x-t slice through the space-time cube. Orientation in the x-t slice is the horizontal component of velocity. Motion is like orientation in space-time, and spatiotemporally oriented filters can be used to detect and measure it.*

weights are balanced, so the operators give no output for a constant intensity stimulus. Rather, their responses are proportional to stimulus contrast, for stimuli that vary in intensity over space and/or time.

The spatiotemporal weighting function of a linear operator determines its selectivity (e.g., for orientation or direction of motion). A linear operator is direction selective if its subregions are tilted along an oblique axes in space-time. For example, Figure 4(c) illustrates the weighting function of a direction selective operator, that responds preferentially to rightward motion.

A spatial array of identical linear operators (sampling the entire visual field) can be thought of as a linear filter that performs a convolution (over both space and time) with the stimulus,

$$g(x, y, t) * f(x, y, t) = \iiint_{-\infty}^{\infty} g(\xi, \eta, \tau) f(\xi - x, \eta - y, \tau - t) \, d\xi \, d\eta \, d\tau,$$

where $*$ means convolution.

Space-time filters and the gradient method Following Adelson and Bergen (1986) and Simoncelli and Adelson (1991b, 1991a), we now show that the gradient-based solution can be expressed in terms of the outputs of a set of space-time oriented linear operators. To this end, note that the derivative operators may be written as convolutions. Furthermore, we can prefilter the stimuli to extract some spatiotemporal subband, and perform the analysis on that subband. Consider, for example, prefiltering with a space-time Gaussian function. Abusing the notation somewhat, we define:

$$f_x(x, y, t) \equiv \frac{\partial}{\partial x}[g(x, y, t) * f(x, y, t)] = g_x(x, y, t) * f(x, y, t),$$

where $*$ is convolution and g_x is the x-derivative of a Gaussian. In words, we compute f_x by convolving with g_x, a spatiotemporal linear filter. We compute f_y and f_t similarly.

Note also that derivatives in oblique space-time orientations can be expressed as linear sums of f_x, f_y, and f_t. For example, the derivative of a Gaussian in a diagonal spatial orientation is given by:

$$g_p = (g_x + g_y),$$

where g_p is a diagonally oriented derivative operator. Finally, note that products of derivatives in the x-, y-, and t-directions can be written as combinations of the obliquely oriented derivatives. For example,

$$4f_x f_y = (f_x + f_y)^2 - (f_x - f_y)^2$$
$$= [(g_x + g_y) * f]^2 - [(g_x - g_y) * f]^2.$$

Now we rewrite the entries of $\mathbf{M}$ and $\vec{b}$ in terms of a set of squared linear filter outputs:

$$m_{11} = \sum (f_x)^2 \tag{7}$$
$$m_{22} = \sum (f_y)^2$$
$$m_{12} = \frac{1}{4} \sum [(f_x + f_y)^2 - (f_x - f_y)^2]$$
$$b_1 = \frac{1}{4} \sum [(f_x + f_t)^2 - (f_x - f_t)^2]$$
$$b_2 = \frac{1}{4} \sum [(f_y + f_t)^2 - (f_y - f_t)^2].$$

In primary visual cortex, there are no cells with receptive fields that behave like products of derivatives (e.g., $f_x f_y$). Thus, rewriting the solution as in equation (7) brings us closer to a model of the physiology. Each linear filter in equation (7) is orientation tuned, with oriented spatial subregions. Four of the operators are direction selective with weighting functions that are tilted obliquely in space-time, e.g., $(g_x + g_t)$ and $(g_x - g_t)$ are selective for leftward and rightward motion.

The linear operators in equation (7) are, therefore, similar to the receptive fields of cortical cells. There are, however, some important differences. As we shall see (Section 3.1), higher order derivative operators are a better model of cortical receptive fields.

2.3. Using higher order derivatives

In this section, we extend the spatiotemporal filter method to use higher order derivative operators.

Consider using g_{xx}, g_{xy} and g_{yy} as prefilters and writing three gradient constraint equations, in terms of derivatives of each these prefilters:

$$
\begin{aligned}
v_1 f_{xxx} + v_2 f_{xxy} + f_{xxt} &= 0 \\
v_1 f_{xxy} + v_2 f_{xyy} + f_{xyt} &= 0 \\
v_1 f_{xyy} + v_2 f_{yyy} + f_{yyt} &= 0,
\end{aligned}
\tag{8}
$$

where f_{xxx} should be interpreted as $f * g_{xxx}$, and likewise for the other derivatives. Equation (8), written in terms of third derivatives, gives three constraints on velocity.

The gradient constraint, equation (2), is based on the intensity conservation assumption; i.e., it assumes that the stimulus intensity shifts (locally translates) from location to location over time. The third derivative constraints, equation (8), are based on conservation of the second spatial derivatives of intensity, i.e., that (f_{xx}, f_{xy}, f_{yy}) shifts over time.

An advantage of using higher order derivatives is that, in principle, there are enough constraints at a single spatial position. Even so, there are stimuli for which there will not be enough constraints locally. There is still a need, therefore, to combine constraints over a local spatial region.

Combining constraints over a local spatial region gives:

$$
\begin{aligned}
R(v_1, v_2) = &\sum_{x,y} [v_1 f_{xxx} + v_2 f_{xxy} + f_{xxt}]^2 \\
+ &\sum_{x,y} [v_1 f_{xxy} + v_2 f_{xyy} + f_{xyt}]^2 \\
+ &\sum_{x,y} [v_1 f_{xyy} + v_2 f_{yyy} + f_{yyt}]^2
\end{aligned}
$$

The least-squares estimate of velocity, minimizing this expression is

$$
\hat{\mathbf{v}} = -\mathbf{M}^{-1}\vec{b},
$$

where $\mathbf{M}$ and $\vec{b}$ are now defined as:

$$
\begin{aligned}
m_{11} &= \sum [(f_{xxx})^2 + (f_{xxy})^2 + (f_{xyy})^2] \\
m_{22} &= \sum [(f_{xxy})^2 + (f_{xyy})^2 + (f_{yyy})^2] \\
m_{12} &= \sum [(f_{xxx})(f_{xxy}) + (f_{xxy})(f_{xyy}) + (f_{xyy})(f_{yyy})] \\
b_1 &= \sum [(f_{xxx})(f_{xxt}) + (f_{xxy})(f_{xyt}) + (f_{xyy})(f_{yyt})] \\
b_2 &= \sum [(f_{xxy})(f_{xxt}) + (f_{xyy})(f_{xyt}) + (f_{yyy})(f_{yyt})].
\end{aligned}
$$

Note the similarity with equation (5). The solutions using first and third derivatives are essentially the same. The main differences are: (1) that the third derivative solution uses a greater number of linear operators, and (2) that the third derivative operators are more narrowly tuned (with more subregions) for spatiotemporal orientation.

As with first derivatives, each element of $\mathbf{M}$ and $\vec{b}$ may be rewritten as a sum of squared outputs of spatiotemporally-oriented operators. As above, we rewrite the products, e.g.,

$$(f_{xxx})(f_{xxt}) = \tfrac{1}{4}[(f_{xxx} + f_{xxt})^2 - (f_{xxx} - f_{xxt})^2].$$

For the third derivative operators, we also rewrite the spatial cross-derivatives (e.g., f_{xxy} and f_{xyy}) in terms of spatially oriented operators. To this end, we define g_p and g_q to be to be derivative operators in diagonal orientations,

$$g_p = g_x + g_y$$
$$g_q = g_x - g_y.$$

The third derivatives in the diagonal orientations are:

$$g_{ppp} = g_{xxx} + 3g_{xxy} + 3g_{xyy} + g_{yyy}$$
$$g_{qqq} = g_{xxx} - 3g_{xxy} + 3g_{xyy} - g_{yyy}.$$

Spatial cross-derivative operators may then be expressed in terms of the oriented operators:

$$g_{xxy} = \tfrac{1}{6}[g_{ppp} - g_{qqq} + 2g_{yyy}]$$
$$g_{xyy} = \tfrac{1}{6}[g_{ppp} + g_{qqq} + 2g_{xxx}].$$

Using a set of identities like these, we can express the velocity estimate in terms of the squared outputs of a set of spatiotemporally-oriented operators. Figure 6 shows the spatiotemporal weighting functions of a representative set of those operators.

On the other hand, we have no *a priori* theoretical basis for choosing Gaussian third derivatives. Other operators could be used just as well (e.g., third or fourth derivatives of some smooth, unimodal, non-Gaussian function). One set of operators or another may provide a stronger constraint on velocity in different situations, depending on the local image structure. For machine vision applications, we advocate using several prefilters, with different preferences for spatial frequency (scale), different orientation tuning widths, and different (e.g., even and odd) phases.

2.4. Normalization and rectification

The model that we advocate in this chapter is an extension of the spatiotemporal filter method described above. In this section, we briefly describe two additional steps in the computation of the model—normalization and rectification. Both extensions are needed for a realistic model of physiological data.

Rectification The linear model of simple cell physiology is attractive because the response of a linear operator can be completely characterized with a relatively small number of measurements. Unfortunately, the linear model falls short of a complete account of simple cell responses. One major fault with the linear model is that cell firing rates are by definition positive, whereas linear operators can have positive or negative outputs.

A linear cell with a high maintained firing rate could encode the positive and negative values by responding either more or less than the maintained rate. Cells in primary visual cortex, however, have very little maintained discharge so they can not truly act as linear operators.

Rather, the positive and negative outputs can be encoded by two halfwave-rectified operators. One mechanism encodes the positive outputs of the underlying linear operator, and the other one encodes the negative outputs. These two mechanisms are complements of one another, that is, the positive weights of one weighting function are replaced by negative weights in the other. Due to the rectification, only one of the two has a non-zero response at any given time.

In this chapter, we consider half-squaring as an alternative form for the rectification. The output of a half-squared linear operator is given by:

$$A(t) = \lfloor L(t) \rfloor^2, \tag{9}$$

where $\lfloor x \rfloor = \max(x, 0)$ is halfwave-rectification, and $L(t)$ is the linear response defined in equation (6).

Normalization A second major fault with the linear model of simple cells is the fact that cell responses saturate at high contrasts. The responses of ideal linear operators, on the other hand, increase proportionally to stimulus contrast over the entire range of contrasts. To explain response saturation, several researchers (Robson, 1988; Bonds, 1989; Heeger, 1992a) have suggested that cells in primary visual cortex mutually inhibit one another, effectively normalizing their responses with respect to stimulus contrast.

Normalization of striate cell responses is also motivated from a theoretical point of view. It is commonly believed that information about a visual stimulus, other than its contrast, is represented as the relative responses of collections of cells. For example, the orientation of a grating might be represented as the ratio of the responses of two cells, each with a different orientation tuning. Indeed physiologists have found that the ratio of a cell's responses to two stimuli is largely independent of stimulus contrast (see Section 3.1). But cortical cells, unlike linear operators, have a limited dynamic range: their responses saturate for high contrasts. Normalization makes it possible for response ratios to be independent of stimulus contrast, even in the face of response saturation.

Consider a collection of half-squared linear operators with various receptive field centers (covering the visual field) and with various spatiotemporal frequency tunings. Let $A_i(t)$ be the squared output of mechanism i. Normalization is achieved by dividing each output by the sum of all of the outputs:

$$\overline{A_i}(t) = \frac{A_i(t)}{\sigma^2 + \sum_i A_i(t)}, \tag{10}$$

where σ^2 is called the semi-saturation constant. As long as σ is nonzero, the normalized output will always be a value between 0 and 1, saturating for high contrasts.

The underlying linear operators can be chosen so that they tile the frequency domain, i.e., the sum of their squared frequency responses is the unit constant function (everywhere equal to one). In that case, summing the squared outputs over all spatial positions and all frequencies gives the total Fourier energy of the stimulus. The normalization can also be computed "locally" by summing over a limited region of space and a limited range of frequencies.

There is a problem with normalization, as it has been presented thus far. Equations (9) and (10) express the normalization in a feed-forward manner. First, the half-squared outputs are computed, using equation (9). Then the half-squared outputs are combined to give the normalized outputs, using equation (10). However, the unnormalized outputs can not be represented by mechanisms with limited dynamic range (e.g., neurons). The solution is to use a feedback network to do the normalization so that the unnormalized outputs need not be explicitly represented as cell output firing rates (see Heeger 1992a, for details).

3. Results

In the previous section, we describe a model for computing velocity from visual stimuli. In this model, velocity estimates are computed from the outputs of a set of normalized, half-squared, linear operators. The normalized outputs are summed to get the entries of $\mathbf{M}$ and $\vec{b}$. In addition, a small offset (the prior) is added to the diagonal entries of $\mathbf{M}$. Finally, the velocity estimate is given as $-\mathbf{M}^{-1}\vec{b}$.

This section reports on simulations of both physiological and psychophysical experiments. We show that our model explains a variety of experimental results.

3.1. Simple cell physiology

For over thirty years, physiologists have been measuring response properties of simple cells in primary (striate) visual cortex. A longstanding view of simple cells is that their responses can be characterized as a weighted sum (over local space) of the intensity values in a visual stimulus (Hubel and Wiesel, 1962; Campbell et al., 1968; 1969). A currently popular model of simple cells is that they act like halfwave-rectified, spatiotemporal linear operators. However, some experiments have revealed blatant violations of linearity.

The model that we advocate is based on spatiotemporal linear operators, but with two important modifications. First, the outputs of the linear operators are half-squared (not halfwave-rectified). Second, the responses are normalized. Heeger (1992a, b) has demonstrated that this new model, with half-squaring and normalization, is qualitatively consistent with a significantly larger body of physiological data.

In this section, we review some measurements of simple cell responses. First, we compare physiological data with the Gaussian third derivative operators. We conclude that the third derivative operators are a reasonable model for the linear weighting functions that underlie simple cells responses. Then, we demonstrate that response saturation can be explained by the nonlinearities (half-squaring and normalization) in the model.

Responses to impulses Many researchers have used impulses (flashed spots or bars) and white noise stimuli to map simple cell weighting functions (e.g., Hubel and Wiesel, 1962; Heggelund, 1981; Jones and Palmer, 1987; McLean and Palmer, 1989; Shapley et al., 1991). Here, we compare physiological data with the weighting functions of the third derivative operators.

Hubel and Weisel (1962) discovered that simple cells have clearly defined excitatory and inhibitory spatial subregions. Bright (brighter than the mean intensity) light in an excitatory region or dim (darker than the mean) light in an inhibitory region enhances the cell's response, whereas bright light in an inhibitory region or dim light in excitatory region inhibits its response. These results are readily explained by the model. The underlying linear stage of the model predicts that excitation to a bright light is complemented by inhibition to a dim light. Due to rectification, the inhibition can be measured only by first driving the operator to a nonzero response with an excitatory stimulus.

According to the model, cells are direction selective because of the underlying linear stage. McLean and Palmer (1989) and Shapley et al. (1991) measured full 3D spatiotemporal weighting functions of simple cells using white-noise stimuli. They found some simple cells with weighting functions tilted along an oblique axis in space-time, like that illustrated in Figure 4(c). The model predicts that these cells be direction selective, that is, that they prefer motion in one direction over the other. In fact, since a spatiotemporal linear operator is completely characterized by its impulse response, the model allows one to predict a cell's preferred direction and speed of motion from the cell's spatiotemporal weighting function. When McLean and Palmer (1989) measured simple cell responses to moving bars, they could, for most cells, correctly predict the preferred bar motion from the weighting function.

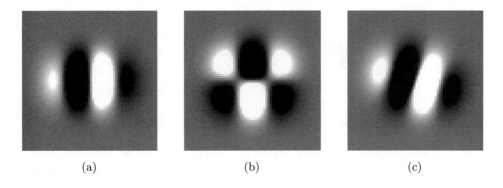

(a)   (b)   (c)

Fig. 5. *Space-time slices through weighting functions of third derivative operators.*
(a) g_{xxx}, the third spatial derivative of a Gaussian, is monophasic and space-time
separable. (b) g_{xxt} is biphasic and space-time separable. (c) $(g_{xxx} + g_{xxt})$ is tilted
in space-time (not space-time separable), and selective for leftward motion.

McLean and Palmer (1989) and Shapley et al. (1991) also found some
simple cells with space-time separable weighting functions. Space-time separable functions can be expressed as the product of a spatial function multiplied by a temporal function. In the model, the direction selective linear
operators are constructed by summing space-time separable operators. For
example, $(g_{xxx} + g_{xxt})$ is a third derivative operator that is selective for leftward motion. This operator is constructed by summing the outputs of two
linear operators, g_{xxx} and g_{xxt}. Figure 5 shows space-time slices through
the weighting functions of each of these three operators. Although g_{xxx} and
g_{xxt} are each space-time separable, their sum is tilted in space-time (not
space-time separable).[2]

Figure 6 shows examples of other linear operators used in the model. The
top row shows spatial slices through the weighting functions, and the bottom
row shows space-time slices through the weighting functions. The operators
depicted in Figure 6 are representative of all of the operators used in the
model. Some of these operators are Gaussian third derivatives (like g_{xxx}
and g_{xxt}), while others are constructed by summing third derivatives (like
$g_{xxx} + g_{xxt}$). The outputs of these operators (and others like them, there
are a total of 46) are half-squared, normalized, and then summed to give
the entries of $\mathbf{M}$ and $\vec{b}$.

[2] Watson and Ahumada (1983, 1985) and Adelson and Bergen (1985) proposed the
quadrature model of direction selectivity, in which direction selective linear operators
are constructed by summing the outputs of two space-time separable subunits. These
subunits are related to one another by a quadrature phase shift both in space and in
time. In our model, the direction selective operators are also constructed by summing
the outputs of two space-time separable subunits, but the subunits are not quadrature
pairs.

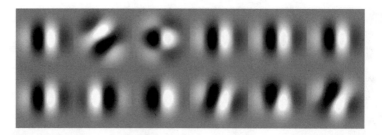

Fig. 6. *Spatial slices (top row) and space-time slices (bottom row) through weighting functions of linear operators representative of the 46 operators used in the model. Some of these operators are Gaussian third derivatives, while others are constructed by summing third derivatives. The operators resemble physiological measurements of simple cell weighting functions.*

For the most part, these linear operators resemble physiological measurements of simple cell weighting functions, such as those measured by McLean and Palmer (1989), Shapley et al. (1991), and others. First, all of the operators in Figure 6 are spatially oriented, with two or more spatial subregions. Second, some of the operators are direction selective (they are tilted in space-time), while others are not direction selective (they are space-time separable). Third, the operators have temporal responses that are either monophasic (like g_{xxx}) or biphasic (like g_{xxt} or $g_{xxx} + g_{xxt}$). And fourth, there is quite a lot of variability in the model's weighting functions[3].

There are, however, some differences between the model operators and simple cell weighting functions. First, some of the operators have irregular spatial structure (e.g., second and third from the left in Figure 6). Second, some of the operators have impulse responses that rotate slightly over time. For example, the operator farthest to the right in Figure 6 has an impulse response that rotates first clockwise by $\pi/8$ radians, and then counter-clockwise by the same amount. Simple cells with this property have not been reported in the literature.

Responses to gratings The response of a spatiotemporal linear operator, to a drifting grating, varies sinusoidally over time with the same temporal frequency as that of the stimulus. A halfwave-rectified linear operator responds over only half of each cycle, remaining silent during the other half-cycle. A half-squared operator also responds over only half of each cycle, but the shape of the response waveform is distorted. Simple cells, like rectified lin-

---

[3] An extension of the model would predict even greater variability in the weighting functions. The model operators need not be Gaussian derivatives. Other operators could also be used (e.g., third or fourth derivatives of some smooth, unimodal, non-Gaussian function). Moreover, different prefilters could be used at different spatial positions. At a given position, the operators must all be derivatives of a common prefilter, but the prefilters at different spatial positions need not be the same.

ear operators, also respond over approximately half of each cycle (Movshon et al., 1978; Andrews and Pollen, 1979; Kulikowski and Bishop, 1981).

Spatiotemporal linear operators, like the linear operators in the model, respond preferentially to gratings with certain orientations, spatial frequencies, and temporal frequencies. In other words, the linear operators are tuned for spatial frequency, temporal frequency, and orientation. The tuning curves of the operators can be computed by taking the Fourier transform of the operator's weighting functions. In this section, we compare simple cell tuning curves with those of first and third derivative operators. In contrast with the third derivative operators, the first derivative operators are not a satisfactory model of simple cell weighting functions for two reasons:

1 There are two few spatial subregions in the first derivative operators. In other words, they are too broadly tuned for orientation and spatial frequency.

2 Researchers have found that a simple cell's spatial frequency tuning (measured with gratings drifting only in one direction) is largely independent of the stimulus temporal frequency. This is not the case for the first derivative operators, but it is very nearly true for the third derivative operators.

Figure 7(a) shows a series of spatial frequency tuning curves, measured from a simple cell (data replotted from Hamilton et al., 1989). Note that the shape of the spatial frequency curves are largely independent of temporal frequency. Other physiologists (Tolhurst and Movshon, 1975; Holub and Morton-Gibson, 1981; Ikeda and Wright, 1975; Foster et al., 1985; Hamilton et al., 1989) have noted this same result, that spatial frequency and temporal frequency tuning curves (measured with gratings drifting only in one direction) are independent of one another[4].

Figure 7(b) shows an analogous series of spatial frequency tuning curves for one of the model's third derivative operators. Like the simple cell data, these simulated tuning curves are largely independent of temporal frequency. Figure 7(c), on the other hand, shows a series of tuning curves for one of the first derivative operators. The spatial frequency tuning of the first

---

[4] Figure 7 demonstrates that spatial and temporal frequency tuning curves (measured with gratings drifting only in one direction) are largely independent of one another. Some researchers have summarized this result by saying that the spatiotemporal frequency tuning is "space-time separable". Note, however, that this is different from requiring space-time separability of an operator's weighting function. The spatiotemporal frequency tuning (for gratings drifting only in one direction) can be separable even if the weighting function is inseparable. The frequency domain measurements (in Figure 7) are separable only when considering one direction of motion. The full spatiotemporal frequency tuning (for gratings drifting in all directions) is space-time separable if and only if the weighting function is space-time separable (i.e., nondirection selective).

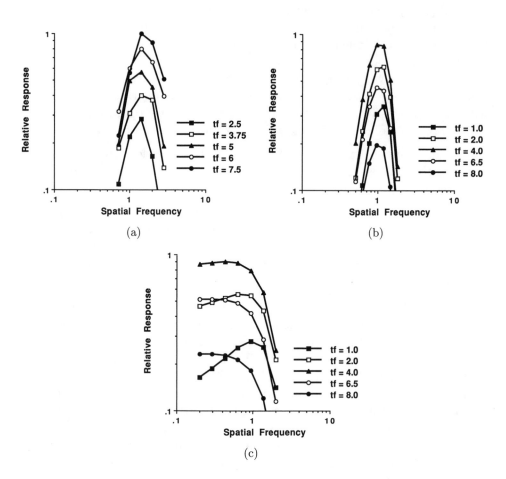

Fig. 7. *(a) Spatial frequency tuning of a simple cell, measured with sine-grating stimuli drifting in the cell's preferred orientation (data replotted from Hamilton et al., 1989). Each curve is for a different stimulus temporal frequency, and each was shifted vertically for ease of viewing. Spatial frequency tuning is largely independent of temporal frequency. (b) Spatial frequency tuning for third derivative operator $(g_{xxx} + g_{xxt})$ is likewise independent of temporal frequency. (c) Spatial frequency tuning for first derivative operator $(g_x + g_t)$ is much broader and varies systematically with temporal frequency.*

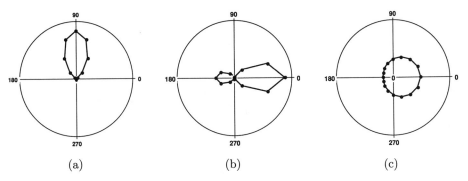

Fig. 8. *(a) Orientation/direction tuning of a simple cell, measured with sine-grating stimuli of preferred spatial and temporal frequency (data replotted from Movshon et al., 1986). Direction of motion is represented by the angular coordinate and relative response is plotted radially. (b) Orientation/direction tuning for third derivative operator $(g_{xxx}+g_{xxt})$ is similar. (c) Orientation/direction tuning for first derivative operator $(g_x + g_t)$ is much broader.*

derivative operator is much broader and it shifts systematically as a function of temporal frequency.

Figure 8(a) shows the orientation/direction tuning of a simple cell (data replotted from Movshon et al., 1986). Figure 8(b) shows an analogous tuning curve for one of the model's third derivative operators. Although there are some differences (the model operator responds slightly to motion in the non-preferred direction), the shape of the tuning curve is quite similar. Figure 8(c), on the other hand, shows that for a first derivative operator, the tuning curve is much broader.

Responses to plaids Movshon et al. (1986) also measured direction tuning curves for sine-grating plaid patterns. Figure 9(a) shows an example of their results, for a typical cell in primary visual cortex. The plaid stimuli consisted of a pair of orthogonal gratings, each of the cell's preferred spatial and temporal frequency. For each different stimulus condition, the entire plaid pattern was rotated so that it moved in a different direction. Figure 9(b) shows an analogous tuning curve for one of the third derivative operators, and Figure 9(c) shows the tuning curve for a first derivative operator. The first derivative operator is so broadly tuned that it does not respond independently to the two component gratings.

Movshon et al. (1986) classified cells into two types (component-flow and pattern-flow) by observing their responses to sine-grating plaid stimuli. Component-flow cells respond independently to each of the component gratings. Pattern-flow cells do not respond independently to the components. According to this classification, the third derivative operator would be classified as a component-flow cell, and the first derivative operator would be classified as a pattern-flow cell. Movshon et al., however, found that all

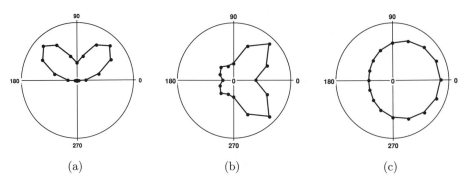

Fig. 9. *(a) Direction tuning of a simple cell, measured with sine-grating plaid stimuli (data replotted from Movshon et al., 1986). Direction of motion of the plaid pattern is represented by the angular coordinate and relative response is plotted radially. (b) Plaid direction tuning for third derivative operator $(g_{xxx}+g_{xxt})$ is similar. (c) Plaid direction tuning for first derivative operator $(g_x + g_t)$ is so broad that it does not respond independently to the two component gratings.*

cells in primary visual cortex are of the component-flow type. Pattern-flow cells were found in a different area of primate visual cortex, area MT.

Figure 9 raises some doubt about the interpretation of these experimental results. Movshon et al. (1986) argued that pattern-flow cells respond to the direction of motion of the plaid as a whole, i.e., to the intersection of constraints direction. The result in Figure 9(c) suggests that this might not be the case. The first derivative operator is not solving for the intersection of constraints. Rather since it is very broadly tuned for orientation/direction, the first derivative operator responds to the average of the two component directions. Moreover, Movshon et al. (1986) did not find a sharp dichotomy between component- and pattern-flow cells. It might be that the continuum of component/pattern types reflects a continuum of orientation tuning widths.

Response saturation The contrast-response function is a plot of response as a function of contrast, typically measured using sine-grating stimuli. Here, we demonstrate that contrast-response of simple cells can be explained by the nonlinearities (divisive normalization and half-squaring) in our model.

Figure 10(a) plots typical experimental contrast-response data, and Figure 10(b) shows results of model simulations. The simulated responses saturate with increased contrast because of normalization.

The hyperbolic ratio function,

$$R = R_{\max}\frac{c^n}{\sigma^n + c^n} + M, \tag{11}$$

has been used to fit contrast-response data, for cells in both cat and primate (Albrecht and Hamilton, 1982; Chao-yi and Creutzfeldt, 1984; Sclar et al., 1990): R, in equation (11) is the evoked response, c is the contrast of the

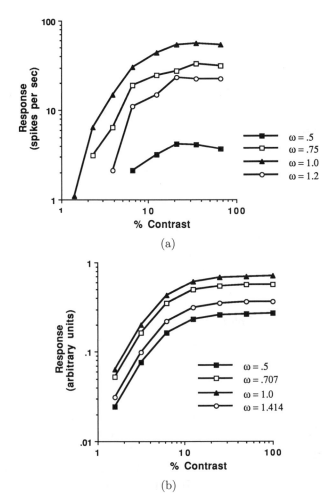

Fig. 10. *Response versus contrast as the spatial frequency, ω, of the stimulus is varied. (a) Data replotted from Albrecht and Hamilton (1982). (b) Model simulation. For both model cells and real cells, the contrast-response curve shifts mostly downward in the log-log plot if the spatial frequency of the test grating is non-optimal.*

test grating, M is maintained discharge, n is a constant exponent, σ^n is the semi-saturation constant, and $R_{\max}$ is the maximum attainable response. From the fits, experimenters have found that the exponent, n, is about 2 on average (Albrecht and Hamilton, 1982; Sclar et al., 1990).

The contrast-response of a model cell is given exactly by the hyperbolic ratio with parameters $n = 2$ and $M = 0$. This is easily demonstrated by recalling that the summation, $\sum A_i(t)$, in the denominator of equation (10) is proportional to c^2. The exponent is 2 in the model because of half-squaring.

In addition, it can be shown that the contrast-response curve of a model cell shifts mostly downward (on log-log axes) if the orientation or frequency of the test grating is non-optimal (see Heeger, 1992a for details). This downward shift is again due to divisive normalization in the model. Downward shifts of contrast-response have been measured physiologically in several labs. Albrecht and Hamilton (1982), for example, measured contrast-response curves for stimuli of non-optimal spatial frequency. Their data is replotted in Figure 10(a), and Figure 10(b) shows the contrast-response curves of a model cell. For both model cells and real cells, the curves shift mostly downward.

This downward shift of contrast-response has important consequences. Consider the response of a linear operator when presented with two different stimuli. If both stimuli are multiplied by the same factor then the ratio of the responses to the two stimuli remains unchanged. The downward shift in figure 10 demonstrates that this is also true for normalized operators and for real cells. In spite of saturation, the response ratio to two different stimuli is largely independent of stimulus contrast. In this way, information about a visual stimulus, other than its contrast, is represented as the relative responses of a collection of cells.

3.2. Perceived velocity of plaids

The perceived velocity of a moving pattern depends on its spatial structure. Adelson and Movshon (1982) conducted psychophysical experiments to study this dependence using sine-grating plaid patterns. Since then, a number of other psychophysicists have measure human velocity judgements using plaids. Stone et al. (1990), in particular, measured the effect of contrast on perceived direction. By varying the relative contrasts of the two component gratings, they found that the plaid motion direction is biased away from the intersection of constraints rule (illustrated in Figure 2b), toward the higher contrast grating. In this section, we show that our model is consistent with their data.

The nominal stimulus in this experiment was a sine-grating plaid made up of two component gratings with equal contrasts and temporal frequencies. This plaid stimulus appeared to move directly upward (in accordance with the intersection of constraints rule). Stone et al. varied both the relative contrast and the relative temporal frequency of the two gratings. These stimuli (with different contrasts or temporal frequencies) appeared to move either slightly right of vertical or slightly left of vertical. The subject's task was to indicate, for each stimulus presentation, whether the plaid appeared to move rightward or leftward.

The total contrast of the plaid was also varied (total contrast was defined by Stone et al. to be the sum of the contrasts of the two components). For each total contrast, Stone et al. varied the contrast ratio of the two components. For each contrast ratio, they adjusted the relative temporal frequency (in a staircase procedure) until the pattern appeared to move directly upward. In other words, they varied the relative temporal frequency to compensate for the bias introduced by the relative contrast difference. Figure 11(a) shows data from Stone et al. (1990), averaged over four subjects. Each curve is the inferred bias, for a fixed total contrast, as a function of contrast ratio.

There are two parameters in the model, the semi-saturation constant for the normalization, and the prior. Both of the parameters in the model contribute to deviations from the intersection of constraints rule. If the normalized responses are small relative to the prior, then there is a large bias. If the normalized responses are large, then there is a small bias. For appropriate values of the two parameters the model behaves like human observers, as shown in Figure 11(b).

On the other hand, there are differences between the simulation results and the actual data. At the highest total contrast (40%) and for small contrast ratios, the human observers often saw the the plaid motion direction biased toward the *lower* contrast grating. This is evident in Figure 11(a) where the 40% curve dips below zero bias. For all of the conditions that we have simulated, the model predicts a bias toward the higher contrast grating.

4. Summary

This chapter presents a model for the computation and representation of velocity information in the primate visual system that accounts for a variety psychophysical and physiological observations. The first stage of the model uses spatiotemporal linear operators to compute a linear sum of the stimulus intensities over a local region of space and recently past time. The outputs of the linear operators are half-squared and then normalized. A slight prior preference for slower speeds is introduced by adding a small offset to two of the normalized outputs. The normalized outputs are then combined, according to a simple formula, to give final velocity estimates.

Our model is consistent with recent psychophysical experiments by Stone et al. (1990) on the perception of sine-grating plaid velocities. When the component grating contrasts are unequal, the velocity estimated by the model is biased toward the higher contrast grating. The bias occurs in the model because the model includes a slight prior (preference) for slower speeds. For appropriate values of the model's two parameters, the model behaves like human observers (Figure 11).

Ferrera and Wilson (1990, 1991) have also measured perceived speed and direction of plaids. We are currently working toward explaining their psychophysical results with the same model (Simoncelli and Heeger, 1992).

Our model is also consistent with physiological data on responses of simple cells in primary (striate) visual cortex. In this chapter, simple cells are modeled as normalized, half-squared linear operators. We consider two sets of linear operators, first and third spatiotemporal derivatives of a Gaussian.

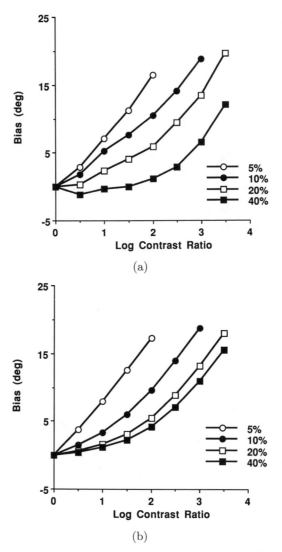

Fig. 11. *Bias of human velocity judgements for sine-grating plaids, as a function of contrast ratio of the two component gratings. (a) Data averaged from four subjects, replotted from Stone et al. (1990). Each curve is for a different total contrast. Relative temporal frequency was varied to compensate for the bias introduced by the relative contrast difference. Inferred bias plotted on the vertical axes is directly related to relative temporal frequency. Inferred bias is the direction that would be seen for that relative temporal frequency (according to the intersection of constraints rule) if both gratings had the same contrast. (b) Results from model simulations. The two parameters of the model were chosen to give the best (least-squares) fit to the data. For these parameter values the model behaves like human observers.*

Although somewhat more cumbersome because of the larger number of filters, the third derivative operators are a better model of simple cells than
the first derivative operators. The third derivative operators are consistent
with a variety of physiological results:

- According to the model, a simple cell's selectivity is due to an underlying spatiotemporal, linear stage. There are a variety of physiological
  results that are consistent with the linear hypothesis (see Heeger, 1992b
  for review). McLean and Palmer (1989), in particular, were able to predict a cell's preferred speed and direction of motion from measurements
  of its underlying spatiotemporal weighting function.

- The third derivative operators in the model resemble simple cell weighting functions (Figures 5 and 6). First, all of the operators are spatially
  oriented, with two or more spatial subregions. Second, some of the operators are direction selective (they are tilted in space-time), while others are not direction selective (they are space-time separable). Third,
  the operators have temporal responses that are either monophasic or
  biphasic. And fourth, there is quite a lot of variability in the model's
  weighting functions.

- Researchers (e.g., Hamilton et al., 1989) have found that spatial frequency and temporal frequency tuning curves are largely independent
  of one another. This is approximately true of the third derivative operators as well (Figure 7).

- The third derivative operators have orientation tuning curves that resemble those of real cells (Figure 8).

- The third derivative operators are sufficiently narrowly tuned for orientation, so that they act like "component-flow" cells (Figure 9), responding independently to each component of a sine-grating plaid stimulus.

- Responses of both model cells and real cells saturate at high contrasts,
  according to the hyperbolic ratio function (Figure 10).

- The contrast-response curve, for either a model cell or a real cell, shifts
  mostly downward for non-optimal stimuli (Figure 10). In other words,
  the ratio of responses produced by two different stimuli is largely invariant with respect to stimulus contrast. In this way, information about
  a visual stimulus, other than its contrast, is represented as the relative
  responses of a collection of cells.

Our model has also been used to compute optical flow fields from image
sequences (Simoncelli et al., 1991). It is important to keep in mind, however,
that the gradient constraint, equation (2), is only approximately valid. The
constraint is based on the intensity conservation assumption, that changes

in intensity are due only to local translation. This ignores possible changes in lighting and reflectance. Moreover, the assumption of local translation is not valid near motion boundaries nor for transparent motions. The gradient constraint is also based on a planar approximation to the (prefiltered) intensity values. The velocity estimated by the model is in error when these assumptions are not satisfied.

In our future research, we plan to extend the model to make it more robust with respect to these assumptions. We also plan to use the model to explain further experimental results. From our point of view, fitting psychophysical or physiological data is not, by itself, a satisfactory goal of computational modeling. The model must also give reliable velocity estimates. Although primates do not always perceive velocity veridically (e.g., Figure 11), we do quite well for most stimuli.

Acknowledgements

This research was supported by NASA RTOP 506-71-51, by NASA-Ames grant NCC2-307, and by the MIT Media Lab. This paper benefited greatly from discussions with Misha Pavel and Lee Stone.

Some recent findings in early vision and focal attention

Bela Julesz

1. Introduction

As I become one of the older active researchers of human vision, the problem arises of what kind of talk I should give. Should I sum up the highlights of my researches spanning over 30 years, or should I prove to you that I am still very active by concentrating on some recent findings I obtained with my coworkers or by myself? Luckily, I do not have to ponder this dichotomy. Indeed, for several years I have been planning to write my second monograph[1] but could not do so, because there were a few unanswered questions that stood in my way. I am happy to report that the most important of these obstacles have been removed by the adequate solution of some difficult problems. As a result, I published a review for the sake of physicists, entitled "Early vision and focal attention" (Julesz, 1991a). I regard this long article as the backbone of my planned second monograph. I will list these scientific hurdles and give some of their solutions. Before doing so, however, I will give some historic account of my researches in what I used to call cyclopean perception, which is currently referred to as early vision.

By the sixties it became clear that the fusion of random dot stereograms (RDS) showed conclusively that, contrary to the common belief at that time, stereopsis was not a local but a global process. Similarly, the discovery of textons in the seventies showed that preattentive texture discrimination was not a global process — based on statistics — but essentially a local one. In the decades following these early insights, others were gained.

2. Some comments on global stereopsis

Thirty years after the introduction of the RDS technique its role in vision research can now be guessed, although it might take another generation to discover its real significance. Stereopsis is a specialized process that yields

---

[1] The first monograph was Julesz, 1971.

relative depth from binocular disparity, whereas recognition of objects (and perspective depth) occurs even in monocular vision. Therefore, if one regards object recognition as the main purpose of vision, one might ask "how strategic is research in stereopsis?" Some answers follow.

1   RDS gave conclusive proof that there is no camouflage in 3-D. Therefore, global stereopsis evolved in our primate (lemur) ancestors to break the camouflage of insects hiding motionless in foliage. Subsequently, stereopsis aided in monocular form perception by performing a very early scene analysis (segmentation) of the environment.

2   Psychoanatomy using RDS is helpful in localizing perceptual processes. For example global (short-range) motion must occur after stereopsis. This can aid neurophysiologists in their tracing of the information flow in the CNS. The demonstration (as early as 1960) that stereopsis can occur in the absence of all monocular form, contour, and depth cues indicated that it must be an early process. Indeed, Hubel and Wiesel switched from form perception to binocular vision after the first demonstration of RDS in 1960. Gian Poggio's neurophysiological findings with dynamic RDS (Poggio and Poggio, 1984) show that cyclopean neurons exist as early as layer IVB in V1 of the monkey cortex (the very input to the visual cortex).

3   The global stereopsis of RDS raises a strategic problem of brain research: the false-target elimination problem. This same problem occurs in the monocular motion perception of random-dot cinematograms.

4   RDS techniques permit sophisticated analysis of visual processes beyond psychoanatomy. For instance, the role of color in stereopsis and in the magno pathway can be studied.

5   RDS permit the first nontrivial linking of a perceptual process with neurophysiology.

6   RDS were amongst the first stimuli that took advantage of the digital computer.

7   Global stereopsis and preattentive texture segmentation are bottom-up processes that, with the addition of focal attention (a top-down process), permit scene analysis without the need for enigmatic semantic information stored in memory. This in turn paves the way for some of the visual algorithms of scene analysis in machine vision.

8   How do top-down processes (depth from shading, pseudoscopy, etc.) influence depth perception of RDS?

3. Some comments on preattentive texture segmentation and texton theory

Although research into RDS was straightforward, my second paradigm—searching for local features that would yield pop-out in iso-second-order texture pairs—involved a much more winding path. My colleagues and I worked for many years to clarify some of its problems, and much additional research is still necessary to settle more conclusively such problems as:

1   The asymmetry problem.

2   Antitextons.

3   Color vs. orientation.

4   Parallel vs. serial scanning and the role of focal attention.

5   Textons vs. nonlinear spatial filters.

4. On scientific style

Before I emigrated to the United States from Hungary in 1956, I was fascinated with thought-experiments and mathematics, two activities that one can pursue in a poor country. For instance, I was fascinated with Einstein's thought experiments with falling elevators that would lead to the theory of general relativity. However, I was aware even then of the limits of such *gedanken* experiments. The original Einstein equations predicted an ever-expanding universe, which Einstein himself regarded as absurd; as a result, he modified his equations. (When Edwin Powell Hubble (1889–1953), at Caltech, discovered the Doppler-shift of the far galaxies, Einstein realized that he had been too hasty in his decision to modify his equations.) It was obvious to me that thought experiments, with their limitations, were only substitutes for real experiments. So, after I arrived in the United States and landed with great luck at Bell Laboratories (one of the miracles of the world) I decided to conduct the most sophisticated experiments I could devise. However, as a devotee of thought experiments, I decided to modify this tool in a constructive way: I would construct experiments (that would require the most complex mathematical and technical tools) in order to obtain a dichotomous question, whose outcome could not be guessed. For instance, could one perceive depth in an ideally camouflaged stereo-pair without monocular contours or form cues? (Such stereograms had to wait until the arrival of the first digital computers permitted their generation, and luckily they arrived at Bell Labs when I did.) Or, could one generate texture-pairs with identical n^{th} order, but different $(n+1)^{\text{th}}$ order statistics, and determine the highest n that could still yield perceptual segmentation without scrutiny? This question led to the texton concept.

The problem still remained of what questions to pose. It was my mentor and former scientific director at Bell, John R. Pierce, who taught me that a good researcher does not attack the problems he likes the most, but rather works on problems that are ripe for solution. Of course, these solvable problems should be challenging, fun to work on, and appear important. Whether a problem is important — perhaps "strategic" is a better term — cannot be assessed at the time of its conception. Only history can distinguish fashionable problems from strategic ones, particularly in psychobiology, a field that is now in a state similar to molecular biology prior to the discovery of the double-helical structure of DNA. Even my two paradigms — the random-dot stereograms and the cinematograms that I introduced in 1960, and the preattentive texture discrimination of texture pairs with iso-second-order statistics of 1962 vintage — are still too recent to be sure of their strategic significance. Nevertheless, these two paradigms — and a third, of spatial frequency channels (which was posed by others, but which we helped pioneer with Charles Stromeyer III in 1972) — kept an entire generation of brain researchers busy. If they had fun as well, then I am partly assured that I accomplished something.

5. Some solved problems of global stereopsis, texture discrimination, and focal attention

At the time that I wrote the aforementioned review for physicists, I also published another article (Julesz, 1991b) in which I tried to separate some metaphysical problems from scientifically ripe ones, and posed approximately forty "Hilbertean" questions that I considered important and solvable.[2] I hope that many of my questions will be solved or proven naïve in the coming decades. I will list and discuss only a few on which I am presently working with my colleagues, (both those at the Laboratory of Vision Research at Rutgers University and those in the Biology Division at CalTech). These problems are particularly important to me. Since some of the findings are not yet published, my discussion will be very brief, to give the flavor of my current interests.

1   Global stereopsis is not color-blind. (In collaboration with Dr. Ilona Kovacs.)

2   Hierarchical processing of color in RDS, random dot cinematograms (RDC), and Glass Patterns. (In collaboration with Dr. Ilona Kovacs.)

---

[2] My reference to David Hilbert, the famous German mathematician, is not immodesty on my part, but rather an allusion to the well-known strategic questions he raised in the first year of this century, many of which were proven *undecidable* during his lifetime by Kurt Gödel, Alonzo Church, and Allen Turing in the thirties.

3   Depth from shading is dominated by stereopsis. (In collaboration with Ms. Jih-Jie Chang.)

4   On the speed of focal attention shifts. (In collaboration with Dr. Jukka Saarinen.)

5   On antitextons. (In collaboration with Dr. Doug Williams.)

6   The asymmetry problem of texture segmentation can be explained by closing the gap in subjective contours. (In collaboration with Dr. Doug Williams.)

7   On the preattentive/attentive dichotomy in texture perception. (In collaboration with Dr. Jochen Braun.)

8   How is the 2-diopter chromatic aberration of the human eye lens compensated? Acuity of blue in the presence of red or green. (In collaboration with Dr. Venkatesh Prasad.)

9   Can non-echolocating primates perceive absolute depth? For instance, stereopsis yields only relative depth. Is relative depth adequate to achieve depth and size constancies? (In collaboration with Dr. Itzhak Hadani.)

10 The mind's-eye looks through a telescope: A suggestion of how movement invariance during eye-movement can be achieved. (In collaboration with Dr. Itzhak Hadani.)

11 Extension of Panum's fusional area by extensive learning: The role of sleep. (In collaboration with Dr. Ilona Kovacs.)

12 Opposing local features (textons) in global perceptual tasks (motion, stereopsis, textural grouping, etc) to assess their perceptual strength. (In collaboration with Drs. Thomas Papathomas and Andrei Gorea.)

Brief discussion:

1 In my first monograph (Julesz, 1971), I reported briefly that polarity-reversed RDS (that cannot normally be fused) *can* be fused if the corresponding reversed gray pixels are similarly colored in the left and right pairs. Thus color can overcome polarity reversal, provided that the reversed contrast is not too large. In spite of this finding that indicated that stereopsis *cannot* be color blind, a series of papers were published using colored RDS at isoluminance (that could not be fused), with the conclusion that stereopsis does not utilize colors. After the difficult technical problems of creating isoluminance (at least for the physical stimulus, but not necessarily over the entire visual field) were solved by Lu and Fender (1972), followed by Ramachandran and Gregory (1978), they reported that stereopsis of RDS portrayed by small pixels did disappear at isoluminance, but for classical stereograms and for

RDS portrayed by coarse pixels, the depth percept lingered. Weird things do happen at isoluminance, but the suggestion that stereopsis is color blind is a non sequitur. Interestingly, only a few researchers have quoted my results as a counterexample to the generally accepted view that stereo is color blind (e.g. De Weert and Sadza, 1983). In hindsight, I understand why this early work of mine was generally ignored. In 1971 computer-controlled color monitors were in their infancy and it was difficult to be sure that by adding colors one would not inadvertently interfere with the contrast settings. So, with Dr. Ilona Kovacs, I have now tried polarity-reversed RDS under complete color and brightness control on a Silicongraphics IRIS computer (the stereo separation was achieved by alternately-switched liquid crystal goggles at 120 frames/sec). The resulting paper will soon be submitted for publication with color stereo plates, so that the interested reader will be able to convince themselves that without color, the polarity-reversed gray RDS cannot be fused, whereas the addition of color re-establishes fusion, without a noticeable change in perceived luminance and contrast. I am glad that my original finding has weathered the test of time, and hope that the difficulties of seeing depth in colored RDS at isoluminance will be understood as not the result of luminance contrast alone. It seems that stereopsis utilizes color, and speculation about stereopsis being primarily a function of the magno system — which might be color deficient (as Livingstone and Hubel (1987) suggested) — is provocative, but probably an oversimplification.

That stereopsis utilizes color is also evident from the work of Diana Grinberg and David R. Williams (1985). They bleached the red and green receptors with a bright yellow light, and showed that dim violet RDS still yielded correct depth percepts. "With the additional assumption that signals from the blue-sensitive mechanism do not contribute to luminance, these results confirm that purely chromatic signals have access to stereoscopic mechanisms" (Grinberg and Williams, 1985). Because of this assumption, the argument for color-sensitive stereoscopic mechanisms is not as direct as we found with our polarity-reversed color stereograms. I hope that we have finally put to rest the idea that stereopsis is color blind.

2 Ilona Kovacs and I have also studied polarity-reversed random-dot cinematograms (RDC) and random-dot moiré (Glass) patterns (RDG). Polarity-reversed RDC are particularly interesting, since they yield inverse-phi motion (as discovered by Anstis, 1970). Adding corresponding colors to polarity-reversed RDC results in correct motion perception! Thus the global (short-range) motion mechanism does utilize color as well. Finally, polarity-reversed RDG patterns in which the global organization cannot be seen, yield the global percept when corresponding color is added to the two patterns that are shifted with respect to each other. I cannot go into details, particularly into the hierarchical questions of how RDS, RDC, and RDG are utilizing color channels, but a paper to be submitted soon will address the

findings of topics 1 and 9. An ARVO Abstract (Julesz and Kovacs, 1992) is presently available.

3 One of the main implications of the global stereopsis of RDS has been the realization that stereopsis is basically a bottom-up process, in which top-down effects of semantics have a minor role, if any. To my knowledge, there are only two perceptual phenomena that challenge this view. One is pseudoscopy — the finding that familiar objects, particularly faces of humans and animals, refuse to appear concave when the left-right views are inverted. This problem is far from being settled, even though van den Enden and Spekreijse (1989) suggested that during pseudoscopy the inverted stereo images still contain strong cues of textural gradients, which remain intact and prevent depth reversals. They present a demonstration in which a human face appears to become concave during pseudoscopic viewing when the textural cues are masked by noise. Unfortunately, the masking noise in their demonstration was not random, but inadvertently contained some opposite disparity cues (as pointed out by several critics afterwards). Nevertheless, I believe that their idea is correct, and that a better masking technique will show that in stereograms without monocular depth cues, as in RDS, pseudoscopic viewing reverses depth, and convex objects become concave, and vice versa.

Another phenomenon that might suggest top-down effects in stereopsis is shape (depth) from shading. Indeed, shaded objects reverse their depth appearance when viewed upside-down (as noted by astronomers generations ago, when they viewed inverted photographs of Moon craters that surprisingly appeared as convex hills). It is most likely that our visual system evolved on Earth (which has only a single Sun); thus, the "belly" of an object is more in shadow than its top, and this fact of illumination has been ingrained in our visual system. Ramachandran (1988) and Kleffner and Ramachandran (1992) argue that shape from shading is an early visual process that might serve as an input to motion perception. In collaboration with Jih-Jie Chang, I showed evidence that global stereopsis does dominate depth from motion. We generated anaglyphs that portrayed convex (concave) spheres defined by shading when monocularly viewed. However, 10–20% of the pixels that portrayed the shading were also RDS that yielded stereoscopic depth, either reinforcing or opposing the depth-from-shading effect. In all cases, stereopsis dominated depth from shading. Even if depth from shading is a top-down process, it does not seem to affect stereopsis. If, however, depth from shading is a bottom-up process, it is even more persuasive evidence that stereopsis operates in the absence of semantics. A demonstration of these stereograms is presented in Julesz (1991b).

4 The problem of the speed of attention shifts has been particularly worrisome for me, as it plays a pivotal role in my theory of preattentive/attentive texture discrimination. Indeed, texton differences that do not pop out have to be searched for with time-consuming scrutiny. We developed this texton theory of texture discrimination by using texture pairs with controlled statistical properties, and using a mask with variable delays (stimulus onset asynchrony (SOA), for details see Julesz, 1981; Bergen and Julesz, 1983; Treisman, 1982; 1985). Others measured reaction time (RT), and found item-by-item search times as fast as 30–50 msec for "conjunction" tasks. With Ben Kröse, I was unable to replicate these fast search velocities. We used targets placed on a circle around the fixation point, and presented visual cues (arrows) pointing randomly to various targets in succession. While we were able to find the first cued target rapidly, the cue became locked on it (as Posner (1978) has reported), and it took more than 150 msec for attention to become unlocked. Weichselgartner and Sperling (1987) used another paradigm, a sort of "visual RT," by presenting a rapid sequence of alphanumeric strings in a window, which they suddenly cued (e.g., brightened) — the observer's task was to report the sequence of the string at and after the cue. Best observers were able to report the cued letter and subsequent ones at a rate of 10 Hz (thus at 100 msec/item scanning speeds). These speeds were much faster than eye-movement speeds, and faster than our speeds with moving cues, but were considerably slower than Treisman's scanning rates (1982, 1985). It seemed that the Sperling method had advantages over RT, but suffered from the fact that the numerals were overlaid and (perhaps due to spatial inhibition) required some time to become visible. Consequently, Jukka Saarinen and I modified the visual RT paradigm, as follows. Instead of presenting the random numerals on top of each other, we placed them as far apart as possible, on a circle around the fixation point, at high rates. Whenever a new numeral was portrayed, the previous numeral was masked simultaneously by an effective masking pattern. We found that at 32 msec/item speeds observers could report four subsequent numerals with good performance, although the correct temporal order was lost (for details, see Saarinen and Julesz, 1991). What surprised us was the rapid attentional scanning rates obtained, as if the transient presentation of the numerals had repelled attentional locking. The 32 msec/frame rate was a technical limitation of computer graphic displays with raster scans; at Rutgers we are now trying new hardware that enables 16 msec/item rates. This new hardware will also enable us to present real-life scenes in place of alphanumeric characters. Obviously, the Saarinen and Julesz study cannot distinguish between the metaphor of "attentional searchlight" and "distributed attention with limited resources." I doubt that psychological methods can decide between these metaphors. However, the finding that the SOA methodology can find the same rates as the RT technique is of considerable interest, and removed one of the last hurdles in my thoughts about attentive vision.

5, 6 Since 1962 I have been interested in another paradigm, the generation of texture pairs side-by-side with identical second-order statistics and the search for effortless (preattentive) discrimination (Julesz, 1962). In these texture pairs the first-, second-, and often even the third-order statistics were identical, and it was shown that in general iso-second-order textures could not be discriminated (Julesz, 1975); therefore, texture segmentation must be the result of local, conspicuous features that I named textons. What these textons really are is difficult to say. For instance, besides quasi-collinearity, elongated blobs and Gabor-patches with given colors, lengths, orientations, and spatial frequencies, there are also white gaps between these elements, giving rise to anti-textons. As I pointed out (Julesz, 1986), it is not only the black (white) textons whose gradients yield texture discrimination; the white (black) spaces between them act as textons too.

In essence, we found that texture segmentation is not governed by global (statistical) rules, but rather depends on local, nonlinear features (textons) such as color, orientation, flicker, motion, depth, elongated blobs, and collinearity, to name the most conspicuous features that are both psychophysically and neurophysiologically accepted as being fundamental. Some less clearly defined textons that occur in the concepts of "corner" and "closure" are related to ends-of-lines or terminators, and are hard to define for half-tone blobs. Particularly important was the realization that — contrary to common belief — texture segmentation cannot be explained by differences in power spectra. On the other hand, it became obvious that instead of searching for higher-order statistical descriptors, the visual system applies a local spatial filtering followed by a nonlinearity, and the results must again be averaged by a subsequent spatial filter stage. In recent years it has become possible to segment textures by computer. Julesz and Bergen (1983) showed how simple linear spatial filters (emulating a Kuffler unit having a 2×2 pixel center of addition with a 2 pixel wide surrounding annulus of subtraction) followed by a nonlinearity (threshold taking) could segment texture pairs with iso-third-order statistics. This was followed by several texture-segmentation algorithms based on linear spatial filters, whose output was processed by squaring or by other nonlinear operations (Voorhees and Poggio, 1988; Adelson and Bergen, 1985; 1986). For a critique that argues that linear spatial filters cannot segment textures, see Julesz and Kröse, (1988) or Julesz (1991b). Recently we showed the nonlinear behavior of human texture discrimination (Williams and Julesz, 1991) as depicted in Figure 1. The undiscriminable iso-second-order texture pair (invented by Caelli et al., 1978) is shown on the right. (This texture pair belongs to the class of rare cases which have iso-second-order statistics without having randomly rotated texture elements.) We were able to decompose this texture pair into the sum of a highly discriminable texture pair and an undiscriminable texture pair, as shown on the left side of Figure 1. The fact that

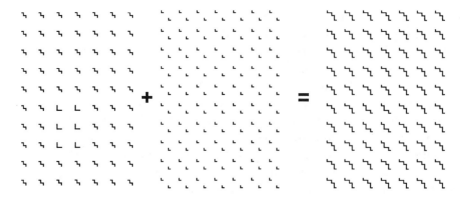

Fig. 1. *Demonstration of the nonlinearity of human texture discrimination. Adding a nondiscriminable texture pair to a highly discriminable texture pair renders the former nondiscriminable, thus the law of superposition is violated. From Williams and Julesz (1991).*

a discriminable texture pair becomes undiscriminable when an undiscriminable texture pair is linearly added shows convincingly the violation of the law of superposition for texture discrimination.

More recently, Fogel and Sagi (1989) and, independently, Malik and Perona (1990) developed texture-segmentation algorithms based on local spatial filters (oriented Gabor-filters) followed by a quasi-local nonlinear operation (simple squaring in the case of Fogel and Sagi and inhibition between neighboring elements in the case of Malik and Perona) and a second spatial filter for final segmentation. It was most impressive that it emulated human texture discrimination performance (as measured by Kröse, 1987), yet could not account for asymmetry. Therefore it is of great significance that Rubenstein and Sagi (1990) extended their model by determining the variances of the local texture elements' distributions after the nonlinear stage, and found these variances asymmetric (particularly when the orientation of the elements was jittered, mimicking human performance). Their model could account for the textural asymmetries reported by Gurnsey and Browse (1987), and probably will be able to handle other asymmetries. It is most heartening that even the textural asymmetry effects that seemed to be based on figure-ground reversals — which in turn depended on enigmatic top-down processes — can be successfully explained by bottom-up processes modeled by relatively simple nonlinear spatial filters.

The Rubenstein and Sagi (1990) model can account for asymmetry by assuming that jitter of line orientation accounts for increase in variance of their filter's output, hence increase in texture discrimination asymmetry. However, the demonstration of Figure 2 clearly shows that, in general, the asymmetry of texture discrimination does not depend on orientational jitter. Indeed, Williams and Julesz (1991) extended the texton theory to include illusory contours and "fill-in" phenomena between gaps and nearby elements,

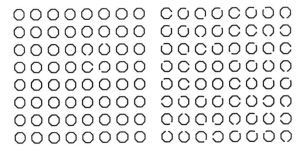

Fig. 2. *Asymmetry of texture discrimination. The perception of a gapped circles in closed circles (left) yields weaker discrimination than vice versa (right). From Williams and Julesz (1991).*

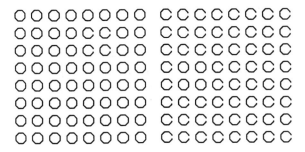

Fig. 3. *Similar to Figure 2, but the position of the gaps is not jittered. This does not reduce the asymmetry. From Williams and Julesz (1991).*

which can be regarded as *anti-textons*. The filling-in of the gaps by subjective contours can account for the asymmetry shown in Figure 2, and in Figure 3, and the fill-in phenomenon between texture elements can explain many other asymmetries.

Textons and anti-textons taken together extend the theory of trichromacy, the only truly scientific theory in psychology. The theory of trichromacy stated that any color could be matched to a combination of three basic colors (red, green, and blue), such that the boundary between the selected color and the combination colors would become minimum (or disappear without scrutiny).[3] When I introduced textons into psychology I desired to extend trichromacy to encompass textures as well as colors. I wanted to know whether any texture could be matched to a finite (and not too large) number of textons, such that the boundary between any textural array and an array containing a mixture of textons would make their boundary perceptually

---

[3] As a matter of fact this theory, postulated by George Palmer in 1777, can be regarded as the *first scientific atom theory*, years before Dalton introduced atoms into chemistry. Palmer's publications are reprinted in a historical collection by MacAdam (1970), and discussed further by Barlow and Mollon (1982).

disappear without scrutiny. It now seems that this can be achieved. The fact that the gamut of colors can be matched by just three colors is in itself amazing. The finding that the infinitely richer variety of 2-D textures could be matched to a mixture of a finite number of textons is even more unexpected!

For the author, who spent much of his scientific career in search of the elusive textons, the fact that quasi-local spatial filters can extract texton gradients without having to specify complex concatenation rules between adjacent textons is anti-climactic (yet most satisfying). I have no doubt that, in the near future, such filters will mimic human preattentive texture discrimination by incorporating several perceptual operations from subjective contours into the filling-in of gaps. The reader familiar with speech research will recognize the similarity between phonemes and textons. Phonemes were never well specified, and complex computer algorithms are now used to cope with the many ad hoc rules of their various concatenations in order to segment speech; nevertheless, crudely defined phonemes permitted the development of phonetic writing, one of the great discoveries of human civilization. Had the development of phonetic speech, millenia ago, coincided with the invention of supercomputers that could automatically segment speech and talk, the skill of writing might never have developed. Of course, the fact that our voice organs limit the number of phonemes to a few dozen aided their universal acceptance. Similarly, the main insight from the texton theory was that of the infinite variety of 2-D textures, only a limited number of textons have perceptual significance, and they are evaluated *quasi-locally* in effortless texture discrimination. (I use the term "quasi-local" instead of "local" because line segments, closed loops, corners, etc., have some finite dimensions.) Even though supercomputers will soon perform automatic texture segmentation, practitioners of visual skills—painters; designers of instrument panels; directors of movies, television shows, and advertisements; and so on—can benefit from the texton theory by manipulating the viewer's eye. Indeed, some of the great artists instinctively knew how to create a strong texton gradient to capture attention, or create a texton-equilibrium for which time-consuming scrutiny is required to discover the hidden images.

As we have shown (Williams and Julesz, 1991), the filling-in phenomena, particularly of gaps, explains the asymmetry phenomena of texture discrimination without the need to evoke complex figure-ground segmentation effects. Furthermore, these phenomena underscore the importance of the blank spaces between textural elements that are themselves elongated blobs, thus, textons. Since so many researchers failed to understand this important asset of the texton theory, for didactic reasons I now refer to these blank spaces as *anti-textons*.

7 With Jochen Braun, I am pursuing the preattentive/attentive dichotomy of texture discrimination, using novel techniques that extend earlier work by

Sagi and Julesz (1985) and Braun and Sagi (1990). We are loading attention around the fixation point by a demanding task (to tell whether several T's contain an L), and simultaneously asking the observer to perform another task — for instance, to determine whether several disks in the parafovea are all of the same color, or to identify the colors of all the disks. We are studying those primitive tokens that can be identified without scrutiny. Now that we know from the Saarinen and Julesz study (1991) that attention can be shifted rapidly, we wish to be certain that attention is fixated to the center during the entire presentation time (say, for 120 msec), and be certain that identification of the parafoveal tasks is indeed preattentive. These are very difficult studies, and the reader must wait for their outcome. In the meanwhile, Barchilon Ben-Av, Sagi, and Braun (1992) reported that perceptual grouping, a phenomenon assumed to be rather elementary, seems to require attention.

8 I have always been fascinated by the problem of how we can perceive that red and blue color patches are equally sharp when there is a more than 2-diopter difference between the sharpness of these two colors, due to the chromatic aberration of our eyes. Obviously, no rapid mechanical fast accommodation of the eye lens can account for this compensation, since middle aged people lose their accommodation powers, yet see red and blue sharply. After Venkadesh Prasad's defense of his Ph.D. thesis (on how to reconstruct depth from the amount of blurring in photographs, due to the limitations of the depth-of-field of optical lenses), it occurred to me to attack the chromatic aberration problem with him.

We found that visual acuity for briefly presented blue targets was excellent (about 1.5 min. arc), but diminished when red or green colors were also shown. Our results will be submitted soon, and are of interest to engineers working on new television standards, particularly high-definition television systems.

9 I have always been puzzled by the fact that stereopsis can only yield *relative* depth, yet one can thread a needle (or hit a nail with an outstretched ruler) better using binocular viewing. That depth perception is not the result of triangulation performed by sensing the convergence angles of the two eyes' axes (and knowing one's interocular distance) was first shown by Dove, just three years after Wheatstone constructed the stereoscope. Dove (1841) presented stereograms tachistoscopically (using an electric spark), and found stereoscopic depth that could not be the result of convergence movements of the eyes (which could not have occurred fast enough). Since then, it has been amply demonstrated that convergence eye movements are inadequate for binocular depth perception, and that a neural machinery performs relative depth processing based on horizontal binocular disparities. Attempts to introduce vertical disparity into psychology to account for absolute depth are improbable, although vertical disparity might be used in machine vision.

Thus, the question of absolute depth in stereopsis remains rather enigmatic. As a matter of fact, I did point out in my first monograph (Julesz, 1971) that stereopsis did not evolve to enable predators to jump on their prey — since no one can jump to a relative depth — but must have evolved to break the camouflage of prey at standstill. It seems that the only role binocular convergence plays in stereopsis is the scaling of perceived depth. The smaller the convergence angle, the larger the perceived depth.

Therefore, I was greatly interested in a question Itzhak Hadani raised recently, proposing that depth judgments during stereoscopic viewing might be strongly correlated with interocular distance (IOD). Because of my belief that stereopsis cannot yield absolute depth judgments, I believed that IOD would also be an absolute distance parameter that could not be appreciated by our visual system. The experiment I performed with Hadani was to align in depth a binocularly viewed physical probe (a thin rod) with the perceived depth of a cyclopean center square and its background in an RDS. The difference (in mm) between the measured square and its background (Z) is related to IOD by the following equation.

$$Z = D.\Delta/(IOD + \Delta) \tag{1}$$

where D is the distance to the nearest target (the cyclopean square) and Δ is the binocular disparity (see also Lappin and Love, 1992). We measured a large pool of observers ($n = 45$), ranging from 7 to 63 years, males and females, with and without glasses, with IODs from 4.9 to 7.3 cm, and found the correlation between their measured Z and their IOD remarkably high. For details, see the published graph in Hadani and Julesz, (1992).

I am not certain that these findings give support to the possibility that absolute depth can be obtained by adding monocular and binocular cues, but I would never have guessed that the exact amount of IOD was known by the visual system. Of course, it might be that information is provided by proprioception, and we know that moving in the environment and manipulating objects establishes an accurate space sense of our own body and its relationship to the outside world.

10 Perceptual constancy, particularly the perceived stability of the visual world during head- and eye-movements is not fully understood. Even if one accepts Helmholtz's notion of outflow signals that nullify movement signals on the retina (or its modern version, the efference copy (von Holst, 1954)), there are unsolved puzzles. How is it possible that objects closer to or farther from a stable surround appear at standstill instead of moving faster or slower than the stable surround? Furthermore, correcting glasses, prisms, and other prosthetic optical devices that slightly magnify or diminish the retinal image, do not affect the stability of the visual world (after a brief adaptation).

In collaboration with Itzhak Hadani, I propose that to achieve stability for objects at different distances from the viewer's eye, the objects must be represented as though viewed via a *1:1 magnification* telescope at *optical infinity*, so that the image projected on the mind's eye is collimated. The simplest 1:1 magnifying collimator is a telescope that requires two lenses of equal focal lengths (of course, more than two complex compound lenses can both collimate the input and correct for many abberations of the first lens). We propose, that one of the lenses of the mind's eye is the optics of our eye, while the cascaded "lens" is provided by either the cortical magnification factor between anatomical mapping of various brain areas from the fovea to V1, V2, and higher visual centers; or neural circuits that can zoom the size of the retinal image. It is this telescopic image which is moved by the corollary discharge. Thus the mind's eye can be conceived of as a "point-wise observer," viewing the world through a 1:1 magnification telescope.

In a sense, this "telescope" idea is merely an isomorphism between the observed perceptual constancy and collimated images, a kind of thought-experiment. Whether it can be converted into a real experiment remains to be seen. For details, see Hadani and Julesz (to be published).

11 For decades I presented brief flash RDS with increasing disparities to summer students who worked in my department at Bell Labs, and noticed that after thousands of trials their performance improved dramatically. Initially, they had a sharp cut-off of binocular disparity, below which they could tell without mistakes whether the briefly flashed RDS followed by a mask portrayed a cyclopean target in front or behind the surround, or an uncorrelated target (a crucial control). At larger disparities, observers' performance rapidly deteriorated to chance guessing. However, after weeks of trials, observers began to identify correctly the RDS that had disparities above the previous cutoff — as though Panum's fusional area had been enlarged. These observations of mine were rather anecdotal, because I had little access to young observers at Bell Labs. At Rutgers I joined forces with Ilona Kovacs and undertook a well-documented study on several observers, young and adult, and found a great plasticity up to 2 arc deg of disparities with training (as though the arborization of disparity-tuned neurons had strengthened with repeated use). Indeed, in real life, large disparity detectors are not used because the convergence movements of our eyes can bring the eyes into alignment. However, in our tachistoscopic task, convergence cannot take place and the neural system is forced to cope with unusually large disparities. An account of these experiments will be published soon.

12 One of my earliest interests was the creation of ambiguous RDS (and RDC), wherein the same random-dot array would portray two independent global organizations (Julesz and Johnson, 1968). In the case of stereopsis, the same RDS would portray two (sometimes even three) different surfaces in vivid depth, and I was interested to discover which would be seen first, whether one could switch global organization at will, and whether both organizations could be perceived simultaneously. In my monograph (Julesz, 1971) I devoted an entire chapter ("Mental Holography") to these problems. Recently, Thomas Papathomas and Andrei Gorea modified the Julesz and Johnson method and, more importantly, opposed the local features in order to see which of them would dominate by yielding the corresponding global organization. In collaboration with them, we have studied stereopsis, motion perception, and texture segmentation by opposing polarity, color, and orientation of local Gabor patches. The hierarchy of these features can be found in several of our papers (Papathomas et al., 1988; 1990; 1991). It is interesting that it has taken a quarter of a century for my two paradigms (the ambiguous RDS, and textons) to be combined into a new research tool. The emerging concept of generalized contrast will be published soon and the model has great predictive power.

6. Conclusion

This article seems to be a hodge-podge of ideas and results of importance to me. Thirty years ago I played with unothodox stimuli of random textures that I presented to one or two eyes, respectively; the implications of those experiments now constitute the field of *early vision*. Whether these newer ideas will coalesce into a more unified whole remains to be seen.

References

Adelson, E. H. and Bergen, J. R. (1985). Spatiotemporal energy models for the perception of motion. *J. Opt. Soc. Am. A*, 2:284–299.

Adelson, E. H. and Bergen, J. R. (1986). The extraction of spatio-temporal energy in human and machine vision. In *Proceedings of IEEE Workshop on Motion: Representation and Analysis*, pp. 151–156, Charleston, S Carolina.

Adelson, E. H. and Movshon, J. A. (1982). Phenomenal coherence of moving visual patterns. *Nature*, 300:523–525.

Adey, W. R. and Noda, H. (1973). Influence of eye movements on geniculo-striate excitability in the cat. *J. Physiol. (Lond).*, 235:805–821.

Albert, B., Beylkin, G., Coifman, R., and Rokhlin, V. (1990). Wavelets for the fast solution of second-kind integral equations. Technical Report DCS.RR-837, Yale Research Report.

Albrecht, D. G. and De Valois, R. L. (1981). Striate cortex responses to periodic patterns with and without the fundamental harmonics. *J. Physiol. (Lond.)*, 319:497–514.

Albrecht, D. G. and Hamilton, D. B. (1982). Striate cortex of monkey and cat: Contrast response function. *J. Neurophysiol.*, 48:217–237.

Albright, T. D. and Desimone, R. (1987). Local precision of visuotopic organization in the middle temporal area (mt) of the macaque. *Exp. Brain Res.*, 65:582–592.

Albright, T. D., Desimone, R., and Gross, C. G. (1984a). Columnar organization of directionally selective cells in visual area mt of the macaque. *J. Neurophysiol.*, 51:16–31.

Albright, T. D., Desimone, R., Gross, C. G., and Bruce, C. (1984b). Stimulus selective properties of inferior temporal neurons in the macaque. *J. Neurosci.*, 4:2051–2062.

Allen, M. J. and Carter, J. H. (1967). The torsion component of the near response. *Amer. J. Opt.*, 44:343–349.

Allman, J., Miezin, F., and McGuiness, E. (1985a). Direction- and velocity-specific responses from beyond the classical receptive field in the middle temporal visual area (mt). *Perception*, 14:104–126.

Allman, J., Miezin, F., and McGuiness, E. (1985b). Stimulus specific responses from beyond the classical receptive field. *Ann. Rev. Neurosci.*, 8:407–430.

Allman, J. and Zucker, S. W. (1990). Cytochrome oxidase and functional coding in primate striate cortex: An hypothesis. *Cold Spring Harbor Symposia on Quantitative Biology*, 55:979–982.

Allman, J. and Zucker, S. W. (1992). Metabolic specializations in cortical processing. *Cerebral Cortex*. (in press).

Aloimonos, J., Weiss, I., and Bandyopadhyay, A. (1988). Active vision. *Int. J. Comp. Vis.*, 1:333–356.

Amigo, G. (1974). A vertical horopter. *Optica Acta*, 21:277–292.

Andersen, R., Snowden, R., Treue, S., and Graziano, M. (1990). Hierarchical processing of motion in the visual cortex of monkey. *Cold Spring Harbor Symposia on Quantitative Biology*, 55:741–748.

Anderson, C. and Van Essen, D. C. (1987). Shifter circuits: A computational strategy for dynamic aspects of visual processing. *Proc. Nat. Acad. Sci. USA*, 84:6297–6301.

Andrews, B. W. and Pollen, D. A. (1979). Relationship between spatial frequency selectivity and receptive field profile of simple cells. *J. Physiol. (Lond.)*, 287:163–176.

Andrews, D. P. (1965). Perception of contours in the central fovea. *Nature*, 205:1218–1220.

Andrews, D. P. (1967). Perception of contour orientation in the central fovea. part i: short lines. *Vision Res.*, 7:1975–1977.

Andrews, D. P., Butcher, A. K., and Buckley, B. R. (1973). Acuities for spatial arrangement in line figures: human and ideal observers compared. *Vision Res.*, 13:599–620.

Anstis, S. M. (1970). Phi movement as a subtraction process. *Vision Res.*, 10:1411–1430.

Anstis, S. M. (1989). Kinetic edges become displaced, segregated and invisible. In *Neural mechanisms of visual perception*, pp. 247–260. Portfolio/Gulf, Houston.

Anstis, S. M., Howard, I. P., and Rogers, B. (1978). A Craik-O'Brien-Cornsweet illusion for visual depth. *Vision Res.*, 18:213–217.

Asada, H. and Brady, M. (1986). The curvature primal sketch. *IEEE Trans. PAMI*, 8:2–14.

Aspect, A., Dalibard, J., and Roger, G. (1982). Experimental test of Bell's inequalities using time-varying analyzers. *Phys. Rev. Lett.*, 49:1804–1807.

Attneave, F. (1954). Some informational aspects of visual perception. *Psych. Rev.*, 61:183–193.

Ayache, N. (1991). *Artificial Vision for Mobile Robots: Stereo Vision and Multisensory Perception*. MIT Press, Cambridge, Mass.

Bajcsy, R. (1988). Active perception. *Proceedings of the IEEE*, 76:996–1005.

Baker, C. L., Hess, R. F., and Zihl, J. (1991). Residual motion perception in a 'motion-blind' patient, assessed with limited-lifetime random dot stimuli. *J. Neurosci.*, 11:454–461.

Ballard, D. H. (1986). Cortical connections and parallel processing: Structure and function. *Behav. Brain Sci.*, 9:67–120.

Ballard, D. H. (1991). Animate vision. *Artificial Intelligence*, 48:57–86.

Ballard, D. H. and Brown, C. (1982). *Computer Vision*. Prentice-Hall, Inc., Englewood Cliffs, N.J.

Balliet, R. and Nakayama, K. (1978). Training of voluntary torsion. *Invest. Ophthal. Vis. Sci.*, 17:303–314.

Banton, T. and Levi, D. M. (1990). Vernier localization in the motion system. *Invest. Ophthal. Vis. Sci.*, 31 (Suppl.):443.

Barbeito, R., Levi, D. M., Klein, S. A., Loshin, D., and Ono, H. (1985). Stereo-deficients and stereoblinds cannot make utrocular discriminations. *Vision Res.*, 25:1345–1348.

Barlow, H. B. (1953). Sensation and inhibition in the frog's retina. *J. Physiol. (Lond.)*, 119:69–88.

Barlow, H. B. (1961a). The coding of sensory messages. In Thorpe, W. H. and Zangwill, O., (Eds.), *Current Problems in Animal Behaviour*, pp. 331–360. Cambridge University Press, Cambridge, England.

Barlow, H. B. (1961b). Possible principles underlying the transformations of sensory messages. In Rosenblith, W., (Ed.), *Sensory Communication*, pp. 782–786. MIT Press, Cambridge, Mass.

Barlow, H. B. (1978). The efficency of detecting changes of density in random dot patterns. *Vision Res.*, 18:637–650.

Barlow, H. B. (1985). Cerebral cortex as model builder. In Rose, D. and Dobson, G., (Eds.), *Models of Visual Cortex*. Wiley, New York, NY.

Barlow, H. B. (1990). Conditions for versatile learning, Helmholtz's unconscious inference, and the task of perception. *Vision Res.*, 30:1561–1571.

Barlow, H. B. and Mollon, J. D., (Eds.) (1982). *The senses*. Cambridge Univ. Press, Cambridge, England.

Barron, J., Fleet, D., Beauchemin, S., and Burkitt, T. (1992). Performance of optical flow techniques. Technical Report TR299, Dept. of Computer Science, University of Western Ontario. (see also CVPR 1992).

Barrow, H. G. and Tenenbaum, J. M. (1978). Recovering intrinsic scene character-istics from images. In Hanson, A. R. and Riseman, E. M., (Eds.), *Computer Vision Systems*, pp. 3–26. Academic Press, New York, NY.

Barrow, H. G. and Tennenbaum, J. M. (1981). Interpreting line drawings as three-dimensional surfaces. *Artificial Intelligence*, 17:75–116.

Bartels, R. H., Beatty, J. C., and Barsky, B. A. (1987). *An Introduction to Splines for use in Computer Graphics and Geometric Modelling*. Morgan Kaufmann, Los Altos, Calif.

Bartlett, J. and Doty, R. (1974). Response of units in striate cortex of squirrel monkeys to visual and electrical stimuli. *J. Neurophysiol.*, 37:621.

Bartlett, J. R., Doty, R. W., Lee, B. B., and Sakakura, H. (1976). Influence of saccadic eye movements on geniculostriate excitability in normal monkeys. *Exp. Brain Res.*, 25:487–509.

Basri, R. (1991). On the uniqueness of correspondence under orthographic and perspective projections. A. I. Memo 1333, Artificial Intelligence Laboratory, Massachusetts Institute of Technology.

Basri, R. and Ullman, S. (1990). Recognition by linear combinations of models. A. I. Memo 1152, Artificial Intelligence Laboratory, Massachusetts Institute of Technology.

Bayes, T. (1783). An essay towards solving a problem in the doctrine of chances. *Phil. Trans. Roy. Soc.*, 53:370–418.

Bell, J. S. (1965). On the Einstein, Podolsky, Rosen Paradox. *Physics*, 1:195–200. reprinted in *Quantum Theory and Measurement*, J. A. Wheeler and W. H. Zurek (Eds.), Princeton University Press, Princeton, 1983.

Ben-Av, M. B., Sagi, D., and Braun, J. (1992). Visual attention and perceptual grouping. *Percept. Psychophys.*, 52:277–294.

Bennett, B., Hoffman, D., and Prakash, C. (1989). *Observer Mechanics*. Academic Press, London.

Bennett, P. J. and Banks, M. S. (1991). The effects of contrast, spatial scale, and orientation on foveal and peripheral phase discrimination. *Vision Res.*, 31:1759–1786.

Bergen, J. R. and Julesz, B. (1983). Parallel versus serial processing in rapid pattern discrimination. *Nature*, 303:696–98.

Bergen, J. R. and Landy, M. S. (1991). Computational modeling of visual texture segregation. In Landy, M. and Movshon, J. A., (Eds.), *Computational Models of Visual Processing*. MIT Press, Cambridge, Mass.

Bertero, M., Poggio, T., and Torre, V. (1987). Regularization of ill-posed problems. A. I. Memo 924, Artificial Intelligence Laboratory, Massachusetts Institute of Technology, Cambridge, Mass.

Beverley, K.I. and Regan, D.(1980).Visual sensitivity to the shape and size of a moving object: implications for models of object perception.*Perception*, 9:151–160.

Binford, T. O. (1971). Visual perception by computer. In *Proceedings IEEE Systems Sci. Cybernet. Conf.*, Miami, Fla.

Binford, T. O. (1981). Inferring surfaces from images. *Artificial Intelligence*, 17:205–244.

Blake, A. and Zisserman, A. (1987). *Visual Reconstruction*. MIT Press, Cambridge, Mass.

Blake, R. and Cormack, R. H. (1979). Psychophysical evidence for a monocular visual cortex in stereoblind humans. *Science*, 203:274–275.

Blakemore, C. and Campbell, F. W. (1969). On the existence of neurones in the human visual system selectively sensitive to the orientation and size of retinal images. *J. Physiol. (Lond.)*, 203:237–260.

Blakemore, C. and Nachmias, J. (1971). The orientational specificity of two visual aftereffects. *J. Physiol. (Lond.)*, 213:157–174.

Blaquiere, A. (1966). *Nonlinear systems analysis*. Academic Press, New York, NY.

Bobick, A. (1987). Natural categorization. A. I. Memo 1001, Artificial Intelligence Laboratory, Massachusetts Institute of Technology, Cambridge, Mass.

Bohr, N. (1949). Discussion with Einstein on epistemological problems in atomic physics. In Schilpp, P. A., (Ed.), *Albert Einstein: Philosopher-Scientist*. The Library of Living Philosophers, Evanston. in *Quantum Theory and Measurement*, J. A. Wheeler and W. H. Zurek (Eds.), Princeton University Press, Princeton, 1983.

Bolles, R., Baker, H., and Marimont, D. (1987). Epipolar-plane image analysis: An approach to determine structure from motion. *Int. J. Comp. Vis.*, 1:7–55.

Bonds, A. B. (1989). Role of inhibition in the specification of orientation selectivity of cells in the cat striate cortex. *Vis. Neurosci.*, 2:41–55.

Bove, M. (1989). Discrete fourier transform based depth-from-focus. In *Optical Society of America Image Understanding and Machine Vision Conference*, pp. 118–121, Falmouth, Cape Cod, Mass.

Braddick, O. J. (1974). A short-range process in apparent motion. *Vision Res.*, 14:519–527.

Braddick, O. J. (1980). Low-level process in apparent motion. *Phil. Trans. Roy. Soc. Lond. B*, 290:137–151.

Bradley, A., Skottun, B. C., Ohzawa, I., Sclar, G., and Freeman, R. D. (1987). Visual orientation and spatial frequency discrimination: A comparison of single neurons and behavior. *J. Neurophysiol.*, 57:755–772.

Bradley, A., Switkes, E., and De Valois, K. K. (1988). Orientation and spatial frequency selectivity of adaptation to colour and luminance gratings. *Vision Res.*, 28:841–856.

Braitman, D. (1984). Activity of neurons in monkey posterior temporal cortex during multidimensional visual discrimination tasks. *Brain Res.*, 307:17–28.

Braun, J. and Sagi, D. (1990). Vision outside the focus of visual attention. *Percept. Psychophys*, 48:45–58.

Brecher, G. A. (1934). Die optokinetische Auslösung von Augenrollung und rotatorischem Nystagmus. *Pflüg. Arch. ges. Physiol.*, 234:13–28.

Bregman, A. S. (1990). *Auditory Scene Analysis: The Perceptual Organization of Sound*. MIT Press, Cambridge, Mass.

Briand, K. and Klein, R. (1987). Is Posner's Beam the same as Treisman's Glue?: On the relation between visual orienting and feature integration theory. *J. Exp. Psych.: Human Perception and Performance*, 13:228–241.

Broida, T. J. and Chellappa, R. (1986). Estimation of object motion parameters from noisy images. *IEEE Trans. PAMI*, 8:90–99.

Brookes, A. and Stevens, K. A. (1989). Binocular depth from surfaces versus volumes. *J. Exp. Psychol.*, 15:479–484.

Brooks, R. A. (1984). *Model-Based Computer Vision*. UMI Research Press, Ann Arbor, Mich.

Brooks, R. A., Greiner, R., and Binford, T. O. (1979). The ACRONYM model-based vision system. In *Sixth International Joint Conference on Artificial Intelligence (IJCAI-79)*, pp. 105–113, Tokyo, Japan.

Brown, P. (1987). *The acoustic modelling problem in Automatic Speech Recognition*. PhD thesis, Carnegie-Mellon University. Also published as IBM Research Division Technical Report RC 12750.

Bülthoff, H. H. and Kersten, D. (1989). Interactions between transparency and depth. *Perception*, 18.

Bülthoff, H. H. and Yuille, A. L. (1991). Bayesian models for seeing shapes and depth. *J. Theoretical Biol.*, 2. Issue 4.

Burbeck, C. A. and Regan, D. (1983). Independence of orientation and size in spatial discriminations. *J. Opt. Soc. Am.*, 73:1691–1694.

Burr, D. J. (1981a). A dynamic model for image registration. *Comput. Graphics Image Process.*, 15:102–112.

Burr, D. J. (1981b). Elastic matching of line drawings. *IEEE Trans. PAMI*, 3:708–713.

Burton, G. J. (1973). Evidence for non-linear response processes in the human visual system from measurements on the thresholds of spatial beat frequencies. *Vision Res.*, 13:1211–1225.

Bushnell, M., Goldberg, M., and Robinson, D. L. (1991). Behavioral enhancement of visual responses in monkey cerebral cortex I. Modulation in posterior parietal cortex related to selective visual attention. *J. Neurophysiol.*, 46:755–787.

Caelli, T. M., Brettel, H., Rentschler, I., and Hilz, R. (1983). Discrimination thresholds in the two-dimensional spatial frequency domain. *Vision Res.*, 23:129–133.

Caelli, T. M., Julesz, B., and Gilbert, E. (1978). On perceptual analyzers underlying visual texture discrimination: Part ii. *Biol, Cybernetics*, 29:201–214.

Campbell, F. W., Cleland, B. G., Cooper, G. F., and Enroth-Cugell, C. (1968). The angular selectivity of visual cortical cells to moving gratings. *J. Physiol. (Lond.)*, 198:237–250.

Campbell, F. W., Cooper, G. F., and Enroth-Cugell, C. (1969). The spatial selectivity of visual cells of the cat. *J. Physiol. (Lond.)*, 203:223–235.

Campbell, F. W. and Kulikowski, J. J. (1966). Orientation selectivity of the human visual system. *J. Physiol. (Lond.)*, 187:437–445.

Campbell, F. W. and Robson, J. G. (1968). Application of Fourier analysis to the visibility of gratings. *J. Physiol. (Lond.)*, 197:551–566.

Canny, J. F. (1983). Finding edges and lines in images. Master's thesis, MIT.

Carney, T. and Klein, S. A. (1989). Parameter free prediction of bisection thresholds. *Invest. Ophthal. Vis. Sci.*, 30 (Suppl.):453.

Cavanagh, P. (1991). Short-range vs long-range motion: Not a valid distinction. *Spatial Vision*, 5:303–309.

Cavanagh, P. and Leclerc, Y. G. (1989). Shape from shadows. *J. Exp. Psychol. Human Percep. Perform.*, 15:3–27.

Cavanagh, P., MacLeod, D. I. A., and Anstis, S. M. (1987). Equiluminance: Spatial and temporal factors and the contribution of blue-sensitive cones. *J. Opt. Soc. Am A*, 4:1428–1438.

Cavanagh, P. and Mather, G. (1990). Motion: the long and short of it. *Spatial Vision*, 4:103–129.

Cavanagh, P., Tyler, C. W., and Favreau, O. E. (1984). Perceived velocity of moving chromatic gratings. *J. Opt. Soc. Am A*, 1:893–899.

Chakravarty, I. (1979). A generalized line and junction labeling scheme with applications to scene analysis. *IEEE Trans. PAMI*, 1:202–205.

Chao-yi, L. and Creutzfeldt, O. (1984). The representation of contrast and other stimulus parameters by single neurons in area 17 of the cat. *Pflügers Archives*, 401:304–314.

Cheung, B. S. K. and Howard, I. P. (1991). Optokinetic torsion: Dynamics and relation to circularvection. *Vision Res.*, 31:1327–1335.

Christ, J. P. (1987). *Shape Estimation and Object Recognition Using Spatial Probability Distributions*. PhD thesis, Carnegie Mellon University.

Chubb, C. and Sperling, G. (1988). Drift-balanced random stimuli: a general basis for studying non-Fourier motion perception. *J. Opt. Soc. Am. A*, 5:1986–2007.

Chubb, C. and Sperling, G. (1989). Two motion perception mechanisms revealed through distance-driven reversal of apparent motion. *Proc. Nat. Acad. Sci.*, 86:2985–2989.

Churchland, P. M. (1988). *Matter and Consciousness. A Contemporary Introduction to the Philosophy of Mind*. MIT Press, Cambridge, Mass.

Churchland, P. S. (1986). *Neurophilosophy. Toward a Unified Science of the Mind/Brain*. MIT Press., Cambridge, Mass.

Cipolla, R. and Blake, A. (1990). The dynamic analysis of apparent contours. In *IEEE ICCV*, pp. 616–623, Osaka, Japan.

Clark, J. J. and Yuille, A. L. (1990). *Data Fusion for Sensory Information Processing Systems*. Kluwer Academic Press, Boston, Mass.

Cogan, A. (1979). The relationship between the apparent vertical and the vertical horopter. *Vision Res.*, 19:655–65.

Cole, G. R., Stromeyer III, C. F., and Kronauer, R. E. (1990). Visual interactions with luminance and chromatic stimuli. *J. Opt. Soc. Am. A*, 7:128–140.

Collewijn, H., der Steen, J. V., Ferman, L., and Jansen, T. C. (1985). Human ocular counterroll. *Exp. Brain Res.*, 59:185–196.

Collewijn, H., van der Mark, F., and Jansen, T. C. (1975). Precise recording of human eye movements. *Vision Res.*, 15:447–50.

Condo, G., Florence, S., and Casagrande, V. (1987). Development of laminar and columnar patters of cytochrome oxidase activity in galago visual cortex. *Soc. Neurosci. Abst.*, 13:1025.

Cormack, R., Blake, R., and Hiris, E. (1992). Misdirected visual motion in the peripheral visual field. *Vision Res.*, 32:73–80.

Cowie, R. I. D. (1983). The viewer's place in theories of vision. In *International Joint Conference on Artificial Intelligence*, pp. 952–958.

Crone, R. A. (1975). Optically induced eye torsion. II. Optostatic and optokinetic cycloversion. *Von Graefes Arch. Klin. Exp. Ophthal.*, 196:1–7.

Crone, R. A. and Everhard-Halm, Y. (1975). Optically induced eye torsion. I. Fusional cyclovergence. *Von Graefes Arch. Klin. Exp. Ophthal.*, 195:231–239.

Culhane, S. and Tsotsos, J. (1992). An attentional prototype for early vision. In *European Conference on Computer Vision*. (in press).

Curtis, S. R. and Oppenheim, A. V. (1989). Reconstruction of multidimensional signals from zero crossings. In Ullman, S. and Richards, W., (Eds.), *Image Understanding*. Ablex, Norwood, NJ.

da Vitoria Lobo, N. and Tsotsos, J. K. (1991). Using collinear points to compute egomotion and detect nonrigidity. In *IEEE CVPR*, pp. 344–350, Maui.

Daubechies, I. (1988). Orthonormal bases of compactly supported wavelets. *Communications on Pure and Applied Mathematics*, 41:909–996.

Daugman, J. G. (1980). Two-dimensional spectral analysis of cortical receptive field profiles. *Vision Res.*, 20:847–856.

Daugman, J. G. (1984). Spatial visual channels in the fourier plane. *Vision Res.*, 24:891–910.

Daugman, J. G. (1985). Uncertainty relation for resolution in space, spatial frequency, and orientation optimized by two-dimensional visual cortical filters. *J. Opt. Soc. Am.*, 2:1160–1169.

Daugman, J. G. (1987). Image analysis and compact coding by oriented 2D Gabor primitives. In *Image Understanding and the Man-Machine Interface, SPIE Vol. 758*, pp. 19–30.

Daugman, J. G. (1988a). Complete discrete 2-D Gabor transforms by neural networks for image analysis and compression. *IEEE Transactions on Acoustics, Speech, and Signal Processing*, 36:1169–1179.

Daugman, J. G. (1988b). Pattern and motion vision without laplacian zero-crossings. *J. Opt. Soc. Am. A*, 5:1142–1148.

Daugman, J. G. (1989). Entropy reduction and decorrelation in visual coding by oriented neural receptive fields. *IEEE Transactions on Biomedical Engineering*, 36:107–114.

Davis, E. T., Kramer, P., and Yager, D. (1986). Shifts in perceived spatial frequency of low-contrast stimuli: data and theory. *J. Opt. Soc. Am. A*, 3:1189–1202.

De Valois, K. K. and Switkes, E. (1983). Simultaneous masking interactions between chromatic and luminance gratings. *J. Opt. Soc. Am.*, 73:11–18.

De Valois, R. L. and De Valois, K. K. (1988). *Spatial Vision*. Oxford University Press, New York, NY.

De Valois, R. L. and De Valois, K. K. (1991). Vernier acuity with stationary moving Gabors. *Vision Res.*, 31:1619–1626.

De Valois, R. L., Yund, E. W., and Hepler, N. (1982). The orientation and direction selectivity of cells in macaque visual cortex. *Vision Res.*, 22:531–544.

De Voe, E. A. and Van Essen, D. C. (1988). Concurrent processing streams in monkey visual cortex. *Trends in Neurosci.*, 11:219–226.

De Weert, C. M. M. and Sadza, K. (1983). New data concerning the contribution of colour differences to stereopsis. In Mollon, J. and Sharpe, T., (Eds.), *Colour Vision*, pp. 553–562. Academic Press, New York, NY.

Dempster, A. P., Laird, N. M., and Rubin, D. B. (1977). Maximum likelihood from incomplete data via the EM algorithm. *Proc. Roy. Stat. Soc.*, B-39:1–38.

Dennett, D. C. (1985). Can machines think? In Shafto, M., (Ed.), *How We Know*, pp. 121–145. Harper & Row, New York, NY.

Dennett, D. C. (1988). Quining qualia. In *Consciousness in contemporary science*, pp. 42–77. Oxford University Press, New York, NY.

Dennett, D. C. (1991). *Consciousness Explained*. Little, Brown and Company, Boston, Mass.

Derrington, A. M. and Badcock, D. R. (1986). Detection of spatial beats: non-linearity or contrast-increment detection? *Vision Res.*, 26:343–348.

Derrington, A. M. and Lennie, P. (1984). Spatial and temporal contrast sensitivities of neurones in lateral geniculate nucleus of macaque. *J. Physiol. (Lond.)*, 357:219–240.

Descartes, R. (1664). *Treatise of Man*. Harvard Univ. Press., Cambridge, Mass. (reprinted 1972).

Desimone, R., Schein, S. J., Moran, J., and Ungerleider, L. G. (1985). Contour, colour and shape analysis beyond the striate cortex. *Vision Res.*, 25:441–452.

Desimone, R., Wessinger, M., Thomas, L., and Schneider, W. (1990). Attentional control of visual perception: Cortical and subcortical mechanisms. *Cold Spring Harbor Symposia on Quantitative Biology*, 55:963–971.

Dobbins, A., Zucker, S. W., and Cynader, M. (1987). End-stopped neurons in the visual cortex as a substrate for calculating curvature. *Nature*, 329:438–441.

Dove, H. W. (1841). Über stereoskopie. *Ann. Phys.*, series 2:494–498.

Downing, C. J. and Movshon, J. A. (1989). Spatial and temporal summation in the detection of motion in stochastic random dot displays. *Invest. Ophthal. Vis. Sci.*, 30 (Suppl.):72.

Duhamel, J. R., Colby, C. L., and Goldberg, M. E. (1992). The updating of the representation of visual space in parietal cortex by intended eye-movements. *Science*, 255:90–92.

Durbin, R., Szeliski, R., and Yuille, A. L. (1989). An analysis of the elastic net approach to the travelling salesman problem. *Neural Computation*, 1:348–358.

Durbin, R. and Willshaw, D. (1987). An analog approach to the travelling salesman problem using an elastic net method. *Nature*, 326:689–691.

D'Zmura, M. and Lennie, P. (1986). Mechanisms of color constancy. *J. Opt. Soc. Am. A*, 3:1662–1672.

Edelman, G. M. (1992). *Bright Air, Brilliant Fire. On the Matter of the Mind.* Basic Books, Harper Collins, New York, NY.

Edelman, S., Ullman, S., and Flash, T. (1990). Reading cursive handwriting by alignment of letter prototypes. *Int. J. Comp. Vis.*, 5:303–331.

Einstein, A., Podolsky, B., and Rosen, N. (1935). Can quantum-mechanical description of physical reality be considered complete? *Physical Review*, 47:777–780. Reprinted in *Quantum Theory and Measurement*, J. A. Wheeler and W. H. Zurek (Eds.), Princeton University Press, Princeton, (1983).

Eisner, A. and MacLeod, D. I. A. (1980). Blue-sensitive cones do not contribute to luminance. *J. Opt. Soc. Am.*, 70:121–123.

Ejiri, M., Miyatake, T., Kakumoto, S., and Matsushiam, H. (1984). Automatic recognition of design drawings and maps. In *Proc. Seventh ICPR*, volume 2, pp. 1296–1305.

Elfar, S. and De Valois, R. L. (1991). Orientation tuning of monkey V1 cells to luminance-varying and color-varying patterns. *Invest. Ophthal. Vis. Sci.*, 32 (Suppl.):1253.

Elfes, A. and Matthies, L. (1987). Sensor integration for robot navigation: Combining sonar and stereo range data in a grid-based representation. In *IEEE Conference on Decision and Control*. IEEE Computer Society Press.

Ellerbrock, V. J. (1954). Inducement of cyclofusional movements. *Amer. J. Optom. Arch. Amer. Acad. Optom.*, 31:553–566.

Emerson, R. C., Bergen, J. R., and Adelson, E. H. (1992). Directionally selective complex cells and the computation of motion energy in cat visual cortex. *Vision Res.*, 32:203–218.

Ericksen, C. and Murphy, T. (1987). Movement of attentional focus across the visual field: A critical look at the evidence. *Percept. Psychophys.*, 42:299–305.

Erkelens, C. J. and Collewijn, H. (1985). Eye movements and stereopsis during dichoptic viewing of moving random-dot stereograms. *Vision Res.*, 25:1689–1700.

Fahle, M. and Poggio, T. (1981). Visual hyperacuity: spatiotemporal interpolation in human vision. *Proc. Roy. Soc. Lond. B*, 213:451–477.

Faugeras, O. D., Ayache, N., and Faverjon, B. (1986). Building visual maps by combining noisy stereo measurements. In *IEEE Conf. Robotics and Automation*, pp. 1433–1438, San Francisco, CA.

Feldman, J. (1991). Perceptual simplicity and modes of structural generation. In *Proc. 13th Ann. Conf. Cog. Sci.*

Feldman, J. (1992). Constructing perceptual categories. *Proc. Comp. Vis. & Pat. Recog.* (to appear).

Feldman, J. and Ballard, D. (1982). Connectionist models and their properties. *Cog. Sci.*, 6:205–254.

Felleman, D. and Van Essen, D. C. (1991). Distributed hierarchical processing in primate cerebral cortex. *Cerebral Cortex*, 1:1–47.

Fennema, C. L. and Thompson, W. B. (1979). Velocity determination in scenes containing several moving objects. *Comp. Graph. Image Proc.*, 9:301–315.

Ferman, L., Collewijn, H., Jansen, T. C., and Van den Berg, A. V. (1987a). Human gaze stability in horizontal, vertical and torsional direction during voluntary head movements, evaluated with a three-dimensional scleral induction coil technique. *Vision Res.*, 27:811–828.

Ferman, L., Collewijn, H., and Van den Berg, A. V. (1987b). A direct test of Listing's law — I. Human ocular torsion measured in static tertiary positions. *Vision Res.*, 27:929–938.

Ferrera, V. P. and Wilson, H. R. (1987). Direction specific masking and the analysis of motion in two dimensions. *Vision Res.*, 27:1783–1796.

Ferrera, V. P. and Wilson, H. R. (1990). Perceived direction of moving two-dimensional patterns. *Vision Res.*, 30:273–287.

Ferrera, V. P. and Wilson, H. R. (1991). Perceived speed of moving two-dimensional patterns. *Vision Res.*, 31:877–893.

Feynman, R. P. (1985). *QED-The Strange Theory of Light and Matter.* Princeton University Press, Princeton, NJ.

Fischer, B., Bach, M., and Boch, R. (1981). Stimulus versus eye-movements — comparison of neural activity in the striate and prelunate visual-cortex (A17 and A19) of trained rhesus-monkey. *Exp. Brain Res.*, 43:69–77.

Fischler, M. and Firschein, O., (Eds.) (1987). *Readings in Computer Vision: Issues, problems, principles, and paradigms.* Morgan Kaufmann, Los Altos, CA.

Fischler, M. A. and Elschlager, R. A. (1973). The representation and matching of pictorial structures. *IEEE. Trans. Computers*, 22:67–92.

Fleet, D. (1992). *Measurement of Image Velocity.* Kluwer, Boston, Mass.

Fleet, D. J. and Jepson, A. D. (1990). Computation of component image velocity from local phase information. *Int. J. Comp. Vis.*, 5:77–104.

Fogel, I. and Sagi, D. (1989). Gabor filters as texture discriminators. *Biol. Cybern.*, 61:103–113.

Foster, K. H., Gaska, J. P., Nagler, M., and Pollen, D. A. (1985). Spatial and temporal frequency selectivity of neurons in visual cortical areas V1 and V2 of the macaque monkey. *J. Physiol. (Lond.)*, 365:331–363.

Freeman, W. T. and Adelson, E. H. (1990). Extensions of steerable filters. *Optical Society of America Technical Digest Series*, 15:25.

French, R. M. (1990). Subcognition and the limits of the Turing test. *Mind*, 99:53–65.

Friedland, B. (1986). *Control System Design.* McGraw-Hill, New York, NY.

Frost, B. J. (1985). Neural mechanisms for detecting object motion and figure-ground boundaries contrasted with self-motion detecting systems. In Ingle, D., Jeanerod, M., and Lee, D., (Eds.), *Brain Mechanisms of Spatial Vision.* Nijhoff, The Netherlands.

Fry, G. A. (1968). Nomograms for torsion and direction of regard. *Amer. J. Optom. Arch. Amer. Acad. Optom.*, 45:631–41.

Fuster, J. (1988). Attentional modulation of inferotemporal neuron responses to visual features. *Society of Neuroscience Abstracts*, 8.5.

Fuster, J. (1990). Inferotemporal units in selective visual attention and short-term memory. *J. Neurophysiol.*, 64:681–697.

Fuster, J. and Jervey, J. (1981). Inferotemporal neurons distinguish and retain behaviorally relevant features of visual stimuli. *Science*, 212:952–954.

Gabor, D. (1946). Theory of communication. *Journal of the Institute of Electrical Engineers*, 93:429–457.

Gallager, R. (1968). *Information Theory and Reliable Communication*. Wiley, New York, NY.

Gamble, E. and Poggio, T. (1987). Visual integration and detection of discontinuities: the key role of intensity edges. A. I. Memo 970, Artificial Intelligence Laboratory, Massachusetts Institute of Technology.

Geisler, W. S. (1984). Physical limits of acuity and hyperacuity. *J. Opt. Soc. Am. A*, 1:775–782.

Geisler, W. S. (1989). Sequential ideal observer analysis of visual discriminations. *Psychol. Rev.*, 96:267–314.

Geisler, W. S. and Davila, K. D. (1985). Ideal discriminators in spatial vision: two-point stimuli. *J. Opt. Soc. Am. A*, 2:1483–1497.

Gelb, A. (1974). *Applied Optimal Estimation*. MIT Press, Cambridge, Mass.

Geman, S. and Geman, D. (1984). Stochastic relaxation, Gibbs distribution, and the Bayesian restoration of images. *IEEE Trans. PAMI*, 6:721–741.

Gershon, R., Jepson, A. D., and Tsotsos, J. K. (1987). Highlight identification using chromatic information. In *IEEE ICCV*, pp. 161–170, London, England.

Giaschi, D., Regan, D., Kothe, A., Hong, X. H., and Sharpe, J. (1991). Multiple sclerosis can degrade detection and/or discrimination of motion-defined form while sparing motion sensitivity. *Invest. Ophthal. Vis. Sci.*, 32 (Suppl.):1282.

Giaschi, D., Regan, D., Kothe, A., Hong, X. H., and Sharpe, J. (1992). Motion-defined letter detection and recognition in patients with multiple sclerosis. *Annals of Neurology*. (in press).

Giblin, P. and Weiss, R. (1987). Reconstruction of surfaces from profiles. In *IEEE ICCV*, pp. 136–144, London, England.

Gibson, J. J. (1950). *The Perception of the Visual World*. Houghton Mifflin, Boston, Mass.

Gibson, J. J. (1956). *The senses considered as perceptual systems*. Houghton Mifflin, Boston. Mass.

Gibson, J. J. and Gibson, E. J. (1957). Continuous perspective transformations and the perception of rigid motions. *J. Exp. Psych.*, 54:129–138.

Gillam, B., Flagg, T., and Finlay, D. (1984). Evidence for disparity change as the primary stimulus for stereoscopic processing. *Percept. Psychophys.*, 36:559–564.

Glassman, R. B. (1978). The logic of the lesion experiment and its role in the neural sciences. In Finger, S., (Ed.), *Recovery from brain damage*, pp. 3–31. Plenum Press, New York, NY.

Gogel, W. C. (1956). The tendency to see objects as equidistant and its inverse relation to lateral separation. *Psychol. Monogr.*, 70.

Gogel, W. C. (1963). A test of the invariance of the ratio of perceived size to perceived distance. *Am. J. Psychol.*, 76:537–553.

Goodenough, D. R., Sigman, E., Oltman, P. K., Rosso, J., and Mertz, H. (1979). Eye torsion in response to a tilted visual stimulus. *Vision Res.*, 19:1177–1179.

Graham, N. (1989). *Visual Pattern Analyzers.* Oxford University Press, New York, NY.

Graham, N. (1991). Complex channels, early local nonlinearities, and normalization in texture segregation. In Landy, M. and Movshon, J. A., (Eds.), *Computational Models of Visual Processing.* MIT Press, Cambridge, Mass.

Granger, E. M. and Heurtley, J. C. (1973). Visual chromaticity-modulation transfer function. *J. Opt. Soc. Am.*, 63:1173–1174.

Gregory, R. L. (1977). Vision with isoluminant colour contrast: 1. A projection technique and observations. *Perception*, 6:113–119.

Grenander, U., Chow, Y., and Kennan, D. (1990). *HANDS: A Pattern Theoretic Study of Biological Shapes.* Springer-Verlag, New York, NY.

Grimson, W. E. L. (1983). An implementation of a computational theory of visual surface interpolation. *CVGIP*, 22:39–69.

Grimson, W. E. L. and Hildreth, E. C. (1985). Comments on "digital step edges from zero crossings of second directional derivatives". *IEEE Trans. PAMI*, 7:121–127.

Grinberg, D. L. and Williams, D. R. (1985). Stereopsis with chromatic signals from the blue-sensitive mechanism. *Vision Res.*, 25:531–537.

Gross, C. G., Desimone, R., Albright, T. D., and Schwartz, E. L. (1985). Inferior temporal cortex and pattern recognition. *Pont. Acad. Sci. Scripta Varia*, 54:179–201.

Grossberg, S. (1991). Why do parallel cortical systems exist for the perception of static form and moving form? *Percept. Psychophys.*, 49:117–141.

Grossberg, S. and Mingolla, E. (1985). Neural dynamics of perceptual grouping: Textures, boundaries, and emergent segmentations. *Percept. Psychophys.*, 38:141–171.

Grzywacz, N. M., Smith, J. A., and Yuille, A. L. (1989). A computational theory for the perception of inertial motion. In *Proceedings IEEE Workshop on Visual Motion*, pp. 148–155, Irvine, California.

Grzywacz, N. M. and Yuille, A. L. (1990). A model for the estimate of local image velocity by cells in the visual cortex. *Proc. Roy. Soc. (Lond.) B*, 239:129–161.

Gurnsey, R. and Browse, R. (1987). Micropattern properties and presentation conditions influencing visual texture discrimination. *Percept. Psychophys.*, 41:239–252.

Guzman, A. (1969). Decomposition of a visual scene into three-dimensional bodies. In Grasseli, A., (Ed.), *Automatic Interpretation and Classification of Images.* Academic Press, New York, NY.

Hadani, I. and Julesz, B. (1992). Interpupillary distance and stereoscopic depth perception. *Invest. Opthal. Vis. Sci.*, 33 (Suppl.):707.

Haenny, P., Maunsell, J. H. R., and Schiller, P. (1988). State dependent activity in monkey visual cortex II. Retinal and extraretinal factors in V4. *Exp. Brain Res.*, 69:245–259.

Haenny, P. and Schiller, P. (1988). State dependent activity in monkey visual cortex I. Single cell activity in V1 and V4 on visual tasks. *Exp. Brain Res.*, 69:225–244.

Hallinan, P. W. (1991). Recognizing human eyes. In *Proceedings of Conference 1570, SPIE*, San Diego.

Hamilton, D. B., Albrecht, D. G., and Geisler, W. S. (1989). Visual cortical receptive fields in monkey and cat: spatial and temporal phase transfer function. *Vision Res.*, 29:1285–1308.

Hampton, D. R. and Kertesz, A. E. (1982). Human response to cyclofusional stimuli containing depth cues. *Am. J. Opt. Physiol. Optics*, 59:21–27.

Hamstra, S. and Regan, D. (1991). Dot lifetime and presentation duration have little effect on orientation discrimination for equally-detectable motion-defined and contrast-defined bars. *Invest. Ophthal. Vis. Sci.*, 32 (Suppl.):1270.

Haralick, R. M. (1984). Digital step edges from zero crossing of second directional derivatives. *IEEE Trans. PAMI*, 6:58–68.

Harrison, C. W. (1952). Experiments with linear prediction in television. *Bell System Technical Journal*, 31:764–783.

Heeger, D. J. (1987). A model for the extraction of image flow. *J. Opt. Soc. Am. A*, 4:1455–1471.

Heeger, D. J. (1988). Optical flow using spatiotemporal filters. *Int. J. Comp. Vis.*, 1:279–302.

Heeger, D. J. (1992a). Half-squaring in responses of cat simple cells. *Vis. Neurosci.*, 9:427–443.

Heeger, D. J. (1992b). Normalization of cell responses in cat striate cortex. *Vis. Neurosci.*, 9:181–197.

Heeger, D. J. and Jepson, A. D. (1990). Simple method for computing 3D motion and depth. In *IEEE ICCV*, pp. 96–100, Osaka, Japan.

Heeger, D. J. and Jepson, A. D. (1992). Subspace methods for recovering rigid motion I: Algorithm and implementation. *Int. J. of Comp. Vis.*, 7:95–117.

Heel, J. (1990). Temporally-integrated surface reconstruction. In *IEEE ICCV*, pp. 292–295, Osaka, Japan.

Heggelund, P. (1981). Receptive-field organization of simple cells in cat striate cortex. *Exp. Brain Res.*, 42:89–98.

Hel Or, Y. and Zucker, S. W. (1989). Texture fields and texture flows: Sensitivity to differences. *Spatial Vision*, 4:131 –139.

Henning, G. B., Hertz, B. G., and Broadbent, D. E. (1975). Some experiments bearing on the hypothesis that the visual system analyzes spatial patterns in independent bands of spatial frequency. *Vision Res.*, 15:887–897.

Herbert, N. (1985). *Quantum Reality*. Anchor/Doubleday, New York, NY.

Hildreth, E. C. (1984). *The Measurement Of Visual Motion*. MIT Press, Cambridge, Mass.

Hildreth, E. C. (1987). Edge detection. In Shapiro, S. C., (Ed.), *Encyclopedia of Artificial Intelligence*, pp. 257–267. John Wiley and Sons, New York, NY.

Hinton, G. E. (1977). *Relaxation and its role in vision.* PhD thesis, University of Edinburgh.

Hinton, G. E. (1989). Deterministic Boltzmann learning performs steepest descent in weight-space. *Neural Computation*, 1:143–150.

Hinton, G. E., Williams, C. K. I., and Revow, M. D. (1992). Adaptive elastic models for hand-printed character recognition. In Moody, J. E., Hanson, S. J., and Lippmann, R. P., (Eds.), *Advances in Neural Information Processing Systems 4.* Morgan Kaufmann, Los Altos, CA.

Hofmann, F. B. and Bielschowsky, A. (1900). Über die der Willkurentzogenen Fusionsbewegungen der Augen. *Pflügers Arch. ges. Physiol.*, 80:20–28.

Hofstadter, D. R. and Dennett, D. C. (1981). *The Mind's I: Fantasies and Reflections on Self and Soul.* Bantam Books, New York, NY.

Holub, R. A. and Morton-Gibson, M. (1981). Response of visual cortical neurons of the cat to moving sinusoidal gratings: Response-contrast functions and spatiotemporal interactions. *J. Neurophysiol.*, 46:1244–1259.

Hong, X. H. and Regan, D. (1989). Visual field defects for unidirectional and oscillatory motion in depth. *Vision Res.*, 29:809–819.

Hong, X. H. and Regan, D. (1990). Visual acuity for optotypes made visible by relative motion. *Optometry and Visual Science*, 167:49–55.

Hooten, K., Myers, E., Worall, R., and Stark, L. (1979). Cyclovergence: The motor response to cyclodisparity. *Albrecht v. Graefes Archiv. Ophthal.*, 210:65–8.

Horn, B. K. P. (1986). *Robot Vision.* McGraw-Hill, New York, NY.

Horn, B. K. P. and Brooks, M. J. (1986). The variational approach to shape from shading. *CVGIP*, 33:174–208.

Horn, B. K. P. and Schunk, B. G. (1981). Determining optical flow. *Artif. Intell.*, 17:185–203.

Horton, J. (1984). Cytochrome oxidase patches: a new cytoarchitectonic feature of monkey cortex. *Phil. Trans. Roy. Soc. London (Biol)*, 304:199–253.

Horton, J. and Hubel, D. H. (1981). Regular patchy distribution of cytochrome oxidase staining in primate visual cortex of macaque monkey. *Nature*, 292:762–764.

Howard, I. P. and Evans, J. (1963). The measurement of eye torsion. *Vision Res.*, 3:447–55.

Howard, I. P. and Templeton, W. B. (1964). Visually induced eye torsion and tilt adaptation. *Vision Res.*, 4:433–437.

Howard, I. P. and Zacher, J. (1991). Human cyclovergence as a function of the frequency and amplitude of cyclorotation. *Exp. Brain Res.*, 85:445–450.

Hu, Q., Klein, S. A., and Carney, T. (1992). Can sinusoidal vernier acuity be predicted by contrast discrimination? *Vision Res.*, 33:1241–1258.

Huang, T. S. and Lee, C. H. (1989). Motion and structure from orthographic projections. *IEEE Trans. PAMI*, 2:536–540.

Hubel, D. H. and Weisel, T. N. (1968). Receptive fields and functional architecture of monkey striate cortex. *J. Physiol. (Lond.)*, 195:215–243.

Hubel, D. H. and Wiesel, T. N. (1959). Receptive fields of single neurons in the cat's striate cotex. *J. Physiol. (Lond.)*, 149:574–591.

Hubel, D. H. and Wiesel, T. N. (1962). Receptive fields, binocular interaction, and functional architecture in the cat's visual cortex. *J. Physiol. (Lond.)*, 160:106–154.

Hubel, D. H. and Wiesel, T. N. (1977). Functional architecture of macaque monkey visual cortex. *Proc. Roy. Soc. Lond. B*, 198:1–59.

Huber, P. J. (1981). *Robust Statistics*. John Wiley & Sons, New York, NY.

Hummel, R. and Zucker, S. (1983). Foundations of relaxation labelling processes. *IEEE Trans. PAMI*, 5:267–287.

Hung, Y.-P., Cooper, D. B., and Cernushi-Frias, B. (1988). Bayesian estimation of 3-D surfaces from a sequence of images. In *IEEE International Conference on Robotics and Automation*, pp. 906–911, Philadelphia, Pennsylvania. IEEE Computer Society Press.

Ikeda, H. and Wright, M. J. (1975). Spatial and temporal properties of 'sustained' and 'transient' neurones in area 17 of the cat's visual cortex. *Exp. Brain Res.*, 22:363–383.

Jackson, F. (1982). Epiphenomenal qualia. *Philosophical Quarterly*, 32:127–136.

Jenkin, M., Milios, E., and Tsotsos, J. (1992). TRISH: The Toronto-IRIS Stereo Head. In *SPIE Applications of AI X, Machine Vision and Robotics Conference*, pp. 36–46, Orlando, Florida.

Jepson, A. D., Gershon, R., and Hallett, P. E. (1987). Cones, color constancy, and photons. In Kulikowski, J., Dickinson, C., and Murray, I., (Eds.), *Seeing Contour and Color*, pp. 768–776. Pergamon Press, Oxford.

Jepson, A. D. and Heeger, D. J. (1990). A fast subspace algorithm for recovering rigid motion. In *Proc. IEEE Workshop on Visual Motion*, pp. 124–131, Princeton, NJ.

Jepson, A. D. and Heeger, D. J. (1991). A fast subspace algorithm for recovering rigid motion. In *IEEE Workshop on Visual Motion*, pp. 124–131, Princeton, NJ.

Jepson, A. D. and Richards, W. (1991). Integrating vision modules. Preprint.

Jepson, A. D. and Richards, W. (1992). A lattice framework for integrating vision modules. *IEEE Trans. Sys. Man. & Cyb.*, 22. (in press).

Johansson, G. (1975). Visual motion perception. *Sci. Am.*, 232:76–88.

Jones, J. P. and Palmer, L. A. (1987). The two-dimensional spatial structure of simple receptive fields in cat striate cortex. *J. Neurophysiol.*, 58:1187–1211.

Julesz, B. (1962). Visual pattern discrimination. *IRE Transactions on Information Theory*, IT-8:84–92.

Julesz, B. (1964). Binocular depth perception without familiarity cues. *Science*, 145:356–362.

Julesz, B. (1971). *Foundations of Cyclopean Perception*. Chicago University Press, Chicago.

Julesz, B. (1975). Experiments in the visual perception of texture. *Sci. Am.*, 232:34–43.

Julesz, B. (1981). Textons, the elements of texture perception, and their interactions. *Nature*, 290:696–698.

Julesz, B. (1986). Texton gradients: The texton theory revisited. *Biological Cybernetics*, 54:245–251.

Julesz, B. (1991a). Early vision and focal attention. *Reviews of Modern Physics*, 63:735–772.

Julesz, B. (1991b). Some strategic questions in visual perception. In Gorea, A., (Ed.), *Representations of Vision: Trends and Tacit Assumptions in Vision Research*, pp. 331–349. Cambridge University Press, Cambridge, England. Proceedings of 13th European Conference on Visual Perception (ECVP) September 4-7, 1990 Paris, France.

Julesz, B. and Bergen, J. R. (1983). Textons, the fundamental elements in preattentive vision and perception of textures. *Bell Syst. Tech. Jour.*, 62:1619–45.

Julesz, B. and Johnson, S. C. (1968). Stereograms portraying ambiguously perceivable surfaces. *Proc. Nat. Acad. Sci. USA*, 61:437–441.

Julesz, B. and Kovacs, I. (1992). Stereopsis is not colorblind (except for green). *Invest. Opthal. Vis. Sci.*, 33 (Suppl.):1332.

Julesz, B. and Kröse, B. (1988). Visual texture perception: features and spatial filters. *Nature*, 333:302–303.

Kass, M. and Witkin, A. (1988). Analyzing oriented patterns. In Richards, W., (Ed.), *Natural Computation*. MIT Press, Cambridge, Mass.

Kass, M., Witkin, A., and Terzopoulos, D. (1987). Snakes: Active contour models. In *Proc. First International Conference on Computer Vision*, pp. 259–268, London, England.

Kass, M., Witkin, A., and Terzopoulos, D. (1988). Snakes: Active contour models. *Int. J. Comp. Vis.*, 1:321–331.

Kayama, Y., Riso, J., Bartlett, J., and Doty, R. (1979). Luxotonic responses of units in macaque striate cortex. *J. Neurophysiol.*, 42:1495.

Kendall, D. G. (1989). A survey of the statistical theory of shape. *Statistical Sci.*, 4:87–120.

Kendall, D. G. and Kendall, W. S. (1980). Alignments in two-dimensional random sets of points. *Adv. Appl. Prob.*, 12:380–424.

Kertesz, A. E. (1972). The effect of stimulus complexity on human cyclofusional response. *Vision Res.*, 12:699–704.

Kertesz, A. E. and Jones, R. W. (1969). The effect of angular velocity of stimulus on human torsional eye movements. *Vision Res.*, 9:995–8.

Kertesz, A. E. and Sullivan, M. J. (1978). The effect of stimulus size on human cyclofusional response. *Vision Res.*, 18:567–571.

Kimura, M., Komatsu, Y., and Toyama, K. (1980). Differential responses of simple and complex cells of cats striate cortex during saccadic eye-movements. *Vis. Res.*, 20:553–556.

Kleffner, D. A. and Ramachandran, V. S. (1992). On the perception of shape from shading. *Percept. Psychophys.* (in press).

Klein, S. A. (1989). Visual multipoles and the assessment of visual sensitivity to displayed images. In *Human Vision, Visual Processing, and Digital Display, SPIE Proceedings 1077*, pp. 83–92.

Klein, S. A. (1991). The duality of psycho-physics. In Gorea, A., (Ed.), *Representations of Vision. Trends and Tacit Assumptions in Vision Research*, pp. 231–249. Cambridge University Press, Cambridge, England.

Klein, S. A. (1992). Channels: bandwidth, channel independence, detection vs. discrimination. In Blum, (Ed.), *Channels in the visual nervous system: Neurophysiology, psychophysics and models.* Freund Publishing House Ltd., London.

Klein, S. A. and Beutter, B. (1992). Minimizing and maximizing the joint space-spatial frequency uncertainty of Gabor-like functions: comment. *J. Opt. Soc. Am. A*, 9:337–340.

Klein, S. A., Casson, E., and Carney, T. (1990). Vernier acuity as line and dipole detection. *Vision Res.*, 30:1703–1719.

Klein, S. A. and Levi, D. M. (1985). Hyperacuity thresholds of one second: theoretical predictions and empirical validation. *J. Opt. Soc. Am. A*, 2:1170–1190.

Klein, S. A. and Levi, D. M. (1987). Position sense of the peripheral retina. *J. Opt. Soc. Am. A*, 4:1543–1553.

Klein, S. A. and Tyler, C. W. (1986). Phase discrimination of compound gratings: generalized autocorrelation analysis. *J. Opt. Soc. Am. A*, 3:868–879.

Klein, S. A. and Tyler, C. W. (1992). The psychophysics of visual detection: A review of Graham's "Visual Pattern Analyzers". *J. Math. Psych.* (In press).

Knill, D. C. and Kersten, D. K. (1991). Ideal perceptual observers for computation, psychophysics and neural networks. In Watt, R., (Ed.), *Pattern Recognition by Man and Machine.* MacMillan, London.

Koch, C. and Ullman, S. (1985). Shifts in selective visual attention: towards the underlying neural circuitry. *Human Neurobiology*, 4:219–227.

Koenderink, J. J. and van Doorn, A. J. (1981). Exterospecific component of the motion parallax field. *J. Opt. Soc. Am. A*, 71:953–957.

Koffka, K. (1935). *Principles of Gestalt Psychology.* Harcourt, Brace and Wood, New York, NY.

Kohonen, T. (1982). Self-organized formation of topologically correct feature maps. *Biol. Cyber.*, 43:59–69.

Kolers, P. and von Gruneau, M. (1976). Shape and color in apparent motion. *Vision Res.*, 16:329–335.

Kooi, F. L. (1990). *The Analysis of Two-Dimensional Luminance and Color Motion Perception.* PhD thesis, University of California, Berkeley, CA.

Kooi, F. L., De Valois, K. K., Switkes, E., and Grosof, D. H. (1992). High-order factors influencing the perception of sliding and coherence of a plaid. *Perception*, 21:583–598..

Krauskopf, J., Williams, D. R., and Heeley, D. W. (1982). The cardinal directions of color space. *Vision Res.*, 22:1123–1131.

Krekling, S. (1973). Comments on cyclofusional eye movements. *Albrecht v Graefes Arch. Ophthal.*, 188:231–38.

Krishnan, G. (1988). *Segmentation and Interpretation of Line Drawings.* PhD thesis, State University of New York at Buffalo.

Krishnan, G. and Walters, D. K. W. (1988). Segmenting intersecting and incomplete boundaries. In *SPIE Applications of Artificial Intelligence VI*, pp. 550–555, Orlando, FL.

Kröse, B. J. A. (1987). Local structure analysers as determinants of preattentive pattern discrimination. *Biol. Cybern.*, 55:289–298.

Kröse, B. J. A. and Julesz, B. (1989). The control and speed of shifts of attention. *Vision Res.*, 29:1607–1619.

Krotkov, E., Brown, C., and Crowley, J. (1992). Active computer vision. In *Tutorial Session M5 Notes, IEEE Int. Conf. on Robotics and Automation*, Nice, France.

Kulikowski, J. J. and Bishop, P. O. (1981). Linear analysis of the response of simple cells in the cat visual cortex. *Exp. Brain Res.*, 44:386–400.

Landy, M. S. and Bergen, J. R. (1991). Texture segregation and orientation gradient. *Vision Res.*, 31:679–691.

Lappin, J. S. and Love, S. R. (1992). Planar motion permits perception of metric structure in stereopsis. *Percept. Psychophys.*, 51:86–102.

le Cun, Y., Boser, B., Denker, J., Henderson, D., Howard, R., Hubbard, W., and Jackel, L. (1990). Handwritten digit recognition with a back-propagation network. In *Advances in Neural Information Processing Systems 2*, pp. 396–404, Los Altos, CA. Morgan Kaufmann.

Leclerc, Y. G. (1989). Constructing simple stable descriptions for image partitioning. *IJCV*, 3:73–102.

Lee, H.-C. (1986). Method for computing the scene illuminant chromaticity from specular highlights. *J. Opt. Soc. Am. A*, 3:1694–1699.

Lee, H.-C. (1989). A computational model of human color encoding. Technical report, Eastman Kodak Report, Imaging Science Laboratory.

Lee, S. H., Haralick, R. M., and Zhang, M. C. (1985). Understanding objects with curved surfaces from a single perspective veiw of boundaries. *Art. Intell.*, 26:145–169.

Legge, G. E. (1981). A power law for contrast discrimination. *Vision Res.*, 21:457–469.

Legge, G. E. and Foley, J. M. (1980). Contrast masking in human vision. *J. Opt. Soc. Am.*, 70:1458–1470.

Leigh, R. J., Maas, E. F., Grossman, G. E., and Robinson, D. A. (1989). Visual cancellation of the torsional vestibulo-ocular reflex in humans. *Exp. Brain Res.*, 75:221–26.

Lettvin, J., Maturana, H. R., McCulloch, W. S., and Pitts, W. U. (1959). What the frog's eye tells the frog's brain. *Proc. Inst. Rad. Eng.*, 47:1940–1951.

Levi, D. M. and Klein, S. A. (1990). The role of separation and eccentricity in encoding position. *Vision Res.*, 30:557–585.

Levi, D. M. and Klein, S. A. (1992a). The role of local contrast in the visual deficits of humans with naturally occurring amblyopia. *Neurosci. Letters*, 136:63–66.

Levi, D. M. and Klein, S. A. (1992b). "Weber's law" for position: the role of spatial frequency and contrast. *Vision Res.*, 32:2235–2250.

Levi, D. M., Klein, S. A., and Aitsebaomo, P. (1985). Vernier acuity, crowding and cortical magnification. *Vision Res.*, 25:963–977.

Linsker, R. (1986). From basic network principles to neural architecture. *Proc. Nat. Acad. Sci, USA*, 83:7508–7512, 8390–8394, 8779–8783.

Livingstone, M. S. and Hubel, D. H. (1984). Anatomy and physiology of a color system in the primate visual cortex. *J. Neurosci.*, 4:309–356.

Livingstone, M. S. and Hubel, D. H. (1987). Psychophysical evidence for separate channels for the perception of form, color, movement, and depth. *J. Neurosci.*, 7:3416–3468.

Loop, C. and DeRose, T. (1990). Generalized B-spline surfaces of arbitrary topology. *Computer Graphics (SIGGRAPH'90)*, 24:347–356.

Lowe, D. G. (1985). *Perceptual Organization and Visual Recognition*. Kluwer Academic Publishers, Boston, Mass.

Lu, C. and Fender, D. H. (1972). The interaction of color and luminance in stereoscopic vision. *Invest. Ophthal. Visual. Sci.*, 11:482–489.

Lucas, B. D. and Kanade, T. (1981). An iterative image registration technique with an application to stereo vision. In *Proceedings of the 7th International Joint Conference on Artificial Intelligence*, pp. 674–679, Vancouver.

MacAdam, D. L. (1970). *Sources of color science*. MIT Press, Cambridge, Mass.

MacKay, D. M. (1976). Perceptual conflict between visual motion and change of location. *Vision Res.*, 16:557–558.

MacKay, D. M. (1978). The dynamics of perception. In Rougeul-Buser, P. B. A., (Ed.), *Cerebral Correlates of Conscious Experience*. Elsevier, Amsterdam.

MacKay, D. M. (1985). The significance of 'feature sensitivity'. In Rose, D. and Dobson, V., (Eds.), *Models of the Visual Cortex*. Wiley, New York, NY.

Maguire, W. and Bazier, J. (1982). Luminance coding of briefly presented stimuli in area 17 of the rhesus monkey. *J. Neurophysiol.*, 47:128–137.

Malik, J. M. A. (1987). Interpreting line drawings of curved objects. *Int. J. Comp. Vis.*, 1:73–103.

Malik, J. M. A. and Perona, P. (1990). Preattentive texture discrimination with early vision mechanisms. *J. Opt. Soc. Am. A*, 7:923–932.

Mallat, S. G. (1987). A theory for multiresolution signal decomposition: the wavelet representation. *IEEE Trans. PAMI*, 11:674–693.

Mansouri, A., Malowany, A., and Levine, M. (1987). Line detection in digital pictures: A hypothesis prediction/verification paradigm. *CVGIP*, 40:95–114.

Maragos, P. (1987). Tutorial on advances in morphological image processing and analysis. *Optical Engineering*, 26:623–632.

Marmarelis, P. Z. and Marmarelis, V. A. (1978). *Analysis of physiological systems: the white noise approach*. Plenum Press, New York, NY.

Marr, D. (1970). A theory of cerebral neocortex. *Proc. R. Soc. Lond. B*, 176:161–234.

Marr, D. (1978). Representing visual information. In Hanson, A. R. and Riseman, E. M., (Eds.), *Computer Vision Systems*, pp. 61–80. Academic Press, New York, NY.

Marr, D. (1982). *Vision*. W. H. Freeman and Company, San Francisco, CA.

Marr, D. and Hildreth, E. C. (1980). Theory of edge detection. *Proc. Roy. Soc. Lond. B*, 207:187–217.

Marshall, J. (1990). Adaptive neural methods for multiplexing oriented edges. In *Proceedings of the SPIE Symposium on Advances in Intelligent Systems*, Boston, Mass.

Matthies, L. H., Szeliski, R., and Kanade, T. (1989). Kalman filter-based algorithms for estimating depth from image sequences. *Int. J. Comp. Vis.*, 3:209–236.

Maunsell, J. H. and Van Essen, D. C. (1983). Functional properties of neurons in middle temporal visual area of the macaque monkey. 1. Selectivity for stimulus direction, speed and orientation. *J. Neurophysiol.*, 49:1127–1147.

Maunsell, J. H. R. (1987). Physiological evidence for two visual subsystems. In Vaina, L. M., (Ed.), *Matters of Intelligence*, pp. 59–87. D. Reidel Pub. Co., Norwell, MA.

Maunsell, J. H. R. and Newsome, W. T. (1987). Visual processing in monkey extrastriate cortex. *Ann. Rev. Neurosci.*, 10:363–401.

Maunsell, J. H. R., Sclar, G., and Nealey, T. (1988). Task-specific signals in area V4 of monkey visual cortex. *Society of Neuroscience Abstracts*, 8.4:10.

Mayer, M. J. and Kim, C. B. (1986). Smooth frequency discrimination functions for foveal high-contrast, mid spatial frequencies. *J. Opt. Soc. Am. A*, 3:1957–1969.

Mayhew, J., Frisby, J., and Gale, P. (1981). Psychophysical and computational studies towards a theory of human stereopsis. *Art. Intell.*, 17:349–385.

McCarthy, J. (1980). Circumscription – a form of non-monotonic reasoning. *Art. Intell.*, 13:27–39.

McDermott, D. and Doyle, J. (1980). Non-monotonic logic. *Art. Intell.*, 13:41–72.

McFarlan, D. (1991). *Guinness Book of World Records*. Bantam Books, New York, NY.

McGuinness, E., MacDonald, C., Sereno, M., and Allman, J. (1986). Primates without blobs: The distribution of cytochrome oxidase activity in striate cortex of *tarsius, hapalemur*, and *cheirogaleus*. *Soc. Neurosci. Abstr.*, 12:130.

McKee, S. P. (1981). A local mechanism for differential velocity discrimination. *Vision Res.*, 21:491–500.

McLean, J. and Palmer, L. A. (1989). Contribution of linear spatiotemporal receptive field structure to velocity selectivity of simple cells in area 17 of cat. *Vision Res.*, 29:675–679.

Merigan, W. H., Byrne, C. E., and Maunsell, J. H. R. (1991a). Does primate motion perception depend on the magnocellular pathway? *J. Neurosci.* (in press).

Merigan, W. H., Katz, L. M., and Maunsell, J. H. R. (1991b). The effects of parvocellular lateral geniculate lesions on the acuity and contrast sensitivity of macaque monkeys. *J. Neurosci.*, 11:994–1001.

Merigan, W. H. and Maunsell, J. H. R. (1990). Macaque vision after magnocellular lateral geniculate lesions. *Vis. Neurosci.*, 5:347–352.

Middleton, D. (1987). *An Introduction to Statistical Communication Theory*. Peninsula Publishing, Los Altos, CA.

Miller, R. and Stout, Q. (1992). *Parallel Algorithms for Regular Structures*. MIT Press, Cambridge, Mass.

Miller, W. H. (1979). Ocular optical filtering. In Autrum, H., (Ed.), *Handbook of Sensory Physiology, vol. 6A*. Springer-Verlag, Berlin.

Mishkin, M., Ungerleider, L. G., and Macko, K. A. (1983). Object vision and spatial vision: two cortical pathways. *Trends in Neurosci.*, 6:414–417.

Mjolsness, E. (1990). Bayesian inference on visual grammars by neural nets that optimize. Technical Report YALEU-DCS-TR-854, Dept. of Computer Science, Yale University.

Moran, J. and Desimone, R. (1985). Selective attention gates visual processing in the extrastriate cortex. *Science*, 229:782–784.

Morgan, M. J. and Aiba, T. S. (1986). Vernier acuity predicted from changes in the light distribution of the retinal image. *Spatial Vision*, 1:151–161.

Morgan, M. J. and Regan, D. (1987). Opponent model for line interval discrimination: interval and vernier performances compared. *Vision Res.*, 27:107–118.

Morgan, M. J. and Ward, R. (1980). Conditions for motion flow in dynamic visual noise. *Vision Res.*, 20:431–435.

Morrone, M. C., Burr, D. C., and Maffei, L. (1982). Functional implications of cross-orientation inhibition of cortical visual cells. I. Neurophysiological evidence. *Proc. Roy. Soc. Lond. B*, 216:335–354.

Motter, B. (1988). Responses of visual cortical neurons during a focal attentive task. *Society of Neuroscience Abstracts*, 8.3:10.

Motter, B. C. and Mountcastle, V. B. (1981). The functional properties of the light-sensitive neurons of the posterior parietal cortex studied in waking monkeys: foveal sparing and opponent vector organization. *J. Neurosci.*, 1:3–26.

Mountcastle, V. B. (1979). An organizing principle for cerebral functions: the unit module and the distributed system. In Schmidt, F. and Woden, F., (Eds.), *The Neuroscience Third Study Program*, pp. 21–42. Plenum Press, New York, NY.

Mountcastle, V. B., Motter, B., Steinmetz, M., and Sestokas, A. (1987). Common and differential effects of attentive fixation on the excitability of parietal and prestriate (V4) cortical visual neurons in the macaque monkey. *J. Neurosci.*, 7:2239–2255.

Movshon, J. A., Adelson, E. H., Gizzi, M. S., and Newsome, W. T. (1986). The analysis of moving visual patterns. In Chagas, C., Gattass, R., and Gross, C., (Eds.), *Exp. Brain Res. Suppl. II: Pattern Recognition Mechanisms*, pp. 117–151. Springer-Verlag, New York, NY.

Movshon, J. A., Thompson, I. D., and Tolhurst, D. J. (1978). Spatial summation in the receptive fields of simple cells in the cat's striate cortex. *J. Physiol. (Lond.)*, 283:53–77.

Mullen, K. T. (1985). The contrast sensitivity of human colour vision to red-green and blue-yellow chromatic gratings. *J. Physiol. (Lond.)*, 359:382–400.

Nachmias, J. and Rogowitz, B. (1983). Masking by spatially-modulated gratings. *Vision Res.*, 23:1621–1629.

Nachmias, J. and Sansbury, R. V. (1974). Grating contrast: discrimination may be better than detection. *Vision Res.*, 14:1039–1042.

Nagel, A. (1868). Über das Vorkommen von wahren Rollungen des Auges um die Gesichtslinie. *Albrecht von Graefes Arch Ophthal*, 14:228–246.

Nagel, H. H. (1987). On the estimation of optical flow: relations between different approaches and some new results. *Art. Intell.*, 33:299–324.

Nagel, T. (1974). What is it like to be a bat? *Philosophical Review*, 83:435–450. reprinted in *The Mind's I*, D. R. Hofstadter and D. C. Dennett (Eds.), Bantam Books, New York, NY (1981).

Nakayama, K. (1977). Geometric and physiological aspects of depth perception. In *Proc. SPIE*, volume 120, pp. 2–9.

Nakayama, K. (1985). Biological image motion processing: A review. *Vision Res.*, 25:625–660.

Nakayama, K. and Mackeben, M. (1989). Sustained and transient components of focal visual attention. *Vision Res.*, 29:1631–1647.

Nakayama, K. and Shimojo, S. (1990). Towards a neural understanding of visual surface representation. *Cold Spring Harbor Symposia on Quantitative Biology*, 55:911–924.

Nakayama, K. and Silverman, G. H. (1986). Serial and parallel processing of visual feature conjunctions. *Nature*, 320:264–265.

Nakayama, K. and Silverman, G. H. (1988). The aperture problem — I. Perception of nonrigidity and motion direction in translating sinusoid lines. *Vision Res.*, 28:739–746.

Nakayama, K. and Tyler, C. W. (1981). Psychophysical isolation of movement sensitivity by removal of familiar position cues. *Vision Res.*, 21:427–433.

Nevatia, R. and Babu, K. R. (1980). Linear feature extraction and description. *Computer Graphics and Image Processing*, 13:257–269.

Newsome, W. T. and Pare, E. B. (1988). A selective impairment of motion perception following lesions of the middle temporal visual area (mt). *J. Neurosci.*, 8:2201–2211.

Ogle, K. N. (1946). The binocular depth contrast phenomenon. *Amer. J. Psychol.*, 59:111–126.

Ogle, K. N. and Ellerbrock, V. J. (1946). Cyclofusional movements. *AMA Arch Ophthal*, 36:700–735.

Oliver, B. M. (1952). Efficient coding. *Bell System Technical Journal*, 31:724–750.

Osterberg, F. (1935). Topography of the layer of rods and cones in the human retina. *Acta Ophthal. Supplementum*, 6:1–103.

Papathomas, T. V., Gorea, A., and Julesz, B. (1990). Juxtaposition of orientation, luminance and polarity in perceptual grouping. *Invest. Ophthal. Vis. Sci.*, 31 (Suppl.):105.

Papathomas, T. V., Gorea, A., and Julesz, B. (1991). Two carriers for motion perception: color and luminance. *Vision Res.*, 31:1883–1892.

Papathomas, T. V., Gorea, A., Julesz, B., and Chang, J. J. (1988). The relative strength of depth and orientation in motion perception. *Invest. Ophthal. Vis. Sci.*, 29 (Suppl.):401.

Parent, P. and Zucker, S. W. (1989). Trace inference, curvature consistency and curve detection. *IEEE Trans. PAMI*, 11:823–839.

Parisi, G. (1988). *Statistical Field Theory*. Addison-Wesley, Reading, Mass.

Pearl, J. (1988). *Probabilistic Reasoning in Intelligent Systems: Networks of Plausible Inference*. Morgan Kaufmann, Los Altos, CA.

Penrose, R. (1989). *The Emperor's New Mind*. Oxford University Press, Oxford, England.

Pentland, A. P. (1986). Perceptual organization and the representation of natural form. *Art. Intell.*, 28:293–331.

Pentland, A. P. (1987). A new sense for depth of field. *IEEE Trans. PAMI*, 9:523–531.

Pentland, A. P. (1989). Local shading analysis. In Horn, B. and Brooks, M., (Eds.), *Shape from Shading*. MIT Press, Cambridge, Mass.

Pentland, A. P. (1991). Cue integration and surface completion. *Invest. Ophthal. Vis. Sci.*, 32 (Suppl.).

Perrett, D. I., Rolls, E. T., and Caan, W. (1982). Visual neurons responsive to faces in the monkey temporal cortex. *Exp. Brain Res.*, 47:329–342.

Perrone, J. A. (1990). Simple technique for optical flow estimation. *J. Opt. Soc. Am. A*, 7:264–278.

Petrov, A. P. and Zenkin, G. M. (1973). Torsional eye movements and constancy of the visual field. *Vision Res.*, 13:2465–2477.

Phillips, G. C. and Wilson, H. R. (1984). Orientation bandwidths of spatial mechanisms measured by masking. *J. Opt. Soc. Am. A*, 1:226–232.

Poggio, G. and Poggio, T. (1984). The analysis of stereopsis. *Ann. Rev. Neurosci*, 7:379–412.

Poggio, T. (1990). 3D object recognition: on a result of Basri and Ullman. Technical Report 9005-03, IRST, Povo, Italy.

Poggio, T., Gamble, E., and Little, J. (1988). Parallel integration of vision modules. *Science*, 242:436–440.

Poggio, T., Little, J., Gamble, E., Gillett, W., Geiger, D., Weinshall, D., Villalba, M., Larson, N., Cass, T., Bülthoff, H. H., Drumheller, M., Oppenheimer, P., Yang, W., and Hurlbert, A. (1990). The MIT Vision Machine. In Winston, P. H. and Shellard, S. A., (Eds.), *Artificial Intelligence at MIT: Expanding Frontiers — Volume 2*, pp. 492–529. MIT Press, Cambridge, Mass.

Poggio, T., Torre, V., and Koch, C. (1985). Computational vision and regularization theory. *Nature*, 317:314–318.

Pollen, D. A. and Ronner, S. F. (1981). Phase relationships between adjacent simple cells in the visual cortex. *Science*, 212:1409–1411.

Posner, M. I. (1978). *Chronometric explorations of the mind.* Lawrence Erlbaum Assoc., Hillsdale, NJ.

Posner, M. I. (1980). Orienting of attention. *Q. J. Exp. Psych.*, 32:3–25.

Poston, T. and Stewart, I. (1981). *Catastrophe Theory and Its Applications.* Pitman, London.

Ramachandran, V. S. (1987). Interaction between colour and motion in human vision. *Nature*, 328:645–647.

Ramachandran, V. S. (1988). Perception of shape from shading. *Nature*, 331:163–166.

Ramachandran, V. S. and Anstis, S. M. (1983). Displacement thresholds for coherent apparent motion random dot patterns. *Vision Res.*, 24:1719–1724.

Ramachandran, V. S. and Anstis, S. M. (1986). Perception of apparent motion. *Sci. Am.*, 254:102–109.

Ramachandran, V. S. and Anstis, S. M. (1990). Illusory displacement of equiluminant kinetic edges. *Perception*, 19:611–616.

Ramachandran, V. S. and Gregory, R. L. (1978). Does color provide an input to human motion perception? *Nature*, 275:55–56.

Regan, D. (1982). Visual information channeling in normal and disordered vision. *Psych. Rev.*, 89:407–444.

Regan, D. (1985). Masking of spatial frequency discrimination. *J. Opt. Soc. Am. A*, 2:1153–1159.

Regan, D. (1986a). Form from motion parallax and form from luminance contrast: Vernier discrimination. *Spatial Vision*, 1:305–318.

Regan, D. (1986b). Visual processing of four kinds of relative motion. *Vision Res.*, 26:127–145.

Regan, D. (1989a). Orientation discrimination and shape discrimination for motion-defined targets. *Invest. Ophthal. Vis. Sci.*, 30 (Suppl.):263.

Regan, D. (1989b). Orientation discrimination for objects defined by relative motion and objects defined by luminance contrast. *Vision Res.*, 29:1389–1400.

Regan, D. (1989c). *Human Brain Electrophysiology.* Elsevier, New York, NY.

Regan, D. (1991a). A brief review of some of the stimuli and analysis methods used in spatiotemporal vision research. In Regan, D., (Ed.), *Spatial Vision*, pp. 1–42. Macmillan, Boca Raton.

Regan, D. (1991b). Detection and spatial discriminations for objects defined by colour contrast, binocular disparity and motion parallax. In Regan, D., (Ed.), *Spatial Vision*, pp. 135–178. Macmillan, Boca Raton.

Regan, D., Bartol, S., Murray, T. J., and Beverley, K. I. (1982). Spatial frequency discrimination in normal vision and in patients with multiple sclerosis. *Brain*, 105:735–754.

Regan, D. and Beverley, K. I. (1978). Looming detectors in the human visual pathway. *Vision Res.*, 18:415–421.

Regan, D. and Beverley, K. I. (1980). Visual responses to changing size and to sideways motion for different directions of motion in depth: linearization of visual responses. *J. Opt. Soc. Am.*, 70:1289–1296.

Regan, D. and Beverley, K. I. (1982). How do we avoid confounding the direction we are looking and the direction we are moving? *Science*, 215:194–196.

Regan, D. and Beverley, K. I. (1983). Spatial frequency discrimination and detection: Comparison of postadaptation thresholds. *J. Opt. Soc. Am.*, 73:1684–1690.

Regan, D. and Beverley, K. I. (1984). Figure-ground segregation by motion contrast and by luminance contrast. *J. Opt. Soc. Am. A*, 1:433–442.

Regan, D. and Beverley, K. I. (1985). Postadaptation orientation discrimination. *J. Opt. Soc. Am. A*, 2:147–155.

Regan, D. and Cynader, M. (1979). Neurons in cat area 18 visual cortex selectively sensitive to changing size: nonlinear interactions between responses to two edges. *Vision Res.*, 19:699–711.

Regan, D., Erkelens, C. J., and Collewijn, H. (1986a). Necessary conditions for the perception of motion in depth. *Invest. Ophthal. Vis. Sci.*, 27:584–597.

Regan, D., Erkelens, C. J., and Collewijn, H. (1986b). Visual field defects for vergence eye movements and for stereomotion perception. *Invest. Ophthal. Vis. Sci.*, 27:806–819.

Regan, D., Giaschi, D., Sharpe, J. A., and Hong, X. H. (1992). Visual processing of motion-defined form: selective failure in patients with parieto-temporal lesions. *J. Neurosci.*, 12:2198–2210.

Regan, D. and Hamstra, S. (1990). Shape and orientation discrimination for motion-defined and contrast-defined objects: Temporal integration. *Invest. Ophthal. Vis. Sci.*, 31 (Suppl.):2578.

Regan, D. and Hamstra, S. (1991). Shape discrimination for motion-defined and contrast-defined form: Squareness is special. *Perception*, 20:315–336.

Regan, D. and Hamstra, S. (1992). Dissociation of orientation discrimination from form detection for motion-defined bars and luminance-defined bars: effects of dot lifetime and presentation duration. *Vision Res.*, 32:1655–1666.

Regan, D. and Hong, H. X. (1990). Visual acuity for optotypes made visible by relative motion. *Opt. Vis. Sci.*, 67:49–55.

Regan, D., Kothe, A., and Sharpe, J. (1991). Recognition of motion-defined shapes in patients with multiple sclerosis and optic neuritis. *Brain*, 114:1129–1155.

Regan, D. and Price, P. (1986). Periodicity in orientation discrimination and the unconfounding of visual information. *Vision Res.*, 26:1299–1302.

Regan, D. and Spekreijse, H. (1970). Electrophysiological correlate of binocular depth perception in man. *Nature*, 255:92–94.

Rehg, J. and Witkin, A. (1991). Visual tracking with deformation models. In *IEEE International Conference on Robotics and Automation*, pp. 844–850, Sacramento, California. IEEE Computer Society Press.

Reichardt, W. (1961). Autocorrelation, a principle for the evaluation of sensory information by the central nervous system. In Rosenblith, W. A., (Ed.), *Sensory Communication*, pp. 303–317. Wiley, New York, NY.

Reichardt, W. (1986). Processing of optical information by the visual system of the fly. *Vision Res.*, 26:113–126.

Reichardt, W., Poggio, T., and Hausen, K. (1983a). Figure ground discrimination by relative movement in the fly. Part II. *Biol. Cybernet.*, 46:1–15.

Reichardt, W., Poggio, T., and Hausen, K. (1983b). Figure ground discrimination by relative movement in the fly. Part III. *Biol. Cybernet.*, 35:81–100.

Reiter, R. (1980). A logic for default reasoning. *Art. Intell.*, 13:81–132.

Remington, R. and Pierce, L. (1984). Moving Attention: Evidence for time-invariant shifts of visual selective attention. *Percept. Psychophys.*, 35:393–399.

Reuman, S. and Hoffman, D. (1986). Regularities of nature: the interpretation of visual motion. In Pentland, A. P., (Ed.), *From Pixels to Predicates*. Ablex, Norwood, NJ.

Richards, W. (1971). Motion detection in man and other animals. *Brain Behaviour and Evolution*, 4:162–181.

Richards, W. (1975). Visual space perception. In Carterette, E. and Friedman, M. P., (Eds.), *Handbook of Perception, Vol. V: Seeing*, chapter 10, pp. 351–386. Academic Press, New York, NY.

Richards, W. and Regan, D. (1973). A stereo field map with implications for disparity processing. *Invest. Ophthal. Vis. Sci.*, 12:904–909.

Risannen, J. (1983). A universal prior for integers and estimation by minimum description length. *Annals of Statistics*, 11:416–431.

Roberts, L. G. (1965). Machine perception of three-dimensional objects. In Tippett, J. P., (Ed.), *Optical and Electro-optical Information Processing*. MIT Press, Cambridge, Mass.

Robinson, D. A. (1963). A method of measuring eye movement using a scleral search coil in a magnetic field. *IEEE Trans Bio-Med Engin*, BME-10:137–145.

Robson, J. G. (1988). Linear and nonlinear operations in the visual system. *Invest. Ophthal. Vis. Sci.*, 29 (Suppl.):117.

Rodman, H. R. and Albright, T. D. (1987). Coding of visual stimulus velocity in area mt of the macaque. *Vision Res.*, 27:2035–2048.

Rodman, H. R. and Albright, T. D. (1989). Single-unit analysis of pattern-motion selective properties in the middle temporal visual area (mt). *Exp. Brain Res.*, 75:53–64.

Rogers, B. J. and Howard, I. P. (1991). Differences in the mechanisms used to extract 3-D slant from disparity and motion parallax cues. *Invest. Ophthal. Vis. Sci.*, 32 (Suppl.):697.

Rose, D. and Dobson, V. G. (1985). *Models of the Visual Cortex.* Wiley, New York, NY.

Rosenfeld, A. (1979). *Picture Languages.* Academic Press, New York, NY.

Rosenfeld, A. (1986). Axial representations of shape. *CVGIP*, 33:156–173.

Rosenfeld, A. and Kak, A. C. (1982). *Digital Picture Processing.* Academic Press, New York, NY.

Rubenstein, B. and Sagi, D. (1990). Spatial variability as a limiting factor in texture-discrimination tasks: implications for performance asymmetries. *J. Opt. Soc. Am. A.*, 9:1632–1643.

Saarinen, J. and Julesz, B. (1991). The speed of attentional shifts in the visual field. *Proc. Nat. Acad. Sci. USA*, 88:1812–1814.

Sachs, M. B., Nachmias, J., and Robson, J. G. (1971). Spatial frequency channels in human vision. *J. Opt. Soc. Am.*, 61:1176–1186.

Sagi, D. and Julesz, B. (1985). "Where" and "what" in vision. *Science*, 228:1217–1219.

Saito, H., Yukie, M., Tanaka, K., Hikosaka, K., Fukada, Y., and Iwai, E. (1986). Integration of direction signals of image motion in the superior temporal sulcus of the macaque monkey. *J. Neurosci.*, 6:145–157.

Salmon, W. (1967). *The Foundations of Scientific Inference.* Univ. Pitts. Press, Pittsburg, PA.

Schiller, P. H., Logothetis, N. K., and Charles, E. R. (1990). Functions of the color-opponent and broad-band channels of the visual system. *Nature*, 343:68–70.

Schlag, J., Schlag-Rey, M., Peck, C. K., and Joseph, J. P. (1980). Visual responses of thalamic neurons depending on the direction of gaze and the position of targets in space. *Exp. Brain Res.*, 40:170–184.

Sclar, G., Lennie, P., and DePriest, D. (1989). Contrast adaptation in striate cortex of macaque. *Vision Res.*, 29:747–755.

Sclar, G., Maunsell, J. H. R., and Lennie, P. (1990). Coding of image contrast in central visual pathways of the macaque monkey. *Vision Res.*, 30:1–10.

Searle, J. R. (1980). Minds, brains, and programs. with open peer commentaries. *The Behavioral and Brain Sciences*, 3:417–457. reprinted with a provocative commentary by Hofstadter in *The Mind's I*, D. R. Hofstadter and D. C. Dennett (Eds.), Bantam Books, New York, NY (1981).

Searle, J. R. (1984). *Minds, Brains and Science.* Harvard University Press, Cambridge, Mass.

Searle, J. R. (1990a). Is the brain a digital computer? In *Presidential Address at Sixty-fourth Annual Pacific Division Meeting of the American Philosophical Association*, pp. 21–37, Los Angeles, CA.

Searle, J. R. (1990b). Is the brain's mind a computer program? *Sci. Am.*, 262:26–31.

Seebeck, A. (1841). Beohachtungen über einige Bedingungen der Entstehung von Tönen. *Annalen der Physik und Chemie*, 53:417–436.

Serra, J. (1982). *Image Analysis and Mathematical Morphology.* Academic Press, New York, NY.

Shafer, S. A. (1984). Using color to separate reflection components. *Color Res. & Appl.*, 10:210–218.

Shannon, C. E. and Weaver, W. (1949). *The Mathematical Theory of Communication.* Univ. of Illinois Press, Urbana, IL.

Shapley, R., Reid, R. C., and Soodak, R. (1991). Spatiotemporal receptive fields and direction selectivity. In Landy, M. and Movshon, J. A., (Eds.), *Computational Models of Visual Processing*, pp. 109–118. MIT Press, Cambridge, Mass.

Sheinberg, D., Bülthoff, H. H., and Blake, A. (1990). Shape from texture. *Perception*, 19:A87b.

Shen, X. and Howard, I. P. (1991). Optokinetic torsion: The effects of the area and position of the visual display. *Invest. Ophthal. Vis. Sci.*, 32 (Suppl.):1020.

Sherk, H. (1986). The claustrum and the cerebral cortex. In Jones, E. and Peters, A., (Eds.), *Cerebral cortex, vol. 5*, pp. 467–499. Plenum Press, New York, NY.

Shipley, T. and Rawlings (1970). The nonius horopter. I. History and theory. *Vision Res.*, 10:1225–1262.

Shulman, G., Remington, R., and McLean, J. (1979). Moving attention through visual space. *J. Exp. Psych.: Human Perception*, 5:522–526.

Siegel, R. M. and Andersen, R. A. (1988). Perception of three-dimensional structure from motion in monkey and man. *Nature*, 331:259–261.

Silverman, M., Grosof, D., DeValois, R., and Elfar, S. (1989). Spatial frequency organization in primate striate cortex. *Proc. Nat. Acad. Sci. (USA)*, 86:711.

Simoncelli, E. P. and Adelson, E. H. (1990). Non-separable extensions of quadrature mirror filters to multiple dimensions. *Proceedings of the IEEE*, 78:652–664.

Simoncelli, E. P. and Adelson, E. H. (1991a). Computation of optical flow: Relationship between several standard techniques. Technical report 165, vision and modeling group, MIT Media Lab.

Simoncelli, E. P. and Adelson, E. H. (1991b). Relationship between gradient, spatio-temporal energy, and regression models for motion perception. *Invest. Ophthal. Vis. Sci.*, 32 (Suppl.):893.

Simoncelli, E. P., Adelson, E. H., and Heeger, D. J. (1991). Probability distributions of optical flow. In *Proceedings of Computer Vision and Pattern Recognition*, pp. 310–315, Maui, HI.

Simoncelli, E. P. and Heeger, D. J. (1992). A computational model for perception of two-dimensional pattern velocities. *Invest. Ophthal. Vis. Sci.*, 33 (Suppl.):954.

Singh, A. (1990). An estimation-theoretic framework for image-flow computation. In *IEEE ICCV*, pp. 168–177, Osaka, Japan.

Skilling, J. (1991). Fundamentals of maximum entropy in data analysis. In Buck, B. and Macaulay, V., (Eds.), *Maximum Entropy in Action.* Oxford University Press, London.

Skottun, B. C., Bradley, A., Sclar, G., Ohzawa, I., and Freeman, R. D. (1987). The effects of contrast on visual orientation and spatial frequency discrimination: A comparison of single cells and behavior. *J. Neurophysiol.*, 57:773–786.

Snowden, R. J., Treue, S., Erickson, R. G., and Anderson, R. A. (1991). The response of area MT and V1 neurons to transparent motion. *J. Neuosci.*, 11:2768–2785.

Sober, E. (1975). *Simplicity*. Oxford University Press, London.

Spetsakis, M. E. (1988). Optimal computing of structure from motion using point correspondences in two frames. In *IEEE ICCV*, pp. 449–453, 684, Florida.

Spetsakis, M. E. (1991). Models of statistical visual motion estimation. Technical Report Tech. Rep. CS-91-06, Dept. of Computer Science, York University, North York.

Spitzer, H., Desimone, R., and Moran, J. (1988). Increased attention enhances both behavioral and neuronal performance. *Science*, 240:338–340.

Srinivasan, M. V., Laughlin, S. B., and Dubs, A. (1982). Predictive coding: a fresh view of inhibition in the retina. *Proc. Roy. Soc. Lond. B*, 216:427–459.

Stapp, H. P. (1972). The Copenhagen Interpretation. *Am. J. Phys.*, 40:1098–1116.

Stapp, H. P. (1990). A quantum theory of the mind-brain interface. Technical Report Report LBL-28574 expanded, Lawrence Berkeley Lab. This article will be published as the lead chapter in Stapp's forthcoming book entitled *Mind, Matter and Quantum Mechanics*, Springer-Verlag, Heidelberg, 1992.

Stensaas, S., Eddington, D., and Dobelle, W. (1974). The topography and variability of the primary visual cortex in man. *J. Neurosurgery*, 40:747–755.

Stevens, K. (1978). Computation of locally parallel structure. *Biol. Cybernetics*, 29:19–28.

Stone, L. S., Watson, A. B., and Mulligan, J. B. (1990). Effect of contrast on the perceived direction of a moving plaid. *Vision Res.*, 30:1049–1067.

Stromeyer III, C. F. and Julesz, B. (1972). Spatial frequency masking in vision: Critical bands and spread of masking. *J. Opt. Soc. Am.*, 62:1221–1232.

Stromeyer III, C. F. and Klein, S. A. (1974). Spatial frequency channels in human vision as asymmetric (edge) mechanisms. *Vision Res.*, 14:1409–1420.

Stromeyer III, C. F. and Klein, S. A. (1975). Evidence against narrow-band spatial frequency channels in vision: the detectability of frequency modulated gratings. *Vision Res.*, 15:899–910.

Sutter, A., Beck, J., and Graham, N. (1989). Contrast and spatial variables in texture segregation: testing a simple spatial frequency channels model. *Percept. Psychophys.*, 46:312–332.

Swain, M. . J. and Ballard, D. H. (1990). Color indexing. Technical Report Technical Report 360, Department of Computer Science, University of Rochester, Rochester, NY.

Swift, D. J. and Smith, R. A. (1983). Spatial frequency masking and Weber's law. *Vision Res.*, 23:495–505.

Switkes, E., Bradley, A., and De Valois, K. K. (1988). Contrast dependence and mechanisms of masking interactions among chromatic and luminance gratings. *J. Opt. Soc. Am. A*, 5:1149–1162.

Switkes, E., Bradley, A., and Schor, C. (1990). Readily visible changes in color contrast are insufficient to stimulate accommodation. *Vision Res.*, 30:1367–1376.

Szeliski, R. (1987). Regularization uses fractal priors. In *Sixth National Conference on Artificial Intelligence (AAAI-87)*, pp. 749–754, Seattle, Washington. Morgan Kaufmann Publishers.

Szeliski, R. (1989). *Bayesian Modeling of Uncertainty in Low-Level Vision*. Kluwer Academic Publishers, Boston, Mass.

Szeliski, R. (1990a). Fast surface interpolation using hierarchical basis functions. *IEEE Trans. PAMI*, 12:513–528.

Szeliski, R. (1990b). Real-time octree generation from rotating objects. Technical Report 90/12, Digital Equipment Corporation, Cambridge Research Lab.

Szeliski, R. (1991). Shape from rotation. In *IEEE CVPR*, pp. 625–630, Maui, Hawaii. IEEE Computer Society Press.

Szeliski, R. and Terzopoulos, D. (1989a). From splines to fractals. *Computer Graphics (SIGGRAPH'89)*, 23:51–60.

Szeliski, R. and Terzopoulos, D. (1989b). Parallel multigrid algorithms and computer vision applications. In *Fourth Copper Mountain Conference on Multigrid Methods*, pp. 383–398, Copper Mountain, Colorado. Society for Industrial and Applied Mathematics.

Szeliski, R. and Terzopoulos, D. (1991). Physically-based and probabilistic modeling for computer vision. In *SPIE Vol. 1570 Geometric Methods in Computer Vision*, pp. 140–152, San Diego, Calif. Society of Photo-Optical Instrumentation Engineers.

Szeliski, R. and Tonnesen, D. (1992). Surface modeling with oriented particle systems. In *SIGGRAPH*, pg. (to appear).

Tanaka, K., Fukada, Y., and Saito, H. (1989). Underlying mechanisms of the response specificity of expansion/contraction and rotation cells in the dorsal part of the medial superior temporal area of the macaque monkey. *J. Neurophysiol.*, 62:642–656.

Tanaka, K. and Saito, H. (1989). Analysis of motion in the visual field by direction, expansion/contraction and rotation cells clustered in the dorsal part of the medial superior temporal area of the macaque monkey. *J. Neurophysiol.*, 62:626–641.

Terzopoulos, D. (1986a). Image analysis using multigrid relaxation methods. *IEEE Trans. PAMI*, 8:129–139.

Terzopoulos, D. (1986b). Regularization of inverse visual problems involving discontinuities. *IEEE Trans. PAMI*, 8:413–424.

Terzopoulos, D. (1988). The computation of visible surface representations. *IEEE Trans. PAMI*, 10:417–439.

Terzopoulos, D. and Fleischer, K. (1988). Deformable models. *The Visual Computer*, 4:306–331.

Terzopoulos, D. and Metaxas, D. (1991). Dynamic 3D models with local and global deformations: Deformable superquadrics. *IEEE Trans. PAMI*, 13:703–714.

Terzopoulos, D., Witkin, A., and Kass, M. (1987). Symmetry-seeking models and 3D object reconstruction. *Int. J. Comp. Vis.*, 1:211–221.

Thomas, J. P. (1983). Underlying psychometric function for detecting gratings and identifying spatial frequency. *J. Opt. Soc. Am.*, 73:751–757.

Thorpe, W. H. (1963). *Learning and Instinct in Animals*. Harvard University Press, Cambridge, Mass. Second edition.

Tigges, J. and Tigges, M. (1985). Subcortical sources of direct projections to visual cortex. In Jones, E. and Peters, A., (Eds.), *Cerebral cortex, vol. 3*, pp. 351–378. Plenum Press, New York, NY.

Tinbergen, N. (1951). *The Study of Instinct*. Clarendon, Oxford.

Tolhurst, D. J. and Movshon, J. A. (1975). Spatial and temporal contrast sensitivity of striate cortical neurons. *Nature*, 257:674–675.

Tomasi, C. and Kanade, T. (1991). Factoring image sequences into shape and motion. In *IEEE Workshop on Visual Motion*, pp. 21–28, Princeton, NJ.

Tootell, R., Hamilton, S., and Silverman, M. (1985). Topography of cytochrome oxidase activity in owl monkey cortex. *J. Neurophysiol.*, 5:2786.

Toyama, K., Komatsu, Y., and Shibuki, K. (1984). Integration of retinal and motor signals of eye movements in striate cortex cells of the alert cat. *J. Neurophysiol.*, 51:649–665.

Treisman, A. (1982). Perceptual grouping and attention in visual search for features and for objects. *J. Exp. Psychol: Human Perception and Performance*, 8:194–214.

Treisman, A. (1983). The role of attention in object perception. In Braddick, O. J. and Sleigh, A. C., (Eds.), *Physical and Biological Processing of Images*. Springer-Verlag, New York, NY.

Treisman, A. (1985). Preattentive processing in vision. *Computer Vision, Graphics and Image Processing*, 31:156–177.

Treisman, A. (1988). Features and objects: The Fourteenth Bartlett memorial lecture. *Q. J. Exp. Psych.*, 40A:201–237.

Troscianko, T., Montagnon, R., Le Clerc, J., Malbert, E., and Chanteau, P. L. (1991). The role of colour as a monocular depth cue. *Vision Res.*, 31:1923–1929.

Tsal, Y. (1983). Movements of attention across the visual field. *J. Exp. Psych.: Human Perception*, 9:523–530.

Tsotsos, J. K. (1988). A 'complexity level' analysis of immediate vision. *Int. J. Comp. Vis.*, 1:303–320.

Tsotsos, J. K. (1989). The complexity of perceptual search tasks. In *Proceedings International Joint Conference on Artificial Intelligence*, Detroit.

Tsotsos, J. K. (1990). Analyzing vision at the complexity level. *Behav. Brain Sci.*, 13:423–469.

Tsotsos, J. K. (1991). Locating and localizing stimuli with an inhibitory attentional beam. Technical Report RBCV-TR91-37, Dept. of Computer Science, University of Toronto.

Turano, K. (1991). Evidence for a common motion mechanism of luminance and contrast modulated patterns: selective adaptation. *Perception*, 20:455–466.

Turano, K. and Pantle, A. (1989). On the mechanism that encodes the movement of contrast variations: velocity discrimination. *Vision Res.*, 29:207–221.

Turing, A. M. (1950). Computing machinery and intelligence. *Mind*, 59:433–460. Reprinted in *The Mind's I*, D. R. Hofstadter and D. C. Dennett (Eds.), Bantam Books, New York, NY.

Tyler, C. W. (1974). Depth perception in disparity gratings. *Nature*, 251:140–142.

Tyler, C. W. and Cavanagh, P. (1991). Purely chromatic perception of motion in depth: Two eyes as sensitive as one. *Percept. Psychophys.*, 49:53–61.

Ullman, S. (1979). *The Interpretation of Visual Motion*. M.I.T. Press, Cambridge, Mass.

Ullmann, J. R. (1972). Correspondence in character recognition. In *Machine Perception of Patterns and Pictures*. Institute of Physics, London, U.K.

Ungerleider, L. G. and Mishkin, M. (1982). Two cortical visual systems. In Ingle, D., Goodale, M., and Mansfield, R. J. W., (Eds.), *Analysis of Visual Behavior*, pp. 549–586. MIT Press, Cambridge, Mass.

Vaina, L. M. (1989). Selective impairment of visual motion interpretation following lesions of the right occipito-parietal area in humans. *Biological Cybernetics*, 61:347–359.

van den Enden, A. and Spekreijse, H. (1989). Binocular depth reversals despite familiarity cues. *Science*, 244:959–961.

van der Horst, G. J. C. and Bouman, M. A. (1969). Spatiotemporal chromaticity discrimination. *J. Opt. Soc. Am.*, 59:1482–1488.

van der Horst, G. J. C., de Weert, C. M. M., and Bouman, M. A. (1967). Transfer of spatial chromaticity-contrast at threshold in the human eye. *J. Opt. Soc. Am.*, 57:1260–1266.

Van Essen, D. C. (1985). Functional organization of primate visual cortex. In Peters, A. and Jones, E., (Eds.), *Cerebral cortex, vol. 3*, pp. 259–330. Plenum, New York, NY.

Van Essen, D. C., Felleman, D. J., De Voe, E. A., Olavarria, J., and Knierim, J. (1990). Modular and hierarchical organization of extrastriate visual cortex in the macaque. In *The Brain*, pp. 679–696. Cold Spring Harbor Lab Press, New York, NY.

Van Essen, D. C. and Maunsell, J. H. R. (1983). Hierarchical organization and functional streams in the visual cortex. *Trends in Neurosci.*, 6:370–375.

van Santen, J. P. H. and Sperling, G. (1984). Temporal covariance model of human motion perception. *J. Opt. Soc. Am. A*, 1:451–473.

van Santen, J. P. H. and Sperling, G. (1985). Elaborated Reichardt detectors. *J. Opt. Soc. Am. A*, 2:300–321.

Vemuri, B. C., Terzopoulos, D., and Lewicki, P. J. (1989). Canonical parameters for invariant surface representation. In *SPIE, Advances in Intelligent Robotics Systems*, Philadelphia, Pennsylvania. Society of Photo-Optical Instrumentation Engineers.

Verhoeff, F. H. (1934). Cycloduction. *Trans. Amer. Ophthal. Soc.*, 32:208–228.

von der Heydt, R. and Peterhans, E. (1989). Mechanisms of contour perception in monkey visual cortex. I. Lines of pattern discontinuity. *J. Neurosci.*, 9:1731–1748.

von der Heydt, R., Peterhans, E., and Baumgartner, G. (1984). Illusory contours and cortical neuron responses. *Science*, 224:1260–1262.

von Helmholtz, H. (1909). *Physiological Optics, Vol 3*. Dover, New York, NY. First published in 1866. The 1909 edition was translated into English by J.P.C. Southall in 1924 and republished in 1962.

von Holst, E. (1954). Relations between the central nervous system and the peripheral organs. *British J. of Animal Behaviour*, 2:89–94.

Von Neumann, J. (1932). *Mathematische Grundlagen der Quantenmechanik*. Springer-Verlag. English translation reprinted in *Quantum Theory and Measurement*, J. A. Wheeler and W. H. Zurek (Eds.), Princeton University Press, Princeton, (1983).

Voorhees, H. and Poggio, T. (1988). Computing texture boundaries from images. *Nature*, 333:364–367.

Waithe, P. and Ferrie, F. (1991). From uncertainty to visual exploration. *IEEE Trans. PAMI*, 13:1038–1049.

Wallach, H. (1935). Über visuelle Wahrgenommene Bewegungsrichtung. *Psychol. Forsch.*, 20:325–380.

Wallach, H. and O'Connell, D. N. (1953). The kinetic depth effect. *J. Exp. Psych.*, 45:205–217.

Walters, D. K. W. (1987). Selection and use of image primitives for general-purpose computer vision algorithms. *CVGIP*, 37:261–298.

Walters, D. K. W. and Fang, C. (1992). Thinning Using a Stylus Generated Image Model. (in preparation).

Walters, D. K. W. and Krishnan, G. (1987). Perceptual significance hierarchy: a computer vision theory for color separation. In *Proceedings of American Association of Artificial Intelligence*, pp. 767–771, Seattle, WA.

Walters, D. K. W. and Weisstein, N. (1982). Perceived brightness is influenced by structure of line drawings. *Invest. Ophthal. Vis. Sci.*, 22 (Suppl.):124.

Waltz, D. I. (1975). Understanding line drawings of scenes with shadows. In Winston, P. H., (Ed.), *The Psychology of Computer Vision*. McGraw-Hill, New York, NY.

Warren, W. H. and Hannon, D. J. (1988). Direction of self-motion is perceived from optical flow. *Nature*, 336:162–163.

Warren, W. H. and Hannon, D. J. (1990). Eye movements and optical flow. *J. Opt. Soc. Am. A*, 7:160–169.

Watamaniuk, S. N. J., Grzywacz, N. M., and Yuille, A. L. (1992). Dependence of speed and direction perception on cinematogram dot density. *Vision Res.* (to appear).

Watson, A. B. and Ahumada, A. J. (1983). A look at motion in the frequency domain. In Tsotsos, J. K., (Ed.), *Motion: Perception and representation*, pp. 1–10. Association for Computing Machinery, New York, NY.

Watson, A. B. and Ahumada, A. J. (1985). Model of human visual-motion sensing. *J. Opt. Soc. Am. A*, 2:322–342.

Watt, R. J. (1984). Towards a general theory of the visual acuities for shape and spatial arrangement. *Vision Res.*, 24:1377–1386.

Watt, R. J., Morgan, M. J., and Ward, R. M. (1983). The use of different cues in vernier acuity. *Vision Res.*, 23:991–995.

Webster, M. A. (1988). *Properties of Spatial Vision with Luminance or Color Varying Patterns*. PhD thesis, University of California, Berkeley, CA.

Webster, M. A., De Valois, K. K., and Switkes, E. (1990). Orientation and spatial frequency discrimination for luminance and chromatic gratings. *J. Opt. Soc. Am. A*, 7:1034–1049.

Weichselgartner, E. and Sperling, G. (1987). Dynamics of automatic and controlled visual attention. *Science*, 238:778–779.

Werner, H. (1938). Binocular depth contrast and the conditions of the binocular field. *Amer. J. Psychol.*, 51:489–497.

Westheimer, G. (1975). Visual acuity and hyperacuity. *Invest. Ophthal. Vis. Sci.*, 14:570–572.

Westheimer, G. (1979). The spatial sense of the eye. *Invest. Ophthal. Vis. Sci.*, 18:893–912.

Westheimer, G. and McKee, S. P. (1977). Spatial configurations for visual hyperacuity. *Vision Res.*, 17:941–947.

Westheimer, G., Shimamura, K., and McKee, S. P. (1976). Interference with line orientation sensitivity. *J. Opt. Soc. Am.*, 66:332–338.

Wetherill, G. B. and Levitt, H. (1965). Sequential estimation of points on a psychometric function. *Brit. J. Math. Stat. Psychol.*, 18:1–10.

Wheeler, J. A. and Zurek, W. H. (1983). *Quantum Theory and Measurement*. Princeton University Press, Princeton, NJ.

White, J. M. and Rohrer, G. D. (1983). Image thresholding for optical character recognition and other applications requiring character image extraction. *IBM J. Res. Develop.*, 27(4):400–410.

Widrow, B. (1973). The 'rubber-mask' technique–I. Pattern Measurement and Analysis. *Pattern Recognition*, 5:175–197.

Wigner, E. P. (1961). Remarks on the mind-body question. In Good, I. J., (Ed.), *The Scientist Speculates*. Heinemann, London. Reprinted in *Quantum Theory and Measurement*, J. A. Wheeler and W. H. Zurek (Eds.), Princeton University Press, Princeton, (1983).

Williams, D. and Julesz, B. (1991). Filters vs. textons in human and machine texture discrimination. In Wechsler, H., (Ed.), *Neural Networks for Perception, Vol. 1 - Human and Machine Perception*, pp. 145–175. Academic Press, Boston, Mass.

Williams, D. W., Philips, G., and Sekuler, R. (1986). Hysteresis in the perception of motion direction: evidence for neural cooperativity. *Nature*, 324:253–255.

Williams, D. W. and Sekuler, R. (1984). Coherent global motion percepts from stochastic local motions. *Vision Res.*, 24:55–62.

Wilson, H. R. (1980). A transducer function for threshold and suprathreshold human vision. *Biol. Cybernetics*, 38:171–178.

Wilson, H. R. (1985). Discrimination of contour curvature: data and theory. *J. Opt. Soc. Am. A.*, 2:1191–1199.

Wilson, H. R. (1986). Responses of spatial mechanisms can explain hyperacuity. *Vision Res.*, 26:453–469.

Wilson, H. R. (1991a). Model of peripheral and amblyopic hyperacuity. *Vision Res.*, 31:967–982.

Wilson, H. R. (1991b). Psychophysical models of spatial vision and hyperacuity. In Regan, D., (Ed.), *Spatial vision*, pp. 64–86. Macmillan, Boca Raton.

Wilson, H. R. and Bergen, J. R. (1979). A four mechanism model for threshold spatial vision. *Vision Res.*, 19:19–32.

Wilson, H. R., Ferrera, V. P., and Yo, C. (1992). Psychophysically motivated model for two-dimensional motion perception. *Vis. Neurosci.*, 9:79–97.

Wilson, H. R. and Gelb, D. J. (1984). Modified line-element theory for spatial-frequency and width discrimination. *J. Opt. Soc. Am. A*, 1:124–131.

Wilson, H. R., Levi, D., Maffei, L., Rovamo, J., and De Valois, R. L. (1990). The perception of form: retina to striate cortex. In Spillmann, L. and Werner, J. S., (Eds.), *The Neurophysiological Foundations of Visual Perception*. Academic Press, New York, NY.

Wilson, H. R., McFarlane, D. K., and Phillips, G. C. (1983). Spatial frequency tuning of orientation selective units estimated by oblique masking. *Vision Res.*, 23:873–882.

Wilson, H. R. and Regan, D. (1985). Spatial frequency adaptation and grating discrimination: predictions of a line element model. *J. Opt. Soc. Am. A*, 1:1091–1096.

Wilson, H. R. and Richards, W. A. (1989). Mechanisms of contour curvature discrimination. *J. Opt. Soc. Am. A*, 6:106–115.

Wilson, H. R. and Richards, W. A. (1992). Curvature and separation discrimination at texture boundaries. *J. Opt. Soc. Am. A*, pg. (in press).

Witkin, A. (1986). Scale space filtering. In Pentland, A. P., (Ed.), *From Pixels to Predicates*. Ablex, Norwood, NJ.

Witkin, A. and Tennenbaum, J. M. (1983). On the role of structure in vision. In Beck, J., Hope, B., and Rosenfeld, A., (Eds.), *Human and Machine Vision*, pp. 481–543. Academic Press, New York, NY.

Wolf, W., Hauske, G., and Lupp, U. (1980). Interaction of pre-saccadic and post-saccadic patterns having the same coordinates in space. *Vision Res.*, 20:117–125.

Wolfe, J. M. and Owens, D. A. (1981). Is accommodation color blind? Focusing chromatic contours. *Perception*, 10:53–62.

Wong-Riley, M. (1979). Changes in the visual system of monocularly sutured or enucleated cats demonstrable with cytochrome oxidase histochemistry. *Brain Res.*, 171:11–28.

Woodham, R. J. (1981). Analysing images of curved surfaces. *A.I. Journal*, 17:117–140.

Wyszecki, G. and Stiles, W. S. (1967). *Colour science, concepts and methods: Quantitative data and formulas*. Wiley, New York, NY.

Yarbus, A. L. (1967). *Eye movements and vision*. Plenum Press, New York, NY.

Yo, C. and Wilson, H. R. (1992). Perceived direction of moving two-dimensional patterns depends on duration, contrast, and eccentricity. *Vision Res.*, 32:135–147.

Yuille, A. L. (1990). Generalized Deformable Models, Statistical Physics, and Matching Problems. *Neural Computation*, 2(1):1–24.

Yuille, A. L., Cohen, D. S., and Hallinan, P. W. (1989). Feature extraction from faces using deformable templates. In *IEEE CVPR*, pp. 104–109, San Diego.

Yuille, A. L. and Grzywacz, N. M. (1988). A computational theory for the perception of coherent visual motion. *Nature*, 333:71–74.

Yuille, A. L. and Grzywacz, N. M. (1989). A mathematical analysis of the motion coherence theory. *Int. J. Comp. Vis.*, 3:155–175.

Yuille, A. L. and Poggio, T. A. (1986). Scaling theorems for zero crossings. *IEEE Trans. PAMI*, 8:15–25.

Zeevi, Y. Y. and Shamai, S. (1989). Image representation by reference-signal crossings. In Ullman, S. and Richards, W., (Eds.), *Image Understanding*. Ablex, Norwood, NJ.

Zeki, S. (1990). Colour vision and functional specialization in the visual cortex. *Discussions in Neuroscience*, 6:1–64.

Zeki, S. M. (1974). Functional organization of a visual area in the posterior bank of the superior temporal sulcus of the rhesus monkey. *J. Physiol. (Lond.)*, 236:549–573.

Zeki, S. M. (1978). Functional specialization in the visual cortex of the rhesus monkey. *Nature*, 274:423–428.

Zihl, J. D., Von Cramon, D., and Mai, N. (1983). Selective disturbance of movement vision after bilateral brain damage. *Brain*, 106:313–340.

Zucker, S. W. (1984). Type i and type ii processes in early orientation selection. In Dodwell, P. C. and Caelli, T. M., (Eds.), *Figural synthesis*, pp. 283–300. Lawrence Erlbaum, London.

Zucker, S. W. (1986). The computational connection in vision: Early orientation selection. *Behaviour Research Methods, Instruments, and Computers*, 18:121–128.

Zucker, S. W., Dobbins, A., and Iverson, L. (1989). Two stages of curve detection suggest two styles of visual computation. *Neural Computation*, 1:68–81.

Zucker, S. W. and Hummel, R. (1986). Receptive fields and the representation of visual information. *Human Neurobiology*, 5:121–128.

Index

adaptation, 11, 16, 37, 155, 156, 159, 297, 406

affine transformation, 60, 61, 129–133, 138, 140–142, 145, 203, 205, 209, 210

amblyopes, 26, 190

amplitude modulation, phase modulation, 64, 67, 69, 75, 77–83, 86, 87

AMPM, *see* amplitude modulation, phase modulation

amygdala, 188, 189

annealing, 134, 138

anti-texton, 401, 403, 404

arborization of disparity, 407

aspect ratio, 269, 300, 303

attention, 255, 313–331, 394–408

attenuation, 152

audition, 15, 16

B-spline, *see* spline fitting

bandlimited patterns, 64

bandwidth, 9, 11, 16, 21, 30, 63, 155, 156, 163, 176, 213, 232, 295, 297

basal dendrites, 218, 219, 226, 227

bats, 187

binocular vision, *see* cyclopean vision, 405–407

bisection experiment, 10, 12, 14, 17, 21

blindness
to motion in depth, 307

blobs, 115, 143, 268, 401, 404

Bohr-Einstein debates, 194–196

Boltzmann distribution, 234

Boltzmann Machine, 136

CAD, *see* Computer Aided Design

camouflage, 281–287, 289, 292–294, 299, 307, 308, 394, 395, 406

Cauchy function, 16–18

causality, 193, 195, 196

center-surround operator, 219

channels, 11, 32, 63, 82, 155, 159, 215, 295, 396
color, xiv, 122, 398

Chinoiserie, 7

chromaticity, 123, 149, 153, 155

cinematograms, 394, 396, 398

coarse to fine, 147

coherent motion, 157, 158, 296, 297, 304–308, 334–337

collapse of the wave-packet, 195, 196, 199

color, 21, 33, 34, 36, 37, 90, 119, 149–159, 185, 191, 229, 251
contrast, 152, 157, 158, 405
defined form, 395, 401
in stereopsis, 394, 396–399, 408

columnar organization, 182, 262, 295

computer aided design, 240, 251

cones, 22, 26, 120, 153, 191, 302

consciousness, 185, 188–190, 194, 197, 199–201

contrast, 24

contrast sensitivity, 17, 23, 150, 152, 156, 294

cortex
medial superior temporal cortex (MST), 162, 309, 310
medial temporal cortex (MT), 161, 162, 309
V1, 34, 161, 162, 189, 267, 311, 394
V2, 34, 161, 162, 182, 407

curvature, 35, 142, 143, 146, 163, 167, 168, 170, 171, 212, 241, 250
cyclodisparity, 350, 351, 355, 361, 363, 364
cycloduction, 350
cyclopean vision, 393–394
cyclophoria, 353
cyclovergence, 355–365
cycloversion, 349, 353–356, 359
cytochrome oxidase, 33–38

depth
    absolute vs relative, 397
    from motion, 39, 229, 399
    from shading, 394, 397
    from stereopsis, 362, 394, 399
    perception, 156–157
Descartes, 192, 193, 196
dichoptic viewing, 349
difference of Gaussians, 45, 61, 212
disparity, see cyclopean vision
DNA, 201, 396
DOG, see difference of Gaussians
Doppler shift, 395

echo-locating, 397
edge, see representations, edge based
    detection, 89, 90, 237, 250, 263, 326, 339
edge detection, 258
eigenvalue, 42, 48, 50, 52, 54, 55
Einstein, 32, 194
energy
    law of conservation, 192
    metabolic, 34
epipolar lines, 203, 209
epipolar plane, 235
evoked potential, 386
eye, 120, 367
    movement, 15, 21, 287, 315, 405
    of origin, 189, 190
    rotation, 349, 350
    template, 85, 339
    torsion, 351

face, 10, 83, 399
feature detection, 83, 89, 91, 93, 333, 337
filter
    bandpass, 69
    orientationally tuned, 163, 169, 296, 297

spatial, 9–11, 61, 163, 165, 288, 296
spatiotemporal, 174, 297, 334, 336, 367, 368, 373
filter interaction, 64
fixation direction, 120
fixation point, 45, 152, 330, 349, 351, 355, 359, 400, 405
focal attention, 397
focal length, 41, 44, 51, 59, 407
foreshortening, 337
Fourier analysis, 16, 64, 161, 215, 379, 383
fovea, 152, 163, 173, 177, 178, 292, 302, 312, 350
fractal, 234
fronto-parallel plane, 346

Gabor filter, 17, 87, 402
ganglion cells, 86
Gaussian
    distribution, 43, 54, 105, 127, 129, 133, 235, 335
    filter, 17, 171, 369, 375, 377, 380, 382, 389
    noise, 44, 234–236
gaze, 349
gedanken experiments, 190, 197, 395
geometric modeling, 107, 128, 230, 244, 261, 262, 267
geometric modelling, 245
Gestalt Psychology, 334
Gibbs distribution, 128, 234, 241, 246, 335, 339, 342
Gibson, 120, 367
Glass patterns, 396, 398
gluons, 192
gradient
    based systems, 367, 368, 373, 374
    constraints, 239, 376, 391
    descent, 132, 215, 233, 347

Heisenberg's uncertainty principle, 194
Helmholtz, 281, 282, 350, 406
Hering, 350
Hilbertean questions, 396
hippocampus, 188
homunculus, 185, 189, 192–194, 197–200
hyperacuity, 22, 23, 26, 32, 302
hypercolumn, 35, 36, 317, 322
hyperplane, 103, 105
hysteresis, 225, 226

ideal observer, 22, 26, 117, 118
ill-posed problem, 333
interblob, 34–37
interocular distance, 406
interpolation, 56, 211, 212, 216, 217, 219,
      228, 231, 234, 236, 243
IOD, *see* interocular distance

JND, *see* just noticable difference
just noticeable difference, 19, 27

Kalman filter, 211, 219–228, 235–237,
      246
   extended, 240, 241
knowledge-based systems, 257
Kuffler unit, 401

Lambertian surface, 344
Laplacian of a Gaussian, 81
Lateral Geniculate nucleus, 310, 311
LD, *see* lumenance defined form
linear subspace methods, 39
luminance defined form, 283, 291, 293,
      295, 296, 307

macaque monkey, 36, 163, 331
magic, 188
magic lantern, 282
magnocellular, 309, 310
Markov, 143, 145, 223–225, 230, 234
Marr, 90, 91, 96, 104, 231, 258, 281, 333,
      334, 347
matching, 78, 127, 128, 132, 147, 203,
      209, 241, 245, 336, 337, 340
memory, 268
mind-body problem, 185, 192, 193, 196,
      197, 200
miracle, 395
modulation, *see* demodulation, 45,
      63–65, 68, 87
moiré patterns, 398
Monte-Carlo simulation, 82, 235
motion, 39, 77, 120, 150, 158, 353, 371,
      372, 386
   analysis, 33, 40, 161, 171, 174, 179,
      183, 209–210, 237, 333
   defined form, 281, 283, 285, 288, 290,
      291, 293–295, 302, 304
   detection, 281–282, 359, 367, 368,
      394
Mr. Data, 186
MST, *see* cortex

MT, *see* cortex
multiple sclerosis, 304, 305
music, 15, 16

navigation, 229, 235
von Neumann, 196
neural network, 127, 175, 176, 186
Newton, 32, 75, 193
nonius lines, 350, 359–361, 364, 365
Nyquist rate, 165

object-based systems, 129, 130, 133, 135,
      141
Observer Mechanics, 105
observer motion, 39, 41, 106
occlusion, 56, 90, 359
OKN, *see* optokinetic nystagmus
opponent process, 176, 294–299, 303
optic flow, 161, 230, 237, 242, 245
optokinetic nystagmus, 359
orientation
   selectivity, 34, 35, 69, 78, 87, 151,
      154–155, 284, 287, 383
   tuned, 36, 130, 156, 351, 369, 386, 391
   tuned filters, 9, 21, 27, 28, 31, 82, 159,
      163, 164, 168, 169, 175, 181, 358,
      375, 377
origami, 256, 257

pain, 186, 187
Panum's fusional area, 365, 397, 407
parafoveal, 289, 405
pattern discrimination, 163, 165, 171
pattern recognition, 128
perceptual significance hierarchy, 252,
      254–256
perturbation, 52, 102, 353
phase, 10, 14, 15, 17, 21, 31, 65, 69, 84,
      158, 168, 170, 291, 377, 381
   lag, 352–354
   modulation, 63, 64, 80
phonemes, 404
photon, 22, 195
plaids, 78, 157–159, 171, 173, 178, 179,
      182, 367, 368, 371, 385–386, 388,
      389
Posner, 318, 400
primate, 33, 34, 90, 162, 181, 295, 309,
      310, 315–317, 368, 386, 389, 394,
      397
PSH, *see* perceptual significance
      hierarchy

quadrature, 87, 215, 381
qualia, 185–191, 195, 197, 200
quantum mechanics, 185, 192–197

random dot cinematogram, *see*
    cinematogram
random dot stereogram, 393–408
RDC, *see* cinematogram
RDS, *see* random dot stereogram
rectification, 164, 169–171, 174, 176,
    179–181, 377, 378, 380
recursion, 215, 217
reflectance, 102, 106, 121, 149, 150, 159,
    231, 344, 392
regularization, 211, 212, 219, 228, 231,
    234, 333, 335, 342
relaxation labeling, 314
representations
    contour based, 92, 120, 249, 251, 335
    edge based, 10, 90, 152, 167, 245, 246,
        250, 263, 371
    multiscale, 35, 214, 272, 340, 377
    pixel based, 44, 220, 284
    ribbon model, 259, 263–267
    two and a half D, 229
retina, 14, 26, 86, 90, 112, 255, 281, 350,
    359, 406
ribbon model, *see* representations
robot vision, 394, 405

saccade, 315
scale space, *see* representations, scale
    space
Schroedinger wave equation, 194
segmentation, 45, 128, 157, 249, 250, 252,
    256, 275, 345, 346, 394, 395, 397,
    401, 402, 404
shadow, 90, 150, 159, 399
shape from rotation, 241
signal to noise ratio, 50, 52
simple cells, 87, 164–169, 269, 367, 368,
    378–388

sine wave grating, 157
SNR, *see* signal to noise ratio
spline fitting, 127, 128, 131, 240
square wave, 167–170
stereo, 393–408
stereomotion, 157
stereopsis, 156, 157, 393, 394
superquadrics, 240

template matching, 22, 85, 127, 337
Template Observer, 22–29
texton, 31, 393, 395
texture, 63–87
    discrimination, 30, 31, 393, 394
thought experiments, *see* gedanken
    experiments
torsional alignment, 349, 353, 355–357
torsional eye movements, 351
tracking, 242, 287
transparent, 157, 392
Turing test, 185–187

uncertainty models, 229

V1, *see* cortex
V2, *see* cortex
velocity field, 335, 336
vergence, 349–351, 356, 360, 361, 364
vestibular, 120, 349
voiceprint, 16

Waterfall illusion, 292
wavelet, 17, 211, 213, 218–220, 223, 225,
    226, 228
winner take all, 313–315, 319
WTA, *see* winner take all

Zeki, 33, 161, 308
Zeki Hypothesis, 34
zero-crossing, 78, 81, 90, 245
zimbo, 189
zombie, 189